Urban Design and the British Urban Renaissance

Urban Design and the British Urban Renaissance

Edited by John Punter

LONDON AND NEW YORK

First published 2010
by Routledge
2 Park Square, Milton Park, Abingdon, Oxon OX14 4RN

Simultaneously published in the USA and Canada
by Routledge
270 Madison Avenue, New York, NY 10016, USA

Routledge is an imprint of the Taylor & Francis Group, an informa business

Typeset in Goudy by Prepress Projects Ltd, Perth, UK
Printed and bound in Great Britain by MPG Books Group, UK

This book is the outcome of an ESRC Seminar Series entitled 'Urban design and the British
urban renaissance: contribution and critique' (RES–451–26–0409). The assistance of the
Economic and Social Research Council in bringing together the contributors to this volume
in four regional seminars with a wide range of local design and regeneration practitioners,
planners and amenity activists is gratefully acknowledged.

British Library Cataloguing in Publication Data
A catalogue record for this book is available from the British Library

Library of Congress Cataloging-in-Publication Data
Urban design and the British Urban renaissance/edited by John Punter.
p. cm.
1. City Planning–Great Britain. 2. Urban Policy–Great Britain. I. Punter, John. HT169.
G7U674 2009
307.1'2160941–dc22
2009013224

ISBN13: 978–0–415–44304–3 (hbk)
ISBN13: 978–0–415–44303–6 (pbk)
ISBN13: 978–0–203–86920–8 (ebk)

ISBN10: 0–415–44304–0 (hbk)
ISBN10: 0–415–44303–2 (hbk)
ISBN10: 0–203–86920–6 (ebk)

Contents

Plates

Figures

Tables

List of contributors

Mike Biddulph is Senior Lecturer in the School of City and Regional Planning at Cardiff University and works with the Design Commission for Wales on design training.

Philip Booth is Reader in the School of Town and Regional Planning at Sheffield University and Chair of the City of Sheffield's Conservation Advisory Group.

Matthew Carmona is Professor of Planning and Urban Design and Head of Department at the Bartlett School of Planning at University College London, and Associate Editor of the *Journal of Urban Design*.

Sarah Chaplin is Professor of Architecture and Urbanism at the University of Greenwich, and Deputy Director of the Urban Renaissance Institute.

Michael Edwards is Senior Lecturer in the Bartlett School of Planning at University College London and has worked with the King's Cross Railway Lands Group for many years.

Leslie Forsyth is Head of School and Coordinator of the Postgraduate Programme in Urban Design at Edinburgh College of Art.

Tim Heath is Professor of Architecture and Urban Design and Head of the School of the Built Environment at Nottingham University.

Michael Hebbert is Professor of Town Planning at Manchester University, a Founder of Vision for London, and Editor of *Progress in Planning*.

Marilyn Higgins is Lecturer and Coordinator of the Postgraduate Urban Studies Programme at the School of Built Environment, Heriot-Watt University and an Enabler for Architecture + Design Scotland.

Joe Holyoak is Director of the MA Urban Design course at Birmingham City University, a practising urban designer and a CABE representative.

Tony Lloyd Jones is Principal Lecturer in Urban Design and Development at the School of Architecture and the Built Environment at the University of Westminster and Senior Manager of Research and Consultancy at the Max Lock Centre.

Ali Madanipour is Professor of Urban Design at the School of Architecture Planning and Landscape, University of Newcastle upon Tyne.

William J. V. Neill is Professor of Spatial Planning in the Centre for Planning and Environmental Management, University of Aberdeen.

Lora Nicolaou is a Principal with DEGW in London and part-time Professor at the Urban Renaissance Institute at the University of Greenwich.

John Punter is Professor of Urban Design at Cardiff University and a Director and Design Review Chair of the Design Commission for Wales.

Marion Roberts is Professor of Urban Design at the School of Architecture and the Built Environment, University of Westminster.

Henry Shaftoe is Senior Lecturer in the School of the Natural and Built Environment at the University of the West of England.

Lindsay Smales is Lecturer in the Centre for Urban Development and Environmental Management at Leeds Metropolitan University.

Andrew Tallon is Senior Lecturer in Urban Policy in the School of the Natural and Built Environment at the University of the West of England.

Steve Tiesdell is Senior Lecturer in the Department of Urban Studies at the University of Glasgow and a member of the Glasgow Urban Design Panel.

Rachael Unsworth is Lecturer in Geography at the University of Leeds and works with the Leeds Initiative on behalf of the University.

Preface

In 1998 the Deputy Prime Minister, John Prescott, commissioned the eminent architect and Labour peer Sir Richard Rogers to Chair an Urban Task Force (UTF). He charged it with the task of 'establishing a new vision for urban regeneration founded on the principles of design excellence, social well-being and environmental responsibility within a viable economic and legislative framework' (UTF 1999a: 1). A year later the 313-page report, *Towards an Urban Renaissance*, recommended 'design-led' urban regeneration, 'placed within its economic and social context' to ensure sustainability, as the way of accommodating rapid household growth in England and revitalising its major towns and cities (1999a: 7). The report helped to reshape British planning, housing, and regeneration policies over subsequent years, placing a particular importance on the role of urban design, which was seen as a key factor in improving the quality and longevity of development, while becoming a major component of the progression towards zero-carbon development and more sustainable cities.

In late 2006, when this research project was conceived, it was acknowledged that it was too early to thoroughly evaluate the impacts of the urban renaissance. The renaissance of British cities was at least a thirty-year project rather than something that could be accomplished in a decade, especially when many of the major cities had been suffering population decline for the better part of a century. Some members of the Task Force themselves reviewed policy progress in their 2005 report, *Towards a Strong Urban Renaissance*, producing a strongly critical report on the implementation of their recommendations, but they did not have the time or space to explore the particularities of urban design. It was felt that it would be useful to assess in more detail the ongoing physical transformation of the largest cities, the urban design dimension of planning, and the quality of development and urbanism that was being achieved.

The end of Tony Blair's leadership of New Labour seemed a good point at which to attempt an appraisal, particularly with the Chancellor of the Exchequer taking over as Prime Minister, and with the Treasury agendas of driving urban economic competitiveness, tackling housing supply shortages, speeding up infrastructure delivery and reforming development taxation being brought to the fore. But by late 2007 to 2008, when the research conferences that underpin this book were under way, the focus was shifting as the effects of the collapse of the American sub-prime mortgage market, the Northern Rock and Bradford and Bingley rescues, the sharp decline in house prices and the collapse of the buy-to-let market all impacted upon the UK. These events emphasised that the urban renaissance had been primarily driven, and significantly distorted, by an exceptionally long economic boom (1993–2006) characterised by rampant property and wider financial speculation, over-lending by the banks and unsustainable increases in commercial, governmental and household debt. Nonetheless, an evaluation of renaissance progress over the previous decade was still considered to be opportune given the obvious end to the economic cycle.

The academic research context

The Economic and Social Research Council's (ESRC) 'Cities: Competitiveness and Cohesion' research programme (1999–2004) had generated a large body of work that had helped shape understanding of contemporary British urbanism and current policy initiatives. It posited a 'new conventional wisdom' of urban governance with strong public–private partnerships; an urban competitiveness ethos to improve economic performance; and an emphasis upon social cohesion to reduce socio-economic polarities (Buck *et al.* 2005). Urban design was noticeable by its absence from that research programme, but it was recognized as an important mechanism in the reimaging and place-marketing of cities, thereby enhancing their competitiveness. Urban design's wider contribution to physical regeneration was not clearly articulated, and elsewhere was widely contested, while the 'new conventional wisdom' underplayed the urgent need to pursue more sustainable cities. The reduction of carbon emissions, particularly through energy conservation in buildings and reductions in private car use, the creation of more walk/cycle routes and safer places, the maintenance of urban biodiversity, and the general encouragement of more sustainable household behaviours were all areas where better urban design could make a significant contribution.

Other research had explored these 'new uses of urban design' across Europe, and had shown how it has become a key tool in economic development (Gospodini 2002). This acknowledged the potential tensions between avant-garde and iconic architecture and place identity, and recognised how the use of design will vary across the urban hierarchy, and according to each city's economic centrality–peripherality. Other international observers had argued that urban design had taken on an inflated, yet superficial, role in urban policy making (Cuthbert 2004) with urban planning down-graded in favour of 'designing' to deliver flagship projects, iconic architecture and cultural projects, and spectacular new sites of consumption replete with 'designer spaces' (Harvey 1989a,b; Hannigan 1998; Miles and Miles 2003). There had been strong criticisms of the shallowness of design and culture as regeneration agents (Evans 2003; Julier 2005), of city branding, and 'quarterisation' (Bell and Jayne 2003) and of urban design as an agent of gentrification (Lees 2003). Accordingly, urban design faced many challenges, not only to become an integral component of public policy, but also to remain a socially progressive and environmentally conscious force in the face of intensifying neoliberal governance (Cuthbert 2006; Madanipour 2006). These were some of the bigger questions that the analysis of individual cities' urban design initiatives hoped to embrace alongside the evaluation of individual developments and their cumulative impact upon urban form and quality.

Researching and writing the book

Having established the rationale and scope of the book the editor approached some fifteen urban design, or design-interested, academics to contribute chapters to a broadly defined template that still allowed each author scope for individual interpretation and focus. Most of those approached had collaborated before in smaller groups and in a range of research, writings and seminar series with a development/design remit, and most were closely engaged in local urban design practice as activists, commentators, consultants, design advisers or review panellists and/or had written about aspects of their city in academic and professional journals or in other formats.

An ESRC Seminar Series award was used to bring together a group of academics for a series of mini-conferences to debate contemporary urban design as public policy in each of the major UK cities. Additional support and advice was provided by the three national design bodies (the Commission for Architecture and the Built Environment, Architecture and Design Scotland and the Design Commission for Wales). Four two-day seminars held in Cardiff, Manchester, Glasgow and London each debated progress in four cities/boroughs. The seminars were organised to create a well-informed, intense, cross-professional, and cross-sector debate about the progress made 'Towards an Urban Renaissance' in each of the thirteen largest cities in the UK. Although urban renaissance is strictly speaking only an English urban policy a decision was made to include the largest cities in the devolved administrations of Scotland, Wales and Northern Ireland. They were undergoing very similar development pressures and changes in urban governance, while being subjected to rather different planning policy regimes. They were seen as providing a counterpoint to English policy and experience, while facilitating the development of a UK-wide perspective on urban regeneration and urban design.

In each seminar the local urban renaissance was introduced by a local authority representative and then critiqued by the academic author. Three local practitioners then commented upon both presentations, offering their own perspectives on design achievements. The discussion was then thrown open to general discussion with specific interventions from other local experts and activists who had been invited to offer their particular take on events and outcomes. The result was a very lively and well-informed debate (for summaries of the seminar proceedings see Carmona 2008; Hebbert 2008; Punter 2008; Tiesdell 2008). It is the task of this book to capture these wide-ranging analyses and debates, to consider their implications for current and future design policy and practice, and to raise questions about the future direction of the urban renaissance and urban design.

Structure of the book

The book is structured into eighteen chapters, the first being a general introduction reviewing the recommendations of the Urban Task Force, their adoption, modification and implementation, and their translation and absorption into the varied strands of planning, housing, regeneration, and local government policy. There then follow the individual case studies divided into three sections, each with a short introduction. We begin with the English 'Core Cities' of Birmingham, Manchester, Leeds, Sheffield, Liverpool, Bristol, Newcastle upon Tyne and Nottingham. Four studies of parts of London then follow, embracing Central London, King's Cross, The Isle of Dogs and the Thames Gateway. Finally the four principal 'Celtic' cities – Edinburgh, Glasgow, Cardiff and Belfast – are examined to compare and contrast their experiences of renaissance under similar economic conditions but slightly different urban policy and planning regimes. A longer concluding chapter draws together the case studies and the discussion that ensued in the four regional seminars. It returns to the original set of research questions to draw together the evidence of the case studies, to comment on outstanding renaissance issues, and to offer an assessment of the positives and negatives and what remains to be achieved.

The audience for the book

This book is aimed at a wide audience of undergraduate and postgraduate students of urban design, planning and architecture; of academics and practising professionals in each of these disciplines; and of politicians, urban activists and amenity group members who are also engaged in the process of shaping the quality of the cities in which they live and work. The book will probably be of most use to undergraduate and postgraduate students seeking an introduction to the urban renaissance and an understanding of how it has shaped, and been shaped by, government policy over a decade. The individual city chapters will provide an accessible overview of regional progress, and hopefully will encourage students to write essays and dissertations about local design and development issues, and to visit as many of these cities as possible, to see for themselves what has been achieved and what remains to be done.

However, the editor and authors hope the book will be of equal interest to professional practitioners and urban activists with its strong practice orientation. It provides a broad national policy context within which to locate the design dimension of the urban renaissance, to understand the very wide range of initiatives that have followed in its wake, and to appreciate the full range of policy, guidance and research which is advancing practice and developing critique. It is a full-time job keeping track of policy pronouncements and the flow of advice and best practice, even in the relatively narrow field of urban design, and this book should help busy professionals in this process. The book also echoes a wide range of informed views on the strengths and weaknesses of the urban renaissance and urban design as public policy as aired by practitioners in the research seminars.

The main body of the book consists of the individual city chapters, which represent an attempt to reach a verdict on each city's practice of urban design as public policy. Each chapter draws on the competing views of those shaping individual cities from both the public and private sides. These verdicts are hoped to be well-informed, but they are necessarily simplified, selective and personal, and written from outside the processes of politics, planning and development where all the messy compromises have to be made. They will, it is hoped, provoke local professional and activist debate, help practitioners reach and express their own verdict on events, and give each city a chance to compare and contrast their experiences and learn from each other (as they already regularly do).

Acknowledgments

As editor of this volume I would like to express my thanks to all those who have contributed, particularly to my fellow authors, who have subjected themselves to complex organisational tasks for each seminar and responded positively to editorial comments. I would especially like to thank my three colleagues, Steve Tiesdell, Mike Hebbert and Matthew Carmona, who helped refine the original proposal for a seminar series to inform the writing of the book, and who not only contributed a chapter, but took on the responsibility for coordinating and hosting one of the regional mini-conferences, and also commented on the final chapter. With some thirty to forty-five speakers at each conference, and the need to precirculate powerpoints and coordinate presenters and respondents, the organisational task was immense. In this task we were greatly assisted by Sue Jones and Margaret Roberts (Cardiff), Debra Whitehead (Manchester), Georgiana Varna (Glasgow) and Elena Besussi (London).

A particular debt is owed to the ESRC for financial support to hold four regional seminars where the progress towards an urban renaissance in each of the thirteen cities could be debated. Under their Research Seminar Series programme the ESRC funded the authors, and a similar number of graduate students and young researchers, to attend the seminars, allowing all of us to benefit from a wide range of informed views from public and private practitioners. Our thanks are also due to the Chief Executives of the national bodies who promote architectural and urban design quality who also supported the seminars financially and practically. Richard Simmons (Commission for Architecture and the Built Environment), Sebastian Toombs (Architecture and Design Scotland) and Carol-Anne Davies (Design Commission for Wales) also found the time to contribute to the proceedings and encouraged their staff to attend.

Special thanks should go to all those who presented at the seminars (whose names are listed below) and our other speakers from the floor and invitees, some 160 people in all, who funded themselves to attend one or more of these events, and who made important contributions to the debate from the floor. Our thanks go to our respective University Schools for hosting the mini-conferences and providing administrative and audio-visual support all free of charge.

The authors would like to acknowledge the contributions of the following who gave presentations to the ESRC seminars on one of the cities. *Birmingham*: Chris Crean, Nick Ebbs, Adrian Passmore. *Manchester*: Tom Russell, Shelagh McInerney, Barbara McLoughlin, Mick Timpson. *Leeds*: Philip Crabtree, John Thorp, Irena Bauman, Jonathan Morgan. *Liverpool*: Nigel Lee, Beatrice Frankel, Trevor Skempton, Paul Sheppard. *Sheffield*: Simon Ogden, David Topham, Andy Topley, John Pringle. *Bristol*: Alastair Brook, George Ferguson, Keith Hallett, Gerry Hicks, David Farnsworth. *Newcastle upon Tyne*: Harvey Emms, Eric Morgan, Michael Crilly, Tony Wyatt.

Nottingham: Nigel Turpin, Adrian Jones, Jim Taylor. *Central London*: Terry Farrell, Adrian Pen-fold, Alistair Huggett, Jim Monahan, Graham King; *King's Cross*: Peter Bishop; *Isle of Dogs*: Jamie Ounan, Howard Dawber, William Roberts; *Thames Gateway*: Tobias Goevert, William McKee, David Balcombe, Caroline Lwin. *Edinburgh*: Ricardo Marini, Ian Wall, Terry Levinthal, Sebastian Toombs. *Glasgow*: John Bury, Gerry Grams, Stephen Tucker, Niall Murphy. *Cardiff*: Alan Francis, Mark Hallett, Nigel Hanson, Pat Thompson. *Belfast*: Marie-Therese McGivern, Bill Morrison, Karen Latimer.

In addition the following each chaired a seminar session: Richard Simmons, Jonathan Davies, Carole Anne Davies, Kevin Murray, Eric Sorensen, Tom Lonsdale.

As editor I would like to thank Liz Mills for her help with editing Chapters 1 and 18 and supplying critical commentaries on the seminar proceedings and on the European dimension of the urban renaissance. Special thanks are due to Heather Morecroft for managing the assembly and formatting of the chapters, including the bibliographies and references, and Jan Edwards, who assembled, checked and amended all the illustrations as necessary. At Routledge I would like to thank Catherine Lynn for guiding the book through the production process and at Prepress Projects, Evelyn Wilkins for copy-editing and Leah Gourley for typesetting and project management.

The authors would also like to thank all those who gave permission to use particular illustra-tions, all of which are acknowledged in the relevant captions.

Common acronyms

A+DS	Architecture and Design Scotland
ASC	Academy for Sustainable Communities; now part of HCA
ATLAS	Advisory Team for Large Applications Service
BIDs	Business Improvement Districts
BREEAM	Building Research Establishment Environmental Assessment Mechanism
CABE	Commission for Architecture and the Built Environment 2000–
CBD	Central Business District
CIL	Community Infrastructure Levy
CSH	Code for Sustainable Homes
DCfW	Design Commission for Wales
DCLG	Department of Communities and Local Government 2006–2007; now CLG
DETR	Department of the Environment, Transport and the Regions
EH	English Heritage
EP	English Partnerships; now part of HCA 2008
ESRC	The Economic and Social Research Council
HC	Housing Corporation; now part of HCA 2008
HCA	Homes and Communities Agency 2008–
LAA	Local Area Agreements
LDF	Local Development Frameworks 2004–
LPA	Local Planning Authority
LSP	Local Strategic Partnership
NDC	New Deal for Communities 1998–
NSNR	National Strategy for Neighbourhood Review 1998–
ODPM	Office of the Deputy Prime Minister 1999–2006
PAS	Planning Advisory Service
PDG	Planning Delivery Grant
PFI	Private Finance Initiatives
PPG	Planning Policy Guidance Notes 1992–2002
PPS	Planning Policy Statements 2004–
RCEP	Royal Commission on Environmental Pollution
RDA	Regional Development Agency
SCS	Sustainable Community Strategy
SDC	Sustainable Development Commission
SRB	Single Regeneration Budget
UDP	Unitary Development Plan 1992–2004
URC	Urban Regeneration Company 2000–
UTF	Urban Task Force 1998

1 An introduction to the British urban renaissance

John Punter

Introduction

This book examines the urban design dimension of the urban renaissance promoted in England by Lord Rogers' Urban Task Force report of 1999, and the urban design advances that have taken place in the thirteen major cities in the UK since that date.

In this introductory chapter the background to, and recommendations of, the report are introduced alongside the more academic and professional debates which surrounded its launch and subsequent implementation. The report is dissected into four components – design excellence, housing delivery and design, urban environmental management, and local governance and delivery – and the extent to which the recommendations have been realised is assessed. The chapter concludes with the research questions that guide the sixteen city case studies in the book, and which provide the structure for the concluding chapter.

The urban renaissance is an English government policy that has also been influential in Northern Ireland because planning there is still a central government responsibility. It is not Welsh or Scottish policy, but the studies of the Celtic cities – Edinburgh, Glasgow, Cardiff, and Belfast – assess the wider UK influence of the Task Force report on devolved government policy and the planning and design practices in their major cities. Suffice it to say that in both Scotland and Wales the report has had some influence, and their largest cities have been subjected to largely identical development pressures, while their administrations have closely observed the English Core Cities and their promotion of urban renaissance.

Defining urban design and its recent evolution in the UK

Urban design has come to occupy an increasingly prominent role in planning, housing, regeneration and environmental improvement practices in the UK over the last decade. The English government's key policy pronouncement, *Planning Policy Statement* (PPS) *1* now states that 'good design is indivisible from good planning', and that 'high quality and inclusive design . . . should be the aim of all those involved in the development process' (DCLG 2006a: paras 33–35). The Government's definition of urban design, adopted as the foundation for this research, is as follows:

> Urban design is the art of making places for people. It includes the way places work and matters such as community safety, as well as how they look. It concerns the connections between people and places, movement and urban form, nature and the built fabric, and the processes for ensuring successful villages, towns and cities.

Urban design is a key to creating sustainable developments and the conditions for a flourishing economic life, for the prudent use of natural resources and for social progress.

(DETR/CABE 2000: 8)

This is a definition that recognises the increasingly important sustainability agenda, but only hints at important issues such as biodiversity, sustainable drainage, public health and inclusive design. It does not explicitly encompass social inclusion, community participation or management, all of which are becoming key design concerns (RCEP 2007), as this study will confirm.

In this study the primary concern is urban design as public policy (Barnett 1974, 1982), a distinctive element and ethos of planning policy embedded in development plans/frameworks and development control practice (as recognised in the quotations from *PPS 1* above). But urban design also has to be seen by local government as a corporate activity, a way of 'joining up' its diverse functions and injecting a design quality and 'place-making' dimension as it builds highways, pedestrianises streets, calms traffic, furnishes and lights public spaces, conserves green space, creates parks, disposes of land and builds all manner of public facilities. In both these roles urban design is 'second order design' (George 1997): it does not directly design the buildings and spaces or settlements but it shapes the 'decision environments' of all those who are involved in the process, working cross-professionally, collaborating with developers, public agencies and the wider public. In the words of the Urban Task Force 'design is a core problem solving activity that not only determines the quality of the built environment but also delivers many of the instruments for the implementation of the urban renaissance' (UTF 1999a: 39).

Reconstruction, redevelopment, renewal, regeneration, renaissance: the evolution of British urban policy

Where does the urban renaissance fit into recent planning and urban policy? A concise conceptualisation of post-war urban policy describes it as successive decades of reconstruction, revitalisation, renewal, redevelopment, regeneration and renaissance (Roberts and Sykes 2000: 14). This summary reveals some of the key shifts in urban development practices, but it also obscures the complexities of central and local government intervention in the built environment.

The Thatcher years: urban policy under the Conservatives

At the end of the 1970s, with the election of Margaret Thatcher's Conservative Government, urban policy shifted dramatically towards property-led regeneration utilising the Urban Development Corporations and Enterprise Zones to drive new investment. But by the early 1990s the negative externalities of both laissez-faire planning policies and a-social regeneration approaches had forced the Conservative Government to introduce a more plan-led system to refocus development around existing urban centres (see *Planning Policy Guidance Note 6 (PPG6)* in DoE 1996a), and to begin to encourage a shift from private to public modes of transport (see *PPG13* in DoE 1996b). A restatement of urban containment and concentration policies was spurred on by the 1992 household projections for England, which suggested that 4.4 million new homes would be required in England by 2016. A national target of 50 per cent of development on brownfield land was set. In regeneration an emphasis upon community participation, public–private partnership and local empowerment returned, though often not targeted on the areas of greatest social need, and funding was often disbursed by competitive bidding (Cullingworth and Nadin 2006:

366–371). Environment Ministers such as Chris Patten and especially John Gummer asserted the need to embrace urban design as a means of delivering better quality development, and set in motion the production of a national design manual (DETR/CABE 2000).

New Labour and the Third Way

New Labour under Tony Blair came to power in 1997, committed to 'Third Way' politics that sought to find the middle ground between the neoliberal economic and social policies of the Conservatives (deregulation, privatisation and specialist development agency-led) and the Keynesian welfare state (Tiesdell and Allmendinger 2001: 904). The aim was a more caring public policy balancing competitive individualism and personal freedoms with notions of social justice and the creation of a more socially inclusive and engaged community (Giddens 1998: 65). As in the late 1960s, Labour's regeneration aspirations were driven by a desire to address widening inequalities through programmes of social inclusion, neighbourhood renewal and community involvement. However, these were tempered by a strong thrust towards reductions in welfare dependence, downplaying poverty as the main cause of social deprivation (Kearns 2003: 52–54).

A communitarian doctrine underpinned much of New Labour's social welfare and urban policy (Johnstone and Whitehead 2004: 10). The neighbourhood was the 'foundational principle' of urban regeneration, through which anti-social behaviour and poor housing conditions in the most deprived communities could be addressed by the government's Social Exclusion Unit. The wider regeneration of the cities and the delivery of 'sustainable communities' would be pursued through 'urban renaissance' policies (Whitehead 2004: 59–66) espousing the same ethos of vitality, social mix and community in order to encourage and accommodate an influx of more affluent residents into the inner city, though in turn creating obvious social tensions and further implementation challenges (Cochrane 2000).

New Labour had more of a 'big city' focus and a clearer aspiration for the qualities of continental European cities (Rogers and Fischer 1992; Rogers and Power 2000). Whereas their first urban policy moves were to tackle social exclusion and the regeneration of deprived inner-city neighbourhoods, in 1998 the Deputy Prime Minister established the UTF (chaired by the Labour peer and eminent architect Richard Rogers) to devise an urban revival based on 'co-ordinated action [and] the joint principles of design excellence, economic strength, environmental responsibility, good governance and social wellbeing' (UTF 1999a: 3). This gave a massive boost to the urban design dimension of planning and development.

At the same time the government sought to modernise local government and reinvigorate local democracy through an emphasis upon 'citizenship', though it focused far more on the former (service delivery) than the latter (political participation) (Wilson and Game 2006: 353). It created a performance management culture replacing Compulsory Competitive Tendering with Best Value Indicators and later Comprehensive Performance Assessments (Stoker 2005: 86–107; Wilson and Game 2006: 353–375). It sought more dynamic local leadership through the introduction of elected mayors and cabinets, and more community re-engagement through reforms to voting and more extensive public consultation. 'Partnership' and 'joining up' were the keys to a multi dimensional approach to citizen and community needs, along with new powers to ensure community wellbeing and major initiatives on crime and anti-social behaviour to 'civilise' the inner city.

The net result of a very wide range of reforms has been a bewildering array of overlapping urban policy initiatives; frequent changes in programmes, departmental names and responsibilities; and national and local schemes funded by a multiplicity of agencies. New legislation has no sooner been digested than new White or Green papers have proposed more reforms, and all of this legislative and policy development has been set within a performance management and audit culture. Even ministers acknowledge that what was once a 'patchwork quilt' of urban policy has become a 'bowl of spaghetti' (Lord Rooker quoted in Cullingworth and Nadin 2006: 379). The *Guardian* coined the term 'initiativitis' (quoted in Johnstone and Whitehead 2004: 14) to describe the frenzied press releases and policy announcements, the frequent repackaging of policies and the presentation of existing funding streams as new resources. They all became integral to political spin. This state of affairs was perhaps an inevitable result of embarking on major programmes which had ten- to twenty-year time horizons (thirty years in the case of the urban renaissance) whereas political cycles demanded faster responses to public concerns and rapid results 'on the ground'.

The bigger issue, however, was that New Labour came face to face with the impossibility of balancing a 'dynamic capitalist economy, so coveted by the New Right, with the egalitarian city and community-based metropolis desired by the Old Left' (Johnstone and Whitehead 2004: 15; cf. Callinicos 2001: 29) as they continued to 'make obeisance at the shrine of deregulation, liberalism, privatisation, low taxes and the minimal state' (Hutton 1998: 2). By late 2007 this very problem and associated issues was threatening the whole future of the government and indeed the future prosperity of the nation.

Towards an urban renaissance: the agenda of the Urban Task Force

The remit of the UTF was to identify the causes of urban decline and to recommend practical solutions. They were 'to establish a vision for our cities, founded on the principles of design excellence, social wellbeing and environmental responsibility within appropriate delivery, fiscal and legal frameworks' (UTF 2005: 2). The Deputy Prime Minister recognised the potential for an urban renaissance based on the need to accommodate a projected 3.8 million additional households in England by 2021, and the already confirmed 60 per cent brownfield target for new housing. The Task Force Chair stressed the 'need to create the quality of life and vitality that makes urban living desirable', arguing that 'regeneration has to be design-led . . . but to be sustainable . . . [it] has to be placed within its economic and social context' (UTF 1999a: 7). Lord Rogers recognised that social issues vital to regeneration lay outside his remit, but his continental European vision of 'well-designed, more compact and connected cities, with integrated public transport and supporting a range of diverse uses, allowing people to live at close quarters within a sustainable and adaptable urban environment' (UTF 1999a: 8) was always intended to be socially inclusive.

Michael Keith has distilled four principles which underpin the rhetoric and these might be précised as follows:

- by building densely it should be possible to maximise land values;
- by maximising land values it should be possible to levy significant amounts of social value against enhanced profit, and to translate this into social housing;
- a rational planning framework can harness the self interest of profit and the equity of affordable housing to deliver mixed development and communities;
- a sustainable municipal revenue base generated from Section 106 agreements and enhanced

revenue from property and business taxes will fund a high quality public realm and the future re-engineering of the city.

As Keith concluded tersely 'at least this is the script' (2008: 57–58).

The UTF Report included 105 recommendations grouped under ten key headings of urban design, connections, management of the environment, urban regeneration, skills and innovation, planning, land supply, recycling buildings, and finance (UTF 1999a). These are set out in Table 1.1 alongside a very brief headline summary of their achievement drawing on a wide range of evidence. The subsequent *Urban White Paper* (ODPM 2000), which was a much wider statement about government urban policy, gave an explicit response to each UTF recommendation, demurring at only nine of these (mainly fiscal measures relating to taxation of work-place car parking, vacant land, removing Value Added Tax (VAT) on refurbishments, and removing Council Tax exemptions on empty properties – the last introduced more recently). In 2005 many members of the original UTF team collaborated on an independent stock take of achievements six years on. *Towards a Strong Urban Renaissance* (UTF 2005) contained further recommendations designed to 'stimulate public debate and encourage new thinking' and these remain very relevant to future reforms.

Critiques of the Urban Task Force report

The urban renaissance report received a warm welcome from many quarters, notably from architects, planning and urban design professionals, local government and some countryside lobbyists. There was widespread support for the clear articulation of a positive urban agenda (countering decades of English anti-urbanism), for a reassertion of the central role to be played by local government in regeneration (particularly through stronger planning policies), and for an emphasis on community involvement and community development to address deprivation and improve social cohesion (Robson 1999; Amin *et al.* 2000). Some criticised a 'physicalist' urban design view of cities with its limited understanding of the complex social worlds of the city or of the implications of participatory governance (Healey 2004). Even urban designers on the UTF doubted the extent to which the urban renaissance could be 'design-led' as Rogers had suggested, and there was professional recognition that good design was a necessary, though not sufficient, condition for successful urban regeneration (Crookston 2001). There was some suspicion of the proliferation of the new breed of urban design professionals in government bodies and consultancies and their capacity to listen to the community, and debates as to whether a quality public realm was a tool for, or an outcome of, social cohesion (Holden and Iveson 2003). Others questioned the notion of 'sustainable local communities' and whether social mix and local community could be delivered, and at what scale and with what scope (Colomb 2007).

There was widespread criticism in professional, academic and political circles of many of the Report's assumptions and recommendations. Some saw it as a classic restatement of European urban romanticism celebrating the aesthetic, cultural and environmental virtues of the west European city (Amin *et al.* 2000). They argued that it promoted the myth of harmonious inner-city communities rather than the reality of constant struggles over employability, housing affordability, public service quality, security, neighbourhood identity and amenity. Others emphasised the weakness of the economic analysis in the UTF report and argued that the sharp decline of urban employment, and the continuing decentralisation of jobs, would not be reversed by consumption-oriented economies (Turok 1999: 268–269). Some recognised post-war British

Table 1.1 Selected Task Force recommendations and their achievement

Task Force recommendation 1999	Achievement by 1 January 2007
1 Require local authorities to prepare a single strategy for the public realm and open space, dealing with provision, design, management, funding and maintenance	Community strategies to embrace this CABE space developing ideas/good practice New PSA8 introduced 2004 to improve public space Review of Liveability (2006) reports some progress Minimum achievement
2 Introduce a national programme to create comprehensive green pedestrian routes around and/ or across each of our major towns and cities	No specific action on green routes PPG13 (1999): Local Transport Plans (2000) and guidance Safe Routes to School 2003 (£50m) and School Transport Plans Walking and Cycling Action Plan 2004: ambitious targets Three Demonstration Cities: Peterborough, Darlington, Worcester Cycling Cities 2008 Minimum achievement
3 Revise planning and funding guidance to: (a) discourage LPAs from using 'density' and 'overdevelopment' as reasons for refusal (b) presume against excessively low-density urban development; and (c) advise on use of density standards, linked to design quality	PPG3 (2000) advocates densities 30–50 du/ha: average densities of new housing increased to 40 du/ha PPG3 *Better Places to Live* (manual) 2001 PPS3 (2006) retains 30 du/ha minimum, but argues local density policy: significant retreat CABE reports on housing design quality achieved suggest persistence of urban design major failings Significant achievement
4 Introduce a mandatory double performance rating for houses combining a single environmental rating and a single running cost rating so that house-buyers know what they are getting for their money	Energy Performance Certificates in Home Information Pack Mandatory introduction June 2007 in line with EU Directive 2002/91/EC on the Energy Performance of Buildings Major energy initiative introduced 2006: targets carbon neutrality of new residential in 2016 Existing buildings need more attention and incentives for energy efficiency Achieved
5 Make public funding and planning permissions for area regeneration schemes conditional upon the production of an integrated spatial masterplan, recognising that public finance may be required upfront to pay for the masterplanning	EP/HC *Urban Design Compendium* (2001, 2007) CABE *Creating Successful Masterplans* (2004c). Only advice: no requirements, generally poor masterplanning according to CABE Minor achievement
6 and 94 All significant area regeneration projects should be the subject of a design competition. Funds should be allocated in any regeneration funding allocation to meet the public costs of such competitions. Design competitions for all significant public buildings	Used in Millennium Communities Programme Best advice in GLA (Architecture and Urbanism unit) *Commissioning a Sustainable and Well-Designed City* (R94) Wider use of competitions in public building commissions Minor achievement

Table 1.1 (continued) Selected Task Force recommendations and their achievement

Task Force recommendation 1999	Achievement by 1 January 2007
7 Develop and implement a national urban design framework, disseminating key design principles through land use planning and public funding guidance, and introducing a new series of best practice guidelines	PPG1 (1997) revised PPS1 (2005) *By Design* (2000) manual, PPG3 manual (2001) CABE established as National Design Advisory Body (1999) *Safer Cities* (2004) Accessibility *Manual for Streets* (2007) Achieved
8 Building on the Millennium Communities initiative, undertake a series of government-sponsored demonstration projects, adopting an integrated approach to design-led regeneration of different types of urban neighbourhood	Millennium Community Experiments *Preparing Design Codes* (2006) manual Minor achievement
9 Establish local architecture centres in each of our major cities. There should be minimum network of twelve properly funded centres, fulfilling a mix of common objectives and local specialisms	Achieved
10, 12 and 13 Place local transport plans on a statutory footing. Develop explicit targets for reducing car journeys and increasing year on year the proportion of trips made on foot, bicycle and public transport. Prioritise walk/cycle/public transport, ensure connections. Increase their share of transport investment to 65 per cent: allow RDAs to fund transport	Achieved but targets not being met in any locations
11 Introduce home zones in partnership with local communities, based on a robust legal framework, using tested street designs, reduced speed limits and traffic-calming measures.	Transport Act 2000 empowers LAs Nine pilots: £30m funding (2003): Pilot Clear Zones introduced to reduce traffic in more deprived centres Minor achievement
19–20 Set a maximum standard of one car parking space per dwelling for all new urban residential development. Charge all forms of private non-residential car parking	PPG3 (2000) advises 1.5 cp/du as maximum PPS3 (2006) retreats and advises local car parking standards *Manual for Streets* (2007) replaces Design Bulletin 32 and initiates design-led road layout planning: major advance EP best practice advice on car parking *Not achieved* (but much better design advice)
21–29 Increase the resources for urban environmental management, assign strategic role to LAs, establish a single point of contact, create town improvement zones and pilot new models of neighbourhood management, increase sanctions and fines and review performance indicators	Funding increased by 3 per cent for first three years, and management experiments via the NSNR. Performance indicators reformed. Good progress with park improvement. Mixed success with public realm: funding inadequate. Varied achievement – minor to significant

Task Force recommendation 1999	*Achievement by 1 January 2007*
30–31, 36–37 New commitment to regeneration: combined government spending. UPAs and partnerships for regeneration; special powers/incentives for neighbourhood renewal; establish housing regeneration companies; new UPA committees to speed decisions	Green Paper *Quality and Choice: Decent Homes for All* Half of the unfit homes upgraded 2005 (1 million) Trebled Housing Corporation budget 1997–2007 Increased investment in social housing (up 57 per cent) Minimum achievement
32–35 Establish urban regeneration companies, Housing regeneration companies and LA regeneration companies as single delivery regeneration vehicles	(R26) URCs established including three in Scotland and one each in Wales and NI by 2005 but lack requisite powers HCA to start work in 2009 combining social housing and regeneration powers in single national agency Some achievement
41 Produce detailed planning policy guidance to support the drive for an urban renaissance: ensure policies are implemented in RSS, LDFs and planning decisions; enable full involvement of local communities in the urban planning process	PPS1 Delivering Sustainable Development PPS3 Housing PPS6 Planning for Town Centres PPS12 Local Development Frameworks PPS13 Transport Achieved
42 Strengthen regional planning guidance on integrated spatial planning and accessibility, brownfield, etc.	Made statutory 2004 and new PPS11: spatial vision with integrated regional transport strategy and housing strategy and implementation plan plus sustainability appraisal. CABE advice on RSS design content. Achieved
43 Simplify local development plans with a stronger emphasis on strategy to create a more flexible basis for planning. The plans should avoid including detailed site-level policies	PPG12 (2000) then Planning and Compensation Act (2004) institutes new but more complex development plan system Reforms proposed in White Paper 2007 Achieved
44 Achieve comprehensive development plan coverage in England by the end of 2002. Where necessary, government regional offices should work alongside underperforming local planning authorities to ensure that the deadline is met	LDF production rates have slowed further Not achieved (new monitoring and performance targets introduced)
45 Support a more streamlined planning process in urban priority areas by enabling the Secretary of State to take action against authorities that consistently fail to deliver planning permissions within a reasonable time period	Improvements to speed of processing through 'Best Value' targets and PDG incentives. Performance still very uneven across LPAs but overall major improvement: 75 per cent of all LPAs meet all three targets Major achievement
46 Require local planning authorities to conduct a review of all local rules, standards and procedures to enhance urban development	Deregulation of householder applications impacted 2008 Some achievement

Table 1.1 (continued) Selected Task Force recommendations and their achievement

Task Force recommendation 1999	Achievement by 1 January 2007
47 Devolve detailed planning policies for neighbourhood regeneration, including urban priority areas, into more flexible and targeted area plans, based upon the production of a spatial masterplan and the full participation of local people. Strengthen SPG where necessary	Elements included within new LDFs (see R43) Guidance now available (see R5) Not achieved
48 Review regional employment land and accelerate release for housing	Addressed through regional guidance Not achieved
49–51 Revise and relax national guidance on the use of planning agreements; 'fast track' process for the conclusion of agreements; standardise system of impact fees for local environmental improvements and community facilities. Consider environmental impact fees	Await specific proposals for CIL in 2008 for implementation 2009 No achievement
52–53 Review the mechanisms by which LPAs use planning gain to secure affordable 'social' housing to ensure mixed-tenure neighbourhoods; enable more mixed income housing projects to proceed	Taken forward in PPG3/PPS3. Research into the use by LPAs of their powers to seek affordable housing contributions has been commissioned and good practice guidance will be published 2008. Some achievement: 40 per cent of schemes deliver affordable component. Trebled Housing Corporation budget 1997–2007: extra 10,000 social homes annually. Low-cost home ownership schemes 230,000, 1997–2005. Design for Manufacture low-cost homes scheme 2005 Belatedly achieved but problems and shortages persist
54 Establish clear procedures under the proposed 'plan, monitor and manage' system for assessing future housing demand, to ensure the early correction of an emerging undersupply or oversupply of housing.	Taken forward through PPG3 and 11, PPS3 and regional planning guidance Sustainable Communities Plan prioritised supply increases Achieved
55 Oblige all LPAs to carry out regular urban capacity studies on a consistent basis	Taken forward through PPG3/PPS3 Achieved
56 Formally adopt a sequential approach to the release of land and buildings for housing, supported by a system of regional and subregional reconciliation of housing needs and demand. Planning guidance should specify monitoring procedures for every LPA to apply	PPG3 and PPS3 Achieved

Task Force recommendation 1999	Achievement by 1 January 2007
57–62 Set ambitious targets for the proportion of new housing to be developed on recycled brownfield land in urban areas where housing demand is currently low; remove allocations of greenfield land for housing from development plans where no longer consistent with planning policy; retain presumption against development on designated green belt; inventories and increased release of public vacant land	Taken forward through PPG3/PPS3 72 per cent achieved by 2004 Achieved Green belts currently under review
64–71 Vacant land taxation and foreclosures, temporary uses facilitated, compulsory purchase reforms and resolve contaminated land glitches, revolving funds for land assembly	Compulsory purchase being used again but still difficult Financial accounting frameworks have made land assembly more difficult No achievement
72–78 Improve environmental regulation systems for land, water, waste and agree standards, minimise risk, pilot condition statements, clean-up campaigns, enforce liability on owners who add to contamination	Landfill Directive has increased costs. Contaminated land legislation still lacks comprehensive guidance and appropriate and economic thresholds significantly increasing costs. Remediation allowances have been provided and some simplification of licenses Some achievement but increased costs
79–80 Maintain empty property and market unpopular housing	No statutory duty introduced on empty homes. Decent Homes for All and housing market renewal areas market unpopular housing Some achievement
81 Introduce new measures to encourage the restoration and use of historic buildings left empty by their owners: PPG15 review of building regulations and an end to the business rate exemptions on empty listed buildings	PPS15 awaited Not achieved
82 Review and enhance the role of civic amenity societies in planning the reuse of historic buildings and in securing regeneration objectives	Heritage White Paper 2007 promises more public involvement in designations and pre-application discussions Not achieved
83 Facilitate the conversion of more empty space over shops into flats by providing additional public assistance	£80m package to encourage conversions including tax relief Significant achievement
84 Harmonise VAT rates at a zero rate in respect of new building, and conversions and refurbishments	Rejected by Treasury Not achieved

Table 1.1 (continued) Selected Task Force recommendations and their achievement

Task Force recommendation 1999	Achievement by 1 January 2007
85–86 Provisions for increasing the resources for local government including allowing Council Tax on empty homes, review of LA spending formula, longer-term spending strategies, retention of proportion of the Council Tax and business rate uplift. Renaissance Fund for repairs	Still largely under consideration although Council Tax on empty homes in 2007 budget. Neighbourhood Renewal Fund changed aspects of the funding formula. Better use of EBMOs to reduce empty homes Very minor achievement
87–91 Establish new public–private investment funds for regeneration projects, pilot PFI on estate renewal, new instruments for investment, tax incentives for regeneration sites/buildings	Private investment limited by shortfall in public investment First regional regeneration investment company established in East Midlands. Evidence-based research has demonstrated good returns Minor achievement
92–93 Include regeneration funding in annual Comprehensive Spending Review. Create PSA for urban renaissance	Disconnection of regeneration funding by agencies and government offices limits effectiveness
95–98 Review government's LA spending formulae, provide longer-term capital finance, funds for school building. Allow LAs to recycle Council/Business Tax uplift in regeneration areas	No action by central government on major reforms, though Lyons Review and other reports have affirmed their desirability. No achievement
99–102 Combine Single Regeneration Budget with EP land and property funds, give RDAs flexible funds, simplify funding, review Lottery Fund impacts	Disconnection of regeneration funding by agencies and government offices limits effectiveness. Formation of English Communities links regeneration and social housing together. RDAs? Minor achievement
103–105 Enable housing stock transfer via ALMOs, incentivise more mixed social housing, new home improvement loans for private owners in regeneration areas	> 50 per cent of social housing now owned by housing associations. Stock transfers (248) and ALMOs (44) in majority of urban LAs: twelve Pathfinder Housing Market Renewal projects in the north tackle areas of market collapse Significant achievement

Notes
ALMO, arm's-length management organisation; CABE, Commission for Architecture and the Built Environment; CIL, Community Infrastructure Levy; EBMO, Empty Buildings Management Order; EP, English Partnerships, now part of HCA, Homes and Communities Agency 2008; GLA, Greater London Assembly; PDG, Planning Delivery Grant; PFI, private finance initiative; PPG, Planning Policy Guidance Notes 1992–2002; PPS, Planning Policy Statement; PSA, Public Service Agreement; LA, local authority; LDF, local development framework; LPA, local planning authority; NSNR, National Strategy for Neighbourhood Renewal; RDA, Regional Development Agency; RSS, Regional Spatial Strategy; SPG, Supplementary Planning Guidance; UPA, urban priority area; URC, Urban Regeneration Company.

planning's familiar rhetoric of 'containment' of urban sprawl and 'protection of the countryside', and wondered about the equity implications of the promotion of an 'urban idyll' as a counter-weight to the longstanding rural idyll (Hoskins and Tallon 2004).

Other critics argued that the UTF report ignored the essentially suburban culture and housing preferences of the English (Oc 2002; Price 2002) and the need to build more compact (New Urbanist) new suburbs in southern England (Hall 2002). Some saw the UTF report as a 'gentrifier's charter' (Lees 2003), promoting the return of the middle classes to the city to rebuild neighbourhoods, generate consumption-led jobs, revive sociability, create a café culture and improve local amenity, while simultaneously inflating house prices and deepening social exclusion. Others questioned the notion that good design would attract people back to the city when the primary reasons they had left were access to good state schools, urban crime rates, and race relations (Williams 1999). Many saw architectural determinism at the heart of the urban renaissance project, particularly perhaps the idea that 'compact city' living would reduce car use and deliver more energy efficient and less polluted cities and suburbs (Haughton 1999). Others posited the counter view that the proposed densification of cities and suburbs would undermine urban sustainability by reducing urban green space and residential amenity (Hall 1999; Lock 1999).

Perhaps Allison Ravetz best encapsulated the broadly sympathetic, yet critical, reception of the report with the observation that:

> much as I savour good design and would like to share the report's pious belief that it is 'essential for successful social, economic and environmental regeneration', history reminds me that environmental quality is the result rather than a determinant of a well functioning society.
>
> (1999: 279)

Despite the numerous references to individual European cities in the UTF report, it did not draw a great deal on the urban policy work which had taken place at European level during the 1990s. This includes the European Commission's Expert Group on the Urban Environment (a forum in which the UTF report was discussed), the Member States' Urban Exchange Initiative (in which the Department of the Environment, Transport and the Regions (DETR) was fully involved), and work leading up to the Commission's adoption of its Framework for Action on sustainable urban development (Mills 1998), which underpinned subsequent European funding for urban regeneration. In making its recommendations the Task Force, it seems, was largely unaware of – or simply discounted – EU-wide policy measures supportive of its cause, including a raft of legislation relating to the environment. Moreover, the availability of substantial EU funding for regeneration received only a passing mention, and the opportunity to promote EU programmes for cooperation and exchange of experience was missed.

Delivering on UTF recommendations

We now turn to an assessment of what has been delivered in terms of the Task Force's agenda on urban design, housing, the public realm and governance. Reference is made to the key design recommendations made in the UTF Report, and the assessment is amplified by reference to the partially reconstituted Task Force's 'independent report based on the personal experiences of . . . members' (UTF 2005). There are four dominant themes. Under *design excellence* the creation of a national design framework, new style development plans, reforms to development control, and new forms of design guidance (including masterplanning, residential street design and design coding) are all considered. *Housing delivery* issues include supply and affordability, urban compactness, the creation of sustainable communities, the delivery of mixed communities, the design quality of both medium- and high-density housing, and the whole question of sustainable construction. *Public realm and urban environmental quality* concerns are linked through the drive to improve urban liveability, through public realm strategies, better street and public space design, traffic management and transport and green infrastructure provision. Finally, under *governance and delivery*, issues of local government leadership and resources, infrastructure and regeneration funding and the shortage of design/delivery skills are all discussed.

Table 1.1 outlines selected Task Force recommendations that are most relevant to design and planning and assesses their level of achievement. It acts as a reference point for the discussion of all individual recommendations. Table 1.2 lists all key legislation, reports and policy/guidance that impinge upon the renaissance and have shaped planning and urban regeneration since 1999, to allow the reader to understand the broader evolution of policy and practice over the last decade as the renaissance agenda has been reshaped.

Design excellence and the national urban design framework

In line with Recommendation 7 (R7) (see Table 1.1 for selected UTF recommendations), the government has developed *a national urban design framework*, which sets out the principles, processes and practices through which national design standards can be raised. Where previously the Circulars and PPG Notes had preached restraint and non-intervention in design matters, now the PPS 1 encouraged local authorities to seek 'high quality and inclusive design' (DCLG 2006a: para 33), a message reiterated in subsequent PPSs on biodiversity, open space, housing and town centres. A proactive approach to design was driven by comprehensive design advice founded on the manual *By Design* (DETR/CABE 2000) and reinforced by detailed statements on access (ODPM 2003a), safer places (ODPM/Home Office 2004) and residential street design (DfT/DCLG 2007). Much valuable advice has been produced by the Commission for Architecture and the Built Environment (CABE) founded by the government in 1999 (and run by the former UTF Secretary for the first five years), which has become indispensable to the development and delivery of best practice in urban design. CABE's key advice includes collaborations with English Heritage on contextual design in conservation areas and on tall buildings policy (EH/CABE 2002, 2003 (updated 2007); POS/EH/CABE 2002), as well as guidance developed from design review (CABE 2004a, 2005a). These documents have been supplemented by contributions from the design and planning professions (Carmona *et al.* 2002; UDG 2002) and English Partnerships, the latter's *Urban Design Compendium* (EP/HC 2007) being especially valuable for its second volume on implementing design quality. If local authorities have the political will to raise design standards they now have unequivocal government support and comprehensive advice on which to found their efforts.

Important work has also been done to demonstrate 'the value of urban design' (CABE 2001, 2003a, 2006c) and 'quality regeneration' (EP/HC 2007) to both the private and public sectors. Both English Partnerships and the Housing Corporation (HC 2007) (now absorbed into the new Homes and Communities Agency 2008) have adopted substantive design quality standards, the former's embracing quality places, quality buildings (with Building Research Establishment Environmental Assessment Mechanism (BREEAM) sustainability standards), construction quality and project delivery, including community engagement and long-term management (EP 2007a).

Table 1.2 The urban renaissance agenda and government policy streams 1997–2009

	EU	UK regional/local government	Planning	Design	Housing	Urban Policy and regeneration	Environmental sustainability and transport
1997	Towards an Urban Agenda in the EU (CEC)	Labour government elected (May 1997)	PPG1 Policy and Principles (revision) (issued under Conservatives)	Urban Design Alliance established (UDAL)	Millennium Communities Programme (ODPM)	Social Exclusion Unit established A National Strategy for Neighbourhood Renewal	UK National Air Quality Strategy
1998	5th Framework 1998–2002: City of Tomorrow and Cultural Heritage Sustainable Urban Development in the EU: Framework for Action (CEC) Urban Exchange Initiative	Modernising Local Government: Local Democracy and Community Leadership Enhancing Public Participation in Local Government (DETR) Building Partnerships for Prosperity	Planning for the Communities of the Future Circ. 6/98 Future of Regional Planning Guidance (DETR) Planning for Sustainable Development (DETR)	Places, Streets and Movement (DETR/DoT)	Circ. 6/98 Planning and Affordable Housing	New Deal for Communities: 10-year Programme Neighbourhood Renewal Fund Regional Development Agencies Act Action Zones for Health, Education, Employment	New Deal for Transport Sustainable Local Communities for the 21st Century: LA21 Strategy
1999	Proposed Community Framework for Cooperation to promote sustainable urban development European Spatial Development Perspective Urban Exchange Initiative II Sustainability Urban Form	Local Leadership: Local Choice	PPG13 Transport PPG12 Development Plans PPG11 Regional Strategies PPG10 Planning and Waste Management	Commission for Architecture and the Built Environment (CABE) established	Household Projections (DETR)	Opportunity for All: Tackling Poverty and Social Exclusion (DSS) Towards an Urban Renaissance (ODPM)	Transport: The Way Forward (DETR) A Better Quality of Life: A Strategy for SD in the UK Quality of Life Counts: Indicators for SD (DETR)

Table 1.2 (continued) The urban renaissance agenda and government policy streams 1997–2009

	EU	UK regional/local government	Planning	Design	Housing	Urban Policy and regeneration	Environmental sustainability and transport
2000	Structural Funds Objective 1 and 2 – 2006 Urban II: Framework for Action – 2006	Local Government Act Freedom of Information Act Preparing Community Strategies: Draft Guidance (Local Strategic Partnerships)	PPG 3 Housing Residential Development on Greenfield Land Direction	Survey of Urban Design skills in Local Government Training for Urban Design By Design: Urban Design in the Planning System Urban Design Compendium (EP/HC) Better Public Buildings	Quality and Choice: A Decent House for All (DETR) Housing Market Renewal Pathfinder	New Deal for Communities: Delivering Change Better Town and Cities Public Service Agreements (eight targets established) Business Improvement Districts introduced	TRANSPORT ACT Transport 2010: the 10 Year Plan Pollution Control and Prevention Act Not Too Difficult: Economic Instruments to Support SD (UKRTSD) Sustainable Urban Drainage Manual (CIRIA)
2001	Euro Governance (EC) White Paper 428 (CEC) A Sustainable Europe for a Better World: EU SD Strategy ('Gothenburg')		Green Paper: Planning: Delivering a Fundamental Change (ODPM)	Better Public Buildings Campaign (PM) Better Places to Live: by Design (PPG 3) Urban Design Skills (CABE survey) The Value of Urban Design (CABE)		Our Towns and Cities: The Future: An Implementation Plan (ODPM) A New Commitment to Neighbourhood Renewal: (Cabinet Office) Local Strategic Partnerships established ODPM Urban Policy Unit set up Neighbourhood Renewal Unit established	Home Zones Funding

continued overleaf

Table 1.2 (continued) The urban renaissance agenda and government policy streams 1997–2009

	EU	UK regional/local government	Planning	Design	Housing	Urban Policy and regeneration	Environmental sustainability and transport
2002	Environment 2010: Our Future: Our Choice (CEC) 6th Environmental Action Programme 2002–2012 (7 themes) CIVITAS 2002–2006 Cleaner and better transport in cities (19 cities)	Participatory Plans for Sustainable Communities (ODPM)	Sustainable Communities: Delivering through Planning (ODPM) Planning Obligations: delivering a Fundamental Change (ODPM) PPG17 Open Space	Building for Life Manifesto (CABE etc.) Paving the Way (CABE) Building in Context (EH/CABE) Protecting Design Quality in Planning (CABE) Better Public Buildings Program	Community Chest		Green Spaces Better Places (DTLR)
2003	Urban Policy Working Group: Strategies for Financing Urban Regeneration	Local Government Act (Prudential Borrowing)	The Relationship between Community Strategies and Local Development Frameworks (ODPM)	Planning and Access for Disabled People Councillors Guide to Urban Design The Value of Housing Design and Layout Make Space (all CABE) Guidance on Tall Buildings (EH/CABE)	Sustainable Communities: Building for the Future (ODPM) Building Sustainable Communities: Actions for Housing Market Renewal (CABE)		Our Energy: Our Future: Creating a Low Carbon Economy (ODPM) SC Liveability Fund (ODPM) Accessible National Greenspace Standards (EN)

Table 1.2 (continued) The urban renaissance agenda and government policy streams 1997–2009

	EU	UK regional/local government	Planning	Design	Housing	Urban Policy and regeneration	Environmental sustainability and transport
2004	Towards a Thematic Strategy on the Urban Environment 60 (EC) Urban Audit 2004 report (189 cities)	The Future of Local Government: A 10 Year Strategy (ODPM) Local Area Agreements Pilots Community Involvement in Planning (ODPM)	Planning And Compulsory Purchase Act Review of Heritage Protection (DCMS) Compulsory Purchase and Compensation Procedure PPS12 LDFs PPS11 RSS PPS22 Renewable Energy	Safer Places (Home Office/ODPM) Local Authority Design Champions (CABE) Creating Successful Masterplans (CABE) Circ 5/94: Planning out Crime	Housing Act Barker Review of Housing Supply (Treasury) The Northern Way: Housing Market Renewal	Single Community Programme (NRU) Making it Happen. Core Cities (ODPM) Urban Regeneration Companies Act Our Cities are Back (ODPM)	Biodiversity by Design (TCPA) Walking and Cycling Action Plan (DfT) The Future for Transport (DFT) Green Space Strategies (CABE) Planning and Climate Change: A Guide to Better Practice Cleaner, Safer, Greener Communities (ODPM) Egan Review Skills for Sustainable Communities
2005	Review of the EU SD Strategy (Directorate General Environment) CIVITAS II 2005–2009 17 cities Bristol Accord on Sustainable Communities Urban Housing Intergroup: promotes European Charter for Housing	Citizen Engagement and Public Services Why Neighbourhoods Matter (HO)	PPS 6 Planning for Town Centres Circ 5/2005 Planning Obligations PPS9 Biodiversity and Good Planning PPS3 Updates Public Sector Minimum Standards for Procurement	Design Coding: Testing its use (ODPM) Design Quality and PFI Making Design Policy Work Start with the Park Creating Successful Neighbourhoods Housing Audits (all CABE)	SC: Homes for All (ODPM) New Growth Points Initiative Code for Sustainable Homes Barker Review: Interim (Treasury) SC: People, Places, Prosperity: A 5 Year Plan (ODPM) SC: Delivering Sustainable Communities (ODPM)	Urban Task Force: Independent Progress Report	Academy for Sustainable Communities established Securing the Future: Delivering UK Sustainability Strategy (DEFRA)

continued overleaf

Table 1.2 (continued) The urban renaissance agenda and government policy streams 1997–2009

	EU	UK regional/local government	Planning	Design	Housing	Urban Policy and regeneration	Environmental sustainability and transport
2006	Thematic strategy on the urban Environment 718 (CEC) Urban Sprawl in Europe: EEA Cohesion policy and cities: the urban contribution 385 (CEC)	A Framework for City Regions Strong and Prosperous Communities Loosening the Leash (APUDG)	PPS13 Transport PPS1 Delivering Sustainable Development PPS3 Housing Government Response on Planning Gain Supplement Biodiversity duty on public bodies	Preparing Design Codes (DCLG) The Principles of Inclusive Design Transforming our Streets Design and Access Statements Design Champions (all CABE)	Barker Review Final Report (Treasury) From Decent Homes to Sustainable Communities Callcutt Review of House Building Delivery Delivering Affordable Housing	State of the English Cities Reports (ODPM/DCLG)	New Building Regulations (Part L Energy Saving) Stern Review of Economics of Climate Change Code for Sustainable Homes Enhancing Urban Green Space NAO (ODPM) The Eddington Transport Study Green Infrastructure (RCEP)
2007	First State of European Cities Report URBACT II: funds exchange between cities Leipzig Charter on Sustainable European cities adopted by ministers Green Paper on Adaptation to Climate Change (0354) (CEC)	Place Shaping: A Shared Ambition for the Future of Local Government (Lyons)		Manual for Sheets DFT			

Table 1.2 (continued) The urban renaissance agenda and government policy streams 1997–2009

EU	UK regional/local government	Planning	Design	Housing	Urban Policy and regeneration	Environmental sustainability and transport
		Heritage Review (DCMS) Planning for a Sustainable Future (CLG) PPS1 Climate change additions PPS 4 Economic Development PPS 12 LDFs revised Shaping and Delivering Tomorrow's Places (RTPI) Changes to Permitted Development In Depth Review of Sustainable Community Policy (UKSDC)	Manual for Streets (DFT/CLG) Urban Design Compendium Vol. 2 (EP/HC) Sustainable Development, Climate Change and the Built Environment Paved with Gold: the Real Value of Street Design (all CABE) Revised Guidance on Tall Buildings (EH/CABE) Actions for Housing Growth (CLG)	Decent Homes for All Homes for the Future (Green Paper) Revised Housing Projections Future Role for Social Housing Delivering Affordable Housing New Growth Points Initiative		Carbon Challenge: Zero Carbon Homes PPS1 Supplement: Climate Change Building Regulations: Energy efficiency requirements The Urban Environment (RCEP)

continued overleaf

Table 1.2 (continued) The urban renaissance agenda and government policy streams 1997–2009

	EU	UK regional/local government	Planning	Design	Housing	Urban Policy and regeneration	Environmental sustainability and transport
2008	DG Environment launch European green capital award	Empowerment White Paper	Killian Pretty Review Ten ecotowns announced Draft Heritage Bill: delayed Planning Reform Bill proceeding	Code for Sustainable Homes L3 mandatory for grant-aided homes Housing and Regeneration Act (implements Green Paper)	Homes and Communities Agency established (EP/HC/ASC)	Manchester congestion charge rejected	
2009	2nd State of European Cities Report	Community Infrastructure Levy introduced					London western congestion zone rescinded

Notes
APUDG, All Party Urban Development Group; ASC, Academy for Sustainable Communities; CABE, Commission for Architecture and the Built Environment; CEC, Commission of the European Communities; CIRIA, Construction Industries Research and Intelligence Association; CIVITAS, CIty-VITAlity-Sustainability; DCLG, Department of Communities and Local Government 2006–2007, now CLG; DCMS, Department of Culture, Media and Sports; DETR, Department of the Environment, Transport and the Regions; DFT, Department for Transport; DTLR, Department for Transport, Local Government and the Regions; DoT, Department of Transport; DSS, Department of Social Services; EEA, European Environment Agency; EN, English Nature; EP, English Partnerships now part of HCA 2008; HC, Housing Corporation now part of HCA 2008; HO, Home Office; LDF, Local Development Framework; NAO, National Audit Office; ODPM, Office of the Deputy Prime Minister; PPG, Planning Policy Guidance Notes 1992–2002; PPS, Planning Policy Statement; RCEP, Royal Commission on Environmental Pollution; RSS, Regional Spatial Strategy; RTPI, Royal Town Planning Institute; SC, Sustainable Communities; SD, Sustainable Development; UKRTSD, United Kingdom Round Table on Sustainable Development.

The foundation for urban design as public policy has to be *the development plan system* (R41–R44). In England the government has instituted Regional Spatial Strategies to shape the pattern of regional development, creating a role for strategic urban design (CABE 2004b) that needs further development. Under a new system for local spatial planning established in 2004, every English local authority must establish a Sustainable Community Strategy (SCS) setting out the strategic vision for the place, and prepare a Local Development Framework (LDF) in line with this strategy. Central to the LDF is a visionary Core Strategy for future development. In the new system the focus is on action plans for areas of change, but less attention is paid to detailed development (and design) control. So far the rate of production and content of Core Strategies has been disappointing, and they have often lacked both vision and strategy. So, by November 2008, far from having a situation where all English local authorities had delivered new LDFs (R42), only thirty-four had their Core Strategies declared sound by the Planning Inspectorate, about one tenth of the total (Planning Inspectorate 2008).

The implementation tools for delivering large scale regeneration have received considerable attention. There has been much good advice (CABE 2004c) and valuable experimentation with *masterplanning* (R5) as a means of securing improved design. Close attention has been paid to participation, design preparation, economic feasibility and implementation issues, with the introduction of design coding (CABE 2004d; DCLG 2006b) to strengthen quality control, particularly on larger scale, multi-phased developments. The UTF will have been disappointed with the limited use of design competitions (R6), but these should always be used selectively. Regrettably design briefs are still poorly developed and neglected as a tool when they could underpin a positive, proactive approach to design control (see Hall 2007).

Great progress has been made in speeding up *development control decision-making* (R45), with 71 per cent of local authorities now meeting government targets, a result in part of judicious use of Planning Delivery Grant (PDG) as an incentive (DCLG 2007a). The government has recently moved to reduce control on minor development (R46) to free up resources for a better service on major applications. But there remain deep concerns about the time that development control officers have to offer pre-application discussions and to 'add value' to applications, and whether enough of them have the design and negotiation skills needed routinely to 'add value' in design terms (R38–R40). A haemorrhaging of talent from local authorities to planning consultancies has weakened the public sector's application improvement and negotiation capacity (Holden and Iveson 2003: 66–67; RIBA 2007). National, regional and local design review panels, design champions, large application teams such as the Advisory Team for Large Applications Service (ATLAS) and other measures are all being deployed to address the skills deficit, some with local and even national success (PAS 2006). Again CABE has provided valuable advice on design for both controllers and councillors and promoted the idea of design champions to create a stronger design culture in planning and development processes (CABE 2002a, 2003b, 2006b).

The national urban design framework has made huge strides over the last eight years, fully meeting all the requirements set out by the UTF. The problem is that the majority of local authorities lack commitment to, and are unwilling or unable to staff and implement these best practices on the scale required to make a major difference to design quality. Whether this is the case in the major cities will be explored in subsequent chapters.

Housing supply, affordability, quality and sustainability: policy innovations and some changed priorities

The UTF's housing recommendations addressed only a specific subset of national housing policies. Their focus was the accommodation (by 2024) of 3.8 million new households in existing built-up areas where new residents would revitalise and diversify declining communities. There was a strong commitment to better designed, more energy efficient housing in higher density, mixed tenure neighbourhoods served by public transport. Other recommendations elaborated on New Labour's social inclusion and area regeneration initiatives that preceded the UTF report, notably the New Deal for Communities (NDC) (SEU 1998) and the 2001 National Strategy for Neighbourhood Renewal (NSNR). Particularly important were the UTF commitments to 'mixed communities' and improving the supply of affordable housing.

As regards *housing delivery*, many of the UTF's key aspirations have been met in quantitative if not necessarily qualitative terms. Seventy-four per cent of housing development now takes place on brownfield land (R57), while average densities have increased to forty-one dwelling units per hectare (R3) (DCLG 2007a). PPG3 (DETR 2000a) was the critical document prioritising brownfield urban sites and implementing a sequential approach to the release of housing land (R55–R56) and a 'plan, monitor, manage' approach to delivery (R54). Restraints on higher density development were removed (R3), but while good advice was provided on the design and control of medium-density development (ODPM/CABE 2001), the particular requirements of high-density development were neglected (R3). PPG3 proved to be very effective in securing rapid implementation of denser forms of housing development (Hull 2004). However, the government has recently back-tracked on its drive for higher average densities in PPS 3 (DCLG 2006c), leaving it to local discretion, while rejecting the targets of 75 per cent brownfield and forty dwellings per hectare minimum density proposed in the second UTF report (UTF 2005). This is because of fears that adopting these targets could slow down overall house building rates and reduce the supply of family housing, an argument made by Peter Hall in his critically important dissenting note to the second UTF Report (UTF 2005: 19). The government has also softened its stance on reducing car parking standards, contrary to UTF recommendations (R19).

A major government effort has been made to *regenerate existing housing* (R30–R31), and particularly to improve the quality of social housing and the services and amenities of the most deprived housing estates, which was New Labour's first urban priority. One million social housing units had been brought up to the new 'decent homes' standard by 2005, and eighty-eight of the most deprived areas have benefited from intensive neighbourhood renewal schemes 'joining up' housing investment with joblessness, health, education/skills and community safety programmes, though many of these have not yet implemented plans for physical transformation (Gallent and Tewdwr-Jones 2006). The UTF's goal of *socially mixed communities* and estates, and particularly the desegregation of large social housing estates, by levering in private house building (R103–R105), has been a major government priority, but it has also been controversial and its notions of mix ambiguous (Colomb 2007). Desegregation of social housing is widely recognised as an important step towards reducing social exclusion (Kintrea 2007), but it is acceptable only as long as an adequate supply of affordable housing is assured, and this is far from the case across much of the south and east of England, in particular. How such estates are redesigned, whether there is genuine consultation and partnership, how careful is project management, how extensive are improvements to community facilities and services, and how well different tenures are integrated are all critical issues (R47) (Bailey 2007).

As regards *housing affordability* the UTF recommended a review of Section 106 agreements as a means of improving the delivery of affordable housing (R52–R53) and ensuring more mixed communities, and there is clearly scope to dramatically extend their use on smaller scale development and in all local planning authorities (LPA) (Whitehead 2007). The government has relied heavily on the private sector to supply affordable housing (it now provides about half of all such supply) but it has taken a long time to recognise that it needs to boost the supply of social housing more directly, recently promising that at least a third of all annual production will be affordable by 2010 (70,000 units), and two thirds of this will be social housing (DCLG 2007b).

The UTF recognised the need to improve the *energy efficiency of housing* (R4) but not the urgency for such improvement. After several false starts, the government embarked on a much more ambitious programme of energy efficient housing construction, some of this driven by the requirements of EU legislation (e.g. Home Energy Certificates). The Code for Sustainable Homes (CSH) (DCLG 2006d) aims to deliver all new housing to zero carbon standards (in energy consumption terms) in three stages by 2016, an extremely ambitious target. Social housing has to meet the first stage standards immediately. The responsibility has been placed on the house builders to deliver this carbon reduction, passing on the cost to house-buyers.

Improving the *quality of housing design* was at the heart of the UTF's aspirations. The comprehensive housing audits completed by CABE (2004e, 2005b, 2007a) across England revealed that less than a fifth of all the medium-density schemes surveyed met what experts within the industry, community and professions considered to be a good standard across a wide range of urban design factors, and over a quarter were classed as poor (see Table 1.3). There has undoubtedly been an increase in the number of exemplar schemes, and some house builders are

Table 1.3 CABE evaluation of new housing in the English regions 2004–2005.

	Very good (BfL > 80%)	Good (BfL > 70%)	Average (BfL > 50%)	Poor (BfL < 50%)	Survey date
London	15	6	66	15	2003
South-East	3	18	54	24	2003
East	3	9	60	27	2003
South-West	0	6	76	18	2005
East Midlands	3	0	42	55	2005
West Midlands	3	12	38	47	2005
Yorkshire and Humber	0	0	86	14	2004
North-East	3	3	63	31	2004
North-West	7	7	62	24	2004
Totals (%)	5	13	53	29	

Source: CABE (2004d, 2005b, 2007a).

Notes
The Building for Life (BfL) assessment criteria awarded points in the range +3 to –3 for each of sixteen audit criteria embracing sense of place, appropriation of enclosure, safety, legibility, exploitation of site assets, avoidance of highway dominance, promotion of non-car travel, car parking, servicing, movement, integration, bespoke design, architectural quality, public amenity, public realm quality adaptability and access to public transport.

Those in the poor category are classed as unworthy of planning consent. Total sample size is 293.

Assessments made by urban design specialists through site visits. BfL methodology now includes 20 questions with one point for compliance and zero for non-compliance, the total converted into a percentage score.

committed to achieving consistently higher standards of design, while a number of niche developers have emerged for whom urban design quality is a given (Biddulph *et al.* 2004). However, many volume builders do not aim above design mediocrity, perhaps because housing demand has so far outstripped supply (at least until the onset of the 'credit crunch' in 2007).

Undoubtedly the biggest design challenge is the *quality of the highest density housing*, which is widely criticised for its poor architecture and urban design, lack of energy efficiency, limited social mix, and inadequate management and amenities (CABE 2005c). The Task Force was careful to argue for medium densities and to note that higher densities could be achieved without necessarily building high (UTF 1999a: 60–64), but this view has been widely ignored, and there is a growing clamour for more appropriate design approaches that can address issues of mixed communities at the project and the neighbourhood level (R3c) (see DfL 2007).

Meanwhile, in the *mature suburbs* the UTF was quite explicit about the need for densification in those areas best served by public transport, and emphasised the value of mixed-use district centres and neighbourhood nodes offering diverse and convenient services and workplaces (UTF 1999a: 50–55, 64–66). However, suburbanites have been very resistant to development proposals (see Kochan 2007) and few LPAs have yet developed positive intensification strategies in the mature suburbs.

The urban renaissance housing agenda has been very much overtaken by events and by the recognition on the part of the Treasury that *household growth has been far outstripping housing supply*. This is particularly evident in south-east England with very rapid house price inflation threatening labour mobility, economic growth and social inclusion (Barker 2005a,b). The 2003 *Sustainable Communities Plan* (ODPM 2003b) was launched to increase the supply of housing in four growth areas of the south-east, and to activate a *Housing Market Renewal* (HMR) programme ('The Northern Way') across the cities of northern England. Criticisms of the plan helped to shape more positive, design-led approaches to large-scale housing development and sustainable urban extensions (TCPA 2007a), but not before valuable opportunities had been missed (SDC 2008). The 2007 Housing Green Paper (DCLG 2007b) consolidated plans to deliver 3 million new homes by 2020, addressing the historic problem of undersupply. However, the enlarged Growth Areas and New Growth Points initiatives that have been introduced (DCLG 2008a) both have an inevitable suburban, greenfield emphasis, whereas the proposed Eco Towns (10 schemes with at least 5,000 homes designed to new levels of sustainability; DCLG 2008b) are largely exurban, further promoting dispersal, undermining urban renaissance (Power and Houghton 2007) and attracting fierce NIMBY (Not In My Back Yard) opposition.

Quality of the public realm and the urban environment

The UTF sought to raise the general quality of urban environments so as to attract new households to urban areas. Their report expressed particular concern with the quality and connectedness of the urban public realm and its capacity to encourage sustainable movement patterns, especially walking. They stressed the value of 'traditional streets' and of public spaces as 'outdoor rooms' and the necessity of managing the urban environment so as to tackle common problems – crime, hooliganism, litter, graffiti, noise – which were especially prominent in the inner and larger cities. Its recommendations focused on better *design of the public realm, reducing traffic and improving public transport and walking conditions* in towns and cities, *better management of the urban environment* as a whole and *improving urban green space*.

The recommendations for the *public realm* and *comprehensive green pedestrian networks* (R1 and 2) concentrated on the development of a single strategy to link design, funding, management and maintenance at the local authority level. Few, if any, such strategies have materialised, although many small-scale initiatives and experiments such as the introduction of Home Zones (R 11) have contributed to a range of good practice (Biddulph 2001; DfT 2005). CABE have researched the barriers to design quality in urban streets and made recommendations for more design-informed corporate management (CABE 2002b, 2007b). Work to promote less risk-averse approaches to highway engineering continues. The Manual for Streets (DfT/DCLG 2007) has laid the basis for major improvements in residential street design, and a parallel initiative is under consideration for more heavily trafficked arterials and 'high streets'. CABESpace has championed design and management excellence in public spaces, streets and green spaces (CABE 2005d, 2005e, 2007b). However, funding remains a major constraint for all these initiatives, which often have to call upon already stretched highway budgets or at best Section 106 monies. A failure to allocate available European Regional Development Fund monies for these kinds of improvements in most UK cities previously eligible for Objective 1 and 2 funds is worth noting (Mills 2005a).

The Task Force recommended increased resources for *urban environmental management*, new models of neighbourhood management and new performance indicators (R21–R29). Some new government money was forthcoming. A 'Cleaner–Safer–Greener' programme (ODPM 2002a) was introduced to improve local government performance across the range of urban management responsibilities. An urban Liveability Fund was launched and a new Public Service Agreement 8 introduced to deliver higher standards of management of the public realm. However, by 2003 only 17 per cent of authorities had adopted integrated strategies for managing public space (ODPM 2004a), while coordinated management and community involvement were sporadic (Carmona and de Magalhaes 2006). The paucity of enhancement budgets has meant that significant public realm improvements outside central areas are comparatively rare, though an exception has been the improvements made to public parks after decades of underinvestment (NAO 2006).

The government is now committed to close monitoring of liveability and this has been given considerable prominence in the State of the Cities reports (ODPM 2006a,b; DCLG 2006e). Although the cleanliness of air, streets and open spaces has improved, there has been little systematic improvement in the quality of place (Table 1.4). Crime has fallen but anti-social behaviour increases. Generally, substantive evidence of an urban renaissance in the public realm remains thin (DCLG 2006e: 37).

The general failure to *reduce traffic levels and create alternatives to the car* was another key conclusion of the urban liveability survey (DCLG 2006e). The Task Force made recommendations to reduce car use, reclaim road space for pedestrians and improve walking, cycling and use of public transport (R10–R13), increase parking charges and reduce its supply in towns and cities (R19–R20). The reversal of the long-term disinvestment in public transport and traffic calming has begun, but is only slowly having a positive effect, though rail use is now growing rapidly. Regrettably the government remains ultra cautious on large-scale congestion charging and investment in light rail, and only central London and Durham have taken advantage of the former, and Greater Manchester, Nottingham, Edinburgh and south London the latter.

Walking and cycling have been encouraged through initiatives such as Safe Routes to School and school travel plans. The government rashly promised to treble cycling levels by 2010 in its 2000 Transport Plan but has funded demonstration projects in fifteen towns and cities (Cullingworth and Nadin 2006: 415; *Guardian* 2008: 17). Further local innovation and positive experimentation

Table 1.4 Urban liveability indicators and trends 1999–2005

	Indicator	Trend	
A	***Environmental quality***		
1	Noisier–quieter?	↘	
2	Dirtier–cleaner?	↗	
3	More or less congested?	↘	
4	Building quality, better or worse?	↗	(?)
B	***Place quality (physical)***		
5	Quality of the built environment 'product'	↔	(?)
6	Levels of derelict land	↗	
7	Quality of parks and green spaces	↗	
8	Public realm quality	..	(?)
C.	***Place quality (functional)***		
9	Pedestrian journeys: easier- or harder?	..	(?)
10	Public transport quality	↔	(?)
11	Vitality and viability of services	↗	(?)
D	***Safer places***		
12	Crime levels	↗	
13	Antisocial behaviour	..	(?)

Key

↘   Poor or worsening trend.

↗   Good or improving.

↔   Unclear/ambiguous – no clear trend.

··   Unable to make an indicative assessment based on judgement;

(?)   Insufficient data/research to support judgement – trend based on anecdotal evidence and/or professional judgement.

have been co-financed through EU programmes (e.g. CIty-VITAlity-Sustainability (EC initiative; CIVITAS) 2002–2009). However, resources have been insufficient to achieve a marked modal shift towards walking and cycling.

The UTF displayed only a limited grasp of the importance of the natural environment in urban areas – including its role in making urban areas more liveable. Although they called for more urban green routes (R2), issues such as biodiversity, the maintenance of ecosystems and the contribution of green space to air quality and water management were largely neglected, though very well understood in many of the European cities that the UTF admired, and relevant for pressing compliance with EU Environmental Directives. The Green Spaces Task Force (ODPM 2006c), CABESpace (CABE 2005d), Countryside Agency (2005) and Town and Country Planning Association (TCPA 2004) have helped to promote green space strategies (and most recently green infrastructure strategies and measures; TCPA 2008) to integrate improved park management, wider open space protection, nature conservation and countryside access programmes as well as hydrological management. The Sustainable Communities and Housing Market Renewal programmes provide an important opportunity to develop this kind of thinking at subregional, authority-wide and community levels (CABE 2004b, 2005d). The TCPA (2004) has developed prescriptions for multifunctional green infrastructure and sustainability measures in their *Biodiversity by Design* guide, linking these to national and local Biodiversity Action Plans, and seeking to embed green space strategies at all levels of plan-making. Such design imperatives will be vital to the proposed Eco-towns, but they also need to be an integral part of urban regeneration and suburban intensification programmes linking in to the wider public health and well-being agendas (Goode 2006; RCEP 2007). As residential densities are increased and urban compaction proceeds, such green space strategies become increasingly important to the enhancement of the urban environment. Moreover, they are now recognised as key tools for the adaptation of urban areas to climate change.

Overall there have certainly been improvements in the design, maintenance and management of streets, public spaces and especially parks, but the scale of improvement has been modest and focused on city centres (DCLG 2006e). There has been real progress in developing government guidance, disseminating best practice in design and management and publicising exemplar projects and practices, but when local authorities contemplate such initiatives they can rarely fund them on any scale. There is perhaps most disappointment with the failure to reduce urban traffic levels, especially by extending congestion charging, a win–win measure which would also serve to fund improvements to public transport and the public realm.

Resources for local government and regeneration, performance management processes, staff skills and the place-making role

Most of the above-mentioned UTF recommendations depend for their implementation on the activities of local authorities in their role as providers of local services and infrastructure. One of the great strengths of the UTF Report was the key role it gave local authorities to foster their own urban renaissance, whereas over previous decades they had been largely by-passed by Conservative regeneration programmes. In taking this stance the UTF was closely in tune with thinking at European level. The original UTF Report (1999) recognised that major improvements were necessary in the political and professional leadership of local authorities and in their resourcing/funding and legal powers, to allow them to play an effective role in large-scale urban revitalisation (see also NAO 2007a). Specific recommendations to these ends included reforms to Council Tax and Business Rates and potential new taxes (R85–R86), new spending formulae and long-term capital financing (R95–R98), and new public–private investment funds for regeneration (R87–R91). New means to reuse abandoned and empty property (R81–R83), and for the compulsory purchase and assembly of land (R64–R71) were also recommended. The UTF Progress Report (2005) reaffirmed this wish list, but observed that while there had been much discussion and official reports, there had as yet been little action on the key resource recommendations.

Most commentators agree that significant *fiscal reforms to local government* are a necessary foundation for any lasting urban renaissance. The UTF made the review of the spending formula for local government one of its key proposals, but not one of its specific recommendations on this topic has yet been implemented. The most obvious measures, set out clearly in the Lyons Report (ODPM 2007),would be the revaluation of housing to reflect current values, the introduction of new higher bands of Council Tax to yield more from the highest value homes, a local Business Rate Supplement to provide funds to invest in urban improvements, and the introduction of tourist and sales taxes. The UTF Progress Report recommended pilots of tax increment funding to further incentivise growth agendas and create funds for new infrastructure, but these have not materialised either. As a result local authorities continue to have very limited funds to invest in infrastructure to support new development, are forced into maximising financial returns when disposing of their land assets, and are increasingly having to retreat to their statutory functions because of very tight annual financial settlements from central government.

On the specific issue of *infrastructure funding* the UTF favoured standardised environmental impact fees (R49–R51). The policy debate on this topic became more focused in the wake of the Barker reports on housing supply (Barker 2005a,b) and progressed through various notions of a Planning Gain Supplement and a 'roof tax' before the Treasury decided on a Community Infra-structure Levy (CIL: placed on the landowner at the point of commencement of the development; DCLG 2008c) as the key tool and an integral component of the LDF system. The government has funded major infrastructure investment in the Growth Areas under the *Sustainable Com-munities Plan* (£14 billion in 2007), established a Community Infrastructure Fund (£300 million over three years), and provided additional funding for the *New Growth Points Initiative* (DCLG 2008a). However, although these monies will improve the quality of the suburban extensions, they do not contribute to the urban renaissance as such.

The *simplification of regeneration funding* and consolidation of participating agencies also remains unresolved (R99–R102) and, at least at the local level, the bewildering complexity of funding sources and financial controls continues to undermine coherent action (Leunig *et al.* 2007: 27–34). The UTF recommendation for single-purpose delivery bodies that could coor-dinate all relevant funding schemes reporting directly to the mayor or Cabinet (R35) would have given local authorities much more effective agencies with which to drive regeneration and better design. There has been some shift of responsibility for the management of key regenera-tion budgets to regional bodies – the Regional Development Agencies (RDA) in England and the devolved administrations. New streamlined arrangements are expected – possibly for the *subregional* level – but for the moment the picture is unclear.

More independence of action is widely considered likely to spawn greater enterprise and innovation, as cities in other European countries (most enjoying powers of general competence) demonstrate (URBED 2008). Both the UTF and New Labour were committed to *strong leader-ship at the local level*, particularly to the direct election of City Mayors. However, local councillors have been reluctant to embrace the idea, and only eleven mayors have been elected since 1999. The *Lyons Inquiry into Local Government: Final Report* recently conceded that 'too strong a focus on the leadership of one individual for every area risks losing some of the strengths of the current system' and recommended the retention of local choice as regards models of leadership (Lyons 2007: 9).

The UTF Report called for a 'systematic and sustained *investment in urban development skills*' (1999: 157, my emphasis) and made recommendations for Architecture Centres for public and professional debate (R9), for the development of Centres of Excellence for regeneration in association with regional universities, and for an Academy for Sustainable Communities (ASC) (R38–R39) with a wider remit for public education in regeneration and sustainability matters. These have all been implemented, and are contributing to the provision of much more cross-professional training, multi-skilling, and awareness-raising amongst the wider public and councillors. However, these initiatives are not directly addressing the skills deficit in local authori-ties, and evidence suggests a dramatic loss of skilled planning practitioners from the public sector as planning becomes progressively privatised (Durning and Glasson 2006; Durning 2007). The

UTF also recommended that the government establish a five-year programme of international secondments. This has not been implemented, although there are secondment opportunities in the EU Lifelong Learning programme, and EU programmes such as INTERREG (Innovation and Environment Regions of Europe Sharing Solutions) provide opportunities for local government officers to work with their counterparts outside the UK (ASC 2006).

The parlous state of local government leadership, finances, regeneration expertise and skills, strategic and local planning capabilities undermine the ambitions of the UTF for a locally driven urban renaissance. They are major barriers to the wider strategic role for local government set out by the Lyons Report (2007), promoting the general well-being of citizens, building local identity, maintaining cohesiveness, improving the economy and the environment and responding to community needs and preferences. This *place shaping* role described by Lyons has been developed in the 2007 Planning White Paper (DCLG 2007a), but it contrasts sharply with the widespread, though not universal, failure to create a common understanding of the importance of spatial planning among leading officers and members at the top of many local authorities. Here the common separation of planning's regulatory (development control) and plan-/policy-making functions, and the relegation of the former to a backbench role while vision and strategy become the preserve of the Executive, undermine both forward planning and a more proactive, value-adding 'development management' (IDOX 2007).

The drive for urban economic competitiveness, the boosterist mentality of city councils, and the determination to lever in as much investment and development as possible has tended to sideline planning and urban design in many local authorities. Although the UTF report was weak on the urban economy, once it became clear to the Treasury and the Department of Trade and Industry (DTI) that British urban competitiveness was lagging well behind that of much of north-western Europe, economic imperatives began to reshape the renaissance and planning agendas (ODPM/HMT/DfT 2003; ODPM 2004b; ODPM/HMT/GOER 2004) and league tables of economic performance indicators became key measures of renaissance success locally as well as nationally. Thus when the ODPM (2006a,b) completed a comprehensive monitoring of the progress of the urban renaissance (itself a response to a Task Force recommendation) it was dominated by economic performance measures, though it did also attempt to measure liveability (Table 1.4) and social cohesion. The same report emphasises the importance of economic development perspectives over those of physical regeneration, and serves as a reminder of how a better performing urban economy can reduce levels of deprivation and help achieve wider social goals. Nonetheless the report continues to argue that although quality of life, liveability and design quality are not 'critically important drivers of economic competitiveness' they are 'an increasingly important part of economic decision-making' (ODPM 2006a: 61, 166) in retaining and attracting residents and investment.

Preliminary conclusions on renaissance progress

With the all-important exception of the governance and regeneration funding recommendations, the 105 recommendations of the UTF have been largely implemented, albeit with varying degrees of success (Table 1.1; see also UTF 2005). The recommendations have been absorbed into the different spheres – some might say 'silos' – of government activity: wider urban policy, urban regeneration, neighbourhood renewal and (social) housing improvement, planning, housing and local government, and the pursuit of environmental sustainability (Table 1.2). Each of these policy areas has its own momentum and shifts in response to global and local events, economic and social trends and changing political imperatives.

The concept of a more holistic 'urban renaissance' has receded in importance, or changed its focus from time to time, as specific problems such as urban economic competitiveness, housing supply and affordability, and crime and security have come to the fore. Sometimes new initiatives and policies have threatened the core ideas of the urban renaissance (an example is the greenfield/urban extension-oriented Sustainable Communities Plan; ODPM 2003b), and at other times they have deepened them (the pursuit of carbon neutrality in new buildings). However, the renaissance programme, together with the spatial planning and place-making agendas, continue to offer a means by which these various initiatives can be 'joined up' so as to be mutually reinforcing in the pursuit of sustainable urbanism. The urgent need to address climate change could serve to re-establish just such a holistic renaissance agenda.

In this introductory chapter the urban renaissance agenda has been examined under four headings with particular resonance for urban design. The preliminary general conclusions are as follows:

- A sophisticated national urban design framework with a range of instruments to improve design outcomes has been successfully put in place, but it is now set within a reformed system of plans that is being delivered very slowly. Although development control efficiency improves nationally, there are major concerns about local authority design skills and the capacity to add value to planning applications and to handle the new challenges of zero-carbon buildings and infrastructure levies. CABE and other agencies in England – and their equivalents in Wales, Scotland and Northern Ireland – purvey excellent design advice, but the delivery of design quality is very uneven within both the development industry and local authorities.
- A significant, but insufficient, increase in housing supply has been delivered within existing built-up areas and on brownfield sites, and at higher densities. But it is of very uneven design quality, with the highest density housing now causing particular concern. Significant regeneration of the social housing stock and deprived neighbourhoods has been achieved, but concerns remain as to the wider social mix, integration and quality of life achieved. A housing affordability crisis has intensified as demand continues to outstrip supply, and although the 'credit crunch' has stifled demand temporarily it does not alter the long-term household formation–housing supply imbalance. The government has recognised the need to significantly increase the supply of affordable housing, and a major drive to deliver zero-carbon housing by 2016 has been launched.
- Improvements to the public realm (through design, maintenance, management and control) have contributed to 'liveability' and amenity, but these improvements have been concentrated largely in selected parks and city centres because of a lack of new funding. Cross-departmentally integrated public realm strategies are rare, but new design guidance should lead to steady improvements in residential street design. Innovations in traffic management and calming, and other measures to foster more sustainable patterns of movement – including congestion charging – need to be implemented much more widely. More attention is being paid to green infrastructure – vital to sustainability in cities and for addressing and adapting to climate change – but again funding is inadequate. These are all areas in which European funds and good practice lessons could be more advantageously deployed.

- The initial welcome for a positive role for local authorities in leading the urban renaissance has to be tempered by the failure to deliver long promised fiscal reforms, financial incentives for growth and adequate infrastructure funding. In England, at least, the Sustainable Communities Plan is well-resourced, but promises of important reforms to regeneration funding bodies have not yet materialised. However, the establishment of the new Homes and Communities Agency (HCA) to bring social housing provision, urban regeneration and skills improvement programmes together is a positive move, as is the enhanced financial control over regeneration to be exercised by the Regional Development Agencies. A challenging place-shaping agenda is now being legislated, but it is threatened by the general skills deficit in LPAs, and there are fears that the strengthening of these central agencies will further undermine local initiatives.

The cities' renaissance experiences

Having set the scene, we turn in the following chapters to examine the experience of the urban renaissance in the thirteen major cities of the UK. Although the contributing authors were allowed the scope to explore particular local issues and areas of interest, the accounts are structured around a common set of research questions developed to guide contributors to the seminar series on which this volume is based, namely:

- What are the most significant changes in the built form, public realm and urban character of British cities? Is there an appreciable improvement in the quality of the built environment?
- How has the property market responded to the urban renaissance? Are developers recognising 'the value of urban design'?
- Is local government adequately equipped to lead the urban renaissance? Do new city visions and partnerships demonstrate a deeper commitment to public participation and design quality? Is there evidence of a collective corporate commitment to good design?
- What is the effectiveness of the new statutory plans/frameworks alongside design strategies, masterplans, briefs, design policy and design control? Do they have adequate political support, resources and skilled support?
- What are the emerging critiques of the new urban landscape?
- What are the sustainability implications of the emerging urban forms? How might a deeper, more sustainable urban renaissance be created?

The city case studies are organised into three sections, each commencing with a short introduction to set their specific renaissance policy context. The 'Core Cities' of England are discussed first, the eight largest provincial cites, in order of population size of the built-up area. London with its four case studies follows, with the four 'Celtic Capitals' (and separate introductions to policy in Scotland, Wales and Northern Ireland) completing the case studies. In the final chapter the responses to the above-mentioned research questions are summarised, drawing on the city case studies, and the positives and negatives of the renaissance identified.

The English 'Core Cities'

An introduction

The eight largest English regional cities are very different cities in terms of administrative boundaries and geographical scope. Manchester, Nottingham and Bristol have very tightly drawn boundaries that have shorn them of much of their suburbs and 'edge city', whereas Sheffield and Leeds incorporate extensive tracts of countryside and numerous villages. Each city also has very different economic characteristics, with Bristol, Leeds and Nottingham displaying stronger economic performance (GDP), and Manchester and Birmingham competing strongly to be recognised as the UK's 'second city', measuring themselves against Barcelona, Lyon, Hamburg and Milan. A number of these Core Cities have reversed decades of population decline, and are now experiencing population growth, along with steady growth in Gross Value Added and reductions in unemployment. Liverpool, Manchester and Sheffield each have public–private Urban Regeneration Companies (established in 2000) working alongside the local authorities.

Two of these cities played a major role in moving urban design onto the British planning agenda in the 1990s (Birmingham and Manchester) while Nottingham quietly followed Birmingham's lead and Liverpool set out to emulate Manchester's achievements in new retailing. Sheffield used its tram to begin to upgrade its city centre, while Leeds and Bristol developed excellent design policies and strategies. Collectively the Core Cities (along with Glasgow) shaped many ideas and practices absorbed by the Urban Task Force (UTF), and provided important British precedents to set alongside European and American urban renaissance exemplars.

The 'Core Cities' came together in 1995 as a cross-party and cross-city alliance to collaborate on economic development and other matters, and to lobby central government for more powers and resources. They now have eight work streams looking at transport, innovation, skills and employment, culture and creative industries, finance and industry, governance and partnerships, sustainable communities, and climate change (Core Cities Group 2006). They have collaborated with central government and the Regional Development Agencies to examine ways of improving their economic performance and to develop the idea of city regions (ODPM/HMT/DfT 2003).

The ODPM have celebrated the collective urban renaissance achievements of the Core Cities in several recent publications, each with a relentless economic competitiveness rhetoric (ODPM 2004b,c). These have emphasised a number of common features driving the renaissance, including the establishment of Local Strategic Partnerships (LSP) to prepare Community Strategies, and good ratings for all cities under the Comprehensive Performance Assessment of local service provision. These reports also provide an overview of each city centre's renaissance, the improvements made in the local authority housing stock, and the progress made in tackling multiple deprivation. Examples of each of their 'iconic urban renaissance and public realm investments' have been used to demonstrate how they are raising their profiles and competitiveness (ODPM 2004c). But it is recognised that these improvements are only a beginning and 'have to be at the front end of a wider renaissance which progressively and systematically extends advantages to cover all areas and all communities' (ODPM/HMT/GOER 2004: 19), a point that many of the subsequent chapters will echo.

The government claimed that within the Core Cities 'a firm trend has been set towards greater devolution and delegation of powers' (ODPM 2004b: 18). But apart from the measures to introduce Business Improvement Districts there was no serious effort to increase the local financial autonomy needed to progress the urban renaissance. The Core Cities continue to campaign strongly for greater influence over all levels of transport investment; improvements to place-making through more integrated strategic planning at the city-region level; and single-pot funding for their investment programmes (Core Cities Group 2006).

A recent review of their urban design progress, written by city spokespersons, emphasised the very different approaches adopted by each city towards the renaissance agenda (see Murray 2007: 16–35). In his introduction to the articles the Director of the Core Cities set out the corporate intention and rationale and intoned the mantra that is now characteristic of British urban visioning and place-marketing.

> The image, identity, feel and functionality of a city are defined to a large extent by its built environment and by the quality of design used. The world judges a city by its centre and even a fleeting glance at the Core Cities will tell you that they are international, world class places in the making . . . What is common is a desire for transformation, quality that is fit for purpose, and a real understanding of the relationship between design, the built environment and economic growth . . . business attraction – and more importantly retention and growth – is closely related to this complex interplay of quality design across the piece. The Core Cities have understood that vibrant, exciting and well made places are those that will succeed in the next phase of global evolution. A commitment to design excellence and to the long term has and will continue to be central to economic success.
>
> (Murray 2007)

Does this place-marketing hype translate into place-making practice? What are the urban design achievements, and where must further improvements and innovations be made? Each city is now explored in turn, in order of the total population of their built-up area, recognising that city size is a critical factor in renaissance, and ignoring the fact that their administrative boundaries are arbitrary and often perverse.

References

Core Cities Group (2006) *A Century for Cities, The Priorities for Future Success of the Core Cities of England* (London: CCG).

Murray, C. (2007) The Economics of Design; Transforming England's Core Cities. *Urban Design*, 107 (16) (Special Issue on the Core Cities).

2 Birmingham

Translating ambition into quality

Joe Holyoak

The biggest and the best

Birmingham competes in the urban race under the handicap of being the second biggest city in the country. It compares itself with the capital and finds itself, unsurprisingly, wanting. This might not be so bad were it to be placed on the Tyne, say, or even on the Mersey. But positioned 120 miles away from London, the capital is too near for Birmingham to confidently acquire the regional independence of Newcastle upon Tyne or Liverpool.

One understandable response to this feeling of inferiority is ambition expressed in size. When the International Convention Centre was being built in the 1980s, a large city council sign on Broad Street exhorted citizens to *THINK BIG*. The misconceived equation of size with quality has been a characteristic of planning and development in Birmingham, at least since the Second World War. It can be traced back to the legacy of Herbert Manzoni, who was the powerful Surveyor, Engineer and Planning Officer of the city council from 1935 to 1963. He was the creator of the Inner Ring Road and the immense comprehensive redevelopment of the inner city, both of which were implemented between the 1950s and the 1970s.

Responses to decline

By the mid-1980s, Birmingham had, as a consequence, acquired a reputation for brashness: ambitious, but with little understanding of what constituted a high-quality environment. In a city dominated by highways and motor vehicles, the use of a drawing of the Birmingham Super Prix, a motor race held on city centre streets between 1986 and 1990, as the frontispiece to the city council's *City Centre Strategy* publication (undated), was unwittingly ironic. This environmental brashness coincided in the 1970s and early 1980s with the collapse of the city's manufacturing economy. Around 200,000 jobs were lost between 1975 and 1985. Birmingham had always prided itself on its responsive industrial practicality: *we may not be pretty*, it reasoned, *but we are a place that makes things, and the world comes to buy them*. But after 1985, this compensation no longer operated. The city was not only ugly, but now unemployed as well.

The city's two responses to this plight in the 1980s were critically important. First, like many other cities in a similar post-industrial situation, it resolved to reinvent itself as a location for the service economy and what it called business tourism. The flagship of this policy was the EU-funded International Convention Centre (ICC), planned in the 1980s and opened in 1991 – a huge fortress building which is a prime example of the obsession with bigness.

The building of the ICC generated an argument which, in varied forms, has continued since: whether or not big, 'prestige' city centre projects are created at the expense of the poorer citizens who are not likely to use them. Beyond the ICC lies a large area of council housing in Ladywood, one of the five inner city Comprehensive Redevelopment Areas built between the 1950s and early 1970s, and characterised by all the indicators of social and economic deprivation. The city council recognised the anomalous relationship of the two when in 1989 it instigated the Ladywood Regeneration Framework, which over the next seven years spent £35 million, funded by the government's Estate Action programme, on improving the estates.[1]

The city council claimed that the construction of the ICC would bring new jobs for Ladywood residents, and that the gradual spread of new development, which it hoped the ICC would generate, would generally spread new wealth around. But these claims were challenged in 1990 in a report written by Patrick Loftman, a researcher at Birmingham Polytechnic (Loftman 1990).[2] Loftman argued that many of the projected jobs deemed suitable for local residents would be of poor quality and with low pay. Moreover, he maintained that council tenants living close to the ICC would bear the costs of the city's economic rebirth through rising land and property values, the loss of sites to commercial property developments and the gentrification of the housing stock. His conclusion was that the ICC, as an engine of economic regeneration, was likely to lead to an increase in poverty and social polarisation. Eighteen years on, Loftman's charges appear justified. Ladywood is still one of the most deprived urban areas in the country,[3] and the spread of new private apartments in the west end of the city centre has resulted in considerable gentrification.

The second response to decline was apparently more minor, but was to prove of huge significance. It was a weekend workshop in March 1988, which came to be known as the Highbury Initiative, named after Joseph Chamberlain's house, where the event took place. Urban design consultants DEGW and Urban and Economic Development Ltd (URBED) organised the event for the city council, and invited eighty participants: a spread of local people plus design experts from Britain, the USA, Japan and the Netherlands. From the Highbury weekend emerged a number of resolutions which have formed the basis of the planning and development of the city centre for twenty years. There was widespread agreement that both the reality and the image of the city centre were dreadful: 'a city in a tearing hurry, addicted to instant success, biggest, first, pragmatic, profitable, confusing, incoherent and monotone' was how one workshop group put it (DEGW 1988). Three fundamental recommendations were that:

1 The definition of the city centre should be enlarged from eighty hectares (inside the Inner Ring Road) to 800 hectares (inside the Middle Ring Road; Figure 2.1).
2 The Inner Ring Road was a physical and perceptual barrier, and its severance should be greatly reduced.
3 Inside the Inner Ring Road, pedestrians should have priority over motor vehicles.

After twenty years, in which we have seen the publication of the Rogers report (UTF 1999a) and the foundation and growth of the Commission for Architecture and the Built Environment (CABE), these resolutions now seem very orthodox. But they were hard-won at the time. Two significant commissions followed to Highbury participants. To the American landscape architect Don Hilderbrandt and his firm LDR, the task of producing a pedestrianisation strategy for the city centre was given. This has since been implemented piece by piece, transforming the city centre experience. Francis Tibbalds was asked to write urban design guidance for the city centre. His *Birmingham Urban Design Study* was published in 1990, and has been described as the best of its kind produced by a British city.

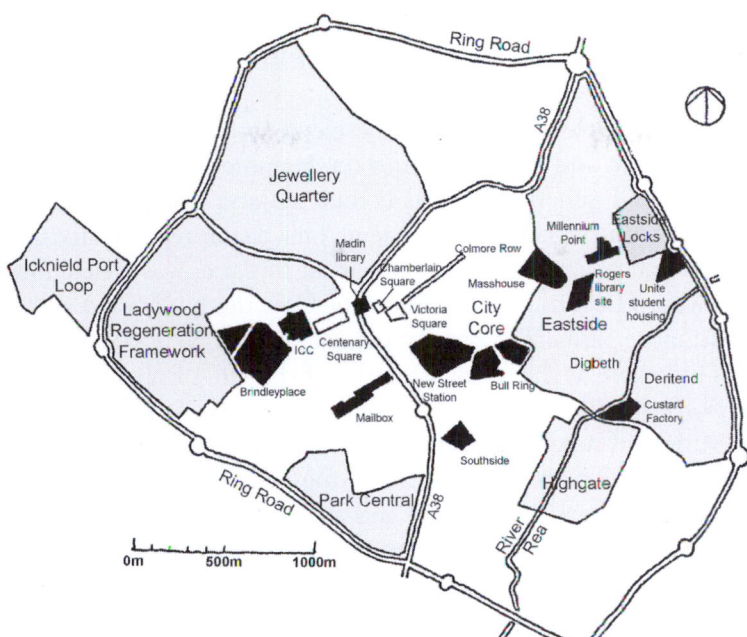

The rebuilding of the Bull Ring

So, in urban design terms at least, Birmingham entered the 1990s with a sense that it was again reinventing itself, but this time with design standards more enlightened than those which had guided the enormous reshapings of the 1950s and 1960s. But within the Council and the city's professional and business institutions, the old attitudes – a mixture of vain ambition and utilitarianism – were still much in evidence. The story of the redevelopment of the Bull Ring, the most celebrated feature of the new twenty-first-century Birmingham, which extended from the public launch of the proposals in 1987 to the eventual opening of the development in 2003, illustrates the distance which had yet to be covered.

The old Bull Ring Shopping Centre, opened in 1964, was the epitome of Birmingham's desire for the big, brash and new. Its inflexibility doomed it to failure both economically and environmentally (Marriott 1967). In 1987, its new owners, the London and Edinburgh Trust (LET), announced their scheme for its replacement, The Galleries. Double the size of the 1964 development, it was in the form of an introverted three-level mall, 500 metres long, described shortly after by its architect as 'a huge aircraft carrier settled on the streetscape of the city' (Pullman 1988). In the national economic recession of the time, Birmingham was desperate for big private sector investment, yet had no urban designers to write guidance. The functions of planning and economic development were combined into one department, under the direction of Graham Shaylor, and the imperatives of economic investment were frequently given priority over good planning and urban design.

Over the next few years a public campaign, led by the citizens' group Birmingham for People, which published in 1989 a counter-proposal to The Galleries, *The People's Plan for the Bull Ring*, succeeded in changing this priority to a significant degree.[4] *The People's Plan* proposed a permeable, mixed-use development, which recreated at its centre a version of the market square of the pre-1964 Bull Ring. The two most significant elements of *The People's Plan* were proposals for a central pedestrian space, recreating the historic view and connection between New Street and St Martin's church and the markets, and, most controversially, the closure of the Inner Ring Road to allow that connection to be made (Holyoak 2004).

Having received and overcome considerable resistance, these elements were incorporated into a later version of the LET development, and eventually into the Hammerson development (called Bullring), which succeeded the LET scheme and was completed and opened in 2003. Judged against modern urban design criteria the completed scheme fails to impress. A mixture of uses, which was required by city council policy for a development of this size, was resisted by the developer and has not been achieved. The initial monolith of The Galleries has been divided into two halves by the pedestrian axis: more permeable, but not permeable enough. Its deep-plan blocks will ultimately prove to be as inflexible as the mega-structure of the 1964 Bull Ring. The architectural treatment by Hammerson's architects, Benoy, is the usual undistinguished dressing-up of internalised volumes, using a variety of superficial forms and materials.

Much attention has been focused upon the one piece of Bull Ring not designed by Benoy: the Selfridges store designed by Future Systems. Its singular and striking external form, eminently photogenic and easily identifiable, fulfils the client's instruction to his architect to design a building that needed no sign attached. Regrettably, the seductive attraction of having a star retail name in the city, and of having an architectural novelty that could promote the city's identity, distracted the Planning Committee from considering the urban design shortcomings of the building. Its two street elevations, to Park Street and Moor Street, are blank, with no public entrances, forming a hostile edge to the Bullring development (see Plate 2.1). This creates not only local damage, but also a strategic problem, as the Selfridges edge of the Bull Ring should be responsible for connecting the development to the future growth area of Digbeth, which begins on the opposite side of Park Street. Owing to the blank edge, this growth is made more difficult to achieve.

This is a critical illustration of a continuing failure in city council planning: the commissioning and writing of very good policy documents, and the ignoring of their policy requirements when it is expedient to do so. The *Birmingham Urban Design Study* (Tibbalds 1990) explicitly requires city centre blocks to provide active ground floor edges to the street, a now orthodox plank of the urban design agenda. Yet one of the most prominent city centre buildings, on a strategically

Plate 2.1 Birmingham: the blank street level of Selfridges on Park Street, contravening city design policy on active street frontages.

important site, is given planning approval despite the fact that it contravenes the council's own policy.

Another important step in the transition of Birmingham to a place where the importance of environmental quality was realised was the appointment of Les Sparks in 1991 as Director of Planning and Architecture, succeeding Graham Shaylor. He brought together the previously separate council architects and planners, and appointed the first urban designers to the council. For the first time, the city had a planning officer who understood what constituted quality, who was prepared to demand it from developers, and who could persuasively promote the importance of a high standard of design among his fellow chief officers and his elected members. He was instrumental in helping to reverse the easy acquiescence of his predecessors towards LET's short-sighted commercialism in The Galleries, whose revised version was approved in 1996, but he had left the council before Hammerson's Selfridges was approved in 2000.

Brindleyplace

One of Sparks's earliest tasks was to assist in the rescue of the ill-starred development of Brindleyplace, the eight-hectare private sector complement to the ICC. He oversaw the production of the masterplan by Terry Farrell and Partners which set the development on the road to success, despite the subsequent bankruptcy of their client Rosehaugh. Once the site had been bought from the administrator by Argent in 1993, and the masterplan revised by Farrell's former partner John Chatwin (Figure 2.2), Sparks ensured that the Brindleyplace masterplan became a flexible and responsive planning tool, able to accommodate market-driven changes to the development form, without any compromise to the essential masterplanning principles. Brindleyplace, with its concentration on good-quality, well-connected public space (albeit totally privately owned and managed), its economic success, and its diverse yet coherent architecture, is the best example of

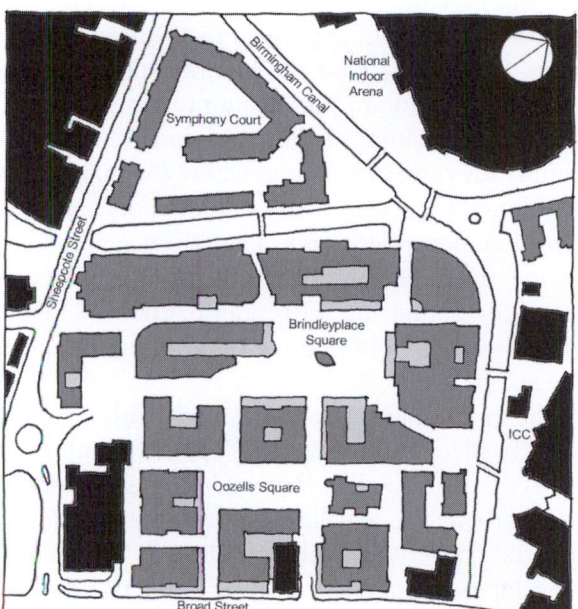

Figure 2.2 Birmingham: the 1999 masterplan by John Chatwin for Brindleyplace, indicating the primacy of the spatial network, and the independence of the building blocks.

modern urban design so far achieved in Birmingham (Latham and Swenarton 1999). It is surprising and ironic that although it is hailed nationally as a model, and led to Argent's appointment as developers for King's Cross in London, its lessons appear not to have been more widely learnt and applied in Birmingham.

The one big anomaly in the success of Brindleyplace is the residential element. Chatwin's masterplan originally envisaged apartments in a number of locations, mostly along canal frontages, integrated with other land uses. The residential developer chosen by Argent, Crosby Homes, was prepared to build only if it could have the detached part of the site, enclosed on two of its three sides by the canal, to itself. The result, named Symphony Court, is a gated, single-use development that is physically separated from the rest of Brindleyplace, thus contradicting the masterplan's intentions. Despite this shortcoming, Crosby's boldness at Symphony Court initiated the city centre residential boom which continued until 2006. Moreover, unlike all other subsequent developments, it included family houses as well as apartments (Barber 2007).

The quarterisation of the city centre

Under Sparks's leadership, the production of quarter plans for the subdivisions of the enlarged 800 hectare city centre continued. The zone outside the city core (beyond the old Inner Ring Road) was subdivided into six quarters. For each one a policy document was produced, which made proposals for future growth and development in a way that strengthened the area's inherent identity.

The results were only partially successful, because quarter designations were imposed rather than occurring organically. The Jewellery Quarter was the only genuine quarter, with a distinctive character and identifiable boundaries, deriving from its historic and particular manufacturing processes and building types. Ironically, it was the last inner area to receive a quarter plan. This was commissioned from the consultants EDAW, and was published in 1998 under the name *The Jewellery Quarter Urban Village Plan* (EDAW 1998).

The consequences of the Urban Village Plan demonstrate some of the problems of quarterisation: the tendency for the identification of the area's special quality to turn into theming, and for that theming to produce a process of gentrification (Bell and Jayne 2004). The Urban Village Plan encouraged the development of new city centre housing in the Jewellery Quarter, on empty sites and in buildings where the manufacturing business had contracted. A target of 2,000 dwellings was set. But with the jewellery and precious metal industries in a vulnerable economic position, dependent upon low-rent accommodation, and with a growing market for city centre living, the large difference in land value between a site in industrial use and the same site with planning permission for residential development put great pressure on the indigenous industry. The result was a huge growth in new apartments, and an industry feeling threatened and under siege.

Such was the concern felt, both within the quarter and within the council, at the impact of new residential development upon the industry that a significant reversal of policy took place in 2001, with English Heritage playing an influential role. The three conservation areas covering parts of the Jewellery Quarter were amalgamated into one, and a new Management Plan for the conservation area published. This plan divided the quarter into zones, with differing development controls for each. In the two zones where most of the manufacturing businesses are concentrated, which it named the Industrial Middle and the Golden Triangle, new residential development, except for live work units as part of a mixed-use development, was prohibited.

This interesting reversion to the policy of land use zoning, which the new urban design ortho-doxy of mixed-use districts had previously declared outdated, was welcomed within the quarter. But it remains under pressure from developers, who have continued to submit planning applica-tions which are contrary to policy, hoping that development pressure will eventually break the resistance of planning restrictions. So far the line has held, and if the city centre apartment market has reached saturation, which it appears to have done, a more consensual approach to the future of the Jewellery Quarter may emerge.

City centre living

Elsewhere in the city centre, the growth in city centre apartments following Symphony Court has not caused the antagonism experienced in the Jewellery Quarter. Concentrated mainly in the expanding west end, near the ICC and Brindleyplace, and taking advantage in many cases of canal-side frontages, the developments have been in locations already ex-industrial. Within a planning policy that generally encourages the repopulation of the city centre, development has been market driven, with little attempt made to create any city centre housing policy. The result has been development consisting almost entirely of one- and two-bedroom apartments for sale, with the addition of the statutory proportion of rented apartments managed by a housing association in partnership with the commercial developer.

Approximately 10,000 apartments have been built since 1993, and sales up to 2007 remained buoyant. But the resulting narrowness of the demographic profile, and the inherently shifting nature of a predominantly young population, has caused concern. Even the numbers are not what they appear to be. A significant proportion are bought and rented out by investors and businesses, with a correspondingly unstable and intermittent pattern of occupancy (Barber and Blackaby 2008).

Judged architecturally, the new city centre apartments are mostly of a decent standard, but are unexceptional. Symphony Court, if one overlooks its gated plan and its neo-Dutch Revival styling, is a substantial piece of architecture with a distinct identity. The apartment buildings which have succeeded it are mostly formulaic in design. Moreover, some developments, in the desire to maximise the profits which could be made from the high sales prices that were earlier being achieved, are arguably overintensive, with little if any communal realm. The conviviality of urban living evoked in Richard Rogers's *Towards an Urban Renaissance* (UTF 1999a) is absent in these places.

The one significant exception to the domination of new apartments in the city centre is the development on the southern edge of the city centre known as Park Central. This is an invented name, a marketing creation to replace the discredited housing estate of Lee Bank (itself a name invented in the 1950s, as one of the five Comprehensive Redevelopment Areas which ringed the city centre). The modernist estate of Lee Bank was a failure, measured in terms of both its physical environment and also the social and economic deprivation suffered by its residents. Two community-led initiatives in the 1990s, to obtain Estate Action and Single Regeneration Budget funding to regenerate Lee Bank, both failed.

Following the successful transformation of the peripheral council estate of Castle Vale, whose council tenants in 1994 voted to replace their city council landlords with a new Housing Action Trust, the city council in 1999 offered Lee Bank tenants the opportunity to create a new housing association, in partnership with a national developer, with funding to rebuild the estate. Optima Housing Association and Crest Nicholson have since given Lee Bank an almost entirely new shape: demolishing high-rise blocks, replacing the dysfunctional open space at the centre of the estate with the eponymous park and building 1,600 new houses and apartments (Figure 2.3). Park Central and Symphony Court are the only locations within the city centre where family houses have successfully been built within the past ten years.

Political changes and political appointments

Les Sparks left the city council in 1999, becoming a CABE Commissioner and then Chair of the CABE Design Review Panel. The matter of his succession did not go happily. The city council twice advertised his post, as Chief Architect and Planner, and twice failed to find a person it was willing to appoint. The expedient response to this failure was to split Architecture and Planning, reversing Sparks's amalgamation, and to appoint Sparks's previous Assistant Director, Emrys Jones, as Director of Planning. Jones was a town planner, and did not have Sparks's holistic capacity to combine the processes of planning, urban design and conservation into a comprehensive programme. The architects were included in a new department which combined surveyors, quantity surveyors, engineers and building maintenance officers, and which, extraordinarily, at the insistence of the then Chief Executive, Michael Lyons, was named the Urban Design Department. It contained no urban designers (they remained in Planning), and it did no urban design!

Following this unhappy disintegration, in 2003 the council created a new post, that of City Design Adviser. Philip Singleton, then Director of the regional centre for architecture, MADE (Midlands Architecture and the Designed Environment), was appointed. The intention was that the City Design Adviser would focus on design quality within the planning process, both from within the council and from the private sector. The City Design Advisor is now, in addition, Assistant Director of Planning, and heads the City Centre Design Team, composed of urban designers and landscape architects. He runs a very effective team, and is the coordinator of the Big City Plan commissioned from Urban Initiatives in 2007. But it is difficult to maintain that the quality of what is produced in the city by the private sector has improved significantly since his appointment.

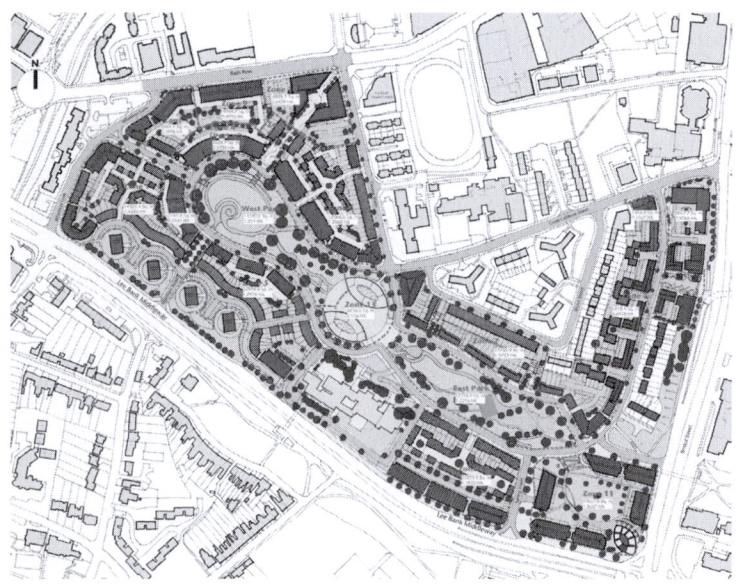

Figure 2.3 Birmingham: the plan of the Park Central redevelopment of the Lee Bank estate, showing the new park surrounded by new housing (Courtesy Crest Nicholson). © Crown Copyright. All rights reserved. Licence number 100049043.

One area where a significant measure of quality has been achieved is in the housing developments assessed in the CABE Housing Audit (CABE 2007a). While the West Midlands overall did very poorly, with only 12 per cent of schemes assessed rated either good or very good, four of the six Birmingham schemes assessed were in these categories, and the other two slightly below. This has been attributed to the input at design stage by the city council's urban designers.

True to its traditions of pragmatism, Birmingham has rarely experienced extremes of political ideology. Over the past half-century, political control of the city council has swung from Labour to Conservative and back again, but there has mostly been a fairly narrow ideological gap between a right-wing Labour group and a left-wing Conservative group. The building of the ICC illustrates the pragmatic continuity which has been the norm. Instituted by the ruling Conservative group in the 1970s in response to economic decline, when it was succeeded by the Labour group in 1983, the project continued without a hitch. From 1983 the Labour Party enjoyed a long period of control, during which it laid the foundations for the reinvention of the city that had been created in the 1950s and 1960s, both economically and environmentally. There was much it had to learn about urban quality, and much was learnt during the sagas of the planning of the Bull Ring and Brindleyplace.

In 2002, the city council, since 1999 under the leadership of Sir Albert Bore, commissioned the Richard Rogers Partnership to design a new library for the city, to replace the Central Library – the 1972 Brutalist concrete building designed by John Madin. The new library was to be sited outside the city core in the regeneration area of Eastside, opposite the city's Millennium Lottery-funded Millennium Point, a big but rather dull science- and technology-themed building designed by Grimshaw Architects, and, like it, intended to become a major catalyst for new development there. But in the local election of 2004, Labour, while remaining the largest party in the city council, lost its overall majority. Control passed to the Conservative Party in coalition with the Liberal Democrats, and with respect to the new library the bipartisan tradition exemplified by the building of the ICC abruptly ended. Rogers's design would have produced one of the best library buildings in the world, and its location would have been a major contribution to the enlargement of the city centre, as determined by the Highbury Initiative. But the commission was scrapped by the incoming administration, headed by the new leader, Mike Whitby.

Whitby is a businessman, a civic booster and, even more than the business-aligned previous Labour administration, his council is assertively promoting Birmingham as a player on the world stage, and as a place for the world to do business. His rhetorical slogan is 'A global city with a local heart'. As ever, there is no shortage of ambition, including its expression in architecture. As well as the new library commission, there is the commission to Foreign Office Architects for the rebuilding of the embarrassingly gloomy, uncomfortable and dysfunctional New Street Station. But a city cannot be made from landmark buildings, even if their absence was suggested by Jeremy Isaacs, chair of the judges, as one of the reasons why Birmingham failed in 2003 to become European Capital of Culture 2008. As the prominent local architect Glenn Howells has emphasised, 'the challenge facing Birmingham is . . . to create a coherent fabric of modern buildings of lasting quality. It is much easier to deliver landmarks than to raise the standard of the context' (Howells 2004; see Plate 2.2).

The headline reason given for the rejection of the Rogers library scheme was that it was expensive, and that nobody knew where the money was to come from. But behind the headline was a cooler attitude by the new administration towards the Eastside project as a whole. Eastside was perceived as a child of the previous Labour regime, and of Albert Bore in particular. The development of alternative strategies for the library replacement proceeded erratically from 2004

Plate 2.2 The Southside housing designed for Crosby Homes by Glenn Howells Architects; normative urban fabric comparable to Georgian streets of the eighteenth century.

to 2007, until it was decided to build on a council-owned surface car park site on Centenary Square, close to the ICC: very central, but really too small to accommodate the projected library. In 2008 the Dutch architects Mecanoo were appointed, with a budget of £193 million, more than the previously calculated cost of the Rogers library.

Both political regimes, before and after 2004, have calculated that a large part of the cost of the new library will come from the sale of the land at Paradise Circus on which the Madin library currently stands, adjacent to the Grade I listed Town Hall and the 1879 Council House. The intention is that private sector offices will be built there, and initial development studies have indicated that it is necessary to build high in order to realise the potential value of the land. But building high in the centre of Birmingham is not simply a matter of economic calculation. Both the Labour and the Conservative groups when in power have promoted the idea that high buildings on the skyline are signs of prosperity and dynamism, and are to be encouraged. There is a Supplementary Planning Document on tall buildings policy, whose sound advice on positioning tall buildings on the city centre ridge derives from Francis Tibbalds's 1990 *Birmingham Urban Design Study*. But, as noted earlier, good planning policy is not always followed in practice. There continues to be a tension between the priorities of economic investment, on the one hand, and urban design and environmental quality, on the other, and often expediency wins.

There are several cases of this happening with tall buildings. One of the most recent is 103 Colmore Row, where the planning committee in 2008 approved a proposal by British Land to build a thirty-five-storey office tower. Colmore Row does lie along the city centre ridge, but it is at the heart of the eponymous conservation area, and is the most architecturally coherent street in the city centre. The north side of the street is very regularly composed, of four- and five-storey nineteenth century buildings, culminating in the Council House at the end, and the conservation area Management Plan states that no new buildings should be significantly higher than others. The city council's conservation strategy document, published in 1999, is called *Regeneration through Conservation*, and it is significant that the title suggests that conservation is not an autonomous process supported by its own values, but is justified by being a tool of regeneration (BCC 1999). Where conservation can support and contribute to economic regeneration, the two processes can be complementary. But where they come into opposition, as at 103 Colmore Row, conservation values become the casualty. Another tall building proposed in a conservation area is part of the Beorma Quarter development in Digbeth, given planning approved in 2009. Compared with 103 Colmore Row, this development makes much more effort to relate contextually in grain and character to relate to the original burgage plot pattern. Nevertheless, the height of the proposed tower is a radical departure from the prevailing scale of the block, and contravenes planning policy (see Plate 2.3).

In 2005, Emrys Jones retired as Director of Planning and was succeeded by Clive Dutton, now Director of Planning and Regeneration. Dutton has a background in urban regeneration and commercial development, and is well equipped to translate Whitby's political agenda into action. He is equally assertive: remarkably, when 103 Colmore Row came before the planning committee, he directly addressed the committee and instructed them that it was vital for the city's commercial credibility that they approve the scheme.

Following the departure of Sparks in 1999, the arrival of Whitby as leader in 2004, and Dutton in 2005, the attitude of the city council towards development and regeneration has tilted more towards prioritising the economic dimension, as it did under Graham Shaylor in the 1980s. In most instances, this priority can be successfully accommodated with appropriate urban design, and the skills are in place to do it, which they were not before the Highbury initiative. In addition to its urban design team, Birmingham is unusual, if not unique, in having a Chair of the Planning Committee who possesses an MA in Urban Design. Although it is too early to be sure, and although its generation has so far been disrupted by disagreements between landowners and withdrawals by developers, just as at Brindleyplace, the plans for the first of Dutton's proposed inner city 'Eco-towns', at Icknield Port Loop, are very encouraging in this respect. But the fetishisation of tall buildings, even when in unsuitable places, as though a tall building has some kind of economic power not possessed by lower buildings, is an example of where economic development is sometimes at the expense of good urban design. Another example is the recent moves in the development of Eastside.

Plate 2.3 Proposed Beorma Quarter development adjacent to the Bull Ring, in the Digbeth Conservation Area, including a 30 storey tower (Courtesy of Salhia Investments Limited).

Eastside

The Eastside regeneration area, 170 hectares of industrial and ex-industrial land on the eastern edge of the city core, was initiated by the Labour group in the late 1990s. The ICC and Brindley-place, and smaller commercial developments consequent to them, had expanded the city centre westwards in the 1990s. Eastside was a deliberate strategy to do the same on the less promising eastern edge. A dedicated planning team was set up, led by the ex-Director of Economic Development, Richard Green. Its importance was emphasised by its physical separation from the rest of the department, located strategically at the top of a high-rise building overlooking the whole of Eastside. Its first act was to remove a large part of the 'concrete collar' – the elevated section of the ring road that separated Eastside from the city core – replacing it with a tree-lined boulevard on the ground (see Plate 2.4).

The Eastside development had aspirations towards sustainable design and construction, and two sustainability advisors were appointed as part of a programme named Sustainable Eastside. But, as so often happens in Birmingham, the ambition was not matched by the necessary urban design moves. Following the successful precedent of Brindleyplace, one might have expected a comprehensive masterplan for Eastside to have been produced. The architects HOK were commissioned to produce what was called a masterplan, but which was in fact nothing of the sort, merely an aspirational illustration of what might happen. The city council published a *Design and Movement Framework* for Eastside in draft in 2003, which left unanswered as many questions about future planning policy as those that it answered. It has never been completed.

The northernmost half of Eastside, adjacent to the city core, was divided into a number of large development sites, for which designs have proceeded independently. One of them was the site for Richard Rogers's library, which now will be occupied by a new campus for Birmingham City University. At the time of writing in 2008, two developments are partly complete: the mixed-use Masshouse development, designed and built by the developer McLean, and canal-side student housing at Curzon Gateway. Both of them are clumsy in their planning and appearance, and neither fulfils the aspirations of the city for a world-class new urban quarter. Two more recently

Plate 2.4 The new boulevard of Moor Street, replacing an elevated part of the Inner Ring Road, with the Masshouse development to the right.

planned developments, Eastside Locks, by the developer Goodman, and Pettifer Estates' 'vertical theme park', were both heavily criticised in 2007/2008 by the CABE design review panel.

Lower Eastside, consisting of Digbeth and Deritend, is a very different place. This is a network of small industrial premises on small streets, mediaeval in origin, crossed by the River Rea, canals and railway viaducts. Most of it is within two contiguous conservation areas. Creative industries, in such forms as The Bond, the Custard Factory, the Ikon Gallery and Maverick Television, have moved into old buildings, rubbing shoulders with metal pressing and car repair businesses. In 2006 the city council commissioned Professor Michael Parkinson to write a socio-economic brief for the future of the city centre, on which a physical masterplan (now called the Big City Plan) would be based (Parkinson 2007). Parkinson was eloquent about the potential of Digbeth and Deritend, writing: 'This is one of the most exciting parts of the city, which has authenticity, grit, great buildings, waterways. In other cities it would be a jewel'.

But there is as yet no planning policy in place which could ensure that this promise is fulfilled. The danger is that the subtle virtues of complex, gritty, fine-grained districts like this, lacking the headline simplicities of high-rise landmark buildings, will not be appreciated, and that, in the absence of an effective plan, ad hoc development will gradually erode the special quality of Digbeth and Deritend.

Changes in Eastside planning management are not encouraging. Since coming to power in 2004, the Conservative and Liberal Democrat administration has run down the Eastside team, before closing it altogether in 2007. Responsibility for Eastside planning now rests within Philip Singleton's City Centre Design Team. There is no longer a Sustainable Eastside programme. It remains to be seen whether or not Professor Parkinson's vision for the special place that Lower Eastside could become will be recognised within the forthcoming Big City Plan.

Public spaces

Post-Highbury, one of Birmingham's great urban design successes has been its new public spaces, whose development was instigated by Don Hilderbrandt's plan for pedestrianisation in the city centre. It is now possible to walk, from St Martin's church in the Bull Ring, over a mile to the furthest side of Brindleyplace, without crossing a vehicular route, and passing through a number of attractive public spaces on the way. The best and most celebrated is probably Victoria Square, which before 1992 was a traffic island with the queen's statue in the centre. Spaces such as this, Centenary Square and Brindleyplace Square have transformed the city centre into a place to enjoy, not just to work and shop. It is now commonplace on a weekend to see families strolling, doing a British version of a *passeggiata*, and pointing out the sights to their visitors.

But the imagination which has been put into the creation of these urban spaces by one part of the city council is not complemented by the imagination shown by the other part which is responsible for managing them. Part of the message of the urban renaissance, that well-designed urban space has a value in its own right, as space, does not appear to be fully recognised. Instead, it appears that the purpose of urban space is perceived to be as a receptacle into which something else can be put. Big wheel, ice rink, beach, German market – all of them worthwhile and enjoyable installations, but the implication is that empty urban space is put there in order to be filled.

The same managerial attitude was visible in the case of the notorious Big Screen. During the renovation of the Town Hall in 2004/2006, temporary planning permission was granted for the placing of a large public TV screen addressing Chamberlain Square, primarily intended to show the football World Cup. When the work was completed and the scaffolding came down, the planning permission was extended. What had previously been a dignified civic space became the urban equivalent of a living-room dominated by a loud TV that could not be switched off. Despite protests, the city council gave approval for a permanent screen in the adjacent Victoria Square. At the time of writing in 2008, construction has been halted by a legal injunction brought against the council by the occupants of the adjacent building.

Entrepreneurialism

While the city council obviously has the key role in setting the direction of the new city, it is not always responsible for initiating the significant moves. Creative entrepreneurs sometimes spot development opportunities which set things moving in a direction which the council had not anticipated. Indeed, the council often claims credit for noteworthy enterprises such as, for example, Selfridges, in whose creation it played no strategic part at all. Two prominent examples of entrepreneurial development worthy of attention are the Custard Factory and the Mailbox.

The developer Bennie Gray bought the disused factory of Alfred Bird, whose father invented egg-less custard powder, in 1990. It is a large complex of buildings in the industrial area of Deritend, part of Eastside. Working incrementally, and converting industrial spaces simply and cheaply into a large number of rentable studios, Gray has over twenty years turned a derelict site into an incubator of small businesses and a centre of rather bohemian activity in an area which had few other reasons to be on people's mental maps. Converted studios have been joined at different times by bars and cafes, shops, a theatre, a dance studio, a violin maker, a Sunday market, a night club, and a new building containing more workplaces. Gray has now bought more redundant industrial buildings in streets beyond the Custard Factory. He has created a diverse pool of economic activity, the biggest concentration of activity in this part of the city, in a way which could not perhaps have been planned from the top down.

Similarly, the transformation of the 1970s Post Office letter-sorting building into the Mailbox was also the result of developers spotting a place that was off-pitch, in a location that was not on the planners' priority list of places where development was expected or encouraged to happen. The letter-sorting office was only three minutes' walk from New Street Station, but, critically, it was on the wrong side of the Inner Ring Road, and therefore perceived to be not part of the city centre. Alan Chatham and Mark Billingham, who had been directors of Brindleyplace plc before it was bought by Argent (Holyoak 1999), bought the redundant building in 1998. Not only was it in an unpromising location, it was a very unpromising building; a huge heavyweight concrete box with deep floor plans and high floor-to-floor dimensions. It now claims to be the biggest mixed-use building in the UK, containing shops (including the sought-after Harvey Nichols), two hotels, bars and restaurants, apartments, and the British Broadcasting Corporation's (BBC) regional headquarters. The key move was to cut a pedestrian street through the middle of the building, leaving two halves with manageable floor depths, and to build a footbridge over the Worcester Canal to connect the street with the towpath. In this way the Mailbox has created a circuit which joins it up with the nightlife area of Broad Street and Brindleyplace beyond. This is a highly significant urban design move, the result not of a quarter plan or any other planning policy, but of enlightened private enterprise.

The response to the urban renaissance

As detailed on the preceding pages, Birmingham's response to the government's urban renaissance programme has been inconsistent. In the years following Highbury and Les Sparks's appointment, Birmingham could claim to be in the vanguard of urban policy among British cities, having started from a very low point. But, as Professor Parkinson noted, the initiative of those days faltered, the progress has not been maintained to the same standard, and a lot of responsibility is currently placed upon the Big City Plan to re-establish Birmingham's eminence.

The government's failure to support extensions of the single rapid transit metro line, between Birmingham and Wolverhampton, has not helped. Birmingham's love affair with the motor car is still alive. Pedestrianisation and the removal of parts of the ring road have transformed parts of the city centre, but public transport remains in the dark ages.

Ambition and pragmatism, uneasy bedfellows, continue to typify Birmingham's approach to regeneration. The lessons of LET's Bull Ring, in which the Council snatched at a major development proposal without considering its urban design implications, have still not been completely absorbed, as Eastside's unhappy Masshouse development, among others, shows. A proposed development's promise of notional new jobs can still override issues of urban design and architectural quality, as shown by 103 Colmore Row. It is telling that the city's daily newspaper, *The Birmingham Post*, devotes complete supplements every week to property, but has no architectural correspondent.

There is much good design policy, but not always implemented consistently. The rhetoric of civic-boosterism can sometimes take precedence over sensible but undramatic improvements. The management of the urban design process suffers from discontinuities. There is an excessive importance placed upon headline-grabbing landmark buildings, but less attention paid to more significant shapings of normative urban fabric such as Glenn Howells Architects' Southside housing.

The Big City Plan

The Big City Plan, preceded by Michael Parkinson's 2007 report, is allegedly the biggest urban design commission to be made in the UK. Urban Initiatives were commissioned by the city council in 2007, to produce a framework for the future growth and development of the city centre. Parkinson wrote that Birmingham, post Highbury, had had a successful first act, but that the momentum had faltered, and that there was now a need for a second act of a distinctly fresh nature. Urban Initiatives' task is to describe what that second act will consist of. Until the much delayed public consultation material is unwrapped, it is premature to judge the content.

The eighty-hectare city core will presumably be subject only to incremental improvement, with the one big exception of the promised improvement of New Street Station, for which the third scheme in recent years was announced in 2008, designed by Foreign Office Architects. Change will be concentrated on the inner city post-Highbury quarters, with the industrial part of Highgate in particular identified as the location for new family housing, to be promoted under a programme called *The Birmingham House*. While the recognition of the inadequacy of the market-led apartment building process is welcome, there is in Highgate, as in adjacent Digbeth and Deritend, a danger of the displacement of indigenous small-scale industry and the consequent gentrification of the area.

It is not another cycle of big gestures that Birmingham requires from the Big City Plan. What is required most of all is an end to what Liam Kennedy calls the 'creative destructiveness' which has characterised the planning and development of Birmingham over the past sixty years (Kennedy 2004); the inbuilt obsolescence which has led to continuous, destabilising change. It is hoped that the Big City Plan can deliver a framework that can accommodate necessary change, but which can primarily offer stability – a coherent, distinctive and enduring background for living.

Notes

1 The author was community planning consultant to the Ladywood Community Forum, representing Ladywood residents, which was the partner with Birmingham city council in the Ladywood Regeneration Framework.
2 Birmingham Polytechnic subsequently became the University of Central England which in turn, in 2007, was renamed Birmingham City University.
3 In 2007, 50 per cent of the ward population was among the most deprived 5 per cent of Super Output Areas (SOAs) in England (Office of National Statistics, *Index of Multiple Deprivations* 2007).
4 The author was a founder-member of the group, and was instrumental in the production of *The People's Plan*.

References

Barber, A. and Blackaby, B. (2008) *Living in Birmingham's City Centre: A Second Independent Review* (Birmingham: Birmingham University, Centre for Urban and Regional Studies).

BCC (Birmingham City Council) (1999) *Regeneration through Conservation* (Birmingham: Birmingham City Council Planning Department).

BCC (2003) *Design and Movement Framework for Eastside (Draft)* (Birmingham: Birmingham City Council).

BCC (undated) *City Centre Strategy* (Birmingham: Birmingham City Council Development Department).

Birmingham for People (1989) *The People's Plan for the Bull Ring* (Birmingham: Birmingham for People).

DEGW (1988) *The Highbury Initiative: Proceedings of the Birmingham City Centre Challenge Symposium*, 25–27 March 1988.

EDAW (1998) *Jewellery Quarter Urban Village Plan* (Birmingham: Birmingham City Council).

Holyoak, J. (1999) City Edge: Before Brindleyplace. In I. Latham and M. Swenarton (eds) *Brindleyplace: A Model for Urban Regeneration* (London: Right Angle Press) pp. 16-25.

Holyoak, J. (2004) Street, Subway and Mall: Spatial Politics in the Bull Ring. In L. Kennedy (ed.) *Remaking Birmingham: The Visual Culture of Urban Regeneration* (Abingdon: Routledge) pp. 13–24.

Howells, G. (2004) Making the Ordinary Extraordinary. In L. Kennedy (ed.) *Remaking Birmingham: The Visual Culture of Urban Regeneration* (Abingdon: Routledge) pp. 41–44.

Kennedy, L. (2004) The Creative Destruction of Birmingham. In L. Kennedy (ed.) *Remaking Birmingham: The Visual Culture of Urban Regeneration* (Abingdon: Routledge) pp. 1–10.

Latham, I. and Swenarton, M. (1999) *Brindleyplace: A Model for Urban Regeneration* (London: Right Angle Press).

Loftman, P. (1990) *A Tale of Two Cities: Birmingham the Convention and Unequal City. The International Convention Centre and Disadvantaged Groups*, Research Paper No. 6 (Built Environment Development Centre: Birmingham Polytechnic).

Marriott, O. (1967) *The Property Boom* (London: Hamish Hamilton).

Parkinson, M. (2007) *The Birmingham City Centre Masterplan: The Visioning Study* (Birmingham: Birmingham City Council).

Pullman, J. (1988) Bull Ring Scheme 'Lacks Humanity'. *Birmingham Post*, 10 March.

Tibbalds, M. K. (1990) *Birmingham Urban Design Study* (Birmingham: Birmingham City Council).

3 Manchester

Making it happen

Michael Hebbert

Critics who saw New Labour's 1999 urban renaissance vision as just the 'predictable outcome of a report by a group of metropolitan designer luvvies' may have missed the point about design (Crookston 2001: 90) but they were onto something about metropolitan bias. The Urban Task Force (UTF) was certainly London-centric. Almost all its members lived in the capital enjoying the advantages of a compact connected city on a daily basis. Their faith in the city as a place of aspiration, which people with choice will choose for living, leisure and work, reflected the realities of social geography in London as nowhere else.

It was not that they lacked first-hand knowledge of the world beyond Watford. Manchester in particular was well represented: David Lunts, the only member with a background in local politics, had chaired the City Council Housing Committee; Jon Rouse had spent his student years in the city; Martin Crookston and Sir Peter Hall had Mancunian connections; Anne Power had studied East Manchester's problem estates; and many of the working group members were Manchester-based – Mike Appleton (AMEC), Tom Bloxham (Urban Splash), Brian Robson (University of Manchester), Tom Russell (Manchester City Council), Michael Ward (Centre for Local Economic Studies) – and one of the main sources of property advice within the delivery group was Chris Brown of AMEC. *Towards an Urban Renaissance* mentioned the redevelopment of Hulme, Manchester's rising city centre population, and its new tram. Yet the prevailing image, seen through a London telescope, was of the physical and social dereliction depicted in a half-page aerial photograph of East Manchester (UTF 1999a: 30) and the uniquely bleak 'postcard from Manchester' which Alan Cherry of Countryside Properties contributed to the earlier *Urban Renaissance – Sharing the Vision* (UTF 1999b: 23).

Perceptions would shift rapidly. When Richard Rogers reconvened the Task Force for a follow-up in 2005, Manchester was high on its list of successes (UTF 2005). Chosen to host the 2005 Urban Summit, the city had become celebrated as a paragon of urban renaissance, much visited, often cited and widely admired as much for the quality of its leadership as for its physical transformation. This chapter explains how, why and when Manchester made it happen.

Manchester, the basics

We should start with the map of the location and size of the City of Manchester. In the conurbation with a population of 2.5 million, which was the world's first industrial metropolis, the core city has only 9 per cent of the metropolitan territory and 17 per cent of the population. No other municipality in this book is so tightly confined by its neighbours. Manchester's Victorian Gothic Town Hall is a fabulous seat of government, worthy of a world city, with a ceiling adorned with the coats of arms of its global trading partners, but the reality is that the local authority boundaries lie only half a mile (three blocks) west, three miles east, four miles north, and in an eight-mile strip due south, which includes the dynamic city centre and the airport, but misses most of the suburban wealth. It also, crucially, includes large areas of industrial and residential development that were gravely affected by the city-region's relatively late and steep deindustrialisation.

So the core city has a poor population – England's third most deprived after Tower Hamlets and Hackney – with twice the national average rate of residents on income support. Yet it also possesses the regional centre for a fifty-mile catchment of 10.5 million, with powerful clusters in retailing, sport, culture, health and education, and its finance and service-based economy jostles with Geneva, Lyon and Lisbon in the ranking of Europe's top twenty business destinations (Cushman and Wakefield 2007). The city has sunbelt productivity trends but a rustbelt poverty profile, high workplace earnings but low household income (ODPM 2006a). That is why the Casino Advisory Panel, in its wisdom, saw Manchester as a uniquely suitable location for Britain's first authorised mini-Las Vegas under the Gambling Act 2005 (CAP 2007: 51).

The socio-economic profile explains a third fact about Manchester – its political and policy stability under a hegemonic Labour council. Sir Richard Leese, leader since 1996, was preceded by Graham Stringer MP, who took over in 1984 after a seismic struggle ending years of internal Labour division. He concentrated decision-making in a powerful central executive, where it has remained ever since. Sir Howard Bernstein became Chief Executive in 1998 and his hand had been on the helm for many years before. Through an unspoken policy of internal appointments he has built around him a cadre of highly able senior officers who – like him – have made entire careers within Manchester Town Hall.

This close-knit executive, unique in British local government, single-mindedly pursues a core strategy to enhance economic competitiveness while spreading benefits through the resident population (MCC: 2007d). The mechanism is partnership with private enterprise. The Manchester Model, as it is known, has been pursued with extraordinary consistency ever since the council rejected leftist politics and adopted the motto 'Making It Happen' in 1984. Two early initiatives which did not happen were the city's bids to host the 1996 and 2000 Olympic Games: both were short-listed despite lukewarm support from the UK government, and though the 1996 Games went to Atlanta (ranking Manchester behind Athens, Toronto and Melbourne) and the 2000 went to Sydney (ranking Manchester third behind Beijing but ahead of Berlin and Istanbul), the bids brought a pay-off of more than £200 million of infrastructure investment, including the second terminal at the airport. Immediately after the failure of the 2000 bid the city relaunched its partnership under the banner of City Pride and bid successfully to host the 2002 Commonwealth Games. This time the eventual pay-off would be more than £2 billion (CGF 2006). Then came the Millennium Task Force, the New East Manchester (NEM), the Piccadilly Partnership, the Mosley Street Partnership, the Spinningfields Partnership, to name just five (Robson 2002; Bernstein 2005). Manchester's track record of collaborative delivery with the private sector is a remarkable achievement considering the only resources the council can bring to the table are political vision, land ownership, regulatory powers, negotiating skill – plus access to central government and European money. For their part Whitehall and Brussels appreciate a reliable municipal performer and have consistently underwritten the city through successive funding regimes. The Manchester Model has acquired a Rolls-Royce reputation: even more than the logic of economic statistics, what impressed the Casino Advisory Panel was the quality of executive commitment demonstrated by Sir Howard Bernstein's team and the will to succeed when others were equivocating (CAP 2007: 53–54). The State of the Cities Report singled them out as the council 'brave enough to focus on priorities and lead' (ODPM 2006b: 107).

Finally we should say a word about the distinctive culture of Mancunian urbanism. Although it got little acknowledgement in UTF's 1999 report, Manchester was an early convert to positive urban design. As soon as the local political élite made its break from Old Labour it had looked for inspiration to European progressive municipalities which took architecture and urbanism seriously (Taylor *et al.* 1996). In Steve Quilley's striking phrase 'the new urban left played mid-wife to the new urbanism' (2002: 76). Councillors visited Barcelona in the run-up to the 1992 Olympics and admired the flair of its street-based design, so different from the low-density, use-segregated solutions offered by their own planners. Reference to continental models increased as Manchester became an active player within Interreg and Eurocities networks in the mid-1990s. With awakened awareness of the city's role on the European and world scene came appreciation of its taken-for-granted but remarkable legacy of Victorian and Edwardian warehouses, clubs and street architecture (see Plate 3.1).

American New Urbanism was another significant reference point. In Hulme, the failed estate of 1960s mega-structures just south of the centre, the regeneration partner was Sir Alan Cockshaw of AMEC. His experience in the London Docklands led to the early hiring of the Toronto-based consultant Joe Berridge, whose masterplan concept for Hulme was developed through a Seaside-style design guide, drawn up by local architect George Mills and based on a partial reinstatement of the nineteenth-century street grid (MCC 1994). The Hulme guide aimed for housing densities of ninety dwellings per hectare, with the highest concentrations along major roads and at focal points. Streets were to be designed to encourage walking, with conventional crossroads at grid junctions, and there were to be no cul-de-sacs, only high streets, secondary streets, and residential roads, each with its codified parameters of building height and separation, frontage line, design speed, visibility splays and kerb radii (Rudlin and Falk 1999).

Ivor Samuels (2004) rates Hulme with Seaside as one of the seminal experiments in New Urbanism. It had to be fought for. Developers tried to stop it and so did the council's own planning and highways professionals and the Greater Manchester Police. But executive centralisation enabled the leadership to circumvent them and offer fast-track planning consents to developers

Plate 3.1 Manchester: a great European city: Cross Street looking west from the Royal Exchange. An ordinary street scene in the irregular grid, illustrating the variety and quality of the city's street architecture.

willing to comply. Encouraged by the outcome, they asked the planner Barbara McLoughlin to develop a similar guide for the city as a whole. She convened an advisory panel which included the architects George Mills, Jim Chapman and Ian Simpson, the planning consultant David Rudlin and two academics: the sociologist Ian Taylor and the geographer Brian Robson. Their *City Development Guide*, issued for consultation in May 1995, spelt out a detailed urban design formula to realise the city's image of a walkable, liveable European city (MCC 1995). Once again the hierarchy of streets provided the framework for everything else. High streets, including the radial roads into the city, were to be subject to rigorous urban principles and lined with mixed-use buildings in block form, built up to the street junctions with visual emphasis at corners (in the Victorian manner). The height of street-facing buildings was to be proportional to the width of the boulevard – the suggested enclosure ratio (building height : frontage-to-frontage width) was 1:5. Secondary streets were to have an enclosure ratio of at least 1:2.5 with most frontage buildings at least three storeys tall. Minor streets were to be less rigorously urban but still aim for an enclosure ratio of at least 1:2 (Rudlin 1999).

In a city known for its crime rate and gun culture it took political guts to encourage on-street parking and direct access to buildings from the street. Overriding police recommendations for target hardening and cellular urban form, the guide insisted on security protection through 'eyes on the street' and a permeable grid. Despite the experience of a major terrorist bomb during the consultation period, the council stuck to its urbanist principles when the code came to be adopted in January 1997:

> Manchester can be made a more secure city without resorting to the obtrusive and offensive spectre of universal barbed wire, bollards, shutters and other crime-prevention devices. The creation of fortified territories is a confession of defeat. We see the application of many such architectural approaches to public security as negative and an inhibition to the City's creativity.
>
> (MCC 1997a: 7)

So by 1997 Manchester was already committed to street-facing design, active frontage, respect for the building line, and a clear distinction between public and private space. The UTF was pushing at an open door. With advice again from Joe Berridge and a masterplan (Figure 3.1) led by Jason Prior of EDAW, rebuilding of the bomb-damaged city centre would become the first great demonstration project of New Labour's urban renaissance (Williams 2003).

The remainder of this chapter follows the renaissance since 1999. We will start thematically with three key ideas of design-led regeneration – integration, quality and density – and then take a circular tour. The chapter ends with a brief stock-taking of the Manchester case within the common agenda of the book.

Integration

The Task Force's most important message was about integrated design: integration of land use and transport, integration of building and street. Manchester could do more about the one than the other.

Towards an Urban Renaissance offers a marvellous exposition, beautifully illustrated by Andrew Wright Associates, of the integration of three-dimensional urban form with a seamless web of efficient public transport. Integration could be seen working for European municipalities who

Figure 3.1 Manchester: Millenium Quarter showing the designated area of the Millenium Task Force (1996–2000), and the principal outcomes of the EDAW masterplan (drawn by Graham Bowden). © Crown Copyright. All rights reserved. Licence number 100049043.

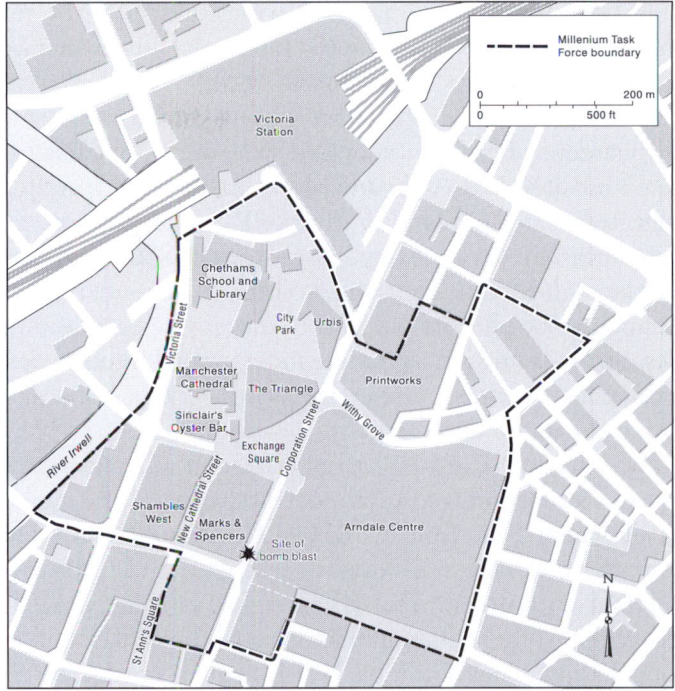

combined transport and planning powers, and they work in London too. England's other cities have almost no control over private bus operators, and very limited ability to initiate and finance tram or light rail alternatives. The UTF held back from recommending a London-style regulated franchise transport system for provincial cities (1999: 99). Six years on they recognised this as the only way to bring certainty to public transport planning and delivery and 'enable developers and regeneration agencies to have some confidence in the public transport systems around which they are being asked to structure higher density mixed-use development' (UTF 2005: 8).

Manchester proves the point. Bus services in the conurbation are operated by thirty-one companies, whose competing vehicles jam the centre. The original 1992 tram connections to Altrincham and Bury were only poorly extended to Eccles in 2002, leaving thirty-six miles of expansion to Ashton, Oldham, Rochdale and Wythenshawe planned since 1998, delayed and then axed by central government in 2004. The city's inability to control its own transport futures can be seen in the weed-grown track-bed at Bradford and the mothballed interchange at Colly-hurst. In 2008 a Transport Innovation Fund bid promised to unlock the impasse with £3 billion of investment as well as an increase in local control. But the deal depended upon the introduction of a road congestion charge to balance the costs. A referendum was held and voters rejected the package by four to one after a vigorous 'no' campaign from a business and motoring lobby led by Peel Holdings, owner of the out-of-town Trafford Centre (Hetherington 2008). Whatever the future holds, the period covered by this chapter was one of municipal impotence in integrated planning of land use and transport.

By contrast the Task Force's message about architectural scale integration of building and street was immediately relevant and deliverable. The *Guide to Development in Manchester* had already determined that new development should conform to a consistent back-of-pavement building line, offering active street frontages, forming street blocks, and accentuating corners. The use of cul-de-sacs was discouraged, and so was passive provision of landscaping. Greenspace should be purposefully integrated with building in the form of gardens, parks and greenways. The ground rules were elaborated for special areas, such as the *Supplementary Planning Guidance for the Bomb Damaged Area* (MCC 1997b), or the *Supplementary Planning Guidance for Ancoats Urban Village* (MCC 1999). They were applied to admirable effect in the refurbishment of Piccadilly Gardens, the insertion of One Piccadilly at the head of Portland Street (a subtly contextual mixed-use design by Allies and Morrison, Plate 3.2), and Argent's exemplary development of the neglected triangle of land in front of Piccadilly Station. Equally, the guidance laid the basis for the refurbishment of the city's large stock of Radburn-layout estates, for example in Beswick and Chorlton-on-Medlock, causing housing to be reoriented to face the public realm, and shopping precincts to be plucked out of the centres of estates and realigned along outer main road frontages. Street-facing precepts were incorporated into site design briefs, and applied consistently in development control. The consequences can be seen all over the city, wherever roadside sites have come up for development.

Six years after the adoption of the *Guide to Development in Manchester* the council convened stakeholder meetings to take stock and consider how much to carry forward into its new-style Development Plan Framework (MCC 2003a, 2004b). The main positive outcome was judged to be the city-wide transformation of gaps and voids into streetscapes – a rapid process and remarkable to witness. The design regime had encouraged the emergence of a 'new Manchester vernacular' giving contemporary form to the traditional urban disciplines of street architecture: frontage line, block form, back-of-pavement entrances, corner features, active frontage, mixed use (see Plate 3.3). These features in turn had stimulated street life and, for the first time, pavement cafes. Developers accustomed to regard mixed use as risky for office lets had learned how it could enhance value. For Peter Stewart, head of design guidance at CABE, Manchester had led the nation in 'sending out the message about the importance of good design and the contribution it can make to the creation of welcoming, enjoyable but effective cities and city centres' (MCC 2004b: 16).

Criticisms of the city's design regime came from two sides. Some wanted more detailed guidelines with local variation based on character analysis of the city's diverse neighbourhoods, especially suburban areas under pressure for infill. Others wanted less direction altogether. With the property boom putting a premium on visual impact, the design and development fraternity

Plate 3.2 Manchester: Piccadilly Gardens. A new office building by Allies & Morrison gives the Gardens a better sense of enclosure.

Plate 3.3 Manchester: Beswick's new frontage onto Ashton Old Road. Outward-facing family homes. In 2004 this view was a landscape of grass and trees screening distant back fences.

preferred buildings to be 'stunning' rather than to fit meekly into the street wall. However, the code has suited Manchester's way of doing things. The city likes to have broad policies for urban integration that are not map-based or tied to land allocations, and can be negotiated case by case: so a diluted version of the design guide remains as a Supplementary Planning Document within the Local Development Framework (LDF; MCC 2007a).

Quality

Richard Rogers's most personal contribution to the Task Force was the conviction that declining cities need good-quality architecture to recover their reputation as places to live. The UTF envisaged no conflict between the strong urban design regime required for urban integration and the pursuit of architectural excellence. Urbanism and architecture would be made to mesh through three-dimensional masterplans, development briefs, design competitions, new procurement practices and a well-informed public awareness, based on a CABE-type national framework and a network of Local Architecture Centres (UTF 1999a: 70–83).

In retrospect we can see two flaws in the UTF doctrine of design excellence. First, it underestimated the gap between urbanist and architectural cultures in Britain, a gap which has tended to widen despite the combined efforts of CABE, the Prince's Foundation, the Urban Design Group and the Academy of Urbanism. Second, Lord Rogers's team underplayed the role of the built heritage in establishing quality and distinctiveness (UTF 1999a: 251). Conserving old buildings and designing new ones to complement and enhance them has turned out to be a vital issue for every case study in this book. It too has been complicated in the past decade by the pressures of a property boom and the disconnection of architectural aesthetic from context.

The quality debate has a particular resonance in Manchester, with its extraordinary wealth of historic sites and buildings (Hartwell 2001; Hartwell *et al.* 2004). Like other rustbelt cities it has mixed feelings about the past (Lowenthal 1985: 403; Savitch and Kantor 2002: 45). On the one hand industrial poverty and blight are still sufficiently close to encourage an instinctive preference for shiny new-builds over conservation of old brick and masonry, an attitude embodied in Sir Howard Bernstein at the heart of the executive. On the other, the city's heritage has been a palpable asset. The marketing strategy of Peter Saville, the council's global positioning adviser, succinctly defines the Manchester brand in terms of historical uniqueness as the original modern city:

> It does not have an icon like the Eiffel Tower, the Sydney Harbour Bridge or the Empire State Building which immediately denotes the city of origin. Its icon is the entire cityscape of new and older buildings
>
> (MCC 2004a: 17)

Renaissance has been literal in the sense of building reuse and figurative in the reborn sense of Manchester's place in the world – the two have run together.

A local bookie, Jim Ramsbottom, set the pace when he bought up the scrap-yards and industrial slums of Castlefields and revealed the eighteenth-century canal basin on the site of the original Roman fort. This evocative site also contained the terminus of the world's first passenger railway (1830) and the majestic iron viaducts of the world's first suburban commuter line (1849). Once conserved, they became the nucleus for a potential World Heritage Site extending linearly along the Bridgewater Canal (1765) to the coal mines of Worsley, and up the Rochdale canal (1805) through ten locks to the great cotton spinning mills of Ancoats (UNESCO 1999). By the measure of global significance the designation could also have included the Royal Exchange, the Free Trade Hall, the John Rylands and Portico libraries, and the extensive district of nineteenth-century warehouses where the products of Cottonopolis were displayed and marketed for global export (Taylor *et al.* 2002).

The early successes of the Manchester Model capitalised on this heritage. The top local architectural practices grew their reputations on buildings that were at once modern, chic and contextual, often knowingly reviving the city's nineteenth-century traditions of street architecture (Hebbert 2008a). Designers explored the traditional material palette of industrial architecture – cast iron, stone flags, exposed brickwork – in their building conversions for developers such as Urban Splash, Bruntwood and Artisan. A Manchester Civic Society was formed and its meetings and widely disseminated newspaper, *Forum*, helped stir Mancunian enthusiasm at a time when Sir Neil Cossins, as chair of English Heritage (EH), was encouraging greater national recognition of the collective memory of the industrial era. High-quality synthesis of old and new was the trademark of Manchester regeneration: in the Gay Quarter bars along Canal Street, in the top-end retailing around St Ann's Square, in stylish infill schemes in the Northern Quarter, in China Town in the warehouse quarter, in the urban village of Ancoats, and above all in the Millennium Quarter, where the city council held out for it in the post-bomb reconstruction against the pressure from landowners for quick and easy reinstatement (Williams 2003).

The approach re-established Manchester's collective reputation as a place of quality and paid dividends to owners too. Innovative rehabilitations of the existing building stock realised investment values that were off the radar of London-based portfolio managers. Conversions exploited the mixed-use potential of these street-based buildings, especially the warehouses with their large floor plates and good daylight. Guy, Henneberry and Rowley (2002) illustrate the process with the Urban Splash conversion of the Smithfield Building in the Northern Quarter, a project also profiled in the UTF report (1999: 252). The design by Stephenson Bell achieved quality on three parameters: in heritage terms as a recycling job within a conservation area; urbanistically, as a perimeter block which cleverly provides active frontage on all sides; and stylistically, as a chic piece of contemporary design.

But a gap opened between these parameters of quality as land prices climbed after 2000, pitting conservation and context against property values and building height. Encouraged by the city's posture of ambivalence, developers sought cleared sites. In contrast to Leeds, Manchester had no Local List and was not proactive on buildings at risk. There were serious lapses in the handling of conservation aspects in, for example, the Free Trade Hall hotel conversion and the Shude Hill Transport Interchange. The most controversial case, ably analysed by Short (2007), was the 171 metre Beetham Hilton (Plate 3.4), which at a stroke torpedoed Manchester's prospects for United Nations Educational, Scientific and Cultural Organization (UNESCO) designation, yet was granted planning consent without any analysis of its impacts on the World Heritage Site or the Scheduled Archaeological Monument of the Roman fort at Castlefield.

Several other cities in this book had their own Beetham projects and all were playing the same competitive game with proposals for would-be iconic towers. But none was better fitted for this type of competition. The Manchester MIPIM Partnership outdid all its rivals at the glitzy Marché International des Professionnels de l'Immobilier (MIPIM) each March in Cannes, with a stand on the balcony over the main entrance of the Palais des Festivals, a yacht in the Vieux Port, and a gala dinner to celebrate the latest crane-count (MIPIM 2008). While the boom lasted the city took what it could get – with both hands.

Quantity

The UTF's clearest message was that successful urbanism needs density. Richard Rogers and Anne Power hammered it home at every opportunity, often citing Manchester to make their point (e.g. Rogers and Power 2000). From a London perspective the most striking thing about

Plate 3.4 Manchester: Beetham Tower from Whitworth Street West. An idiosyncratic building of quality which set the precedent for inferior towers, and had unfortunate consequences for Manchester's World Heritage Site designation.

Manchester was its stock of voids and empty land – Ian Simpson quoted Peter Cook's reason for hating the place as 'too much space and not enough buildings' (Kucharek 2006: 41). The 2001 Census showed Greater Manchester's gross residential density to be less than half that of Greater London: the City of Manchester's 3,400 people per square kilometre compared with inner London's 8,700 and Tower Hamlet's 9,900, and population numbers were still sinking. David Rudlin exhibited giant figure-ground maps showing how the built fabric had become a moth-eaten blanket (URBED 2000). Ten years on and a development boom later the picture had shifted and so had the issues. We got densification, but was it the right type and mix?

Manchester willingly responded to the UTF's encouragement to rebuild population numbers. The well-preserved street grid of the centre offered clear potential for city living: flat conversions of warehouses and offices were already booming in 1998 and were soon overtaken by the wave of new apartment construction that dominated the decade. Flat completions in the city centre averaged 2,000 annually, peaking at 3,000 in 2005. As in other cities, urban apartments became a hot market, with construction and investment sustained by international investment consortia who bought off-plan in bulk and at discount, financing the costs of construction and selling on through investment clubs to absentee landlords on buy-to-let mortgages. In the push for densification developers were allowed to dictate the dwelling mix, which consisted almost entirely of one- or two-bedroom flats in the size range of 50–60 square metres. The authority relaxed its former overlooking standard of twenty-two metres between habitable rooms and applied no internal floorspace standards or requirements for provisions of external amenity space. In the drive for visible architectural impact, developers were encouraged to pursue apartment schemes of more than twenty storeys, sometimes getting 'soft' consents, without obligation to provide community benefits, in return for increases in density and height. By 2006 Manchester had approved more than twenty apartment towers in and around the centre and had as many as forty further schemes under discussion. Refusal of planning consent was practically unheard of.

Manchester was the only major British city to be so permissive. The national advice on tall buildings drawn up by CABE and EH warns that free-for-all policy encourages property speculation and spreads development pressure in the wrong places (EH/CABE 2003: 2). Manchester saw evidence of this as the local average price of land for flats climbed towards £6 million per hectare (VO 2008). The willingness of developers to pay fabulous sums on slivers of land threw a blight over small-scale and incremental development in areas such as the Northern Quarter. But the city council offered no clarification in its 2007 plan revision, maintaining with studied Mancunian insolence that any such proposals should be presented in the context of the joint CABE/EH guidance – the guidance it had itself disregarded (MCC 2007a: 50). The 2007 plan revision did accept the need for minimum space requirements and improved environmental performance, and the council also introduced policies to boost the proportion of family housing in new schemes (MCC 2007c: 26). But these changes came too late to affect the mass of city centre accommodation created in the apartment boom.

The result was a worrisome legacy of small flats with poor specification and high vacancy rates, and a new source of unwelcome media coverage (Brignall 2008). Yet empty buy-to-lets were only half the picture. London journalists tended to miss the other story beyond the Mancunian Way. Most new housing in the inner ring has continued to be built for families, and intensification still follows the Guide to Development's distinctive model of design-led regeneration. The next section offers a quick sample of both worlds (Figure 3.2).

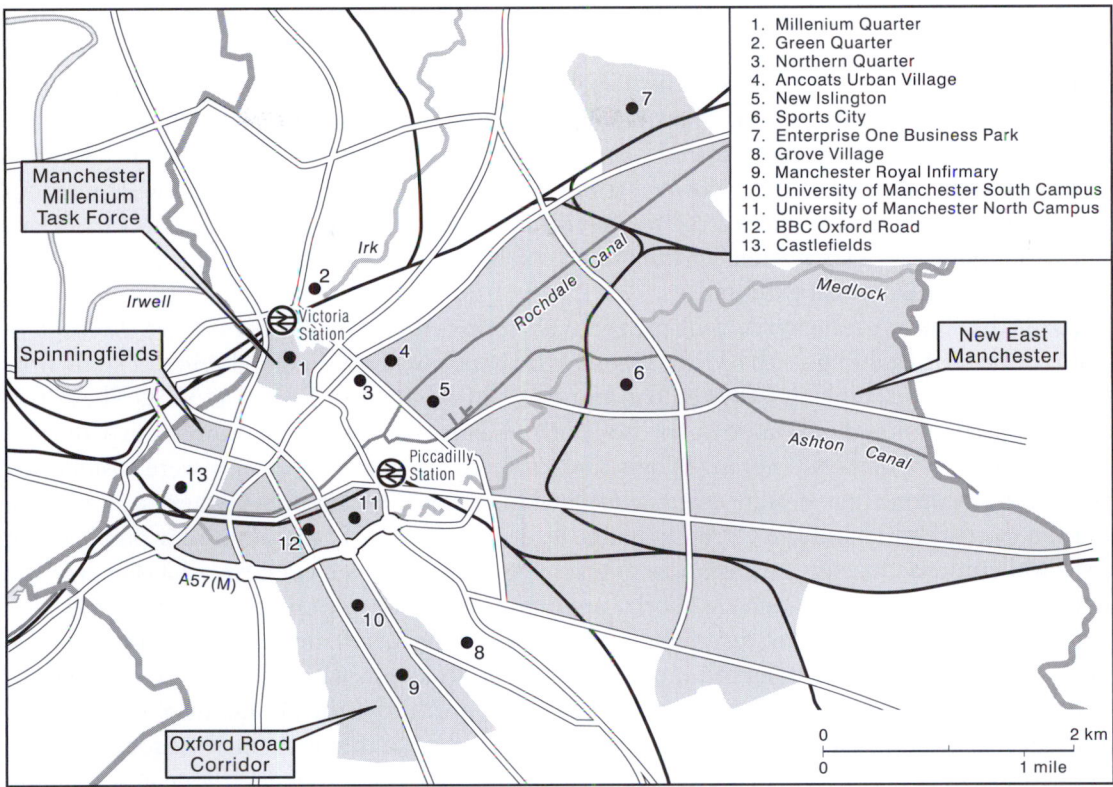

Figure 3.2 Manchester: circular tour of regeneration sites (drawn by Graham Bowden). © Crown Copyright. All rights reserved. Licence number 100049043.

A circular tour of regeneration sites

We begin at the corner of Corporation Street where the Irish Republican Army (IRA) detonated 1,500 kilograms of explosives on Saturday 15 June 1996. Nobody died but the blast caused extensive damage throughout the city centre. The bomb was located precisely between the Arndale Shopping Centre and Shambles Square, two mid-twentieth-century comprehensive redevelopments which had cut off the modern city centre from the mediaeval core containing Manchester's fifteenth-century cathedral and the sixteenth-century Chetham's School and Library (the oldest public library in England), as well as the Corn Exchange and Victoria Station. Rather than just repair the 1,200 damaged buildings, the city used the reconstruction to reintegrate the historic nucleus while cannily expanding the central shopping district in the face of imminent competition from the 100,000 square metre out-of-town centre in neighbouring Trafford. Williams (2003) provides a comprehensive narrative of this complex exercise in design-led regeneration (Figure 3.1).

The city council acted swiftly after the bomb, set up a task force, held design competitions, and coordinated a comprehensive redevelopment covering twenty-four hectares and forty-nine development projects, to a masterplan by EDAW. The massive retail mall of the Arndale Centre was allowed to remain intact but the superblock was reconfigured to create shop windows and entrances around its external façade. The adjacent deck of Shambles Square was demolished and replaced by two new urban blocks and a curving New Cathedral Street, which re-established the historic connection – though not the visual link – between the eighteenth-century St Ann's Square and the cathedral quarter. The street emerges onto Exchange Square, a triangular space framed by Selfridges store, the restored Corn Exchange and the new Arndale façade. Ramped tiers express the change of level down a water sculpture with stepping stones, which articulates the curving boundary line of the mediaeval core. A television mega-screen on the Corn Exchange façade and a ferris wheel encampment on the ramps have cluttered Martha Schwartz's over-sophisticated landscape design.

Across the square to the north-west the red sandstone cathedral tower rises above a deceptive cluster of historic buildings – the Mitre Hotel (1815) and two half-timbered relics of sixteenth-century Manchester, Sinclairs' Oyster Bar and the Old Wellington Rooms (1552). These two survivors used to stand 200 metres to the south and in the 1960s had been jacked up and installed on the Shambles podium. When that came to be demolished they were dismantled and reassembled on their present site – a forgivable solecism in the circumstances. A passage between the cathedral and the Corn Exchange leads into City Park, the other new public space in the Millennium Quarter. This triangle of grass planted with silver birch trees has become the regional gathering place for teenage 'Goths', who punish the again too-clever landscaping. The Corn Exchange and cathedral lie to the south of the park. Chetham's – a mediaeval college of priests, now a school for talented musicians – sits to the west, with its wonderful sixteenth-century chained library, and Victoria Station lies to the north. But the dominant presence along the east side of the park is the featureless glacial slab of Urbis, an urban-themed visitor attraction designed by Ian Simpson (2000). It was one of the first examples of the much-repeated ski ramp profile, a cliché that rarely produces good street architecture. In this case the shiny peak offers a landmark to the city centre while Victoria Station gets a back view of service entrances and rubbish bins.

The Corn Exchange is the unifying centre of the Millennium Quarter, its triangular form marking the original boundary of the mediaeval core known as the Hanging Ditch. Renamed 'The Triangle', the galleried Edwardian space with its glazed roof has become part of the extending web of central shopping and leisure streets. Across Corporation Street shop-fronts have opened around the façade of the Arndale Centre. Across Withy Grove in the former *Daily Mirror* printworks an ersatz pastiche of Manhattan, with steam ducts and fire escapes, leads up through restaurants and bars to a multiplex cinema, all bringing footfall to spaces previously dominated by traffic and parking. The continuing outward spread of regeneration demonstrates the success of the Millennium Quarter masterplan in its primary objective of breaking the barriers – physical and psychological – which restricted and divided the city centre.

Tower cranes to the far side of Victoria Station mark an attempt to break another barrier and extend the city centre boom across the River Irwell where it meets the River Irk, at the foot of Cheetham Hill. The Green Quarter by Crosby Lend Lease is a high-density, mixed-use bridgehead into a low-value industrial area, with almost 1,500 flats and a hotel, offices and shops on a site of 3.2 hectares. The cluster of vertical towers seems intended to make a visual declaration, but future residents will pay the cost through living densities well in excess of 900 persons per hectare. The flats are small, internal dimensions are tight, and the building heights mean that the small external amenity spaces – less than 0.61 square metres per capita – will enjoy little sunlight. Green Quarter is the largest of several similarly problematic projects across the north of the city centre and across the river in Salford (Brignall 2008).

Going clockwise from here, a series of rivers, canals and roads radiate from the city centre, interdigited with tightly gridded industrial districts. Immediately to the east of the city centre the great mills of Ancoats – built in the Napoleonic period and derelict for many years – have been restored to structural soundness and are being converted into flats, offices and hotels, with financing from ING Bank and the Royal Bank of Scotland. The Ancoats grid contains Manchester's only example of traffic-calmed highway engineering. Adjacent to the south between the Rochdale and Ashton Canals, a semi-derelict and crime-ridden housing estate has been demolished and replaced with the New Islington Millennium Community, an architectural showcase of 12.5 hectares, master-planned by Will Alsop in characteristic whacky style, heavily subsidised through English Partnerships (EP) and developed by Urban Splash as one of New Labour's model sustainable settlements. It contains some interesting experiments in terraced family housing and self-build homes, and its neighbourhood services include a new clinic. It is a pampered project, not really model or sustainable – but fun anyway.

The regeneration of the entire sector from the city centre eastwards has been orchestrated through the partnership structure of NEM, founded in 2000 as an Urban Regeneration Company in direct response to the UTF (Parkinson *et al.* 2006). NEM is a comprehensive initiative which touches on all aspects of employment, education, crime prevention and community development over an area of 1,900 hectares. Major schemes include: (three kilometres out from the Town Hall) the extensive brownfield site redeveloped as SportsCity around the stadium built for the 2002 Commonwealth Games, as well as a major Asda-Walmart superstore and the site earmarked for the unsuccessful super-casino bid; and (four kilometres out) the Enterprise One Business Park. Both regeneration sites focus on tram stations and demonstrate the frustrating impacts of externally imposed Metrolink delays. That apart, NEM has been remarkably successful in implementing its 2001 masterplan *A New Town in the City* (MCC 2001). The masterplan is based on a clear philosophy of physical consolidation around a revived street grid, with local centres relocated onto main road frontage, and free-flow green space transformed into a series of spaces that are all enclosed and 'owned' (Hebbert 2008b). The impact of the regeneration is closely monitored through a score of key performance indicators. They starkly show how difficult it is to shift the basic profiles of unemployment, physical incapacity, crime, low educational achievement, and teenage conception. But resident satisfaction with the area as a place to live climbed steadily from 46 per cent in 2000 to 75 per cent in 2005. The changed perception of liveability reflects NEM's attention to physical transformation of East Manchester's nineteenth-century gridded workers' terraces and post-war Radburn social housing. So far the population has only just stabilised, but NEM is on target to build 12,500 new homes in the area by 2010, mostly for families. The city continues to apply Hulme-type principles of perimeter block design and street hierarchy (Figure 3.3) in its long-term aim – as the NEM Interim Evaluation puts it – of making East Manchester 'normal' (Parkinson *et al.* 2006).

Continuing clockwise under the vast railway viaducts that lead into Piccadilly Station we come to the city centre's southern rim. This area contains the original exemplar of design-led regeneration in Hulme as well as a good example of Private Finance Initiative (PFI)-funded estate improvement in Grove Village, where Gleeson is the city's partner in a £90 million make-over of Radburn layout council housing into a street-based neighbourhood of perimeter blocks and pocket parks (Figure 3.3). Oxford Road is due to become Manchester's main zone of transformation in the next ten years as the British Broadcasting Corporation (BBC) relocates to Salford Quays, the universities reorganise their campuses, the National Health Service (NHS) Trust expands, and various sites currently used for car parking become ripe for development. In a classic

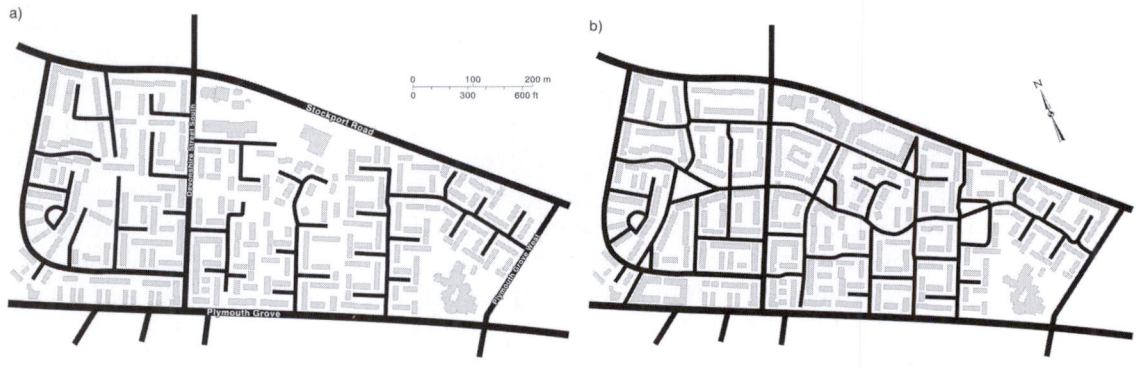

Figure 3.3 Manchester, Plymouth Grove housing: (a) as built in the 1970s by the council housing department and (b) revamped in 2006–2009 and rebranded as Grove Village by M. J. Gleeson, Harvest Housing Group and Nationwide Building Society under the Ardwick Private Finance Initiative.

demonstration of the Manchester Model the city has taken the initiative and set up a City South Partnership, which links these pieces into a compelling narrative based on strategic response to globalisation and expansion of the knowledge economy, city and universities, combining around an ambition to create a UK centre of excellence in maternal and paediatric, biomedical and neuroscience research (MCC 2003b; MCC 2006). Sir Terry Farrell, who had already done the strategic plan for the University of Manchester, has been master-planning the arc from Piccadilly Station westward around the elevated Mancunian Way. Unlike his urban designing for Newcastle, Edinburgh or London, the Manchester work is not in the public gaze: as Sir Terry explained to *Property Week*, 'Howard Bernstein likes to build up an intellectual understanding of the opportunities and we're an aid to help in that thinking process' (McConnell 2007).

Continuing clockwise again, the Bridgewater Canal and the River Irwell lead south-west into the docklands, which have brought development bonanzas to the adjacent municipalities of Trafford and Salford. The City of Manchester is tightly bounded by the Irwell on its western side, but the 500-metre space between Deansgate and the river has yielded another ambitious partnership project, Spinningfields, marketed as the region's premium financial and business services destination. A deceptively large site of twelve hectares has been assembled out of car parking areas, a former Higher Education college campus, commercial acquisitions and compulsory purchase. The city's partner this time is Allied London Properties and the object is a fully managed £1.25 billion business district with 220,000 square metres of flexible offices and potential for 25,000 jobs. The masterplan by Foster and Partners includes a 200-bed five-star hotel, some 400 flats along the river and five new public squares (MCC 2007b). Though the scheme is not due for completion until 2012, the squares are already coming to life (see Plate 3.5). The John Rylands Library and the Pump House People's History Museum, both newly refurbished, provide cultural anchors. So far, the main landmark is the Civil Justice building by the Australian practice Denton Corker Marshall, a grey slab block with yellow extrusions. The largest judicial complex built in Britain since the Royal Courts of Justice in 1882, it lacks the urbanity and humanism of G. E. Street's complex on the Strand but is a striking architectural object and has won nomination for the Royal Institute of British Architects (RIBA) Stirling Prize.

Plate 3.5 Manchester: Hardman Square, Spinningfields. One of five ERDF-funded squares. The visual axis leads only to po-mo medocrity on the Salford bank of the Irwell. Manchester still needs a decent riverfront.

Spinningfields offers yet another example of the vitality of the Manchester Model. Public–private partnership has transformed the Deansgate backwater into a business quarter of large-floorplate, flexible office buildings, that put Manchester on a par with its European competitors.

The city's property newsletter puts it well:

> the development has been designed to be an exemplar of how the national urban renaissance and competitiveness agendas can be translated into tangible action on the ground.
>
> (MM 2005: 2)

Where better to end our tour!

Conclusion

The City of Manchester is a fascinating case study in the larger themes of this book. It demonstrates how a well-managed and purposive local authority can – as the UTF argued – lead urban renaissance and 'make it happen' (1999 44). The local authority is famously entrepreneurial, opportunistic and market-oriented, and has built a very strong reputation as being good to do business with (Williams 2003). The executive does not like to be constrained by statutory planning and thanks to electoral geography is politically unchallenged and has no need to use planning as a collaborative medium. So, by comparison with, say, London, Leeds, Birmingham or Edinburgh, we have little public debate about urbanism and an LDF which is as noncommittal as it can be about building density, height or land use, allowing hope values to roam freely and the city to negotiate developments case by case. Design review is handled internally by council officers.

Yet Manchester does take urban design quite seriously. It hires world-class consultants to provide it – Joe Berridge, Terry Farrell, Jason Prior, Norman Foster – though much of their work is for internal not public use. Its consistent application of New Urbanist principles of street-facing development, mixed-use and active frontage has completely transformed the city centre and some large inner-city estates and at least begun to uplift the vitality of district centres. It had moral and practical support from the local design élite until they grew bored with contextualism and height-to-width ratios. The tall buildings boom marked a new phase in design-led regeneration, in which the city has attached great importance to getting into the premier league of built objects. Most cities try to cluster their towers for good visual and economic reasons. In Manchester, where urban design is done behind closed doors in pre-application negotiations, the scatter-pattern suggests some contrary desire to disperse landmarks to the end of sightlines – along Deansgate to the Beetham Tower, along Corporation Street to the Green Quarter, up Shude Hill to Skyline Central, along Newton Street to the tower called Sarah's Village, and along Store Street to the abortive Gravity Tower. As Sir Terry Farrell was heard to observe in his keynote speech to the Annual Conference of the Urban Design Group in Manchester in November 2004, the logic of building tall in Manchester may be more psychological than economic – 'I see it as an expression thing not a reality based thing'.

Looking back to the UTF, what is interesting about *Towards an Urban Renaissance* is that it never fell for the architectural fallacy – academic critics of the designer-luvvies got this wrong. The UTF's concept of renaissance subordinated design to the larger project of place-making, led by local government and inspired in equal measure by ecological imperatives, economic ambition, and a commitment to social integration. It is a difficult balance for any city to achieve. Manchester has done better than most.

Acknowledgements

With thanks (subject to usual disclaimers) to Martin Crookston, Lyn Fenton, Sir Peter Hall, Warren Marshall, Barbara McLoughlin, Brian Robson, Tom Russell, Michael Short, and to our many Masters students whose dissertations can be read in the Kantorowich Library, especially Eve Bailey, Charlotte Brooks, Ian Love and Lisa Mutch – and many thanks too to Graham Bowden for his cartography.

References

Bernstein, Sir H. (2005) *The Regeneration of Manchester: The Rebuilding of a City*. The Fourth Happold Medal Lecture, 4 April (London: Construction Industry Council).

Brignall, M. (2008) Pop Goes the Property Boom. *The Guardian*, 16 February.

CAP (Casino Advisory Panel) (2007) *Final Report of the Casino Advisory Panel* (London: Department of Culture, Media and Sport).

CGF (Commonwealth Games Federation) (2006) *Manchester 2002: The XVII Commonwealth Games Post Games Report* (five volumes). Online. Available at: http://www.commonwealthgames.com (last accessed 1 September 2008).

Cushman & Wakefield (2007) *European Cities Monitor*. Online. Available at: http://www.cushmanandwakefield.com (last accessed 4 September 2008).

Guy, S., Henneberry, J., and Rowley, S. (2002) Development Cultures and Urban Regeneration. *Urban Studies* 39 (7): 1181–1196

Hartwell, C. (2001) *Manchester (Pevsner Architectural Guides)* (London: Penguin Books).

Hartwell, S., Hyde, M., and Pevsner, N. (2004) *Lancashire: Manchester and the South-East (The Buildings of England)* (New Haven, CT: Yale University Press).

Hebbert, M. (2008a) An Everyday Unity, the Art of Street Architecture. In C. C. Bohl and J.-F. Lejeune (eds) *Modern Civic Art: Sitte Hegemann and The Metropolis* (London: Routledge) pp. 237–248.

Hebbert, M. (2008b) Re-Enclosure of the Urban Picturesque: Green-Space Transformations in Postmodern Urbanism. *Town Planning Review* 79 (1): 31–59.

Hetherington, P. (2008) Disaster Zone? *The Guardian* (Society Guardian supplement 3), Wednesday 17 September.

Kucharek, J.-C. (2006) The Greater Good (Unreal Cities: Manchester). *RIBA Journal* 113 (10): 38–42.

Lowenthal, D. (1985) *The Past is a Foreign Country* (Cambridge: Cambridge University Press).

McConnell, T. (2007) The Mancunian Way. *Property Week,* 21 May.

MCC (Manchester City Council) (1994) *Rebuilding the City: A Guide to Development in Hulme* (jointly published with Hulme Regeneration Ltd) (Manchester: Manchester City Council).

MCC (1995) *City Development Guide: Consultation Draft* (Manchester: Manchester City Council).

MCC (1997a) *Guide to Development in Manchester* (Manchester: Manchester City Council).

MCC (1997b) *Supplementary Planning Guidance for the Bomb Damaged Area* (Manchester: Manchester City Council).

MCC (1999) *Supplementary Planning Guidance for Ancoats Urban Village* (Manchester: Manchester City Council).

MCC (2001) *New East Manchester: A New Town in the City* (Manchester: Manchester City Council).

MCC (2003a) *Guide to Development Review Event, August 22nd 2003* (feedback report) (Manchester: Manchester City Council).

MCC (2003b) *Manchester Knowledge Capital, Manchester* (Manchester: Manchester City Council). Online. Available at: http://www.manchesterknowledge.com (last accessed 1 September 2008).

MCC (2004a) *Marketing Plan for the City of Manchester 2004/5–2006/7* (Manchester: Manchester City Council).

MCC (2004b) *City Development Event Final Report* (Manchester: Manchester City Council).

MCC (2006) *Manchester City Region Development Programme* (Manchester: Manchester City Council).

MCC (2007a) *Guide to Development in Manchester* (Supplementary Planning Document) (Manchester: Manchester City Council).

MCC (2007b) *Spinningfields Masterplan* (Report to The Executive, 27 June) (Manchester: Manchester City Council).

MCC (2007c) *Providing for Housing Choice: Planning Guidance* (Manchester: Manchester City Council).

MCC (2007d) *Manchester City Council Core Strategy: Issues and Options Consultation* (December 2007) (Manchester: Manchester City Council).

MIPIM (2008) *Manchester at MIPIM 2008.* Manchester MIPIM Partnership Online. Available at: http://www.manchesteratmipim.com (last accessed 3 September 2008).

MM (Marketing Manchester) (2005) Spinningfields. *Manchester Update,* October, p. 2.

Parkinson, M., Evans, R., Meegan, R., Karecha, J., and Hutchins M. (2006) *New Evaluated Manchester: Interim Evaluation of NEM* (Liverpool: European Institute for Urban Affairs, John Moores University).

Quilley, S. (2002) Entrepreneurial Turns: Municipal Socialism and After. In J. Peck and K. Ward (eds) *City of Revolution: Restructuring Manchester* (Manchester: Manchester University Press) pp. 76–94.

Robson, B. (2002) Mancunian Ways: The Politics Of Regeneration. In J. Peck and K. Ward (eds) *City of Revolution: Restructuring Manchester* (Manchester: Manchester University Press) pp. 34–49.

Rudlin, D. (1999) The Hulme and Manchester Design Guides. *Built Environment* 25 (4): 317–324.

Samuels, I. (2004) An Anglo-American Postscript. In P. Panerai, J. Castex, J. C. Depaule,. and I. Samuels (eds) *Urban Forms: The Death and Life of the Urban Block* (Oxford: Architectural Press) pp. 168–199.

Savitch, H. and Kantor, P. (2002) *Cities in the International Marketplace* (Princeton: Princeton University Press).

Taylor, I., Evans, K., and Fraser, P. (1996) *A Tale of Two Cities* (London: Routledge).

Taylor, S., Cooper, M., and Barnwell, P.S. (2002) *Manchester, the Warehouse Legacy* (London: English Heritage).

Unesco (1999) *Manchester and Salford (Ancoats, Castlefield and Worsley) Submission to Tentative List by Department of Culture, Media and Sport,* 21 June. Online. Available at: http://www.whc.unesco.org/en/tentativelists/1316/ (last accessed 1 September 2008).

URBED (Urban and Economic Development Ltd) (2000) *Organic Cities* (Manchester: URBED).

VO (Valuation Office) (2008) *Property Market Reports Valuation Office.* Online. Available at: http://www.voa.gov.uk (last accessed 3 September 2008).

Williams, G. (2003) *The Enterprising City Centre: Manchester's Development Challenge* (London: Spon).

4 Leeds

Shaping change and guiding success

Rachael Unsworth and Lindsay Smales

Introduction

Leeds is a city that has experienced a long period of sustained renewal, driven by strong economic forces. Views about the impacts of changes in the built environment differ widely. Some people are simply impressed by the scale and pace of change and make the assumption that it must be good for the city to move on in this vibrant way. Others are more critical in their appraisal. Although Leeds made great strides in the late twentieth century in terms of vitality, public realm, identity, diversity and mix, the city has made less certain progress in recent years under extreme development pressure. The city has seen the construction of a range of mediocre buildings, the dominance of private capital, the sidelining of environmental concerns, and a failure to add new green open space.

Leeds: the development of the city to the twenty-first century

Leeds is the regional capital of Yorkshire and the Humber, having been the foremost and the most diverse industrial city of the West Yorkshire conurbation. According to the 2001 Census, the Leeds Metropolitan District population had at that time reached 715,000, although this figure includes quite separate settlements such as Otley and Wetherby to the north and Morley and Methley in the south. This extensive boundary with a large rural hinterland makes it a different kind of place from any other major English city (Unsworth *et al.* 2004). It was the only one of the eight 'core cities' to show growth in the 1990s and its employment total is fourth in England, behind London, Birmingham and Manchester (ODPM 2006a,b).

Even in the 1990s, Leeds was considered to be the archetypal northern industrial city (Smales and Whitney 1996). The importance of the city's manufacturing base has declined until it now accounts for only 9 per cent of the workforce, while service industries make up over 80 per cent (LCC 2007a). Leeds has emerged as the service centre for its city region and beyond – its legal, financial and business services sector expanded to employ more than 100,000 people by 2005 – and it is also a significant centre for healthcare provision and higher education. This change in economic and employment structure is reflected in the new and refurbished buildings of the city, with offices and other service sector uses taking over sites and buildings previously occupied by factories, warehouses, wharves and railway yards (Stillwell and Unsworth 2008).

Though some notable historic buildings have been retained (Wrathmell 2005), patchy demolition, substantial rebuilding and radical road remodelling in the post-Second World War era led to the urban grain becoming coarser in scale and less intricate, with some street frontages lost or made less coherent (Figure 4.1). In his 1979 history of the city, *Leeds: The Back to Front, Inside Out, Upside Down City,* Nuttgens pointed out that by then it had something of an image problem as a place that was difficult to read and understand. He lamented the fact that the potential of the River Aire was not realised: 'Where after all, is the river? It's not very obvious: most of the time not even visible; certainly not yet exploited as one of the assets of the city – people in Leeds often don't even know it is there' (1979: 1). The late 1970s was perhaps the nadir of the city in urban design terms. But Leeds did not suffer the scale of economic collapse that afflicted many other cities, and in the 1980s some of the redundant sites and buildings were recycled even as de-industrialisation continued. With a fundamentally robust economy, including, as ever, a wide range of activities (Burt and Grady 1994), Leeds moved less painfully into the post-industrial era than was the case with many of its peers.

Much of the new development in the 1980s was uninspiring architecturally: pseudo-Victorian buildings constructed using local brick, local stone and pitched slate roofs, a style which came to be known as 'The Leeds Look' (Smales and Whitney 1996). Critic Kenneth Powell damned the Leeds approach to development control with faint praise in *The Architect's Journal* in an article titled 'The Offence of the Inoffensive' (Powell 1989). It took a series of public debates convened by Leeds Civic Trust before this very prescriptive and limiting approach was challenged and the

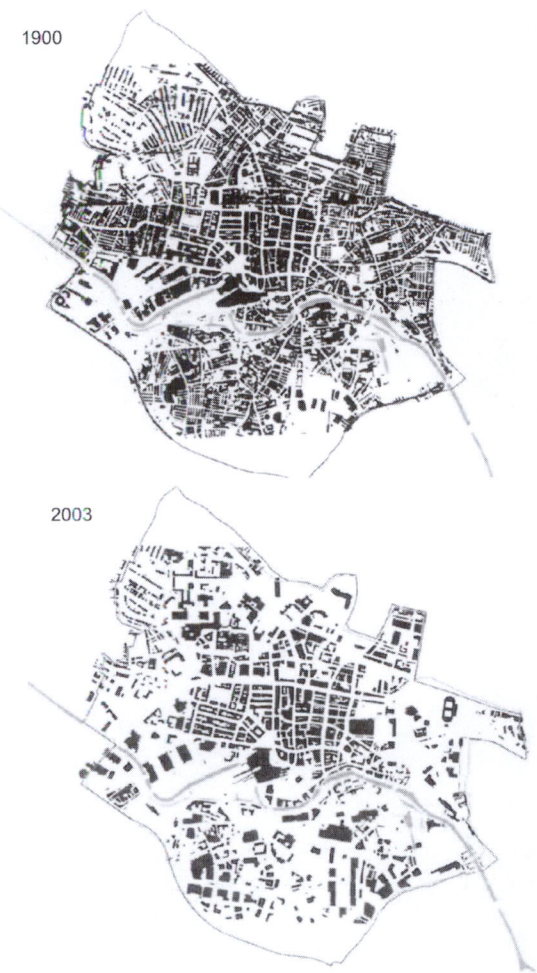

Figure 4.1 Leeds in 1900 and 2000: changing urban grain (Courtesy of Leeds City Council).

city council was prepared to grant planning permission, once again, for more overtly modernist buildings.

The city council – Labour controlled for many years until 2004 – has intervened in the redevelopment process in a variety of ways over the last two decades. In the early 1990s, council leader Jon Trickett promoted the twenty-four-hour city initiative and personally oversaw the Landmark Leeds streetscape project, introducing postmodern street furniture, new lighting and contemporary paving into the central retail core. After Trickett, who acted like a European-style mayor, there has been less charismatic political leadership and more reliance on planning policy and design guidance. An incrementalist approach to regeneration has followed, continuing since 2004 under a joint Conservative–Liberal Democrat administration.

As well as Trickett's city centre initiatives, a number of key development projects were completed on the waterfront and acted as catalysts for further regeneration (see Plate 4.1). These included a new Asda headquarters beside the River Aire just south of the railway station, Barratt's Victoria Quays housing scheme and St James Securities' Embankment office development (both reusing warehouses) and the successful enticing of the Royal Armouries to locate its new museum at Clarence Dock. Once these four major players had rediscovered the urban waterfront, many previously wary investors followed their lead. These developments took place within one of the two Thatcher government-imposed Urban Development Corporation (UDC) areas, but it is considered that the waterfront and nearby area might well have been redeveloped without this central government intervention because shortage of space in the established business district

Plate 4.1 Leeds: Waterfront transformation. The River Aire from Crown Point Bridge – 1960s and 2008 (top photo Courtesy Leeds Civic Trust).

was already creating pressure for outward extension. The UDC simply speeded up the process (Robson *et al.* 1998).

The city centre continued to expand in the 1990s (Figure 4.2), as allowed for in the Unitary Development Plan (UDP; LCC 2001), and redevelopment has come to more and more sites, including Wellington Street and Whitehall Road to the west, Holbeck Urban Village to the south, and around the Armouries Museum to the south-east. Existing public spaces have been improved, some central streets have been pedestrianised, and the retail quarter is generally highly acclaimed. Office stock has been upgraded and expanded, warehouses and mills have been sensitively converted, some less cherished 1960s buildings have been reclad and reused, old bridges have been improved and three new footbridges constructed. This has created a better-functioning city centre with more economic activity, more occupiers and a greatly improved image.

But the story has its less impressive and more contentious elements: of uneven development and the supremacy of the economic growth agenda, and of an overstretched planning system with insufficient powers and with developers calling the tune. The UDP had been too long in gestation (UTF 1999a): a consultation draft appeared in 1992 but the plan was only adopted in 2001, by which stage the circumstances had changed and the plan was lacking in specific guidelines to steer development, especially of city centre residential projects (Unsworth 2007a). Consequently, there is an oversupply of small apartments, as in all major UK regional cities, and a shortage of good-quality, environmentally sound new buildings accessible to the broadest range of users.

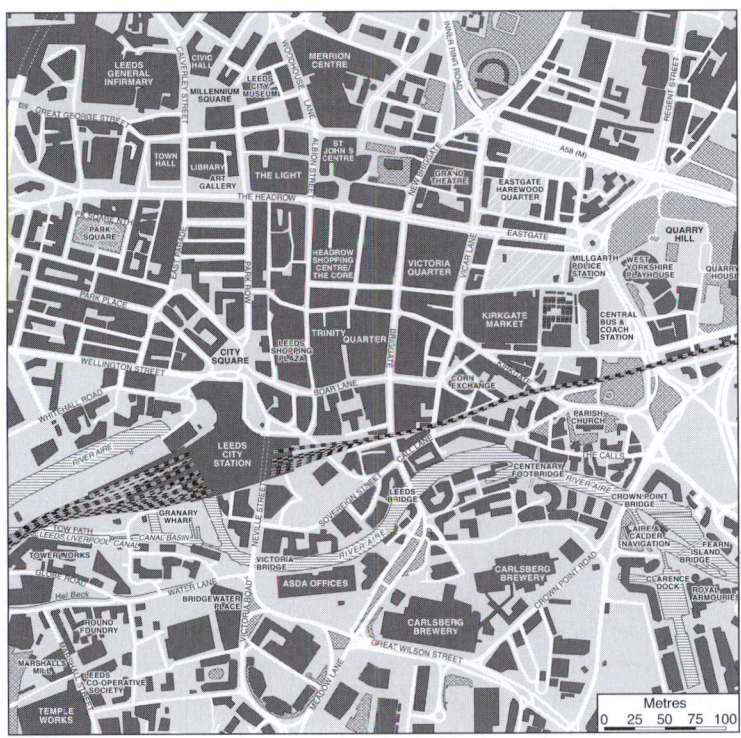

Figure 4.2 Leeds city centre (drawn by Alison Manson). © Crown Copyright. All rights reserved. Licence number 100049043.

Another problem is that, rather than the incremental approach to planning and urban design being a strength, it has become a weakness. And while the economic success of Leeds is much lauded, the local and subregional transport system is overloaded and underfunded, with much of the centre still dominated by traffic. Ironically, Leeds, with its diverse economy and regional capital status has been perhaps too successful for urban design quality to be really high. The pace of change has been frantic and, compared with cities that suffered much greater economic failure in earlier recessions, Leeds has been at a distinct *disadvantage* in not having access to the level of grant money that has been such a boon to other northern cities.

Current urban planning and design policy

Urban planning and design issues are presently the remit of the City Development directorate which, since 2007, has included: transport, land use, economic development and employment, environment, arts, heritage, libraries, sports and active recreation, parks and countryside, highways management, design services and asset management. This enhances the chances of integrated policy development and service delivery, but there are still problems of linkage and coherence between the activities of the main built environment sections.

In 2000, after a decade in which urban design had gradually become more prominent both nationally and locally, Leeds City Council published the *Leeds City Centre Urban Design Strategy* (LCCUDS; LCC 2000). The draft document was exposed to a wide-ranging consultation process which incorporated the views and expertise of, amongst others, Leeds Civic Trust, the Victorian Society and local members of the Urban Design Alliance (UDAL). It also drew on the research work of students on design courses at Leeds Metropolitan University (Smales and Burgess 1999) and took their detailed analysis of the visual and physical qualities of the nine separate areas within the city centre as the foundation for a series of case studies and principles aimed at informing the design of future development.

LCCUDS built on the emphasis placed on matters of design by the city's political leadership and was a timely intervention, demonstrating that the Department of Planning and the Environment possessed officers with the urban design skills required to both analyse and guide the city's future development. Adopting a set of principles grouped around the headings Form, Movement, Space and Use, the aim of the strategy was to 'provide a working tool which can be used to encourage good distinctive design proposals appropriate to Leeds City Centre' (LCC 2000: 2).

Somewhat less prescriptive than contemporary documents with a similar spatial remit (Punter 1999) the LCCUDS was constrained by being unable to include any policies not already in the UDP. Nevertheless, it became a 'must-read' publication for existing owners of buildings and land, as one of the UK's most comprehensive and concise appraisals of a major city centre, and sent out the clear message to developers that the council had a very good appreciation of the character of its city. The implication was that would-be applicants and their architects would therefore have to raise their game, not least in development control negotiations.

Coming less than a year after the publication of the initial Urban Task Force (UTF) Report, LCCUDS was commended in the annual Royal Town Planning Institute (RTPI) Planning Awards for its quality and content, and for the innovative way in which it brought together the ideas of a wide range of local agencies with a long-standing and vested interest in matters of design quality.

The city council has also undertaken a range of schemes for improving the public realm in the city centre, such as the pedestrianisation of the main shopping street, Briggate (part-funded by Yorkshire Forward), the redesign of City Square and the creation of the first new public open

Plate 4.2 Leeds: Millennium Square. Formerly a mix of roads, car parks and municipal gardens, this slightly sloping, paved space can host staged performances as well as civic ceremonies, exhibitions and street entertainment.

space in Leeds city centre since the Victorian era. Millennium Square (see Plate 4.2), completed in 2000, consists of reworked and new spaces and buildings on the north side of the city centre between the Town Hall, Leeds General Infirmary, Civic Hall, the Mechanics' Institute (opened as the City Museum, September 2008) and the Carriageworks Theatre complex. Undoubtedly, the whole area has greater coherence and is more usable in its new form, while considerable private sector investment has been attracted to the periphery of the square.

Negative notes are sounded by some citizens who are sensitive to the fact that not all activities and types of people are made equally welcome. The space is somewhat dominated by a large screen which, whilst important when used to project cultural events, is intrusive and distracting at other times. Further valid criticisms of the design are that the bespoke stainless steel seating is suitably robust but, in consequence, relatively uninviting, and that the use of grey granite for plinths and low walls goes against local tradition and is alien to the Leeds context.

Nevertheless, the best thing about the square is that it exists at all. At a time when most cities were making proposals to the Lottery to fund museum projects based on dying local industries, Leeds City Council's bid had a clear urban design focus and a new public open space with adjacent public institutions was created for the use of this and future generations. However, compared with similar initiatives in Sheffield and Birmingham, Millennium Square and its sister spaces are modest, relatively bland examples of civic design.

Design beyond the city centre

Whilst beginning to address urban design in the high-profile city centre, the city council remained clearly aware that its authority stretched to encompass a wide variety of built environments and communities, ranging from market towns such as Otley and Wetherby, to commuter villages: from deprived inner-city estates to gentrified Victorian suburbs. In the late 1980s and early 1990s nearly all these urban areas began to receive growing numbers of applications for residential development, most of which were deemed to be for housing schemes that lacked any kind of local distinctiveness.

As a consequence, Mark Burgess, the author of LCCUDS, was encouraged by politicians to update the authority's derivative 'residential design aid' leaflets and produce a sophisticated guide for residential areas across the whole of the city district. *Neighbourhoods for Living* (LCC 2004) aimed to provide clarity for prospective housing developers regarding the principles of residential design and the existing character of Leeds housing. It included indicative case studies deploying the type of site analysis that was to be expected as part of future planning submissions for medium to large residential schemes.

As well as producing this district-wide document, the city council also recognised the need to address the development concerns of those living in the forty villages identified in the LCCUDS as being candidates for Village Design Statements (VDS). For the last decade the council has actively sponsored the writing of a series of VDS and has helped produce a range of such documents, most of which are good examples of their kind.

In 2005 a new model of how to guide and influence the future development of part of the Leeds district was put forward, with the publication of *Headingley Renaissance: The Community's Vision for a Balanced and Sustainable Future* (Central Headingley Strategy Group 2005). This initiative was championed by local ward councillors, keen to tackle the growing concerns of the established members of a middle-class Victorian suburb that had become a national exemplar of the problems associated with, what is now called, 'studentification' – a term coined by a Leeds academic (Smith 2002).

The initial intention was to consider the option of getting the publication adopted as a Supplementary Planning Document, but it contained a number of proposals that challenged rather than championed existing council policy. Its community authors were happy to settle for a city council endorsement on its first page stating that the authority acknowledged it as representing 'an expression of the views and aspirations of the local community groups, businesses and residents who took part in the Community Planning Events' (Central Headingley Strategy Group 2005: 2), and therefore being in accordance with 'recent alterations to the planning agenda'. The council also suggested that the document 'be read in conjunction with the relevant policies of the Leeds UDP' (ibid.). Even when out for consultation in draft form, this 'vision' was used by a planning inspector to dismiss an application to develop a key corner site at the heart of the Headingley area, as it did not conform to the community's wishes.

Following the launch of this document, the Central Headingley Strategy Group went on to form The Headingley Development Trust (HDT), one of whose first initiatives was to negotiate to buy the former primary school building for conversion into The Headingley Enterprise and Arts Centre (HEART; see HDT website, www.headingleydevelopmenttrust.org.uk).

This document, and the participatory process through which its objectives and contents came to be established, represents a new way of addressing the development issues facing the communities of inner-city Leeds. Although it has yet to be tried in a part of the city not dominated by middle-class residents (the next area adopting this approach being the relatively attractive Kirkstall ward) it provides a paradigm of how to engage local communities in taking ownership of their neighbourhood and getting their priorities onto the city's planning agenda.

One other design-led initiative for a key area on the fringe of Leeds city centre is the Holbeck Urban Village (HUV) Revised Planning Framework (LCC 2006), a joint initiative by the city council and Yorkshire Forward. This document is essentially a site-specific design brief and sets out a strategy for the regeneration of a relatively small area to the south of the central railway station, whose elevated viaduct effectively severs Holbeck's connections with the city centre.

It was produced because 'it was clear from early schemes to redevelop the area a decade or so ago that this was not happening and that the special quality of the area was being lost' (LCC 2006: 3). This refers to the fact that this part of Holbeck came under the planning remit of Leeds Urban Development Corporation (Haughton and Williams 1996), which failed to see the potential of the area and helped to build anywhere-type 'crinkly tin shed' industrial units. The HUV includes the remarkable Grade I-listed Temple Mills, a building of high quality and local significance. But no viable new uses have yet been found and structural decay has been accelerated. Although beautifully produced, the hard-backed planning framework is a fairly typical, relatively uninspiring example of its kind – not least in its omission of a sophisticated implementation strategy. It is, however, a document designed to entice the private sector into seeing the potential of the place, following on from the highly successful Round Foundry scheme, a small-scale, mixed-use redevelopment incorporating existing Victorian industrial buildings.

The city centre: urban design workshops, the Renaissance Project and the City Centre Area Action Plan

Proceeding chronologically, the most difficult topic of all is now encountered: the way that the planning and urban design of the city centre is handled within the statutory planning system, and within the locally specific Renaissance Project, that has a high profile, but no statutory status. This project is still evolving and is only gradually being published.

One strand of the background to the Renaissance Project begins in the mid-1990s and relates to the work of the Civic Architect, John Thorp, who has attempted to give urban design more prominence in the city. Enthusiastic councillors, most notably Liz Minkin, helped to bring the Leeds Architecture and Design Initiative (LADI) into being. From 2001, major planning proposals were subject to much closer scrutiny in design terms through detailed discussion in urban design workshops as part of the pre-application process. Previously, a detailed application was submitted, the different officers wrote their view on design, conservation, transport and other relevant matters, and a planning officer advised elected members whether to grant permission. With the new system, the relevant parties meet before the proposal is finalised so that the different elements can be worked into the scheme *before* coming to the formal stage. Members of the Plans Panel (which replaced the former 'planning committee') often want to view the context of a proposal before making a decision.

But this process does create a problem: at what stage should the deliberations become part of the publicly accountable planning procedure? The Civic Trust has reported that critical views have been excluded from the design process. Though many schemes should have gone to the Commission for Architecture and the Built Environment (CABE) for urban design input, the volume of proposals has been so high (150 major proposals in the four years from spring 2003) that senior officers have decided with CABE which ones should be submitted.

The second strand explaining the genesis of the Renaissance Project started considerably later, in 2003. In the Yorkshire and Humber region, Yorkshire Forward, the regional development agency, established a Renaissance Towns and Cities programme to work with local communities to address town centre revitalisation. Initiated in 2001 in six Yorkshire towns, the programme eventually involved nineteen towns, each with a 'town team' whose members represented amenity, business and political interest. Yorkshire Forward also made available world-class expert advice through inviting architectural and urban design practices to apply to be on a Renaissance Panel. With this guiding hand, each team developed a vision and a masterplan to suit its own circumstances. The team then moved on to develop implementation plans, including the identification of a portfolio of prioritised urban design projects with defined delivery mechanisms and timescales. The overall goal was to deliver better places to live, work and visit, and to do so by working with the existing diverse urban fabric (Simpson and Hancock 2003).

Yorkshire Forward was surprised to find that Leeds had no city centre masterplan. Alan Simpson, architect and urbanist leading the Yorkshire Forward initiative, initially wanted a 'streets and spaces' study for the retail quarter of the city centre. But Leeds politicians did not want to focus only on the city centre with the 'town team' approach used elsewhere. Leeds Initiative is too large a partnership body to act as a 'town team'. In any case, the relative prosperity of Leeds meant that growth stimulation was unnecessary and also meant that there was no time for a more considered approach to the city centre. Developers were all too keen to come forward with schemes, confident in the expectation of market demand. The Civic Architect argued that, as development could not be halted while a masterplan was devised, a pragmatic approach was needed to deal with this development pressure.

Yorkshire Forward funded exploratory work jointly carried out by the Civic Architect and Koetter Kim, consultants from Boston, Massachusetts, during 2003. From then until 2007, John Thorp built on the innovative insights and suggestions of Koetter Kim and worked on The Renaissance Project maps, while still working long hours on scores of development proposals. Meanwhile a project board, made up of key public sector actors, provided a conceptual framework for the proposed spatial development of the city. A vision for the whole district, with special focus on the 'core' – the most central area – it aims to rediscover and reinstate the urban grain and remake streetscapes and spaces wherever the opportunity arises when sites are the subject of development proposals. This is referred to by John Thorp as 'dynamic patience'.

It is said to be 'an emerging narrative, a search for understanding', not dogma. The role of the Renaissance team is seen as that of guiding and encouraging, using the so-called 'principles' of (re)connecting greening, covering and adding to the water front, skyline and cultural offer. But this is not instructing or ordering action and priorities, nor is it setting a vision from the top which then has to be adhered to in every detail within a set time frame. It allows for creativity within the framework and recognises the need for compromise between the different interests. Shapes and juxtapositions of future development are suggested as well as the potential for reconnecting parts of the whole, based wherever possible on existing but sometimes obscured or blocked lines of movement (Renaissance Leeds 2004).

The Renaissance team does not focus only on the prosperous city centre. Close by, there are problems of inner-city dereliction, crime, poor-quality housing and social exclusion (Stillwell and Shepherd 2004). The city council and its partners are well aware of the need to 'narrow the gap' between the city centre and 'the rim' of the inner city, to draw more people into sharing the prosperity that has been generated and to attract more regeneration activity to the inner city (Leeds Initiative 2004). Much was done under the now discontinued Neighbourhood Renewal Fund regime between 2001 and 2008, though the level of spend was paltry compared with the amount of private sector money that has flowed into the city centre (Thomas 2004). There are now special efforts under way in west Leeds, Beeston and Holbeck, East and South East Leeds (EASEL) and the Aire Valley, with members of the City Development Department urban design team actively involved. A new departure in the Aire Valley is a proposed eco-settlement.

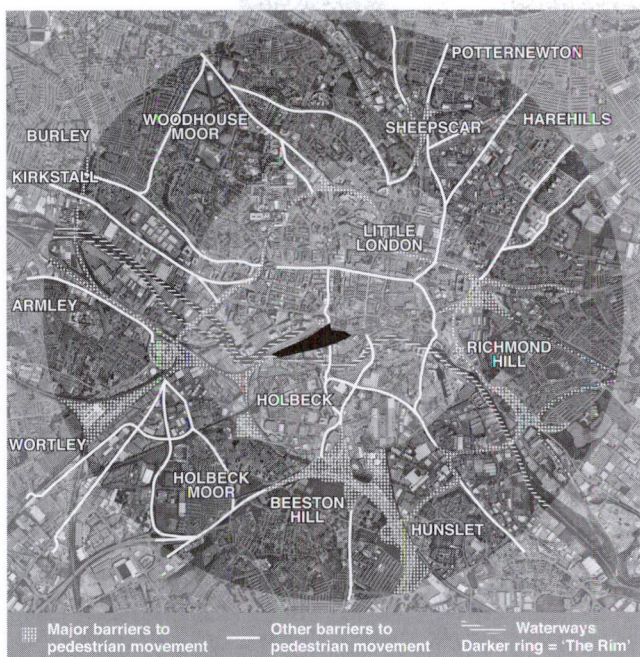

Figure 4.3 Leeds city centre and 'the rim of discontinuity' (Leeds Renaissance Partnership).

The links to the surrounding inner city have been a priority since the outset (Unsworth and Smales 2004). In 2006 a study was commissioned to map the land use and ownership of the one-kilometre band immediately adjacent to the city centre. This 'rim study' (still unpublished at time of going to press; see Figure 4.3) is to be followed by much more detailed work so that a sensitive approach can be taken to upgrading within the rim: refurbishment of terraced housing, additional development and selective replacement of some housing that cannot be appropriately upgraded. Large-scale demolition is not appropriate for social and environmental reasons; refurbishment can also make more sense in financial terms (Power and Houghton 2007). But it is much harder to realise schemes in parts of the city where markets are weaker, so it will take many years to achieve significant change.

Critique of the Renaissance Project

The Renaissance Project is full of attractive, colourful sketches which quite literally draw comparisons between the plan form of Leeds and the seductive patterns of nature, especially flowers and petals. As such, it is substantially different from its more policy-based, perhaps more pragmatic, design guidance cousins. The approach to *Imagining Leeds* (LCC 2003) can only be described as plan-centric, being an example of urban designers looking down on a city from above and finding linkages, routes and attractive shapes which do not necessarily exist in the three-dimensional reality of traffic-clogged roads and built environments that are far from being walkable and pedestrian friendly.

The formally labelled Renaissance Project, set up only in 2003, came relatively late into the most recent era of change. It is not yet entirely clear how the renaissance thinking should be used by civic leaders, policy-makers or the target local communities, or how it fits with the statutory land use planning process. The principles (perhaps more accurately 'themes' or 'aspirations') were certainly not clearly articulated in the first version of the City Centre Area Action Plan section of the Local Development Framework (LDF). A Renaissance officer says it 'occupies a space above the planning system' (personal communication). Undoubtedly, the Civic Architect's involvement in design workshops on all the major development schemes over many years means that elements of this thinking have been threaded into final versions of schemes, though until 2007 none of the Renaissance Project work was published. It is intricate and provides a sensitive analysis of the way that the city fits together on its physical base. But many people with concern for urban design within the city – architects, the Civic Trust (and some of its property developer members) as well as academics – view the Renaissance Project as too descriptive and malleable. It relies on urban design emerging from the 'piece by piece' reworking of the mosaic rather than giving a firm steer for the development process that will enable greater coherence to be generated. No city can reinvent itself in an ideal way or in an ideal order; there has to be realism in fitting around existing buildings and developing sites that happen to become available. The Civic Architect has called this 'collective improvisation'. But there are also chances for site assembly, safeguarding sites for particular functions and greater use of Compulsory Purchase Orders, the latter being an instrument that Leeds City Council, like most councils, is extremely reluctant to use. In very recent times, the Renaissance Project mapping does seem to be moving onwards to generate some strategic thinking across the boundaries of the 'mosaic' pieces, especially with respect to creating and joining up green spaces and creating or enhancing cycling and walking routes. But a great deal of development has occurred without sufficient regard for this higher level of urban design.

Despite John Thorp's seeming strong influence over many years, it is alleged that the former Chief Planning Officer pushed some schemes through for the sake of the economy rather than either rejecting them outright or working to improve their design quality. So it is perhaps unfair that some of the less good buildings are labelled as products of the urban renaissance process, as they came through the system before the Renaissance Project had come to fruition and despite the Civic Architect's attempts to influence design quality. But this returns us to the criticism that the more intensely urban design-orientated thinking of the Renaissance Project came too late in the boom, has not been thoroughly connected into the planning system, was too dependent on the input on one key officer, and for all these reasons has not had sufficient influence on the shaping of the city.

There is some thought given in the Renaissance Leeds document to how tall buildings would sit within the local topography and in relation to each other, an acknowledgement that this might well become a future issue for the city. It is this very topic that has since become the latest subject of the city council's burgeoning portfolio of design guidance.

The Consultation Draft *Tall Buildings Design Guide* (TBDG; LCC 2008a) is a curious document. Its purpose is stated as: 'to establish clear principles and advice to steer them to appropriate locations and ensure they are well designed' (2008a: 6). It takes on board much of the accepted good practice in the design of tall buildings previously issued by CABE and English Heritage (2003) and aims to apply these to the Leeds city centre context. It adopts a systematic and mostly visual approach to the issue of tall buildings in the city and the findings of a Tall Buildings workshop held in 2003. Since then, the city council has granted planning permission for a number of tall buildings, and in 2007 the city marketed itself at the international property fair at Cannes with the line 'Europe's newest skyline'. There is some support for an interesting juxtaposition of contrasting building types, scales and materials, and a sense that so-called 'iconic' buildings will help to achieve the strategic aim of 'going up a league' (Leeds Initiative 2004),

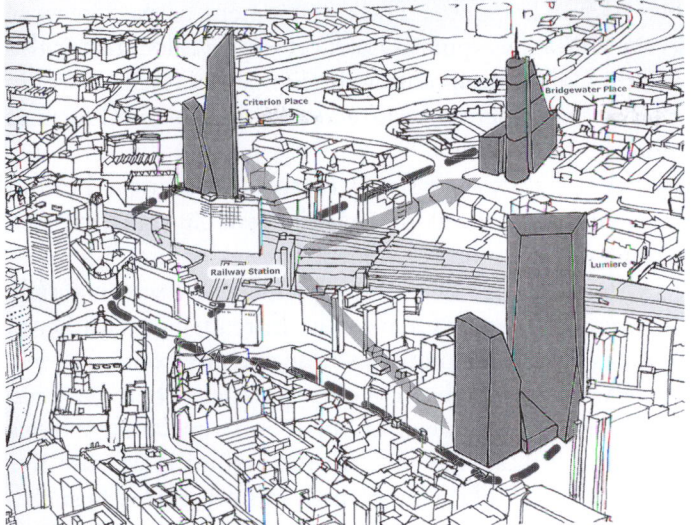

Plate 4.3 Leeds: City Council's draft *Tall Buildings Design Guide* (2008) supposedly showing the relationship between Bridgewater Place and two other proposed tall developments. While suggesting a deliberately planned tripartite symmetry, this is a purely accidental result of developers' decisions (Courtesy Leeds City Council).

Plate 4.4 Leeds: The Plaza, a private sector student hall of residence. The complex, on a prominent site, is criticised for its poor design and materials.

though it has never seemed a strong argument in a provincial market that can absorb only a moderate amount of space each year. The TBDG attempts to justify the siting and visual impact of these structures retrospectively when, in reality, their location is the product of the private development sector's efforts to secure sites and build on whichever bit of the city centre they can option in order to maximise returns. The attempt in the guide effectively to 'retrofit' Lumière (fifty-five storeys), Criterion Place (forty-five storeys) and Bridgewater Place (thirty-two storeys) into planning policy does not work and is in direct contravention of best practice, whether this be in the TBDG's 'clustering' of tall buildings (see Plate 4.3) or previous efforts to establish a Tall Buildings Strategy (LCC 2000). The latter is exemplified by the purpose-built, private sector student halls of residence on the high point on the northern edge of the city centre, creating a forbidding presence just above the Georgian houses of Queen Square (see Plate 4.4).

From mid-2007, changed economic conditions made development finance harder to obtain and sharply reduced the availability of residential mortgages. At the same time, a period of steeply increasing resource prices pushed up building costs. The development of the largest of the tall buildings extensively justified in the TBDG was put on hold, creating a dilemma for this competitive city. It is now highly unlikely that all the proposals with planning permission will in fact go ahead. Indeed, it may well be that none of them is resurrected in their original form as market conditions enter a wholly new phase.

If a guide to tall buildings is now no longer necessary as no such structures are going to be built in the near future, this begs the question: what form of development will Leeds City Council wish to 'guide' next time around? One answer might be found in a reflection on the fate of a major site that has singularly failed to meet its potential. An element of the city centre which should have made a major contribution to its urban renaissance is Quarry Hill. Instead, large swathes of this site remain undeveloped (though subject to various proposals) and the city council's 1990 masterplan for the area, produced by Terry Farrell, has not been put into practice. There has been some development, led by BDP's Quarry House, a new College of Music and a speculative block of flats, but the area remains the traffic island it was when the West Yorkshire Playhouse was opened in 1990. The playhouse itself is also a big part of the problem as it is orientated in such a way that its unattractive and inhibiting service area confronts the city centre.

In Leeds city centre, piecemeal regeneration has led to pockets of good design, such as the Victoria Quarter and the Round Foundry, but there is a clear need for a more sophisticated approach to controlling development in order for the city to be a match for the continental European cities it aspires to emulate.

Despite the failure of Quarry Hill, it is in handling applications on larger sites that the city council urban designers have perhaps been able to have the most influence. There is masterplanning at a certain scale but not for the whole city centre. In the last three years major schemes have been put forward for a new mixed-use quarter to the north of Kirkgate Market, the Eastgate/ Harewood development – with another masterplan by Terry Farrell, the Trinity Quarter shopping centre by Enric Miralles and a mixed-use New West End. The Miralles scheme aims to maximise pedestrian connectivity through a series of covered malls which wrap themselves around the Georgian Trinity Church on Boar Lane.

Higher density and better connectivity: city living and transport planning

As in other cities, a completely novel element of this latest phase of change has been the return of residents to the city centre to live in apartments in converted buildings and new blocks. This phenomenon has largely happened in spite of, rather than because of, land use planning. The whole process has been developer led – in turn responding to demand from buy-to-let investors – and the timing has been unfortunate. The UDP had been adopted in 2001 just before the pace of development proposals picked up, and there was no real policy steer at that time to give a sense of how city living would be slotted into the existing urban landscape and how supporting facilities and green space would be encouraged and integrated. Some of the new blocks have been pinpointed as potential 'slums of tomorrow', though it seems that housing associations may be prepared to take charge of unsold blocks to house those unable to afford market rents.

As more people live in these moderately dense, mixed-use central areas, working within walking distance, there should be a significant reduction in demand for travel, and this should have a positive impact on energy demand, road congestion and air pollution. But although the properties may be welcomed as reused sites and/or buildings, and often contribute mixed-use schemes to mixed areas, in every other regard they have not been constructed or refurbished according to sustainable design and construction principles. A Supplementary Planning Document (LCC 2007b) to influence environmental performance is still not adopted policy. Also, city centre occupiers have not been sufficiently encouraged to live a car-free lifestyle, and survey findings show even more importance being attached to the availability of car parking spaces than was the case previously (Fox and Unsworth 2003; Unsworth 2005, 2007a). Over 10,000 apartments are now completed or under construction. In spring 2007, planned schemes, around half with consent, totalled nearly 12,000 units (Unsworth 2007a), but the financial crisis of 2008 resulted in all proposed schemes being postponed.

A cancelled project seen as crucial to the future of the city was the proposed 'Supertram'. The strategic aims were to ease congestion, improve accessibility and air quality and act as a regeneration stimulus, but government funding was not made available. Although congestion in Leeds is much less intense than in the south-east of England, steep growth in commuter traffic has been experienced and cannot endlessly be accommodated. The metro system of rail and bus services connects Leeds to surrounding towns and rural areas in West Yorkshire, but many routes now run at above 100 per cent capacity in the rush hour and additional capacity is urgently needed. Proposals for enhancements are in the pipeline, but funding is unresolved. Whatever the quality of urban design, sustainable urban regeneration cannot be achieved without improved accessibility, reduced congestion, reduced pollution and the associated improved quality of life in the central streets and spaces. A transport system that works well enhances the value of property, and means that developers can afford to provide better-quality development because occupiers are prepared to pay more for it.

A city which once aimed to segregate pedestrians and vehicles by building a network of first-floor walkways – elevated concrete channels that were even intended to encircle the Town Hall and Corn Exchange (Smales and Whitney 1996) – has yet to come thoroughly to terms with this urban dilemma. Visitors exiting Leeds railway station are immediately confronted with busy roads to cross and a wall of 1970s development to navigate before they can access the office or retail quarters. This is not an appropriate initial experience or welcome for a city with aspirations to place itself towards the top of the European urban hierarchy. Solving the problems of this aspect of the urban experience, as Gehl has convincingly demonstrated (Gehl and Gemzoe 2004), is the next obvious step on the path to creating a true urban renaissance in Leeds. Hoping that the private sector will provide it, given the right form of encouragement and a bit of gentle prodding, is unrealistic. The issue of moving in and around the city centre from the perspective of those on foot is being addressed in a legibility study commissioned by the City Centre Management team (LCC 2008b). There is strong support for a car-free city centre from many citizens and commuters (though some people continue to call for additional and cheaper parking.) Leeds Civic Trust (2008) has developed some initial ideas for reducing the negative effects of the inner road 'loop' and hopes to influence the city council in its thinking.

The City Centre Area Action Plan and 'visioning'

Planning strategy in Leeds seems to have been running hard to catch up with development for much of the last two decades: the painfully slowly developed UDP had not long been adopted before the LDF process had to be started. One of the 'family' of documents under this new system covers the city centre. The 2007 consultation draft of the City Centre Area Action Plan (CCAAP; LCC 2007c) was widely felt to lack vision and to be strangely separate from the already well-developed renaissance thinking. The statutory process and the Yorkshire Forward-inspired renaissance process were allowed by officers and councillors to run on separate tracks without early consideration for how they would mesh. In response to the dissatisfaction with the inadequacy of the CCAAP, and the need to integrate more strategic thinking, the City Centre Management Team hosted an event in the town hall in early 2008 bringing together more than 300 influential people from business, local government and community organisations. This aimed to combine experience and ideas and generate a vision and prospectus for the development of the city centre up to 2020. It started a process of thinking about the longer-term shape of the city centre, and stimulated a wide range of opinions about the following questions:

- What should our aspirations be for the city centre over the next five to twenty years?
- How can we ensure that the city centre is simultaneously a major driver for the regional economy and a key influence towards closing the gap between the 'haves' and 'have nots'?
- How can we communicate better about the great qualities of the city centre?
- How can we create a city centre that is appealing to all our senses – a 'must go there' destination for all Leeds residents as well as for investors, businesses, retailers, shoppers and visitors?
- How can we make it a place where all Leeds residents can feel connected to the city and its prosperity?

The visioning event was well received and provoked many heart-felt ideas from those who attended, but there was a limit to how much could be achieved in a single day. Some further workshops were held within the council (for councillors and senior officers), but there was a long gap before a draft prospectus setting out some potential answers to these questions was published for consultation in November 2008 (Leeds Initiative 2008). The way that Leeds shapes up the thinking set out in this slim prospectus will be a crucial determinant of the city's functioning and appearance.

One aspiration is worth picking out. As well as the car-free city centre idea mentioned above, there is strong support for improved city centre green space – expressed both at the city centre visioning event 2008 and in the city surveys carried out in 2005 and 2007. A striking and substantial city centre park would meet many aims: improved quality of life for city centre residents, workers and visitors; a green lung for the city; and an additional component of the city's image. Many cities around the world are finding the space, the political will and the resources to create new kinds of parks (Cumberlidge and Musgrave 2007), and Leeds would further a number of aims if this were to be made a priority. The city council has started to consider what a park might be like and where it might be. One suggested site for a park is on the south side of the river, using the land where Asda Head Quarters now stands and extending to adjacent sites. This idea is an element of a creative, integrated approach from engineers Arup for enhancing greenspace, connectivity and flood management in 'City Centre South' (Leeds Chamber of Commerce 2009). The stimulus for this thinking was to find a way to reduce the potential negative impacts of high flood defences in the city centre (proposed by the Environment Agency and to be funded by the Department of Environment, Food, Rural Affairs; DEFRA). Wall heights coud be reduced if a new flood channel reroutes Hol Beck and carries a proportion of flood water when run-off is excessive. This would also require/enable reworking of part of the road network and additional benefit would come from positioning bus and taxi interchange facilities on the south side of the station. These infrastructure changes would be the platform and framework for creating an attractive, accessible new mixed-use district. But rules on cost-benefit assessment, funding limits and time horizons may make this unrealisable.

Conclusions

The latest phase of physical change in Leeds has been a whirlwind of development control activity with policy struggling to keep up, let alone firmly controlling the nature, location, amount and style of development of various kinds, while prioritising sustainable development. The number of planning applications, rising to a peak of around 7,500 by 2006 to 2007, has overstretched the development control system. The sheer amount of development in the city centre means it is perhaps too early to tell what impact this has had on the city as a whole. Although urban planning historians believe they can now effectively interpret the explicit and implicit values behind the plans for the city put forward by previous generations, an accurate assessment of the constantly changing contemporary urban scene is a major challenge for any observer. But it can be said that while successes have been achieved, there have been many shortcomings in terms of the urban renaissance process and the results on the ground.

The City Development Department has produced an impressive array of guidance documents which aim to inform and educate, cajole and inspire. In the absence of any detailed research which tracks the effectiveness of these guides in helping to shape the city for the better, it is difficult to assess their value. It is similarly challenging to envisage what Leeds and its constituent parts would be like if they had never been written. Of late, there is concern that recent developments, including some city living apartment blocks and the growing number of private sector student flats, are of poor architectural quality (Stillwell and Unsworth 2008).

As we have seen, Leeds City Council has a curious relationship to the development of its city. It seems to oscillate between adopting a bold and aspirational stance and being timid and accepting. It is caught between the need to encourage as much development as the local economy can accommodate and the desire to be selective and discerning on the grounds of quality. There is a wide gap between the ambition of being a truly European city and the reality. Those who aspire to be in control of urban change in Leeds are more at its mercy than they would like to think or have us believe.

References

Burt, S. and Grady, K. (1994) *The Illustrated History of Leeds* (Derby: Breedon Books).

Central Headingley Strategy Group (2005) *Headingley Renaissance: The Community's Vision for a Balanced and Sustainable Future* (Leeds: Central Headingley Strategy Group).

Cumberlidge, C. and Musgrave, L. (2007) *Design and Landscape for People* (London: Thames and Hudson).

Fox, P. and Unsworth, R. (2003) *City Living in Leeds 2003* (Leeds: University of Leeds and KW Linfoot plc.).

Gehl, J. and Gemzoe, L. (2004) *Public Spaces, Public Life* (Copenhagen: The Danish Architectural Press).

Haughton, G. and Williams, C. (1996) *Corporate City: Partnership, Participation and Partition in Urban Development in Leeds* (Aldershot: Avebury).

LCC (Leeds City Council) (2000) *Leeds City Centre Urban Design Strategy: Improving Our Streets, Spaces and Buildings* (Supplementary Planning Guidance) (Leeds: Leeds City Council).

LCC (2001) *Leeds Unitary Development Plan, Volume 1: Written Statement* (Leeds: Leeds City Council).

LCC (2003) *Imagining Leeds: Phase One Report of Urban Design Studies*, unpublished, part of Leeds Renaissance Project (Leeds: Leeds City Council).

LCC (2004) *Neighbourhoods for Living: A Guide for Residential Design in Leeds* (Leeds: Leeds City Council).

LCC (2005) *Creating the Place: A Design Guide for Aire Valley* (Leeds: Leeds City Council).

LCC (2006) *Holbeck Urban Village Revised Planning Framework* (Leeds: Leeds City Council).

LCC (2007a) *Leeds Economy Handbook 2007* (Leeds: Leeds City Council).

LCC (2007b) *Sustainable Design and Construction* (Leeds: Leeds City Council). Online. Available at: http://www.leeds.gov.uk/files/Internet2007/2007/week29/inter__6f1086a2–2cc3–4109-b32a-805ac0ee57e0_1961ecd4–635a-4a63–8ca0-aa7778579118.pdf (last accessed June 2008).

LCC (2007c) *Local Development Framework City Centre Area Action Plan: Preferred Options Main Report,* April 2007 (Leeds: Leeds City Council).

LCC (2008a) *Tall Buildings Design Guide: Draft SPD* (Leeds: Leeds City Council). Online. Available at: http://www.leeds.gov.uk/Business/Planning/Planning_consultations/Tall_Buildings_Design_Guide__draft_SPD_(LDF).aspx (last accessed 20 May 2009).

LCC (2008b) *Legible Leeds: Wayfinding Strategy: Revised Draft* (Leeds: Leeds City Council, unpublished).

Leeds Chamber of Commerce (2009) Leeds City Centre South: Giving Shape to the Vision. *Fusion,* April/May/June 2009: 6–9.

Leeds Civic Trust (2008) *Linking the Station to the City: Crossing 'The Loop' and More* (Leeds: Leeds Civic Trust).

Leeds Initiative (2004) *Vision for Leeds 2004–2020* (Leeds: Leeds Initiative).

Leeds Initiative (2008) *Leeds City Centre 2020: A Prospectus for our Future* (Leeds: Leeds Initiative). Online. Available at: http://www.leedsinitiative.org/WorkArea/showcontent.aspx?id=8332 (last accessed 20 May 2009).

Nuttgens, P. (1979) *Leeds: The Back To Front, Inside Out, Upside Down City* (Otley: Stile Books).

Powell K. (1989) The Offence of the Inoffensive. *The Architect's Journal,* 189 (18): 124–126.

Punter, J. (1999) Urban Design Strategies in Britain: The Key Questions. *Built Environment,* 24 (4): 371–385.

Renaissance Leeds (2004) *Transformation and Continuity in a Diverse, Dynamic City.* Koetter Kim and Associates Inc., Architecture Urban Design and Leeds Civic Architect (unpublished).

Robson, B., Bradford, M., Deas, I., Fielder, A., and Franklin, S. (1998) *The Impact of Urban Development Corporations in Leeds, Bristol and Central Manchester* (London: Department of the Environment, Transport and the Regions).

Simpson, A. and Hancock, H. (2003) *Regional Renaissance Towns: Beginnings* (Leeds: Yorkshire Forward).

Smales, L. and Burgess, M. (1999) Tapping Into Local Talent: The Production of the Leeds City Centre Urban Design Strategy. *Built Environment,* 25 (4): 300–316.

Smales, L. and Whitney, D. (1996) Inventing a Better Place: Urban Design in Leeds in the Post-War Era. In Haughton G. and Williams C. (eds) *Corporate City? Partnership, Participation and Partition in Urban Development in Leeds* (Aldershot: Avebury) pp. 199–218.

Smith, D. (2002) Patterns and Processes of 'Studentification' in Leeds. *The Regional Review,* 12 (1): 14–15.

Stillwell, J. and Shepherd, P. (2004) The 'Haves' and 'Have Nots': Contrasting Social Geographies. In R. Unsworth and J. Stillwell (eds) *Twenty-First Century Leeds: Geographies of a Regional City* (Leeds: Leeds University Press) pp. 127–146.

Stillwell, J. and Unsworth, R. (2008) *Around Leeds: A City Centre Reinvented* (Leeds: Leeds University Press).

Thomas, K. (2004) *Regeneration Funds in Leeds: A Quick and Dirty Guide.* Presentation to Leeds Central Labour Group, November 2004.

Unsworth, R. (2005) *City Living in Leeds 2005* (Leeds: University of Leeds and KW Linfoot plc.).

Unsworth, R. (2007a) *City living in Leeds 2007* (Leeds: University of Leeds: KW Linfoot plc. and Morgans City Living).

Unsworth, R. (2007b) City Living and Sustainable Development: The Experience of a UK Regional City. *Town Planning Review,* 78 (6): 45–67.

Unsworth, R. and Smales, L. (2004) Form, Movement, Space and Use: Land-Use Planning and Urban Design. In R. Unsworth and J. Stillwell (eds) *Twenty-First Century Leeds: Geographies of a Regional City* (Leeds: Leeds University Press) pp 319–344.

Unsworth, R., Stillwell, J., Stephens, P., and Carey, G. (2004) Twenty-First Century Leeds. In Unsworth, R. and Stillwell, J. (eds) (2004) *Twenty-First Century Leeds: Geographies of a Regional City*, pp. 365–384 (Leeds: Leeds University Press).

Wrathmell, S. (2005) *Leeds (Pevsner Architectural Guides)* (London: Yale University Press).

5 Sheffield

A miserable disappointment no more?

Philip Booth

Introduction

If there is one thing that is clear about Sheffield it is that its external public image has – at least traditionally – been unremittingly bleak. From the eighteenth century onwards, the city was for most of its visitors 'a damn'd bad place', in George III's memorable dictum, a city that lay under a pall of smoke and had few of the attributes of other places of distinction within the kingdom. This was in stark contrast to the quality of the surrounding landscape whose beauty has been extolled in direct proportion to the vilification heaped on the city. The very idea that Sheffield might be characterised by the quality of its urban design would, until very recent times, have seemed risible: the achievements of the past decade in these terms look remarkable.

Like all received wisdoms, the traditional view of Sheffield as an inconsequential place before it became a grimy centre of the industrial revolution needs qualification, for all that it represents a substantial truth. Sheffield was in its origins essentially a medieval settlement, which had developed expertise in cutlery making based on the availability of raw materials and water power. From the middle years of the seventeenth century the cutlery industry began to expand rapidly to become the major source of the city's livelihood, and the industrial character of the city was already being noted by visitors. Urban growth to accommodate the expansion was largely haphazard, though one or two attempts to regularise the street layout appear from the later eighteenth century. The major expansion of Sheffield occurred in the later nineteenth century with the development of a highly innovative steel industry. None of this was the occasion for grand architecture, however, and Sheffield's industrial and commercial buildings were modest brick-built structures often organised around an internal courtyard, with only the occasional pediment or Venetian window making a gesture towards higher architectural sensibilities.

It is perhaps not surprising, then, that Nikolaus Pevsner, in his West Riding volume in the *Buildings of England* series, was to declare that Sheffield was 'a miserable disappointment' where an impoverished urban environment contrasted with a 'promising site' (Pevsner 1967: 446–447). There would be good reason for disagreeing with Pevsner's assessment of the city, as Harman and Minnis (2004) in their updated *Pevsner Architectural Guide* have done, but he had a point: Sheffield did not compare with cities like Manchester, Liverpool or Leeds in the scale of its development or the grandeur of its architecture.

The city of dreams: Sheffield and the modern movement

This historical preamble is necessary as a context for what has happened in Sheffield in the past ten years. But it would be incorrect to think that Sheffield has only 'discovered' urban design in the past decade. Visions for the city as a whole began to emerge much earlier, and perhaps the most significant was a direct result of the Second World War , in which Sheffield suffered badly from bombing. This, coupled with a large legacy of unfit housing that had not been demolished before the war and had not been bombed, presented the city with an urgent need to restructure its fabric. The major advance came about with the city's failure to extend its boundaries in 1951 (and so carry on with a strategy of peripheral housing estates that had been developed before the war), and the appointment of a convinced modernist, J. L. Womersley, as City Architect in 1953. His vision for reconstruction in the areas immediately adjacent to the city centre included dramatic designs for Netherthorpe, Burngreave and, above all, Park Hill.

Much has been written about Park Hill and the two young architects, Jack Lynn and Ivor Smith, whom Womersley appointed to design the scheme. That they were intent on interpreting and applying the ideas of Le Corbusier is well known. What is perhaps less well known is the extent to which they envisaged the scheme as being a vital part of Sheffield as a whole, not simply something that was of intrinsic merit as the realisation of a new Jerusalem, which would sweep away an old order. Both Womersley and Lynn, in describing the design task at Park Hill, made overt reference to Capability Brown (Lynn 1962; SCC 1962; Womersley 1963). This romantic insistence on *genius loci* is curiously at odds with the rationalism of the project itself, and clearly derives from a picturesque tradition that was also being revived in the post-Second World War period, in works such as Kidder-Smith's *Italy Builds* (1955) or Ian Nairn's and Gordon Cullen's explorations of townscape (Cullen 1961; Nairn 1964). Park Hill (see Plate 5.1), Burngreave and Netherthorpe were very much about creating a visual identity for the city as well as providing satisfactory living conditions for its citizens.

This vision was not to last. The departure of Womersley in 1964 and a loss of faith in the virtues of modernism were both factors in its demise. Far more critical, however, was the spectacular collapse of the steel industry from the late 1970s onwards, a collapse whose legacy was an

Plate 5.1 Sheffield Railway Station in 2004, with the inner ring road confronting travellers: Park Hill flats are being emptied on the ridge behind.

industrial wasteland in what had been the steel industry's heartland, the Lower Don Valley, as well as a demoralised population.

The crisis and its aftermath

There is little doubt that the city council, which had traditionally left the economy of the city to industrialists in order to concentrate on improving housing, welfare and education, was bereft of solutions given the gravity of the crisis. Steps were taken to promote partnership between the council and private enterprise but, to the council's chagrin, were not considered sufficient to address the problem by the Thatcher government, and in 1988 an Urban Development Corporation (UDC) was created to deal with the Lower Don Valley.

Much has been written about the work of the Sheffield Development Corporation (SDC) and need not be rehearsed here (but see Seyd 1993; Dabinett and Ramsden 1999; Booth 2005). As with all the UDCs, the SDC engaged in property-led regeneration and to that end produced a planning framework, even if the only formal planning powers given to UDCs were in development control. The SDC had the misfortune to start work at the beginning of what was to be a major crisis in real estate development, but in the nine years of its existence it claimed credit for achieving a good deal of redevelopment. The outcome was a series of individual building projects, some of them impressive, not least those for the World Student Games held in 1991, which was not actually a project initiated by SDC. But these did not demonstrate an integrated *design* strategy for the Lower Don Valley. The one project in the area that did suggest an integrated approach to the urban environment was the gradual opening up of a footpath and cycleway along the eight kilometres of the River Don, a scheme originally proposed by the city council and undertaken not by the SDC or the city council, but by a charitable trust (Five Weirs Walk Trust 2005).

The legacy of this first phase of urban regeneration was far from an unmitigated success, in terms of either the city's economy or its impact on the urban environment. The World Student Games was financially disastrous and its management was questionable (Seyd 1993), while we have already noted that the physical redevelopment was not informed by an overarching view of the nature of the place to be created. Nevertheless in retrospect this focus on physical development can be seen as something new in the city's approach to urban regeneration, which was to find its first full expression in two further major projects in the 1990s.

Supertram

The full history of the development of a modern tramway system in Sheffield cannot concern us here. It was a project whose origins go back some way and was a product neither of the city council nor of the SDC, but of the South Yorkshire Passenger Transport Executive. Parliamentary approval had been achieved in 1985 and work began on the system in 1991. The network was opened in phases in 1994 and 1995.

Supertram was used to generate a series of linked public spaces in the city centre. The cathedral forecourt was remodelled and integrated into Church Street. More dramatic was the change to Castle Square, which had been part of the Womersley modernist project, a roundabout with a lower-level shopping arcade, loved and scorned in equal measure by Sheffielders as 'th'hole in t'road'. It was entirely recast, with the lower-level shopping arcade filled in and traffic routes realigned to create a more pedestrian-friendly environment. More generally, much thought was given to the design detailing of the tram stops and public art was commissioned for the major spaces that were remodelled as part of the process. From now on Sheffield could consider itself in the same league as Manchester or Newcastle, or, on a European scale, Grenoble, Dortmund or Vienna. It was without question an important precursor of the urban regeneration that was to follow.

The Heart of the City

Supertram began to suggest what could be achieved in the improvement of public open spaces and gave the city some experience in handling a complex project implemented by the private sector. The second project of the 1990s was at least as ambitious and was wholly a creature of the city council, unlike Supertram. The significance of the Heart of the City project is not just that it foreshadowed the work of urban regeneration after 2000; it established the basis for all subsequent work within the city centre.

In 1991 and 1992, the city council had failed in its bid to secure City Challenge funding, largely because the government doubted the effectiveness of the city's partnership arrangement through the admittedly rather cumbersome Sheffield Economic Regeneration Committee. In order not to suffer the same problem with the Single Regeneration Budget programme, which succeeded City Challenge, the city set up a new partnership body in the form of the City Liaison Group, whose membership was smaller than that of the Sheffield Economic Regeneration Committee and which represented not only private sector commercial and industrial interests but also the universities and the Sheffield Health Authority as well as the SDC (Dabinett and Ramsden 1999). With the creation of the City Liaison Group, the focus of attention shifted away from the Lower Don Valley back to the city centre, and the revitalisation of the centre now seemed to be the priority for the city council.

The start of this process appears to have been an academic study which looked at how Sheffield might capitalise on national trends and which called, rather ambiguously, for the city to aim for quality in regeneration (Foley and Lawless 1992). It was backed by another report which aimed to show what might be learnt from the experience of regeneration in Glasgow.

Some of the thinking behind these studies was taken forward in a strategy for the city centre that was prepared jointly by the city council and the SDC (SCC 1994). The involvement of the SDC was on the face of it rather odd, given that the centre was not part of its area of intervention. But it indicates the importance that the SDC attached to the economic vitality of the centre as a factor in the success of the strategy for the Lower Don Valley. The strategy presented a 'vision' of the city centre that was multifunctional, knowledge based and offered a new sense of place. It laid particular emphasis on the quality of public spaces as an essential element in the regeneration of Sheffield's economy, a connection which was to underpin all subsequent work. It was then backed by a city business plan produced by the council for the City Liaison Group, which among other things proposed a concentration on two pedestrian axes, one running more or less due west from the railway station and a north–south route, both of which would be the focus of work to the public realm (Sheffield City Liaison Group 1996).

The Heart of the City project that was to emerge from the City Centre Strategy was designed as an audacious bid to the Millennium Commission (SCC 1995). It was based on the perception that, in spite of what had been achieved in the building of Supertram, much of the city centre was indeed a 'miserable disappointment', a compound of piecemeal decision-making and urban decay. In particular, those arriving in the city by train were, on leaving the station, brought face to face with a scruffy car park and a roundabout on the inner ring road whose hazards were only to be avoided by using an unpleasant subway, later abandoned in favour of unsatisfactory light-controlled crossings (Plate 5.1). The crossings led in turn to an unattractive route up Howard Street, flanked on one side by semi-derelict sites, before the city centre proper was reached by another subway.

The occasion for taking a strategic approach to a route through the city centre that could eventually link it to the railway station, was compounded by the desire to replace a 1970s extension to the town hall. The extension, which was dubbed, not entirely affectionately, the 'egg-box' on account of its massive and clumsy precast projecting window units, was due for replacement. This in turn offered the prospect of redesigning the Peace Gardens, which was even then one of the key open spaces within the city centre, linking it to a series of buildings and public spaces back to the station. Finally, the proposal incorporated an intention to downgrade two major roads: Arundel Gate, designed as dual carriageway in the 1960s with pedestrian underpasses; and Pinstone Street, passing in front of the town hall down towards the Moor.

Improvements to the public realm were only the first of four key components of the Heart of the City bid. As important was the proposal for a Millennium Centre which would include the 'northern presence of a major national museum'. The other two components were commercial developments of 500,000 square feet, to include a replacement for the town hall extension, and the concentration of Sheffield Hallam University's operations on the central campus. The proposal was, in other words, predicated on the creation of a high-quality public realm which would be financed in part by commercial development – specifically offices and a hotel – on sites adjacent to the public spaces created (SCC 1995).

The bid to the Millennium Commission was approved in 1996 and the architects Allies and Morrison were commissioned to draw up a masterplan. The plan now included proposals for two major public buildings linked as part of a route from the station into the Peace Gardens. The Millennium Centre had become the Millennium Galleries, no longer the northern presence of a national museum but an exhibition space housing both permanent collections (in particular the Ruskin collection) and temporary exhibitions from the Tate and the Victoria and Albert Museums. New to the project was a proposal for a Winter Gardens, a temperate greenhouse which would serve, it was hoped, as a covered meeting place for residents of the city, to complement the external public spaces (see Plate 5.2). This particular element of the project was almost certainly suggested by a former Head of Parks at the city council, Jon Bauer.

The Heart of the City was innovative in its approach to urban design, but its birth was not an easy one. It came into existence from the combination of a group of committed officers, and a powerful triumvirate in the form of the then leader of the city council, Councillor Mike Bower, the Head of Planning, Narendra Bajaria, and (from 1997) a new Chief Executive, Robert Kerslake, who staved off a major loss of confidence on the council's part in 1997. At the outset, officers realised that such an ambitious project would not succeed without a dedicated team willing its realisation. The solution was to create the City Development Agency, which operated at arm's length from the city council and was wholly focused on the project. It was in effect a precursor of the Urban Regeneration Company (URC) that was to be formed in 2000.

The Heart of the City was undertaken in stages, and quite deliberately the first parts completed were the public realm projects. First, was the revamped Peace Gardens in 1998 (later slightly extended when the commercial development was finished), designed not by Allies and Morrison but by a city council team, followed by the Millennium Galleries and then the Winter Gardens in 2001. This was followed in turn by the construction of the St Paul's Hotel and the first phase of St Paul's Place along the eastern side of the Peace Gardens. Still under construction

Plate 5.2 Sheffield Winter Gardens: a spectacular indoor public space connected to the hotel and Millenium Galleries.

are the final phases of St Paul's Place which include a thirty-two-storey and a nine-storey tower, as well as a multistorey car park (Creative Sheffield 2007).

The Peace Gardens was remodelled in the form of a shallow amphitheatre focused on fountains which rise from the floor of the space, with the southern flank of the town hall acting as backdrop. Large urns on the outer edge of the amphitheatre cascade water down channels between raised lawns (see Plate 5.3). Above the amphitheatre is a paved area that gives access to bus stops and has been partly colonised by tables and chairs from the cafés that surround the gardens to the east and south. The Millennium Galleries has an L-shaped plan with a block fronting a downgraded Arundel Gate and a long block perpendicular to it running westwards towards the town hall. At the western end and at right angles to the Millennium Galleries is the Winter Gardens, a spectacular glass-roofed space formed by laminated timber parabolic arches (see Plate 5.2).

The remodelled Peace Gardens, the Winter Gardens and the Millennium Galleries were an immediate popular and critical success. Critics praised the high quality of the buildings designed by Pringle Richards Sharratt and the layout and detail of the public spaces. The Peace Gardens, which had always been well used, now became a major focus in the city centre (Plate 5.3). The fountains were an inevitable magnet for children who, to the city council's credit, have never been prevented from playing in them. No less popular was the Winter Gardens, which provide a mildly exotic space importantly protected from the elements.

Between its completion in 2001 and 2004, the Winter Gardens was visible as a whole from the Peace Gardens and hence from the city centre in the vicinity of the town hall. When work started on the St Paul's Hotel, there was an immediate outcry that a fine and by now much loved building would be obscured by something which was held to be considerably inferior in design

Plate 5.3 Sheffield Peace Gardens: redesigned and slightly extended by council designers and animated with fountains.

quality. Much the same was true of the first phase of the St Paul's Place commercial develop-ment, which completed the eastern edge of the Peace Gardens. In one respect, the criticisms were ill-founded in that the original Allies and Morrison master plan had always envisaged that the Winter Gardens would lie alongside a hotel building, which would form part of a necessary (in urban design terms) enclosure for the Peace Gardens. Yet the completion of the thirty-two-storey tower may yet be the occasion for further outcry.

The city council was not wholly deaf to such criticisms and, concerned that the sudden and unparalleled upsurge in development in the city centre could lead to incoherence, commissioned a design study from the landscape architectural firm of Gillespies – the *Urban Design Compendium* – which would offer an analysis of the city centre's existing character and a guide for its future development (Gillespies 2004). This has proven to be a particularly robust assessment of both the historic built fabric and the potential for, and constraints on, new building. The *Compendium* divided the city into quarters and identified the character of each, as well as proposing general design policies for the city centre as a whole. It does indeed provide an important model for policy-making in urban design. A second step intended to meet the criticisms was the creation of an Urban Design Review Panel, which was to meet monthly to consider schemes both before and after they had been submitted for planning permission. Chaired by John Pringle, whose architectural practice had designed the Millennium Galleries, the panel brings together design expertise from around the country. But the *Urban Design Compendium* and the panel appeared after another important step in the process of urban regeneration in the city centre to which we must now turn.

'Sheffield's time has come': Sheffield One and the rebirth of the city centre economy

The early successes with the Heart of the City project led to a yet more ambitious attempt to tackle the problems of the city centre through the medium of a URC of the type proposed by the Urban Task Force (UTF 1999a) and later taken up by the *Urban White Paper* (DETR 2000b). The city had already set up a separate agency dedicated to implementing the Heart of the City; the advantage of a URC would be the direct involvement of English Partnerships and the Regional Development Agency as shareholders with the city council, thus completing the expertise required to carry forward development on the scale that was now envisaged. The city's contribution was to be the transfer in its entirety of the City Development Agency. The urban regeneration company, set up in 2000 and baptised Sheffield One, was chaired by Sir Peter Middleton, chairman of Barclays Bank.

Sheffield One's first task was to a commission a masterplan for the whole of the city centre. The premise on which this master plan was based was that the city centre would be the motor for the city's and the subregion's economy. Revitalising the city centre through development was therefore a priority. The masterplan set about identifying seven key areas for development, each of which represented a critical element in the regeneration of the economy. Four particular concerns lay behind the choice of these areas. The first was the will to improve the city's performance as a retail centre, which had been undermined by the development of Meadowhall: by 2002, Sheffield was lower (in thirtieth place) than Meadowhall in the Experian ranking of British retail centres (White Young Green 2003). The second was the desire to encourage high-technology industry that would draw on the expertise of the city's universities, through the development of an 'e-campus'. The third was a general intention to develop a commercial office market in Sheffield, something that had been conspicuously absent. And underlying all three concerns was a fourth: to improve the quality of the public realm as an essential contributor to the economic regeneration of the city. Indeed, the masterplan report identified eight key public realm projects, of which four were already part of the Heart of the City project (Koetter Kim 2000; Figure 5.1).

Of the seven projects identified in the 2000 masterplan (not in fact approved until February 2001), the Heart of the City was already under way and was continued under the control of

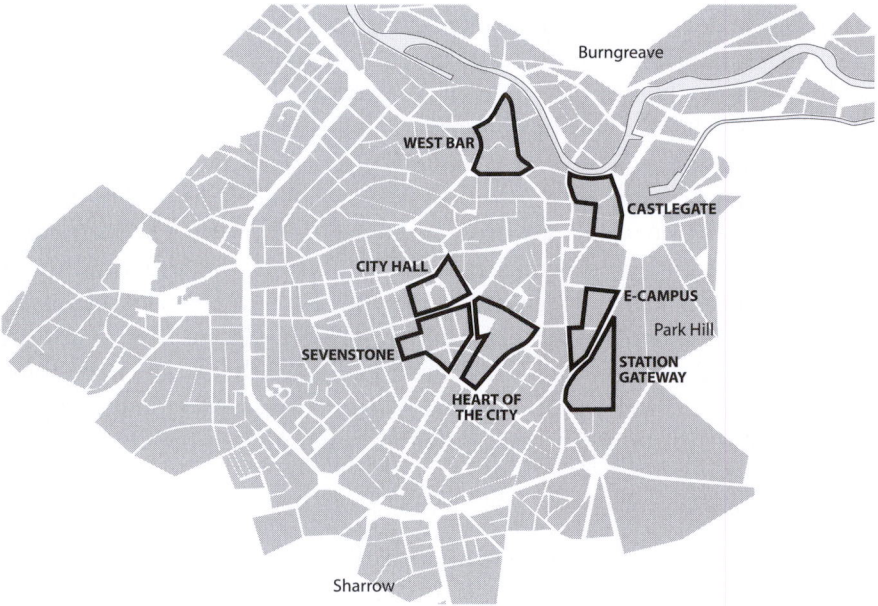

Figure 5.1 Sheffield City Centre: the Masterplan and the 'Magnificent Seven' (drawn by Paul Coles and Graham Allsopp). © Crown Copyright. All rights reserved. Licence number 100049043.

Sheffield One. Indeed, what had now become the 'gold route' through the Heart of the City project was extended, by the focus on the 'station gateway' and the city hall area as two of the seven projects. In front of the station the realignment of the inner ring road and the removal of the roundabout made room for a new open space: Sheaf Square opened in 2006, protected from traffic by a steel wall, symbolising Sheffield's expertise, and adorned with basins and cascades to perpetuate the water theme (Plate 5.4). The railway station itself, a listed building whose frontage dates from 1905, has also undergone a spectacular refurbishment. Sheaf Square was then linked to the centre by Howard Street, relaid as a pedestrian space that arrives at Arundel Gate opposite the Millennium Galleries. At the other end of the 'gold route', the restoration of the city's premier concert hall, a major, and surprisingly late, neo-classical building, and the redesign of the Barker's Pool open space which it fronts, completes the succession of public open spaces.

The most ambitious and probably the most controversial of the seven projects was to be the creation of a new retail quarter, now named by the developer Sevenstone. Hammersons was selected as the developer on the basis of a limited competition, and a masterplan for the area was drawn up by the architects BDP. The plan envisaged a major restructuring of the city centre on the other side of Pinstone Street from the Peace Gardens, with a new store for the John Lewis Partnership as the anchor and a new pedestrian street leading from it. Both Sheffield One and Hammersons declared their intention that this should not be just another shopping mall but would be a development that was fully integrated into the fabric of the city. The new street would therefore be a public thoroughfare, not privatised space. Hammersons also, from the outset, divided the site into blocks that would be handed to different architectural practices, with the stated intention of introducing variety into the scheme. Construction, which was due to begin in 2008, has now been deffered by a year as the result of the recession.

The masterplan has now been revised after a rather longer process of consultation and the approved version was published in 2008. New projects have been identified but the general philosophy of creating a high-quality public realm remains the same. But where the 2000 masterplan limited itself to projects within the core of the city centre, the 2008 masterplan talks of an increase in economic activity and an extension of the area in which it will take place. The

Plate 5.4 Sheffield: Sheaf Square. More fountains and stainless steel water features create the eastern end of the 'Gold Route' (Courtesy Sheffield City Council).

whole of the area around the Moor, the principal shopping street that runs south-westwards from the town hall, is designated a business area. A second business area is identified as linking the Castlegate redevelopment (one of the original seven projects in the 2000 masterplan) and the Victoria Quays at the end of the canal linking Sheffield and Rotherham. But the 2008 masterplan is no longer couched so much in terms of discrete projects and emphasises, rather, the theme of connectivity. To the 'gold route' have now been added a 'steel route', from the edge of the Lower Don Valley south-westwards along the Moor to the boundary of the city centre with the Sharrow, and a 'blue route' running more or less east–west by the Don from Park Hill to Kelham Island (Figure 5.2). This opens up the prospect of further public realm improvements, with areas such as Moorfoot at the end of the Moor ripe for remodelling (EDAW 2008).

2008 has also seen institutional change to match the revised planning vision. Sheffield One has been subsumed into a new organisation, Creative Sheffield. It describes itself as the country's first 'city development company' and combines the physical development expertise of Sheffield One with a remit to act as the lead marketing agency for the city as a whole and 'to develop initiatives that promote the city's scientific, creative and cultural and knowledge base' (Creative Sheffield 2008).

The urban renaissance in Sheffield: an evaluation

The first point to be made about the achievements in Sheffield over the past decade is that, although they clearly conform to many of the prescriptions in the Urban Task Force report, the thinking that lay behind those achievements predates the UTF, as the chronology of events will have made clear. The public realm works in connection with Supertram, although modest by comparison with what was to come, were an indication of a new philosophy; the Heart of the City, dating from the mid-1990s, is already a mature expression of a particular view of the role

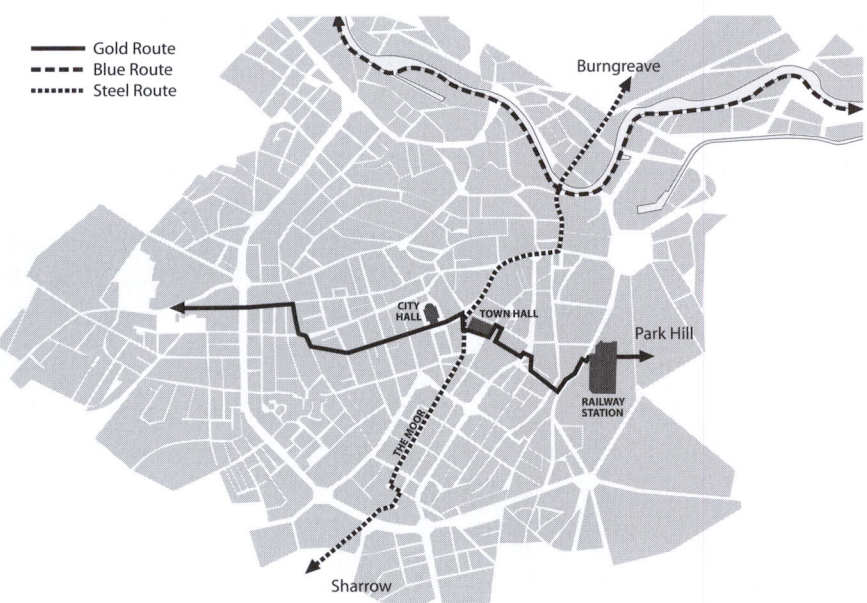

Figure 5.2 Sheffield City Centre: The 'Gold', 'Steel' and 'Blue' Routes (drawn by Paul Coles and Graham Allsopp). © Crown Copyright. All rights reserved. Licence number 100049043.

of urban design in urban regeneration, albeit for a limited area. If there was a model here, it was the Birmingham of Brindley Place and the Jewellery Quarter. Sheffield was in the vanguard, particularly in respect of the financing and realisation of such projects.

But what of the results? The quality of the public spaces and buildings created in the Heart of the City project has been widely commented on. More or less for the first time since the building of Park Hill, Sheffield has been in the national public eye and its experience held up as an example to others. At the same time, the popular success of the Peace Gardens, the Winter Gardens, Sheaf Square and the Millennium Galleries is evident from the extent to which all are used by the public at large and the way in which these spaces appear to have extended the hours during which the city centre is actively used.

There is little doubt that the care and quality of the design itself is a major factor in these spaces' success. Careful selection of materials – sawn sandstone paving, granite setts, a range of specially designed street furniture to include lamp standards and seating – is part of the equation. Water has been used as a thematic feature throughout the spaces: water cascades from urns at the edge of the Peace Gardens; a descending series of basins flank the path through Sheaf Square to the station; other smaller fountains punctuate the spaces. At Sheaf Square the space has been protected from a remodelled inner ring road by a steel wall, an attempt to symbolise the city's former prowess in producing steel implements. Perhaps as important has been the thinking about spaces in sequence and in terms of use, so that connections are as vital as the internal design of the spaces themselves. It is also clear that the design of the Millennium Galleries and the Winter Garden has brought architecture of a very high order to Sheffield's city centre.

Apart from the quality of the public realm, there is evidence that the will to introduce new commercial floor space to the city centre, and in so doing to stimulate a market in office floorspace, has in fact worked. At least part of the success has been attributed to the public investment in the public realm. But success is also due to the increasing quality of the offer, and St Pauls Place has, according to a report, been instrumental in benchmarking quality in the office sector (Knight Frank 2007), although quite how quality is defined is left ambiguous. The general perception of Sheffield as an attractive place has gained currency and the cliché that nothing succeeds like success seems to hold good.

The very success of the Heart of the City project and the work that has now evolved from it raises questions, however. We have already noted that, if the public realm has had unqualified praise from both within and outside Sheffield, the quality of some of the architecture has been contested. The St Paul's Hotel, located immediately next to the town hall, and the first phase of the St Paul's Place office development have attracted a good deal of criticism. There will doubtless be further criticism when the Sevenstone blocks start emerging, and already there has been concern that the employment of a series of separate architectural practices to work on the scheme will lead not to satisfying diversity, but to incoherence.

The commercial success of Sheffield has also led to a spate of proposals for tall buildings. The first of these has been City Lofts' development of St Paul's Tower, already referred to above, which when complete will be the tallest structure in Sheffield. The Allies and Morrison masterplan envisaged an eighteen-storey tower, but the developers came forward with a proposal for a thirty-two-storey building, on the grounds that at that height the resulting building could be less squat. What the visual impact of such a high building in that location on the rest of the city would be was never fully analysed, however, but the project became inescapable because it would be the way in which part of the costs of the public realm improvements in the Heart of the City project were to be financed. There was evidently some tension within the city council and a first version of the tower was refused planning permission, before a slightly modified scheme was approved. At the time of writing, construction is well under way.

The *Urban Design Compendium* was later to identify other areas in which high buildings would be acceptable, and proposals were matched by an analysis of existing landmarks and views into and out of the city. This at least provided criteria against which the accelerating rate of applications could be judged, but the St Paul's Tower had already received planning permission by the time the compendium was published. Later, the Urban Design Review Panel was to be critical of at least some of the proposals, which had applied too loosely the concepts of 'gateway' and 'landmark', that the compendium used to justify the locations of tall buildings. And none of this matches the concern shown in the 1960s to relate buildings to a dramatic topography.

The second area of concern is the extent to which the urban design effort has been concentrated on the city centre. It is true that the central area, which became Sheffield One's responsibility, was widely drawn to include the whole of the area within the inner ring road; however, by no means all of the area was involved in the projects of even the second masterplan. The result has been that, without much input from either the city council or Sheffield One, a good deal of mainly residential development has taken place within the central area, partly as a result of the revival of the city's economic fortunes, but no doubt at least as much due to the prolonged boom in residential property values from 1999 to 2007. Its architectural quality has often been mediocre and, in particular, the concentration of provision for student housing has raised fears that the new residential development will not lead to sustainable communities.

The contrast between prestige central projects and other development is even starker in neighbourhoods beyond the central area. Some of Sheffield's most deprived areas lie immediately adjacent to the city centre and display, as for example in the case of Burngreave to the north, not only a manifest disparity in wealth and wellbeing, but a contrast in the quality of the physical environment too. There is no specially selected paving and the roads remain pot-holed. Burngreave was made a New Deal for the Communities (NDfC) project in 2001 and as part of the project, physical renewal of buildings and a project to improve the streetscape in the neighbourhood's main thoroughfare, Spital Hill, has taken place (Burngreave NDfC 2007) But the scale remains small in relation to work in the city centre. What is true of inner districts is true of outlying suburbs too, particularly those very large areas of council housing that lie to the north and east of the city. There have been prolonged programmes of intervention, notably under the Single Regeneration Budget, but the contrast with a manicured city centre remains striking. Not only is it a question of high-quality materials and the design expertise lavished upon the city centre spaces, it also the high level of management that has been an important part of the approach adopted. Litter does not drift ungathered in the Peace Gardens and planting is not left weed choked and unpruned.

Of course, the transition from Sheffield One to Creative Sheffield may lead to a renewed interest both in the inner-city suburbs and in the outer areas. Attention has begun to turn to the urban design qualities of inner districts such as Burngreave and Sharrow – the latter now experiencing its own property boom with all the attendant problems of erosion of historic environments and inappropriate development, but without the commitment to spending on the public realm. Some energy is being devoted to design qualities of the physical environment through the Housing Market Renewal area that covers a large swathe of north and east Sheffield. Transform South Yorkshire, the Housing Market Renewal Pathfinder partnership, has launched a programme with the Commission for Architecture and the Built Environment (CABE) entitled Delivering Design Quality, and has pointed to improvements in the public realm under this programme (Transform

South Yorkshire 2006). But much of the effort, inevitably, has been put into sustainable housing design. The city council, meanwhile, has published policies for open space in east Sheffield, with some emphasis on design (SCC 2008). But in neither case does urban design appear to be central to thinking in the same way as in the city centre.

There is one striking exception to this general pattern. Park Hill, feted in 1960 as the purest expression of Corbusian ideals in Europe, sinking lower and lower in public estimation as age began to take its toll on the fabric, has seen a dramatic reversal of its fortunes (see Plate 5.1). The starting point was its Grade II listing in 1998, although this did nothing to resolve the structural problems to which it has been prey. In 2003, the city council in conjunction with English Partnerships appointed the developer Urban Splash to undertake the rehabilitation and conversion of the buildings, with some 634 of a total 880 flats being offered for sale. The scheme will make some important modifications to the building itself: the original brick infill panels are to be replaced and the areas of glazing to each flat increased. The scheme is also intended to bring major improvements to the public spaces, which will in effect be an extension of the public realm improvements of the city centre. Park Hill is exceptional for, although it lies outside the area covered by Sheffield One, it is immediately adjacent to the city centre. It has now been incorporated into the revised masterplan.

The third area of concern is the impact of the city centre projects on the historic environment. Sheffield disappointed Pevsner because of its lack of the heroic architecture of the industrial revolution that characterised other parts of the West Riding, or Liverpool and Manchester. But Sheffield has a legacy of historic buildings which are of considerable significance as a witness to its industrial past, modest though those buildings often are. Their qualities reside in their particular arrangement and layout, in their architectural detailing, and in the scale and grain of the industrial areas in which they are grouped. Many of the most important groupings of historic buildings are within the city centre, in areas in which major change has been proposed. There have, it is true, been some notably successful examples of restoration and conversion, as for example in the case of Butcher's Wheel (Harman and Minnis 2004; see Plate 5.5). However, as much is at risk, and one of the considerable concerns with Sevenstone is that it will lead to the

Plate 5.5 Sheffield: Butcher's Wheel Works, now restored for residential and commercial uses. (Courtesy J.F Finnegan & Son Ltd.).

loss of several notable but unlisted metal trades buildings and, as importantly, the transformation of an area as a whole. At stake is the grain of the area west and south of the city hall, with a major recasting of the street pattern. And perhaps most contentious of all, is the proposal to build a multistorey car park on the site of the Kangaroo Works, one of the metal trades buildings referred to above.

Urban design in the British urban renaissance: the Sheffield experience

These concerns about the process of regeneration, and the particular way in which the question of design is being handled, give rise to more general questions. It is important, first of all, to recognise that the Sheffield experience, for all that it shares much in common with the UTF's vision for a renewed public realm, has been independent of the UTF's work. We have noted that the philosophy that underpins the central area improvements was in place well before 1999. For its part, the UTF was advised by one city council officer and was impressed by the existence of a degree programme in urban regeneration at Sheffield Hallam University, but otherwise the report does not refer to Sheffield (UTF 1999a).

Second, the successes in Sheffield in transforming the city centre have come about through innovative approaches, to both management and policy-making. There is little doubt that Sheffield could not have achieved this transformation without the creation of a dedicated agency, first in the form of the City Development Agency and then later the Urban Regeneration Company. That these organisations have been highly effective is not in doubt. But they do raise, as do the Local Strategic Partnerships set in place by the Local Government Act 2000, real questions of accountability and democratic control. As for policy-making, Sheffield has demonstrated the virtues of both masterplanning and the use of design policy documents. What is conspicuous by its absence is any reference to the formal hierarchy of development plans, either in the old form or in the new order created by the Planning and Compulsory Purchase Act 2004. In the Sheffield case, it is clear that the Sheffield Development Framework will become a kind of gathering of otherwise discrete policy documents and in this way may provide a useful strategic overview of the city's development. But the framework does not itself appear to be innovative or productive of new approaches to urban design.

Third, much is made of creating distinctive urban places through this process of regeneration. But how distinctive are the places being created? What has tended to emerge in Sheffield, as elsewhere, is a vision of urban living promoted by the UTF: a vaguely 'Mediterranean' lifestyle that revolves around a 'café culture', a cliché which is already becoming monotonous by repetition. And yet, the individuality of the urban realm being created in Sheffield is nevertheless worthy of comment: the Winter Gardens and Millennium Galleries provide unique covered public spaces and the Peace Gardens are the source of real delight. These are probably more important than the proliferation of pavement cafés.

Fourth, who exactly is this effort in the creation of an immaculate public realm in the city centre actually intended for? The very fact that a great deal of effort has gone into creating a route from the railway station to the town hall suggests that it is, to a large extent, about creating the right image for visitors to the city. The element of marketing and the desire to modify external perceptions are very strong in this particular approach to place-making. What then of its impact on citizens of Sheffield? We have noted the popular appeal of the new spaces created, but there is a real danger that what happens in the city centre becomes increasingly less relevant to residents in the suburbs. This is partly a matter of an image that is sharply at odds with the reality of everyday life, and partly one of lifestyle predicated on high spending.

Finally, it is worth observing how far the perception of urban design in the city has changed in the current round of regeneration. In the 1950s and 1960s there was a clear vision of how the city might be that was based on a marriage of rationalism in the architectural realisation of buildings, to a picturesque sense of form in relation to topography. It was a vision that took a long view but, it might be argued, was less concerned with the micro-management of space. In the early twenty-first century the approach seems to have been reversed. Urban spaces have been treated with sedulous care and to often excellent effect, but the overall vision of the city and its form is lacking.

References

Booth, P. (2005) The Contradictions of Partnership: Sheffield from Steel to Urban Regeneration. In Booth, P. and Jouve, B. (eds) *Metropolitan Democracies: Transformations of the State and Urban Policy in Canada, France and Great Britain* (Aldershot: Ashgate) pp. 83–98.

Burngreave NDfC (New Deal for Communities) (2007) *Burngreave Community Project*. Online. Available at: http://www.bndfc.co.uk/projects (last accessed 20 August 2008).

Creative Sheffield (2007) *Top Ten Developments*. Online. Available at: http://www.creativesheffield.co.uk/developinsheffield/keydevelopments (last accessed 20 August 2008).

Creative Sheffield (2008) *Top Ten Developments*. Online. Available at: http://www.creativesheffield.co.uk/CorporateInformation (last accessed 4 September 2008).

Cullen, G. (1961) *Townscape* (London: Architectural Press).

Dabinett, G., and Ramsden, P. (1999) Urban Policy in Sheffield: Regeneration, Partnerships and People. In Imrie, R., and Thomas, H. (eds) *British Urban Policy and Evaluation of the Urban Development Corporations* (London: Sage) pp. 168–185.

EDAW (2008) *Sheffield City Centre Masterplan: Review and Roll Forward* (London: EDAW).

Five Weirs Walk Trust (2005) *Five Weirs Walk: The Trust*. Online. Available at: http://www.fiveweirs.co.uk/ (last accessed 20 August 2008).

Foley, P. and Lawless, P. (1992) *2010: A Vision of Quality: The Sheffield Central Area Study* (Sheffield: University of Sheffield and Sheffield Hallam University).

Gillespies (2004) *Sheffield City Centre: Urban Design Compendium* (Sheffield: Sheffield City Council).

Harman, R. and Minnis, J. (2004) *Sheffield (Pevsner Architectural Guides)* (New Haven, CT: Yale University Press).

Kidder-Smith, G. E. (1955) *Italy Builds: Its Modern Architecture and Native Inheritance* (London: Architectural Press).

Knight Frank (2007) *Sheffield Central Area Activity Report* (London: Knight Frank).

Koetter Kim and Associates (2000) *Masterplan Report* (London: Koetter Kim and Associates).

Lynn, J. (1962) Park Hill Redevelopment, Sheffield. *Journal of the Royal Institute of British Architects*, 62 (12): 447–461.

Nairn, I. (1964) *Your England Revisited* (London: Hutchinson).

Pevsner, N. (1967) *Yorkshire, the West Riding* (2nd edn) (Harmondsworth: Penguin).

Seyd, P. (1993) The Political Management of Decline 1973–1993. In C. Binfield, R. Childs, R. Harper, D. Hey, D. Martin, and G. Tweedale (eds) *The History of the City Of Sheffield 1843–1993: Vol. 1, Politics* (Sheffield: Sheffield Academic Press) pp. 151–185.

SCC (1962) *Ten years of housing in Sheffield* (Sheffield: Sheffield City Council).

SCC (1994) *A New City Centre: Sheffield's City Centre Strategy* (Sheffield: Sheffield City Council and Sheffield Development Corporation).

SCC (1995) *Remaking the Heart of the City* (Sheffield: Sheffield City Council).

SCC (2008) *East Sheffield Green and Open Spaces Study* (Sheffield: Sheffield City Council).

Sheffield City Liaison Group (1996) *Sheffield City Centre Business Plan* (Sheffield: Sheffield City Council).

Transform South Yorkshire (2006) *Annual Report* (Sheffield: Transform South Yorkshire).

White Young Green (2003) *Sheffield Retail Study* (Bristol: White Young Green).

Womersley, J. L. (1963) Appraisal of the Park Hill Redevelopment, Sheffield. *Journal of the Royal Institute of British Architects*, 70 (7): 281–286.

6 Liverpool

Liverpool's Vision and the decade of cranes

Mike Biddulph

Introduction

This chapter considers the extent to which Liverpool has experienced a renaissance in its urban design and development fortunes following a period of very severe economic decline. The chapter is based on a review of recent documents related to development including design policy and guidance, two recent site visits to reflect on the developments of the last decade and a series of ten extended interviews undertaken with people closely associated with design and development in the city. This recent work complements eight years of living and working in the city during the 1990s.

The chapter starts with a discussion of the state of the city during the late 1980s and early 1990s – a period that forms a prelude to the Urban Renaissance report. Then it introduces changes to city governance occurring at the start of the 1990s, which provide a context for subsequent developments. The chapter then discusses urban design policies and guidance and a number of design-related initiatives introduced during the period. It then considers some of the city centre developments and the processes through which they have emerged, before moving out of the city centre to look, in particular, at the impact of housing renewal initiatives on the quality of developments emerging in designated neighbourhoods. Finally, we will return to discuss what the experience of Liverpool might contribute to the themes of this book. Figure 6.1 provides an overview of some of the sites referred to in this chapter with places shown on the map indicated by a number in italics in the text.

The environmental legacy of economic decline

The book *Seaport* by Quentin Hughes (1964) illustrates the proud Georgian and Victorian legacy of Liverpool before it stumbled through the later decades of the twentieth century. Within a few years it had gone from being one of Britain's most successful cities to one of Britain's least, and this experience for its people was written firmly into the cityscape. Images from the late 1970s and early 1980s show Britain's largest group of Grade I-listed historic buildings, the Albert Dock (*1*), derelict, but at least still standing, in a sea of otherwise unused docklands.

This commercial decline was translated into the harsh realities of life across the city. In Liverpool's poorest communities, particularly (but not exclusively) in north Liverpool, Granby, Toxteth, Kensington, the Dingle and Garston, it was possible to see the legacy of decline not only in the old nineteenth-century bylaw housing and commercial streets, but also in the gap sites created by post-war road schemes or the new and unpopular social housing schemes built just

Figure 6.1 Liverpool City Centre: key locations discussed in the text. © Crown Copyright. All rights reserved. Licence number 100049043.

decades earlier. Rapid population decline also left the city struggling with an over-large public infrastructure, particularly a legacy of fine Victorian Parks. Low demand saw what would be an attractive and popular stock of large Georgian and Victorian homes in many other more affluent cities taken over and cheaply subdivided by social and private landlords, or just left to become derelict, whilst the housing market for bylaw housing stagnated, particularly in parts of the city with the greatest social problems.

Historic commercial buildings in the city centre survived a collapse in demand for office space, but the city centre's streets were not well maintained, and former commercial areas, such as London Road (*2*) or the area between Bold Street (*3*) and Duke Street (*4*), just off-centre from the commercial core, went into serious decline. Post-war comprehensive developments of St Johns (*5*) and Paradise Street (now the site of Liverpool One; *22*) cut off traditional connections across the city, and so cast an ugly and depressed economic shadow over neighbouring environments, whilst the schemes themselves quickly became dated and unpopular.

It was not all bad, however. Parts of the city had managed to hold on to their character and vitality, and it has always been possible to live in the city and not really encounter on a day-to-day basis the true extent of the poverty experienced by others. The environment around Liverpool University (*6*), the northern edge of Canning, itself in some respects ravaged by a poorly conceived campus development plan from the post-war period, managed to dodge the economic effects of such a recession. In addition, suburbs to the south of the city centre around and beyond Sefton Park, and also areas in neighbouring authorities in Sefton and Wirral, tended to maintain their affluence, and a good, affordable, quality of life could be had.

The prelude to renaissance: Liverpool in the late 1980s and early 1990s

Developments from the previous decade (1990–1999) illustrate that the city was turning itself around, albeit at a slow pace and with mixed degrees of success. Positive trends included investment in the universities, the emergence of the city as popular with students and the appearance of private student housing providers near the campuses. These developments introduced a new population to the city centre, albeit in schemes that were not always of a high quality. Related to this were the emergence of a strong night-time economy and the creative exploitation of cheap buildings for youth culture. Design-led developers Urban Splash started to create new types of flexible business space in the city centre for small creative industries, whilst also subsequently acknowledging the commercial value of good public space. Concert Square (7), a new successful space surrounded by bars and apartments, was private, but popular with young people, and it was managed heavily, given the extent of its use, in ways which a city council could not sustain or justify (see Plate 6.1). This suggested new ways of creating and managing space which the city could consider. The period also saw the slow emergence of a city centre private, and subsequently social, housing market, starting again around Concert Square. The city started to take advantage of its heritage through the ripple effects of the Albert Dock, and the establishment of new heritage and cultural venues, such as the Tate Gallery (8), Conservation Centre (9) and Merseyside Maritime Museum (10) which, when added to the pre-existing museums and galleries on Merseyside, easily surpass the cultural offer of cities of a similar size. The uses in the Albert Dock also started to reconnect the city with its river frontage. The city's heritage also formed the backbone of a successful bid for United Nations Educational, Scientific and Cultural Organization (Unesco) World Heritage Status for the waterfront and commercial district during the subsequent years.

Away from the city centre in Speke and Garston a Single Regeneration Budget Partnership started creating employment opportunities around former automotive sites and the former aerodrome, next to the revitalising and renamed John Lennon Airport. Although little can be said in design terms about much of the development, the Matchworks, a small business centre in a converted Bryant and May match factory by Urban Splash, and the conversion of the former Art Deco airport terminal building and hangar into a hotel and leisure club, are noteworthy. Environmental improvements along the Speke Boulevard have made a significant improvement to the approach to the city from the south.

On a more negative front, during this period there was a very low commitment to new commercial office development, whilst existing space continued to lose value relative to that available

Plate 6.1 Liverpool: Concert Square, Ropewalks: one of the earliest public space projects in the UK to realise the economic and cultural value of adjacent properties, undertaken at the initiative of Urban Splash.

in other cities. Strand House (*11*) was one of the only schemes approved in the city, and is a poor addition to the cityscape in a highly visible location. The city also slipped significantly down the retailing hierarchy compared with similar destinations, with shoppers going instead to Manchester, the Trafford Centre or Chester. The city also saw the development of inappropriate forms of inner-city housing, with no regard to appropriate densities, whilst in places they were unable to meet the most basic of urban design expectations such as at the City Challenge funded scheme of new-build homes at St Andrew's Gardens (*12*) (see Plate 6.2). Finally, the city also retained a persistent number of very significant sites around the city centre which remained totally derelict, whilst its public realm remained generally neglected.

Governance for development

Liverpool was certainly the type of city to which the Urban Task Force (UTF) report was directed, and so it had plenty of reason to embrace the report and its recommendations, not least because in commercial terms the previous approaches to regeneration were not leading to significant levels of private investment. Two things that have driven change, however, have had little to do with national policy. The first has been the availability of European Objective One money to the city as a result of its status as one of the weakest-performing regions of the older European Union grouping. The second was a change in governance in the city following the success of Liberal Democrats in the local elections in 1998 (Morgan 1998). This resulted in the introduction of a new council leader and the employment of a new chief executive. The team used Objective One funding (funnelled through the North West Regional Development Agency: NWRDA) and city council and English Partnership (EP) funding, to establish an Urban Regeneration Company (URC), Liverpool Vision. Such companies were a recommendation from the UTF report and in Liverpool's case focused exclusively on promoting developments in and around the city centre. URCs have no significant funding or planning powers; instead they are partnership organisations established with the task of identifying development opportunities, formulating strategic plans and drawing on the expertise of existing agencies to facilitate development. The culture of Liverpool Vision was to be 'market facing, business friendly and private sector oriented and led' (Parkinson 2008: 12). The city council and Liverpool Vision felt that the company formed a

Plate 6.2 Liverpool: Housing at St Andrews Gardens illustrates the inappropriate, defensive and suburban form of housing emerging around the city centre during the 1990s as a result of worthy public involvement exercises.

useful interface with developers and funders who were less confident about dealing directly with the city council on matters relating to development. The agency essentially took over the development of strategic thinking for its area and created mechanisms to deliver resulting projects that would subsequently be part-funded by Objective One monies.

Policy and guidance

Together, the city council and Liverpool Vision have become engaged in producing, using and shelving design-related policies and guidance that have evolved over the decade, leading to a relatively complete set of documents, albeit with some significant gaps. This is, however, a significant improvement on the previous decade when urban design did not figure very highly in city council policy.

Liverpool's current urban development plan was adopted in 2002. Design is considered in reasonable *motherhood* policies, but the emphasis in the plan is on the traditional themes of heritage and conservation. In general, the feeling is of a council with a strong concern for conserving its built past but a less proactive concern for shaping the future form of the city.

Subsequently, the city did commission the production of the *Liverpool Urban Design Guide* (LCC 2003a). The document emerged after the employment of a new head of the regeneration department in Liverpool, who had previously worked in Manchester. Knowing the influence of the Hulme Guide to Development (Hulme Regeneration Ltd 1994) and the Guide to Development in Manchester (MCC 1997) he imported the idea into Liverpool, and updated it by employing consultants to apply the principles of the recently published *By Design* to the city (DETR/CABE 2000). The document contains no strong policy or guidance and was designed to be a coffee table publication which could be sent to developers, partly to promote the potential of the city, whilst also employing the newly fashionable language of urban design (interviews). The document highlighted the need for more detailed forms of guidance which might subsequently be adopted through the planning process, but none of this guidance has materialised.

Ropewalks (*13*), the area between Bold Street and Duke Street, had been the target of a successful Single Regeneration Budget-funded strategy coordinated by the Ropewalks Partnership in the late 1990s (Couch and Dennemann 2000). In urban design terms this strategy saw the development of new spaces modelled on the success of Concert Square, the creation of new routes linking the area more fully back to Bold and Duke Streets, and a very high-quality plan for the public realm. The original Integrated Action Plan for the area was supplemented by a public realm handbook produced by BDP. In 2005, as the city council took responsibility for Ropewalks from the Ropewalks Partnership, a new Supplementary Planning Document was adopted to maintain the strategic clarity which the area had previously enjoyed (LCC 2005).

Liverpool Vision has subsequently been very proactive in establishing a policy framework for action very similar to that previously adopted by the Ropewalks Partnership, and it is this organisation that has delivered the strategic spatial thinking which has subsequently promoted and shaped development on the ground in other parts of the city centre. Its initial document was the Strategic Regeneration Framework (Liverpool Vision 2000), which has stood the test of time and is regarded as a positive legacy of its first chief executive. The document established agreed action areas for which more detailed plans would be drawn up, including specific objectives for developments in what have become the recognised character and land use areas of the city centre – Pier Head (*14*), the commercial district (*15*), the historic centre around Castle

Street (also referred to as the live/work area (*16*)), the cultural quarter around the main centre of museums (*17*) including the Lime Street gateway, the retail core (*18*), Kings Dock (*19*), and Hope Street (*20*) – whilst also drawing out the need for particular initiatives in relation to movement and the quality of the public realm.

Emerging from this document has been the Liverpool City Centre Movement Strategy, a document initiated by Liverpool Vision, but heavily shaped by both the city council, as highway engineers, and Mersey Travel, as the main service operators. Urban designers in the public sector have worked hard to maintain an awareness of urban design and development concerns through a process of briefing for and implementing an important series of highways and public transport projects, with plans for a protected strip for a future tramline being particularly contentious.

A more detailed concern for the quality of the public realm was advocated by an early planning manager working at Liverpool Vision, and he initiated a never completed City Centre Urban Design Guide, and wrote a Public Realm Implementation Framework. This highlighted the hierarchy of streets and public spaces within the city, established a set of standards for surfaces and street furniture, and then encouraged the City Centre Projects Team to adopt the framework and develop detailed projects on the basis of the guidance.

More specifically, Liverpool Vision has developed a series of masterplans and frameworks for a number of larger project sites within the city. These not only identify the areas of development potential for outside investors, but also establish links back to their broader strategy for the city centre, creating site-specific spatial strategies for land use, travel and built form, formulating development principles and establishing development criteria. These documents are typically adopted as supplementary planning documents for use when considering planning applications, and the Liverpool Commercial Quarter Master Plan (Urban Initiatives 2004) (*21*) has also been awarded outline planning permission, whilst the city council has backed up this document with an adopted Special Planning Document (SPD) (LCC 2006).

In principle, this would seem to demonstrate good, coordinated and committed planning of the area, but the Government Office for the North West reacted badly to the proliferation of SPDs and required Liverpool to halt the adoption of any similar documents until its Core Strategy is produced as part of the new Local Development Framework (LDF) process. This has left planners working lower down the planning hierarchy wondering how to shape change on specific sites that require development briefs, whilst it also highlights a rift between the site-specific strategic work of Liverpool Vision and the slower work of the planning authority, which is now, in terms of adoption, also forced to distance itself a little from the outputs of the regeneration company.

Gaps in policy and guidance relate specifically to themes that tend to remain within the city council's jurisdiction, including residential layouts and tall buildings. Both were suggested to the city council by the *Urban Design Guide*, along with a specific design guide for the city centre. Tall building and city centre guides have been produced in draft (the former was not very comprehensive), but have not made it through the politics necessary for adoption, whilst there has never been any obvious concern for design in residential areas away from the city centre. The adoption of the historic core as a World Heritage Site also led to a somewhat embarrassing call for a more rigorous adopted SPD for the area, and this is the only supplementary document that the Government Office will now accept owing, somewhat depressingly, to the international pressure.

Better working practices

In addition to these strategic initiatives, it is evident that over the last decade Liverpool Vision and the city council have together enhanced their in-house skill and knowledge base with regard to urban design. This is important because the city council and Liverpool Vision are commissioning outside consultancies to produce their strategic frameworks and thinking, and if they are to be understood and implemented then there must be 'buy-in' from council staff and members. During the 1990s the city employed one architect to comment on specific buildings coming in for planning consent. Today, using the Planning Delivery Grant, the city has an urban design manager, as well as the previous architect and one additional urban designer involved in dealing with statutory planning matters. This is not a large urban design team compared with other cities, but it is a significant improvement. Liverpool Vision, however, also has a planning manager with a strong commitment to urban design, and also a part-time urban designer who comments on significant schemes within the city centre. The city has also retained a preplanning application negotiation process which will utilise these professionals, although, like other people working in a discretionary planning system, they sometimes feel powerless to effect positive design improvements to schemes in a strongly pro-development political context.

There is a distance between these design professionals and those people employed to implement projects, particularly for the public realm. The city has passed over its highway and public realm design and construction work to a public sector service delivery partnership, Liverpool 2020, whilst city centre projects are delivered by the City Centre Projects Team. There are some complaints that engineers working in development control agree well-designed schemes whilst engineers delivering the projects lose the qualities somewhere along the way. However, within the city centre, good schemes have been delivered by the Projects Team assisted by the consistent message of the Public Realm Implementation Framework.

Other initiatives to promote design quality

Three additional initiatives have also tried to secure a good quality of development for the city. Liverpool was early to adopt the urban renaissance notion of a design champion – a person who scrutinises approaches to securing quality in design and development in all aspects of local authority and private sector activity occurring in the city. In contrast to cities such as Edinburgh, Liverpool's design champion was firmly embedded in the city and its local politics. The post was created by the new council leader and chief executive and was paid for using planning agreement and councillor fees. A particular achievement has been the greater involvement of the Commission for Architecture and Built Environment (CABE) in the city, by establishing a locally based CABE manager to liaise with the central office, whilst the design champion has also been involved in the design review processes in the city. More recently, because the current champion has changed political allegiances, the formal position of champion would appear to have lapsed. This illustrates how politicised the post has been in Liverpool – to be design champion you have to be a member of the governing party – something that should not automatically follow. It also suggests a lack of corporate and political commitment to the position in the longer term, because the lack of a champion does not appear to be at the top of anyone's agenda and no one locally knows if the position will be renewed.

In addition to the design champion, the establishment of CABE as a significant contributor to national debate on design quality has run in parallel with the decade of initiatives occurring in

Liverpool, and it has certainly influenced the direction that the city has taken. Within Liverpool, CABE established Design Liverpool, a regional pilot whose job it is to ensure that the national objectives of CABE are met within the city. Through this organisation CABE is an advocate for design quality at development-related events, and also within any partnership working arrangements. It is gauging interest in establishing an architectural centre within the city. It also comments on draft design-related policies and guidance produced by the city council or Liverpool Vision. Prior to the urban renaissance agenda and the influence of CABE it is acknowledged that the quality of design and development did not appear to be high on the city's list of priorities (interview). Consequentially, design training has also been offered through CABE in the form of Liverpool 50, a programme of seven months of one-day workshops and exercises, targeted at a very wide range of professionals, including development control planners, engineers, housing, parks and public realm professionals, the police and council members.

Finally, as design-related initiatives go, the process of design review cannot be ignored. The Liverpool Urban Design and Conservation Panel was established in 1999, prior to many similar national or regional organisations. Made up of a collection of local volunteer design experts, the panel has typically reviewed projects late in the planning process, and minutes of their meetings have been presented in relevant planning committee reports. Subsequently, CABE established its well-funded national design review panel, and tensions have resulted when schemes reviewed in London at an early stage of the design process by CABE are treated differently by the local panel. The reported tendency has been for the Liverpool planning committee to disregard the comments of its local volunteers, and the local opinions are somewhat lost when a national panel has already had a chance to encourage positive changes to any development.

Recently, both CABE and the city's design champion have pushed for changes to the local panel, building on the design review work done by Places Matter, an architecture and built environment centre for the north-west of England. Places Matter was established in 2007, funded by Renew North West, and it is supported in principle, but not endorsed, by CABE. The national and regional organisations agree which schemes they might review, thus removing any scope for duplication. However, Liverpool chose not to send its schemes to Places Matter for comment, preferring to maintain its own arrangements, even if they cannot be as well resourced. Locally there is an acceptance that a newly constituted panel might offer a better service if it can adopt standing orders and produce fuller reports, in line with regional and national practices. Still, the tension remains between the timing of comments, and conflicts between national and local opinions, whilst the increasingly formal procedures and demand for lengthy reports may test the resolve of the local volunteers.

A decade of city centre developments

The city centre of Liverpool has seen a turn-around in its fortunes, and despite some large schemes that will be discussed below, it is worth noting that a significant number of smaller developments have also been completed. Mapping of derelict sites in 1997 gives some impression of the overall picture at the time, with large empty sites at King's Dock, around Paradise Street, behind Central Station and beyond the then rather depressed office quarter to the north of the city centre. A group of sites to the east also mark the line of a proposed road to complete the inner ring: a plan that was refused planning permission at the end of the 1990s.

Using City Centre Development Updates produced by Liverpool Vision between 2001 and 2008, a summary can be made of all of the developments in the city centre since 2000, a period

Figure 6.2 Liverpool City Centre: all developments 2001-2008 (Information from Liverpool City Centre Development Updates). © Crown Copyright. All rights reserved. Licence number 100049043.

that has seen the development of all the major sites, but also a significant preponderance of smaller projects, particularly in the Ropewalks and in the old historic commercial centre around Castle Street (Figure 6.2). The majority have been mixed use, containing a combination of retail, office and, in particular, residential buildings by a diversity of developers, the vast majority being relatively small and local. In terms of sites a few names, such as Frenson, Liverpool University, Maritime Housing Association, Urban Splash and the Iliad Group, appear repeatedly. Interesting also is the role of regional developers such as Downing and Neptune, Iliad and Urban Splash, as well as the active nature of housing associations such as Maritime Housing Association and the Liverpool Housing Trust, proving that Liverpool city centre, at least, is not being developed exclusively with 'yuppie' apartments.

Liverpool One

The key scheme in Liverpool city centre is Liverpool One (*22*), a mixed-use scheme by Grosvenor Estates. It is designed to lift Liverpool back up the national retail hierarchy, and attract shoppers from within its older catchment who had been shopping in Manchester, the Trafford Centre or Chester instead. With a value of £920 million it marks a national sea change in the way city centre retailing developments might be approached (Plate 6.3).

The site forms a significant link between the main shopping streets, the Ropewalks area (*13*) and the Albert Dock (*1*). Undeveloped since the war, Chavasse Park had a development brief produced by the Merseyside Development Corporation in 1993, and a proposal for a shopping centre designed by the acclaimed architect Philip Johnson was submitted by The Walton Group. The scheme was rejected in 2002 because it was inward looking and it was thought that it would fail to deliver regenerative effects within the wider context. This was a bold move for a city desperate for development and on a site of this scale and importance.

Plate 6.3 Liverpool One is the most significant new development in the city, and forms a new 'retail triangle' with two new anchor stores, whilst also connecting (elaborately) with Marks and Spencer on Church Street.

Instead the city commissioned a retail study by Healey and Baker to examine the state of retailing in the city, and assess more broadly the potential for development. Using the results, it sought development partners for not only the Chavasse Park site, but a wider area embracing neighbouring streets and gap sites owned by a range of landowners. A bid by Grosvenor was successful, with Grosvenor acknowledging the changing political and investment climate in the city. As partners, the city council and Grosvenor employed BDP as masterplanners, and they developed the scheme together, with Grosvenor underwriting the scheme and the city using its compulsory purchase powers to secure the land necessary to create a very comprehensive development. The partnership established a planning process approved both by CABE and the Government Office for the North West, and the city employed an urban designer to work exclusively alongside BDP to establish a masterplan that was given outline planning consent. Following this, sixteen architecture firms were employed to design schemes for twenty-six separate sites, with Herbert's Bling Bling building by CZWG (23) already a celebrated landmark.

Rather than adopting an internal mall, the scheme re-establishes streets which, although privately owned and managed, are fully open to the public. The masterplan creates a 'retail circuit' embracing the city's existing anchor stores across a range of levels, and includes an impressive new, largely green, public space built over car parking, linking the site across to the Albert Dock and the waterfront. The scheme contrasts significantly with the monolithic mall projects so common in other cities, but there is a firm commercial rationale behind the form. Grosvenor observed that rents on traditional streets have held up better than those in shopping centres over the longer term; that the middle classes tend to dislike malls; that traditional anchor stores, such as C&A, House of Fraser and Marks and Spencer, have not performed well economically during the past few years; and they wanted to make it easy to adjust the form over future decades as markets change and evolve (interview).

Other sites

Office development has also started to re-emerge within the Commercial Quarter with some success. The city celebrated investment yields down to 4.7 per cent and rents of over £200 per square metre for the first time in Class A office space developed in St Paul's Square (*24*), whilst mixed-use commercial projects like The Plaza (*25*), The Unity (*26*), the Beetham (*27*) and West Towers (*28*) have added a certain flair to the formerly depressed streetscape along Old Hall Street. Princes Dock (*29*) remains a little sterile and lacking vitality but, after decades of dereliction, new commercial buildings are enclosing the water and a Malmaison boutique hotel (*30*) has established some exclusivity to the location. Within the historic commercial streets the city has seen new vitality with some smaller hotel developments such as the Hard Days Night Hotel on North John Street (*31*), introducing a new use into the area, and mixed-use conversions of former (often listed) buildings, such as the scheme by Urban Splash at Old Haymarket (*32*; see Plate 6.4), award-winning social housing in a converted mill in Preston Street by Maritime or the sympathetic but interesting conversion of an old fire station at Eden Square on Hatton Gardens by Downing (*33*). In terms of retailing the story is not confined to Liverpool One, with the listed post office on Victoria Street and Whitechapel being successfully converted for £70 million by Milligan to an exclusive mall of fashion boutiques now called The Met Quarter (*34*).

Along with the historic commercial streets, Ropewalks has seen the highest density of development proposals, and the public realm works and Supplementary Planning Document have helped maintain, to some extent, the momentum of development in the area. The FACT Centre (*35*; cinema, arts and café) and the conversion of the Tea Factory on Wood Street by Urban Splash were early significant developments (*36*). East Village on Kent Street (*37*), by the consortium of David McLean, Iliad and Maritime Housing Association, added new public spaces and a rich mix of uses in a sympathetic new-build scheme covering a few blocks, whilst twenty separate development proposals have seen the significant rejuvenation of Duke Street (*4*). The conversion of St Peter's Church on Seel Street (*38*) by Urban Splash has received acclaim, whilst Argyle Street, Campbell Square and Henry Street have seen a rich mix of small-scale contemporary developments integrated with converted mill and warehouse buildings to a good standard, whilst retaining the distinctive character of the area (*39*).

Mount Pleasant has seen an excellent public realm project providing a much needed civic space and entrance to the Metropolitan Cathedral, replacing what was formally a grass bank.

Plate 6.4 Liverpool: Old Haymarket. A development by Urban Splash, illustrates the smaller-scale, mixed-use developments appearing within the old commercial district, and forms part of a group of refurbishments which uplift the entrance into the district from the Queensway tunnel.

This is successfully framed by new 'science park' incubator units developed by the Neptune Group for new businesses, emerging from the Universities (*40*). The new Hope Street Hotel takes advantage of an admirable position amongst Georgian buildings and between the cathedrals and theatres, creating a new commercial hub around the junction between Hardman and Hope Streets (*41*).

After Liverpool One the most significant strategic development is the Arena and Convention Centre located on Kings Dock (*42*). After decades of indecision, and a failed bid to build a new stadium for Everton Football Club on the site, the new building by Wilkinson Eyre sits well on its site and seems to have been well received. It is a shame that the remaining developments on the site do not sit so comfortably with the emerging public realm, and although the site is masterplanned, the residential schemes emerging do not seem to provide an intimacy and purpose to the public realm that a good masterplan should prescribe.

Finally, Liverpool is also starting to see the result of protracted attempts to develop Mann Island (*43*). A scheme by Neptune and Countryside is emerging on the site of the failed Fourth Grace project to build a new iconic building on the waterfront. The scheme by Broadway & Malyan includes a £65 million Liverpool Museum building and £120 million apartment and office buildings that are also striking in form, although the forms sit statuesquely on their site with a certain ambiguity about the purpose of the public realm and the orientation of buildings to it. Possibly helping to overcome this is one of the most interesting if unsung projects – the building of a new canal through the scheme and in front of the existing Three Graces linking the Leeds and Liverpool Canal back-up with the River Mersey via the Albert Dock. If this is managed well it will bring a bit more boating life back to the area, albeit on a small scale.

New Heartlands: housing market renewal

The success of the city centre is not without its critics. Some local commentators are concerned that the new jobs in the city centre will not solve the deeper employment crisis that the city has endured, whilst development of new residential apartments in the centre is not contributing to a much needed reinvigoration of the housing markets in the older housing stock where market values have stagnated for decades. As a response, the city council supported the principles of, and subsequently also participated in, the Housing Market Renewal (HMR) initiative set up by national government to re-establish private and rented sector housing markets within inner-city areas. Within Liverpool, funding exists for ten to fifteen years to reverse the collapsed private sector market for homes within the extensive areas of Victorian bylaw housing, which form a ring just beyond the city centre. The city has approximately 200,000 terraced houses, and the initiative targets approximately 70,000, of which 20,000 are vacant (interview). The project aims to demolish 15,000 homes, and 12,000 homes will be built by the private sector to replace them (LCC 2003b). The Liverpool initiative forms part of a wider Merseyside project called New Heartlands, reflecting the wider state of the housing market within the region as a result of depopulation and economic decline.

Within the HMR areas a very significant amount of public funding is being invested, with £120 million being spent between 2003 and 2007, combining HMR initiative money with local Housing Capital Programme funds (LCC 2008). Public funding for the fifteen-year lifetime of the project is anticipated to be £423 million, and this it is hoped will attract private investment of about £1 billion – impressive, but still only the value of the new shopping centre (LCC 2003b). This funding is being targeted at a comparatively large area, and is being spent on renovating properties but also, and controversially, demolishing existing bylaw homes. It is also being spent on building new houses and apartments which, it is argued, meet contemporary standards, particularly with regards to insulation, gardens and parking. Within Liverpool a housing development Supplementary Planning Document focuses on the level of residential provision in the city on development sites within the HMR pathfinder area, with a particular focus on subareas called 'zones of opportunity' in Anfield and Breckfield, Kensington, Picton, Granby, Lodge Lane and Princes Park. In addition, the HMR Strategic Investment Framework (LCC 2003c) outlines in more detail the substance of the programme and includes a *bolt-on* statement relating to the forms of development that might secure the necessary quality. Unfortunately, there were no initial place-specific studies and, despite the initial aspiration, the city has awarded preferred developer status to a private sector developer and a social housing provider in each of three designated areas. This means that the developers have a monopoly over the development within their area. One rationale for this was argued to be that a developer could offset the risk of difficult sites against the potential returns of good sites, thus making the prospect of working in the area more attractive (interview). The approach contrasts with that adopted in other HMR areas, where developers must compete for sites and design quality criteria can be more effectively enforced by trained and motivated design professionals.

Initial plans for the Anfield, Picton and Edge Hill areas received a very negative response from CABE, as it objected to proposed compulsory purchase orders that would lead to selective demolitions in all of the areas. It dismissed a 'masterplan' for Edge Hill West at national design review because of its lack of detail and its unconvincing layout. In general, CABE doubted that the HMR programme would deliver the market transformation that the government spending

Plate 6.5 Liverpool: Clevedon Park. New housing as part of the HMR project, built on sites created by demolished by-law terraces. The new houses are not much larger or of a higher quality than those that are being replaced. (Courtesy John Stonard, Design Liverpool.)

ought to achieve, and it lacked faith in the quality of the places and homes emerging through the established processes. CABE withdrew its objections only once it was agreed that the HMR sites and partners would be subjected to a design-enabling programme involving recognised design experts and community representatives working with the developers to improve the schemes. More recent CABE design review comments for the scheme in Anfield and Breckfield have been more cautiously positive, suggesting that CABE's involvement has finally seen a greater concern for urban design being introduced into the process, even though at the time of writing this process has some way to go.

Housing Market Renewal is essentially still at the planning and design stages. Early schemes like Clevedon Park in Granby have been well received despite controversy about replacing homes in the nearby 'Welsh Streets' (see Plate 6.5), but despite some smaller interventions on easy-win sites the project has not yet delivered enough new-build development to deserve a full evaluation. Interviewees repeatedly referred to the mundane nature of some homes and environments, and more importantly to the extent to which the programme has blighted large areas due to the potential use of compulsory purchase powers, the scale of potential interventions and the uncertainty generated by the 2007–2008 housing market collapse.

Reflecting on Liverpool's achievements

Liverpool's decade of development has left a very positive impact on the city, although compared with the scale of problems in the city, following decades of severe decline, there is still plenty to do. Notable has been the role of key individuals in the promotion of development and in encouraging a concern for design, and in this respect the new administration's council leader and chief executive were pivotal. They set up Liverpool Vision and separately secured the role of Grosvenor in Liverpool One, whilst also establishing a new market confidence for development in the city centre. While this is to be applauded, questions still remain as to whether the design agenda will be sustained at the top level, and the demise of the design champion could be evidence of reducing commitment.

Liverpool Vision has also established a clear strategic plan which, in a productive partnership with the city council, it has successfully delivered. In some respects it is the people in Liverpool Vision who are the strategists, overcoming the reactive nature of an under-resourced city planning department. But most of these strategies have embraced the urban design agenda fully, with the support of senior planning managers who, throughout the lifetime of the organisation, have maintained a concern for design as developments have come through. In particular, it has been impressive to see the integrated hierarchy of documents setting out a clear strategy for the city centre, including works to highways and the public realm that have now been delivered.

It is heartening to see urban design skills improving within the planning department through training and the employment of dedicated staff, but the ambivalence of the city council to its Urban Design Guide is cause for concern. Meanwhile the lack of residential design guidance and a highway adoption practice which is limited to asphalt probably means that the door will remain open to poor volume housing schemes away from the spotlight of the city centre. In this respect CABE has been pivotal, particularly in the HMR areas where the approach to development has given monopoly development powers to four developers in four areas. This is a set-up that will not guarantee a good quality of design or development.

Liverpool has led the way in the UK in terms of embracing its outstanding cultural institutions, recognising its heritage and, after learning the lessons of Concert Square from Urban Splash, understanding the value of a good public realm. The city is also at the forefront of mixed-use development and the city centre residential population has been booming. New privatised public spaces in Liverpool One had already been criticised even before they were opened (Minton 2006). But the quality of the public spaces is very high in a city that struggles to justify investment against political priorities which lie elsewhere, and this is in a city where, unfortunately, vandalism has often undermined many good intentions. No doubt the debate will continue, as it should, but at the moment the spaces seem to work.

Liverpool One should also set a benchmark in the UK for open street systems and a more urbane form of comprehensive development. The city council was right: the developers have seen the commercial merit of being connected firmly back into the rest of the city and allowing for change in an uncertain future through the development of smaller blocks. Other local authorities should also learn from the regenerative effects of schemes such as this upon their contexts. The developer of Liverpool One is proud of the fact that following its opening the owners of The Beatles Story in the Albert Dock, about a mile away, noted a significant increase in trade because the city was now closer to the waterfront (interview). Large self-contained malls do not deliver such effects. Some might bemoan the impact of comprehensive schemes on cities and the scale of the money involved, but in Liverpool at least that level of investment was necessary, whilst the 'old money' of Grosvenor should remain committed to the area's success.

Finally, although it is easy to be seduced by the major schemes, it is also worth noting that the city centre is being developed by smaller companies and individuals, and their schemes are certainly constrained, but improved, by the heritage in the city centre which requires complex schemes that also deliver interesting design solutions. There have been some blunders, but in general most developments have made a positive contribution to the city, whilst a strong pattern of Victorian and Georgian streets has created a robust framework for new developments. When compared with a previous decade of poor housing, and a total absence of investment in retail or office development, the last decade has seen a significant turn-around, but get out of Lime Street and walk in any direction for about half an hour and it is obvious that there is still plenty to do.

References

Couch, C. and Dennemann, A. (2000) Urban Regeneration and Sustainable Development in Britain: The Example of the Liverpool Ropewalks Partnership. *Cities*, 17 (2): 137–147.

Hughes, Q. (1964) *Seaport: Architecture and Townscape of Liverpool* (London: Lund Humphries).

Hulme Regeneration Ltd (1994) *Rebuilding the City: A Guide to Development in Hulme* (Manchester: HRL).

LCC (Liverpool City Council) (2003a) *Liverpool Urban Design Guide* (Liverpool: Liverpool City Council).

LCC (2003b) *Strategic Integrated Investment Framework* (Liverpool: Liverpool City Council).

LCC (2003c) *Inner Core Strategic Investment Framework (North and South Sectors)* (Liverpool: Liverpool City Council).

LCC (2005) *Ropewalks Supplementary Planning Document* (Liverpool: Liverpool City Council).

LCC (2006) *Commercial Quarter Supplementary Planning Document* (Liverpool: Liverpool City Council).

LCC (2008) *Housing Market Renewal in Liverpool Annual Report 2006/07* (Liverpool: Liverpool City Council).

Liverpool Vision (2000) *Strategic Regeneration Framework*, (Liverpool: LV).

Liverpool Vision (2001–2008) *Liverpool City Centre Development Update* (various annual documents) (Liverpool: LV).

MCC (Manchester City Council) (1997) *A Guide to Development in Manchester* (Manchester: Manchester City Council).

Morgan, B (1998) *The Local Elections of 7 May 1998 and the London Referendum, House of Commons Research Paper No 98/59* (London: House of Commons).

Parkinson, M. (2008) *Make No Little Plans: The Regeneration of Liverpool City Centre 1999 – 2008* (Liverpool: Liverpool Vision).

Urban Initiatives (2004) *Liverpool Commercial Quarter Masterplan* (Liverpool: Liverpool Vision).

7 Bristol

Not a design-led urban renaissance

Henry Shaftoe and Andrew Tallon

Introduction: staggering forwards

Bristol is the sixth largest city in England, with a population of just under 400,000, although it serves a 'city region' of about 1 million (Tallon 2007). Since the abolition of Avon County Council in 1996, the actual conurbation of Bristol overflows into South Gloucestershire's jurisdiction to the north and east and, to a lesser extent, North Somerset to the west, and Bath and North-East Somerset to the south (Figure 7.1). This has led to problems of strategic area coordination, particularly in relation to transport and public service provision (see Lambert and Oatley 2002; Lambert and Smith 2003; Boddy *et al.* 2004). For a large English city, Bristol has been relatively economically prosperous during recent decades, perhaps because it has always had a mixed economy which has not been overly reliant on declining manufacturing industries (see Boddy 2003; Boddy *et al.* 2004). However, there are pressures of economic and population growth in the city region, linked to concerns for sustainability and affordability. These coexist with long-standing social problems which remain entrenched in parts of the inner city and peripheral estates. Bristol, as a post-industrial city, continues to witness ambitious urban regeneration projects in the city

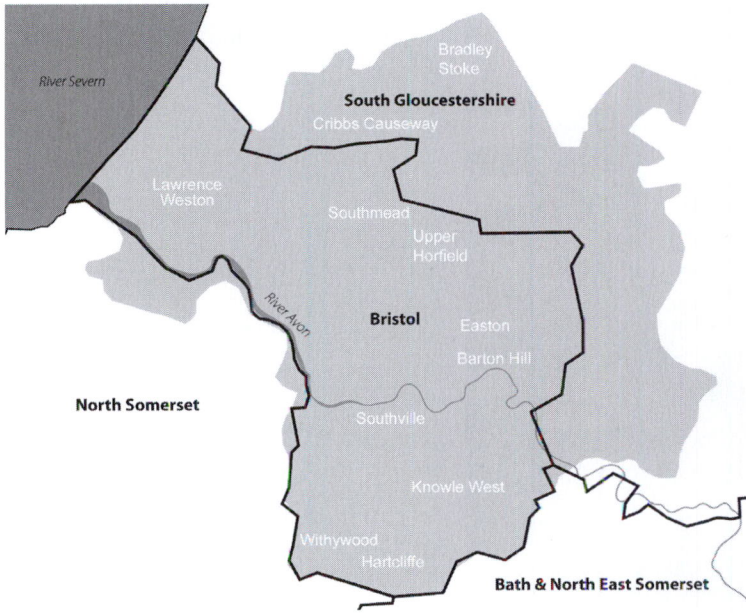

Figure 7.1 Bristol: city boundaries and neighbouring authorities (drawn by Jamie Roxburgh). © Crown Copyright. All rights reserved. Licence number 100049043.

centre, continued expansion within the northern fringe of the city and social policy interventions targeted at the most deprived areas of the city.

This chapter explores the design-led renaissance in Bristol over the last couple of decades by focusing on approaches and developments not just in the city centre, but in the inner suburbs, mature peripheral suburbs and estates, and at the city edge. Key themes within these four sections of the city include design and renaissance of public spaces, central city urban regeneration projects, policy interventions in the inner and mature suburbs, smaller-scale but enlightened developments in the inner city and suburbs, and transport issues. In pursuing an urban renaissance, the process of gentrification has been promoted, as witnessed in new-build city centre developments, and in the refurbishment and upgrading of housing in the inner and outer suburbs of the city.

The city centre

Bristol has long had a reputation for being a 'laid-back' city where things are slow to happen. This has continued to be the case in terms of design-led regeneration over the last twenty years. Bristol has not experienced the spectacular and glossy city centre transformations witnessed in Birmingham and Manchester. Instead, the city has inched forward, for example with the Harbourside redevelopment (see Plate 7.1) and Broadmead expansion, and has sometimes slipped backwards, as in the case of the aborted Performing Arts Centre (see Griffiths *et al.* 1999; Bassett *et al.* 2003; Tallon 2006). In some ways this could be seen as a more positive incremental approach, where consultation is thorough and lessons are learnt piece by piece. However, the quality of resulting developments, particularly on the Harbourside, the edges of the city and in the suburbs, does not suggest that this dragging of feet has produced particularly positive results.

Following large-scale destruction of much of the historic centre during the Second World War, a new shopping centre named Broadmead was constructed during the 1950s (Figure 7.2). Characteristic of post-war redevelopment in many British cities, the design was functional and modernist, and the landscape became dominated by bland retail and office blocks, multistorey car parks and a ring road system. At the same time, radical proposals for large-scale office and housing development around the old docks almost led to the loss of the character of this historic

Plate 7.1 Bristol: Harbourside. Apartments frame the view corridor from the south dockside to Bristol Cathedral.

Figure 7.2 Bristol city centre (drawn by Jamie Roxburgh). © Crown Copyright. All rights reserved. Licence number 100049043.

industrial zone (see Punter 1992; Tallon 2006). The creation of the Unitary Bristol City Council in 1996 provided the opportunity to formulate a comprehensive city centre strategy (BCC 1998). This resulted in the emergence of three foci for regeneration: Broadmead shopping centre, the former docks around Harbourside, and Temple office and housing quarter, to the west and north of Temple Meads railway station (Tallon 2007).

Associated with the focus on city centre regeneration, there has been some success in increasing the density of the city through brownfield redevelopment and repopulation of the central city (Lambert and Boddy 2002; Boddy 2007; Bromley *et al.* 2007). The idea of mixed-use neighbourhoods has also been pursued in the city centre to an extent. Indeed, the population of Bristol city centre increased by 66 per cent in the decade from 1991 (Bromley *et al.* 2007). Social housing and small work units, have, on the whole, been token additions to tracts of high-end apartments and office blocks (see Bromley *et al.* 2005, 2007). As Boddy comments:

> What is evident in Bristol and elsewhere is a complex and powerful process of capital investment and the remaking of the urban landscape . . . The occupiers of these new residential developments are from relatively better off strata; provision of affordable housing has been limited, and developments have had little if any positive impact on deprived neighbourhoods.
> (2007: 103)

More strongly, Slater asserts:

> In Bristol, it is hard to get beyond the bare fact that the new developments . . . are appearing both in reaction to and to stimulate further demand from a specific class of resident – the middle-class consumer . . . and they are moving into new-build residential developments – built on formerly working-class industrial space – which are off-limits to the working classes.
> (2006: 745)

Similar to Edinburgh, but less like most other British cities, Bristol has always maintained a reasonably affluent residential population close to the city centre, such as in the Georgian suburbs of Clifton and Kingsdown, with most of the urban poor being hidden away on peripheral estates such as Hartcliffe and Withywood to the south, and Southmead and Lawrence Weston to the north and north-west.

One of Bristol's problems, from an urban design and morphological point of view, has been the 'hole in its heart', resulting from odd spatial redevelopment after the Second World War bombings. Rather than densely rebuilding the area around the ancient 'Bristol Bridge' river crossing and the ancient castle site, the city council took the opportunity to clear any buildings that had survived the Luftwaffe and created a new green space called Castle Park. Although this was no doubt created with the best of intentions, the result is a fragmented city centre. As Phillips observes:

> Although there are certainly plenty of historic sites to visit . . . it takes time and effort to unearth the city's treasures. It is not the kind of place which suits the high speed instant tourism of the weekend break or coach trip. There is no focus; no obvious place to stand.
>
> (1999: 69–73)

There has been considerable progress in reclaiming public space from the motor vehicle. Queen Square (see Plate 7.2) and College Green, both of which had become major vehicular through routes as a result of post-war traffic planning, have been reclaimed and new spaces have also been created (Millennium Square and The Centre Promenade) (see Shaftoe 2008: 122–124). Bristol city centre now has an abundance of public open spaces, many of which are underused, especially at night and out of season. Further new 'reclaimed' spaces lie in the planning pipeline at St Mary Redcliffe and Redcliffe Wharf, yet it is not clear how these will be qualitatively different and thereby well-used and valued (perhaps by making them more controlled and managed than the other entirely open spaces).

The Bristol Legible City initiative has been an innovative project incorporating new mapping and signage to make the admittedly confusing morphology of Bristol easier to navigate around on foot, and to forge a stronger neighbourhood identity for the various city centre 'quarters' (see

Plate 7.2 Bristol: Queen Square, the inner ring road diagonal removed and the Queen Anne square restored.

Kelly and Kelly 2003). The trouble is that it merely overlaid itself onto the existing confusion of road signs and street apparatus, rather than being integrated into a new comprehensive clean sweep of urban furnishing.

There has also been a limited introduction of public art, such as a sculpture of Cary Grant (who was born in Bristol) in Millennium Square, but this has not been as substantial an investment as in some other British and Continental cities, despite the publication of the city council's *Public Art Strategy* in 2003 (BCC 2003). The strategy aims to integrate public art into the specific sites of new and existing development and may consist of temporary installations and events. These are also rolled out to the various outlying neighbourhoods, particularly those with 'renewal' status (see Griffiths *et al.* 1999; Bassett *et al.* 2003). Ironically, the public art interventions that have, arguably, had the most impact on the appearance of the city are the works of graffiti artists, most notably Bristol's own Banksy. Controversial though they may be, they have undoubtedly brightened up a few dank corners of the city.

The most substantial 'renaissance' in urban design terms has been the redevelopment of a string of redundant industrial sites along the banks of the Floating Harbour and the River Avon. As explained in *Design Control in Bristol* (Punter 1990), this started in the 1970s with various office block infill and continued in the 1980s with the construction of Rownham Mead (an entirely residential low-rise development of fairly traditional brick-built houses enclosed by four-storey flats), followed quickly by the similar Baltic Wharf and Bathurst Basin developments (see also Punter 1991, 1992; Tallon 2006). Subsequently, the Poole's Wharf site, one of the last commercial dock facilities in central Bristol, was cleared for residential development, being completed in the late 1990s. All these residential developments are primarily private houses with small or non-existent quotas of socially rented accommodation (Tallon 2006; Bromley *et al.* 2007). They have remained highly desirable places to live, with the only significant change since their completion being an increase in buy-to-let properties. In the new millennium, The Point and Harbourside have been constructed in two of the remaining parcels of old dockside space. They are different from their predecessors in so far as they are of higher density and more modernist in design and incorporate a small amount of mixed-use (mostly leisure and retail) facilities.

However, if anything, these have become even more exclusive than their predecessors, being mostly made up of expensive apartments owned or rented by well-off professionals (Boddy 2007). This is reflected in the proportion of the higher managerial and professional class in the city centre, which increased by 34 per cent between 1991 and 2001, and remains on an upward trajectory (Bromley *et al.* 2007). Further upstream are two more brownfield redevelopments. The first is Temple Quay, which is the area backing on to Temple Meads Station – the main railway station for Bristol. This has been developed almost entirely with large office blocks for various service industries, with one rather bleak public space partially enclosed by a shop and cafés (see Plate 7.3).

Behind this 'prime real estate' is the deprived inner-city residential area of the Dings, which has been partially upgraded through the introduction of a homezone and through its designation as a New Deal for Communities (NDC) urban policy area. Bridging the two is a new residential development called The Zone, which, although primarily consisting of homes for sale, also has a proportion of shared ownership properties.

Considering its size, Bristol has relatively few tall buildings, either commercial or residential. The gothic church spire at St Mary Redcliffe, at eighty-seven metres, is still the tallest structure in the centre. The tall buildings that do exist were mostly constructed in the 1960s and 1970s and are generally of mediocre quality (see BCC 2005a). The city council produced a Supplementary

Plate 7.3 Bristol: Temple Quay office quarter. Standard issue office blocks surround a stark open space – not a place for the public to enjoy.

Planning Document on tall buildings which, in response to public consultation, favoured a case-by-case approach to approval. Apart from the construction of some new blocks along the Temple Quay area, the only significant developments since the guidance came out have been the demolition of the unloved Tollgate House, the construction of a new high-rise apartment complex as part of the new Cabot Circus mega-retail redevelopment, and the recent recladding of one of Bristol's formerly most hated buildings, the old Bristol and West Building Society tower, which has been transformed into a luxury hotel (see Plate 7.4). Indeed, the number of new hotel bed spaces created over the last ten years has been remarkable, with both new-build and change of use resulting in a vast increase in both budget and high-end hotel options in the city.

In an attempt to coordinate the various 'renaissance' opportunities in central Bristol, the 1998 *City Centre Strategy* (BCC 1998) was followed up in 2005 by *The Bristol City Centre Strategy and Action Plan 2005–2010*. The strategy and action plan divides the city centre into nine neighbourhoods including the core Broadmead, Harbourside and Temple zones, and nine topics, including physical environment, but also covering such aspects as employment, tourism, transport and culture (BCC 2005b).

In addition to the mixed results at Temple Quay and Harbourside, the biggest regeneration opportunity identified in the strategy was the revitalisation of Broadmead, Bristol's central shopping area, which was developed after the Second World War on land that had been mostly cleared by the Blitz. It had been pedestrianised but not renewed, despite the addition of The Galleries (a new-build tiered internal mall) in the 1990s, and was losing trade to the out-of-town regional shopping development at Cribbs Causeway (which is administratively in South Gloucestershire, rather than Bristol). This was approved following a twenty-five-year planning saga involving three public inquiries, and despite intense opposition from Bristol City Council (Walker 1996; Tallon 2007). With financial investment from two of the UK's largest retail developers, the 'New Broadmead', renamed 'Cabot Circus', has risen from an extension to the existing site, involving a minor diversion of the inner ring road.

Although undoubtedly a boost to the fortunes of the city centre, the new development is still primarily a monolithic shrine to consumerism despite rhetoric about creating a 'mixed community'. Out of a fairly desultory 300 new housing units built, only thirty are designated as affordable, and they back directly onto the multistorey car park for the whole development (see

Plate 7.4 Bristol: The Centre promenade remodelled over the Floating Harbour, not the public's preferred solution, with the re-clad Bristol and West office building now a hotel.

Tallon 2008). Cabot Circus has undoubtedly contributed to a retail renaissance in the centre of Bristol, exhibiting high-end retailers and good-quality and unique interior design, and it connects well with the existing streets of Broadmead. It has also propelled Bristol up the retail rankings and complements the existing retail area. But it is unclear how much of a positive effect this new development will have on the surrounding deprived areas of St Phillips and St Pauls, or whether it will constitute an even harder edge than the inner ring road, particularly as the design does not easily flow into these neighbourhoods (see Clement 2007). Concurrent with the Cabot Circus development, the run-down existing shopping area has been subject to upgrading, funded by the Broadmead Business Improvement District (BID). This is undertaking public space improvements including new street paving and furniture, and renewed shop frontages, all aimed at integrating the existing Broadmead more effectively with the new mega-development (Tallon 2008; see also Symes and Steel 2003).

The gentrification of the central city

According to Punter (1992) and Slater (2006), the majority of the design-led urban renaissance of Bristol city centre since the early 1980s can be criticised for demonstrating the characteristics of gentrification. In this case, gentrification is defined as the upward social and economic trend of an area which embraces the development of new-build commercial and residential buildings on former industrial sites, as well as 'traditional' displacement of residents from existing and refurbished housing (see Davidson and Lees 2005; Slater 2006). In essence, former industrial and working-class areas such as Harbourside have been transformed into high-end places of consumption (Tallon 2006).

In Bristol city centre, retail, leisure, entertainment, cultural and housing developments over the last couple of decades have largely been carried out by the private sector. The social profile of new residents is skewed towards the professional classes and owner-occupation of housing. New retail, leisure, entertainment and cultural landscapes cater for the affluent middle-class consumer. Lower-status commercial activity and residents have been directly or indirectly displaced from the regenerated centre to elsewhere in the city (Slater 2006).

However, Lambert and Boddy (2002), Tallon and Bromley (2004) and Boddy (2007) have argued that the process at work in Bristol city centre is one of urban development and 'residentialisation' rather than traditional gentrification, albeit with the characteristics of unaffordability, exclusion and privatisation. According to Boddy 'the extension of the term "gentrification" to embrace such forms of development stretches it beyond the point at which it retains utility or meaning'(2007: 86). Whether defined as 'gentrification' or otherwise, the powerful and complex set of urban processes at work has inevitably favoured certain sections of the middle classes and private developers in Bristol city centre's design-led renaissance.

The inner city

Turning to the inner city, one of the most noticeable features is the number of small-scale developments by local entrepreneurs and alternative groups, which contrast sharply with the products of the commercial developers and the volume house builders in the city centre. One of the most interesting new developments from an urban design and urban village point of view has been the Paintworks, developed along Bristol's inner-city watersides (see www.paintworksbristol. co.uk). This is an industrial estate of mostly nondescript brick buildings that is being gradually revamped by a private developer (Verve Properties) to create a mixture of apartments, studios and workshops.

There has been considerable attention to detail in the refurbishment of the buildings, and there is a clever incrementalism in the way in which the site is being gradually upgraded without the usual wholesale clearance and rebuild. The social heart of the new Paintworks is a hugely successful bar and restaurant which has been carved out of a minimally adapted ex-industrial building. Elsewhere in Bristol's inner city, another 'alternative property developer' operating with considerable success is the P G Group. This was set up by the Reverend Gregory Grant as a result of his experience of renovating a deteriorating church site in east Bristol. Their project with the biggest impact has been the St Peter's Court development in Bedminster, just south of the city centre. This collection of Victorian buildings was redeveloped to contain a new library, doctors' surgery, eighty-seven apartments, a restaurant, retail, offices and a community art gallery. Much of the profit from their development activities goes into a charitable trust. Similarly, another space that has been renovated to accommodate a large number of artists is the Spike Island Studio Complex, adapted from an old tea-packing factory just to the south of the Floating Harbour. Run as a non-profit cooperative by the artist residents themselves, this is a good example of how creative spaces can be produced outside of the normal development system (see www. spikeisland.org.uk).

By contrast, the interventions of the ill-fated Bristol Development Corporation, which operated from 1989 to 1996, to the immediate north-east of the Paintworks, and incorporating sections of the city centre and inner city, resulted in little more than an elevated 'spine road' which whisks motorists to an American-style mall of the dreariest design, consisting of a huge car park surrounded by discount stores, chain restaurants and a commercial multiplex cinema. Conflict between the Conservative central government and Labour-controlled local authority, along with community opposition and an economic recession, effectively neutered the plans of the Bristol Development Corporation, which had included large-scale office and housing development. Part of the former Bristol Development Corporation area has subsequently been developed as the Temple Quay office quarter (Plate 7.3; see Oatley 1993; Oatley and May 1999; Deas *et al.* 2000).

An even more problematic regeneration area has been the Stokes Croft area on the northern edge of the city centre, located on the main A38 route to the northern suburbs (see Plate 7.5).

The last section of this, before it arrives at Broadmead and the new Cabot Circus, has been a seedy and semi-derelict area since the mid-twentieth century. As one of the main 'gateway' routes into the centre of Bristol, one might have thought it would have been more of a priority for improvement. As the *Bristol City Centre Strategy and Action Plan* notes: 'some approaches/ gateways to the city centre are marred by poor quality environments with no sense of arrival. Promoting their improvement should be given greater priority' (BCC 2005b: 74). At face value, the area has potential for investment and gentrification due to its proximity to the city centre. Similar issues are being experienced in the inner eastern areas of St Phillips and Easton, which continue to experience deprivation and lack of large-scale regeneration. However, despite exhibiting a similar housing stock and built environment and being a similar distance from the city centre, the northern and eastern inner-city areas have not prospered like the southern inner suburbs of Southville and Bedminster, which have undergone substantial gentrification.

If anywhere in central Bristol needed a 'renaissance' it would be Stokes Croft, given that thousands of people pass along it every day, yet the city council has singularly failed to achieve any substantial improvements, despite at least one speculative masterplan for the area and increasing pressure from the surrounding community. Some people became so frustrated with official inaction over a potentially great asset (there are a large numbers of artists and cultural activities in the vicinity), that they established the People's Republic of Stokes Croft (PRSC; see www.prsc.org.uk) and have produced their own alternative plan for the area. They have also made some provisional improvements by brightening up derelict buildings with murals (see Plate 7.5). One of their slogans is – 'don't redevelop Stokes Croft: let it develop' – an inspiring alternative approach, which would build on its existing assets and diversity, rather than the usual 'clean sweep' of clearance and redevelopment favoured by commercial property developers. In this way, the PRSC is, consciously or not, adopting the 'weak thought planning' philosophy of urban sociologist Yves Chalas that is being put into practice in the incremental regeneration of inner-city Brussels (Cohen and Plissart 2007).

Another interesting alternative approach to incorporating creativity into the urban fabric has been the Artspace/Lifespace project. This has come out of the critical mass of artists and other creative people in Bristol. Essentially it has consisted of a sequence of licensed squats in interesting old buildings awaiting redevelopment. During their time of occupancy (in an old

Plate 7.5 Bristol: Stokes Croft, a half century of decay in a Conservation Area.

Volkswagen garage, the semi-abandoned Bristol Catholic Cathedral and the central Bridewell police station), the Artspace/Lifespace collective has not only provided studio space, but has patched up and redecorated the building interiors in truly imaginative ways and staged a programme of cultural events. Theoretical support for such ventures, as a contribution to urban vitality, can be found in the concept of 'loose space' (Franck and Stevens 2007). This particular project uses interior space temporarily, but an equally fascinating temporary revitalisation of exterior space can be found in Bristol's annual Street's Alive event, where a section of inner-city streetscape is transformed into a huge outdoor living room with carpet, comfortable chairs and entertainment (www.streetsalive.net). These alternative cultural developments are a valuable contribution to the urban renaissance, and represent a contrast with the mega-scale commercial development witnessed elsewhere in the city centre.

One inner-city suburb that has seen a remarkable renaissance is Southville, which, as its name suggests, is the area just to the south of central Bristol. This renaissance has been less to do with urban design and more to do with 'overspill' of professional people wanting to be near the centre, but unable to afford the prices of properties in the suburban northern ring. Although the pleasant Victorian terraced housing has been an attraction, the area received a huge boost with the opening of the Tobacco Factory as an arts centre, bar and restaurant. Again this was a private initiative, by architect George Ferguson, and it has had a huge ripple effect, leading to the opening of more bars and eateries in the area. As with the Lake Shore development in Hartcliffe (see page 125), it can be accused of leading to gentrification and the gradual pricing out of the traditional working-class inhabitants of the area (see Lambert and Boddy 2002; Slater 2006). As Davidson and Lees put it, such developments 'have acted like beachheads from which the tentacles of gentrification have slowly stretched into the adjacent neighbourhoods' (2005: 1186). However, the development has again produced a better social mix and reinvestment in an area that was beginning to get a bit frayed around the edges.

The mature suburbs

As with most British cities, Bristol's suburbs consist of a patchwork of various demographic and socioeconomic clusters, with the more affluent areas generally being to the west and north. An exception to this rule is Southmead – a large low-rise council estate surrounded by predominantly owner-occupied areas.

An intriguing approach to suburban regeneration has been undertaken with the rebuilding of the Upper Horfield estate in north-east Bristol. This huge council estate consisted mostly of precast concrete semi-detached houses which had started to corrode, and a decision was made to demolish them all. As this was quite a low-density development, the rebuilding was partly funded by allowing housing developers to increase the housing density and to sell off the 'extra' homes resulting from this. This also allowed for diversification of housing tenure and type. This has only been partly successful as many of the private homes have been bought by speculators who then let them out, which was not the original intention. Although the new houses are fairly bland in design, there have been attempts to create home zones in some of the streets, although even these have been only partly successful, as some residents have complained about people (mostly young) hanging around in these spaces.

On the other side of the city, the outer suburbs of south Bristol are dominated by disadvantaged social housing estates, still suffering from geographical isolation and lack of employment resulting from the closure of the big factories (mostly tobacco) that the housing was clustered around (see Malpass 1994). Regeneration has mostly consisted of partially successful environmental improvements and the introduction of new 'shed' retailers into the area, thus transferring the area's industry from production to consumption uses. For example, Symes Avenue in Hartcliffe (the site of a riot after two young local men died as a result of a police car chase in the 1990s) has been cleared of its small shops to be replaced by a large Morrison's supermarket – a doubtful benefit from a social and economic point of view.

However, the wider south Bristol area has also benefited from bottom-up, youth-focused and community-led regeneration in the form of the EU Urban II programme, which ran from 2002 to 2008 (see www.bristolurban.org.uk). This has seen £7.4 million of European Regional Development Funding directed at over forty projects including the flagship and innovative Knowle West Media Centre run by the Archimedia group, and the Withywood community centre. Furthermore, the youth community group Spacemakers redesigned, remodelled and regenerated a largely dilapidated, neglected, and nefarious local authority park to create an attractive and popular public space.

One bold but controversial new development in south Bristol has been the renovation, by the property developers Urban Splash, of the derelict former headquarters of Imperial Tobacco in Hartcliffe, into a trendy new apartment complex known as Lake Shore. This mixed tenure and price development in a formerly disinvested neighbourhood, an example of a design-led renaissance, has been criticised by locals and by Slater (2006), amongst others, for favouring middle-income residents and developers rather than working class or low-income tenants, but it is introducing a wider social mix into an area that has hitherto been almost entirely working class.

Easton (a multiracial suburb close to the east of the city centre) continues to struggle with social disadvantage and exclusion, but there have been a couple of design revitalisation successes. The first is the environmental improvement programme that managed to upgrade the streetscape in a mixed tenure residential area. The second, and arguably most visible success, has been the revitalisation of St Mark's Road, a shopping street rather off the beaten track, which has a growing reputation as an 'alternative' location for buying and eating produce from other parts of the world. Nearby Mivart Street studios (an old factory building, now rented out in small units to artists of all kinds) has also helped to add to the mix and vitality of Easton.

Three of Bristol's suburbs have been sites for small but promising self-build housing schemes. Two of them (in Knightstone Close, Hartcliffe, and Walter Street, Southville) were initiated by housing associations and allowed tenants building their own homes to benefit from 'sweat equity'. The third, at Ashley Vale, St Werburghs, came about through a cooperative of self-builders who clubbed together to purchase a brownfield site where they constructed an intriguing development of low-energy dwellings. In all three cases the resulting architecture has more character than the standard volume house builders' product and has provided affordable housing in an innovative way.

Most of the limited improvements in the fortunes of Bristol's social housing estates have, arguably, come from social regeneration rather than physical regeneration, through community-led organisations such as the Hartcliffe and Withywood Community Partnership, the Knowle West Development Trust and the Barton Hill NDC (see Bassett *et al.* 2003; Tallon 2007). The most vivid example of a community improving itself through social interventions, with virtually no design-led improvements, has been the formerly notorious Southmead estate (http://environment.uwe.ac.uk/commsafe/southmeadconts.asp).

Apart from the inevitable rash of new supermarkets, the other striking new development in the suburbs has been a tranche of rebuilt schools. For many years Bristol's state schools have languished towards the bottom of the government's national league tables. It has been argued that this is less to do with the overall standard of education in Bristol and more to do with the fact that aspirational and better-off parents (of whom there are many in this prosperous city) send their offspring to one of the many private schools in the city, or bus them out to more reputable state schools in the surrounding shires, thus leaving inner-city teachers with a particularly challenging group of pupils to deal with. There appears to have been a 'salvation by bricks' philosophy taken by the city education authorities, with almost every state school in Bristol being rebuilt and/or transferred to 'academy' status (whereby a faith or other ideologically based organisation part-sponsors the running of the school). A range of spectacular new buildings has arisen as a result of this approach, some funded through the controversial private finance initiative (PFI). Some of these new schools or academies are clearly flourishing, whereas others are already proving to be not fit for purpose, with design flaws impeding the ability to teach and manage students. There are also concerns about high maintenance costs and the long-term maintenance implications of PFI buildings, where contracts have been sold on to other commercial outfits with little interest in the expensive upkeep of heavy-use buildings.

Edge city

Part of the urban renaissance problem for Bristol is that significant chunks of the built-up area come under the separate (and often non-cooperative) administrations of South Gloucestershire and North Somerset (Figure 7.1). Nowhere has this been more contentious than on the northern fringe of the city, where massive retail and office developments have been approved by South Gloucestershire Council, with little consideration of the effect this would have on the rest of Bristol (Lambert and Smith 2003). On the positive side, this has provided considerable employment opportunities, but, on the other hand, it has put a huge strain on the transport infrastructure and has arguably had a detrimental effect on Bristol city centre retail and office market viability. This is particularly apparent with the Cribbs Causeway regional shopping centre, other retail parks and a multileisure and entertainment complex (Tallon 2007). The last straw for many Bristolians was the relocation to this new mall of the John Lewis department store, which had previously been located in the centre of Bristol. Opportunities to make Cribbs Causeway more accessible by public transport, by providing a new station on the adjacent railway line or a tram link from central Bristol, were not implemented for commercial and political reasons, with the result that the site is dominated by (free) car parking spaces. It has been argued that 'fragmentation and frustration' characterise inter-authority relations in the city-region in terms of strategic planning and policy (Lambert and Smith 2003; Boddy *et al.* 2004).

One of the most controversial developments in the city-region over the last twenty years has been Bradley Stoke. Although within the greater Bristol conurbation, this massive private housing development of over 8,500 properties (allegedly the largest new estate in Europe) is within the local authority of South Gloucestershire and located within the edge city area (see Figure 7.1). Originally conceived by a consortium of private developers with absolutely no content other than housing for commuters, there has been a subsequent retrofitting of retail and community facilities. Initial occupancy of Bradley Stoke coincided with a national downturn in the value of housing in the late 1980s/early 1990s, resulting in many owner-occupiers finding themselves in negative equity and the sarcastic renaming of the area as 'Sadly Broke'.

Overall Bristol's edge city can be summed up as a partial economic success but an environmental liability, with pressures for further housing and commercial growth, and problems of transport and congestion (see Lambert and Oatley 2002; Lambert and Smith 2003; Stewart 2003; Boddy *et al.* 2004; Tallon 2007).

Transport

The aspect of Bristol that the average Bristolian finds most problematic, along with crime and state school education, is almost certainly transport. Repeated city administrations have consistently failed to implement any improvements for citizens attempting to travel around Bristol, by whatever means. Indeed, both public and private transport circulation has actually worsened over the last two decades. The opportunity has been consistently missed to introduce a tram network and, as suburban railways are virtually non-existent, all travellers have to use the same road network, with consequent congestion however you travel.

It is also apparent that motorised transport still has priority in terms of layout of the urban realm of the city centre, although road capacity was reduced with the remodelling of The Centre, and the removal of a major road through historic Queen Square, allowing for it to be restored to its original state. Footpaths are consistently obstructed by road signs and pedestrians are forced (by barriers along the side of pavements or by off-set pedestrian crossing points) to make detours and face delays for the convenience of motor traffic. For example, a new pedestrian crossing to access the new Cabot Circus development, across the diverted inner ring road, requires those on foot to negotiate three separate light-controlled stages.

The only visible progress with transport has been the encouragement of bicycle travel, with the introduction of a limited number of (inconsistent) cycle lanes and the 2008 nomination of Bristol as the UK's first 'cycle city', attracting over £11 million of government funding. This will be matched by a similar amount from the city council, for innovations including cycle lanes, facilities and a bicycle rental network. However, it should be noted that Bristol is probably one of the British cities (along with Edinburgh) *least* physically suited to cycling, as a result of its hilly topography.

The latest strategy of introducing 'showcase' bus routes (where buses get priority down existing streets) is attempting to open up the accessibility and attractiveness of the shopping areas collectively known as Eastside. These routes might not produce the desired results unless the virtual monopoly of bus ownership by one company, not known for its efficiency and economy, is changed. However, public transport in the city-region is set to benefit from £42 million of funding recently announced by central government for the Greater Bristol Bus Network, and increased to around £70 million with local authority and private sector contributions to be spent on infrastructure and vehicles. The city council's only other transport policy appears to be to reduce the number of city centre parking spaces and increase the charges for those that remain – a deterrent that is reasonable only if a cheap and reliable public transport network is available as an alternative.

An even bigger transport failure in Bristol has been the ideological infighting within the council, and rivalry with the surrounding local authorities, which has delayed the implementation of a dedicated public transport network for the whole city region (see Lambert and Oatley 2002; Lambert and Smith 2003; Boddy *et al.* 2004). This delay means that, even if agreement could be reached for the construction of a tram, metro or light railway web, it would probably now be unaffordable.

Urban design and the Bristol urban renaissance: key issues

Quality

With the exception of some of the new waterside housing and a few new public spaces, there is a lack of high-quality new development or redevelopment in Bristol. There are no 'iconic' new buildings that people would travel to see and no redeveloped areas comparable to Temple Bar in Dublin, the Jewellery Quarter in Birmingham or Manchester's Canal Basin area, which are destinations in themselves. The nearest thing that Bristol has to this is the Broad Quay/Narrow Quay area at Harbourside, but as with the similarly revamped Mermaid Quay in Cardiff Bay, it is dominated by corporate chain bars and nightclubs, consistent with the experience across the UK's city centre spaces (see Chatterton and Hollands 2003). The one chance that this area had to become a unique and iconic destination was scuppered when the Arts Council withdrew, at the last minute, its funding for the construction of the spectacular Performing Arts Centre, which to this day remains an empty site overlooking the Floating Harbour. An international design competition for the centre was won by Behnisch and Behnisch Architects, who came up with a truly striking design, which would have put Bristol on the modern architectural pilgrimage route, along with such iconic buildings as the Lowry Centre in Salford and the Sage in Gateshead.

Consumption

Nearly all of Bristol's urban 'improvement' has come from an increasing number of facilities for consuming food, drink, clothes or popular culture. The epitome of this is manifest in the new Cabot Circus development, which is completely dominated by corporate retailing, media and restaurant chains, offering an up-market opportunity to consume. Of course, this is a common pattern across the developed world, but it does seem, given Bristol's reputation for creativity and the extraordinary concentration of artists and musicians, that this productive and distinctive potential has not been capitalised upon by the city authorities. There are exceptions, such as the Spike Island studio complex, run by artists *for* artists, which also holds public events and open days, and the Paintworks development. It appears that the people who are most successfully producing more mixed and inspiring developments in Bristol are alternative property developers such as Verve (responsible for the Paintworks) and the PG Group (responsible for St Peter's Court and the St Patrick's Church site in Redfield). Organisations such as Urban Splash (Lake Shore in Hartcliffe), Urban Creation (the old pro-cathedral site in Clifton) and Urban II in south Bristol are also managing to come up with creative design solutions in derelict structures and spaces.

Consultation

No Bristolian can complain that they are not consulted about the future of their city. The city council has all kinds of consultative mechanisms, including an innovative citizens' panel of randomly selected lay consultees. The problem is that it is not clear how much of the feedback from consultation is actually heeded, with the result that many Bristolians are cynical and fatalistic. A classic example was the redevelopment of the central area just north of Broad Quay, where two options were presented at a series of high-profile public consultation exercises. The public overwhelmingly supported option 2, but the city council went ahead with option 1 anyway (a new 'promenade' – see Plate 7.4).

Compromise

The reason why the city council went ahead with option 1 for the remodelling of The Centre was apparently because it was the quicker and cheaper option. The result has been a city centre promenade of dull water features and uninspired seating engulfed in a roar of circulating traffic (Plate 7.4), when what the public most wanted was a reinstatement of the harbour that lies beneath this site. This is a microcosm of what has happened all too often during attempts to regenerate Bristol. The crucial central Harbourside site known as Canon's Marsh lay dormant for decades whilst various proposals, objections and counter-proposals were wrestled with by the local authority (see Bassett *et al.* 2002; Tallon 2006). It was assumed by many that the final masterplan would have to be good after so much protracted debate. Yet the actual development is proving to be of remarkably mundane appearance and use – mostly corporate office blocks, standard chain leisure facilities of the type found in any other city, and expensive but anonymous apartment blocks.

It would appear that any aspirations on the part of the city council and urban design campaigners to come up with something unique and classy for Bristol have been undermined in too many cases by the economic and political pressures of big businesses. This outcome has been witnessed in the large-scale regeneration developments at both Cabot Circus and Harbourside. There has been an extraordinary plethora of plans, neighbourhood strategies, guidance documents and consultative exercises undertaken by the city council, consultants and amenity groups in Bristol over the last twenty years, but (and Canon's Marsh is a prime example) much of this work has been compromised by the harsh pressures of commerce and expediency in promoting urban renaissance (see Bell and Jayne 2003; Hoskins and Tallon 2004; Colomb 2007).

Complacency

Possibly because Bristol has been a relatively prosperous and successful city for many years (Boddy *et al.* 2004), there appears to have been a general lack of incentive to significantly change or improve the place (unlike, say, Birmingham, which has experienced massive upheavals over the last fifty years; see Loftman and Nevin 1995; Kennedy 2004). Changes, often for the worse, such as Broadmead, the Cumberland Basin multi-gyratory road system and the inner ring road, have been, on the whole, grudgingly accommodated, and very little has been learned from either mistakes made or successes achieved. Bristol's real assets (for example as a potential tourist destination and a major arts powerhouse) have hardly been capitalised upon (in contrast to, for example, Glasgow, which has been successful in promoting itself as a cultural destination; see Booth and Boyle 1993; Paddison 1993).

Campaigning

As a prosperous city, with a large professional class and two universities, Bristol has a number of articulate, influential and well-informed voluntary and community groups with an interest in the quality of the built environment. An alliance of Bristol's neighbourhood groups has recently objected to the Preferred Development Strategy of the new Local Development Framework, and ensured the rewriting of the Statement of Community Involvement to improve their ability to be heard in the planning process. Indeed, many of the positive urban design achievements in Bristol have occurred as a result of interventions by the Bristol Civic Society (www.bristolcivicsociety.

cjb.net) and other voluntary neighbourhood-based groups, either by resisting poor-quality council or developer proposals or by proposing alternative schemes.

Conclusion

It cannot be claimed with any substance that Bristol has had a substantially urban design-led renaissance. Admittedly, there have been some significant improvements to the urban fabric, most notably the reclaiming of parts of the inner ring road for public space and the proliferation of new buildings overlooking the extensive Floating Harbour, linked to new public walkways along the harbour's edge. However, the urban renaissance, particularly in the city centre, has been exclusionary in terms of who can afford to live in the regenerated landscape. It can also be argued (and is by many, including the Bristol Civic Society and many neighbourhood-based environmental groups) that most of Bristol's new or renewed urban fabric is remarkable only for its consistent mediocrity. That Bristol still remains a prosperous and popular city seems to be more to do with the fact that it was a desirable city from many years ago and that it has an amazing topographical setting, with its many hills and waterways. Perhaps therefore Bristol did not need an 'urban renaissance' because, unlike post-industrial cities such as Birmingham, Glasgow and Manchester, it was never in any real danger of 'dying'. For many, Bristol remains a good place to live and work *despite* the limited achievements of its planners, developers and regeneration initiatives.

References

Bassett, K., Griffiths, R., and Smith, I. (2002) Testing Governance: Partnerships, Planning and Conflict in Waterfront Regeneration. *Urban Studies*, 39: 1757–1775.

Bassett, K., Griffiths, R., and Smith, I. (2003) City of Culture? In M. Boddy (ed.) *Urban Transformation and Urban Governance: Shaping the Competitive City of the Future* (Bristol: Policy Press) pp. 52–65.

Boddy, M. (2003) *Urban Transformation and Urban Governance: Shaping the Competitive City of the Future* (Bristol: Policy Press).

Boddy, M. (2007) Designer Neighbourhoods: New-Build Residential Development in Non-Metropolitan UK Cities – The Case Of Bristol. *Environment and Planning A*, 39: 86–105.

Boddy, M., Bassett, K., French, S., Griffiths, R., Lambert, C., Leyshon, A., Smith, I., Stewart, M., and Thrift, N. (2004) Competitiveness and Cohesion in a Prosperous City-Region: The Case of Bristol. In M. Boddy and M. Parkinson (eds) *City Matters: Competitiveness, Cohesion and Urban Governance* (Bristol: Policy Press) pp. 51–69.

Booth, P. and Boyle, R. (1993) See Glasgow, See Culture. In F. Bianchini and M. Parkinson (eds) *Cultural Policy and Urban Regeneration: The West European Experience* (Manchester: Manchester University Press) pp. 21–47.

BCC (Bristol City Council) (1998) *Bristol City Centre Strategy – Section 1: Introduction and Summary* (Bristol: Bristol City Council).

BCC (2003) *Public Art Strategy* (Bristol: Bristol City Council).

BCC (2005a) *Supplementary Planning Document 01: Tall Buildings* (Bristol: Bristol City Council.

BCC (2005b) *Bristol City Centre Strategy and Action Plan 2005–2010 – Section 1: Introduction and Summary* (Bristol: Bristol City Council).

Bromley, R., Tallon, A., and Thomas, C. (2005) City Centre Regeneration Through Residential Development: Contributing to Sustainability. *Urban Studies*, 42 (12): 2407–2429

Bromley, R., Tallon, A., and Roberts, A. (2007) New Populations in the British City Centre: Evidence of Social Change from the Census and Household Surveys. *Geoforum*, 38: 138–154.

Chatterton, P. and Hollands, R. (2003) *Urban Nightscapes: Youth Cultures, Pleasure Spaces and Corporate Power* (London: Routledge).

Clement, M. (2007) Bristol: 'Civilising' the Inner City. *Race and Class*, 48: 97–105.

Cohen, M. and Plissart, M. (2007) *Brussels on our Doorstep: Architecture in Neighbourhood Contracts* (Brussels: Brussels Capital Region, Urban Regeneration Department).

Davidson, M. and Lees, L. (2005) New-Build 'Gentrification' and London's Riverside Renaissance. *Environment and Planning A*, 37: 1165–1190.

Deas, I., Robson, B., and Bradford, M. (2000) Re-Thinking the Urban Development Corporation 'Experiment': The Case of Central Manchester, Leeds and Bristol. *Progress in Planning*, 54: 1–72.

Franck, K. and Stevens, Q. (eds) (2007) *Loose Space: Possibility and Diversity in Urban Life* (London: Routledge).

Griffiths, R., Bassett, K., and Smith, I. (1999) Cultural Policy and the Cultural Economy in Bristol. *Local Economy*, 14: 257–264.

Kelly, A. and Kelly, M. (2003) *Building Legible Cities 2: Making the Case* (Bristol: Bristol Cultural Development Partnership).

Kennedy, L. (ed.) (2004) *Remaking Birmingham: The Visual Culture of Urban Regeneration* (London: Routledge).

Lambert, C., and Boddy, M. (2002) *Transforming the City: Post-Recession Gentrification and Re-Urbanisation* (ESRC Centre for Neighbourhood Research, Paper 6).

Lambert, C. and Oatley, N. (2002) Governance, Institutional Capacity and Planning for Growth. In G. Cars, P. Healey, A. Madanipour and C. de Magalhaes (eds) *Urban Governance, Institutional Capacity and Social Milieux* (Aldershot: Ashgate) pp. 125–141.

Lambert, C. and Smith, I. (2003) Reshaping the City. In M. Boddy (ed.) *Urban Transformation and Urban Governance: Shaping the Competitive City of the Future* (Bristol: Policy Press) pp. 20–31.

Loftman, P. and Nevin, B. (1995) Prestige Projects and Urban Regeneration in the 1980s and 1990s: A Review of Benefits and Limitations. *Planning Practice and Research*, 10: 299–315.

Malpass, P. (1994) Policy Making and Local Governance: How Bristol Failed to Secure City Challenge Funding (Twice). *Policy and Politics*, 22: 301–312.

Oatley, N. (1993) Realizing the Potential of Urban Policy: The Case of the Bristol Development Corporation. In R. Imrie and H. Thomas (eds) *British Urban Policy and the Urban Development Corporations* (London: Paul Chapman) pp. 136–153.

Oatley, N. and May, A. (1999) Out of Touch, Out of Place, Out of Time: A Valediction for Bristol Development Corporation. In R. Imrie and H. Thomas (eds) *British Urban Policy: An Evaluation of the Urban Development Corporations*, (2nd edn) (London: Sage) pp. 186–205.

Paddison, R. (1993) City Marketing, Image Reconstruction and Urban Regeneration. *Urban Studies*, 30: 339–350.

Phillips, T. (1999) What are Cities for? Bristol on the Eve of the Millennium, Part 2. *Contemporary Review*, 2 January.

Punter, J. (1990) *Design Control in Bristol 1940–1990* (Bristol: Redcliffe Press).

Punter, J. (1991) The Long-Term Conservation Programme in Central Bristol 1977–1990. *Town Planning Review*, 62: 341–364.

Punter, J (1992) Design Control and the Regeneration of Docklands: The Example of Bristol. *Journal of Property Research*, 9: 49–78.

Shaftoe, H. (2008) *Convivial Urban Spaces: Creating Effective Public Spaces* (London: Earthscan).

Slater, T. (2006) The Eviction of Critical Perspectives from Gentrification Research. *International Journal of Urban and Regional Research*, 30: 737–757.

Stewart, M. (2003) Towards Collaborative Capacity. In M. Boddy (ed.) *Urban Transformation and Urban Governance: Shaping the Competitive City of the Future* (Bristol: Policy Press) pp. 76–89.

Symes, M. and Steel, M. (2003) Lessons from America: The Role of Business Improvement Districts as an Agent of Urban Regeneration. *Town Planning Review*, 74: 301–313.

Tallon, A. (2006) Regenerating Bristol's Harbourside. *Town and Country Planning*, 75: 278–282.

Tallon, A. (2007) City Profile: Bristol. *Cities*, 24: 74–88.

Tallon, A. (2008) Mega-Retail-Led Regeneration. *Town and Country Planning*, 77: 131–137.

Tallon, A. and Bromley, R. (2004) Exploring the Attractions of City Centre Living: Evidence and Policy Implications in British Cities. *Geoforum*, 35: 771–787.

Walker, G. (1996) Retailing Development: In Town or Out of Town? In C. Greed (ed.) *Investigating Town Planning: Changing Perspectives and Agendas* (Harlow: Longman) pp. 155–180.

8 Newcastle upon Tyne

In search of a post-industrial direction

Ali Madanipour

The Urban White Paper *Our Towns and Cities: The Future* advocated 'a vision of an urban renaissance which will benefit everyone, making towns and cities vibrant and successful places where people will choose to live, and helping protect the countryside from development pressure' (DETR 2000b: 5). It hoped for 'people shaping the future of their community'; 'living in attractive, well-kept towns and cities'; 'good design and planning' contributing to environmental sustainability; creating and sharing prosperity; and 'good quality services' (ibid.). Looking at the experience of Newcastle during the past decade, how far has this vision been realised, and what contribution has urban design, broadly defined, made to this process? To find some answers, we will need to find out what institutional relationships were at work, and what economic strategies and design philosophies were pursued, with reference to some major urban projects in the northeast of England.

A new strategy: competition or collaboration

The story of urban renaissance in Newcastle does not start with the publication of the Urban Task Force (UTF) report (1999) or the policies of the New Labour government: the decline and revival of Newcastle is a much longer story. A new episode started in the 1980s with a decisive drive for deindustrialisation, deregulation and stimulation of property markets, preparing the ground for the emergence of a service economy. As in other British cities, the underlying trend was radical marketisation under Margaret Thatcher, and social adjustments by the following governments. It coincided with the emergence of urban design as a forward-looking, development-friendly enterprise that could help give material shape to this agenda, erasing the traces of industrial decline and putting in place the necessary infrastructure for a new economy (Madanipour 2006).

Newcastle's management and development since the 1980s is characterised by tensions between city and suburbs, between neighbouring authorities, between local and central governments, between public and private sector roles in urban development, and between joined-up and piecemeal management of change. The main issue at stake has often been whether different geographies and institutions should collaborate or compete with one another. The impacts of these tensions are evident in the shape and nature of developments that were undertaken, reflecting the linkages between institutional change and physical transformation.

A fragmented and weak regional governance has been an obstacle to developing the region's capacity for growth (OECD 2006). The abolition of the Tyne and Wear as an administrative unit in the 1980s was followed by a period of disjointed development, whereby neighbouring authorities competed with one another to attract investment. Rather than deciding at a strategic level about what was needed for the urban region, it was competition that defined the way they related to each other.

The tension between the city centre and suburbs reflects a competition between neighbouring local authorities for jobs, new development and an increase in their tax base. During the 1990s, the city lost 15,000 residents, who went elsewhere for work, or left the city to live in the surrounding areas (Office for National Statistics 2008). Most of the new developments were on the outskirts, where a large out-of-town shopping mall (Metro Centre) now undermined the livelihood of secondary town centres and threatened Newcastle's centre, which worried about losing its hold on the region. In response, existing facilities were improved (Eldon Square, Northumberland Street) and major schemes (Quayside, Grainger Town) launched to revitalise the city and strengthen its core (see Figure 8.1). While most housing continues to be located on the periphery, retail and leisure have been the key to the centre's success, dramatically transforming its character.

The competitive trend was partly reversed by New Labour's promotion of joined-up working, and some collaboration between neighbours can be detected. A significant case is Newcastle–Gateshead collaboration on their joint bid for the European city of culture. Although unsuccessful, the two authorities started closer relationships, most significantly with a new footbridge (Gateshead Millennium Bridge) that connects the two sides together (see Plate 8.1). Competition, however, remains a major force, as evident in competitive bidding for project funding, and more

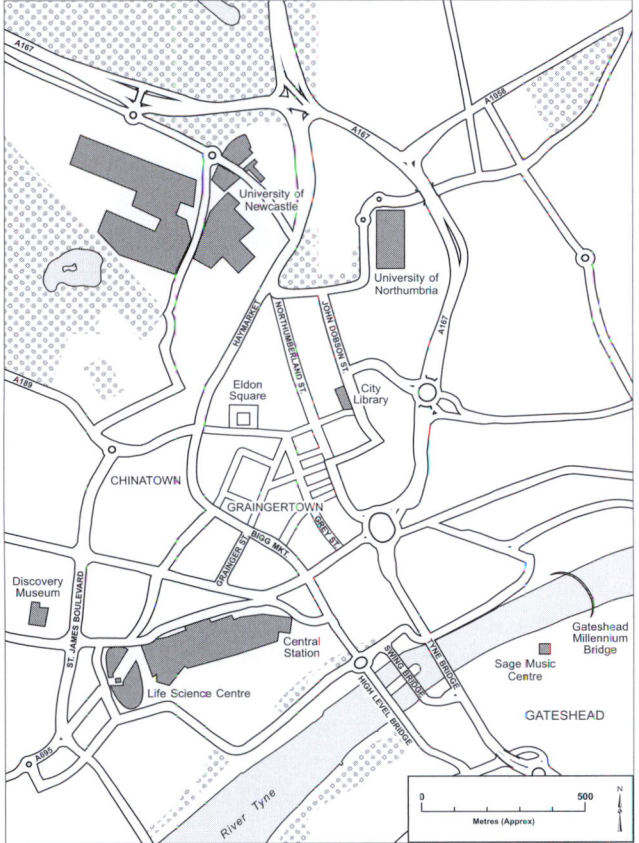

Figure 8.1 Newcastle city centre: street map (drawn by Jan Edwards). © Crown Copyright. All rights reserved. Licence number 100049043.

Plate 8.1 Newcastle: Gateshead Millennium Bridge is an award-winning footbridge that connects the two sides of the River Tyne, reflecting the start of collaboration between neighbouring authorities.

directly in competition for upmarket housing, to the extent that thousands of new houses are being controversially built on Newcastle's green belt (Great Park). The drive to establish an elected regional assembly was rejected in a referendum, but the agenda of city-regions has been pursued through collaboration with Gateshead, and now more widely through a multiarea agreement between the region's local authorities.

The tension between the local and central governments was at its peak in the 1980s, when the Labour local authority and Conservative central government had opposing views on how to manage and develop the city. The central government had installed a powerful regeneration agency (Tyne and Wear Development Corporation), which was not responsible to the local government. The battleground was the future direction of this area: should it return to manufacturing industries, as the local administration promoted, or move into a new, somewhat unknown future. Land reclamation and infrastructure development paved the way for a complete change of urban environment along the riverside, which is now largely judged to be a success, although the strength of the feelings and ideological battles that were fought at the time are difficult to depict. After a period (1997–2004), the central and local government in Newcastle are once again from different parties, and their relations are managed by a local area agreement (LAA).

The debate about competition or collaboration between public authorities drew on a larger tension around the roles and relations of the state and the market. Post-war urban development had been led by the public sector, able to mobilise large amounts of money and productive power. From the 1980s on, however, the public sector was unwilling or unable to take the lead, arguing that there was a need to engage the private sector. The major urban regeneration schemes brought public funds to pave the way for attracting private sector investment.

The result has been public–private partnerships, as a new format for funding urban development (Quayside, Grainger Town). Partnerships have also become the new format for planning the city, whereby it is expected that different stakeholders collaborate, rather than compete with each other, to envisage and implement the future of the city. The Newcastle Partnership produced its first and second Newcastle Plans in 2001 and 2004. Its most recent plan has devised a Sustainable Community Strategy (SCS) and LAA for 2008–2011 (Newcastle Partnership 2008). It envisages the creation of a City Development Company as a partnership between Newcastle,

Gateshead and the regional development agency, to lead the economic regeneration of the urban core.

The change from comprehensive planning and public sector urban development to private sector urban development is best seen in the project-based nature of change. Rather than thinking long term and conducting coordinated development, much of new development in the city, especially in its early regeneration efforts, has been short-term and project based. This has been partly due to the nature of funding, based on fixed-term public funding schemes. It has also been due to the changing fashions in design, particularly from historicist to high-tech design. The result has been piecemeal and incoherent development, with schemes that do not always relate to one another. In response, much has been talked about joined-up thinking and acting. However, this has not yet led to the development of a more coherent urban environment.

Erasing the industrial landscape: reclaiming the riverside

Newcastle was built on the banks of the River Tyne; since Roman times, a bridge (now the Swing Bridge) has connected the two sides of the city. When manufacturing industries took control of the river, as their main transport route and sewerage, the rest of the city grew away from the river, developing uphill towards the north. A number of bridges that connected the hilltops and avoided the riverside reinforced this process: High Level Bridge was built to carry train connections in the nineteenth century and Tyne Bridge in the twentieth century to carry motor cars. As industries declined, the riverside became derelict and dilapidated. The regeneration efforts refocused attention on the river as an axis for the city. New civic buildings, cultural landmarks, offices, flats, hotels and restaurants on both sides have turned the river into a vibrant part of the city once again. Rather than turning its back to the river, the city now looks on it as an asset, and embraces it as an integral part of the urban fabric, although much remains to be done outside a renovated core. The new riverside has become a promenade, a destination for cultural and leisure activities (see Plate 8.2).

Plate 8.2 Newcastle: Quayside. The regeneration of the riverside has turned it into a promenade, a destination for leisure and cultural activities.

This transition from industries to culture and entertainment caused concern over the structural change of the economy from production to consumption, and a shift from working to middle-class users, effectively gentrifying the quayside. The absence of a resident population limited the impact on local communities, but some displacement was caused by the relocation of activities from the city centre to the riverside. Some artistic activities, which had found low-rent space in the dereliction of the riverside, now had to migrate to the other side of the river to Gateshead, or to more marginal parts of the city centre, such as the Ouseburn Valley. When the wave of development encroached upon these areas, there was fierce opposition from the Ouseburn community to the style of regeneration that had gone before. Meanwhile, there has been continuous criticism of city centre regeneration efforts for their disconnection from the inner city. The types of activities and jobs provided are often seen to be good for the middle classes, and new developments look inwards to the centre, rather than out towards the low-income inner-city areas. In some respects, political pressure from the latter has prevented the city centre from encroaching into their space, resulting in a tight boundary around the city centre for regeneration activities. The strong divide between the city centre and the inner city reflects the city's social divide and polarization, which has not been easy to address even after years of economic boom and high employment in the country.

While the city centre and the riverside have been considerably improved, there are dissenting voices that raise their concerns about the character of these improvements. Some people prefer a more modest, old-fashioned industrial image and environment, hating changes that they see as imposed from outside, driven by the preferences of investors, and expressed in a corporate architectural language, rather than by the needs of the people expressed in the local idiom. These improvements are criticised for promoting the vision of the development industry, rather than that of local communities, and for erasing the memory of the past, and undermining the diversity and richness of the local culture which is deeply rooted in the industrial era.

In earlier stages of regenerating the city centre, a key concern was about empty upper floors and entire buildings, which showed the oversupply of built space in the city centre. With the movement of several major institutions to the riverside (the law courts) and financial services to other cities (Leeds), low demand was exacerbated. Some were arguing that the best solution would be to reduce floor space in the city centre and a number of the new regeneration schemes were following this advice, building at lower densities and leaving large open spaces in between buildings (East Quayside). Sometimes the effects of this approach appear to be spaces that are not well defined or articulated (Times Square, International Centre for Life). Following the Grainger Town conservation project, private housing started to flourish in the city centre, primarily new and converted flats. The heated city centre housing market in the country also affected Newcastle, leading to an oversupply of flats, which could not be sold in the following economic downturn.

Transition to a post-industrial imagery

The attempts to erase the memories of industrial decline have emphasised the historic character of the city and established late-modernist landmarks.

There is a high concentration of historic buildings in central areas, many listed for architectural and historic significance. A regeneration scheme (Grainger Town) injected massive public funds into the area, substantially improving the physical fabric (de Magalhaes *et al.* 2002; Healey *et al.* 2002; see Plate 8.3). The emphasis was on changing the image of the city, reviving memories of the pre-industrial past. Other towns and cities may have been known for their historic character, but not Newcastle; therefore, now was the time to correct this misconception. Historic referencing was one of the hallmarks of the postmodern architecture, which was the main form of expression for many regeneration projects, from major buildings to street furniture (East Quayside office buildings, Monument Mall, Haymarket bus station).

The key challenge was how to deal with the past, both recent and remote. Should attempts be made to harmonise efforts with the legacy of the past, or should this past be eradicated and new contrasting spaces and images be constructed? Both these trends have been at work, depending on the period and the target of deliberation. The main city centre regeneration project (Grainger Town, 1997–2003) started life as an effort by conservationists to save the declining core of the city. When regeneration was combined with conservation, it was possible to attract public funds, though not without compromises such as facadism (Lloyds Bank), whereby the façade was kept and the interior completely redeveloped. This was not enough to satisfy conservationists; it was using the image of buildings without keeping their essence. Historical references seemed to be used only for marketing. Historicism subsided when the tide of high-tech, late-modernist architecture arrived in several prestige developments (St James football ground, Sage music centre, Gateshead Millennium Bridge).

The idea of flamboyant entrances to the city has seemed to fascinate the authorities. In the nineteenth century, the railway station's grand architecture produced an impressive entrance at the heart of cities (Central Station). The main entrance to the city was for years from across the river Tyne, marked by bridges (Tyne Bridge) and key buildings (Swan House). Now the entrance to the north of the city centre is being marked by a new landmark (Haymarket Metro Station), and the entrance to Chinatown by another (ceremonial gate, see Plate 8.4). The urban region now enjoys an entrance landmark in Gateshead that has quickly become associated with the north-east (Angel of the North). Emphasis on iconic imagery has been extended to building heights. Tall buildings were used for the 1960s' public housing, as well as marking the entrance to the city. Some of these buildings apparently were never fully occupied, as they were built as a display, rather than as a utility. Some parts of the city centre are now being earmarked for taller buildings (St James Boulevard, Discovery Quarter). The notion of landmark buildings appeals to developers, who wish their buildings to stand out, and to city authorities, who want to prove

Plate 8.3 Newcastle, Grey Street. The city centre's high concentration of listed buildings were improved in a major regeneration project, Grainger Town (1997–2003), to change the image of the city, and raise the quality of its environment.

Plate 8.4 Newcastle: Chinatown's main core has been resurfaced and embellished with lanterns and other Chinese features, including a ceremonial arch, part of the rebranding of city districts in the drive for a new image.

their effectiveness. Whether through expressive architecture, or the height of buildings, many landmark buildings have an uneasy relation to their surroundings. Some are individually beautiful, while others merely resort to exaggeration, screaming for attention, and create a fragmented urban environment, a collection of pieces rather than a coherent whole.

The change of image has been somewhat effective, as Newcastle and its neighbour Gateshead have been given more favourable reports in the national and international media. The result has been the rise of tourism in Newcastle, a phenomenon that barely existed before. The new imagery, however, continues to trouble parts of the local population who cannot identify with it. While the image of the city has changed significantly, its real social and economic conditions are still a long way from being fully successful.

Similar to the riverside, the central area improvements (Grainger Town) are seen as attempts at erasing the city's memory of centuries of industrial life, and returning to a pre-modern past. It is a palimpsest in which selective layers are kept and others are erased. The central area improvements are also subject to criticism for becoming too upmarket, pushing the less well-off out of the city centre, as fewer places cater for the low-income groups. City centre improvements have used expensive building materials, and have given space to chain stores, specialist shops and expensive outlets. The places that catered for the low-income groups (Grainger Market) are constantly under pressure to change their functions, and their clientele are at the risk of eventually being pushed out of the centre altogether. While new public and private investments have dramatically improved the quality and character of the city centre, they have also led to gentrification and displacement, and a change of identity.

Pedestrians and public spaces

The city of Newcastle was once reorganised to accommodate cars. Following the modernist recipe for city planning, fast movement across the city was given priority, and the city was reshaped to allow for maximum mobility. Much of the shape of the city was, therefore, remodelled to provide ease of access, tearing down the old urban fabric and maintaining isolated buildings that were considered worthy. In their places, the city's shape, particularly in central areas (Central Motorway), was radically transformed, with multi-level, fast roads to allow for car access to the heart of the city. This tide, however, has been turning and pedestrians have been given increasing recognition in the city, as evident in the way the city's inner ring road (St James' Boulevard) was completed. This road is developed in the form of a boulevard, with an urban speed of thirty miles per hour, with wide pavements and islands in the middle. The wide tree-lined pavements of St James' Boulevard are flanked by buildings and land uses that are expected to create a vibrant street environment.

One of the key aims of post-war development was segregation of pedestrians from vehicles, which was met through multilevel access systems. Flyovers, decks, and underpasses (City Library, Swan House Roundabout) were erected to provide separate access for pedestrians. These created unpleasant and windswept environments. In response, the decks have been removed (John Dobson Street), and cars and pedestrians once again share the space of the street. At one point, the idea of creating upper-level decks was so fashionable that a number of buildings were built in the city in the form of bridges over the roads. These buildings, however, have recently been removed, opening up the space of the street, and creating an unbroken street line (University's King's Road, Westgate House).

Segregation of cars and pedestrians, however, continues in other forms. In the 1970s, an indoor shopping mall had been built in the city centre to create a protected pedestrian environment (Eldon Square). Subsequently, new parts of the city centre have been pedestrianised, including the main shopping street (Northumberland Street), and other parts of the city centre (Grey's Monument area). Attention to pedestrians has even been extended to the river crossing, where a new foot bridge connects Newcastle and Gateshead (Millennium Bridge). At the same time, more restrictions are being placed on cars through the introduction of no-car lanes in the approaches to the city centre, and slowing down the limited speed in parts of the centre. Earlier, public transport was boosted by the construction of an underground network of trains (Metro), which connects the city centre to neighbouring towns and cities (Gateshead, Sunderland), as well as to the international airport (Newcastle Airport).

Recognition of pedestrians and putting new restrictions on cars have coincided with improvements to the public spaces of the city. New public spaces have been created (Blue Carpet – see Plate 8.5; Times Square), while existing spaces have been improved (Grey's Monument). Public

Plate 8.5 Newcastle: Blue Carpet Square, completed 2002, one of the new city centre public spaces. Part of the Grainger Town project, colour and surface treatments were used to create a sense of cohesion and character.

art, new street furniture and new paving material have been used to improve the overall atmosphere of public places (Quayside, Grainger Town). Part of the drive to improve the city centre's public spaces has focused on the detailed level of the pedestrian experience, as well as on presenting a new image for these spaces. Attention to street furniture and paving material has been increasing (Grainger Town). This attention has also been expressed in the form of public art, used to embellish parts of the city (Paolozzi in Central Square, Grainger Street, Grey's Monument, St James' Boulevard). Gateshead has historically been more sensitive than Newcastle in this regard, which is evident in its important symbol for the region (Angel of the North), as well as its attention to the quality of landscaping and public spaces (Gateshead Metro station) and its quayside regeneration.

Overall, a new balance has been created between cars and pedestrians. Whereas at one time transport engineers determined the fate of the city centre, now urban designers have found more influence. The result is that more attention is paid to the details and the quality of the urban environment to enrich the pedestrian experience of the city. The car, though, is still a major influence on the shape and character of the city, and the way it is linked to its surroundings.

Clustering and mixing of land use

Despite the emphasis on mixed use, regeneration efforts seem to have encouraged a reduction in diversity. The centre, which once housed a more diverse range of land uses and social groups, has become primarily a place for shopping and leisure.

During the day, shopping dominates the city centre. The city's high street (Northumberland Street), which has been recently pedestrianised, is reported to be the most expensive shopping street outside London, with an annual rent of £1,742 per square metre (BBC 2004). An indoor 1970s shopping mall (Eldon Square) is continuously being upgraded to compete with out-of-town shopping malls (Metro Centre). The new city centre improvement schemes (Grainger Town) also helped create new upmarket shopping outlets in the city centre. The concentration of shopping in the centre maintains the city's position as the regional capital, where shoppers come from all over the region, and even from other countries, such as Norway. This concentration, however, has limited the diversity of land use in the central areas. At times, the city centre appears to be one large shopping mall, where most people present are either shoppers or shopkeepers. Emphasis on upmarket shopping has reduced its social diversity, with exclusionary effects on some social groups (Akkar 2003), although some efforts have been made to make spaces accessible to the disabled. The impact on the city centre appears to be gentrification: general improvement as well as exclusion and a loss of diversity.

At night, the city centre is dominated by leisure. Traditionally, many pubs and bars were concentrated in one part of the city centre (Bigg Market). But the development of new bars and restaurants (Quayside, Osborne Road, Gosforth High Street), casinos, theatres and cinemas (The Gate) has spread entertainment to new parts of the city centre. Notions of a night-time economy and a twenty-four-hour city have been at the forefront of city centre regeneration, creating new demand for parts of the city and generating new resources. At the same time, they have changed the character of the city centre, becoming dominated by young drinkers, at the expense of older people, ethnic minorities, and families, who may feel vulnerable.

Leisure and retail account for most of the land use in the city centre. However, many upper floors of buildings have been empty for years, as residential population in the city has been very small. Major efforts have been made to bring people back to the city for living in flats, converting old buildings and building new ones, often for higher-income groups. With the oversupply of small and expensive flats, and a weakened housing market, the possibility of encouraging mixed use in the centre has been jeopardised. Furthermore, there are tensions between a city centre devoted to leisure and one in which a residential population can live. There are no schools or everyday shops to support families, so most of the new population tend to be young or old individuals or small households. Even this population's needs are not the same as those of the entertainment industry. Pubs and restaurants are nervous about running their businesses next to homes, as they know that in case of disputes housing tends to win.

Diversity, therefore, may decline in economic and social terms; it tends to find an aesthetic expression in the range of goods to consume and in rebranding parts of the town. The examples of rebranding include renaming parts of the city (Grainger Town), and associating them with a particular character (Chinatown (Plate 8.4), Theatre Village, Discovery Quarter). These seem to be mainly driven by marketing initiatives, to change the image of the city and its parts, so that they become more fashionable and appealing in the eyes of visitors and investors (Newcastle Chinatown: 2008). This exercise is partly due to a general trend of promoting distinctiveness in different districts of the city. An important issue is whether this form of districting, which partly draws on a notion of legibility (Lynch 1960), helps the urban environment's enrichment or simplification (Madanipour 2001).

One of the key debates in the city is the shape of its future economy. After industrial decline, the city needs to find a new basis for its economy. For a while the regional economic development strategy was trying to attract international firms by providing a skilled industrial workforce, financial incentives, and low costs of production. Inward investment was the main vehicle for attracting new resources to the region. This approach, however, has suffered from a setback, as lower-cost regions in the world can effectively compete with the north-east of England. The only way open to this region, and regions like it, is now considered to be the path of knowledge economy (i.e. moving up the chain of production and being engaged in research and development, in design and innovation).

Two areas have opened up for future: culture and science. New cultural facilities have been set up (Baltic Gallery, university's cultural quarter) to support the development of cultural activities and industries. Science has also been boosted, through the establishment of new scientific facilities (International Centre for Life) and designation of the city as a Science City by the government. A major new site (former Newcastle Brewery) has been bought jointly by the university, city council and the regional development agency, as a site for the interface between university and industry. Newcastle and Northumbria Universities and Newcastle College have made large investments in new buildings and campus improvement schemes, and Gateshead College has been given a new site near the riverside as part of Gateshead regeneration. The region's universities have been seen as an asset in its future economic growth (OECD 2006). Science and culture may appear to occupy different parts of the city, at different times of the day and with different types of activity. There are, however, tensions between the two, in the overall image of the city, as well as the use of its spaces (Minton 2003).

Participation and social mixing: renaissance in the inner city

An aspect of partnership has been participation by citizens, which has been widely promoted, though not always implemented. The quayside did not have a residential population to be involved in regeneration. The city centre has a small residential population, and the regeneration process

(Grainger Town project) made sure to involve it in the process of change. Through business and citizen forums, those working and living in the city centre were represented. The city centre, however, belongs to the city as a whole, an aspect which was not sufficiently taken into account in its regeneration.

For decades, Newcastle's local governance was characterised by clientelism, paternalism and fragmentation. In 1997, the Labour council initiated an agenda for reforms, which brought in Kevin Lavery, a senior management consultant from Price Waterhouse in London, as the new chief executive. The strategy for reform was based on applying private sector methods of management to make the local council outward-looking and market-friendly, overcoming departmental boundaries and embracing an integrative and flexible approach. A strategic approach to regeneration was adopted, which was linked to the new framework of area governance formed by a Local Strategic Partnership and councillor-led area committees (Johnston 2006).

In 2000, Newcastle City Council published draft masterplans for the east end and west end of the city, which became known as Going for Growth. It explicitly used the language of urban renaissance, and even employed Richard Rogers, the chair of the UTF, to prepare the plans. The initiative set out a vision for the year 2020, specifically focused on 'the renaissance of the inner area – West and East' (NCC 2000: 1).

The document made a case for radical change: Going for Growth was 'not an option' but 'a necessity' (NCC 2000: 6). These areas were losing population, despite the large amounts of public investment during thirty years of regeneration policies and programmes. The west end had lost 40 per cent and the east end 30 per cent of its population, so that schools were becoming unviable. While £500 million had been spent on the regeneration of the west end in the previous twenty years, people still were leaving. Private investment was rare, and council services spent £10 million a year managing decline in the west end (ibid.). The solution was thought to be a radical shake-up of these areas through large-scale redevelopment: demolishing 6,600 existing homes and building 20,000 new ones in mixed housing areas, in the hope of attracting 15,500 new residents and generating 30,000 new jobs. In addition to two district masterplans for the west end and east end, a number of community area plans were also envisaged, so that the city-wide strategy could be completed. There was a need to 'clarify the community structure', enhanced through the provision of district and neighbourhood centres, providing essential facilities for residents.

The renaissance of the inner areas, therefore, aimed at the renewal of market confidence in these areas, to stimulate the growth of population and economic activity, and reduce the public sector burden of housing maintenance and management of decline. The radical nature of the plans, however, was controversial. Resident groups started fighting the demolition plans, arguing that perfectly useful houses and streets were being threatened by these plans. It appeared to be a top-down solution, which had not shown enough sensibility to the needs and aspirations of local communities. The controversies in local government reorganisation and its regeneration strategy led to the departure of Kevin Lavery in 2001. The city council started a process of community participation and setting up community networks. But mistrust had set in, and it took several years before any new masterplans could be developed and accepted. Community networks were enabled to participate in selecting developers and comment on the plans (Madanipour and Merridew 2004). Area committees, however, could not function well, as the process was too long, participation not fully open to community representatives, and private sector and organisational representatives preferred to participate in the city-wide forum (Johnston 2006).

The turbulence of reorganisation and radical reform proved fatal for the Labour group. In 2004, there was a historic change of political administration, in which Labour lost control of the city council after a generation. The incoming Liberal Democrat administration undertook a structural reorganisation of the council and an overhaul of all major projects. Compared with Labour's emphasis on affordability, Liberal Democrats emphasised sustainability and community involvement. There was little difference in their vision for the future of the city. Their major differences lay in the methods of implementation: top-down methods of the old administration were contrasted with the community-friendly methods of the new. Area committees were abandoned and ward committees were strengthened in 2006 to allow for participation and scrutiny of the regeneration process. Now project boards are being established to manage the area-based regeneration schemes (NCC 2007). The city moved to an 'executive director' model, in which a small executive team is in charge of strategic direction and corporate leadership.

Going for Growth was based on a notion of 'positive' gentrification, in which the low-income areas are made welcoming to the middle-income buyers, so as to generate a mixture of different social classes living in the same area (Cameron 2003). The idea of social mixing was thought to be a way of confronting the phenomenon of 'sink estates' and social exclusion. It was thought that the arrival of middle classes would coincide with better-quality services and avoidance of new ghettos in the city. The problem in Newcastle, where demand is lower than supply, is that this social mixing is harder to achieve. In Walker, despite much public subsidy, the new homes have not found a positive market response, a situation worsened by housing market decline. In other words, the middle classes have not been persuaded to buy homes in an area where schools are not considered to be strong and where negative stigma still lingers.

In 2002, a housing market renewal pathfinder called Bridging NewcastleGateshead was set up as a partnership between the two councils, covering around 77,000 properties in the area. In February 2008, it was given £95 million by the central government to continue its housing improvement work for another three years (Bridging NewcastleGateshead 2008).

Different interpretations of urban renaissance

A key problem of urban renaissance has been the differences of opinion about its meaning, reflecting a divide between quantitative and qualitative interpretations. For some decision-makers and their advisors, quantitative indicators matter most: the number of houses redeveloped or renovated, densities achieved, new floor spaces developed, etc. For others, including urban designers, however, quality of development is equally important. The culture of targets, pressure for accountability and the difficulty of measuring quality have all encouraged decision-makers to vouch for quantity. However, as the 1960s had shown, quantity could not guarantee success in urban transformation.

In early stages of regeneration, as the city was struggling to develop its economy, little attention was given to the quality of design and development. Owing to low demand and absence of investment, any development was welcomed, no matter what its quality and impact on the surrounding urban environment (Manor's business park, The Gate). Larger developers, who are responsive to their shareholders, are often accused of not paying enough attention to the quality of their development, which requires long-term commitment. A similar short-term perspective has sometimes been shown by career-minded professionals, as well as by politicians, who have an eye to simplifying the agenda, so that it can be easily communicated through the media. In contrast, some niche developers have shown that, by taking risks and investing in the quality of their output, they can succeed even in a weak market (Central Square). As the process matured and a market was established, the city council could start expecting higher-quality development, even though some developers saw the pressure for quality as an obstacle to development. As much of the regeneration work takes place on public land, the local authority has become both an advocate and a regulator of development, hence performing an internal division in enabling and controlling change, making the quality of development more difficult to achieve.

Quality is sometimes equated with following - national standards and guidelines. It is thought that if a checklist is followed, the quality of design is ensured. The problem, however, is that these guidelines may reflect the growth management requirements of the south, rather than the regeneration needs of the north. The application of these standards in a local context such as Newcastle may be in the form of paternalist pressure by quangos (quasi non-governmental organisations), rather than working with the physical and cultural grain of the locality. Furthermore, innovation in urban design has suffered from the emergence of a culture of checklists and narrow guidelines, which assumes that the essential features of a desirable urban environment can be fitted into a brief list. The result has become a rather rigid application of checklists that are not particularly suited to Newcastle's specific context.

Quality is sometimes equated with celebrity: if well-known consultants were hired, it is sometimes assumed, the quality of their work must be high. This, however, has not been always the case. Large firms of consultants often front the project with their high-calibre staff, but they can only work on their large number of projects by means of an army of junior staff. The quality of their work, therefore, sometimes leaves much to be desired. There is also a disconnection between the landmarks designed by celebrity architects and the surrounding context, resulting in the loss of quality of the urban space.

The definition of urban design has been broadened during the past decade: whereas in Grainger Town, urban designers were expected to focus on street furniture, in Going for Growth they were engaged in masterplanning and community development, and in Scotswood in enabling sustainable development. This broadening has embedded urban design in the work of the city council, rather than being confined to a specialist and separate section. From a phase in which urban designers were expected to provide nice images as ornaments for documents, they are now engaged in the process of developing visions and plans. Strategic thinking, however, has brought forward the need for design skills necessary to address smaller-scale issues of the urban environment as well.

The general pattern appears to be encouraging local authorities to recruit and manage private consultants, rather than develop and maintain their in-house urban design expertise. The higher prestige and pay of the private sector, therefore, has had a negative effect on the city's urban design capacity. Following a period of uncertainty and insecurity in the city council, structural changes instigated by the new administration, combined with competition from the private sector, led to the departure of a number of key urban design staff to take up positions in private consultancies.

A paradigm shift in achieving quality in design has been the current initiative for the establishment of the UK's first housing exposition at Scotswood, a low-income area in the west end, aiming at diversifying housing tenure, raising the profile of the area and the city, and leaving a lasting physical legacy for the city (NCC 2006). Signing up well-known architects, the city council hopes that at its 2010 completion, the sixty-five-hectare Expo will provide a model for housing market renewal (Dosanjh 2006).

Newcastle reborn?

The city's physical environment, as well as it economy and society, have undergone major changes in the last three decades. As one of the birthplaces of the Industrial Revolution, the loss of manufacturing industries has been painful and turbulent, associated with managing decline and searching for a new economic rationale for the region. Through decades of structural change, services have emerged as the linchpin of the economy, transforming the institutional and physical landscape of the city. The models of development and management, the sense of identity of people, as well as the character and quality of urban space, have considerably changed in line with these structural changes over the lifetime of a generation. The overall strategy has been to embrace the methods and resources of private enterprise, with which to bring land and labour back to the marketplace and make the public administration more effective. Regeneration of the urban environment has followed this strategy, enabled through public policy and resources used for infrastructure development, confidence-building and market-making. While significant efforts have been made to spread the benefits, these changes have inevitably been more beneficial to those better placed in the market.

By the time the White Paper was published, Newcastle's riverside regeneration had already been ongoing for more than a decade, and two of its most important projects, Grainger Town in the city centre and Going for Growth in the inner city, had already started. The language of renaissance, however, was embraced and continues to be employed in the region, as shown by the Regional Spatial Strategy promoting a wide ranging renaissance for the region (GONE 2007: 17).

Like other medium-sized cities, Newcastle faces a serious challenge to find a place in the global economy (OECD 2006). During the past decade, the overall conditions in Newcastle have improved, as evidenced by the stabilisation of the urban population in 2001 and its growth in 2005 and 2006 (Newcastle Partnership 2008: 9). This improvement is also shown by the Index of Multiple Deprivation, which covers income, employment, health, education, housing, environment and crime (DCLG 2007c). According to these indicators, between 2004 and 2007, Newcastle showed an improvement of 9.2 per cent; the neighbouring areas of Gateshead and North Tyneside also improved (by 11.1 per cent and 9.5 per cent respectively) (Pinney 2008). Although the north-east has experienced substantial economic growth over the past decade, other regions have grown faster, and therefore the region's relative position in the UK has remained weak and the gap with the richer regions has widened (Robinson *et al.* 2007) The region's economic strategy aims to narrow this gap by moving from 80 per cent to 90 per cent of the national average GVA (gross value added) per head by 2016 (ONE 2006).

While manufacturing has continued to decline, public sector services have made a strong contribution to the region's economic revival, making its economy vulnerable to any reductions in public expenditure. With the credit crunch and economic slowdown, the north-east region has been hit hardest by the withdrawal of private sector investment, which is looking for safer markets in the south, resulting in a drop of 6 per cent in planned businesses and homes, or more than a thousand projects (Pearson 2008). As the developers warned, this in turn has eroded the local authorities' ability to use Section 106 agreements as a way of securing necessary services.

Conclusion

The city of Newcastle, and its centre in particular, has gone through a major structural change in its economy and society. From a manufacturing industrial city, it has turned into a place of retail and leisure, with aspirations for the development of cultural and scientific sectors in the future. This dramatic change has created a series of tensions about whether and how to change. Should it keep its recent identity and its associated memories, buildings and imagery, or should it eradicate them and move in a new direction? The answer to this question has been largely given, and there are foundations for the future that are being laid, though the shape of this future is unknown. This is shown in the tension between culture and science, between night-time economy and upmarket shopping, on the one hand, and inclusiveness and diversity, on the other hand. These changes have noticeably improved the physical and economic conditions of the city centre. The new spaces and images, however, are contested by some on social and aesthetic grounds, as being corporate and elitist, and not responsive enough to the local character and needs, and not sufficiently subtle or coherent. There are strong pressures to reduce the diversity of the city centre, causing concern about the type of urban environment that might emerge as a result.

Overall, the urban renaissance process in Newcastle has taken many positive steps, leading to a substantial transformation. To become sustainable, this transformation needs to spread socially and geographically, become more diverse in economic sectors and funding sources, and become more confident to demand higher quality of design and development.

How far are the new conditions in line with the vision of urban renaissance laid out in the White Paper? The new developments have certainly created a vibrant city, though this is still concentrated in the city centre and so it has not yet benefited everyone. New developments such as the Great Park also show that the countryside has not been protected as promised, as a sizeable part of the green belt has gone under construction. After almost a decade, therefore, Newcastle's renaissance may score highly on vibrancy, with a considerable contribution from urban design activities, but less successfully on the social and environmental consequences of such vibrancy.

References

Akkar, Z. M. (2003) *The Publicness of the 1990s Public Spaces in Britain, With a Special Reference To Newcastle Upon Tyne*. Unpublished PhD thesis, School of Architecture, Planning and Landscape, Newcastle University, Newcastle upon Tyne.

BBC (British Broadcasting Corporation) (2004) *Fifth Avenue Tops Shops Rich List*. Online. Available at: http://news.bbc.co.uk/1/hi/business/3954649.stm, 26 October, (last accessed 22 July 2008).

Bridging NewcastleGateshead (2008) *Government Announces £Millions for Market Renewal in NewcastleGateshead*. Online. Available at: http://www.bridgingng.org.uk/news_latest_036.htm (last accessed 22 July 2008).

Cameron, S. (2003) Gentrification, Housing Redifferentiation and Urban Regeneration: 'Going for Growth' in Newcastle upon Tyne. *Urban Studies*, 40 (12): 2367–82.

de Magalhaes, C., Healey, P., and Madanipour, A. (2002) Assessing Institutional Capacity Building in a City Centre Regeneration Partnership: Newcastle's Grainger Town. In G. Cars, P. Healey, A. Madanipour and C. de Magalhaes (eds) *Urban Governance, Institutional Capacity and Social Milieux* (Aldershot: Ashgate) pp. 45–62.

Dosanjh, A. (2006) Newcastle Signs Up Big Names for Housing Expo. *Building Design*, 29 September.

GONE (Government Office for the North East) (2007) *North East of England Regional Spatial Strategy* (Newcastle upon Tyne: GONE).

Healey, P., de Magalhaes, C., Madanipour, A. and Pendlebury, J. (2002) *Shaping City Centre Futures: Conservation, Regeneration and Institutional Capacity, Regeneration in Grainger Town Newcastle* (Newcastle upon Tyne: Centre for Research in European Urban Environments, University of Newcastle).

Johnston, A. L. (2006) *My Voice: My Place: Managing Citizen-Council Interactions.* Unpublished PhD dissertation, School of Architecture, Planning and Landscape, Newcastle University, Newcastle upon Tyne.

Lynch, K. (1960) *Image of the City* (Cambridge, MA: MIT Press).

Madanipour, A. (2001) How Relevant is 'Planning by Neighbourhoods' Today? *Town Planning Review,* 72 (2): 171–91.

Madanipour, A. and Merridew, T. (2004) *Neighbourhood Governance: Capacity for Integration, Walker Case Study, New-castle* (three reports) (Brussels: European Commission).

Minton, A. (2003) *Northern Soul: Culture, Creativity and Quality Of Place in Newcastle and Gateshead* (London: RICS & Demos).

Newcastle Chinatown (2008) *Newcastle Chinatown website.* Online. Available at: http://www.newcastlechinatown.co.uk/ (last accessed 28 July 2008).

NCC (Newcastle City Council) (2000) *Draft Masterplans for the East End and West End of Newcastle: Consultation and Participation* (Newcastle upon Tyne: Newcastle City Council).

NCC (2006) *Scotswood Housing Expo, Newcastle upon Tyne* (Newcastle upon Tyne: Newcastle City Council).

NCC (2007) *Newcastle in 2021: A Regeneration Strategy for Newcastle* (Newcastle upon Tyne: Newcastle City Council).

Newcastle Partnership (2008) *Newcastle 2021: Taking the City Forward, Newcastle Partnership's Sustainable Community Strategy and Local Area Agreement (2008–11)* (Newcastle upon Tyne: NP).

OECD (Organization for Economic Cooperation and Development) (2006) *Building a Competitive City Region: The Case of Newcastle in the North East* (Paris: OECD).

Office for National Statistics (2008) Census 2001. Online. Available at: http://www.statistics.gov.uk/census2001/ (last accessed 28 July 2008).

ONE (2006) *Leading the Way: Regional Economic Strategy 2006–2016* (Newcastle upon Tyne: ONE).

Pearson, A. (2008) Homes Slow-Down Hits Region Hardest. *The Journal,* 1 September 2008.

Pinney, L. (2008) A Game of Two Halves. *Regeneration and Renewal,* 18 July, pp. 16–21.

Robinson, F., Zass-Ogilvie, I., and Jackson, M. (2007) *Never Had It So Good? The North East Under New Labour 1997–2007* (St Chad's College: Durham University).

9 Nottingham

'A consistent and integrated approach to urban design'

Tim Heath

Nottingham has, like all of England's 'Core Cities' Group, and indeed most UK cities since the late 1990s, undergone a period of significant change with regard to its public realm and urban fabric (ODPM/HMT/GOER 2004). Indeed, the urban landscape of Nottingham has been transformed through a process that has responded to the city's problems and created an environment that has been able to adapt to emerging and future needs. The national phenomenon of the 'urban renaissance' is readily associated with the Urban Task Force (UTF) final report *Towards an Urban Renaissance* (UTF 1999a). However, Nottingham City Council had been laying the foundations for its own renaissance since the early 1980s. In contrast to many cities, Nottingham has quietly got on with its regeneration activities through a consistent, persistent and opportunistic approach.

Nottingham is one of the largest cities in the UK not to have had an Urban Development Corporation or large-scale European Regional Development Funding for urban regeneration. The lack of vast swathes of derelict industrial land in addition to the city council's opposition to designation led to the government dropping the idea of a development corporation for the city. Instead, the local authority's desire to retain its planning powers and the prospect of government intervention led to the creation of Nottingham Development Enterprise (NDE) as a public–private partnership to pioneer major development in the city. Through one of its many initiatives, NDE established its own 'urban task force' and the city readily embraced a period of significant investment in infrastructure, public transport, the public realm and buildings.

Evolution of the city: capital of the East Midlands

Situated on the River Trent – the historic dividing line between the north and the south of England – Nottingham's conurbation, with a population of around 650,000, is the seventh largest in the UK, but fewer than 300,000 live within the city boundaries. As a result, most of the city's suburbs are located within neighbouring political districts, thereby giving the city council the opportunity to focus predominantly on the city centre and inner residential estates. The downside of these political boundaries has been that the city of Nottingham has traditionally included very few affluent residential neighbourhoods and this has resulted in extremely poor publicity in terms of its position on both crime and education league tables.

The city, with its first evidence of settlements dating back to pre-Roman times, has long been a centre of governmental, commercial and cultural life. The city centre retains a complex structure as a result of its evolution from two separate towns: an Anglo-Saxon borough on the hill to the east, which is now the location of The Lace Market, and a Norman borough around the castle on an outcrop to the west of the current city core. The old city wall and most medieval buildings have long since disappeared, but the castle – not however in its original form – and St Mary's Church in the Lace Market are still prominent on the city's skyline (Powell 2006).

Nottingham did not expand beyond its medieval boundaries, approximately the line of the current inner ring road, until after 1845, when it was engulfed by the Industrial Revolution (Barley and Cullen 1975). At the time, the city's prosperity was founded on the textile industry and it was an internationally important centre of lace manufacture. The city was extremely prosperous in the 1930s and suffered little damage during the First and Second World Wars. It reached its zenith as an industrial city in the 1950s and 1960s when bicycle manufacturing (Raleigh Cycles), tobacco (John Player) and pharmaceuticals (Boots the Chemist) were the major industries.

Post-War planning: the first thirty years

The confidence that stemmed from its prosperous industry in the years following the Second World War led to a period of town planning in Nottingham that reflected the spirit of the age. A mid-war housing programme began to address the stock of outdated Victorian terraced homes just outside of the city centre in the Meadows and St Anns, with slum clearance continuing through until the mid-1970s. Most of the cleared areas were squalid and depressing places, but many robust and liveable homes were also demolished. A huge programme of comprehensive redevelopment projects was undertaken with massive system-built deck access complexes or inner-city Radburn-type estates. The associated decanting and redistribution of communities at this time has subsequently concentrated many social problems in these inner-city areas. From the late 1950s through to the early 1970s, the city also planned a new highway network that would 'slice' up the city centre. Indeed, the four-lane inner ring road of Maid Marian Way destroyed much of the Georgian quarter that previously existed between the castle and Old Market Square.

The 1970s reaction to the radical 1960s transport and development plans

The pressure to abandon the proposed urban motorways had begun in 1970, when the government rejected the proposals for the Eastern Bypass and Sherriff's Way. The plans were finally scrapped in 1972, when the city council adopted a new transport policy. Fortunately, the historic core itself had been relatively untouched and became the focus of a major pedestrianisation scheme which won the European Architectural Heritage Award in 1975 (Barley and Cullen 1975). This policy shift signalled a change in emphasis away from the private car towards public transport that has continued through to the present. As such, park and ride schemes and cycle routes were introduced and the bus network expanded, although some of this new impetus was lost when in 1974 Nottinghamshire County Council took over responsibility as the transport authority from the city council.

In addition to transport measures, the 1970s also saw a number of built environment initiatives introduced to either halt or remedy the planning decisions of the previous decade. Relatively early for the UK, a strong conservation ethos was established by Nottingham City Council that led to the establishment of conservation areas which covered most of the city centre. Barley and Cullen (1975: 43) identified at an early stage the role that refurbishment and adaptive reuse of historic buildings could play in the regeneration of the city: 'The material may be old, but still of good quality, some of it ordinary but pleasant: the historic buildings of every age and quality. Some of the material has to be new, but the pieces must fit into the overall design.' There was also a major focus on the regeneration of deprived inner-city areas with innovative use of the Inner Urban Areas Act 1978, especially the Operation Clean Up programme (DoE 1978). Significantly, many of the structurally and socially failing system-built deck access developments, built only in the early 1970s, were demolished by the mid-1980s.

The revitalisation of the city: preparing for the twenty-first century

Following the decline of the textile industry after the Second World War, the 1980s saw a collapse of the other traditional industries in the city. Greater diversity and less reliance on a single industry, however, meant that the economic and social impact was less dramatic than in many other cities. In spatial terms it led to large amounts of redundant industrial buildings, but few large vacant sites became available due to the predominance of light industry. In 1980, manufacturing employment accounted for around 50 per cent of jobs in the city and the downturn resulted in high levels of unemployment, particularly amongst unskilled males. This exacerbated the underlying social problems of a low-wage economy and poor educational achievements in the inner-city areas.

Nottingham City Council was quick to recognise the need for economic restructuring. As such, it began a strategic economic development programme focused upon establishing the city as a regional service centre. The onus was on attracting inward investment, with the city centre being identified as major economic asset and the focus of this strategy. The city council identified that key employers wanted city centre locations and the relatively intact pedestrianised historic core was promoted as an ideal location for expansion or relocation. In addition, large-scale redevelopment projects were focused outside the historic and commercial centre in the transitional areas vacated by industry to the south and east of the city core. To facilitate this process, Nottingham Regeneration Limited (NRL) was established as a public–private partnership in 1998 to manage urban regeneration in the city and the wider city region of Greater Nottingham. NRL's board consisted of members from the city council, East Midlands Development Agency, English Partnerships and the private sector.

In the late 1980s and early 1990s, the city made full use of the Urban Development Grant scheme, City Grant and Partnership Investment Programme to incentivise private investment to regenerate historic buildings, particularly in the Lace Market (DoE 1993). Public–private sector initiatives have always been important to the city's regeneration projects, and Boots was a major partner in the City Challenge project in St Anns and Sneinton that attracted a £37.5 million grant in the mid-1990s. Nottingham's economic base had significantly changed by the mid-1990s with the influx of new service sector employers such as the Inland Revenue, Experian and Capital One. Indeed, by 2000 manufacturing employment at 13 per cent was proportionately less than a quarter of that in 1980.

A vision for the city

Recognising the need for an attractive and vibrant city centre to draw new investors and to serve existing communities, the city council launched its City 2000 strategy in 1990 (NCC 1990). This provided a framework for the growth of the city centre with a strong focus on the quality of the public realm, re-establishing the historic street pattern and further curbing the dominance of traffic. The key elements of City 2000 included (NCC 1990):

- creating attractive, people friendly streets and spaces;
- expanding the commercial centre by downgrading the inner ring road and removing all of the subways;
- identifying development opportunities whilst protecting the historic core;
- redeveloping the 1970s' Broad Marsh Shopping Centre to re-establish the historic axis from the Old Market Square to the Midland Railway Station;
- promoting residential development in the city centre;
- developing a new tram system and public transport priorities; and
- increasing park and ride schemes and discouraging commuter car parking in favour of shopper and visitor use.

The first phase of the implementation of City 2000 saw a number of physical enhancement projects such as the pedestrianisation of many historic east–west streets linking the Lace Market to the castle. The measures also included the restoration of many key Lace Market buildings such as St Mary's Church and the conversion of the Adams Page Building into a further education college and of the Shire Hall into a museum. The city council also focused upon the creation of new 'urban quarters' such as Castle Wharf on the Nottingham Canal and the former General Hospital site adjacent to the Castle. In addition, the importance of detailed design briefs and competitions for key developments was established (NCC 2006a). This investment of resources by the city council prior to the preparation of design proposals can save considerable time in the initial stages of planning applications for local authorities, landowners, developers and designers by adding some certainty to the planning process.

Humanising the city: the integration of urban design and transportation

Nottingham has always been at the forefront of public transport initiatives, being among the first to adopt bus priority systems, park and ride and integrated cycle networks in the early 1970s. Significantly, after a period of twenty-four years, the City of Nottingham became a unitary council again in 1998, and the formation of the Greater Nottingham Transport Partnership led to better coordination of transport across the city. This enabled a new integrated organisational and management structure to be established, with planning, transportation and highways becoming the responsibility of one department within the city council. The importance of stability should also not be underestimated in Nottingham's achievements to date. Indeed, the consistent and complementary development of strategy, policy and implementation has to a large degree been the product of a dominant Labour-controlled city council and a single Director of Planning, Transportation and Highways from 1997 to 2007. In addition, the previous director has continued to have a close relationship with the city council and play a key role in the city's regeneration through a role at NDE.

The urban renaissance and enhancement of urban design in Nottingham has been intrinsically linked to the development of an efficient and safe transport system. Other activities influencing the urban renaissance can be identified in four other thematic areas: the public realm, housing, commercial investment, and education and culture. The City 2000 initiative was updated in 2005 and relaunched as the *Nottingham City Centre Masterplan 2005–2015* (NCC 2005a; see Figure 9.1). This provided a coherent context for the major developments and demonstrated how these projects would link together through a coordinated public realm. Demonstrating the 'joined-up' approach to urban design, the city centre masterplan also outlined the importance of

Primary pedestrian routes
Pedestrian priority streets
Squares
Planned squares

Figure 9.1 Nottingham: the city centre masterplan placed a major emphasis upon the creation of a high-quality public realm. A system of pedestrian dominated routes has reconnected key landmarks and created a network of public squares (Courtesy Nottingham City Council). © Crown Copyright. All rights reserved. Licence number 100049043.

expanding public transport infrastructure to support economic growth and development. This approach included the redesign of the strategic highway network to enable a safer pedestrian-friendly public realm throughout the city centre.

To improve the design quality of buildings and the public realm and raise awareness of the built environment, the city council, with a number of partners such as Nottingham Regeneration Limited and the East Midlands Development Agency, launched Design 2006. This was a comprehensive Commission for Architecture and the Built Environment (CABE)-backed strategy that included the launch of the Lord Mayor's Awards for Urban Design and a broad programme of high-profile events. This has subsequently been followed by even higher-profile campaigns with Design 07 and Design 08. Through a process of encouraging the involvement of diverse stakeholders, increasing public awareness and raising the level of concern for quality issues, these initiatives identified barriers to achieving quality and developed a strategy to secure good design. In this framework, seminars and workshops have been organised and a training programme delivered to architects, planners and councillors in order to improve their design skills. An important part of this initiative is to raise the design awareness, knowledge and skills of planning officers, councillors, developers and practice-based professionals.

In addition, the city council launched an Urban Design Forum in 1999 comprising representatives from professional, academic and interest groups in the city. Significantly, the city council appointed CABE Commissioner Les Sparks as chair of the Forum. As former Director of Planning and Architecture at the City of Birmingham, he had overseen the remodelling of Birmingham's public realm in the 1990s. The initiative was relaunched as the Nottingham Design Review Panel in 2007 to provide expert, constructive, independent and consistent advice to developers and clients on schemes (CABE 2006c). The panel has a structured process that examines the architectural and urban design quality of proposals following guidelines established in Planning Policy Statements and reports such as *By Design* and the *Urban Design Compendium 2* (DETR/ CABE 2000; DCLG 2005, 2006c; EP/HC 2007).

In 2007, the city council, in partnership with Nottingham Regeneration Limited, also commissioned a team of consultants led by Urban and Economic Development Ltd (URBED) to prepare a new design guide for the city centre of Nottingham to build upon the city centre masterplan. The guide will include a tall buildings strategy, provide generic design advice for the city centre and focus upon creating a coherent new townscape in development areas around the fringe of the central core.

A network of squares and pedestrian-friendly streets

The city council has acknowledged the importance of high-quality public spaces and the public realm more generally for the life and economic activity of the city. Building upon initiatives dating back to the mid-1970s, priority has been given to pedestrians. Indeed, a safe and attractive walkable environment has been created with one of the most extensive networks of pedestrianised and pedestrian-friendly streets in Europe. This has made the urban experience safer, livelier and more accessible for locals and the many tourists who visit the city.

The *City Centre Masterplan 2005–2015* identified twelve new or redesigned public squares to supplement the nine that had been created or refurbished in the previous decade (NCC 2005a). The project for the Old Market Square has been the most prominent of these proposals. The square is nearly a thousand years old; however, at the end of the twentieth century it was clear that it had lost much of its original integrity and purpose. Limited space, owing to level changes and landscape, restricted the size of events that could be hosted and prevented easy movement for pedestrians. The symbolic role of the Old Market Square within the city made political decisions and social acceptance of changes to the square difficult. Nevertheless, in 2004 the city launched an international design competition. This process was enabled and supported by CABE, and following a public consultation process Gustafson Porter was appointed as designers. The 'new' Old Market Square was opened in March 2007 and the design is intended to be emblematic of the city's emphasis on design quality in new developments (see Plate 9.1). The

Plate 9.1 Nottingham: Old Market Square. The completion of the re-landscaping of the square in 2007, the second largest in England, has improved pedestrian permeability and created a space capable of hosting a wide range of public events.

design provides pedestrian routes that bring life to the centre of the square, extends sitting areas, allows the flexible arrangement of markets and encourages events and leisure activities. Since its reopening, the Old Market Square has hosted a large ice-rink, the 'Nottingham Eye' big wheel, music concerts, firework displays and numerous other public events and markets (*Nottingham Evening Post* 2007).

The Lace Market Square and Trinity Square, both having opened in 2008, are two of the most interesting of the new squares that have been created. The Lace Market Square (see Plate 9.2) was originally proposed in reports on the area in the late 1980s and early 1990s, and its completion nearly twenty years later has given the Lace Market its first urban public place to complement the green spaces at St Mary's Church and Barker Gate Rest Garden (Conran Roche 1989; Tibbalds *et al.* 1991). The square creates a link from the commercial core through to the heart of the Lace Market and forms part of a new mixed-use redevelopment project accommodating housing, leisure and creative industries. The new space attracts people from New College Nottingham's adjacent Adams Page Building – a converted 1855 lace warehouse – and the busy Fletcher Gate with its new tram stop. The retail and residential redevelopment at Trinity Square replaces a 1960s car park and includes a new square near to Victoria Shopping Centre. Trinity Square was achieved as a result of a planning brief, which demanded a design solution that would create a sense of place, respect existing buildings and street patterns and provide a high-quality public space. Extended pedestrian areas also enhance the retail environment and create better links between Nottingham Trent University and the city centre. The project was closely integrated with associated highway measures that have relieved heavy traffic from adjacent roads to facilitate pedestrian permeability in the area (NCC 2003a).

Plate 9.2 Nottingham: the Lace Market Square mixed-use development was completed in 2008. The space, one of the city's network of new and re-landscaped public squares, connects the city centre to the historic Lace Market, and is a focal point for local workers and students at the neighbouring college.

Creating a connected transportation network

The integrated approach to planning and transportation has enabled the city to clearly assess its problems and to develop appropriate strategies for best use, maintenance and enhancement of the transport system. The result is a humanised highway network and an advanced public transport system with future plans for an expanded tram network, a multimodal transport interchange and workplace parking charges.

Securing funding and government approval for the Nottingham Express Transit (NET) tram project in 2001 took more than ten years to achieve. Learning from earlier projects in the UK (Manchester and Sheffield) and other European countries, the brief emphasised quality and design from the outset in order to create a new public transport system that enhanced the streetscape. Having opened in 2004, NET has consistently exceeded its passenger targets, assisted by its integration with the bus network, in terms of routes, ticketing, timetabling and real-time travel information. The NET has become a highly popular symbol of Nottingham as an attractive 'European' city, and its success has led to government approval for two further lines connecting further suburbs and local towns (Figure 9.2). The expansion is seen as a key driver for economic development and will be an integral part of a proposed transport interchange following the renovation and expansion of the Midland Railway Station.

Government approval for the NET system also led to major improvements to the city's traffic network. These included the introduction of a Clear Zone around the Old Market Square in 2001 that allowed only public transport to access the city core. In addition, major projects along the inner ring road reduced the volume and speed of traffic whilst creating a permeable and pedestrian-friendly environment (CABE 2007; DfT 2007). One of the more significant

Figure 9.2 Nottingham: public transport oriented since 1974, the plans only really came to fruition when the city council became a unitary authority again in 1998. The NET system is coordinated with the bus network, and an extensive park and ride/glide network (Courtesy Nottingham City Council) © Crown Copyright. All rights reserved. Licence number 100049043.

projects transformed Maid Marian Way using Local Transport Plan (Department for Transport) and Regional Development Authority funding. This busy dual-carriageway inner ring road, constructed in 1964, was voted the fourth worst street in Britain (CABE 2002c). The replacement of unpleasant subways with surface-level pedestrian crossing points, broader pavements and landscaping has recreated attractive pedestrian-friendly routes from the Old Market Square to Nottingham Castle, and it is now upheld as an exemplar project (CABE 2005). These improvements followed many of the guidelines outlined in CABE's Paving the Way campaign (CABE 2002b), and in the *City Centre Streetscape Design Manual*, which advocates street design that promotes environmental quality and sustainability, encourages cycling and assures road safety (NCC 2004a).

A further government-funded project called the Turning Point Scheme was launched in 2005 with the aim of optimising the traffic system (NCC 2005b). Subsequent improvements have transformed problematic roads with heavy traffic into pedestrian-friendly areas with routes for cyclists and buses. This has seen the northern section of the inner ring road restricted to buses and essential access, thereby also reconnecting the Old Market Square to Victoria Shopping Centre, Nottingham Trent University, the Royal Concert Hall, the Theatre Royal (see Plate 9.3), Nottingham Playhouse and St Barnabas Cathedral.

The Local Transport Plan for Greater Nottingham states the transport objectives and describes the necessary investment through to 2011 (NCC 2006b). The objectives include improving accessibility, road safety and air quality, reducing congestion and supporting regeneration by stimulating investment and development. Achieving a high-quality, comfortable public transport system is also central to future plans, with initiatives such as the Big Wheel aiming to make Nottingham a cleaner and greener city (NCC 2008). This initiative and marketing campaign is supported by the Greater Nottingham Transport Partnership and involves both private and public sector partners to promote the efficient application of the Local Transport Plan.

Creating the city as a place to live

As with most towns and cities across the UK, Nottingham has experienced considerable development pressure for city centre housing since the late 1990s. Developers were not slow to recognise

Plate 9.3 Nottingham: a NET tram in front of the Theatre Royal and Royal Concert Hall complex. The remodelling of Theatre Square is a key part of the downgrading of the inner ring road to increase pedestrian permeability and reconnect the Old Market Square to other important parts of the city centre.

the opportunity to transform some quarters of the city centre, and with the government's encouragement, through PPG1 (Planning Policy Guidance Notes), PPG3 and the Urban White Paper, (DETR 1997, 2000a, 2000c), to build at higher density on central brownfield sites. Indeed, the opportunities for development have enabled the city to surpass the government's policy expectations and 'new build residential development in the City exceeds the PPG3 recommended range of densities, averaging 53 dwellings per hectare over the last 10 years' (NCC 2005c: 20).

The end of the twentieth century has seen the emergence of a number of new residential quarters in the city. Since the emergence of city centre living, the Lace Market and Hockley have also become fashionable residential areas with many conversions and new-build apartments. In the eighteenth century, the area was a place for fine lace-making, and the nineteenth century saw lace merchants redevelop the area on the original street pattern, with the huge brick warehouses that dominate the quarter today (Tiesdell *et al.* 1996). The Halifax Place development was the first major housing project completed in 1982, but it was not until the end of 1990s that the revitalisation of the area really began (Bell and Jayne 2004; Lowe and Smart 2007). By 2006, the area had once again become a vibrant quarter of the city centre with a mix of residential, entertainment, leisure, education, tourist and commercial activities coexisting within the historic townscape. Similarly, in the Ropewalk and Canning Circus quarter of the city, several Victorian buildings have been converted into apartments complemented by a number of new-build apartment developments on infill sites and on the former General Hospital site at Royal Standard Place.

Alongside the Nottingham Canal just to the south of the city core there have also been many new-build projects exploiting the waterside setting, the Park Rock development on Castle Boulevard being upheld as an exemplar project. This contemporary interpretation of the Victorian villa typology is located on the site of former industrial buildings at the boundary of a small Victorian park with archaeological importance. The concentration of development on brownfield sites has enabled the City of Nottingham to significantly exceed government expectations (DETR 1998a, 2000c). Indeed, the Nottingham Local Plan (NCC 2005c: 15) notes that 'regional planning guidance contains a target of 60% of new dwellings to be built on previously used sites by 2008. Over the last five years, about 93% of residential development in the city has occurred on previously used land.'

The resident population of Nottingham's city centre increased gradually from 1,500 in 1971 to 4,000 by 1998. The subsequent boom in residential development and student accommodation saw the population of the city centre increase to nearly 14,000 by 2007. Significantly, the completion of schemes currently in the development pipeline, or proposed in regeneration areas, is likely to see the total exceed 22,000 within the next ten years. Market analysis indicates that 59 per cent of inhabitants of Nottingham city centre are between the ages of twenty and thirty-four, predominantly students or young professionals. One- and two-bedroom apartments dominate the market reflecting the majority of either single people or childless couples living in the city centre and, significantly, the private rented sector accounts for over 60 per cent of the market (FHP City Living 2006; Knight Frank Residential Research 2007). A 2006 survey also indicated a high level of satisfaction with the city centre living environment. Accessibility to leisure facilities and the convenience of location related to work, university and transport links were highlighted as significant factors in the choice to live in the city (NCC 2006c). Many respondents did, however, highlight problems such as noise and inadequate and expensive parking. Safety issues and concerns relating to the drinking culture of the city centre were also mentioned, but proved to be lower than expected.

The future of city centre housing

Like most city centres, the level of demand for apartments has begun to fall below the level of supply since late 2006, and this is reflected in rising vacancy levels. As such, there are concerns regarding the existing high prices and the limited range of apartment types, with the majority of new city centre homes being small two-bedroom apartments that appealed to property investors. Volume house building has often resulted in low-quality schemes and, in many cases, standardised products that do not respond to context and do not address the needs of a sustainable community. Despite the encouragement of campaigns, such as the DTLR (Department for Transport, Local Government and the Regions) and CABE's Better Places to Live: By Design, innovative ideas have either rarely been proposed or not found willing supporters to achieve their materialisation (DTLR/CABE 2001). Indeed, having recognised the potential in the city living market, large-scale house builders have often built 'standardised' residential products in sensitive city centre locations (Hardill *et al.* 2003). During times of rapid development a shortage of staff resource with relevant design skills deployed in planning departments can often make it difficult to secure quality and ensure that the commitment to an urban renaissance can keep pace with development activity. This has especially been the case in relation to the city centre housing boom of the early to mid-2000s, where there has been a fast rate of growth and a need for volume production.

Furthermore, the pursuit of affordable and 'green' housing, advocated by the Housing Green Paper, does not necessarily aim at design quality (DCLG 2007b). Social and environmental pressures can also transform affordability and sustainability into political instruments, and all too often quality is compromised for quantity, which actually results in the obstruction of urban regeneration processes. In order to create sustainable inner-city housing, the market has to be wider and include family housing and live–work units. Improved accessibility to good schools, food stores and health services, provision for off-site parking and noise reduction would also maintain the interest in city living on a more sustainable basis. The regeneration proposals for Nottingham continue to promote the development of city centre and city fringe residential schemes, but an increasing emphasis is being put on the achievement of a greater mix of residential types and tenures. Indeed, a number of large new residential projects are in the development pipeline – particularly in the Southside, Eastside and Waterside masterplan areas – to serve the demand likely to be created by the growing business services sector and the expansion of retail, cultural and leisure activities (NCC 2005a).

Neighbourhood regeneration: targeting disadvantaged communities

Nottingham has been undertaking a number of neighbourhood regeneration programmes in its less affluent residential areas. Many of the social, economic and physical problems stem from comprehensive redevelopment projects undertaken in these areas in the 1960s and early 1970s. The recent renewal initiatives began with the successful City Challenge project bid for St Ann's and Sneinton estates in the mid-1990s. These two communities border the current Eastside Regeneration area that aims to connect them to the affluent city core. More recently, the city has formed the Neighbourhood Development Company to manage the £55 million funding secured under the New Deal for Communities Programme in March 2000 for the Radford and Hyson Green neighbourhoods, just to the north of the city centre. In addition, the city obtained £77 million from the government between 2001 and 2008 from the Neighbourhood Renewal

Fund (ODPM 2000; Cabinet Office 2001a). This funding is coordinated through three strategic regeneration frameworks, covering the north, east and south of the city, that have established local partnerships to enable the most deprived neighbourhoods to share in and contribute to the city's economic growth. Initiatives include increasing housing quality and choice, creating a sense of place and community, breaking down barriers and improving education, employment, training and skills. Like most UK cities, the challenge of its inner-city neighbourhoods is one which Nottingham continues to tackle and will be at the forefront of urban policy in the next decade as the city attempts to spread the successes of the city core to its less affluent areas.

Extending the commercial heart of the city

Nottingham has always established a strong relationship with its business community, and this has helped to attract new employers and inward investment. Improvements to the public realm, infrastructure and transportation together with new housing developments aimed at young professionals have helped to stimulate growth in both the service and retail sector. In addition, a number of key projects have supported the urban regeneration initiatives and contributed to the city's image as a financial services centre.

One of the first significant successes was the relocation of the Inland Revenue headquarters to Nottingham. The development, which was completed in 1995, actually creates a new urban quarter on the previously neglected Nottingham Canal just below Nottingham Castle. The initial government plan for the area in 1989 did not meet the expectations of the city council and also received the disapproval of the Civic Society and the Royal Fine Art Commission. Despite the risk that Inland Revenue might abandon the project, the city council did not compromise on its expectation of a high-quality design proposal. Fortunately, it was agreed to hold an international architectural competition, and as a result the project was awarded to Hopkins Architects.

Further along the canal-side, the Castle Wharf regeneration project has also helped to reconnect the city to its waterfront whilst providing space for a variety of activities (see Plate 9.4). A number of major employers such as Nottingham Evening Post, British Telecom and Nat West

Plate 9.4 Nottingham: the conversion of the British Waterways warehouse, and new-build projects at Castle Wharf, have created a mixed-use development alongside the Nottingham Canal. The scheme has brought this neglected waterfront back to life throughout the day and into the evening.

have been accommodated in Castle Wharf, along with bars that bring life and activity throughout the day and night. A little further along the canal, next to Midland Railway Station, is the European headquarters of US credit card company Capital One. This project includes the conversion of the 1950s Boots Printing Plant and the development of a large new office complex completed in 2002.

Enhancing the retail experience

Despite considerable pressure, Nottingham resisted the temptation to allow large out-of-town shopping centres throughout the 1980s and 1990s in favour of concentrating its efforts on enhancing its reputation as a city centre retail destination. As a result, Nottingham remains in a healthy sixth position in the UK retail league table behind London, Birmingham, Manchester, Glasgow and Leeds (CACI 2008). The retail offer received a further prestigious boost in 2004 when local fashion designer Paul Smith – having launched his first shop in the city in 1970 – opened his flagship store in the restored eighteenth-century Willoughby House on Middle Pavement (Powell 2006).

The next phase in the retail enhancement of the city will be the redevelopment of the Broad Marsh Centre. This 1970s development has proved to be an inappropriate and unfortunate monolith that has created a barrier rather than an entrance to the city centre. The new development will include robust urban blocks and a permeable network of pedestrianised streets to create a new and important connection between the city centre and the railway station. The project has now been approved and the necessary Compulsory Purchase Orders have been secured to enable the development. However, the complexity of this process and the longevity of the orders demonstrate that the lack of an efficient process of land assembly causes delays and problems in the implementation of large schemes.

Strengthening the knowledge base

Nottingham is a growing educational centre where research and innovation are the main drivers for future development. The University of Nottingham and Nottingham Trent University have an important role in this process, bringing over 50,000 students into the city, and they are major employers and generators of spending. Moreover, inter-university collaboration has been encouraged and has contributed to the development of a strong scientific base. Important links have also been developed with local companies to enhance the applications of research carried out in the universities to enable knowledge transfer. Designated as one of the UK's six Science Cities in 2005, Nottingham is creating a knowledge-based economy where science-based industry is acting as a catalyst for regeneration at a local and regional level (Hardill *et al.* 2003). Although Boots itself is no longer a research-based pharmaceutical company, a combination of former Boots researchers and university spin-off companies have spawned a thriving pharmaceutical and biotechnology sector. The creation of BioCity, the UK's largest bioscience innovation and incubation centre, on the eastern edge of the city core, has created a centre for thirty science-based companies. This evolved from a partnership between the two universities and the East Midlands Development Agency to create research and development laboratories, conference and office space.

Nottingham has also attempted to promote the expansion of cultural activities in the city. Creative industries have been a driver for the regeneration of areas such as the Lace Market and

Hockley, which initially provided large low-rent spaces in former industrial buildings. Indeed, cultural production and consumption firms play a significant part in the Lace Market's business community, accounting for over 400 companies (around 80 per cent) within the quarter. Also in the Lace Market, the Centre for Contemporary Arts, designed by Caruso St John Architects, was completed in 2009. This project, again, resulted from a design competition for one of the largest venues for contemporary performance and object based art in the UK. A significant addition to the leisure and cultural offer is the National Ice Centre, which was completed in 2000 on the site of the previous ice stadium on the eastern edge of the Lace Market. The development consists of an ice-arena, a second rink and a public square at the front. The centre houses the Trent FM Arena and caters for sports and cultural activities, with a 10,000 people capacity venue for conferences and live music events. Although some of the project's weaknesses, such as its parking provision, result from its central location, the centre is easily accessible and has been a generator of life and activity in this area, and has therefore contributed to the renaissance of the city centre.

A coherent framework for future regeneration

Since 2000, the city council has been preparing with consultants a number of strategic master-plans for the remaining major redevelopment areas on the fringe of the city core, outlined in interim planning guidance (NCC 2001, 2003b, 2004b). Three masterplans – Waterside, South-side and Eastside – create a coherent framework for this regeneration process whilst striving to link the deprived inner-city communities back to the prosperous city centre and to reunite the city with the River Trent (Figure 9.3).

The Waterside Masterplan aims to create a 100-hectare mixed-use urban quarter on former industrial land that incorporates existing sports venues. The plan advocates the creation of a sustainable district that will provide space and facilities for employment, leisure and new housing

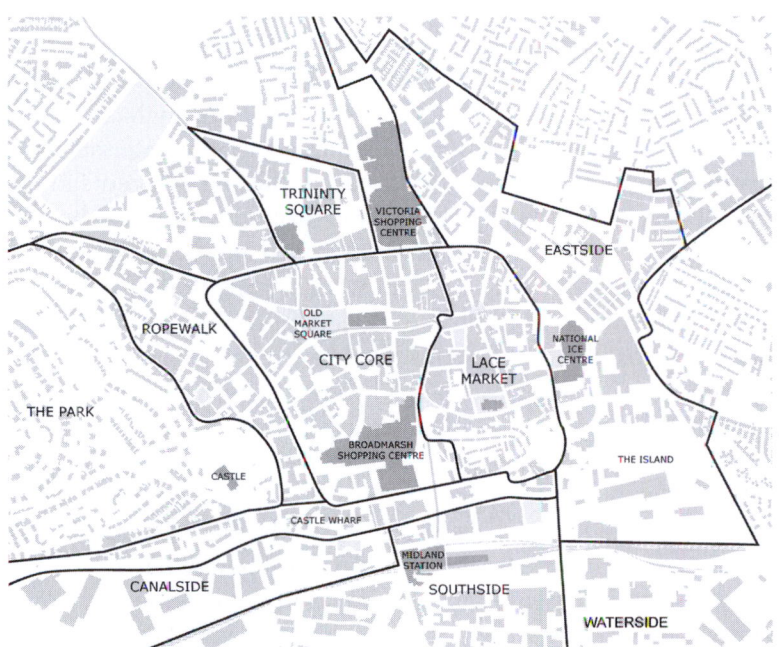

Figure 9.3 Nottingham: major regeneration areas. Eastside, Southside and Waterside are being coordinated through a series of masterplans, collaborative/coordinated working, long-term vision, and improving connections with neighbouring inner-city communities (Courtesy Nottingham City Council). © Crown Copyright. All rights reserved. Licence number 100049043.

types to accommodate different needs. The Southside Masterplan covers forty hectares and is based on the improvement of the transport system and the creation of stronger connections between the city centre and the disadvantaged Meadows area. The transformation of the railway station into a multimodal transport interchange – with new NET lines and the Channel Tunnel link that will connect Nottingham with Europe – will subsequently be a driver for further new development. The Eastside Masterplan is planned to be a fifty-six-hectare extension of the city centre providing space for office and leisure developments, creative industries and residential accommodation. Already, in the northern part there are conversions of old industrial buildings into apartments and office space, and new buildings also combine student housing and leisure facilities. The area also includes BioCity, and at the neighbouring Island Site there is a plan to create a huge £900 million mixed-use development with an efficient network of pedestrian and cycle routes.

Achieving an urban renaissance: achievements, problems and barriers to implementation

Nottingham has been successful in transforming itself from a city reliant upon manufacturing to a service sector and knowledge-based economy. This, however, has been achieved not through a sudden input of resources or investment but through a consistent and long-term strategy. Indeed, the City 2000 strategy was originally seen as a ten-year plan when it was launched in 1990 and, although most of its aims and objectives have been achieved, some are still in the pipeline nearly twenty years later. Achieving an urban renaissance does not, however, lack obstacles and problems. Nottingham, for example, has never had an Urban Development Corporation or major European funding, and this lack of large-scale investment has led to the involvement and crucial role of the private sector. Nevertheless, this was turned into a strength, and the fostering of strong relationships, dialogue and collaboration with the business community and new investors through public–private partnerships has been crucial to the process. The result has been greater local buy-in and a sense of ownership from the private sector, which has led to a more considered and incremental approach to achieving the long-term goals in the city's regeneration.

Coherent design solutions that have carefully integrated improvements to the public realm and the public transport and highway network, have been at the forefront of Nottingham's urban renaissance. The importance of the planning, urban design and transportation being under the remit of one coordinating section of the local authority is evidenced by the achievements in the city. This has ensured that what happens in between buildings and around the city is the first consideration in the urban regeneration agenda and in all major planning and design proposals. Another result is a coordinated public transport system of buses and trams that coexist with pedestrians in the city core, where private vehicular traffic is excluded. In addition, on the fringe of the city core, the traffic volume and speed has been controlled to give primacy back to the pedestrian through the re-establishment of historic routes, and those connecting key destinations, to create a permeable and accessible city.

A design-led approach to planning and transportation in Nottingham has been at the forefront of initiatives during the 2000s. There has been an emphasis on design competitions for major and sensitive schemes since the Inland Revenue project in the early 1990s (NCC 2006a). Other significant measures in raising the aspiration for design quality in the city have been the preparation of detailed planning briefs for all key sites and the promotion of three-dimensional design briefs for particularly important development opportunities. Their role has been to stimulate investment and development and to contribute to significant time savings and certainty for developers in the design and planning phase of the projects. These aspirations for good design will guide the future development of the built environment.

It is important to note that Nottingham's pursuit of design quality and the process of setting and implementing the regeneration agenda has encountered problems. Overall, however, the revitalisation of Nottingham's city centre and the associated improvements to the public realm can be considered a success. As such, there are many lessons for other cities that can be identified that relate first to the city's governance and implementation of regeneration, and second the tools and methods utilised in this process.

Governance and implementation

- stability of political control (certainty of aims and objectives);
- continuity of policy (realisation of the need for long-term planning);
- consistency of approach (key planning officers);
- partnerships between public and private sector.

Tools and methods

- wide use of architectural and urban design competitions;
- detailed development briefs and three-dimensional design guidance;
- establishment and central role of a design review panel;
- coordinated masterplans for the city centre and key regeneration areas;
- initiatives to raise the skill levels and the awareness of design quality.

There have clearly been many other tools and methods at the city's disposal; however, Nottingham's success primarily stems from its ability to approach the city's renaissance over the long term rather than seeking short-term fixes. This created the opportunity for a coordinated approach that is particularly visible in the integration of the city's public realm and transportation network to create an accessible and permeable city centre. Nottingham, like all cities, however, still has a number of urban regeneration challenges that will have a major impact on the next phase of its urban renaissance. Opportunities in its three ongoing masterplan areas will need to be grasped to ensure the realisation of a sustainable and economically prosperous city. In addition, having transformed its city centre, the next phase has to deal with the problems of crime, deprivation and social exclusion on its inner and outer residential estates. The objective for the next twenty years, therefore, needs to be the transformation of its neighbourhoods into socially sustainable communities that can access the city's prosperity.

References

Barley, M. W., and Cullen, R. (1975) *Nottingham Now* (Nottingham: Nottingham Civic Society).

CABE (2005) Case Studies: Maid Marian Way Nottingham (London: CABE). Online. Available at: http://www.cabe.org.uk/case-studies/maid-marian-way (last accessed 1 June 2009).

CABE (2007) This Way to Better Streets: 10 Case Studies on Improving Street Design (London: CABE). Online. Available at: http://www.cabe.org.uk/files/this-way-to-better-streets.pdf (last accessed 1 June 2009).

CACI (2008) CACI Retail Footprint, October. Online. Available at: http://www.caci.co.uk/188.aspx (last accessed 5 October 2008).

Conran Roche (1989) *Nottingham Lace Market: Detailed Proposals and Impacts* (Report for NCC) (London: Conran Roche).

FHP City Living (2006) *Nottingham City Centre Residential Market Report January* (Nottingham: FHP).

Hardill, I., Crampton, A., and Ince, O. (2003) *Nottingham's Urban Renaissance: An Exploration of the Role of Housing and Labour Markets,* The Nottinghamshire Research Observatory Occasional Paper Series.

Knight Frank Residential Research (2007) *Central Nottingham Housing Market Analysis,* Produced for Nottingham Regeneration Ltd and the City Development and Housing Strategy, NCC. Online. Available at: http://www.nottinghamregeneration.ltd.uk/downloads/CNHMAFull.pdf (last accessed 5 October 2008).

Lowe, D. and Smart, A. (2007) The Lace Market. *Nottingham Evening Post,* 10 March.

NCC (Nottingham City Council) (1990) *City 2000* (Nottingham: Nottingham City Council).

NCC (2001) *Waterside Regeneration Interim Planning Guidance* (Nottingham: Nottingham City Council). Online. Available at: http://www.nottinghamcity.gov.uk/CHttpHandler.ashx?id=718&p=0 (last accessed 1 June 2009).

NCC (2003a) *Trinity Square Development Brief* (Nottingham: Nottingham City Council). Online. Available at: http://www.nottinghamcity.gov.uk/CHttpHandler.ashx?id=717&p=0 (last accessed 1 June 2009).

NCC (2003b) *Southside Regeneration Interim Planning Guidance* (Nottingham: Nottingham City Council). Online. Available at: http://www.nottinghamcity.gov.uk/CHttpHandler.ashx?id=710&p=0 (last accessed 1 June 2009).

NCC (2004a) City Centre Streetscape Design Manual (Nottingham: Nottingham City Council). Online. Available at: http://open.nottinghamcity.gov.uk/reports/Intelligence/Transport%20and%20streets/Planning/city%20streetscape%20design%20guide.pdf (last accessed 5 October 2008).

NCC (2004b) *Eastside Regeneration Interim Planning Guidance* (Nottingham: Nottingham City Council). Online. Available at: http://www.nottinghamcity.gov.uk/CHttpHandler.ashx?id=693&p=0 (last accessed 1 June 2009).

NCC (2005a) *Nottingham City Centre Masterplan 2005–2015* (Nottingham: Nottingham City Council). Online. Available at: http://www.nottinghamcity.gov.uk/CHttpHandler.ashx?id=7137&p=0 (last accessed 1 June 2009).

NCC (2005b) *Turning Point Scheme* (Nottingham: Nottingham City Council). Online. Available at: http://www.nottinghamcity.gov.uk/index.aspx?articleid=2805 (last accessed 5 October 2008).

NCC (2005c) *Nottingham Local Plan* (Nottingham: Nottingham City Council). Online. Available at: http://www.nottinghamcity.gov.uk/CHttpHandler.ashx?id=536&p=0 (last accessed 1 June 2009).

NCC (2006a) *Design 06: Design Competitions in Nottingham* (Nottingham: Nottingham City Council). Online. Available at: http://www.design-nottingham.org/websitefiles/competitions_handbook(1).pdf (last accessed 1 June 2009).

NCC (2006b) *Local Transport Plan for Greater Nottingham 2006/07 to 2010/11* (Nottingham: Nottingham City Council and Nottinghamshire County Council). Online. Available at: http://www.nottinghamcity.gov.uk/CHttpHandler.ashx?id=1755&p=0 (last accessed 1 June 2009).

NCC (2006c) *City Centre Living Survey* (Nottingham: The University of Nottingham Survey Unit). Online. Available at: http://www.nottinghamregeneration.ltd.uk/downloads/CityCentreLivingSurvey2006.pdf (last accessed).

NCC (2008) *Get on the Big Wheel: Turning Transport Around in Nottingham* (Nottingham: Nottingham City Council). Online. Available at: http://www.thebigwheel.org.uk/ (last accessed 1 June 2009).

Nottingham Evening Post (Newspaper) (2007) *The City's Pride: Celebration of the New Market Square* (Special Supplement), 24 March.

ODPM (Office of the Deputy Prime Minister) (2000) *Factsheet 9: New Deal for Communities, Neighbourhood Renewal Unit,* (Wetherby: The Stationery Office).

Powell, K. (2006) *Nottingham Transformed: Architecture and Regeneration for the New Millennium* (London: Merrell Publishers Limited).

Tibbalds, F., Colbourne, C., Karski, A., Williams, M., and Monro, R. (1991) *National Heritage Area Study: Lace Market* (Nottingham: TCKWM & NCC).

London and the Thames Gateway

An introduction

London had to be central to any examination of the British urban renaissance as the only British city of genuine 'world city' status, the national capital and the primary 'engine of growth' of the national economy (the City and financial services), and the focal point of the richest region in the European Union (Carmona 2008). Nonetheless, it was argued at the research seminars that the Urban Task Force (UTF) report was not directed at, or especially relevant to, London since it already exhibited many of the good urbanist principles enshrined in the renaissance agenda, had very little brownfield land, and its renaissance was largely assured. However, this view down-plays the city's steady population decline until the early 1990s (ODPM 2006a), and its relatively poor performance on many international liveability and economic competitiveness indicators (ODPM 2004b). Of course, London's renaissance experience is quite different from other cities in this book by virtue of its particularly intense competition with New York and Frankfurt and other global capitals of finance.

London's economic renaissance has been dramatic since the mid-1990s, and its share of national wealth is now 50 per cent greater than its share of population. It has captured more than one-third of all national population growth since 1991, reversing a long slow population decline. It also performs well on all economic performance measures (almost invariably in the top five English cities). Its development pipeline is extraordinary, delivering seventeen times more office floor space annually than the second city (in this case Edinburgh: CBRE 2006), although even before the 'credit crunch' its completion rates had begun to fall significantly as a result of major oversupply. Its housing completions reached nearly 29,000 in 2007, of which 34 per cent were affordable, and they are being built at steadily increasing average densities (averaging 137 dwelling units per hectare on current permissions).

This growth has come at a significant price. Although London has lower overall depriva-tion scores than all but the most prosperous small towns, this hides increasing disparities in employment, income, housing and liveability and significant concentrations of deprivation, espe-cially in the East End (ODPM 2006a). Tower Hamlets is the third most deprived local authority in the country despite being wedged between the primary centres of wealth creation, the City and Canary Wharf, and three other inner London boroughs are among the ten most deprived in the country. London is steadily becoming a more middle-class city, with growth in the profes-sional and managerial classes especially in inner London, while the biggest declines have been in the manual working class (Butler and Hamnett 2009: 51–55). Inequality has widened and much of inner London has now been gentrified and the middle class are pressurising housing markets out towards the east (Imrie et al. 2009).

London was one of the few cities where New Labour was able to deliver an elected mayor, its preferred model for local government leadership. The election of Ken Livingstone, Labour leader of the Greater London Council until its abolition in 1986, was originally contested by the government but eventually accepted as the people's choice. As leader of the Greater London Assembly (managing strategic planning, transport, environment, economic development, etc.) Livingstone made an immediate, major contribution to London's urban renaissance by introducing the public transport 'smartcard' (Oystercard), establishing the London Congestion Zone (2004: extended 2007), insisting on high levels of affordable housing (50 per cent sought and 34 per cent achieved), and promoting higher levels of energy efficiency in buildings (Mayor of London 2008). His London Plan, adopted in 2004, included a set of strategic, new urbanist design principles seeking a compact city, with world-class architecture and design, a high-quality public realm, encouragement of building reuse and the promotion of inclusivity and multi-ethnicity. It promoted tall and large-scale buildings 'where acceptable in terms of design and local impact', and a new 'view management framework' was a major part of the plan (Mayor of London 2004).

As if to confirm the relevance of the renaissance agenda to London, Livingstone appointed Richard Rogers as his Chief Adviser on architecture and urbanism. Design for London (DfL) was established to deliver a 'vision for London's urban renaissance' and to enhance design quality, working with the London boroughs to deliver design strategies, area plans, infrastructure projects and design training. Meanwhile, in the thirty-two London boroughs and the City quite distinctive planning and design regimes operate with different commitments to elements of the urban renaissance (see, for example, Raco and Henderson 2009), while a range of cross-borough and public–private partnerships have had to be established to deliver wider public realm and infrastructure improvements.

Livingstone's cronyism and candour, combined with the deep unpopularity of the Labour government nationally, saw him defeated in the May 2008 election. London lost a leader with real urban design zeal, notwithstanding his uncritical positions on very tall buildings and developers' aspirations generally. His successor immediately confirmed a more positive interest in the future of London's suburbs, a more critical stance towards tall buildings and an abandonment of both Livingstone's public squares project and his western extension of the congestion charging zone.

Choosing four case studies to encapsulate London's urban renaissance was not easy. Central London had to be covered, and the contributors have defined this as the expanded Congestion Zone, which includes the City and the West End, but with some discussion of the South Bank. The Isle of Dogs, focusing particularly on the maturing of Canary Wharf and its immediate impacts, covers both the second great pole of commercial growth and focuses on the high-rise housing boom, all set in the most deprived local authority in London. King's Cross was selected as an example of a single, major redevelopment project, one that had taken two decades to gain planning permission. The final case study selected, the Thames Gateway, is outwith London and the urban renaissance policy frame, but it casts a particular light on both. As one of the four growth areas in the Sustainable Communities Plan (ODPM 2003b, 2005a), which has been established to tackle major housing shortages in the south-east of England, it represents something of the nemesis of the urban renaissance in abandoning the policy of concentrating development on brownfield sites in existing large cities. There is much discussion of the Gateway as the means to sustain the 'entirely unsustainable economy' of London by providing significant amounts of affordable housing (35 per cent), particularly for key workers in the service sector who have been priced out of the city in their pursuit of decent housing. Furthermore, the notion of a 'Sustainable Communities Plan' (an oxymoron in some commentator's eyes: De Angelis 2008), of which it is a part, is critical especially to the next phase of UK urban development, while the Gateway poses special environmental and social challenges in terms of its predominantly flood plain character and complex social geography.

References

Butler, T. and Hamnett, C. (2009) Regenerating a Global City. In R. Imrie, L. Lees and M. Raco (eds) *Regenerating London: Governance, Sustainability and Community in a Global City* (London: Routledge) pp. 40–57.

Carmona, M. (2008) Urban Design and the British Urban Renaissance, part 4: King's Cross, Central London, Docklands and the Thames Gateway. *Urban Design* 109 (Winter): 9–13.

De Angelis, M. (2008) Thames Gateway Oxymorons: Some reflections on Sustainable Communities and Neoliberal Governance. In P. Cohen and M. J. Rustin (eds) *London's Turning: The Making of the Thames Gateway* (Aldershot: Ashgate) pp. 67–82.

Imrie, R., Lees, L., and Raco, M. (eds) (2009) London's Regeneration. In R. Imrie, L. Lees and M. Raco (eds) *Regenerating London: Governance, Sustainability and Community in a Global City* (London: Routledge) pp. 3–23.

Mayor of London (2004) *The London Plan* (London: GLA).

Mayor of London (2008) *London Plan Annual Monitoring Report* (London: GLA)

Raco, M. and Henderson. (2009) Local Government and the Politics of Flagship Regeneration in London: The Development of Paddington. In R. Imrie, L. Lees and M. Raco (eds) *Regenerating London: Governance, Sustainability and Community in a Global City* (London: Routledge) pp. 112–131.

10 Central London

Intensity, excess and success in the context of a world city

Marion Roberts and Tony Lloyd Jones

Introduction

Central London entered the period following the publication of the Urban Task Force (UTF) report from a substantially different base from other city centres in the UK. The task force ascribed this difference to London's importance as a global centre for finance and business. Pursuing Hebbert's (1998) conclusion that London possessed many of the qualities aspired to by the New Urbanists and by implication 'the urban renaissance', the report commended central London's mixed-use areas. The new spectacular projects of the Tate Modern and the IMAX cinema were enthusiastically anticipated. On other matters the report was silent, other than noting a lack of coherent governance for London as a whole (UTF 1999a).

Richard Rogers had, of course, been anything but quiet on the topic of London and the issues facing its development. The publication of his book *A New London* in 1992, set out a manifesto for London's improvement (Rogers and Fisher 1992). This book was not alone in its concern for the state of London as an urban centre and its call for investment, democratic government and a reinvigoration of its urban qualities (Coopers and Lybrand Deloitte 1991; Thornley 1992). These texts regretted the deteriorating state of London's infrastructure, its creaking public transport system, the poor state of its public realm, the lack of investment in the arts and culture and the mediocre quality of much of the new speculative building that had taken place in the city. The Thames was noted as key public space in London that had been woefully neglected.

Broadly speaking, the agenda set out in the UTF report described a consensus developed amongst the urban design professionals, educationalists and activists throughout the 1990s. The concentration of design professionals in London meant that many of the key development sites in the central area were the subject of debate and proposition, some of it offered speculatively. Terry Farrell, for example, has consistently offered a series of urban design proposals for different elements within London, almost 'as a hobby' (Farrell 2007). As the 1990s progressed, awareness of urban design in the capital heightened. Journalists such as Jonathan Glancey and Rowan Moore wrote articles in the *Independent* and the *Evening Standard* newspapers, widening debate beyond sterile discussions over architectural style to urban design preoccupations.

Nevertheless, the issues that faced central London at the end of the 1990s had moved on. Around the world, cities were repositioning themselves in a new global hierarchy in response to the 'new economies' of information and knowledge, tourism and culture (Castells 1989; Zukin 1995; Sassen 2001) Commentators pointed to the importance of reframing the 'symbolic economy' of cities in order to maintain their attraction to international business. Urban design clearly had a significant role to play in this reimaging. The growth of international travel encouraged mass tourism as well as business mobility.

With the decline of manufacturing in inner London and the rise of a new pragmatism on the part of local politicians, tourism became an accepted component of economic development in the 1990s. The reconstruction of Shakespeare's Globe Theatre, following twenty years of campaigning by Sam Wannamaker, is an example of this volte-face. Established media and film companies located in central London's Soho during the 1980s, an area that remains a 'premium location' to this day (GVA Grimley and Burns Owen Partnership 2007). Pressures were growing from the expansion of the creative and knowledge-based industries of the new economy. The architectural and heritage qualities, low rent and flexible spaces of many of the recently vacated industrial buildings provided a natural home for the creative enterprises of the 'new economy'. London's new economy districts were drawn to the 'city fringe' neighbourhoods of Clerkenwell and Shoreditch, Hoxton, and a small enclave on Bermondsey Street in Southwark (Hutton 2004).

The 1990s saw a revival of London's economy that placed new pressures on its core areas. Living in central London regained fashion and, as residential property prices moved upwards, converted lofts competed with studios for warehouse space (Dyckhoff 2003). The approaching millennium promised to place an international spotlight on London. London's position within the global hierarchy would be judged in physical as well as economic terms. This chapter reviews the most significant changes that have taken place in terms of the physical experience of urban design within central London. There is not space here to do justice to recently completed buildings of high architectural quality (Hardingham 2001), nor to consider developments that have only recently been included in the core area such as Paddington Basin and Bishopsgate Goods Yard. The detailed complexities of urban management are similarly excluded, but we start with a brief discussion of policy and governance to inform our account.

Policy and governance

The key events that form this background were the abolition of the Greater London Council (GLC) in 1986, the various business-led initiatives that took off in the 1990s, followed by central government involvement and culminating in the formation of a newly constituted strategic authority and a directly elected mayor in May 2000. A mayor for London, empowered as far as key strategic issues such as transport were concerned, and a new Greater London Authority (GLA) that was substantially enfeebled relative to its GLC forerunner have provided a different setting for the governance of London. However, the thirty-two London boroughs and the Corporation of London continue to wield considerable authority over most local development issues. The first directly elected mayor, Ken Livingstone, a left-winger, had two terms of office but lost the election in May 2008 to the Conservative politician Boris Johnson.

Three interrelated themes dominate the strategies that have evolved with regard to urban design in central London. These are a concern to establish and maintain London as a leading world city, the expansion of London's central district and the complex partnership relationships that form the implementation mechanism for project delivery and management. Added to this are the detailed policies of the boroughs that constitute 'central London', which have a major impact on the capital's urban qualities.

London's position as a world leader preoccupied advice from the London Planning Advisory Committee's *Strategic Guidance* onwards (LPAC 1994). Central government, the central London boroughs and business supported world city status and facilitated policies and projects that would secure pre-eminence. The 1994 guidance was prepared at the end of an economic downturn, when the office market was in decline. This situation had reversed by 2001, when the mayor's office was preparing the Spatial Development Strategy, or London Plan. Mayor Livingstone faced two alternative options with regard to London's development. These were either to pull back on growth and to pursue a policy of dispersal, thereby 'fitting' the population and activities to the existing infrastructure, or to encourage further growth and economic development in the central area and use the revenues raised and other arrangements to fund improvements. Livingstone and his advisers chose the latter (Newman and Thornley 2005). The policy for growth in the central area incorporated a commitment to improving the quality of life as a prerequisite for raising London's attraction as a centre for business, commerce, tourism and the arts. Therefore, improving London's urban design quality was seen as essential to boosting its economic growth.

Mayor Livingstone was equally committed to the reduction of social exclusion as to growth. The potential contradiction between these two objectives has provoked comment and criticism. There are also tensions within the objective of promoting growth and economic development, and ensuring a high quality of urban design. Richard Rogers was appointed as the mayor's advisor and he headed up his own Architecture and Urbanism Unit. The GLA does not have a planning department, but instead has a London Plan team, planning advisers and a decision unit. Hence the two interpretations of urban design, originating from the different fields of architecture and planning, were never fully integrated within the Greater London Assembly itself.

In 2007 this separation was partially resolved with the setting up of Design for London in the London Development Agency, an organisation with direct contact with the mayor that was intended to oversee design policies and interventions within the capital. More recently, Mayor Johnson decided to subsume Design for London within a new, larger Land and Infrastructure Directorate. Views over the impact of its demise vary, but this clearly represented a sidelining of the influence of Richard Rogers and his Barcelona-influenced vision for London (Henley 2008).

A key tension present in the design policies of the London Plan created by the former mayor resides between the concept of 'world-class architecture' and innovative design (4B.2) and the objective of being sensitive to context (4B.1) (Mayor of London 2008). Further frictions revolve around maximising the potential of sites, raising densities, incompatibilities between different uses, overcrowding and high buildings.

The expansion of London's core area helped to ease some of these difficulties. This area had already increased to incorporate the South Bank of the Thames in the 1994 guidance. This district, the Central Activities Zone (CAZ), was further expanded in the 2004 London Plan to include the areas further to the east in the city fringe. Central London, as a concept, was further redefined when the congestion charge was implemented in April 2003 but, although the charge zone included the South Bank, it extended westwards only as far as Victoria. The 2008 alterations to the London Plan made further additions, primarily westwards, but also to the east (Mayor of London 2008). The CAZ, as currently designated, therefore incorporates all of the jurisdiction of the City Corporation of London, the greater part of the City of Westminster and parts of Camden, Islington, Southwark, Lambeth, Tower Hamlets, Hackney and the Royal Borough of Kensington and Chelsea (Mayor of London 2008: 353; see Figure 10.1).

The boroughs shared a commitment to world city status (Newman and Thornley 2005). Integration was achieved through the setting up of collaborative 'regeneration' bodies, spurred on by the previous Conservative government's advocacy of London, the opportunities offered through Single Regeneration Budget funding and facilitated by strategic networking on the part of the

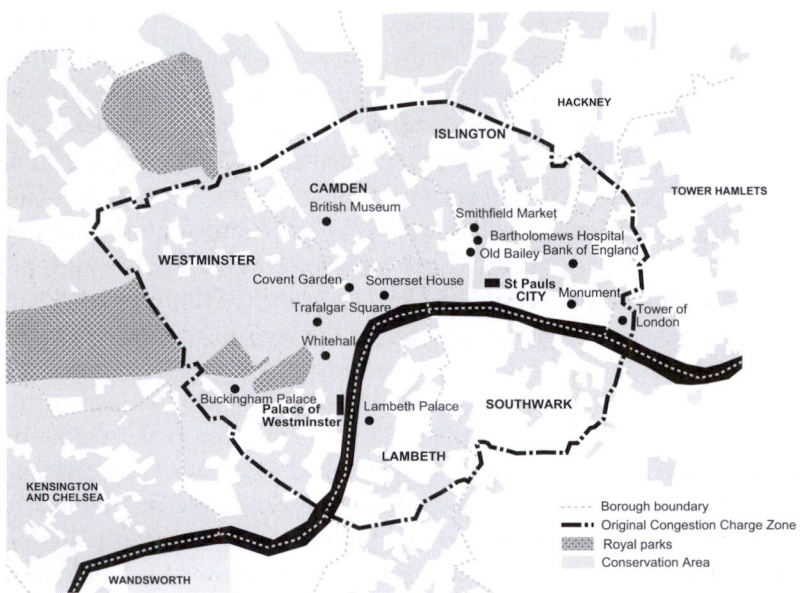

Figure 10.1 Central London: extent of conservation areas (drawn by Budhi Mulwayan).

Government Office for London (GOL). Partnership has formed a theme to virtually all of the urban design initiatives taken since the mid-1990s in central London, either through a combination of different public agencies or through public–private partnerships. The most significant of these, in the context of this chapter, have been the Cross River Partnership (CRP), the Central London Partnership and the Cityside Regeneration Partnership. The CRP is supported by the City Corporation, Southwark, Lambeth and Westminster and has coordinated the transformation of the South Bank of the Thames in relation to the south of Westminster (CRP 2006). The Central London Partnership (CLP), prior to the setting up of the GLA, provided strategic advice and subsequently supported other reports and initiatives. The CLP hosted the Circle Initiative, a government-backed pilot of six business improvement districts (BIDs), in central London. Cityside Regeneration assisted in the regeneration of Brick Lane and the area around Spitalfields Market. Cityside and CLP have since been dissolved and the CRP is due to finish in 2009.

At the local level each borough's Unitary Development Plan (UDP) within the CAZ sets its own requirements for detailed design policies. Each is therefore making its own reconciliation between world city priorities and the principles of the urban renaissance. The two major central authorities, Westminster and the City Corporation, have adopted different strategies for accommodation. Both the City Corporation and Westminster City Council have written urban design policies . In practice, however, the City Corporation is more laissez-faire and has looser policies regarding detailed architectural design. While 76 per cent of Westminster's area within the CAZ is covered by detailed conservation policies with 11,000 listed buildings, in the City it is less than half (City of London 2002: Chapter 10; City of Westminster 2007: Chapter 10).

Further alterations to planning in central London have come from external sources. Although terrorist attacks might have been expected to have an impact on urban design policies in central London, central and local politicians have adopted a 'business as usual' stance with regard to high buildings. The camera technology associated with the implementation of the congestion zone has provided greater opportunities for surveillance, and the only visible responses have been some further 'target hardening', softened with a heritage aesthetic, around sensitive government buildings in Whitehall (Coaffee 2004). Climate change was also seen as a key external threat and the 2008 alterations to the London Plan specifically addressed this issue.

The emergence of strategic leadership for London coincided with a development boom. The expectations on urban design have been high: to deliver both an urban renaissance with 'world city' architecture and masterplanning, all within the context of business-friendly high densities. Mainstream contextual urban design orthodoxies, now embedded in planning policy, have had to engage with the resurgence of international modernism – a 'late modernism', sometimes characterised by an exuberance bordering on the extreme.

The competing voices of the different stakeholders, developers, investors, occupiers, regulators and users have been held together through a complex network of policies, partnerships and initiatives. Evaluation of the transformation that central London has been through in the last decade is made difficult by this lack of hierarchy within and between projects. The main theme that emerges is that of intensity. Central London is a 'compact city' within a city, and the pressures within it have been growing steadily. Improvements have come, but at a pace and price that is dizzying with regard to the large scale, and too slow with regard to the small scale. Meanwhile, old conflicts that come with a booming property market, such as overdevelopment, high buildings and incompatible uses, reasserted themselves alongside market resistance to new thinking, such as mixing uses in the same building.

Delivering the renaissance

In this discussion we concentrate on the aspects of change that most clearly relate to an urban design agenda, highlighting changes to the public realm, movement and connectivity, concentrations of activity and the configuration of built form (see Figure 10.2 for location examples discussed in the text).

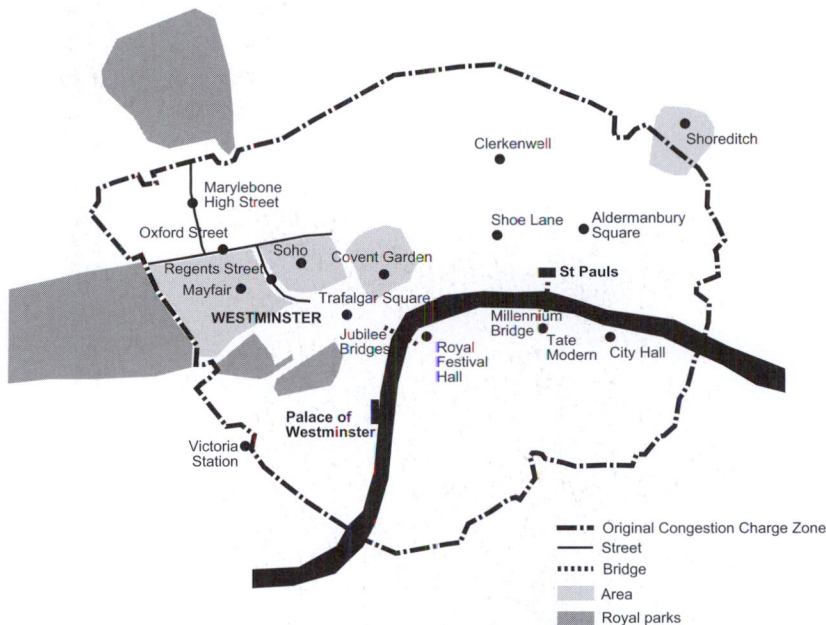

Figure 10.2 Central London: locations discussed in the text (drawn by Budhi Mulwayan).

World Squares

The 'World Squares for all' project provides a direct response to the criticisms of the dire state of London's public realm. The project started in 1996, with a study commissioned by a partnership formed between GOL (now superseded by the GLA), Westminster City Council, English Heritage and key stakeholders from the parliamentary and royal estates. Foster and Partners published a masterplan for the spaces most associated with ceremonial and national functions – Trafalgar Square, Whitehall and Parliament Square.

Trafalgar Square was the first of the spaces to be completed in 2003. The transport and urban design arm of Atkins provided the detailed design for the square, drawing on research on pedestrian movement provided by the Space Syntax unit at University College London. Improvements to the square included the radical step of removing traffic from its north terrace, thereby allowing visitors to the National Gallery direct access to the central spaces of the square (Powell 2003; see Plate 10.1). Following its remodelling, Trafalgar Square has continued in its historical functions as a focus for national celebration and demonstration. In addition, the mayor's cultural programme has expanded the cultural elements of the square's functions encompassing high culture, as in the contemporary art on the fourth plinth, to the carnivalesque. Mayor Johnson has halted work on Parliament Square, explaining that its part-pedestrianisation would increase traffic congestion and turn 'a green glade of heroes into a vast, blasted, chewing-gummed piazza' (GLA 2008a).

Transformation on the South Bank of the Thames

The restructuring of central London within the global hierarchy necessitated its expansion beyond the confines of Westminster onto the South Bank of the river. The Thames has always been a barrier to movement between the two sides, and its central London section was underprovided with crossings in comparison with, for example, Paris. It was only following the successful competition of the Tate Modern that the funding was raised for a new central London bridge, the first to be built for a century. A consortium comprising Foster & Partners, engineers Ove Arup & Partners and the artist Anthony Caro won a competition with an innovative design, marketed

Plate 10.1 London: Trafalgar Square remodelled. The north terrace in front of the main gallery is now pedestrianised.

as 'The Blade of Light'. The pedestrian bridge, connecting Tate Modern to St Paul's Cathedral opened in June 2000. Despite the bad publicity associated with its early structural problems (Sudjic 2001), the Millennium Bridge provides a significant addition to the iconography of London, linking an ancient symbol of religion and royal ceremony to a contemporary temple of culture. In terms of connectivity, the reconstruction of two pedestrian walkways running alongside – the Hungerford railway bridge, connecting Waterloo, and the Royal Festival Hall with Charing Cross Station – is a more significant link for tourists and commuters. Lifschutz Davidson and WSP Ltd won a competition with an elegant design for these two footbridges, properly named the Jubilee bridges. The completion of the Jubilee Line Extension (JLE) to the underground in 2000 provided further connectivity between both sides of the river, although Southwark is the only completely new station in the central zone.

The bridges and new stations contribute to the reframing of central London as a contemporary global city and pull the spaces of the South Bank into that revised symbolic order through the use of aestheticised technological advancement. They enhance the ease with which tourists can access key sites (as well as shopping and leisure facilities north and south of the river) within a hierarchy of global cultural attractions (see Plate 10.2). The integration of the South Bank of the Thames into central London cannot be ascribed solely to one iconic building or artefact for, as Teedon (2001) points out, the strategy was 'design rich'. The designation of the Thames Path in the 1970s provided a foundational concept to which a series of masterplans for events along the route could relate. The CRP was able to marshal substantial funds to provide the necessary linkages between the various points on the popular route, which now runs from Westminster Bridge to Tower Bridge.

Key urban design events on the route are the London Eye, the South Bank Centre, the Tate Modern and City Hall. The London Eye, originally given temporary planning permission for five years, has achieved an iconic status. Both Farrell and Rogers had provided masterplanning ideas for the South Bank Centre. Rick Mather's later masterplan steered a course between Farrell's commercialism and Rogers's ambition (Powell 2003). An office block built alongside the railway line with shops and restaurants beneath has assisted in funding the refurbishment of the Royal Festival Hall, together with the conversion of its undercroft for more shops and restaurants.

Plate 10.2 London: South Bank. The success of the revitalisation of the south bank of the Thames demonstrates the power of an urban design approach linking iconic buildings with public uses to everyday activities. The whole is greater than the sum of its parts.

Whatever the misgivings of architectural critics (Glancey 2008), it is proving to be overwhelmingly popular and the spaces around the concert hall are regularly thronged with people.

The conversion of the former Bankside Power Station into the Tate Modern Gallery of Modern Art by Herzog and de Meuron architects has also surpassed expectations in terms of its popularity. In the five years between 2002 and 2007 it received 20 million visitors, twice the number anticipated. Although it now seems inevitable that the Tate Modern should be on the South Bank, the reality was more complex. The decision was the result of a change in political direction on the part of Southwark Council, strategic use of a £50,000 grant to secure the site and a judicious decision not to apply for listing for the historic Sir Giles Scott building (Newman and Smith 2000). CRP funding provided for a masterplan to relate the revamped building to the Thames and the Millennium Bridge.

Commercial buildings dominate the South Bank between London Bridge and Tower Bridge. Fosters were the architects for More London, which is an extensive set of office buildings that effectively joins Hays Galleria to the west to City Hall, also designed by Foster, to the east. The complex has shops, restaurants, a hotel and a children's theatre. The development has many of the positive features of 'groundscrapers' in that it has fully public routes through it and is not overly high when compared with the Victorian terraces it faces across Tooley Street (Carmona and Freeman 2005). Yet, it is curiously corporate in ambience, a feeling that is compounded by the fact that the shops and services are all representatives of major chains. The failings of this complex are replicated in new commercial developments across London, for example at Tower Place, Cardinal Place (see Plate 10.3) and Exchange Square. Functionally they fulfil their planning requirements to provide public access, public space and mixed uses at ground floor level. The anonymity of their styling, the ubiquitous use of glass and granite and the corporate 'cloned' replication of chain bars and chain stores at ground level rob these new insertions of any character. The labyrinthine nature of London, its greyness and mysterious dark passageways, so beautifully evoked by Ackroyd (2001), is in danger of disappearing in a brave new world of crystal transparency.

Plate 10.3 London: Cardinal Place, Victoria Street. An award winning, mixed-use 'groundscraper'. Westminster Cathedral is behind the photographer, the endpoint of a visual and pedestrian axis.

Other public realm projects

One of the successes of the last decade has been the number of small public spaces in central London that have been the subject of improvement schemes. Award-winning small urban spaces now complement important historic buildings, of which the space outside the Old Bailey is a fine example. Westminster, the City Corporation and Southwark have detailed streetscene guidance documents (City of Westminster 2004; City of London 2005; Southwark Council 2006). These documents are advancing innovation in public realm design by seeing the street as an urban space, rather than a road with attached pedestrian areas. Streetscene improvements that create seating and greenery, take away unnecessary clutter and give pedestrians priority over traffic are beginning to appear in significant numbers across the CAZ.

One of the most advanced improvements to appear nationally is a product of a partnership between Camden Council and the Seven Dials Monument Charity. The charity is a local association that has been campaigning for over twenty years to improve the area around Seven Dials in Covent Garden. It worked with major landowners to bring buildings back into use and to make street improvements. The monument itself is a sundial pillar set at the centre of seven radiating streets in a conservation area, which were laid out in the seventeenth century with Christopher Wren's guidance (BBC 2008). The traffic management scheme takes out through-traffic around the monument but allows pedestrians and local traffic to co-mingle across the piazza. Seven Dials is now regarded as a leading example of a shared space approach to public realm design (Hamilton-Baillie 2008).

Some improvements have been property led. Planning obligation money has been used to particular advantage by the City Corporation and has funded a number of innovative schemes such as in the Shoe Lane Quarter and Aldermanbury Square (City of London 2006). Although BIDs have been subject to criticism in the USA for social exclusion and domination by private business (Zukin 1995), the pilot projects in the Circle Initiative have created public spaces in Bankside and central Westminster that are fully open to the public and well managed. The St Christopher's Place development to the north of Oxford Street, now managed by the New West End Company, provides a pleasant animated square surrounded by cafés and restaurants, with a much needed public toilet below.

The revitalisation of Marylebone High Street could be criticised for gentrification, although market forces have ensured that this has been part of Westminster's history since the eighteenth century. Here the investment was careful management by the street's main freeholder, the Howard de Walden Estate. Howard de Walden is one of the 'Great Estates' that made up eighteenth-century London, and has considerable land holdings nearby. Their decision not to give tenancies to the shops that would pay the highest rent, but to attract 'stylish tenants' such as up-market clothes shops and organic grocery stores has created a unique street that is a counterpoint to the chain stores of Oxford Street nearby (Kay 2007). A similarly long-term view has been taken by the Crown Estates in the refurbishment of Regent Street. In these instances, London's global city status and enlightened private interest have worked together to support the urban renaissance ideal of a walkable, human-scaled lively street environment, albeit one that requires an above average salary to participate in fully.

Sustainability and transport

The most remarkable achievement of the last decade has been the introduction of the Congestion Charging Scheme across central London. This scheme has been controversial in that it imposes a road charge on vehicles entering the zone area between 7 a.m. and 6 p.m. The latest monitoring report found that the total volume of cars entering the zone in 2008 was reduced by 21 per cent from its 2003 level. This amounts to 70,000 fewer cars in the original zone and 30,000 fewer in the western extension. Congestion, measured as the time taken to make a vehicle journey, initially dropped but rose again in 2007/2008 to its 2002 levels in the central zone, and with no improvement in the western extension (TfL 2008). Transport for London (TfL) has attributed this to the number of road works, in particular those associated with the ongoing renewal of the capital's ageing water mains infrastructure.

Air quality has improved in the congestion zone. In addition, Livingstone introduced a Low Emission Zone (LEZ) that covers the whole of the Greater London Area. The most polluting lorries, buses, large vans and minibuses either have to upgrade their engines or pay a toll of up to £200 a day to enter into the LEZ. This scheme started in February 2008 and is anticipated to reduce dangerous levels of nitrogen dioxide and fine particulates in the atmosphere (GLA 2008b).

London's public transport system is famously one of the most expensive of the global cities. Ken Livingstone lost his battle with central government over the privatisation of the underground. He therefore made investment available for the part of the transport he could control, the bus network. A major proportion of the money raised annually from the congestion charge, £137 million in 2007/2008, has been reinvested in the bus network (TfL 2008). The improvements have been far-reaching, with increases to the number of routes and frequency, ticketing improvements, reduction in fares as far as feasible, modernisation of vehicles, and improvements in information for passengers, security and staff training and conditions. The image of buses has been improved such that the growth of new bus users has been most marked amongst working males between thirty-five and forty-four years of age who are car owners (Hendy 2005). Bus passenger levels have increased, with over 100 million more passenger trips recorded in 2004 than in 2001(TfL *et al.* 2004).

The improvements to cycling are impressive, with a daily increase in cycle journeys of 83 per cent in 2007 compared with 2000. Transport for London produced a London Cycling Action Plan in 2004 that proposed to extend the network of cycle lanes and routes from 150 kilometres to 900 kilometres by 2010. Implementation was by the individual boroughs and the results in central London have been somewhat fragmented, with cycle lanes abruptly ending at borough boundaries. Walking has not been ignored, with the production of *The Walking Plan* (Mayor of London and TfL 2004), guidance for developers, a walking strategy and proposals for wayfinding (TfL 2005). A CLP- and TfL-sponsored study of central London's main streets was carried out by Jan Gehl (Gehl Architects 2004). His team documented the now familiar problems of overcrowded pavements, traffic dominance, noise, clutter, conflicts between traffic and pedestrians and lack of seating and public toilets.

The problems of central London's main streets are emblematic of the issues facing the urban renaissance in this area in a wider sense. There are conflicts between different uses, and different tiers of governance (and sectors of government) on top of the stress caused by intensity of use. TfL has taken over responsibility for maintaining traffic flows on the main arterial streets from central government (the Department of Transport) but does so, often, at a serious cost to the pedestrian experience and quality of life, as for example in Marylebone Road, the most polluted street in Britain. TfL's improvements to the bus services, resulting in 200,000 people a day alighting or boarding in Oxford Street and Regent Street, has been at the cost of their suffering ever more congested pavements when they get there. The City of Westminster is extending pavements widths in planned improvements to Oxford Street and creating pedestrian 'oases' at various points along its length. However, the fundamental problem of the heavy concentration of bus routes along Oxford Street, based on a logic from over fifty years ago, remains unresolved.

Conflicting agendas

Whilst there may be strategies for each physical element and activity, these cannot be combined into a meaningful design unless choices are made and some activities or qualities given priority over others. This is a perennial issue for urban design practice, but the situation of central London makes the conflicts more acute. It is to these that we shall turn to next, taking the examples of conflicts of use and high buildings.

London as a place to live and play

In contrast to many provincial cities in the UK, the central areas in London house a substantial population. For example, the first congestion zone ring, which contains all the central London functions such as government buildings, museums, retailing, royal palaces, parks and the City, accommodates 230,000 people in its twenty-one square kilometres. Even the least populated portion, the square mile of the City Corporation, has 9,000 residents. The City of Westminster jealously protects all of its residential areas, including wealthy Mayfair and Belgravia (City of Westminster 2007). Their quiet leafy squares form a significant part of London's character (Rasmussen 1982). It is not only the super-rich, however, who inhabit central London. Whereas narratives from the USA recount wholesale displacement (Smith 1996), the UK's legacy of social housing has assured a continuity of housing for low-income residents in estates and blocks across the central area. Meanwhile, the cost of private residential renting has soared.

Local authorities in central London, including Camden, Westminster City Council and others, have in place planning policies that require new development to be mixed use and requiring a proportion of any residential component to be affordable housing. Ken Livingstone's requirement that all new housing should have a 50 per cent affordable element proved unenforceable in practice and has been quickly abandoned by Mayor Johnson in favour of a more modest quantitative target for London as a whole. This is despite the strong increase in the resident population of central London, due primarily to in-migration. The City of Westminster's population, for example, is estimated to have increased by more than 25 per cent between 2001 and 2005 (City of Westminster 2007). Because of the high demand for affordable accommodation by low-paid immigrant workers in the service industries (GOL 2004), central London has proportionately more than its share of the problems of tenants living in overcrowded and temporary conditions. The affordable housing targets set by Mayor Livingstone did not include any provision for the West End and Victoria.

Additional affordable housing has been delivered through Section 106 agreements between the planning authorities and developers in partnership with registered social landlords. In practice, this represents a relatively small addition to the historical stock, of which by far the biggest proportion was built in the inter- and post-war period by the local authorities themselves. On top of the council tenants' right-to-buy legislation, changes to regulations now permit registered social landlords, such as the Peabody Trust, to sell and let vacant property at market rents, undermining the pressure to maintain and increase the proportion of affordable housing for rent.

Glancey (2001:15) somewhat unkindly characterised the pre-1980 central London population as the 'rich, those living on old money and trust funds, the bohemian, the mad, the newly immigrant and the hopelessly poor'. This too has left a legacy of groups of residents who are active campaigners not only for their own conditions, but also for a wider agenda of liveability and social inclusion across the central area. Campaigns to maintain the quota of affordable housing continue. At the time of writing, the redevelopment of the blocks adjacent to St Giles' Circus is a source of contention.

The ideals of the 'compact city' and of the urban renaissance set out the virtues of a city that is a centre for habitation, work and leisure. Whereas nineteenth-century reformers fought battles to regulate incompatibilities between residential areas and noxious industry, in the late twentieth and twenty-first centuries the fracture lines have shifted, to conflicts between entertainment uses and the remaining life of the city. Westminster has been at the forefront of this conflict for three reasons: its pre-eminence as a centre for entertainment, its sizable residential population and because, alongside Manchester, it was the first authority in Britain to permit late-night licensing (Lovatt *et al.* 1994).

A combination of a concern to boost tourism and the ideas of urban theorists about the 'twenty-four-hour city' lay behind the city council's liberal attitudes towards the granting of liquor licences and permission to operate into the early hours of the morning in the 1990s. An unprecedented expansion in the number of premises, their sizes and operating hours resulted from changes in the structure of the drinks industry, a booming economy and higher disposable incomes. The number of people on the streets late at night increased, as did noise, vandalism, verbal abuse, fighting, acts of violence, street fouling, overall disorder and antisocial behaviour (Roberts and Turner 2005). Local resident groups in the West End protested to the council and prompted a change in leadership, and subsequently a change in policy.

Westminster introduced the concept of 'stress areas', where the numbers, type and size of alcohol-related entertainment uses are limited. The notion of the 'stress area', although initially resisted by central government, after further lobbying was included in the Guidance to the Licensing Act 2003 (Hadfield 2006). It is now called a 'Special Policy Area' or 'Cumulative Impact Zone'. Westminster has recently adopted a highly sophisticated Statement of Licensing Policy that will be dovetailed with a Supplementary Planning Document on entertainment. The West End Stress Area covers 4.5 per cent of the city council's area, contains 4,027 residential properties (Westminster City Council 2007: 147–148) and along with two other stress areas, Bayswater and Edgware Road, accommodates 36 per cent of the authority's 2,960 licensed premises. In addition to its detailed policies, Westminster also implemented a number of measures to manage the 250,000 to 500,000 people who appear on its streets late at night (Westminster City Council 2007).

The GLA took a more distant approach to clashes between entertainment and residential uses in their initial approaches to the London Plan. The authority published its own best practice guidance (GLA 2007) and included more detailed reference to the night-time economy in its alterations to the London Plan (Mayor of London 2008: Figure A2.10). The neighbouring boroughs of Camden and Southwark have also had to deal with licensing and planning issues. The City escaped night-time economy problems until recently. Crime and disorder has risen, causing concern to residents and business tax-payers (House of Commons 2008). Speculatively it would seem that promoters and operators, deterred by close regulation in Westminster, have moved eastwards to the City and the City fringe.

High Buildings: pressure for commercial development

The economic growth that was associated with financial deregulation in the City also fuelled a steep rise in demand for commercial premises. The City Corporation self-consciously promoted the renewal of the square mile during the financial boom of the 1980s, including the massive development at Broadgate, north of Liverpool Street Station, and Richard Rogers's famous Lloyd's Building, allowing the reconstruction of almost 70 per cent of the area not covered by conservation policies. A decade and a half later, a substantial proportion of this area has either been rebuilt or is in the process of reconstruction. As the architectural critic of the *Financial Times* comments, this has happened 'somehow on the quiet without anyone noticing' (Heathcote 2008).

The main beneficiary of the 'Big Bang' of 1986 was the development of London's new financial centre at Canary Wharf, some way to the east of the Square Mile and now home to the UK's three tallest buildings. This took pressure off the City, as discussed in Chapter 12. Although its developers, Olympia and York, went bust with the collapse of the property market in the early 1990s, the huge increase in office space that came online with this development, together with the downturn in the market, kept up the pressure on the City. With the revival of the boom in the later part of the 1990s and into the new millennium, the corporation has continued to encourage renewal and the construction of tall buildings, within the framework of strategic view protection and its own conservation area policies, which cover significant parts of the City.

Many of the new properties are quiet, well-mannered buildings that observe the street line and surrounding building heights. Others are less successful. They neither fall into the category of contextual insertions nor are skyscrapers articulated separately from the street, but sit somewhat uncomfortably in between. While the greatest impact on the streetscape of central London has been felt through the insertion of new mid-height buildings of variable quality, it is very tall buildings that have led to the fiercest debate and most prominent urban design policy shifts. As a major city that was largely developed before the advent of the technology that permitted the construction of very tall buildings, London's experience of skyscrapers has not been an entirely happy one. For 300 years the dome of St Paul's loomed over a skyline that rarely rose above six storeys, but recent decades have seen dramatic changes.

Although the Victorians came close with the Victoria Tower at the Palace of Westminster in the mid-nineteenth century, it was not until the 1960s that its height was surpassed by the Shell Building on the South Bank in 1961.[1] This heralded the period of something of a free-for-all, with more than 300 high-rise buildings of more than fifty metres, or twelve storeys, being built in the 1960s and 1970s. This period of intensive, but largely uncoordinated, construction of both residential and commercial towers spread across central London and into the inner suburbs, inevitably leading to a backlash once the boom, and the development pressures that led to it, subsided in the 1980s.

With the London boroughs individually responsible for planning policies relating to tall buildings within their jurisdiction, and with widely different approaches taken by, for example, the City Corporation and the City of Westminster, it fell to central government to set out a strategic framework for tall buildings policy in central London as a whole. This was provided by the Regional Planning Guidance (RPG) 3, published in 1991 (GOL 1991). This is the nearest there was to a tall buildings policy for central London and worked on the basis of the protection of strategic views of the key landmarks of St Paul's Cathedral and the Palace of Westminster from a series of high points in the landscape north and south of the river. In 1999, LPAC issued its *Supplementary Advice on High Buildings and Strategic Views in London*, retaining the ten strategic views, but making English Heritage a statutory consultee for all new high buildings in London and introducing the concept of important local views, panoramas or prospects (LPAC 1999). In 2003, English Heritage produced its *Guidance on Tall Buildings*, which was revised jointly with CABE in 2007 (EH/CABE 2003). As with urban design guidance provided by local authorities, written policies are good in intent but not specific enough, and open to a wide range of interpretation in planning briefs and design proposals. With the recent spate of tall buildings proposals, where CABE has often lent its support to many controversial proposals, English Heritage has maintained an almost across-the-board objection to tall buildings (Carney 2007: 201).

In its enthusiasm for pushing London's skyline upwards and from a position of growing power within the global financial network, the City of London found an unlikely ally in left-wing Mayor Livingstone. A supporter of tall buildings, Livingstone commissioned a study of the Strategic View Framework by DEGW (2002), and replaced it with a Special Planning Guidance supplement to the London Plan, the *London View Management Framework* (Mayor of London 2007). Although providing a more complex and nuanced set of guidelines, the net effect was a radical reduction in the width of many of the viewing corridors. There were reservations from some of the central London boroughs, principally Conservative-led Westminster, but also Labour-led Camden. South of the river, however, cash-strapped Lambeth and Southwark joined forces with

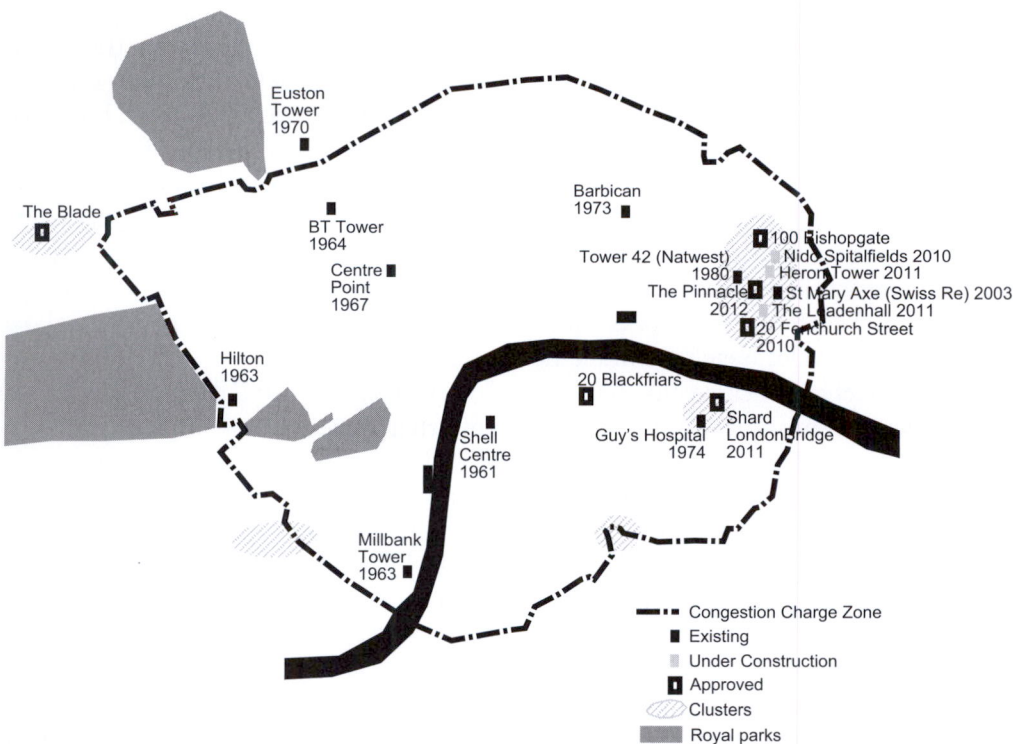

Figure 10.3 Central London: existing and proposed high buildings across the central area (drawn by Budhi Mulwayan).

the Tory-led City Corporation in pushing a liberal approach to the tall buildings agenda (Figure 10.3).

The new Mayor, Boris Johnson, advised in planning matters by the former leader of Westminster City Council, Sir Simon Milton, is using his powers to review major developments to call in many of the proposed tall buildings in sensitive locations. He has also indicated his preference to return broadly to the original viewing corridors set out in RPG3. The proposals principally affected are those along the river on the South Bank, such as Ian Simpson's fifty-one-storey Beetham Tower on Blackfriar's Road and the adjacent forty-two and twenty-three-storey towers by Wilkinson Eyre, which had all been given planning approval by Southwark Council at the time of writing (Stewart 2008). Lambeth and Southwark are relying on the major Section 106 contributions from these projects and Renzo Piano's sixty-six-storey Shard at London Bridge (aiming to be London's tallest building at 306 metres, if completed as scheduled in 2011) to fund badly needed social provision. Clearly, there are conflicting demands behind the pressure to build higher and the resistance to it, leading to such unlikely political alliances.

One of the main criticisms levelled against London's planning policies with regards to tall buildings, particularly at the strategic level, is that these have been largely negative, saying where tall buildings should not go, rather than where they should go and how they should be designed (Burdett *et al.* 2002). Now that precedents have been established, London is unlikely to avoid future incursions on its skyline. If the many high-rise projects that have already been approved go ahead then the skyline will look altogether different in four years' time. This is unlikely to happen in its entirety because the property slump is, at the time of writing, already claiming major victims such as Richard Rogers's 'Cheesegrater' building at 122 Leadenhall (Lazell 2008).

The emerging consensus is to permit high-rise development in clusters, rather than a random sprinkling that evokes Prince Charles's proverbial carbuncles (Booth 2008). This certainly formed part of Ken Livingstone's approach, with the London Plan emphasising the importance of siting intensified development around well-connected transport nodes. The current argument is over how many clusters, with Boris Johnson proposing to narrow it down to the City, Canary Wharf, Stratford and Croydon town centre. The City Corporation, meanwhile, by a process of elimination of areas covered by strategic viewing corridors and/or conservation areas status, has identified two clusters within the Square Mile itself (City of London 2002). Prince Charles joined those struggling unsuccessfully to preserve the Tower of London World Heritage site against the encroachment of city 'monsters' like Raphael's Viñoly's 36-storey 'Walkie Talkie' building at 20 Fenchurch Street, whose much wider footprint does more damage (Booth 2008). Even Charles, however, does not suggest that all tall building construction should halt, or simply be banished to a single cluster in Canary Wharf.

In all of this there is little talk of a coherent urban design approach to the design of tall buildings. In the City, Foster's 'Gherkin' building at 30 St Mary Axe, however its architectural merits are judged (Jenkins 2006), has established itself as a key London landmark. It is due, however, to be crowded out by a rash of new developments each trying to shout louder than the next (see Plate 10.4). It is hard to avoid the impression that the City skyline will become an ill-mannered architectural 'zoo'. A particular case in point is the 288-metre Pinnacle Building in Bishopsgate by Kohn Pedersen Fox Associates, the so-called 'Helter Skelter', a massive curving glass edifice that will crash into the streetscape like something out of a sci-fi movie. This is ironic given the same architects have designed a still massive but somewhat better articulated, environmentally conceived and slightly more street context-conscious building, the Heron Tower, just up the road.

Plate 10.4 London: 'City cluster,' showing proposed new development adjacent to 30 St Mary Axe (The Gherkin). The 'credit crunch' casts doubt on how many of these projects will be achieved (Courtesy Miller Hare © 2008).

An urban design approach to tall buildings would preclude a free-for-all within a given area and instead require new buildings to relate to one another and to the street, with more than an offhand gesture to the public realm. The opportunity to shape a well-designed cluster, in which slender and well-articulated towers are mediated by intermediate height buildings or podia that bear some considered relationship to surrounding streets, is being lost. Hedge funds are prepared to pay a premium for headquarters in Mayfair where the City of Westminster has maintained its historic morphology and the quality of its public realm and services, with shops, side streets, cafés and places to meet. Whilst the City Corporation faces different pressures and requirements, it sometimes appears to be lost on those guiding its development that these self-same qualities, its cultural capital, are among its major attractions.[2]

Concluding comments

Development pressures have pushed the concepts that make up the 'urban renaissance' to the limit within central London. There has been no strategic approach to urban design, but this has not impeded some qualitative improvements. The transformation of the South Bank of the Thames, from County Hall to Tower Bridge, counts as a real achievement of the last decade, although bland commercial development and various uncoordinated proposals for high buildings along the waterfront threaten to undermine the quality of the Thames as the major public space at the heart of central London. The make-over of Trafalgar Square demonstrates that London is still capable of making a grand gesture. Various smaller-scale public realm improvements have added to the enjoyment of, and pleasure in, the city. The City of Westminster's conservation policies have preserved its essential qualities, and Rasmussen would recognise many of the squares and streets whose virtues he extolled. The centre is certainly easier to get around, by bike and bus and, away from the main streets, walking has become more pleasurable with the reduction in traffic levels.

London has famously resisted large-scale plans, and this has been one of its virtues (Hebbert 1998). This is not to say that an urban design strategy would not have been an improvement on the free-for-all that has resulted from loosening the restrictions on high buildings in the City and in north Southwark. The positive improvements to the public realm might also have added up to be more than the sum of their parts had they only been part of a grander concept, as with Farrell's as yet unbuilt proposal for a 'Nash Ramblas'. Where there has been a strategy, as with the Thames Path on the South Bank, with its connections to the North Bank via the Jubilee and Millennium Bridges, the result has surpassed expectations.

The most disappointing aspect of the last decade has been that, in the midst of a property boom in the centre of the fifth largest economy in the world, so little has been captured for the average Londoner in the London's oldest quarter, the square mile of the City. The pressures on this financial centre to become 'the world city', outstripping Tokyo and New York, have encouraged the construction of ever larger, ever shinier corporate buildings, ever more elaborate in form, competing against one another for attention. Their polished granite plazas, lined by franchised coffee bars, have an anonymous, hard quality. External forces are having a similar detrimental effect on other aspects of London's character across the whole central area. The upwards spiral of residential property prices means that, gradually, the super-rich are taking over, and Livingstone's affordable housing policy will have made only a small dent in that process. Jonathan Raban comments that the London he inhabited in *Soft City* no longer exists in central London and to find it means journeying much further out into the suburbs (Raban 2008). Processes of gentrification and globalisation are not, of course, unique to London, but it seems more could be done to resist them in protecting low-income housing and local shops and services.

The efforts made by Westminster City Council, the GLA and Camden illustrate the strengths of adopting new cooperative ways of working within boroughs, between agencies and with the involvement of businesses. The new regeneration partnerships have proved their worth too, working across the traditional divides between the poorer boroughs of the fringe and the wealthy centre.

The Mayor and the central London authorities have produced a wealth of site-specific detailed urban design guidance in the last decade. The use of masterplans and design briefs is standard practice for developments in which the public sector is a stakeholder, such as for King's Cross (see Chapter 11). Design competitions for major sites and structures, such as the bridges, have produced innovative and imaginative proposals. Yet, despite this, the boroughs still lack detailed general urban design guidance that goes beyond written policies. In the overheated London property market, case law has a tendency to set precedents and values and policies have to be crafted around this expensive contestation. At the time of writing established UDP policies are being reworked into the new local development framework structure, and only time will tell if these new documents will cover the ground effectively against insensitive speculative development. The 2008 alterations to the London Plan imposed 'cheese slice' subregional wedges around the capital, with the suggestion that each portion of the CAZ related to the portion of the wedge adjacent to it. In response to this, six of the central London boroughs in the CAZ have formed a new partnership, Central London Forward (City of London 2008). It is to be hoped that this organisation will include an urban design strategy as part of its mission.

The financial crisis that began in 2007 has created uncertainty for the property market in London. The downturn will give Mayor Johnson and his advisors a breathing space in which to ask themselves the same questions that faced Ken Livingstone at the start of his term of office. Once the property market takes off again, however, the issues of concentration, expansion and/ or dispersal will once again become pressing. It would seem that hard choices between keeping central London's existing street layout and pattern of development, and responding to the needs of the global financial markets, will have to be faced anew. Perhaps this time new policies, more sensitive to London's historical form and physical qualities, will emerge.

Notes

1 Data on tall buildings in London, both historical and current or proposed, are drawn from the buildings database of Emporis.com (http://www.emporis.com/en/).
2 We would like to thank Graham King for his helpful comments on this chapter. The views expressed are our own.

References

Ackroyd, P. (2001) *London: The Biography* (London: Vintage).

BBC (2008) London Places: The Rise and Fall . . . And Rise Again of Seven Dials. Online. Available at: http://www.bbc.co.uk/print/london/content/articles/2008/09/01/seven_dials_feature.shtml (last accessed 30 September 2008).

Booth, R. (2008) Charles Does it Again: Skyscraper Boom a Rash of Carbuncles. *Guardian*, 1 February. Online. Available at: http://www.guardian.co.uk/uk/2008/feb/01/design.architecture (last accessed 29 August 2008).

Burdett, R., Firth, K., and Travers T. (2002) *Tall Buildings: Vision of the Future or Victims of the Past* (London: London School of Economics).

Carmona, M. and Freeman, J (2005) The Groundscraper: Exploring the Contemporary Reinterpretation. *Journal of Urban Design*, 10 (3): 309–330.

Carney, I. (2007) The Politics of Design: Architecture, Tall Buildings and the Skyline in Central London. *Area*, 39: 195–205.

Castells, M. (1989) *The Informational City: Information Technology, Economic Restructuring and the Urban-Regional Process* (Oxford: Basil Blackwell).

City of London (2002) *Unitary Development Plan* (London: Corporation of London). Online. Available at: http://www.cityoflondon.gov.uk/Corporation/LGNL_Services/Environment_and_planning/Planning/Planning_policy/udp.htm (last accessed 10 August 2008).

City of London (2005) *City Street Scene Manual* (London: Corporation of London, Department of Planning and Transportation). Online. Available at: http://www.cityoflondon.gov.uk/Corporation/LGNL_Services/Environment_and_planning/Urban_design/Urban±design±publications.htm (last accessed 30 August 2008).

City of London (2006) *Street Scene Challenge: Approved Schemes Update* (London: Corporation of London, Department of Planning and Transportation).

City of London (2008) *Central London Forward*. Online. Available at: http://www.cityoflondon.gov.uk/Corporation/LGNL_Services/Environment_and_planning/Regeneration/Regeneration_partnerships/central_london_forward.htm (last accessed 4 August 2008).

City of Westminster (2004) *Westminster Way: A Public Realm Manual For The City* (London: Westminster City Council). Online. Available at: http://www.westminster.gov.uk/environment/planning/publicrealm/city_wide_guidance.cfm (last accessed 29 September 2008).

City of Westminster (2007) *Unitary Development Plan* (adopted 24 January edn) (London: Westminster City Council). Online. Available at: http://www.westminster.gov.uk/environment/planning/unitarydevelopmentplan (last accessed 10 August 2008).

Coaffee, J. (2004) Rings of Steel, Rings of Concrete and Rings of Confidence: Designing out Terrorism in Central London pre and post September 11th. *International Journal of Urban and Regional Research*, 28: 201–211.

Coopers and Lybrand Deloitte (1991) *London: World City* (London: London Planning Advisory Committee).

CRP (Cross River Partnership) (2006) About Cross River Partnership (London). Online. Available at: http://www.crossriverpartnership.org/ (last accessed 1 August 2008).

DEGW (2002) *London's Skyline: Views and High Buildings (SDS Technical Report 19)* (London: DEGW). Online. Available at: http://www.london.gov.uk/mayor/planning/docs/tr19_high_bdgs_lowres.pdf (last accessed 30 August 2008).

Dyckhoff, T. (2003) Higher and Higher: How London Fell for the Loft. In J. Kerr and A. Gibson (eds) *London: From Punk to Blair* (London: Reaktion Books) pp. 228–235.

Farrell, T. (2007) London Calling: Special Issue. *The Architectural Review*, 222 (1327): 44–100.

Gehl Architects. (2004) *Towards a Fine City for People: Public Spaces and Public Life – London* (London: Transport for

London and Central London Partnership). Online. Available at: http://www.gehlarchitects.dk/images/28780_tfl_public_spaces.pdf (last accessed 11 August 2008).

GLA (Greater London Authority) (2007) *Managing the Night-Time Economy: Best Practice Guidance* (London: Greater London Assembly).

GLA (2008a) Proposal to Part-Pedestrianise Parliament Square is Halted 6-8-2008. *Greater London Assembly Press Release* (404). Online. Available at: http://www.london.gov.uk/view_press_release.jsp?releaseid=18174 (last accessed 26 September 2008).

GLA (2008b) London's Poor Air Quality Tackled With Launch Of Low Emission Zone. *Greater London Assembly Press Release* (072). Online. Available at: http://www.london.gov.uk/view_press_release.jsp?releaseid=15533 (last accessed 11 August 2008).

Glancey, J. (2001) *London: Bread and Circuses* (London: Verso).

Glancey, J. (2008) Why This Year's Stirling Prize is Cooler Than Ever. *Guardian*, 9 September. Online. Available at: http://blogs.guardian.co.uk/art/ (last accessed 31 July 2008).

GOL (Government Office for London) (1991) *Strategic Guidance for London Planning Authorities (RPG3)* (London: GOL).

GOL (2004) *Consultation on the London Housing Strategy 2005* (London: GOL).

GVA Grimley and Burns Owen Partnership (2007) *Westminster's Creative Industries* (London, City of Westminster). Online. Available at: http://www3.westminster.gov.uk/docstores/publications_store/CI_FINAL_REPORT_OCT_2007.pdf (last accessed 30 August 2008).

Hadfield, P. (2006) *Bar Wars: Contesting the Night in Contemporary British Cities* (Oxford: Oxford University Press).

Hamilton-Baillie, B. (2008) Towards Shared Space. *Urban Design International*, 13: 130–138.

Hardingham, S. (2001) *London: A Guide to Recent Architecture* (London: Batsford).

Heathcote, E. (2008) An Era of Urban Visionaries. *Financial Times* (London), weekend, Saturday 9 August: p. 1.

Hebbert, M. (1998) *London: More by Fortune than Design* (Chichester: Wiley).

Hendy, P. (2005) Exemplary Provision of Bus Services: Is London a Model for Other Conurbations? *Public Money and Management*, 25 (3): 195–200.

Henley, W. (2008) 100 Public Spaces Axed in London Design Shake-Up. *Building Design*. Online. Available at: http://www.bdonline.co.uk/story.asp?sectioncode=426&storycode=3119605&c=1&encCode=00000000017e6635 (last accessed 1 August 2008).

House of Commons (2008) *Hansard Debates: Westminster Hall (24 June 2008: Column 54WH)* (London: The Stationery Office).

Hutton, T. A. (2004) The New Economy of the Inner City. *Cities*, 21(2): 89–108.

Jenkins, S. (2006) The Gherkin is Magnificent but it Should Have Been Built Somewhere Else. *Guardian*, 13 January. Online. Available at: http://www.guardian.co.uk/culture/2006/jan/13/society.communities (last accessed 29 August 2008).

Kay, J. (2007) How Private Equity Revamped a London High Street. *Financial Times* (London), 19 December. Online. Available at: http://www.johnkay.com/print/528.html (last accessed 29 September 2008).

Lazell, M. (2008) Rogers' 'Cheese Grater' Melts Under The Crunch. *Building Design*, 14 August. Online. Available at: http://www.bdonline.co.uk/story.asp?storycode=3120514&origin=BDweeklydigest (last accessed 29 August 2008).

Lovatt, A., O'Connor, J., Montgomery, J., and Owens, P. (1994) *The 24-Hour City: Selected Papers from the First National Conference on the Night-Time Economy* (Manchester: Manchester Metropolitan University).

LPAC (1994) *Advice on Strategic Planning Guidance for London* (London: LPAC).

LPAC(1999) *Supplementary Advice on High Buildings and Strategic Views in London* (ADV83) (London: LPAC).

Mayor of London and TfL (2004) *Making London a Walkable City: The Walking Plan for London* (London: Mayor of London). Online. Available at: http://www.tfl.gov.uk/assets/downloads/walking-plan-2004.pdf (last accessesd 11 August 2008).

Mayor of London (2007) *London View Management Framework: The London Plan Supplementary Planning Guidance* (London: Greater London Authority) Online. Available at: http://www.london.gov.uk/mayor/strategies/sds/spg-views.jsp (last accessed 30 September 2008).

Mayor of London (2008) *The London Plan: Spatial Development Strategy for Greater London: Consolidated with Alterations since 2004*, February edn (London: Greater London Authority).

Newman P. and Smith I. (2000) Cultural Production, Place and Politics on the South Bank of the Thames. *International Journal of Urban and Regional Research*, 24 (1): 9–24.

Newman, P. and Thornley, A. (2005) *Planning World Cities: Globalization and Urban Politics* (Basingstoke: Palgrave, Macmillan).

Powell, K. (2003) *New London Architecture* (London: Merrell).

Raban, J. (2008) My Own Private Metropolis. *Financial Times* (London), weekend, Saturday 9 August: p. 1.

Rasmussen, S. E. (1982) *London: The Unique City* (Cambridge, MA: MIT Press).

Roberts, M. and Turner, C. (2005) Conflicts of Liveability in the 24-Hour City: Learning From 48 Hours in London's Soho. *Journal of Urban Design*, 10 (2): 171–193.

Rogers, R. and Fisher M. (1992) *A New London* (Harmondsworth: Penguin).

Southwark Council (2006) *Southwark Streetscape Design Guide* (London: Southwark Council).

Stewart, D. (2008) 'Boris' Threat To Tall Buildings. *Building*, 18. Online. Available at: http://www.building.co.uk/story.asp?storycode=3113210 (last accessed 29 August 2008).

Sudjic, D. (2001) *Blade of Light: The Story of London's Millennium Bridge* (London: Penguin Press in association with the Millennium Bridge Trust).

Teedon, P. (2001) Designing a Place Called Bankside: On Defining an Unknown Space in London. *European Planning Studies*, 9 (4): 449–481.

TfL (Transport for London) (2005) *Improving Walkability: Good Practice on Improving Pedestrian Conditions as Part of Development Opportunities* (London: Transport for London).

TfL (2008) *Central London Congestion Charging: Impacts Monitoring, 6th Annual Report* (London: Mayor of London).

TfL, National Economic Research Associates and MVA (2004) *The Case for Investing in London's Buses: Presenting the Results of the London Buses Strategic Review* (London: Customer Services, London Buses). Online. Available at: http://www.tfl.gov.uk/assets/downloads/businessandpartners/busesstrategicreview.pdf (last accessed 11 August 2008).

Thornley, A. (ed.) (1992) *The Crisis of London* (London: Routledge).

Westminster City Council (2007) *Statement of Licensing Policy 2008–2011* (London: Westminster City Council).

11 King's Cross

Renaissance for whom?

Michael Edwards

Introduction

This chapter examines the planning and development history of the area around King's Cross station on the northern edge of central London, picking up the story in the late 1980s and concentrating on the last decade. In the late 1980s London was in the grip of a major property boom, an outcome of the deregulation of the Thatcher period, in which a speculative surge in office property development was replacing and expanding the building stock of central London, pushing upwards but also outwards and lapping at areas such as King's Cross.

At its core, London is polycentric, with its main concentrations of activity around the Bank of England in the Roman and medieval 'City'; the Westminster focus of government, royalty and diplomacy; and with shopping and entertainment just to the west and north of Westminster. Between these eastern and western poles lie areas in Fleet Street, Holborn and Covent Garden which have transformed dramatically in the twentieth century with the exodus of wholesale vegetable trading from Covent Garden and of newspapers and printing from Fleet Street, and the assimilation of the urban fabric into retail, entertainment and cultural uses in Covent Garden, and with offices in Holborn and Fleet Street strongly linked to the legal profession. The whole of this 'centre' is ringed by the Circle Line of the underground.

King's Cross lies on the northern edge of this centre, extremely well connected by underground and surface railways. However, it had long been a Cinderella district, shunned by big business. It lies in the valley of the River Fleet, which, running from Hampstead to the Thames at Blackfriars, had long been associated with insanitary living conditions, poverty and mess. In the second half of the twentieth century the district suffered severe blight caused by the disinvestment in the railways, and by planning uncertainty about how the awkward traffic intersections should be handled. It was thus, by the 1980s, the lowest-rent area for central London offices and with a commercial building stock mostly unchanged since the nineteenth century. Buildings of the twentieth century were all either social housing – the product of massive building by the London County Council (LCC) and two socialist boroughs – or public buildings, of which the outstanding example was the new British Library. The area was thus densely populated with working-class and other council tenants, and with a distinctive set of local enterprises– virtually none of them corporate – taking advantage of cheap yet accessible premises.

The experience of the King's Cross area merits analysis because it is in many respects a microcosm (Edwards 1992), representative of wider processes going on in the city and in society. The analysis thus has to touch on what has been happening in society at large and its spatial development, on the changing dynamics of the economy and of property development, on the weakening planning and local government system and its continuing reconstitution, since the 1970s, as subordinate to business interests. Within this turbulent history, design and planning ideas and practices have been reformed and have played crucial roles in shaping social, economic and physical outcomes.

The last two decades have indeed been a period of proliferating discourses on urban studies and policy – though often more like parallel worlds than strands in any real debate. Thus, the *urban renaissance* stems from John Prescott's efforts to harness architectural and design ideas to urban policy. At the same time the Home Office and the Cabinet Office were busy developing ideas about *social exclusion* as a new, rather European, way of containing poverty. We also saw the Blair government pursuing its *reform* agenda for local government and, above all, the growing dominance of *competitiveness* as the leading desideratum for all policy, essentially a euphemism for the pursuit of measurable economic growth. There is no space here to disentangle these strands and their languages, but their deeply problematic nature, and the contradictions among them, have been examined elsewhere by Colomb (2007), Harloe (2001) and myself (Edwards 2006), among others.

One major problem in this analysis has been to disentangle the influence of the Urban Task Force (UTF) from the impacts of these other policy regimes and from differing strands of thought – a problem shared with other authors in this book. Another shared problem is that change in the King's Cross area is in full swing at the time of writing (though seriously challenged by the world economic crisis). Indeed, the biggest development project in the area, the redevelopment of the railway lands by Argent, is only just starting, and much of the discussion is necessarily about likely outcomes over the next decade or more.

From a methodological point of view, this chapter should probably be classified as a political economy. Its central concern is with the production and use of the built environment as an important facet of a capitalist society undergoing, since the late 1970s, rapid change. The main thrust of the change is hard to describe in language which is both precise and widely comprehensible. It is common to speak about 'restructuring' in the sense that major features of the social structure have been transformed: trades unions and other working-class organisations weakened, the constraints on capital relaxed and the state sector of the economy transformed through privatisation. But the word sounds very technical, which is misleading, and an emphasis on 'structure' has rightly been criticised for suggesting that we are all the helpless victims of invincible and mechanical forces acting on us. The historian Edward Thompson made this comment most lucidly in his critique of French structuralism (Thompson 1994), and later writers have built a powerful approach, which attaches great importance to the agency of individuals, classes and groups within society, whether in challenging and changing structures of power or in passively reproducing them (Jessop and Sum 2006). This 'structure/agency' approach forms part of the background toolkit of this chapter.

The increasing dominance of 'neoliberal' ideas (Brenner and Theodore 2005; Siemiatycki 2005) is another important strand in this account, being evident at all levels, from the international organisations which regulate trade and investment, through to most of the professionals, officers and councillors in local government today. But this term, too, is deeply unsatisfactory, familiar to only a small coterie of social scientists and hard to explain briefly, though Harvey does it brilliantly and at length, working from the following definition:

> Neoliberalism is in the first instance a theory of political economic practices that proposes that human well-being can best be advanced by liberating individual entrepreneurial freedoms

and skills within an institutional framework characterised by strong private property rights, free markets and free trade . . . Furthermore if markets do not exist (in areas such as land, water, education, health care, social security, or environmental pollution) then they must be created, by state action if necessary.

(Harvey 2005: 2)

This chapter draws on twenty years of engagement with King's Cross, partly through research funded by the King's Cross Partnership (Mutale and Edwards 2003), partly through advisory work with local authorities and developers, but mainly through my own and my students' collaborations with the King's Cross Railway Lands Group, an umbrella organisation of local groups (Holgersen 2008; see www.kxrlg.org.uk). This local work has been strengthened and refreshed through international collaborations with similar struggles elsewhere in the world in two networks – the Bartlett International Summer Schools (BISS 1969–1996) and the International Network for Urban Research and Action (INURA 2004; see www.inura.org) – both modest examples of globalisation from below. The approach is partly indebted to Risebero (1992) and appears to have elements in common with the much more elaborate methodology of Cuthbert (2006).

Was 'urban renaissance' a sound approach?

The report of the Urban Task Force (UTF 1999a), which is the main focus of this book, contains a disparate collection of discussions on a variety of urban questions under the umbrella 'urban renaissance'. Many of these discussions are valuable and bear re-reading a decade later. There is impassioned writing on the potentialities of good design to enrich the living environment. Within that we find a restatement of many of the principles enunciated thirty-seven years earlier by Jane Jacobs (Jacobs 1962): the value of mixed uses for continuous sociability, the merits of short blocks and so on (though no mention of the benefits of mixed tenures or mixed building ages to the diversity of streets and users). There is also a salutary passage on the need to strengthen and reanimate local government in the UK after two decades in which it had been weakened and marginalised.

On the other hand, the report is very weak in some of its central arguments, especially in the justification it offers for two of its main recommendations: increases in urban density and the reuse of 'brownfield land' to minimise development on 'green-field' sites. These two principles have become fetishes in British urban policy-making, and the UTF bears some responsibility for embedding them so thoroughly. Both are gross oversimplifications, or worse, but they are popular with the Council for the Protection of Rural England, and with those who support it in defence of their own use values or property values, or indeed for other motives, including altruistic ones. But there is no recognition of the severe negative effects of Britain's restrictive approach to urban development, raising land, housing and premises costs, and helping to impoverish citizens who are not established owner-occupiers. Such uncomfortable truths are pointed out only by independent-minded welfare economists (Cheshire and Sheppard 2002) or isolated leftists (Edwards 2002), and the Task Force really ducks all the awkward issues of land economics. Equally it avoids confronting the negative features of what Ruth Glass, working here in Islington, termed 'gentrification' (Glass 1964), whereby lower-income people are displaced by wealthier people as urban areas are upgraded. For these reasons the Task Force failed to achieve its lofty ambition to 'identify causes of urban decline' (UTF 1999a: title page) and its recommendations are seriously hazardous, as this chapter will show.

Was the 'urban renaissance' appropriate to London?

In many ways the UTF addressed a stereotype of a British (or perhaps a mid-Atlantic) city, characterised by population decline (at least in core and inner areas), an exodus of prosperous income groups to the suburbs, extensive unused or underused land (formerly industrial), and by a lack of residential or business demand for inner urban space.

This stereotype did not fit London in the late 1990s. The population of central and inner London had already stopped declining and had started growing in the 1980s. Upper-income households had never abandoned central London or the more salubrious parts of inner London and, by the 1990s, were colonising poorer boroughs too. It is true that London, especially inner areas, had been losing middle-income households, especially those at the family formation stage. That, however, is generally viewed as a response to high house prices, to perceived quality of education and of the environment for children. It is an important problem but not amenable to the general strategy of making urban living more attractive to all those with choice (Champion 1989; Buck *et al.* 2002; Butler 2003; Hamnett 2003a; Mayor of London 2008).

For these reasons the UTF's proposals were, essentially, unnecessary in much of London since the 'problems' they addressed were not London's problems or were already, in 1999, on the way to being eradicated. And although London did (and does still) have some unused or underused former industrial land (Doak and Karadimitriou 2007), it almost all lay in the extreme eastern areas where the London Docklands Development Corporation (LDDC) was being wound up, with its job largely complete. Elsewhere such land had largely been redeveloped to satisfy a surging private residential market, and planning authorities were under pressure to release more land from protective 'employment' designations. The issue was becoming one of how to generate or reclassify enough land as brownfield to satisfy developers' demand (Doak and Karadimitriou 2007).

The UTF's ideas were thus, in much of London, and certainly around King's Cross, reinforcing established trends, not reversing them. And it is in this context that we come to King's Cross, zooming in via the international, national and London levels of process.

The international context of change in London

The world economy in the 1990s and in the decade that followed could be characterised as one of strong capital accumulation with growing liberalisation of financial flows and investment (Glyn 2006: 50ff). A great deal of money-capital was (and is) in the hands of investors and had to be channelled by portfolio managers into assets which they expected to be profitable. Investment in the production of goods had been increasingly shifting to authoritarian regimes in the Far East and to lower-wage countries elsewhere, including some of the formerly communist states, while the UK experienced strong investment in financial and property assets. Investment in property assets (ranging from commercial buildings to developable land, from individual houses to mortgage or consumption debt secured against housing) was aimed at capturing a combination of income and future growth in capital values. It was thus, to some extent, self-sustaining: so long as investors continued to believe in future value growth, and continued to invest, prices continued to rise because supply was so limited – especially the supply of property in good locations and especially where the planning regime was restrictive. 'Investors', in this context, comprise not only corporations and institutions but ordinary house-buyers too: all of us are involved in the process either as beneficiaries or losers from the escalation of housing prices.

London's international position in the period had a number of features relevant to the unfolding of urban change at King's Cross. The City of London was, from the big bang of the 1980s, pre-eminent in many of the burgeoning unregulated financial markets, and that led to the dramatic boom in demand for central office space, both in quantity and in scale of floorplates. The transformation of London's office areas, by groundscrapers in the City and skyscrapers at Canary Wharf, is essentially the product of that episode (Fainstein 2001). The UK also played a leading role in spreading the Thatcherite message of neoliberal restructuring and in advising on privatisations and the transformation of former communist societies, generating growth in the management consultancy and related legal professions based in London (Massey 2007). The London region also gained increasing dominance within the UK, draining human resources and investment from elsewhere as regional policy withered away within the country (ibid.) and within other European member states (Dunford 2005).

Thus, by the time the UTF started its work, London was already subject to a strong version of the hegemonic story which could be paraphrased like this: finance and business services are increasingly the dominant sectors in the UK economy, leading the way in productivity (gross value added per worker) and in generating the invisible earnings which enable us to import more and more of the goods we consume. Because London is overwhelmingly the seat of this sector, London must subordinate all other priorities to serving the needs of finance, business services and the related real estate industry. This kind of argument, with added references to 'world city' or 'global city', had been nurtured by the City of London Corporation during the vacuum left by the Greater London Council's (GLC) abolition (Edwards 2001), and later formed the 'vision statement' of national planning documents, of all three versions of the London Plan (Mayor of London 2004, 2006, 2008) and of many borough policy documents including those of Camden (London Borough of Camden 2000, 2006). The same vision formed the opening statement of the presentation of Camden's view on King's Cross at the Economic and Social Research Council (ESRC) seminar in July 2008 (by Peter Bishop, who had been Camden's Director of Environment throughout the period considered here).

London in 1999

By 1999 London was once again in the full flood of boom conditions in its economy and its property markets. The recovery from the crash of 1990 had, interestingly, been led by the housing sector and average house prices in the capital and adjacent regions rose dramatically until the new crash of 2007/2008. The boom spread to office production a little later but, here too, a speculative surge was well under way by 1999 as investors pushed asset values up. Figure 11.1 shows just how strong this growth of asset values in the UK was.

Rather little of the flood of money into the housing market had resulted in new construction, however: most had just driven prices up. At a national level this failure of the market to meet demand led the Treasury to commission a special report by Kate Barker (Barker 2004). The 'market failure' has posed severe problems for the management of the national economy and a major challenge to neoliberal orthodoxy: the free market simply was not delivering (for a discussion, see Edwards 2008). At the London level the severity of the housing shortage preoccupied Mayor Livingstone through successive plans, and in his draft housing strategy produced shortly before

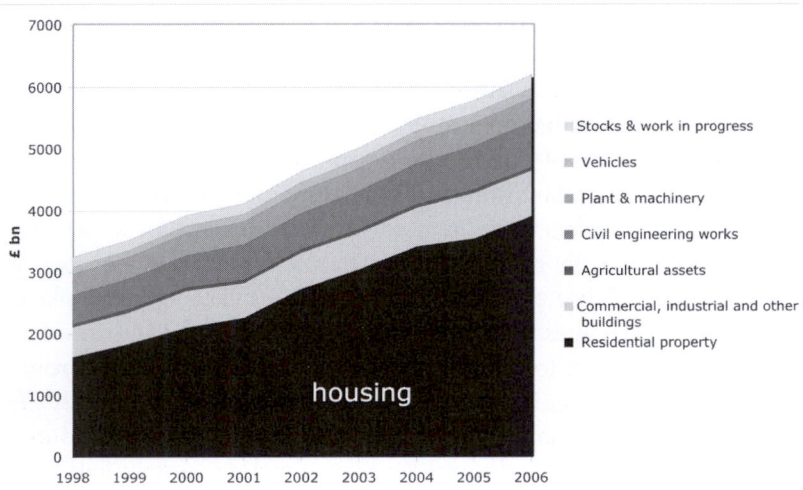

Figure 11.1 Market value of tangible assets in the UK, 1998-2006 (Source ONS 2007).

his defeat (Mayor of London 2007). Production of housing for sale in London had stayed resolutely static through the price boom; housing association output had contributed some growth but had entirely failed to replace the contribution which council house building had made in the 1960s and 1970s. Furthermore, the production of new social housing was not even enough to make up for the losses due to the right to buy (Mayor of London 2007: 23). The housing system in London had become a tremendous wealth machine for established owner-occupiers and investors, and simultaneously a poverty machine for the rest of the population: tenants and new purchasers (Edwards 2004).

King's Cross

This set of conditions underpinned the demands expressed by community groups and many Labour politicians for a major housing development on the railway lands at King's Cross through the 1980s and 1990s. But, as we shall see, this was not to be fully realised.

An earlier round of debate on the future of King's Cross in the period from 1987 is documented elsewhere (Edwards 1992) and is not the subject of this chapter, but it needs to be summarised briefly. In the late 1980s, British Rail, under pressure to behave more like a private firm pending its privatisation, had made a great deal of money from the development of surplus land and air rights at some London termini, notably Charing Cross, Canon Street and the huge Broadgate development at Liverpool Street. It had in mind a sequel at King's Cross, which would gain much of its value from a planned new station for the delayed Channel Tunnel Rail Link (CTRL), then expected to be carved out on a diagonal axis below the listed train shed of King's Cross. British Rail initially kept quiet about this new station plan, but its true intentions were uncovered by local residents, and that deviousness contributed to strong distrust among the area's people.

British Rail, through its property board, invited developers to bid in a design and financial competition for the right to be development partners and reached agreement with Rosehaugh Stanhope, whom it had partnered at Broadgate. A consortium of Rosehaugh Stanhope, with the secondary landowner National Freight Corporation (later UPS Exel Logistics), was formed as the London Regeneration Consortium (LRC) and the architects Foster and Partners were commissioned as masterplanners.

Camden Council, as the local planning authority, was somewhat divided (even among the ruling Labour group) on what its requirements for the development should be, and intense debates took place in 1987–1990 on the content of a planning brief which would guide negotiations with LRC. The main issue was the relative weight to be attached to the long-standing aspirations for large-scale affordable housing, as against the strong corporate office emphasis which the developers favoured. The King's Cross Railway Lands Group (KXRLG), formed in 1987, brought together tenants' associations, resident groups, small and medium businesses, conservation and transport campaigners, a homeless group and others to press for an assortment of demands. It worked with sympathetic councillors and officers (with grant support from Camden) and the combined effect was – in hindsight – a fairly effective episode in consultation, if not full participation. It had some influence on the evolution of the Planning Brief and the LRC/Foster scheme and culminated in the submission of community-generated alternative planning applications pitted against the LRC application (Parkes 1991, 2004): KXRLG won a London Planning Achievement Award from the London Branch of the Royal Town Planning Institute.

In the event, Camden had reached a decision in 1992 that it was 'minded to grant' planning permission for LRC's mainly office scheme, when the scheme effectively collapsed. The collapse was a rather clear example of 'overdetermination' in the sense that multiple factors led to its demise and perhaps any one of them might have been sufficient or decisive. The factors included the collapse of the central London office market, which suffered from massive oversupply and falling demand in the early 1990s. That fact, combined with rising interest rates, drove many developers into bankruptcy or inactivity, including Rosehaugh Stanhope, which ceased trading. Furthermore the British Rail scheme for the CTRL, tunnelling through south-east London and under the listed King's Cross station, was withdrawn following intense campaigning by affected groups along the route, and on cost grounds. In all this, the KXRLG had expected and hoped for the collapse of the office markets, and had anticipated that the struggle to prevent an outright planning permission would bring this outcome, as indeed it did.

The narrative resumes in the late 1990s, after a long period in which the UK and London economies had been recovering. There were three pertinent features of that period: the CTRL Act of 1997, the local initiation of a 'partnership' under the Single Regeneration Budget (Mawson *et al.* 1995) and the Greater London Authority Act of the Blair government. During the 1990s an initiative launched by Mark Bostock of the consultancy Arup led to a new alignment for the CTRL being adopted by government and embodied in the Channel Tunnel Railway Act of 1997. The route crossed under the Thames downstream, between new stations near Bluewater and at Stratford, and arrived (along the route of the North London Line) at St Pancras, which was to be expanded for the purpose, involving an elevated complex of tracks at the final approach. That was to create problems of noise and physical severance for development schemes, and it also greatly reduced the area of land which would be available for development at King's Cross, from fifty-five hectares to twenty-seven hectares. Even more important for the outcome was the financial basis the government designed for the new railway.

In keeping with the neoliberal tenets of Thatcherism, the Major and Blair governments were determined that this should be a private railway. After very protracted negotiations, an agreement was made with a private consortium London and Continental Railways (LCR), that it would build and operate the new railway. But because ticket revenue was not expected to make the railway profitable, a government subsidy was essential, and to reduce the scale of subsidy the consortium was promised the development rights over land at King's Cross, St Pancras, Stratford and Ebbsfleet (near Bluewater) as part of the agreement. The significance of this is that property development at King's Cross was required to generate not just profit on development investment, but also substantial revenues to LCR and government to help offset the costs of the railway. Although the details of these agreements, and of the various parties' profit expectations, are hidden by 'commercial confidentiality', it is clear that they have been important constraints on the composition of the development scheme.

Meanwhile the government financed a 'King's Cross Partnership' with £37.5 million funding from the Single Regeneration Budget (SRB) to run from 1996 to 2003. The significant partners were the railway companies and the Camden and Islington Councils, with 'the community' in a very subordinate role, represented on the board by invited people. It had been expected to operate through the period in which the CTRL construction and related regeneration was going on, but the delays in getting those works funded and launched meant that there was little overlap, and the Partnership was often criticised for not knowing quite what to do. In the event, it spent part of its money on valuable training and education, assisting local people entering the labour market. Otherwise most of its effort was devoted to changing the image of the area through a mixture of psychological and material measures.

The attack on the area's image was an instance of the familiar strategy whereby a locality is first characterised as run-down, dirty, crime-ridden, deprived and so on, and then (perhaps after some actual changes have occurred) it is given a new characterisation as vibrant, creative, safe(r) and desirable. Both parts of this sequence were strongly in evidence at King's Cross (Campkin 2009). The dark picture stressed edgy physical decay, prostitution and drugs (infuriating and alienating many local residents for whom the area was a good enough or valued home). It was associated with heavy investment in CCTV, the relics of which can still be seen around the area, and with a programme of street scene improvements: grants to firms for façade upgrades and the usual replacement of sidewalk paving, street furniture, and so on. A fine new park at Edward Square was perhaps the most tangible legacy.

Meanwhile other improvements were made by local authorities through the Estates Improvement Programme, more substantial in their effects on residents and with less attention to cosmetic impact (see Plate 11.1). Alongside the physical changes, the partnership invested heavily in posters, painted hoardings, website design, leaflets and tourist maps, all designed to present the locality as creative and cultural, visually appealing (with stress on the historic buildings) and, by implication, non-threatening.

Plates 11.1 King's Cross: Cromer Street, Camden Council Estate Improvement in which dwellings were modernised, estate security radically improved, and public and shared areas re-landscaped.

The third important influence from the 1990s was the decision of the Blair government to establish the Greater London Authority (GLA) and to do so on the 'strong mayor' model. When the first elected mayor was the independent Ken Livingstone, it was expected by some that King's Cross might benefit from the same sort of policies which he had espoused for the area as leader of the GLC in the mid-1980s. The GLC's Community Areas Policy had been designed to defend the vulnerable populations and small firms of areas such as King's Cross from the expansion pressures of the central office area. It had proposed expansion of social housing instead of office development and had implemented an industrial zone beside Battlebridge Basin to foster the manufacturing sector, using GLC powers and money (GLC 1985).

In the event, Ken Livingstone as mayor formed a very close relationship with the City of London and property interests, and his approach was fully compliant with the hegemonic vision for world city growth explained above. He showed no residue of his 1980s attempts to protect community interests. King's Cross is shown in the London Plan (Mayor of London 2008) as a northwards extension of the Central Activities Zone (CAZ).

With the planning uncertainties about the area now resolved, a significant set of developments went ahead on sites surrounding the Railway Land (which was designated as an Opportunity Area in the Mayor's and Camden's plans – see Figure 11.2 – and was largely occupied with engineering works until 2007). The owners of these adjacent sites were now in a position to realise the enormous development values of the area – values created by the inherited and forthcoming infrastructure, by the image transformation work of the partnership and by proximity to Argent's forthcoming scheme. The most important of these schemes was the P&O development, now known as Regent Quarter, immediately east of King's Cross station. The site had been assembled speculatively over many years, initially by Joe Levy's Stock Conversion and Investment Trust

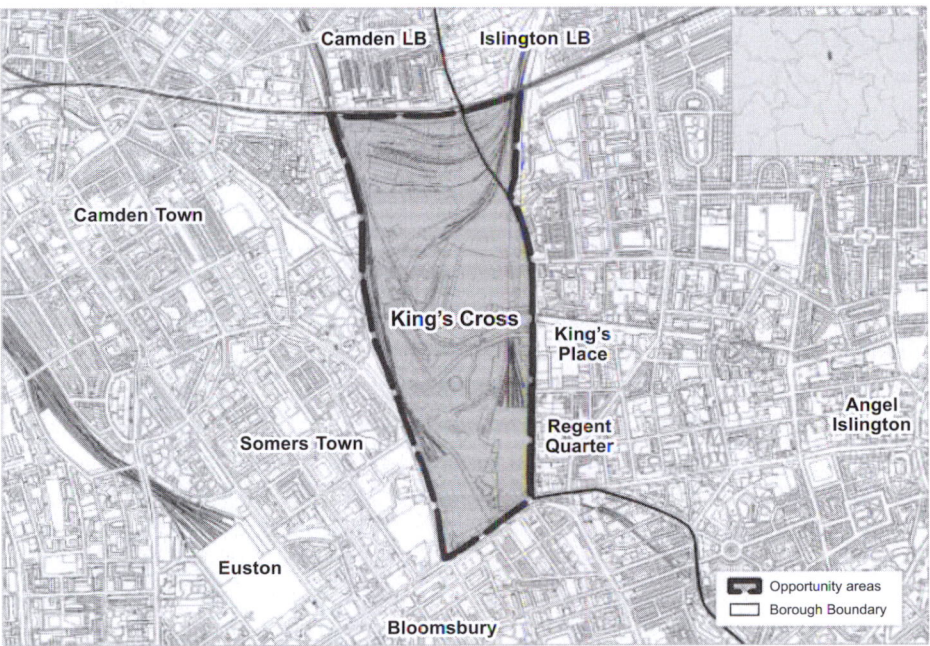

Figure 11.2 London: King's Cross Opportunity Area in context (information from the London Plan 2008) © Crown Copyright. All rights reserved. Licence number 100049043.

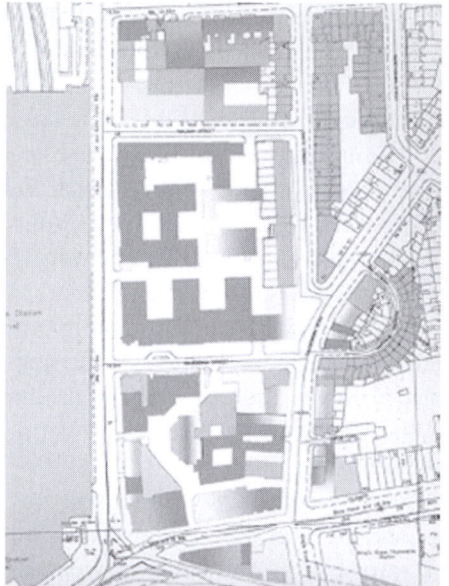 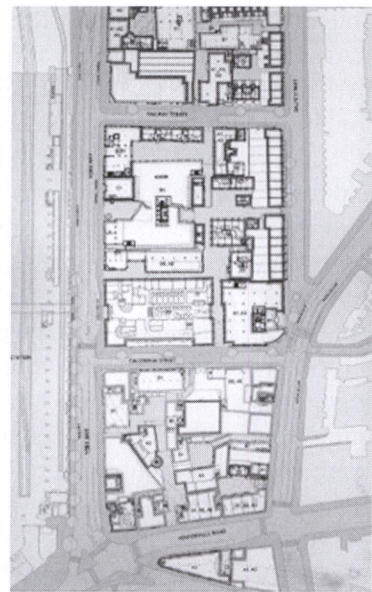

Rolfe Judd master plan, 2000   RHWL master plan, 2001

Figure 11.3 London: Regent Quarter. The original scheme for which permission was refused (left), and the second approved scheme (right). The southern triangular block and the northernmost block remain undeveloped in 2008. (Courtesy P&O Developments.)

and then, after 1986, acquired by P&O. The Borough of Islington prepared a brief for the site in 1998, and in 2000 a planning application was submitted for a predominantly office development designed by Rolfe Judd, architects (see Figure 11.3). The project envisaged the demolition of much of the nineteenth-century building stock, which had been allowed to decay very badly, and its replacement by a series of rectangular blocks, some built behind retained façades, for offices, retailing, a hotel, twenty flats and extensive parking. This scheme met with very strong resistance from a broad array of agents: residents' groups seeking more housing; conservation groups led by the late Lisa Pontecorvo, calling for the retention of more of the old buildings; and the Partnership Board, critical of the design in many respects, especially on conservation.

In the light of these objections, and its Planning Brief, Islington refused permission, whereupon P&O devised an entirely new scheme with RHWL architects in which a very high proportion of the old building stock was retained, interspersed with modern buildings of similar scale; a chain of internal courtyards created (gated) footpaths through all the blocks and the mix of uses was changed to provide much less office space, 138 flats (25 per cent as social housing), a hotel, bars and cafés and only twenty parking spaces for a scheme of 58,550 square metres (see Figure 11.3 and Plate 11.2). Two-thirds of the scheme was completed by 2005 and its housing units were sold very fast at prices that were higher than the developer had expected. The offices let more slowly, but well enough to enable P&O to sell the completed parts to Lasalle Investment Management as it sought to focus on its 'core business' of operating ports and shipping (Vogdopoulou 2006).

The Regent Quarter scheme could be described as a good professional compromise between conflicting forces. The design of the buildings and the intervening spaces are handled in a seamless and careful way which produces something of a Covent Garden atmosphere: intricate in plan and sections, diverse in uses, somewhat mixed in social composition, housing large and small

Plate 11.2 King's Cross: Regent Quarter. Internal views.

firms in varied sectors and sheltered from the thunderous traffic on surrounding roads – which is still a gyratory system. Two small streets remain, cutting through the scheme, but otherwise the spaces created are gated and only public at the discretion of the proprietors. These are supervised and regulated spaces for consumption and the writer has seen visitors being ejected by security staff. The detail is a mix of authentic (but sand-blasted) industrial building and *faux* or repro industrial building, decorated with the occasional cog wheel, as it might be an anchor at the seaside or a crane in Docklands. However, the scheme is regarded as substantially a victory by conservationists and those campaigning for housing and for car-free development.

The other main development now completed at King's Cross is King's Place, further up York Way and filling the space between the street and the Battlebridge Basin of the canal (Plate 11.3). This is the site which, in the 1980s, the GLC had developed for light industry (printing) in single-storey brick sheds and for a pub with a popular canal-side terrace. It was acquired by Peter Millican's Parabola Land, which sought and obtained permission to develop it for the most unusual combination of offices and concert halls. It has bars and cafés on the canal-side, enclosing performance and rehearsal spaces, which are home to a number of orchestras. All of this is surmounted (and paid for) by 28,000 square metres of offices on seven floors (half pre-let

Plate 11.3 King's Cross: Regent Quarter. King's Place, the Regent's Canal and Battlebridge Basin contain the building on two sides; York Way runs along the western side, separating this development from King's Cross Central beyond.

to the *Guardian*) in a design by Dixon Jones, which has attracted accolades. In terms of power relations and bargaining, the developer here secured his permission in recognition of the cultural contribution of the orchestras, including outreach work they are contracted to do in neighbouring schools. This was the substance of the S106 agreement, in contrast to the social housing or other community benefits, which would have been more normal in this area.

There is some dispute among local activists and politicians about the height of the building. One story is that the developer secured greater height in the building than would normally have been permitted alongside the canal under the development plan. Others, however, contend that the building would have been even higher had it not been for effective lobbying by local conservation groups. Whatever the truth on that point, the building is important for its great mass, casting its shadow over the canal and, in winter, over adjoining gardens and flats. Since it gained permission before Argent's proposals for a wall of offices overshadowing the canal were decided, King's Place was regarded as establishing a new de facto benchmark. This episode is an example of a process we have been seeing a lot in the last decade: that the presumption in favour of higher densities – one of UTF's strongest nostrums – works through the ratcheting-up of building heights in this way. Once a new eaves line is established, owners of neighbouring sites can follow.

Regent Quarter and King's Place are the largest of the pilot fish nosing up to the big fish of the King's Cross Central development. But there are many smaller ones, notably to the south-east along the Fleet valley, where a jumble of nineteenth-century workshops, factories, stables and dwellings are being converted piecemeal to new and luxurious uses. A stable becomes a wine bar; a factory becomes the London outpost of New York art dealer Gagosian; various architects convert warehouses as their offices, and so on. This process displaces the old economy of printers, trade unions, campaign groups and charities, including the birthplaces of *Time Out* and *The Big Issue*. The Peace Movement and Housmans bookshop remain only because they are stalwart owners of their freehold and not for sale. So the process we see in these areas is a simple market process of upscale activity replacing downscale activity.

Finally we consider the big fish: King's Cross Central.

King's Cross Central

In the same year as Ken Livingstone's inauguration, LCR appointed as developers Argent plc, an unusual development company which had made its name with an award-winning scheme of corporate offices and mixed uses at Brindleyplace in central Birmingham (Latham and Swenarton 1999). Argent was, in turn, partnering with St George, a house-building firm, part of the Berkeley Homes group, but St George withdrew in 2004 as part of a far-sighted reduction in its portfolio of London projects.

Since the land Argent was to develop would not become available for building until the CTRL construction was completed in 2007, the company had six years or so in which to devise its scheme and deal with local authorities, community groups, and so on. This time was filled by the

Plate 11.4 King's Cross Central. Illustrative model of the outline scheme, southern part (above) in white. King's Cross station far left. Northern part (right). Granary complex (above foreground. Some of the relocated gas holders are visible top left. Both photos looking west.

production of a series of Argent documents, alternating with Camden's production of a draft and then (with Islington) a final planning brief (London boroughs of Camden and Islington 2004) for the site, now renamed King's Cross Central by the developers.

The Argent scheme now has outline permission, and work started on site in late 2008. The scheme can be described as a predominantly office/mixed-use development of twenty-six hectares. The permisssion is innovative in that it allows the developer roughly 20 per cent flexibility to vary the mix of uses within the total 713,000 square metres of floorspace permitted.

The site slopes upwards from the Euston Road in the south to the Regent's Canal, and is then relatively flat as far as its boundaries: a railway embankment to the north and York Way to the east. Roughly the southern half of the site was densely occupied with the structures of the massive transport hub, which grew here from 1800 until about 1930: canal, gas works and gas holders, railways, storage and interchange buildings for rail/cart/boat movement, stables, offices and so on (see Plate 11.4). It was a very distinctive ensemble including some historically important early workers' housing blocks and has been brilliantly documented by Angela Inglis (2007). Much of the ensemble has been lost, but fragments are retained and reused, notably the granary and adjoining buildings which have been pre-let to the University of the Arts. But south of the canal, where the market incentive for Argent is to maximise the quantity of office space and retailing, the whole ensemble has been swept away except for one retained gem of a building, the German Gymnasium and – after much haggling with English Heritage – one of the three blocks of Stanley Buildings, innovative workers' housing of 1864/1865.

The wedge-shaped space between the two train sheds is planned to be filled by predominantly wedge-shaped office buildings, climbing to their maximum height at their northern (canal) end with new streets running through between them. There is no attempt to link eastwards by reinstating the line of Battlebridge Road to reconnect with the Islington street grid, and the decision not to do this (alongside Railtrack's reluctance to pay for a bridge) remains a matter of intense local protest. Camden officers refused to insist on this link being made and, at the relevant planning committee meeting, a Camden officer said 'this is not in anyone's business interest so I don't see it happening' (author's verbatim note). He appeared to have forgotten that a role of the planning system is precisely to insist on elements of the public interest where private commercial interest may not meet these needs.

North of the canal the University of the Arts, occupying the granary complex, will front onto the former canal basin, to be laid out as a large public square, linked with small shops and cafés in the arches below the 'coal drops', and then a grid of new streets is to be laid out across the rest of the land with mixed use buildings. From a design point of view this looks as though it will turn out to be rather 'normal' urban landscape. Its main problem will be in configuration because it is cut off in a broad arc on the north and west by the impenetrable CTRL embankment, to be separated from the development site by a wall of buildings: housing, a CHP plant and a multistorey car park (mysteriously not sited on the main road but well into the back of the scheme). It may prove hard to make the shops and services work well in this situation.

All these judgements about design at King's Cross Central must be very provisional because the scheme has only outline permission and many changes may be made as detailed designs come forward over ten to twenty years. In my view the major issues surrounding the Argent development relate to its composition and to the ownership and process issues.

Conclusions

The composition of the Argent scheme, particularly its limited provision of affordable social housing to rent and its strong provision of corporate office space, has been the main source of conflict. It is a type of conflict which the London planning system and policy handles badly. Regeneration is not seen as primarily a process serving the low- and middle-income people in whose name regneration policy was developed: rather it is seen, in line with the hegemonic discourse summarised earlier, as essentially a business activity aimed at growth and competiveness. Within it, some concessions have to be made to low- and middle-income groups, but that is all they are. The issue is particularly fraught in localities which are already subject to strong gentrification forces (e.g. with private rents perhaps five to ten times the level of council rents) because only massive expansion of social housing could inoculate the area against the pressures. It is an acute conflict of use values and exchange values, social need versus commodification.

Ownership and process issues have been the other main focus of dispute. Ownership is an issue in the sense that there has been no attempt by the authorities to transfer legal or effective ownership of any of the nationally owned land or buildings to collective or municipal control, using land trusts or other mechanisms such as the Coin Street development at Waterloo (Brindley 2000). More generally, the local communities have felt disenfranchised in the decision process, notwithstanding extensive 'consultation'. Both Argent and Camden have prided themselves upon their extensive and innovative programmes of consultation and have won awards for their efforts. Those who remain dissatisfied are essentially reflecting their lack of influence in the consultation process: they are endlessly listened to but have no detectable power to determine the outcome. And it should be added that these feelings of frustration are shared not only by low- and middle-income residents but by back-bench local councillors, who tend to be marginalised in our 'reformed' local councils.

There is perhaps one element in all this that can be chalked up as a victory for local community demands: Camden has insisted that the new streets being created as part of the Argent development will be adopted as public highways and thus subject to normal police powers, rather than private security patrols.

Finally I return to the main issue of this book, the UTF and its urban renaissance. The developments completed and under way at King's Cross are the outcome of multiple influences, and the UTF is probably not a major one. However, we can observe in the new buildings, streets and squares all the strengths and weaknesses of the Task Force's approach. On the positive side we see a strong affirmation of stylish urban settings, lots of careful design and very strong market demand for premises. On the negative side we see few defences against gentrification, few youth clubs or non-commodity meeting places and a very private sort of environment. When we see who can afford to live or do business here in a decade from now we shall surely find a much less socially mixed set of people.

The rethinking of neoliberal assumptions has started at the level of international and national financial regulation but has yet to reach those involved in local development. The structures of economic relationships, political alignments and professional ideas have become overwhelmingly set in a neoliberal mould in the last decade or so. The professionals, politicians and others who could have been active agents in challenging them have failed to do so – yet.

References

BISS (1969-1996) Proceedings of the Bartlett International Summer Schools on the Production of the Built Environment (BISS) (London: Bartlett School, UCL).

Brindley, T. (2000) Community Roles in Urban Regeneration: New Partnerships on London's South Bank. *City*, 4 (3): 363–377.

Buck, N., Gordon, I., Hall, P., Harloe, M., and Kleinman, M. (2002) *Working Capital: Life and Labour in Contemporary London* (London: Routledge).

Butler, T. (2003) *London Calling: The Middle Classes and the Re-Making of Inner London* (London: Berg).

Campkin, B. (2009) *Dirt, Blight and Regeneration: A Study of Urban Change in Twentieth Century and Contemporary London*. Unpublished thesis, University of London (forthcoming).

Champion, A.G., (ed.) (1989) *Counterurbanisation: The Changing Face and Nature of Population Deconcentration* (London: Edward Arnold).

Cheshire, P. and Sheppard, S. (2002) The Welfare Economics of Land Use Planning. *Journal of Urban Economics*, 52: 242–269.

Doak, J. and Karadimitriou, N. (2007) (Re)development, Complexity and Networks: A Framework for Research. *Urban Studies*, 44 (2): 209–229.

Dunford, M. (2005) Old Europe, New Europe and the USA: Comparative Economic Performance, Inequality and the Market-Led Models of Development. *European Urban and Regional Studies*, 12 (2): 151–178.

Edwards, M. (1992) A Microcosm: Redevelopment Proposals at King's Cross. In A. Thornley (ed.) *The Crisis of London* (London: Routledge) pp. 163–184.

Edwards, M. (2001) Planning and Communication in London. *City*, 5 (1): 91–100.

Edwards, M. (2002) Property Markets and the Production of Inequality. In S. Watson and G. Bridge (eds) *A Companion to the City* (Oxford, Malden MA: Blackwell) pp. 599–608.

Edwards, M. (2004) Wealth Creation and Poverty Creation: Global–Local Interactions in the Economy of London. In R. Paloscia (ed.) *The Contested Metropolis: Six Cities at the Beginning of the 21st Century* (INURA, Basel: Birkhäuser).

Edwards, M. (2006) Hamlet Without the Prince: Whatever Happened to Capital in Working Capital? *City*, 10 (2): 197.

Edwards, M. (2008) Blue Sky Over Bluewater. In P. Cohen and M. Rustin (eds) *London's Turning: Thames Gateway: Prospects and Legacies* (London: Ashgate).

Fainstein, S. (2001) *The City Builders: Property Development in New York and London, 1980–2000* (Kansas: Kansas University Press).

Glass, R. (1964) *London: Aspects of Change* (London: Macgibbon and Kee).

GLC (Greater London Council) (1985) *Community Areas Policy: A Record of Achievement* (London: GLC).

Glyn, A. (2006) *Capitalism Unleashed: Finance, Globalization, and Welfare* (Oxford: Oxford University Press).

Harloe, M. (2001) Social Justice and the City: The New 'Liberal Formulation'. *International Journal of Urban and Regional Research*, 25 (4): 889–897.

Harvey, D. (2005) *A Brief History of Neoliberalism* (Oxford: Oxford University Press).

Holgersen, S. (2008) *Class Conflicts and Planning: A Case Study of Contemporary Development at King's Cross in London* (Saarbrücken: VDM Verlag Dr Müller).

Inglis, A. (2007) *Railway Lands: Catching St Pancras and King's Cross* (London: Troubadour).

INURA (International Network for Urban Research and Action) (ed.) (2004) *The Contested Metropolis: Six Cities at the Beginning of the 21st Century* (Basel: Birkhäuser for International Network for Urban Research and Action).

Jacobs, J. (1962) *The Death and Life of Great American Cities* (London: Cape).

Jessop, B. and Sum, N. -L. (2006) *Beyond the Regulation Approach: Putting Capitalist Economies in their Place* (Cheltenham: Edward Elgar).

Latham, I. and Swenarton, M., (eds) (1999) *Brindleyplace: A Model for Urban Regeneration* (London: Right Angle Publishing).

London Borough of Camden (2000) *Unitary Development Plan* (London: LBC).

London Borough of Camden (2006) *Replacement Unitary Development Plan* (London: LBC).

London Boroughs of Camden and Islington (2004) *King's Cross Opportunity Area Planning and Development Brief* (London: LBC).

Massey, D. (2007) *World City* (Cambridge: Polity).

Mawson, J., Beazley, M., Burfitt, A., Collinge, C., Hall, S., Loftman, P., Nevin, B., Srbljanin, A., and Tilson, B. (1995) *The Single Regeneration Budget: The Stocktake* (Birmingham: School of Public Policy, University of Birmingham).

Mayor of London (2004) *The London Plan: The Spatial Development Strategy* (London: GLA).

Mayor of London (2006) *The London Plan: The Spatial Development Strategy With Alterations* (London: GLA).

Mayor of London (2007) *Draft Mayor's Housing Strategy* (London: GLA).

Mayor of London (2008) *The London Plan, Consolidated With Alterations* (London: GLA).

Mutale, E. and Edwards, M. (2003) *Monitoring and Evaluation of the Work of the King's Cross Partnership: Final Report* (London: Bartlett School of Planning for the King's Cross Partnership).

ONS (2007) *Blue Book, National Income and Expenditure* (London: HMSO).

Parkes, M. (1991) *King's Cross Railway Lands: Towards a People's Plan* (London: KXRLG).

Parkes, M. (2004) Community Participation and Urban Regeneration: King's Cross and the Elephant and Castle. In Paloscia, R. (ed.) *The Contested Metropolis: Six Cities At the Beginning of the 21st Century* (INURA, Basel: Birkhäuser).

Risebero, B. (1992) *Fantastic Form: Architecture and Planning Today* (London: Herbert).

Siemiatycki, M. (2005) The Making of a Mega Project in the Neoliberal City: The Case of Mass Rapid Transit Infrastructure Investment in Vancouver, Canada. *City*, 9 (1): 67–84.

Thompson, E. P. (1994) *The Poverty of Theory* (London: Merlin Press).

Vogdopoulou, E. (2006) *Master Plan Evaluation. A Tool to Enhance Successful Urban Regeneration*. Regent Quarter case study, MSc EPDP Thesis, Bartlett School, UCL. http://eprints.ucl.ac.uk/2334.

12 The Isle of Dogs

Thirty-five years of regeneration but have we seen a renaissance?

Matthew Carmona

An impossible dream

The tale of London's Docklands from the 1970s to the property crash of the early 1990s has been told and retold many times. Yet, despite the surfeit of work tracking the period up to the early 1990s, surprisingly little has been written about the area since and, particularly, how it has fared in the UK's post-1997 New Labour era. It seems that, after the crash, many simply lost interest in the area, writing it off alongside the liquidated remnants of Olympia and York (the developers of Canary Wharf) as another planning disaster and the inevitable end to an impossible dream.

But this is not the whole story. As the economy picked up, so did Canary Wharf, which subsequently bounced back with a vengeance. Today, the Isle of Dogs has a very particular and special status in the London Plan as an 'opportunity area' that is seen as having a vital contribution to make to enhancing London's world city role (Mayor of London 2004: Policy 5C.1). Thus, the latest revisions to the plan contain proposals that the Isle of Dogs should accommodate 200,000 new jobs and 10,000 new homes by 2026, making in the process by far the largest contribution to the planned growth of the capital of any location in London (Mayor of London 2008: Table 5C.1). Fifteen years after the crash it can be argued that the impossible dreams are being realised (see Figure 12.1), but in the post-1997 language of regeneration can what has happened be described as an urban renaissance?

This chapter is based on a detailed review of the literature, supplemented by analysis of physical change on the ground, and of the twelve plans that sought to guide development over the thirty-five years and four development waves of the area's regeneration. Space does not permit a detailed review of this material (see Carmona 2009), and instead the findings are summarised using four key questions:

- What forms of planning have we seen?
- What role has design played in this?
- What outcomes have resulted from these processes?
- Have we seen an urban renaissance?

To help interpret the diversity of planning models utilised in this one small part of London, each development wave is viewed through an analytical framework constituting two separate but related continua, from market-led to state-led and from plan-based to opportunity-based modes of planning (Figure 12.2). The chapter begins with a brief overview of the history.

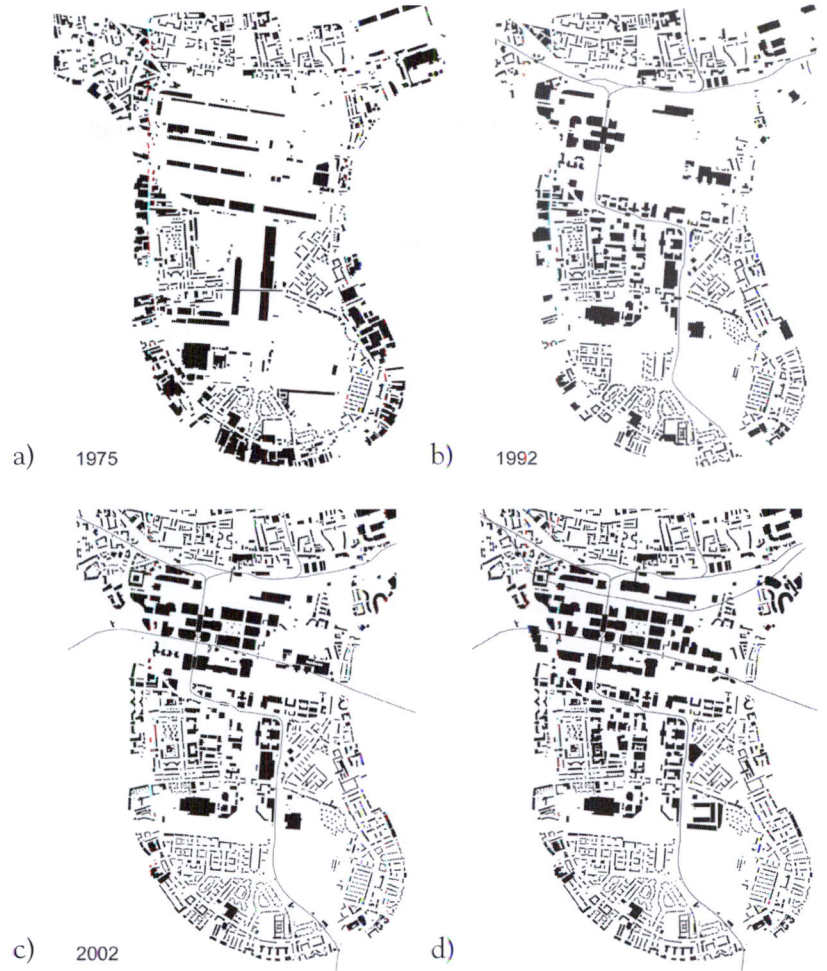

a) 1975

b) 1992

c) 2002

d)

Figure 12.1 Isle of Dogs: a transformed morphology: pre-regeneration 1975, end of wave two 1992, end of wave three 2002, into the future.

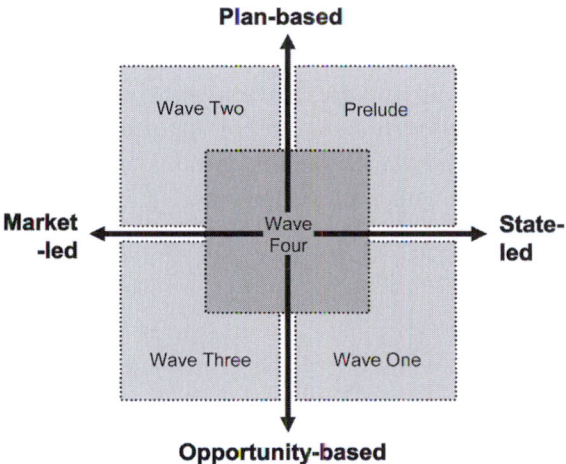

Figure 12.2 The market/state, plan/opportunity continua related to the Isle of Dogs' development waves.

A potted regeneration history

Prelude: 1973–1981

Serious attempts at regenerating Docklands began in 1971 when the Conservative government at the time commissioned private consultants to develop options for the then largely redundant post-industrial landscape. Reacting strongly to what was seen as an attempt to impose national and private sector solutions on local and public problems, the subsequent Labour administration placed control in the hands of a public–community partnership – the Docklands Joint Committee (DJC).

Despite the successful completion of the London Docklands Strategic Plan in 1976 (the only pan-Docklands plan ever to be formally adopted), the period was marked by inaction and failure, with the general economic climate restricting both public sector funds and private sector interest. The latter was also limited by the plan's innate opposition to private investment and support (almost exclusively) for new public housing and industrial regeneration.

The failure of the DJC was in part a failure to understand that the times were changing, and that local government would no longer have the same powerful role that it had occupied in the past. Using the analytical framework described in Figure 12.2, the period can be classified as plan based and state led.

Wave 1: 1981–1985

From 1981 to 1985, a dogmatic preference for public sector solutions gave way to a dogmatic preference for private ones, spearheaded by the designation of an Enterprise Zone on the Isle of Dogs and the establishment of the London Docklands Development Corporation (LDDC) to take control of the wider Docklands regeneration. This first wave of real development was characterised by a design and development free-for-all, with the LDDC largely unaware of the area's potential and almost entirely devoid of any serious vision beyond 'anything goes'.

The only attempt to impose some sort of order came through the commissioning of the townscape-inspired Isle of Dogs Development and Design Guide from (amongst others) Gordon Cullen. The result was quickly dismissed as 'preposterously aesthetic' (Buchanan 1989: 42; see Plate 12.1), whilst the whole exercise was undermined by the absence of any real belief in the plan, which, as a result, was largely sidelined as ad hoc development opportunities came along.

Nevertheless, the state (in the guise of the LDDC) was active, utilising marketing guides, hype, direct public realm investment and fiscal incentives to drive the development agenda. The period can therefore be characterised as state-led but opportunity based (Figure 12.2), whilst on the ground the results were fragmentedly suburban and roundly criticised as 'an architectural zoo' featuring 'a different beast in each plot' (Buchanan 1988: 14).

Wave 2: 1985–1991

With the arrival of Canary Wharf (1 million square metres of commercial offices and ancillary uses) everything changed. Design was seen for the first time not as a barrier to innovation and a cost on investment, but as a means to establish a marketable sense of place. The urban yet starkly private vision that resulted was fixed within a detailed masterplan and series of design codes

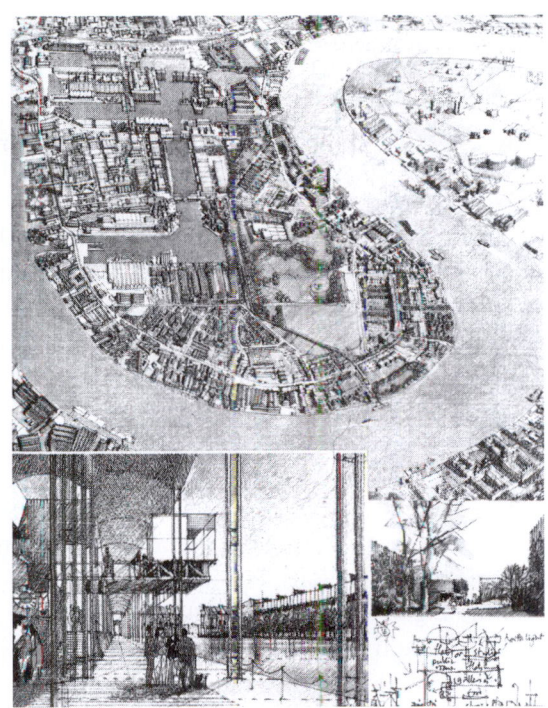

Plate 12.1 Isle of Dogs: Gordon Cullen's townscape vision, criticised as preposterously aesthetic and roundly ignored (Courtesy London Docklands Development Corporation).

Plate 12.2 Canary Wharf, phase one: urban, introspective and private but accessible to the public: designed to contrast strongly with its wider surroundings.

designed to contrast dramatically with the surroundings – economically, physically and socially (see Plate 12.2).

Yet the area remained marginal, not least because of its almost non-existent public transport infrastructure. History shows how Olympia and York overstretched itself and when faced with a major economic downturn in the early 1990s was unable to let enough space to service its spiralling debts. In 1992 it went under.

If the scheme marked a continuation of the lack of interest the LDDC had shown for social and community concerns, it demonstrated the importance of the certainty (up to a point) that goes hand in hand with a robust plan. Finding no such plan in place, the market sought to create one. The period can therefore be characterised as plan based and market led, a new and important departure for the UK development industry (Figure 12.2).

Wave 3: 1991–2002

At this time the public sector stepped in with increasingly large amounts of cash to belatedly put in place the necessary infrastructure to give the area a viable long-term future. This had been envisaged as far back as the various 1970s plans, but in the early 1990s was still largely absent. The extension of the Docklands Light Railway to Bank, and later the building of the Jubilee Line extension (opened in 1999), were truly catalytic for the area, and it was this as much as the recovering fortunes of the markets that led to the gradual re-emergence of Canary Wharf under new owners – Canary Wharf Group – from the mid-1990s onwards.

Critics who had rashly written off the Isle of Dogs were proven incorrect as the original masterplan (with some revision) was completed alongside a second phase on Heron Quays. During this period both the urban design and the architecture matured, the former becoming less introverted and formal and the latter more international and corporate. The combined impact was that a real place began to emerge, albeit still largely disconnected from its immediate hinterland. But although the LDDC began to apply the design-led lessons from Canary Wharf to other parts of the Docklands, it continued to pursue a hands-off marketing-led strategy in the remainder of the Isle of Dogs, with sites marketed as isolated enclave development opportunities (see Plate 12.3).

By 1998, when the LDDC was wound up, the regeneration had delivered 849 hectares of developable land, 75,485 jobs (Kochan 1998: 8), 24,300 new homes, including 6,000 for social housing, with a further 8,000 council units refurbished (Bazlinton 1998: 38). A total of £8.7 billion of private investment had been leveraged in by £2 billion from the LDDC and £2 billion in transport infrastructure (ODPM 2004). But research commissioned by the Isle of Dogs Community Foundation (IDCF) concluded that the island remained an island of two halves, with advantage, wealth and great liveability sitting side by side with exclusion, alienation and squalor. The report argued that this amounted to a catastrophic failure in human and social terms (Inform Associates 1997: 4). Despite this, when the London Borough of Town Hamlets (LBTH) took over from the LDDC, initially it continued the same incrementalist approach to development.

The third wave can be categorised as a market-led process guided by opportunity rather than effective plan-making (Figure 12.2). Thus, the Canary Wharf masterplan was rapidly recast in the light of the new market context, whilst LBTH's 1998 adopted plan represented little more than a borough-wide development control manual.

Plate 12.3 Isle of Dogs: apartment developments, waves 3 and 4. An enclave on the Island's edge, and Millennium Quarter buildings appearing in advance of the public realm.

Wave 4: 2002 onwards

The fourth wave saw urban renaissance ideas begin to influence the area through the auspices of the new London Plan, where intensification and the pursuit of better design were significant themes. The permissive approach to commercial and residential development that this ushered in, alongside sustained economic growth from the mid-1990s onwards, marked a period of major development proposals spreading beyond the confines of the Canary Wharf estate, to areas in the centre of the Island (the Millennium Quarter). These developments look set to gradually sweep away the wave 1 suburban business park developments concentrated there.

A sequence of plans from LBTH latterly attempted to give some structure to both this area and to the island as a whole. These included the Millennium Quarter Masterplan (Figure 12.3), which has been partially successful in the former. However, the Isle of Dogs Area Action Plan looks likely to fail in the latter, having been thrown out by the Government Office for London, alongside the Local Development Framework (LDF) Core Strategy, for lacking any meaningful spatial vision.

Yet this has been a period of huge development on the island, during which a better mix of uses is being achieved as high-rise residential mega-schemes appear in the Millennium Quarter. Permissions for these and equally massive commercial developments in and around Canary

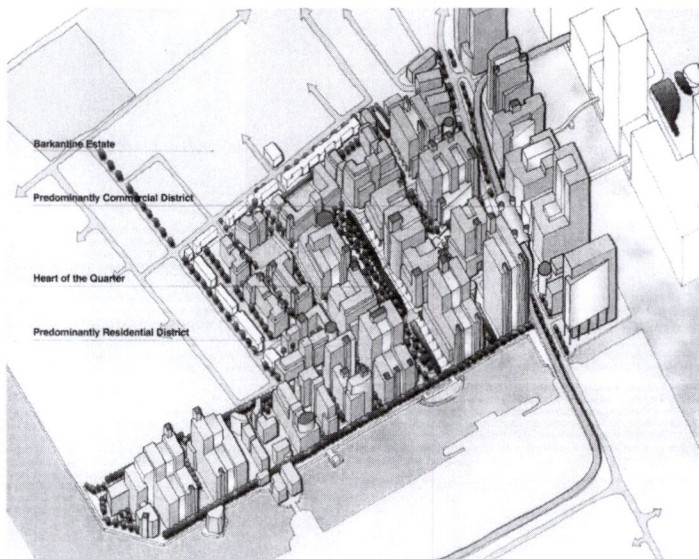

Figure 12.3 Isle of Dogs: Millenium Quarter masterplan (Courtesy London Borough of Tower Hamlets).

Wharf are being delivered with major planning gain packages attached. Through the auspices of the IDCF, these are supplementing continued direct public sector funding (e.g. £3.1 million Single Regeneration Budget funding) to deliver a range of social regeneration benefits.

With a huge pipeline of projects on the horizon, the potential to overcome the still obvious physical fragmentation of the island now also exists (see Figure 12.1d); although with the danger of perpetuating a network of private or pseudo-private landscapes (see Plate 12.3). The period nevertheless demonstrates (perhaps for the first time) a pragmatic planning that is balancing state and market agendas, informed by plan and opportunity combined.

What forms of planning have we seen?

Every sort

An immediate conclusion that can be drawn is that the recent history of the Isle of Dogs has been characterised by multiple and often overlapping forms of planning and associated development processes (see Figure 12.2). Taking Brindley *et al.*'s (1996) six styles of planning to illustrate this and beginning pre-LDDC, this was a period when public authorities aspired to emulate the dominant model of the post-war period, a form of direct public investment planning (in this case with pretensions at popular planning). Ultimately, however, in the absence of any actual public investment (or private market), the approach proved ineffective.

Somewhat perversely, the next period delivered the long-sought-after public investment at a time when a market model was outwardly being favoured. Thus, the LDDC administered a large dose of leverage planning (the use of public sector finance to stimulate investment in otherwise weak markets), which during the first wave was used almost in isolation as an effective (if expensive) means to stimulate a viable private market. Unfortunately, the fact that the area continues to suck in significant public sector funds today emphasises the failure of this investment to tackle the area's endemic social problems.

With the arrival of Canary Wharf, a new model of planning also arrived – private management planning. Since then the private sector has continued to shape and manage the northern part of the Island as Canary Wharf relentlessly expanded during the second, third and fourth waves. Although the closing of the second wave brought with it the demise of Olympia and York and a realisation about the limits of this model of planning, its continued existence ever since, as part of a more mixed planning landscape, can testify to its value in the eyes of blue-chip developer/investor organisations such as the Canary Wharf Group.

For the public sector, trend planning (a hands-off process, with planning seen as a means to better facilitate the actions of the market) has remained the dominant model throughout the LDDC and post-LDDC period. During the first wave the approach featured strongly alongside the leverage model as exemplified by the Isle of Dogs Development and Design Guide. It dominated the third wave, as practised first by the LDDC and almost without change by LBTH.

Regulatory planning (the view that, through regulation, development activity can be positively directed) has increasingly featured in the fourth wave as the confidence of LBTH to address the complex planning and design requirements of the Island has grown, and as the influence of the London Plan's design aspirations, have impacted on development (see below). Yet despite the growing importance of active regulation through development control, this continues to sit alongside a flexible trend-based process of plan-making. In a boom market, the model proved to be effective at delivering private, and increasingly – through planning gain – public goals.

Thus, although the period of the 1980s is often characterised as one of ad hoc, opportunistic and market-led planning, and the antithesis of the more design-led approaches later advocated by the Urban Task Force (UTF 1999a), it was also characterised by Olympia and York's concern to create a new 'place' in the sea of chaos as a means to safeguard its massive long-term investment. Alongside examples such as Broadgate in the City of London and Brindleyplace in Birmingham, the approach taken at Canary Wharf has spearheaded a move back to design-led development.

If the dominance of this model in the commercial development world is anything to go by then, over time, the experience has helped to convince receptive developers that another route to value creation is possible. As a by-product it has been an unheralded inspiration for the urban renaissance.

An indictment on plan-making?

For public sector planning, Edwards (1992: 19) has argued that what happened in the Isle of Dogs marked the end of two centuries of British town planning that began with the great Georgian estates and included the great civic achievements of the Victorians and the utopian social visions of post-war architects and planners (the remnants of whose philosophy could be traced in the plans of the DJC). For him, the assumption that urban development must serve a wider social or environmental purpose came to an end in the 1980s.

The experience on the Isle of Dogs clearly marked a major contrast with that in other major European cities during the 1980s and 1990s. Thus, when Paris was building its *grands projets*, Berlin was masterplanning the *Internationale Bauausstellung* (IBA), and Barcelona (the great urban renaissance exemplar) was planning its Olympic legacy, the Isle of Dogs never possessed a public sector plan that was both visionary and deliverable at the same time. Perhaps because of this there continues to be a failure to deliver anything more than unconnected segments of a high-quality public realm.

Despite this, there has been no shortage of planning if the twelve plans produced over this period (approximately one every three years) are anything to go by. But this plan-making has been largely ineffective. Instead, when plans have been prepared, they have either quickly and quietly been set aside as new developers have come along, demanding ever bigger buildings and more of the water area (Edwards 1992: 43); have failed to engage with the realities of the new Dockland's context; have been relegated to life as development control manuals; or have been overtaken by the process-driven imperatives of central government. This, arguably, represents an indictment on plan-making, just as what we see today represents a triumph of the market, and increasingly (in the absence of a coherent plan) of ad hoc discretionary development control, with every case seemingly judged on its merits. An un-answerable question therefore remains: with a more effective system of plan-making, might we have delivered so much more?

But guided incrementalism is working

Looking back at the period of the LDDC, Florio and Brownill (2000: 58–59) argue that the corporation's legacy can be seen in the role it played in breaking up the opposition to private investment in the inner cities, achieving flexibility in land and labour markets, and establishing a context in which public investment in the built environment now occurs only when it also suits the interests of the private sector. The cost was a growing realisation that property-led regeneration by itself could not solve all the problems of such localities and should occur instead as part of a social contract that would also invest in the social infrastructure. This partnership of interests reflects the neoliberal settlement that in the New Labour era has dominated British politics and which, if evidence from the fourth wave of development on the island is to be believed, is proving effective, combining as it does state and market objectives.

Through evaluating the sequence of ten monographs published by the LDDC in its final year, Florio and Brownill conclude that the LDDC was able to present its use of 'incremental opportunism' as part of a strategic approach to regeneration. They argue that, 'within today's planning world, it has become possible to be very open about practicing incremental opportunism while still maintaining that a strategy is being pursued' (Florio and Brownill 2000: 56). An evaluation by the National Audit Office (2007b: 24–27) broadly accepts the case, and includes Docklands amongst a range of European examples that have achieved a renaissance. They argue that the experience demonstrated clear and strong leadership around a shared vision not of a particular place that would be built, but instead of a brand that could be delivered if the marketing and fiscal incentives were right.

What is clear is that incremental opportunism largely remains the strategy adopted by both private and public actors in the area. In part this is likely to be a legacy of the weakened role of planning which has not had the skills and resources to command real change from a position of vision and power. The rejected LDF reflects this, combining very broad social and design aspirations with a flexibility borne out of a determination not to stifle market opportunism; the goose that (though planning gain) lays the golden eggs.

What role has design played in this?

To design or not to design?

For Hinsley and Malone (1996), although the failure of the early urban design visions for the Isle of Dogs can be put down in part to the antipathy of the LDDC to planning, it also represented a failure of urban design theory and practice. For them, the early urban designers were too concerned with the physical, formal and spatial issues of development, and with the ability of the public realm to provide a unifying framework for investment. As such, the proposals failed to give adequate weight to the pressures exerted by development interests, and 'missed opportunities to provide strategies for Docklands based, in greater measure, on planning, land-use and market criteria' (1996: 51–52).

An interesting perspective on this debate is offered by the LDDC's former principal architect, Charles Attwood (in Hinsley and Malone 1996: 52–53). Attwood argues that the conflict between urban designers and the LDDC revolved around a reluctance of designers to recognise that, in a location where no market exists, there is a need for an introductory development process in which planning is marginalised in favour of development interests. He concludes that a fully developed urban plan was never likely to provide the confidence that an incremental phase would offer as a means to build up momentum, and for the property market to determine an appropriate direction for the redevelopment process to take. For him, Canary Wharf marked the watershed and effectively provided the necessary direction.

Hinsley and Malone, by contrast, suggest that architects and urban designers were involved in the development process of the Isle of Dogs, but the results establish that their form-based preoccupations come up short as a basis for large-scale development. For them, it was the exclusion of planning (rather than design) that undermined the project, and this was manifest in the lack of a spatial framework and adequate public investment programme. As a result, when eventually development was attracted, it sat stranded as an 'island of international capitalism' (1996: 53–57).

Continuing the theme, Gospodini (2002: 61) quotes Harvey's (1989b) assertion that in the postmodern world there is no 'planning', only 'designing', something that resonates with the experience on the Isle of Dogs. Thus, in a context of growing volatility of capital and increasing competition amongst cities, long-term planning can be at odds with the flexibility required to attract investment. For Harvey, two options are possible. Either the responsible authorities need to be highly adaptable and fast-moving to respond to market shifts or they have to be able to mastermind the market shifts themselves by manipulating market tastes, opinions and needs in order to fit into a proposed design scheme. Arguably, the LDDC (initially at least) strongly favoured the first of these options, whilst Olympia and York, and latterly the Canary Wharf Group, have favoured the latter. LBTH today, in common with many planning authorities, makes noises about the latter, whilst actually (consciously or not) pursuing the former. None of these actors has taken a spatial (planning) approach seriously at any stage, although the masterplans of Olympia and York, and latterly LBTH in the Millennium Quarter, confirms that design is on the agenda.

The UTF made the case forcefully for such three-dimensional masterplans, yet over the thirty-five-year period covered by this chapter, the huge amount of development that has occurred on the island has not been guided by a coherent design vision. Thus, Reg Ward, the charismatic first Chief Executive of the LDDC, argued:

> what London Docklands is trying to do is to manage uncertainty. You do not manage it by creating artificial certainties within it, but by accepting the uncertainty by adopting an organic approach which enables one to respond to actuality . . . It is difficult, often uncomfortable but it is totally productive and rewarding in the results that can be achieved.
>
> (1987: 35)

Location, location, location . . . and design

As such, the approach adopted on the Isle of Dogs raises profound questions about the increasingly dominant mantra of governments. These are summed up by Gospodini, who argues that 'while for centuries the quality of the urban environment has been an outcome of economic growth of cities, nowadays the quality of urban space has become a prerequisite for the economic development of cities; and urban design has taken an enhanced new role as a means of economic development' (Gospodini 2002: 60). In the case of the Isle of Dogs, few would question that the truly transformative investment that became Canary Wharf was attracted without any significant urban design vision in place or a high-quality public realm in which to fit; or that the non-planned areas (initially the sites of so many design horrors) over time are gradually giving way to a more coherent urban landscape (see Figure 12.1d).

On the other hand, the Canary Wharf development under different ownerships has consistently pursued a strongly design-based strategy (like it or hate it), one that after the wave 2 crash and (critically) the injection of the necessary transport infrastructure, has recorded unparalleled success in attracting blue-chip footloose tenants. For Bell (2005) the overriding lesson from Canary Wharf has been that design can be used as a means to both create and protect value, by convincing investors and tenants of the merits of a scheme, and by creating quality that will deliver over the long term. Thus, for him, the masterplans that have been produced (even if endlessly modified thereafter) have (in contradiction to Reg Ward's assertion) been used as a means to provide the design and development certainty that, the UTF argued, major investment requires.

The conflicting evidence suggests that the old adage 'location, location, location' still holds true, and the genius of Reg Ward, Paul Reichmann (the original brains behind Canary Wharf – pre-Olympia and York), and others, was in recognising it. To what extent the experience of the island is transferable is therefore an open question, as few other locations have had such untapped locational potential, potential which has been enhanced in the case of Canary Wharf through the design-based strategy, but undermined elsewhere on the island (until recently) because of its absence. With hindsight and recent experience, perhaps the adage can now confidently be modified to 'location, location, location, and design' if, as Gordon (2001: 165) has argued, we should sit up and take notice 'when powerful private developers insist on imposing planning regulations upon themselves'. Again, it leads one to ask, could we have done better?

What outcomes have resulted from these processes?

Design quality

For some, the question 'Could we have done better?' is met by a firm 'yes'. Streetsweeper (2004) argues that few sites ever had so much going for them yet are so characterised by mediocrity. Others confirm the assessment. Ted Hollamby (1990: 12–15) (formally chief architect and planner for the LDDC) argued that the Docklands major asset, its waterscape, was largely ignored as a structuring devise, and, although large areas were preserved, they were done in such a way that they were unable to stamp their character on the new environment. Edwards (1992: 170) concludes that 'The myth that urban quality can be created by private sector developers enjoying unprecedented levels of design freedom should be finally buried by the example of the Isle of Dogs'.

But were these judgements made too soon? Although much remains to be built, or even given planning permission, the evidence from analysis of the fourth wave proposals suggests that, if built out, for the first time the island will begin to possess a continuous, connected urban fabric, and, with the arrival of Crossrail, an enviable public transport infrastructure (see Figure 12.1d). In addition, the area will finally be a major residential, as well as office, location; will benefit from a diversity of (pseudo-) public open and civic spaces; and will possess a unique urban form with a distinct identity, in both London and global terms. As such, although questions of sustainability have hardly featured in plans or debates about the Isle of Dogs, at least some environmental precepts are being met. Plans for the Millennium Quarter promise (on paper at least) to build on this.

A critical question remains, however, whether a high-quality public realm can be replicated in the Millennium Quarter where ownerships are fragmented and LBTH is responsible for coordination (alongside the Mayor of London, whose powers extend to the right to determine all developments over 15,000 square metres or thirty metres in height)? So far developments are contributing to the bigger vision of the Millennium Quarter Masterplan, although in a flexible manner that remains true to the spirit, if not the detail, of the plan. Thus, sites are coming forward in an uncoordinated manner, with no obvious respect for the phasing strategy; schemes are being built to a higher density with a higher plot coverage than envisaged; and some loss of intra-block permeability and use mix is apparent. Analysis of the Mayor's planning reports nevertheless consistently demonstrate a concern for design and that buildings should contribute to the delivery of high-quality animated public space. This strategic intervention has so far strongly reinforced the local drive for quality. Unfortunately, in this part of the island it is too early to assess the outcomes, particularly given the massive transformation that is currently under way (see Plate 12.3 and Figure 12.3).

Wider impacts

Beyond the island the impact is immediately tangible, if indirect, for example on the City of London. Despite unleashing the shackles of its conservation policy in the 1980s in order to deliver a more competitive context for new development (so rivalling and arguably undermining Canary Wharf; Gordon 2001: 153–155), the City has been able to retain a good part of its historic fabric as the pressure for expansion was funnelled elsewhere. Today, Peter Rees, the long-standing City chief planner, is sanguine about Canary Wharf, arguing that the area is now as much part of London as the West End, but with a different character to the City, and one that for him satisfies the short-term and temporary demand for large floorplates (Lemon 2008).

For HRH the Prince of Wales, a still influential voice in debates about the built environment in the UK, the location also represents a major opportunity to save the rest of the capital from what, to him, is the damaging impact of high buildings on the historic fabric: 'New skyscrapers should be built in Canary Wharf, rather than overshadowing Wren's and Hawksmoor's churches' (quoted in Carpenter 2008).

What is clear is that if London was to remain a global financial centre, then it needed to break free from the shackles of the Square Mile. The Isle of Dogs in many respects represented a logical and highly desirable location for this expansion to occur, and it is not surprising that the extent of this need, and the associated opportunity, was first recognised by the private sector, and only later accepted across the public sector, which today unquestioningly accepts the need for a third commercial pole for London. To some degree the conflation of the permissive enterprise culture of the LDDC, and the growing demands of the financial sector were a happy coincidence. The result (2.5 million square metres of commercial space; Gordon 2001: 164) has gone a long way to securing the future of London as a world financial capital. Yet, many commentators believe that in the short term the cost has been high: in social inequity, urban fragmentation, public subsidy and private economic catastrophe.

Has it trickled down?

But if the transformation of the Isle of Dogs has been in the interests of UK plc, has it also been in the interests of the local community? In other words, has trickle-down economics worked? The official government assessment of the regeneration gave the LDDC's time at the helm a clean bill of health, concluding that the amount of new social housing created was higher than would have been created without it, whilst a total of £110 million was spent on social and community development (half on education and training) across the Docklands during the corporation's life (ODPM 2004). Yet, indices of multiple deprivation compiled by government in 2007 demonstrate that LBTH retains the most deprived wards in London (four in the county's top 500; see www.communities.gov.uk), and that deprivation remains evenly spread across the borough, with pockets of severe deprivation in all areas. Drawing on the 2004 version of this work, and at the finer Super Output Area scale, LBTH itself has graphically demonstrated the proximity of very affluent areas on the Isle of Dogs with highly deprived areas, with deprivation focused on and around the island's council estates, which have remained largely untouched by social and economic regeneration (see www.towerhamlets.gov.uk).

Despite this, the community has gradually become less vociferous and more compliant with the changes. It may be that the historic working-class communities have become resigned to the change and weary of struggle, or that increasingly they have become outnumbered by the incomers to such a degree that the original voices can no longer be heard. For Merrifield, adopting Lefebvre's (1991) term, conflict has become 'inscribed' in Docklands space, particularly in the Isle of Dogs, where the landscape that has emerged represents, for him, a spatial inscription of social conflict, and of 'such variegated processes as changing international divisions of labour, the rise of financial capital, structural unemployment and deindustrialisation, shifting relations between central and local government in Britain, and outbreak of community resistance' (Lefebvre 1993: 1261). Alternatively, with 40 per cent of residents now working directly in the financial sector (across LBTH), it may simply be that most residents in one way or another are directly benefiting from the expansion of the sector in the area and no longer see any alternative.

Despite this, Hamnett (2003a: 244)concludes that 'there is little doubt that the redevelopment of Docklands and Canary Wharf has generated winners and losers and that most of the winners are not locals'. For him,

> this does not necessarily undermine the overall success of the venture. Its success needs to be measured in terms of the massive redevelopment of Docklands in a way which was almost unimaginable fifteen years ago . . . It is extremely doubtful that any of the alternative schemes being considered in the 1980s would have been anywhere near as successful.
>
> (ibid.)

Similarly, he argues that the manufacturing-based plans that were being considered in the 1970s were doomed to failure as manufacturing was in terminal decline, whilst what was required was an acceptance that employment growth in a post-industrial era would come from different sources.

The inevitable consequence was a different landscape on the Isle of Dogs, although one which could have paid far more regard to what was already there, in particular to the dire housing needs. He concludes:

> more affordable housing could and should be provided to ensure that the local residents and their children can remain in the area. They should not be reduced to the status of children with their noses pressed against the glass of the new sweet shop but unable to go in and buy.
>
> (ibid.: 245)

Yet, even this most intractable of problems is seeing progress. Thus, in 2005/2006, average residential development densities in LBTH far outstripped those across London at 486 units per hectare (up from 113 just five years earlier), helping to ensure that the borough contributed 2,734 new housing units in 2005/2006 (1,000 more than any other borough), of which 1126 were affordable (600 more than any other borough) and 44 per cent of the total (compared with 31 per cent London-wide) (Mayor of London 2007). With much of this development occurring or planned on the Isle of Dogs, the most recent wave of development is likely to have a significant impact on the social housing stock available to residents, at a time when the affordability of the market stock has climbed well out of reach of many: the average property price in early 2008 rose to a peak of £390,000 (www.upmystreet.com) and this is expected to increase again when the Crossrail effect begins to be felt (Thomas 2007).

On other fronts, work by the IDCF (2004) concluded that 80 per cent of children in Blackwall and 67 per cent in Millwall (the two Isle of Dogs wards) live in households with no or low incomes, that unemployment is more than three times the national average and that the perception of crime is high. Their analysis revealed that the influence of Canary Wharf has been profound in driving up the affluence of the area, so much so that the two island wards, alongside the city fringes, were the least deprived wards in the borough, and clearly outside of the most deprived 20 per cent of wards nationally. However, the high levels of affluence amongst incomers act to mask pockets of extreme deprivation 'which sit side by side with pockets of very significant wealth' (IDCF 2004: 3). Therefore, although the labour market and opportunities have grown, the 13,500 living in the island's social housing estates remain largely excluded from the surrounding economy, with particular disadvantage felt amongst Black and Minority Ethnic (BME) groups (ICDF 2004: 6).

Despite the very obvious physical changes on the island, and the less obvious but still steady social and economic programmes that in recent years have continued to funnel resources into the island's most deprived communities, the area retains the same essentially divided character that the LDDC was so criticised for perpetuating in the 1980s. Ten years after the demise of the LDDC, the gap between the haves and the have-nots on the Isle of Dogs remains larger than ever, although the physical environment of the estates, the availability of affordable units, and training opportunities have all improved. Trickle-down is working, but very slowly indeed.

Have we seen an urban renaissance?

The Isle of Dogs has certainly been physically regenerated, parts of it twice since the 1980s, but whether it has undergone a renaissance will depend on who you ask. If the test is whether

Plate 12.4 Isle of Dogs, still a place of contrasts: café culture comes to Millwall but not for 'the other half.'

developers are willing to invest and financial service sector companies and their workers are prepared to locate in the area, then clearly a renaissance has taken place. If the area has become a haven for cappuccino drinking and alfresco dining, continental style (Plate 12.4), then again, yes, a renaissance has occurred. But if it means that this new wealth and opportunity is being shared by all, and that all sections of society are now able to enjoy a coherent, connected and welcoming urban landscape, then change has occurred, but the Isle of Dogs still has some way to go to achieve a real civility.

Unpacking the urban renaissance

In unpacking New Labour's urban renaissance, Colomb identifies four key themes: the construction of a new urbanity, the concept of social mix as an engine for cohesion, strong local communities, and the idea of good urban design as a precursor to civility and citizenship (2007: 6). Unpacking what has occurred in the Isle of Dogs, one might conclude that, on the first count, a new urbanity has certainly emerged, both physically and, more significantly, in a willingness amongst investors to invest and homeowners to buy in the area. Thus, there has been a huge growth not only in employment, but also in the resident population, now approaching 30,000, up by over 50 per cent since 1991 (LBTH 2006: 14).

On the second count, at the macro scale there is certainly a much greater social mix than ever before, with the majority of incomers holding well-paid jobs and choosing to buy or rent from the burgeoning private rental market. Today, just one-third of homes are in the social rented sector, almost a complete reversal of the situation in the 1970s (IDCF 2004: 31), and new affordable housing is finally being provided, albeit often physically separated in less advantageous locations or sites than their private counterparts. Yet on the micro scale, communities remain starkly divided both physically and socially, and a mix at this level has not so far occurred.

On the third count, although strong long-established communities exist in many of the island's council estates, these sit side by side with the more transient and part-time residents occupying many of the new apartment blocks where a high level of second home ownership and churn is readily apparent. Butler, for example, in his analysis of middle-class gentrification in London, revealed that the typical occupants of the new residential developments felt that where they lived was largely a relationship born of convenience rather than commitment, and 'the attraction of Docklands was its lack of commitment' (Butler 2004a: 275). 'They did not wish to become integrated into their neighbourhoods, or become friendly with their neighbours; rather, they simply wanted 'efficient' living arrangements with minimal commitments' (ibid.: 278). The findings are confirmed by the experiences on the ground of the IDCF (2004: 36), which has reported great difficulty building community capacity in the area.

Finally, on the question of design, analysing the various plans that have signalled the coming and passing of successive phases of the Isle of Dogs experiment, it seems clear that a lack of planning from the very start of the regeneration process has been perpetuated in a lack of convincing plan-making (if not development control) throughout the process, even today. In a very real sense this has been and remains a market-led process, guided in large part by opportunity rather than planning. Even if the intention was that an initial period of market-building and incrementalism would establish a market, after which normal planning service would resume, this does not seem to have happened, at least not if normal planning implies planning based on a coherent public sector vision for the whole island.

Moreover, the initial period led to an incoherent landscape through the subjugation of urban design to market forces, and to a landscape that in many of its essentials is still with us today. As an early Isle of Dogs developer put it:

> the LDDC was Thatcher's instrument to give developers the chance to make money from locations that would otherwise have remained derelict. It worked, but ignored the fact that buildings remain for a long time. The result is a tribute to capitalism but a poor legacy for future generations.
>
> (Preston 1998: 42)

Nevertheless, recent improvements in and around the Canary Wharf estate, and potential improvements in the Millennium Quarter, where the new public realm has yet to emerge, bode well for a less fragmented and more coherent urban fabric in the future.

In assessing the impact of the wider English urban renaissance on the locality, undoubtedly the greatest impact has been in the acceptance once again of higher-density urban living on the basis of better urban design. This philosophy is firmly incorporated in the London Plan and in the emerging (if still problematic) LDF documents of LBTH. It is being delivered through development control processes at strategic and local scales, leading to a host of social benefits (via planning gain) and to the funding of the new public realm that is gradually emerging.

Too soon to judge

The evidence is therefore mixed on whether an urban renaissance has occurred, although undeniably the area has been transformed and now plays an indispensable part in London's global city role. Some sort of renaissance has therefore occurred, even if not of the type envisaged by the UTF some twenty-five years after the redevelopment process of the Isle of Dogs began. In essence, this has been a renaissance born of private initiative and public subsidy, and that once established has only gradually incorporated a more proactive, if as yet still hesitant, public sector contribution to charting its future. Thus, the multiple public sector plans that have been produced over the course of this regeneration have largely been ineffective as a means to establish a clear vision for its future, and have become effective only when the lessons of the highly effective private sector alternative were learnt. These lessons are that, in England today, for planning to succeed requires a clear physical vision (to guide economic and social objectives), sustained commitment to its delivery, and above all private sector buy-in, and thereby resources.

We may yet end up with a well-shaped and cohesive part of the city that has a part to play beyond the very obvious economic role that it currently performs. The high cost of office space in London (the highest in the world: Cheshire and Hilber 2007), the massive planned expansions now on site or on the drawing board, and the new determination of the public sector to shape this development in a more positive manner than in the immediate past all bode well.

But planning of this type needs one more thing to succeed: a buoyant economy. Therefore, as we move into a more uncertain global economic climate, one in which commentators such as George Soros are persuasively arguing that the super-boom of the last sixty years is finally coming to an end (see www.ft.com), and that the financial services on which the island's expansion has been predicated will be hit hardest, all future plans are in doubt. In regeneration of this scale, thirty-five years is still too soon to judge.

References

Bazlinton, C. (1998) Learning to Live Together, in London Docklands, The End of the Beginning. *Building*, March, Special Supplement: pp. 38–39.

Brindley, T., Rydin, Y., and Stoker, G. (1996) *Remaking Planning, The Politics of Urban Change* (2nd edn) (London: Routledge).

Buchanan, P. (1988) What City? Docklands. *The Architectural Review*, November: pp. 38–40.

Buchanan, P. (1989) Quays to Design. *The Architectural Review*, April: pp. 39–42.

Carmona, M. (2009) The Isle of Dogs: Four Development Waves, Five Planning Models, Twelve Plans, Thirty Five Years, and a Renaissance . . . of Sorts. *Progress in Planning* 71 (3): 87–151.

Carpenter, J. (2008) Skyscrapers are a Risk, Says Prince. *Regeneration & Renewal*, 8 February: p. 3.

Cheshire, P. and Hilber, C. (2007) *Office Space Supply Restrictions in Britain: The Political Economy of Market Revenge*, paper presented to the European Real Estate Society Conference, 28 June, London, City University.

Edwards, B. (1992) *London Docklands: Urban Design in an Age of Deregulation* (Oxford: Butterworth Architecture).

Florio, S. and Brownill, S. (2000) Whatever Happened to Criticism? Interpreting the London Docklands Development Corporation's Obituary. *City*, 4 (1): 53–64.

Gordon, D. (2001) The Resurrection of Canary Wharf. *Planning Theory and Practice*, 2 (2): 149–168.

Hinsley, H. and Malone, P. (1996) London: Planning and Design in Docklands. In P. Malone (ed.) *City, Capital and Water*, (London: Routledge).

Hollamby, T. (1990) Docklands, *London's Backyard into Front Yard* (London: Docklands Forum).

Inform Associates (1997) *Responding to Need in the Isle of Dogs, an Agenda for Action* London (Isle of Dogs Community Foundation).

IDCF (Isle of Dogs Community Foundation) (2004) *Regenerating the Isle of Dogs, Update 2004* (London: IDCF).

Kochan, B. (1998) UDCs Hand Over the Regeneration Baton. *Urban Environment Today,* Issue 42, 2 April: pp. 8–9.

LBTH (London Borough of Tower Hamlets) (2006) *Local Development Framework, London Borough of Tower Hamlets Development Plan Document, Isle of Dogs Area Action Plan, Submission Document* (London: LBTH).

Lefebvre, H. (1991) *The Production of Space* (Oxford: Basil Blackwell).

Lemon, R. (2008) An Interview with Peter Rees. *London Calling, The Journal of the London Region of the RTPI,* April: pp. 1–2.

Mayor of London (2004) *The London Plan: Spatial Development Strategy for Greater London* (London: Greater London Authority).

Mayor of London (2007) *London Plan Annual Monitoring Report 3* (London: Greater London Authority).

Mayor of London (2008) *The London Plan: Spatial Development Strategy for Greater London Consolidated with Alterations Since 2004* (London: Greater London Authority).

Merrifield, A. (1993) The Canary Wharf Debacle: From 'TINA' – There is No Alternative – to 'THEMBA' – There Must be an Alternative. *Environment and Planning A,* 25: 1247–1265.

ODPM (Office for the Deputy Prime Minister) (2004) *Regenerating London Docklands* (London: ODPM).

Preston, B. (1998) No Limits: A Developer's Dream, in London Docklands, The End of the Beginning. *Building,* March, Special Supplement.

Streetsweeper (2004) The Isle of Mediocrities. *Urban Design International,* 9: p. 171.

Thomas, M. (2007) Crashing in on the 'Crossrail Effect'. *The Docklands,* 24 October: p. 1.

Ward, R. (1987) View from the Top. *Building Design,* 19 June: pp. 34–35

13 The Thames Gateway
Alive and well?

Lora Nicolaou and Sarah Chaplin

Introduction

The subject of this chapter differs from other contributions focusing on recognised urban entities, in that it deals with a place that is a political construction rather than a physical reality. We are also dealing with a place that has yet to undergo its own urban renaissance, and may not necessarily achieve this end as a total project. The Thames Gateway therefore needs to be contextualised rather differently, as a plan rather than as a place. Moreover, there has been, and continues to be, considerable political will to bring the plan into existence and to champion it as an urban renaissance success story.

In this chapter we will attempt to tell the story so far, and in the process make sense of the complex interwoven arguments for and against the Thames Gateway. We will review the issues faced at national strategic policy-making level through to local delivery, and then consider the prospect for the realisation of the Thames Gateway in the light of recent changes in the UK economy. The chapter will question the notion of the gateway as one place, and how far it is likely to acquire this identity in future. Part of this narrative also requires a discussion as to how and why the Thames Gateway agenda has changed over time, what issues remain unresolved and why, in our view, the focus needs to shift still further.

Over the main period that this chapter covers, our research within the Urban Renaissance Institute (URI) has interfaced closely with the development of the Thames Gateway, particularly in terms of Medway's urban renaissance. URI was part of the SEEDA-funded (South East England Development Agency) project to use outward-facing higher education providers as a key regenerating agent in Chatham, where we have our offices. We have also consulted on energy strategies and workspace capacities within Kent and Essex, which has given us an insight into both the conceptual scope and practical limitations of the Thames Gateway. We were part of a consortium of organisations that bid in 2007 to become the Thames Gateway Institute for the Urban Renaissance, a project that has since been shelved. URI worked with EEDA (East of England Development Agency) to deliver a learning laboratory, and, as part of the University of Greenwich, we have also done work in relation to Greenwich's status as one of the host boroughs for the London 2012 Olympics. Most recently, the Thames Gateway has provided us with a useful context in which to test the notion of strategic urban design, as part of a major piece of work we were asked to carry out for the Commission for Architecture and the Built Environment (CABE).

From corridor to gateway

Ostensibly covering an area of 80,000 hectares, and a distance of roughly sixty kilometres from east to west, stretching from Stratford and Greenwich to Southend and Sheppey, and extending thirty kilometres from north to south, the Thames Gateway has an existing population of 1.6 million, occupying approximately 700,000 households (Figure 13.1). It is an area that has been continuously occupied since pre-history, and since Roman times has played a pivotal role in the development of London as a global port and trading capital.

The inception of the Thames Gateway is invariably attributed to an article by Martin Simmons published in *The Planner* in 1987, in which the author speculated about the future growth potential of the south-east of England once the Channel Tunnel route became established. This idea of treating a high-speed rail corridor as a means to open up a new area for economic development was one that Michael Heseltine adopted when he was made Secretary of State for the Environment in 1991. Heseltine then appointed Sir Peter Hall to be his special advisor on strategic planning and commissioned consultants Llewellyn-Davies to carry out a study of the area's development capacity. Their report was published in 1993, confirming the potential of an East Thames Corridor. The report also made it clear that 'for this to be realised, there needed to be a coherent overall framework for the area and arrangements to ensure that efforts to promote its economic and environmental improvement are properly co-coordinated'. Without such an approach, the report warned that 'past patterns of piecemeal development would be repeated', and that, if so, 'the full scale of the opportunity would not be realised' (Llewelyn-Davies 2006).

Initially, the East Thames Corridor was seen simply as a development eastwards, following the success of London Docklands in the 1980s, and taking in Kent and Essex along the river estuary. Cohen and Rustin (2008a), in their book *London's Turning*, see this as a sea change in emphasis, from the affluent west to the impoverished and neglected east. As an expanded riverside site, it was capable of delivering 'a combination of brown-field and green-field development rather than pure urban regeneration' and would draw on the benefits of its easy access to Europe as well as to London. The National Audit Office confirmed that the area has 3,150 hectares of brownfield

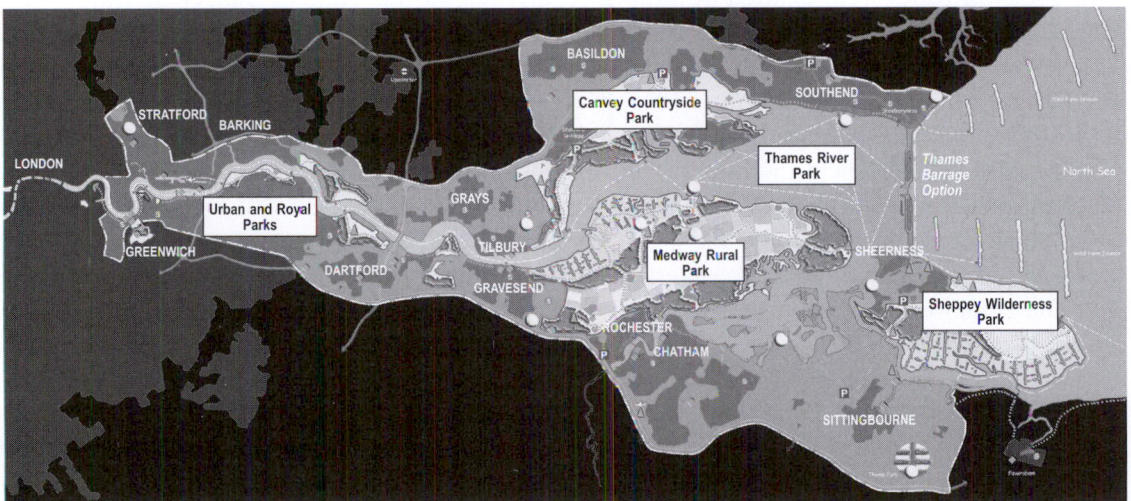

Figure 13.1 Thames Gateway: Parklands Concept (Courtesy Farrells) © Crown Copyright. All rights reserved. Licence number 100049043.

land, representing 17 per cent of the total within the south-east region (NAO 2006). Whilst the notion of a development corridor persisted, ambitions were sensibly confined to a narrow swathe of land, and a ribbon of ongoing development was envisaged. However, when the Department of Environment set up an internal task force to oversee the development of the East Thames Corridor as an area-based strategy, it enlarged the scope and renamed the project 'The Thames Gateway plan for sustainable communities' in 1994.

Where the river itself was concerned, the expansion east of London had already been occurring, in any case, as a natural consequence of the increasing size of commercial vessels needing to dock. In the post-war period, London's upper docks began to close, and new container and passenger ports were built further downstream at Grays, Sheerness and Tilbury, all controlled by the Port of London Authority. By 1981, 150,000 port-related jobs had been lost in London's former docks. The Conservative government established the London Docklands Development Corporation (LDCC) to redevelop the docks into a new banking and finance hub, which served to counter the effects of this decline (albeit addressing itself to a totally different workforce) and enabled the new light rail infrastructure to be built, thereby stimulating new forms of employment and economic activity in the east end of London. Meanwhile, the Port of London, which controls the full ninety-five kilometres of the tidal Thames, moved its focus eastwards, and today supports more than seventy independently owned terminals, employing 35,000 people and contributing £3.5 billion to the economy every year.

Whilst there is a strong sense of historic continuity in the notion of the Thames as a 'gateway', harking back to a time when this would have been quite literally the portal through which all traffic from overseas arrived, the subsequent development of other radial routes into London means that there is now no palpable sense of coherence regionally between Kent and Essex, despite the construction of many tunnels and bridges. Any sense of adjacency experienced by those living and working on opposite sides of the Thames estuary is likely to be limited to visits to their shopping centres: Lakeside at Thurrock and Bluewater at Erith. The River Thames, then, remains more of a boundary than a conduit and is, moreover, one that exponents of the Thames Gateway have yet to adequately overcome, either perceptually or physically. Just as Anglo-Saxon tribes were defined in terms of which side of the Thames they came from, when the English counties were established, the River Thames was the natural boundary that gave Essex, Kent, Middlesex, and other counties further upstream, their county borders. Thus whilst the River Thames itself represents a gateway, the application of the term 'gateway' to apply to a wider regional spatial territory is more problematic to sustain.

This basic geographical disconnect between north and south has given rise to one of the central problems of the Thames Gateway: if it is difficult to conceptualise, it is difficult to endow it with a strong sense of purpose and a core agenda. The area consists of fragmented zones each vying with each other to do business, especially those focusing around environmental technologies and shipping. The Thames Gateway is a heroic appellation for the 'backyard' of London, where the 'spreading out' of the corridor into a wider territory was a political indication that, at least conceptually, a more inclusively defined and progressive project could be staked. The notion of a 'gateway', seen in this light, takes on the sense of a threshold through which the future is to be ushered. It is a territory which could easily be staked, because, at least in terms of levels of affluence, there is less to be lost. Seen another way, as Cohen and Rustin suggest, the heroic ambition of the Thames Gateway to transform the prospects of the region, and not least those communities left behind by the advent of the new economy, is to be translated into social fact on the ground. With so much at stake we cannot afford to fail.

(2008a: 5)

From planning framework to delivery plan

As the Thames Gateway gathered political momentum, the need to formally articulate a strategic overview grew. 1995 saw the publication of *The Thames Gateway Planning Framework* (DoE 1995), which promised to address the steep decline that the area had been experiencing, and acknowledged the fact that 'traditional industries employ far fewer people, or have left the area, leaving unemployment in their wake'. Parts of Thames Gateway's environment show the legacy of past carelessness with damaged land, breakers' yards and overhead power lines. The framework enshrined five core objectives, which were (DoE 1995):

- to improve economic performance, enhancing London's position as a major world and European city;
- to maximize the opportunities for new economic activity and jobs, created by the improving transport connections to continental Europe;
- to work with the market, building on existing economic and community strengths, reinforcing the economic base, and at the same time attracting new economic investment, strengthening existing communities as well as attracting new residents;
- to encourage a sustainable pattern of development, optimising the use of existing and proposed infrastructure and making the fullest possible use of the many vacant, derelict and underused sites which previously supported other activities;
- to safeguard and enhance natural and man-made environmental assets and, where necessary, raise the quality of the local environment; to encourage the highest quality in the design, layout and appearance of new developments .

At the time of its publication, as well as acknowledging that the regeneration and development of Thames Gateway was a long-term, market-led project, stretching for twenty or thirty years into the future, the *Planning Framework* made much of the early wins for the Thames Gateway:

The Thames Gateway . . . has got off to a promising start. Government policies are giving full weight to the area's needs. Swale and the London riverside have gained Assisted Area status, attracting grants to assist job-related investment. Thames Gateway is a priority for English Partnerships, the new agency for regeneration, which can help in restoring derelict land. £8m at Barking Reach is its first major investment. The very first bidding round for the Government's Single Regeneration Budget Challenge Fund produced £54m of Government money for Thames Gateway, levering in a total of £227m towards regeneration projects.

(DoE 1995)

At around the same time, the new regional development agencies came into effect in England, and were given devolved responsibilities to ensure that targets were set for *subregional* development that would deliver to central government agendas, especially with regard to inward investment. The Thames Gateway, straddling the jurisdictions of three regional development agencies – LDA (London Development Agency), EEDA and SEEDA – faced a tall order in making the many different cross-regional partnerships, consortia and forums work, even before any actual development started to take place. These included strategic bodies such as North Kent Success and the Thames Gateway London Regeneration Partnership, as well as area bodies such as the Greenwich Waterfront and Kent Thameside development partnerships. There were many overlapping objectives and agendas with little clarity as to the structure of any overall administrative framework (Figure 13.2). Progress was therefore cautious and slow, in no small part due to the inevitable bureaucracy, conflicting regional policies and priorities, and inadequate coordination of effort.

This is not to say that there was a lack of broad multiparty political support for the Thames Gateway's emergence as the right move for the south-east. It was simply that views on how the project was to be managed and views on the quality of what was planned proved extremely divergent, with much high-profile rhetoric masking the high turnover of senior executives involved, and considerable expenditure on capacity studies and environmental impact assessments, to try to determine which assumptions would prove reliable in the short, medium and long term. Whatever their differences of opinion, all parties involved were conscious that within the Thames Gateway there were still those 3,000 hectares of brownfield land, all ripe for development. Matching this abundance of suitable land, the government set its initial targets high: 120,000 new homes and 180,000 new jobs by 2016. There were supposed to have been 70,000 homes delivered by 2006. It is unclear how these figures were arrived at, as the density and

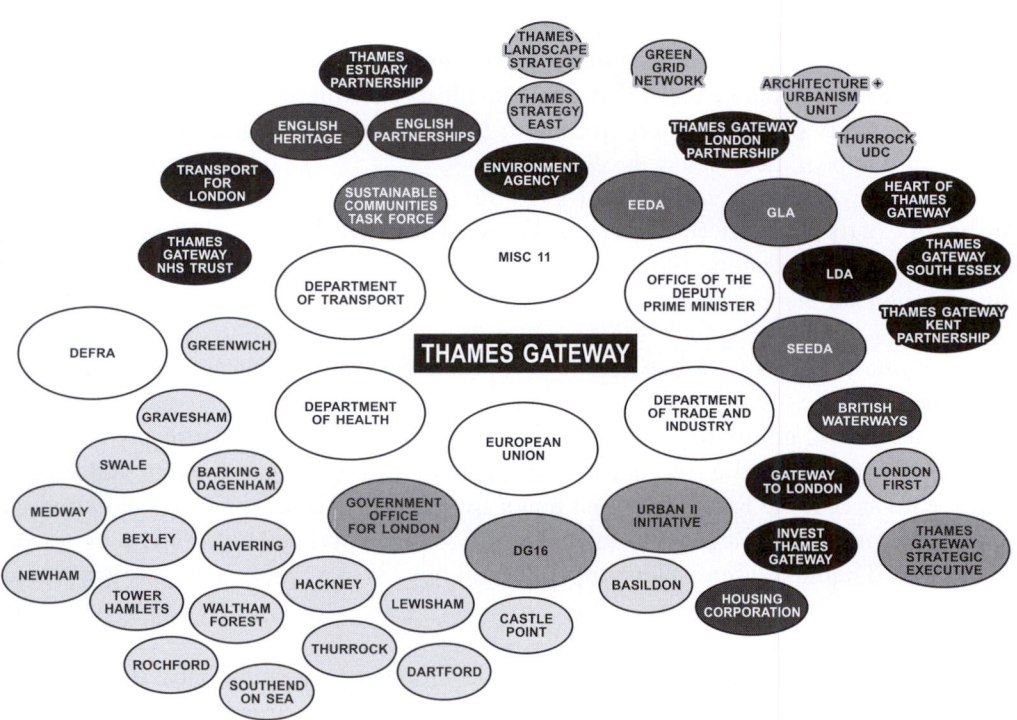

Figure 13.2 Thames Gateway: Multiple Agencies involved in delivery (Courtesy Farrells).

capacity assumptions that lay behind the figures were not disclosed, nor were the specific job sectors to be targeted.

One might infer from the fact that the 2016 milestone is aligned with government directives that all new homes are to be zero carbon by 2016, but these figures were always overambitious. The Campaign to Protect Rural England (CPRE), in its 2006 report, *Compact Sustainable Communities*, commented that:

> Under the 2003 Sustainable Communities Plan, the Government has a target for 120,000 additional dwellings in the Thames Gateway from 2003 to 2016. However, this target was based essentially on the (then) current and planned transport infrastructure capacity limits, rather than on the likely availability of land. It is highly unlikely that the figure represents the true capacity of the Thames Gateway to accommodate new housing in urban areas and there is therefore a danger that the 120,000 figure will be translated into less than optimal density requirements on a site-by-site basis.
>
> (CPRE 2006: 24)

There were certainly no clear indications of need deriving from demographic figures on the Thames Gateway. However, much of the early debate following the announcement of these targets focused not on the actual quantum of development proposed, but on the appropriateness of the location, with insurers in particular criticising the idea of so much housing being built on such a low-lying area with a very high flood risk. The possibility of houses being uninsurable was an early hurdle that the government had to overcome.

Responding to the insurance issue, which was in part a product of new research on rising sea levels as a result of climate change, in 2004 the Environment Agency commissioned some capacity studies of its own, producing strategic flood risk assessments (SRFAs) for the Thames Gateway (Environment Agency 2004). The predictive flood maps that were produced indicated the speed and depth of floodwater, and enabled sites to be categorised into hazard ratings, making it much easier for a planning authority to make appropriate decisions. Once the notion of planned flooding in certain areas was proposed, a degree of resilience was restored, which proved enough for the insurance issue to be discounted. The Thames Gateway's claim to being 'strategically positioned', with excellent infrastructural opportunities and potential to attract inward investment on London's doorstep, was then reasserted.

Inevitably, delivery rates on the housing front slowed while flood risk management continued to be an issue. Roger Tym & Partners was commissioned to produce a report for the government in 2000, suggesting a need for improved delivery mechanisms and quicker implementation within the Thames Gateway area. As a result, the Thames Gateway Strategic Partnership was created later that year, with a remit to engender development and solve delivery issues collaboratively.

It was not until November 2007, in many ways a turbulent moment in the history of the Thames Gateway as behind the scenes its chief executive Judith Armitt was in the process of being replaced, that Gordon Brown unveiled the Thames Gateway Delivery Plan and finally declared that a budget of £9 billion was earmarked for building sustainable communities in the Thames Gateway. With the stakes raised, so too were the targets: now instead of 120,000 homes it was 160,000, and 225,000 jobs were now to be created instead of 180,000. Whilst some definite sites were identified for this activity, there was still a lack of detailed information about the desired housing mix and employment sectors. Penny Bernstock has noted that, to date, 'a reliance on the market to deliver housing across the Thames Gateway is leading to a mismatch between the type of housing delivered and the type of housing that is needed' (Bernstock 2008: 185; Figure 13.3). Now that we are facing a different economic era, the matching of supply and demand is likely to be closer, albeit much more cautiously progressed.

From precedents to prescience

As the Thames Gateway proposals took shape, successive governments and their quangos (quasi non-governmental organisations) have looked to a range of precedents from which to draw inspiration and to learn the lessons of others' experiences. On the one hand, there are the kind of dispersed, peri-urban developments that have created a highly effective networked landscape beyond the boundaries of a major urban centre, such as has taken place in the Randstad in Holland, and between Copenhagen and Malmo in Scandinavia. On the other, there were examples of large-scale reinvention of former industrial landscapes such as Emscher Landschaftspark in Germany. Projects that are often cited as regeneration comparators in terms of the delivery of significant physical change often neglect to highlight certain unique conditions behind each project, and it is these conditions that render them more or less relevant to the Thames Gateway. What has tended to be highlighted are the comprehensiveness of approach in the case of the Randstad, the need for proximity to key nodes of economic activity in Sweden, and central funding with local delivery in the case of Emscher Landschaftspark.

With the Randstad, the government owned almost all the land, and was able to achieve an impressive rate of delivery: 400,000 homes in the space of ten years. It was able to subsidise flagship developments with revenue earned from other less prominent and lower density development. Randstad, under the umbrella of the Phoenix project in the 1990s, represents a truly integrated regional development programme, with sites properly identified upfront, and funding for infrastructure available and in place when it was needed. In hindsight, some regrets have been expressed with regard to design and density decisions, and the quantity of housing that was realised, but on the whole the model worked (OECD 2007). Its relevance, however, for

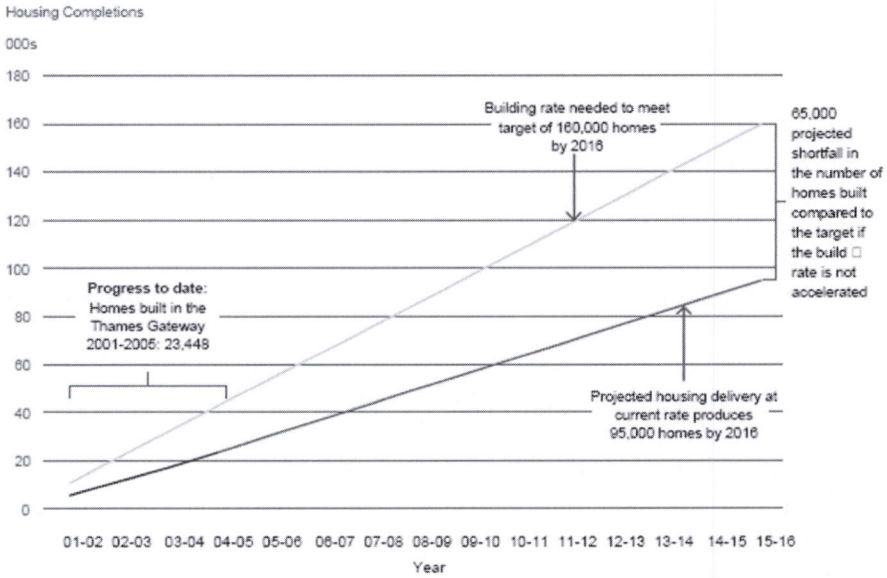

Figure 13.3 Thames Gateway: Housing delivery shortfall as of 2006 (Courtesy National Audit Office).

Thames Gateway is limited: very little land is publicly owned, many sites have yet to be prepared, consents have not been sought and funding is uncertain.

Copenhagen has meanwhile slowly developed the supraregional identity of the Øresund, incorporating Malmo in southern Sweden, and locking the two cities ever more closely together to form a major European centre. Here a stretch of water separating two countries was successfully bridged, and the two cities function virtually as one. Can't the Thames Gateway achieve something similar, binding together its north and south shores? One issue here is that, unlike Copenhagen, relative to the capital, the Thames Gateway was not the only development axis for London to consider, and it did not have a significant urban magnet at the other end of the axis. Development towards Milton Keynes – itself a previous urban growth strategy to take the pressure off London – along an axis containing Corby and Northampton is more likely to succeed in this way. Similarly, development towards Cambridge, with London Stansted Airport en route, produces a more focused programme of development in a corridor to the north-east of London (DCLG 2008b).

Emscher Landschaftspark, as a precedent, appears to have more to teach the Thames Gateway, occupying an area of a similar size in a highly post-industrial part of the Ruhr (see Plate 13.1). Here, the IBA, which advised on strategy and coordinated the accumulation of funding for Emscher Landschaftspark, did not in fact have a delivery responsibility. One fact that is regularly overlooked in relation to this precedent, however, is that the success of the programme was due to the mobilisation of local governments and organisations, which were directly responsible for delivery, a situation which is not replicated in the Thames Gateway.

Other comparators offer compelling legacy stories of previous Olympic and other global event host cities, such as Sydney, Barcelona and Manchester, but the reach of such legacies would be unlikely to affect the whole of the Thames Gateway. Any such benefits (or disbenefits) will be confined to the western end of the region. Nevertheless, the lessons learned here are profound: many global events leave behind a trail of debt and unsustainable or, worse, unusable infrastructure, and the task for the Thames Gateway is to be sanguine and to some extent prescient about the impact of the Olympics. It would be instructive to focus on precedents to do with process

Plate 13.1 Emscher Landschaftspark, Germany (Courtesy Dysturb images).

rather than product, and to look to examplars of leaders who in taking decisions and exerting influence over their development have displayed a remarkable degree of prescience in their own right about future market conditions.

From wasteland to parkland

The Thames Gateway survived the transition from John Major's last term in office to New Labour, but it remained in many ways a weakly articulated intellectual construct. The media was fond of caricaturing the Thames Gateway in the late 1990s as somewhere senior decision-makers had heard of but had never had cause to visit: Jonathan Glancey once described the area as a kind of 'cockney Siberia' full of 'eels and yellowhammers' (Glancey 2003). Tony Blair and John Prescott visited the region only by helicopter.

Lacking a cogent mindset or a clearly articulated official vision, it took the private ruminations of one individual architect, Sir Terry Farrell, to mobilise a single big idea capable of sustaining momentum until delivery started to take place in earnest. Farrell, who claims London to be his 'hobby', produced in *The Architectural Review* a series of provocative and far-sighted ideas with which to tackle London's problems, on both a macro and a micro scale (Farrell 2007). Farrell conceived the Thames Gateway as a new national park, and made a series of propositions for the latent capacities of the Thames Gateway. Unusually, this work was conducted on an entirely voluntary basis, and constituted for Farrell an aspirational vision. Offsetting any ideas that the Thames Gateway was merely a large expanse of underdeveloped land that could be cheaply built out at very low densities, Terry Farrell's visual propositions showed that 90 per cent of the required development could be met with a relatively tiny land take. This left only 10 per cent of the development to be accommodated in the rest of the area, which Farrell therefore envisaged as a vast amenity space, a lush and contiguous terrain.

The arguments for allocating land east of London as the right space to put houses were made largely on the grounds of its plentiful supply of brownfield land. However, the cartographic task of visualising the Thames Gateway as a post-brownfield place simultaneously required a degree of 'greenwash'. By applying the same light-green tone across the piece, extending from the outer east London boroughs to the sea, Farrell's new vision unified and rationalised the Thames Gateway in a new way, and made it seem attractive regardless of whether or not physical development took place. Here was the opportunity, he said, to create a massive amenity space for London, where biodiversity that has largely arisen due to neglect of the land can be brought under management, turning the vast areas of marshland into an attractive leisure resource (see Plate 13.2). Cartographically, the application of a continuous green tone across the Thames Gateway serves to recuperate the land as part of a vast rural rehabilitation project, a proposition that proved deeply attractive with the environmental lobby.

Over the next two years, Farrell's vision for the Thames Gateway gained influence. Asked to review his proposal, CABE's Design Review Panel convened in June 2005 and signalled its support for Terry Farrell and Partners' proposals, in particular that the Thames Gateway be promoted as a conceptual framework for a new national park. The panel admitted it was a proposal that lay outside its usual design review parameters, but welcomed the 'big picture' approach as well as the notion that 90 per cent of housing need could be concentrated in the area nearest to London as high-density suburban development. In the review, there are, however, a number of cautionary comments about the Thames Gateway representing a 'clientless' scheme with 'no single driving force'. CABE also registered that social issues had been somewhat 'downplayed' (CABE 2005).

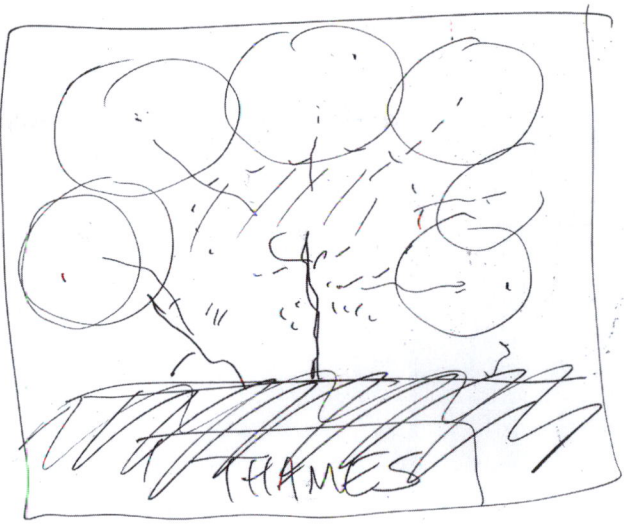

Plate 13.2 Thames Gateway: Sir Terry Farrell's initial sketch for Thames Gateway Parklands (Courtesy Farrells).

Despite having some reservations, CABE continued to give the Thames Gateway positive support, and in 2006 published *Making New Things Happen*, taking a bundle of top-down policy initiatives and channelling them through the Thames Gateway proposition. The publication set out some key precepts that CABE felt the Gateway had the potential to address, namely, redefine work, reconnect with nature, reassert individualism and reinvent identity. CABE's chair, John Sorrell, described the Thames Gateway in this document as a 'pioneering culture', describing it as 'less like a place and more like a journey' (CABE 2006: 6). These pronouncements were not received with uniform levels of commitment, however, and different locations within the Thames Gateway found these 'common themes' less relevant, and in some instances an imposition, which was difficult to accommodate constructively at the delivery end.

Lord Rogers was vocal in his support for Farrell's original vision, claiming that 'it is not only the best idea for the Thames Gateway, it is the only idea'. Significantly, the argument for Thames Gateway as the new national park for London was made on the basis that it made sense in terms of climate change: not only would it give Londoners access to open space and fresh air, but it would also serve to make them less vulnerable to rising flood levels and other effects of global warming. However, the complex issues of land assembly and the subsequent cost of managing such an environment, with its planned flood capacities, were glossed over in a sequence of attractive leisure images.

In the wake of Farrell's timely interventions, by November 2007 the Thames Gateway was effectively rebranded an 'eco-region' by Yvette Cooper, the then housing minister, raising expectations that the area would not just become developed, but would be developed in an exemplary manner. Following through on this renewed commitment to the Thames Gateway, the government then published its *Prospectus for the Thames Gateway as an Eco-region* in November 2008. The headline text makes reference to the need for a 'coherent vision' in responding to the 'specific environmental opportunities' that exist in the Thames Gateway, and claims to describe 'the first steps' of realising the vision. These included a woefully inadequate £35 million being set aside to 'support' the Parklands Vision, commitment for setting up an Institute for Sustainability

Plate 13.3 Thames Gateway: Greenwich Millennium Village, Greenwich Peninsula (Courtesy Farrells).

in the Thames Gateway (replacing the earlier idea of a Thames Gateway Institute for the Urban Renaissance), and other funds aimed at tackling issues of renewable energy and district heating schemes, amongst others. It was a weak offer, despite much plugging of current government imperatives. There were no sticks or sanctions, no special zones were designated, no specific invitations were issued to developers and investors, insufficient funds were committed, and 'moving forward' became an overused phrase.

In June 2008, CABE published its booklet *Thames Gateway Parkland* (2008), with landscape character studies and a reliance on greening, in the hope that the Thames Gateway would be able to retain its attractiveness to investors even in a rapidly cooling market. The Thames Gateway has effectively moved from being sold on the basis of an argument for a much-needed resilient stock of floodable green space, to a way of tackling the proliferation of health problems associated with sedentary lifestyles: here was the means to promote development with a healthier lifestyle concept.

Having reviewed the main trajectories that together characterise the 'story so far' of the Thames Gateway, there are a number of pertinent questions that need to be addressed, in order to gain more insight into some of the delivery issues that are now being faced.

Who is going to live there?

As somewhere to live, the Thames Gateway offers patches of low-lying low-density rural and suburban development, clustered around historic urban centres and coastal functions. Many who have chosen to live in south Essex and north Kent do so because the housing is cheaper and more plentiful than it is in central London, and they must commute to their places of employment. For some categories of cultural producers, the creative classes, there are a few locations, such as Whitstable in Kent and Leigh on Sea in Essex, which can offer the prospect of a high quality of life that is not dependent on the long commute into London. Promoting the enhancement of other such places in the Thames Gateway, with the potential to become as attractive to the UK's cultural producers, should play an important part in current thinking. That said, the task of turning the many small centres within the Thames Gateway into truly self-sufficient places, where people can live and work, is much more difficult to achieve, and may therefore remain an unfulfilled long-term goal.

Conversely, if the Thames Gateway is to fulfil its latest expectations to become an eco-region, delivering commuter homes must come low down on the list of priorities, as unsustainable on all counts. In the short term, the truth is that the Thames Gateway will be home to many lower-paid key workers, leading highly compromised existences, with long hours spent travelling to their place of employment. Targeting this group has not characteristically been a priority for the volume house builders, who are already reneging on some of their commitments to deliver their 40 per cent of affordable housing typically within any given scheme.

Barking Riverside (see Plate 13.4) is one area where the reality of the Thames Gateway is currently being put to the test. Billed as 'a milestone' in *Regeneration and Renewal* magazine, plans were submitted in January 2009 for the first 4,000 homes and district and local centres, which include two new schools and much needed local transport improvements. This is a joint venture between the new Homes and Communities Agency and Bellway Homes, and is the second largest growth point in the overall Thames Gateway growth area: 26,000 people are expected to be living in Barking Riverside by 2031, with 45 per cent of the homes being aimed at families. This seemingly well-founded agenda is not without its political machinations, however. Michael Keith reminds us that 'The British National Party (BNP) campaigned against the Gateway development, against development in and migration to the borough, and against the development of Barking Riverside'. Keith thus believes that 'Barking Riverside provides a litmus test for the interplay of models of city change and London's new multiculture', not least because

> for many existing inhabitants in the borough (of Barking and Dagenham) the Thames Gateway experience thus far has been 'all pain/no gain'. There have been increased pressures on public services and housing – with insufficient new affordable housing in either the private or the public domain, and new jobs which many locals cannot access. Nevertheless, Barking has one of the lowest social housing waiting lists in London, and this 'offers the opportunity to grow the stock for the first time in two decades'.
>
> (Keith 2008: 3.11)

Plate 13.4 Thames Gateway: Visualisation of Barking Riverside (Courtesy squint/opera)

Who is footing the bill?

Despite the bewildering plethora of public and statutory bodies involved in the delivery of the Thames Gateway, there are still relatively few financial instruments at their disposal to even begin to coordinate the kind of building programme that is needed if targets are to be addressed. Where land is already publicly owned, progress can be made, and where Section 106 agreements can be reached with private developers other infrastructure costs can be met. Given the lack of availability of credit in any large quantities for the foreseeable future, the new Homes and Communities Agency will have to confront some difficult decisions in the next couple of years as the government faces the real prospect of little or no development in the Thames Gateway. As one academic from the London School of Economics has observed, 'funds have to be brought together in complex packages where timing can be of the essence and much depends on expectations about land values. Commentators agree that the funds available upfront for infrastructure are simply inadequate' (LSE 2008).

Whilst it will help facilitate a more holistic approach to infrastructure projects in the long term, it is also likely that the newly imposed Community Infrastructure Levy (CIL) will slow down development in the short term rather than escalate it in the Thames Gateway. The CIL is a new charge on development land values introduced in 2008, which local authorities may impose on most types of new development in their area, calculated in relation to the size and character of the development paying for it. The intention is that the proceeds of the levy will be spent on local and *subregional* infrastructure to support the development of the area.

Who is going to create the jobs?

In August 2008, contracts were signed for a Middle-Eastern company to build a new £1.5 billion deep superport in Thurrock, to handle a huge share of Europe's container shipments. This may generate as many as 12,000 new jobs, and is one of the biggest successes for the Thames Gateway in recent months. Other prospects look less promising. GVA Grimley's fourth report (2008) on the Thames Gateway, entitled *Centrifugal Force: The Role of Town Centres in the Thames Gateway*, examined ten towns in the Thames Gateway (Basildon, Barking, Canning Town, Dartford, Grays, Greenwich, Medway, Sittingbourne, Southend and Woolwich) and concluded that the main town centres, which make up 50 per cent of the total Thames Gateway population, are the major employment destinations in the regions. Comparing data on current concentrations of office and retail floorspace, the report indicates that the locus of some 60,000 new jobs over the next fifteen to twenty years is likely to be not in the government's four favoured 'economic transformer' hubs, namely Canary Wharf, Ebbsfleet Valley, London Gateway and Stratford City and the Lower Lea Valley, but in these smaller, more traditional urban centres.

This may appear disappointingly counterintuitive news for the government agencies which have been promoting the new hubs, but makes good sense to many people already living and working in the region. Mike Taylor, one of the authors of the report, commented:

> our research demonstrates the relatively healthy and sustained levels of occupier interest in town centres across the Thames Gateway. The town centres may not be achieving their full potential and many are not on the 'radar' for major occupiers, developers or investors, but there certainly is an underlying strength to these towns.

> (GVA Grimley 2008: 7)

Taylor envisages that, when the market recovers, such places will be able to build upon their core strength to create much more vibrant, healthy and 'visible' town centres.

Unless development is concentrated in this way there will be unsustainable consequences, as CPRE noted in 2006:

> the 120,000 (housing) target requires that strain on transport infrastructure is minimised by creating employment opportunities close to residential areas. There is, however, little evidence that this is happening in any substantial way. There is therefore a serious risk of the Thames Gateway being developed as dormitories for central London workers and of new transport infrastructure catering largely for long-distance travel including by car, instead of local journeys made by other means.
>
> (CPRE 2006: 24)

Who is going to fill the jobs?

Gordon Brown acknowledged that 'there is no point in creating new jobs if there are no skilled workers to fill them'. With this in mind, the LSC (Learning Skills Council) was asked to develop a *Thames Gateway Skills Plan* to help local people develop the skills needed to fill the new jobs on offer, and this plan was published in 2007.

Contractors warned government that its regeneration plans had not been clearly thought out and could lead to severe delays and problems in the longer term, that appropriate management systems for the project were lacking, and that budget implications had been ill-considered. This gave rise to the setting up of a Construction Centre as part of the Thames Gateway, but its managing director, Richard Simmons, said:

> As with all government initiative announcements there is a long way to go before the reality is achieved. The government should rely on the construction industry as a partner and source of help at this stage and not alienate it from proposals. The Thames Gateway regeneration is an ambitious project and needs to be carefully broken down into reasonable sized targets and timescales in order to achieve eventual completion.
>
> (Simmons 2007)

Conclusion

Michael Edwards, writing a prognosis of the Thames Gateway in early 2008, predicted that the Thames Gateway 'is neither bound to succeed nor bound to fail. But it will be hard to make into a great success. It is not the kind of development that the property market, left to itself, would undertake' (Edwards 2008: 290).

At one level, in the fullness of time, the Thames Gateway is likely to be seen as a triumph of pragmatic bottom-up activity over the abstract proclivities of top-down policy. The desired outcomes – lots of houses, lots of jobs – will only be achieved, however, if the policy focus is adjusted in several ways.

The first adjustment relates to workplace geographies, which currently exist in a complex patchwork quilt right across the Thames Gateway. Workplace location affects the local economic situation, which in turn has a social impact, which will tend to have an environmental impact.

Second is the issue of identity: rather than imposing a macro-identity onto a notional region, policy needs to respond more positively to the many discrete places within the Thames Gateway as it is currently delineated, and their individual qualities, including many seaside towns, historic cities, port terminals, industrial estates, regional retail centres and rural hinterlands. If the Thames Gateway is to succeed in its ambitions, the shared identity of such places will need to be amplified in order to attract multiple investors.

The third shift is towards more devolved thinking: the Thames Gateway has been excessively top down for too long, as a government directive will always proceed slowly. Decisions taken locally and expediently, with access to government credit and support structures in place, are more likely to succeed, as they will be based on local drivers and local knowledge, and therefore more likely to deliver steady incremental growth than decisions taken in a larger, more strategic arena. Additional funding and support will be necessary where levels of unemployment creep above 10 per cent.

The Thames Gateway needs to be seen in a much longer-term timeframe of delivery than other growth areas, because the starting point differs considerably where transport and social infrastructure and economic base are concerned. Propositions for development models which allow for a much greater degree of flexibility are needed if the Thames Gateway is to be the '21st century backlands region' in a positive sense. Land needs to be actively identified and reserved for both flooding and development and new models which allow for low-specification, low-cost accommodation, temporary uses and constant transformation of sites are urgently required.

Finally, the Thames Gateway is in need of a shift in emphasis from conceptualisation to realisation. This shift has six components to it:

- re-evaluate the strategic policy focus to allow for a more precise set of regional prioritisations;
- divert resources to facilitate capacity building locally to allow for more bottom-up approaches;
- pay greater attention to particular challenges to delivery programmes and mechanisms;
- pay greater attention to testing and matching of sites and projects;
- allow for pilot testing 'unconventional' accommodation models to suit flexible and temporary needs of the new generation service economies and alternative 'lifestyles';
- consider the possibilities for Thames Gateway to be used as a test-bed for a new model of strategic urban design.

This is not to say that the Thames Gateway does not exist. It does. In 2009, as in previous years, it had a presence at MIPIM in Cannes, but was promoted under the guise of Invest Thames Gateway, a new consortium established in 2008 to achieve a more joined-up approach to attracting investors. Overseas corporate finance may yet pay special interest to the Thames Gateway in the run-up to the 2012 Olympics, not least because building costs, labour and land in the UK will become increasingly cheap. The government may need to step in and control this laissez-faire development, in order to safeguard longer-term community benefits.

Whilst the Thames Gateway remains a non-place without its own internal logic or strong internal connections, it nevertheless remains high on the UK government's agenda and will require new financial incentives, and no doubt unprecedented financial instruments, in order for part, if not all, of the vision to become reality. Lacking revenue funding, the parkland is likely to remain a virtual concept, rather than a managed territory. Cycle paths and riverside walks will make up for the lack of a totally contiguous piece of parkland. Where developers remain active, receipts from Section 106 agreement will suffer immensely in the coming decade and lead to a serious shortfall in the available funding for new public services and infrastructure. Novel forms of centralised investment will be needed in order to deliver health and education facilities and so forth in those areas where developers are prepared to build. In areas where they are not, 'patient' land may be tied up for some time to come, while property values recover sufficiently to justify the build cost. In other places, low-quality development is the only likely means of fulfilling interim housing targets. Expecting zero carbon by 2016 sounds like asking for the impossible, and such directives may need to be eased or even waived and postponed if the UK recession proves as deep and as long as predicted. Foreign investment in the Thames Estuary along the new high-speed train line is perhaps the only tantalising prospect after the Olympics are over.

The Thames Gateway faces many barriers but, much like the Thames Barrier itself, these have a limited lifespan prompted by a much greater sense of event horizon than originally envisaged. In the meantime, accepting the notion of 'no change' remains a serious prospect. Running counter to growth agendas, this could nevertheless function as a positive pause rather than a serious setback, especially if it is used to fundamentally rethink and adjust policy to allow the Thames Gateway to flourish along the lines of what Cohen and Rustin describe as a 'deliberative agency' (2008a: 312). However, deliberations cannot continue for long: an incoming government in the next year or so will have to act swiftly if the small amount of momentum generated over the past twenty years is to be sustained.

References

CABE (Commision for Architecture and the Built Environment) (2005) *Design Review for Thames Gateway*. Online. Available at: http://www.cabe.org.uk/default.aspx?contentitemid=1061.

CABE (2006) *The Thames Gateway Design Pact: Making New Things Happen*. Online. Available at: http://www.cabe.org.uk/default.aspx?contentitemid=2743.

CABE (2008) *Thames Gateway Parkland* (London: CABE).

CPRE (Campaign to Protect Rural England) (2006) *Compact Sustainable Communities* (London: CPRE).

Church, A. and Frost, M. (1995) The Thames Gateway: An Analysis of the Emergence of a Sub-Regional Regeneration Initiative. *The Geographical Journal*, 161 (2): 199–210.

DCLG (2006) *Thames Gateway Interim Plan: Development Prospectus* (London: DCLG). Online. Available at: http://www.communities.gov.uk/publications/thamesgateway/thamesgateway3 (last accessed 8 January 2009).

DCLG (2007) *Thames Gateway Delivery Plan*. Online. Available at: http://www.communities.gov.uk/publications/thamesgateway/deliveryplan (last accessed 8 January).

DCLG (2008a) *Second Round Growth Points* (London: DCLG). Online. Available at: http://www.communities.gov.uk/publications/housing/partnershipsforgrowth (last accessed 8 January 2009).

DCLG (2008b) *Thames Gateway Eco-Region: A Prospectus* (London: HMSO). Online. Available at: http://www.communities.gov.uk/publications/thamesgateway/ecoregion.

DoE (Department of Environment) (1995) *The Thames Gateway Planning Framework*. Online. Available at: http://www.communities.gov.uk/documents/thamesgateway/pdf/147561.pdf (last accessed 12 January 2009).

DoE (1995) *The Thames Gateway Planning Framework* (RPG9a) (London: HMSO). Online. Available at http://www.archive.officialdocuments.co.uk/document/doe/thames/framework.htm (last accessed 5 July 2009).

Edwards, M. (2008) Blue Skies over Blue Water? In P. Cohen and M. J. Rustin (eds) *London's Turning: The Making of Thames Gateway* (London: Ashgate) pp. 283–292.

Environment Agency (2004) *Strategic Flood Risk Assessment for the Thames Gateway*. Online. Available at: www.london.gov.uk/assembly/planning/2007/05sep/item06.rtf (last accessed 4 January 2009).

Farrell, T. (2007) Manifesto for London. *The Architectural Review* (special issue) 222: 1327.

Glancey, J. (2003) *The Thames Gateway: Here be Monsters*. Guardian, 29 October. Online. Available at: http://www.guardian.co.uk/society/2003/oct/29/housingpolicy.g2.

GLA (Greater London Assembly) (2005) *London Under Threat? Flooding Risk in the Thames Gateway*. Report to the Environment Committee. Online. Available at: http://www.london.gov.uk/assembly/reports/environment/flood_thamesg.pdf (last accessed 6 January 2009).

GVA Grimley (2008) *Centrifugal Force: The Role of Town Centres in the Thames Gateway* (London: GVAG).

HM Government (2008) *Prospectus for the Thames Gateway as an Eco-region*. Communities and Local Government Publications. Online. Available at www.communities.gov.uk/documents/thamesgateway/pdf/1074037.pdf (last accessed 30 July 2009).

Keith, M. (2004) The Thames Gateway Paradox. *New Economy*, 11 (1): 15–20.

Keith, M. (2008) Between Being and Becoming? Rights, Responsibilities and the Politics of Multiculture in the New East End. *Sociological Research Online*, 13 (5): 3.11.

Lavery, S. and Donovan, W. (200?) Flood Risk Management in the Thames Estuary Looking Ahead 100 Years. *Royal Society of London Transactions Series A*, 363 (1831): 1455–1474.

LSE (London School of Economics) (2008) *The Thames Gateway: Building a New City Within an Old One?* Online. Available at: http://www.lse.ac.uk/collections/londonDevelopmentWorkshops/lselondondevelopmentworkshops2/thamesGateway/heifThamesGatewayReport.pdf.

LSC (2008) *Thames Gateway Skills Plan*. Online. Available at: http://www.lsc.gov.uk/regions/London/Publications/Latestdocuments/Detail.htm?id=3662a9c9-d17a-4afb-9e15-e1f314b3a1c5 (last accessed 18 January 2009).

NAO (National Audit Office) (2007) *The Thames Gateway: Laying the Foundations*. Online. Available at: http://www.nao.org.uk/publications/0607/the_thames_gateway_laying_the.aspx (last accessed 15 January 2009).

ODPM (2005) *Creating Sustainable Communities: Delivering the Thames Gateway*. Online. Available at: http://www.communities.gov.uk/publications/housing/creatingsustainablecommunities (last accessed 15 January 2009).

OECD (2007) *Randstad Policy Brief*. Online. Available at: http://www.oecd.org/dataoecd/11/25/38246592.pdf (last accessed 5 January 2009).

Simmons, R. (2007) Comments made in Press Release about the the Constructions Centre. Available at http://www.prlog.org/10041622-the-construction-centre-highlights-concerns-over-thames-gateway-regeneration-project.pdf (last accessed 29 June 2009).

The 'Celtic Capitals'

An introduction

The 'Celtic Capitals' embrace Edinburgh, Glasgow (the 'capital of the west of Scotland'), Belfast and Cardiff. With devolved governments since 1999 in both Scotland and Wales, the 'urban renaissance' package of policy proposals (and its subsequent White Paper) did not impact directly upon public policy. However, it did influence government thinking in Northern Ireland by virtue of the centralised planning control exerted by the Department of Environment Northern Ireland (DoENI). The election of Labour administrations in Scotland and Wales, both markedly more 'Old Labour' than 'New', ensured close parallels in urban policy. There was similar commitment to tackling social deprivation through better public services and the creation of more economic opportunities. But urban renaissance and urban design concerns had a rather different genesis and role in urban policy, and they provide comparative examples with which to assess whether the pattern, form, content and quality of urban regeneration in the other parts of the UK are distinctively different from those in England.

Scotland

Scottish urban policy commenced after the war with three decades of decentralisation of households and jobs to New Towns and overspill areas (peripheral estates). It was not until the mid-1970s that the speed of city population decline was fully appreciated and urban regeneration efforts were stepped up. Scotland did not utilise the Urban Development Corporation mechanism, but eleven urban renewal (partnership) initiatives were launched on deprived council estates, later complemented by a dozen priority partnership areas (PPAs), but these initiatives remained largely housing led (Turok 2004). It was not until 2002 that a review of the state of Scotland's six major cities was completed, and the key contribution that they could make to Scotland's future development recognised. *Building Better Cities* (SE 2003) promoted community regeneration and increased social provision and economic opportunities, but it gave urban design far less attention than the Urban Task Force (UTF) had done in England. *Building Better Cities* provided modest funds for infrastructure improvements, and requested that each city-region prepare a 'City Vision', working with relevant organisations and adjacent local authorities (Turok and Bailey 2004: 170, 198). But it was less influential than the UTF report because it was not an externally driven policy document from the heart of government.

Reforms to the planning system were set within a broader agenda of the modernisation of the public sector and public services as a whole, and followed on from the preparation of a national spatial strategy, *The National Planning Framework* (SE 2004; subsequently revised in 2008). *Modernising the Planning System: A White Paper* (SE 2005) placed sustainable development at the heart of national policy (Peel and Lloyd 2006: 100); introduced a new planning hierarchy for national, major, local and minor development decisions; and reasserted the role of the cities, and their regions, as the economic drivers. A more efficient development plan process was a key concern, but so too was public participation, while development control was reframed as a more proactive development management process (Peel and Lloyd 2006). Finally, a new Planning Act was passed in 2006 with the intention of making planning more aspirational, and placing development plans at the heart of the system, the intention being to make them better reflect local character and drive change in the public interest.

If Scotland lagged behind England in national regeneration policies until the late 1990s it was some way ahead in matters of urban design, and its national planning advice notes emphasised a greater commitment to design improvement. A new Planning Act was introduced in 1997 and then, following devolution, a *Policy on Architecture* was launched (SE 2000), closely followed by *Designing Places* (SE 2001), a Scottish version of *By Design* (DETR/CABE 2000; see Cowan 2002). In 2005, Architecture and Design Scotland was established to champion, and promote excellence in, architecture, design and planning, and an update and revision of the Architecture Policy was published in 2007 (SE 2007). So, even if there are few signs of a concerted urban renaissance policy framework, Scotland has certainly established key underpinnings of a 'design renaissance'.

Of course, Scotland has a much stronger urban culture than England, a tradition of much higher-density tenement and apartment living, and a legacy of Georgian and Victorian city planning and civic endowment that is unsurpassed in any of the major provincial cities of the UK. Glasgow led a British revival of urban design in the mid-1980s, and it helped deliver high-quality city centre regeneration particularly, assisted by successful bids for the City of Culture (1990) and City of Architecture and Design (1999). These complemented its celebrated tenement renewal and urban conservation programmes, city centre pedestrianisation and new-build residential (notably New Gorbals). This 'design renaissance' was deepened by the emergence of a 'Glasgow style' and a cadre of talented architectural practices, some of whose best work has been in social housing, emphasising a more inclusive approach to design and local distinctiveness.

While Glasgow recentralised and regenerated, Edinburgh's planning and development challenge was how to create room for growth and change within an urban fabric of outstanding coherence and quality, given international recognition in World Heritage Site designation in 1995. The conservation mentality dictated a very focused pattern of redevelopment through a series of masterplanned developments in the 1990s, the largest in west central Edinburgh (The Exchange), but with significant concentration in the east of the Old Town and around Holyrood (Jenkins and Holder 2005). But intense commercial growth pressures led to the development of Edinburgh Park on the western edge of the city, and then the move to reclaim the waterfront for compact residential and commercial development (Kerr 2005). These and further pressures for suburban development in the south-east of the city have opened up a debate about appropriate visions for the city, and accessibility and social inclusion in their widest sense (Hague and Jenkins 2005).

Both Edinburgh and Glasgow have made major contributions to British urban design as public policy and to the stock of urban renaissance exemplars. But they also retain hugely deprived, often high-rise, council estates and especially problematic peripheral estates. These emphasise the need for a much deeper urban renaissance that can deliver extensive desegregation of large tracts of public housing alongside major improvements in accessibility, employment, services and the living environment.

References

Cowan, R. (2002) Devolution and Urban Design: Scotland. *Urban Design Quarterly,* 84: 25–28.

Hague, C. and Jenkins, P. (2005) The Changing Image and Identity of the City in the 21st Century. In B. Edwards and P. Jenkins (eds) *Edinburgh: The Making of a Capital City* (Edinburgh: Edinburgh University Press) pp. 217–230.

Jenkins, P. and Holder, R. (2005) Creation and Conservation of the Built Environment in the Later 20th Century. In B. Edwards and P. Jenkins (eds) *Edinburgh: The Making of a Capital City* (Edinburgh: Edinburgh University Press) pp. 185–203.

Kerr, D. (2005) Preparing for the 21st Century: The City in a Global Environment. In B. Edwards and P. Jenkins, *Edinburgh: The Making of a Capital City* (Edinburgh: Edinburgh University Press) pp. 204–216.

Peel, D. and Lloyd, M. G. (2006) The Twisting Paths to Planning Reform in Scotland. *International Planning Studies,* 11 (2): 89–107.

SE (Scottish Executive) (2000) *A Policy on Architecture for Scotland* (Edinburgh: SE).

SE (2001) *Designing Places* (Edinburgh: SE).

SE (2003) *Building Better Cities: Delivering Growth and Opportunities*. Online. Available at http: www.scotland.gov.uk/Publications/2003/01/16094/16171.

SE (2004) *The National Planning Framework* (Edinburgh: SE).

SE (2005) *Modernising the Planning System: A White Paper* (Edinburgh: SE).

SE (2007) *Building Our Legacy: Statement on Scotland's Architecture Policy* (Edinburgh: SE).

Turok, I. (2004) Scottish Urban Policy: Continuity, Change and Uncertainty Post-Devolution. In C. Johnstone and M. Whitehead (eds) *New Horizons in British Urban Policy: Perspectives on New Labour's Urban Renaissance* (Aldershot: Ashgate) pp. 111–128.

Turok, I. and Bailey, N. (2004) Twin Track Cities? Competitiveness and Cohesion in Glasgow and Edinburgh. *Progress in Planning* 62: 135–204.

14 Edinburgh

Catching up with the contemporary

Leslie Forsyth and Marilyn Higgins

Introduction: conservation ethic and growth pressure tensions

Edinburgh's geographic and historic context has woven a stunning urban fabric of world-wide fame that serves as a strong backcloth to contemporary urban design debates. The Scottish capital occupies a panoramic setting between the Firth of Forth and Pentland Hills, astride several dramatic extinct volcanoes. A World Heritage Site since 1995, the whole of the city centre and immediate surroundings is a series of conservation areas, containing numerous listed buildings and ancient monuments. The landform and townscape are amongst the city's most famous assets, a major draw for around 3.5 million visitors a year, the second most popular tourist destination in the UK. The city is also a major cultural centre, host to the largest arts festival in the world every August. Edinburgh has the strongest economy of any city in the UK outside London, with unemployment low at 2.2 per cent, and is one of the fastest growing city-regions in Europe. It is largely based around the service sector, including public servants, finance, higher education and tourism. Recent research on Edinburgh and Glasgow confirmed 'strong links between physical assets and competitiveness' (Turok and Bailey 2004: 172).

The capital is relatively compact and contains just under half a million inhabitants. It is tightly confined by the sea to the north and a green belt on its other boundaries. The worst of suburban sprawl has been avoided, but development pressure has spread to surrounding authorities. Scottish urban form has traditionally been higher density than in England. Edinburgh's Old Town retains its medieval street pattern, with relatively high buildings lining the Royal Mile and dense fishbone-like 'closes' running off it. The Georgian New Town, across Princes Street Gardens, and the extensive Victorian suburbs include traditional tenements, and many individual houses have been subdivided. This unique townscape has meant that good-quality housing has kept the city centre populated and vibrant, as well as very expensive.

Edinburgh's city centre has changed less than that of most British cities (Hague 2005: 178). Over the centuries, there has been continuing tension between innovation and conservation, but the city has embraced change without losing its strong sense of identity, connecting political action and artistic aspiration (Edwards and Jenkins 2005). It has been highly influenced by powerful conservation lobbies, including the Cockburn Association, the oldest urban amenity society in the world, founded in 1875. Many of the city's influential citizens have been members over the years, including Patrick Geddes, who advocated 'conservative surgery' to regenerate the city (Rosenburg and Johnson: 2005). Contentious development during the 1960s demolished Georgian squares for new government and university buildings. As a reaction, new buildings from the 1970s hid behind preserved façades or aped the styles of long-gone eras. The best example of the latter is the controversial Scandic Crown Hotel on the Royal Mile, built in 1989.

Although the 'urban renaissance' did not take place in Scotland in the same way as in England, trends have been similar. A significant change occurred in the 1990s, when conservative Edinburgh began to embrace contemporary design: the turning point was the Museum of Scotland. Its opening in 1998 coincided with the new devolved Parliament and Tony Blair's 'New Labour.' The museum exuded a new confidence in contemporary design respecting its context, driven by enlightened trustees who believed in quality. It symbolised a new Scottishness with its castle-like solid geometry and materials, and it established strong visual connections with the rest of the city from the rooftop terrace and carefully placed windows (see Plate 14.1). The new parliament, a contemporary landmark occupying a key site at the foot of the Royal Mile, has been more controversial. The balance has shifted away from conservation and towards development (Turok and Bailey 2004: 167). In line with what one interviewee termed the 'national zeitgeist of Cool Britannia', conservationists began to worry about the prevailing mood of 'new is good and old is bad', which challenged Edinburgh's orthodoxy.

The public realm plays an important role in this capital and festival city. The Royal Mile, Grassmarket and St. Andrews Square (see Plate 14.2) have enjoyed recent improvements, including reclaiming space for public use. Princes Street, with its dramatic setting opposite the castle, has suffered more mixed fortunes. Although it has had successive traffic management schemes over the years, physical improvements have never been radical enough and it remains a disappointing carriageway with street clutter (see Plate 14.3). Traffic and parking bedevil the historic city, and a blow against positive action was struck when a referendum on congestion charging was lost in 2006. Following much debate, a new tram system is forging ahead, linking the coastal expansion areas of Leith and Granton with the city centre and airport to the west.

Development pressure continues to create both opportunities and dilemmas for urban form. There are a growing number of high-quality contemporary infill developments within the historic core. The buoyant residential market has meant that it has been possible to reuse brownfield land and old buildings, often at high densities (Bramley and Morgan 2003: 467). An example is the mixed-use Quartermile development now being built to plans by Norman Foster, with contemporary buildings sprinkled amidst the Victorian Royal Infirmary. Out-of-town shopping, allowed since the 1980s, combined with conservation protection, has hampered the city centre's consumer attractiveness (Turok and Bailey 2004: 156). Plans for new shopping under Princes Street and on top of Waverley Station have been contentious. Proposals to demolish buildings along the Royal Mile as part of the mixed-use Caltongate development have been the subject of a bitter public campaign. Unesco is reported to have had deep regrets about the council's decision to grant permission, seeing it as damaging the integrity of the World Heritage site, and has a growing concern about other unsuitable new developments in Edinburgh (Carrell 2008).

Growth around the city's edge has provoked different dilemmas. A large chunk of western Edinburgh has undergone major expansion, including a new headquarters for the Royal Bank of Scotland at Gogarburn, a major shopping mall and housing at The Gyle, and a business quarter, Edinburgh Park, masterplanned by Richard Meier, all generating car traffic and exposing a fragmented and underfunded system of transport infrastructure (Turok and Bailey 2004: 172–173). Another incursion into the green belt is occurring in the South-East Wedge, including the relocation of the main hospital. Recent research has confirmed that the increase of suburban housing in Edinburgh has been associated with car dependence and the worsening of congestion (Bramley and Morgan 2003: 460). Peripheral post-war public housing estates such as Craigmillar,

Wester Hailes and Muirhouse have been characterised by significant social and economic problems. Although various regeneration initiatives have taken place over the last decades, tensions remain between reconciling economic growth pressures, ensuring improvements for these poorer communities on the edge and achieving high standards of design, connectedness and accessibility (Turok and Bailey 2004: 163). For the city as a whole, major challenges for the future are the provision of more affordable housing, residential land allocation and public transport improvements (Bramley and Morgan 2003).

Urban design influences

An increased awareness of urban design has accompanied this recent building spate. In part, it has been driven by the city council's new entrepreneurial attitude towards investment, with much of it driven by masterplans (Jenkins and Holder 2005). The establishment of the new parliament, focused civic leadership and the growth ambitions of key financial institutions have given Edinburgh a new sense of direction (Turok and Bailey 2004: 183). Several interviewees noted that politicians, some developers and sections of the public have become more sophisticated and discerning. Edinburgh has spawned some high-profile architects who have produced a number of popular contemporary buildings. There has been a growing discontent with the mediocrity and sameness of much new development, and a realisation that it can damage the sense of place, affecting tourism and business investment in the face of increasing international competition (Kerr 2005).

Edinburgh embraced the thrust of the Scottish Executive's *Designing Places* policy (2001) and proactively promoted urban design initiatives that are among the most comprehensive in Scotland. Places as far away as Auckland, New Zealand, have modelled themselves on Edinburgh's actions. There are three main strands to the council's approach: civic leadership; stronger planning policies and guidance; and capacity building, including training, upskilling and improved development management processes (CEC 2002). The Urban Design Working Group, comprising representatives from the public, private and design sectors, produced twenty-five recommendations for action, explicitly acknowledging that the buoyant economy enabled the city to raise standards without fear of frightening away developers (CEC 2003a). An energetic new chair of

Plate 14.1 Edinburgh: The Museum of Scotland, on Chambers Street, marked a turning point for contemporary design in the city.

Plate 14.2 Edinburgh: St. Andrews Square, in the Georgian New Town, has been opened up for public use.

Plate 14.3 Edinburgh: Princes Street has remained a missed opportunity in terms of the pedestrian environment and conservation/re-design of a key architectural façade.

the planning committee was pivotal in appointing Sir Terry Farrell as the city's design champion and a new senior officer as design leader with responsibilities across the council. This echoes the point made in Chapter 1, that key individuals in leadership positions can make a difference. The urban design thrust enjoyed cross-party political support and built on development quality initiatives within the planning department. Although the chair lost his seat in the 2007 election, and the council changed from Labour to a Liberal Democrat–Scottish National Party coalition, the urban design initiative continues to be supported. Farrell has exhorted Edinburgh to engage in 'proactive and creative city making' and not be complacent in the face of its 'albatross of excellence' (Farrell 2008: 3–4).

The *Edinburgh City Local Plan* (CEC 2007a) has an expanded section on design principles to guide new development, although some amenity bodies are worried about the parallel diminution of conservation policies. The new design policies set out broad principles, emphasising issues such as context, connections, active frontages, security, mixed uses, open space and sense of place. While these are based on generally agreed principles to be found in the theoretical and professional literature, they rely on the application of sound design judgement and interpretation of policy when individual proposals are being considered. The city has also produced an impressive array of detailed non-statutory guidance, including city-wide standards for urban design (CEC 2003b), streets (CEC 2006a), trams (CEC 2006b) and sustainable buildings (CEC 2007b). A 2004 landmark case at Shrub Place, Leith, helped build confidence to turn down a proposal on urban design grounds, with the rejection upheld on appeal.

The council maintains an ongoing commitment to design training for both staff and elected members, through in-house workshops and study trips. Dedicated design staff, either architect-planners or urban designers, have been appointed to provide support and advice to case officers dealing with planning applications. Recent research, including a survey of architects and developers, has produced evidence that applicants welcome the role of planning in achieving high quality design, as long as they have confidence in the skills and consistency of the staff involved. The planning committee has noticed an improvement in the design quality of applications as a result of the work of the design officers (Dawson and Higgins 2009).

Method of analysis

Gospodini's classification of European cities puts Edinburgh in the 'small, special' category, characterised by its emphasis on tourism, education and political and administrative institutions; the quality of the built environment is a selling point for visitors and residents alike (Gospodini 2002). She argues that urban design plays an important economic role in 'preserving and enhancing' place identity and quality, particularly in the face of globalisation. Coincidentally, this is the phrase traditionally used in UK heritage legislation to test the appropriateness of new development in conservation areas, making it highly appropriate for the Edinburgh context.

One of the research methods underpinning this chapter has been to identify three distinct areas within the city for more detailed analysis, using 'preservation and enhancement' as the key to considering the impact of recent developments and policy initiatives. The specific geographic areas have been chosen to represent both typical and notable urban design issues, varying in size, location, use, socio-economic characteristics and chronology, thereby enhancing the ability to draw conclusions about the city as a whole. First, Holyrood North is a medium-scale intervention in the historic environment of the Old Town, which preceded the adjacent new parliament. The masterplan slightly predated the urban renaissance agenda, but the authors consider it an example of a successful urban design product and process on a significant site (Figure 14.1). Secondly, Craigmillar is a large-scale regeneration of a public housing estate adjacent to the Green Belt on the south-east edge of the city (Figure 14.2). It suffers from the social, economic and physical disadvantages common to many of Scotland's peripheral estates. The current initiatives are post urban renaissance, although regeneration has been an issue in Craigmillar for much longer. Lastly, the Waterfront is a colossal regeneration of docklands and industrial areas, spreading from Granton to Leith in the north of the city (Figure 14.3). The aim is to reconnect the city to the Firth of Forth estuary, creating a series of new city quarters and providing significant numbers of new homes as well as other major facilities. Although some completed developments predate the urban renaissance, most of the masterplans and proposals have come later.

Consideration of the overarching research questions posed in Chapter 1 has been guided by an analysis of these sample areas, comments from the seminar series, a literature review of recent research and policy and interviews with key individuals from the city council, Architecture +

Design Scotland, national and local amenity societies, private sector developers, built environment professionals and academics. It has also been informed by long-standing involvement by the authors in national and local urban design initiatives and organisations, student projects, research and mid-career professional training.

Holyrood North

Edinburgh Council developed Lothian Regional Council's structure plan for this area in a strategy produced in 1987, which became rooted in a rudimentary site brief within the local plan. When Scottish and Newcastle Brewers decided that the five-hectare site was no longer suited for its operations, the land was bequeathed to the Dynamic Earth Charitable Trust (which operates the millennium visitor attraction across Holyrood Road) because the company's chairman decided to give something back to the city of its headquarters. The trust initiated a redevelopment competition won by the multidisciplinary Development Services Partnership (DSP) in 1993. The masterplanner for the site was John Hope, supported by Campbell and Arnott Architects. Holyrood Development Partnership Ltd was set up to transfer the land from the brewery to end users. The key aims of the proposals were to maximise returns to the trust, create mixed uses and reinstate the historic urban form (DSP 1993: 3). These plans were already in place when the decision was taken to locate the new parliament next door.

The recognisable Old Town urban pattern was embedded in the masterplan (DSP 1993) by reinstating closes (parallel narrow lanes running back from the street) to improve permeability and take advantage of views, reusing some existing buildings, limiting the impact of motor vehicles and ensuring that new layouts conformed to the narrow 'fishbone' pattern of built form along the Royal Mile, creating a variety of public, semi-public and private spaces. The layout evolved after extensive consultation with the local economic development agency, local authority

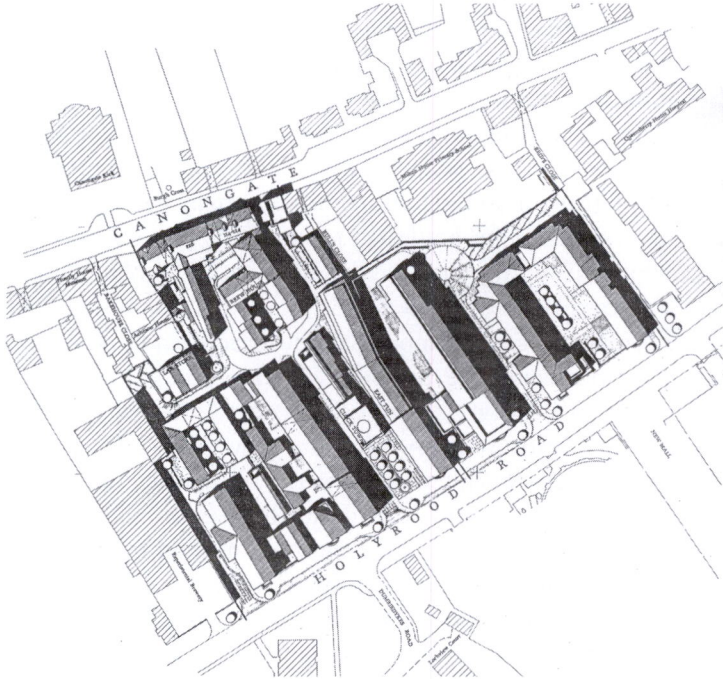

Figure 14.1 Edinburgh: Holyrood North Masterplan (Courtesy John C. Hope Architects).

departments, amenity and conservation bodies and end users. At this stage, a use had been identified for each building and, where possible, a client, tenant or owner with a source of funding.
The uses at this time included 190 residential units, a hotel, a 125-bed student residence, 5,600
square metres of offices and shops, 1,000 square metres of workshops and a bar/pub. Detailed
phasing and revenue production calculations were produced (DSP 1993).

The management of the project was professionally, not contractor, led. Designers were
appointed for each plot, either nominated or approved by DSP, which maintained tight project
management control throughout. The masterplan served as a broad context within which a
variety of designers could participate. The procurement process proposed the assembly of
development packages comprising a targeted end user or developer, a design team and finance,
creating maximum value through splitting the site and phasing development. Various contractors were used, but most buildings were to be procured via design and build to ensure that the
end user was aware of the total commitment. Seven phases were identified, the objective being
to release funding to the trust early and avoid being delayed by a detailed planning application
for the whole site. At this point the projected gross land value was £3.2 million and the total
development costs £24 million (DSP 1993).

Evaluation

The inception of Holyrood North predates the Urban Task Force (UTF) and other design
initiatives in Scotland. However, in terms of design excellence, the process reveals success in
translating an initial concept into a spatial strategy which was carefully implemented, thus proving the success of the original development competition. The scheme was the overall winner of
the Scottish Awards for Quality in Planning 2004. The involvement of the property development
industry was instrumental in the search for a high-quality urban design solution. In response to
the competition, DSP created an organisational framework that ensured that the urban form
respected and enhanced the spatial structure of the Old Town. Within this overall pattern, a
sensitive mix of existing buildings and contemporary interventions illustrates a commitment
to achieving urban design quality. This quality was controlled throughout the process by the
developer, a process similar to the concurrent office project to the west of the city, Edinburgh
Park. In both cases the developer approved individual designs before formal submission for planning approval, ensuring double quality control. This applied to initial designs and any proposed
changes. A genuine variety of uses has been achieved, including the Scottish Poetry Library,
Architecture + Design Scotland, the BBC (British Broadcasting Corporation), an upmarket
hotel and a long-stay apartment-hotel, and many of the buildings were designed by some of the
city's best architects.

Residential uses make up a significant element. One-third of the new residential properties
were developed by the Old Town Housing Association and provision was made for existing tenants. The student accommodation and studio work spaces supported the objective of providing
variety in types of accommodation. The introduction of flats for sale introduced a new tenure
to the area and with it a level of gentrification, though appealing to a variety of income levels.

The masterplan and implementation phases paid particular attention to the quality of the
public realm. It is an excellent example of a design which repairs an urban structure broken down
by the effects of industry in previous centuries. The reintroduction of the closes successfully
increases accessibility and choice. Local distinctiveness is maintained at an architectural level
by the retention of existing buildings with their palette of familiar materials, while the closes

are paved with high-quality stone and recycled building materials. A sense of place is further engendered by dramatic views of Salisbury Crags through the closes and from the flats. Lively ground-floor uses were stipulated along the major road frontages, including shops, cafés and bars.

In environmental terms, the most important aspect of the site is its central location, increasing accessibility by public transport, walking and cycling. Pedestrians have priority within the site, with vehicular access and parking strictly limited to confined areas including under buildings. The briefs for individual sites avoided the use of non-sustainable products and insisted on non-polluting construction materials while reusing materials from demolitions and exploiting solar energy where possible. The high densities accord with both sustainability aims and traditional building patterns in the vicinity.

In terms of governance and resources, council planning strategies were complemented effectively by the landowner's intentions and the project organisation discussed above. Participation with existing inhabitants was not a significant element because the site was previously industrial, but the developers were very careful to involve amenity organisations and conservation bodies in the process. Significant was the way in which end users were involved to ensure that the aims of the project were realised.

Craigmillar

Craigmillar is a suburb three miles south-east of the city centre, primarily inter- and post-war public housing of some 700 hectares, mainly three-storey tenements with some higher blocks of flats. At one point it had a population of 25,000, which dropped to 7,500 in 2004, and the objective is to grow it back to 15,000 (CEC *et al.* 2005: 12). It is a mark of the reputation from which the area suffers that, despite the city's overheated housing market and severe shortage of social housing, there have been high void levels. Most of the original houses have now been demolished, leaving swathes of vacant land. The area is typical of a number of Edinburgh's public sector housing estates where social exclusion is a significant issue.

There have been a number of attempts to regenerate Craigmillar in the past, but none has succeeded in addressing the area's multiple socio-economic problems or generating a sustainable

Figure 14.2 Edinburgh: Craigmillar Urban Design Framework (Courtesy PARC).

neighbourhood. Despite its problems, Craigmillar has always retained a community identity and local pride with well-established community organisations working across employment, training, arts, health and education issues. The Craigmillar Partnership is a social inclusion partnership set up by the Scottish government to help bring about a wide range of improvements to benefit local people, employers and the wider community. Constituted in 2000, its board is made up of a wide range of agencies and individuals who have an interest in regeneration.

The most recent attempt at regeneration is being led by Promoting and Regenerating Craigmillar (PARC), one of six urban regeneration companies currently operating in Scotland. It is a joint venture company (JVC) set up in 2003 between Edinburgh City Council and the Edinburgh Development International (EDI) Group (an arm's-length property company set up by the city in 1988). It is responsible for implementing a fifteen-year mixed development programme of which the main elements defined in the urban design framework are 3,200 houses, 30,000 square metres of commercial floorspace, three new primary schools, one new high school, three new parks totalling 150 acres and one new public library (CEC *et al.* 2005).

The programme aims to create a more balanced tenure mix with 20 per cent affordable housing. The target for family housing is at least 33 per cent, much higher than the city average. Plans include the strengthening of the town centre with new shopping and community facilities including a new secondary school. The programme seeks to achieve better connections into Edinburgh and employment and training linkages with the nearby new Edinburgh Royal Infirmary, associated Bio-Park and the relocated Queen Margaret University.

PARC's role includes land assembly, which it will either carry out itself or project manage. As well as driving this forward, a key role for PARC is to capture and link the income arising from private development to contribute to the funding of the public and amenity projects. The financing of the regeneration relies on five contributors: City of Edinburgh Council £11 million (in kind – land value), EDI £11 million, Scottish Executive £21 million, housing association grant £18 million and private loan finance £62 million.

Evaluation

In terms of design excellence, the property market as represented by EDI through PARC has shown a commitment to achieving good-quality design. The *Craigmillar Urban Design Framework,* commissioned by PARC, is the third masterplan for the area's regeneration in the last ten years, and pays detailed attention to urban design principles (CEC *et al.* 2005). The framework adopts a typological approach using perimeter blocks of mainly two to four storeys and building lines to define public and private space (see Figure 14.2). The adoption of the *Urban Design Framework* as supplementary planning guidance by the council illustrates the commitment of the local authority to ensuring that the implementation of the design is effectively controlled. Within the framework, more detailed masterplans have been developed, including two that recently won first-place awards in the Homes for Scotland Quality Awards 2008.

In terms of housing, one of the key objectives of the regeneration is to introduce a variety of tenures, and this implies a degree of gentrification. The emphasis on mixed tenure and house size and type is welcome but has yet to be fully implemented. Private house sales were going well until the credit crunch of 2008, threatening the proposed tenure mix. Issues to do with tenure, densities and flats versus houses have been emotive.

The framework pays close attention to the public realm, centring around a return to traditional streets but encouraging the use of home zones that give pedestrians priority and include play space. These have begun to be implemented, including around the new schools, which are central to the community. A new primary school integrates Catholic and non-denominational education into one building with separate classrooms but shared communal space. The emphasis on the quality of public open space is welcome, both along the main road and in links to the nearby South-East Wedge and countryside. The clear demarcation between public and private space is a welcome innovation in an area where there has been confusion between the two, and large tracts of poorly managed and unused public space. The introduction of secure private space is to be commended in this context.

Sustainability is a key aim of the *Urban Design Framework*, emphasising public transport connections, biodiversity, sustainable drainage and natural ventilation and minimising the consumption of energy and resources and the generation of pollution. Completed home zones employ innovative design including permeable paving with water infiltration and contaminant removal, the first to be adopted by any local authority in Scotland and probably the largest in the UK (PARC and SEPA 2008). Open spaces are designed to be within walking distance of houses. A comprehensive health impact assessment of the framework commends, amongst other things, the provision of good-quality, energy-efficient housing, a transport network designed to facilitate public transport, walking and cycling and the use of home zones as a way of encouraging people to alter driving behaviour and encourage physical activity (Higgins *et al.* 2005).

In terms of governance, participatory processes have been evident in the initiatives, and PARC has sought a widely shared development agenda, including a three-month public consultation about the development framework. The proposed changes have created degrees of negativity and uncertainty among the existing inhabitants, many of whom have grown cynical from previous waves of regeneration consultation and are reluctant to engage. Although some achievements are on the ground, much more needs to be delivered to convince local people of the success of the initiatives, given Craigmillar's history. There is lingering distrust and worries that current activities are favouring development interests at the expense of the local community. Reaching consensus remains difficult.

In spite of the laudable aims of the Craigmillar regeneration plans, there are fears of an implementation gap. The downturn in the housing market has meant that the scale of private housing and associated planning gain has not materialised, compromising certain planned facilities and improvements. Funding for the tramline to Craigmillar and a new railway station is uncertain. Physical linkages to the new hospital remain tenuous and promised benefits for Craigmillar from development in the South-East Wedge are not yet in evidence. Craigmillar typifies an area where radical and sustained intervention needs to be of such high quality that it overcomes its previous image and attracts people as a place to live. It still has a way to go in reaching this.

Waterfront

Less than three miles from the city centre, the Port of Leith and the industrial area of Granton had the effect of privatising the waterfront, severing it from the rest of the city. Economic decline of port activities led to considerable vacant and derelict land and Forth Ports is relocating the remaining docks to more modern facilities elsewhere in the estuary (Carley and Ferrari 2007: 38). Historically, Edinburgh's waterfront communities have exhibited poor socio-economic characteristics. Leith has been the subject of a major regeneration initiative, first promoted by the Scottish Development Agency in the 1980s, based on mixed uses and a blend of new development alongside old. A new building at Victoria Quay serves as the office headquarters of

Figure 14.3 Edinburgh: Leith Docks and Western Harbour. Aerial image of indicative proposals (Courtesy RMJM Architects).

the Scottish government, completed in 1995. Although it was constructed on environmentally friendly principles, it is an unsustainable distance from the city centre and poorly integrated with its surroundings. Leith's gentrification has included significant growth in private and housing association dwellings, upmarket shops and restaurants, offices and leisure uses. Ocean Terminal, a major multistorey shopping mall with cinema and restaurants with design input from Sir Terence Conran, was opened in 2001. It is the control point for the Queen's former yacht *Britannia*, now a tourist attraction moored in Leith.

Building on these initiatives, there are currently three major regeneration projects along the water's edge. Granton Waterfront was the first of these, planned on 140 hectares of derelict industrial land. A joint venture company, Waterfront Edinburgh, was set up in 2000 by the local enterprise company and Edinburgh Council. It forms part of the larger Waterfront Partnership with Forth Ports and National Grid Property, the major landowners. Development is due to be complete by 2015, including 11,000 residential units (20 per cent of which are affordable), 9,000 new jobs, a new campus for Telford College, offices and retail units, a hotel, parkland, schools and community facilities. The approximate development value is £1 billion. Improvements were conceived in conjunction with the regeneration of adjacent communities. The design was driven by a number of successive masterplans, first a comprehensive one but later ones in conjunction with landowners.

Western Harbour is a forty-hectare dockland where 3,000 new homes are planned with 15 per cent affordable units. A large public park of eight hectares is proposed as central to the development, which also includes 50,000 square metres of commercial/business space and 6,000 square metres of retail space. An early masterplan resulted in three similar private apartment blocks, sixteen storeys at their highest. A waterside path has recently been opened along part of the site (see Plate 14.4). Following commercial and urban design misgivings, Forth Ports subsequently commissioned Robert Adam Architects to masterplan the remainder of the site. This latest plan, based on a study of context and microclimate, proposes tight-knit lower buildings and shorter-perimeter blocks, with facilities and open space within a five-minute walk of houses. It seeks to integrate a hierarchy of circulation spaces and introduce variety to the built form.

More controversially, it also includes non-stylistic design coding, specifying not only height and setbacks but also details such as window proportions, crown and base lines, plot widths, corner features and materials. The design codes were part of the outline planning permission and the code's authors have to approve designs before seeking detailed planning approval. The Congress for New Urbanism gave a Charter Award to the plan in 2008, the only European winner, for 'an urban texture that is much more closely related to the historic fabric of the adjacent historic area', differing from the former masterplan, which 'suffered from a lack of variety and urban form that was set to create an unpleasant and somewhat dangerous neighbourhood'. The award commends attention to climate and ecology to ensure environmental sustainability, walkable areas, controlling the use of vehicles, distributed public transport, and mixed uses including affordable housing. 'Lessons learned' emphasise 'generic coding based on character analysis of each street and space, specific ranges of materials and clear identification type' (Congress for the New Urbanism 2008).

Leith Docks is the largest development of all, 150 hectares, with 15,200 new homes planned, 25 per cent affordable, in addition to retail, commercial, leisure, educational and community services (totalling 200,000 square metres: Figure 14.3). The development value is approximately £2 billion. The *Leith Docks Development Framework* was prepared for Forth Ports by RMJM and adopted by the council as supplementary planning guidance to guide this colossal undertaking (CEC 2005). More detailed masterplans will be produced for smaller areas, the first ones by RTKL, which was involved in the regeneration of Baltimore Harbour. Outline planning permission was given in 2008, following public consultation. A *Planning and Design Statement* suggests that urban design principles have driven the proposals (Forth Properties Ltd. 2007).

Evaluation

Edinburgh's waterfront developments constitute a huge area (330 hectares) of long-term change, involving several billion pounds of investment and a population increase of 70,000 in the next twenty years. The waterfront is a major brownfield opportunity to reconnect the city with the seafront and meet pressing residential and employment needs.

The new *Edinburgh City Local Plan* has a chapter devoted to waterfront regeneration, including 'concept diagrams' and references to particular masterplans, thereby providing statutory weight and firm links with the planning process (CEC 2007a: 138–147). Urban design principles are firmly embedded in development frameworks and masterplans covering all areas, prepared by leading multidisciplinary firms. These emphasise laudable aims such as mixed land uses and housing tenure; lively street frontages; high-quality public realm; security; well-integrated public open space; public transport, pedestrian and cycling links; reduction in car dominance; access to the water; medium to high densities to support sustainability aims; building typology of perimeter blocks and some landmark buildings; strong linkages to existing areas; safeguarding strategic views; and microclimate and orientation. Unfortunately, the initial overarching Llewelyn-Davies Granton masterplan, prepared in 2001, fell apart when individual landowners refused to comply out of self-interest (Kerr 2005:213), commissioning their own plans, which resulted in disjuncture.

An integrative element is the recent *Edinburgh Waterfront Promenade Design Code*, establishing a continuous footpath and cycleway extending for ten miles. Plans for the promenade strengthen connections between the city, sea and movement networks, create activity nodes, promote tourist

Plate 14.4 Edinburgh: Western Harbour. One of the first apartment blocks, and the water-side walkway.

attractions, safeguard nature conservation and historic structures and assist regeneration (CEC 2008). This is a good example of strategic guidance incorporating strong urban design principles combining functional and aesthetic aspects, but it has yet to be implemented.

The recent urban design emphasis contrasts favourably with earlier waterfront developments. The scale of the monolithic retail development at Ocean Terminal works against the shops integrated within residential areas. The public is specifically excluded from the waterside (as with the nearby Scottish government headquarters), and both ends of the development are dominated by multistorey car parking, including the public gateway as approached from the city. Early development in Granton was characterised by a separation between buildings and streets, creating an unfriendly and lifeless feeling, with development not well related to the main roads. At Western Harbour, the scale of recently completed north-facing apartment blocks aggravates the windiness of this exposed peninsula (see Plate 14.4). In reaction, the pendulum has now swung to design codes harking back to a vernacular idiom, with detail going beyond what is generally regarded as urban design.

In order to turn around the negative image of industrial dereliction, an element of place marketing has been inevitable. References have been made to the twenty-first century New Town, the Forth Riviera and the Cool Sea. The reality of the biting wind whipping in from the North Sea and the rainy Scottish climate contrasts sharply with the Mediterranean imagery.

The waterfront proposals are contributing significantly to the city's housing stock and the overall inclusion of around 25 per cent affordable units is to be welcomed, in line with council planning policy. The challenge remains to implement a mixture of housing tenure, size and type. Regeneration efforts in Leith have been criticised for providing accommodation for single people and couples and not attracting families. It remains to be seen whether school provision will attract families and whether the emphasis on medium- to high-density accommodation will fly in the face of the many households, especially families, who prefer more suburban, lower-density living (Bramley and Morgan 2003: 467). What has been built so far is disappointingly representative of the current private housing market and it lacks diversity in terms of price, house types, size and social and demographic groups (Turok and Bailey 2004: 181). Developers themselves are now realising that the market is oversaturated with two-bedroom apartments, and there are plans for more family units, including townhouses. Proposed flats at Leith Docks are mainly five to eight storeys, unlike the early high-rise at Western Harbour.

Turning to the public realm, Edinburgh has traditionally tended to be well served by buses, and it is a positive feature of recently completed development that new bus routes have been quick to emerge. The new tramline linking Granton, Leith, the city centre and airport represents a real opportunity to prove Edinburgh's commitment to sustainable public transport, although the detailed design of the network has been criticised by Architecture + Design Scotland for not knitting in better with the urban fabric.

It is a strength that all the waterfront masterplans incorporate networks of open space, but too early to comment on their detailed design, management and use. An appendix to the *Leith Docks Development Framework* sets out sustainability targets and means of implementation, including drainage, waste, energy generation and use, green travel plans and accessibility.

In terms of governance issues, the waterfront is another example of regeneration initiatives being dependent on public–private partnership. The public sector is reliant on the private sector and has limited leverage over them. Economic development is not proceeding at the same pace as housing. The opportunity for wider links to the rest of the estuary, including ferry travel, has not been fully realised. There have been some genuine attempts at public consultation and visioning over time, but meaningful engagement is difficult when so much of the area has no existing community. It remains difficult to overcome the 'us and them' barriers that persist between new development and existing neighbourhoods. One of Terry Farrell's main design foci was the waterfront, but his limited time does not allow for ongoing detailed involvement. A self-appointed group, Art in Architecture, is promoting an alternative plan for Leith Docks and has stimulated debate at a symposium and on the web (Art in Architecture 2008). This public debate is vital for such an important site, but is it too late?

Conclusions

Tensions continue between integrating new development with the existing urban pattern of Edinburgh and worries that the quality of much new development falls short of the best from the past. The case studies show that a careful integration of old and new, taking advantage of the capital's unique context, is needed to both 'preserve and enhance' the environment. In a city notorious for its strong conservation lobby, a growing number of high-quality contemporary infill developments have spawned a new public confidence in what careful urban design can achieve. There is no doubt that messages about design excellence promoted by the Scottish government and Architecture + Design Scotland are increasingly evident as the city embraces urban design agendas. The city's comprehensive initiatives are making a difference in terms of raising awareness, gaining political support, improving skills levels of at least some staff, providing statutory policies and frameworks and guiding day-to-day planning applications. Planning policy and the development management process should play a crucial role in rejecting poor proposals. Officers and elected members need both the skills and confidence for strategic vision and firm control. Civic leadership and strategic direction are more evident now, supported increasingly by designers and the property industry. It is critical that the urban design agenda continues to receive cross-party support in a fragile political climate; an energetic political advocate has yet to emerge following the last election. Monitoring the practical effects of the new policies and guidance is crucial. The design champion and design leader, while contributing to this growing awareness, have not had the resources to implement significant change. There continue to be concerns about the council's ability to deliver on the ground, including its important client role, and worries that lack of support from senior officers throughout the council limits action.

The case studies show that development frameworks and masterplans for significant proposals are now the norm. They show conclusively that good design also relies ultimately on landowners, investors, developers and designers who understand its benefits. The Holyrood North case study shows what can be achieved by an enlightened developer, while past examples at the waterfront illustrate rampant opportunism. Following a period of ambitious masterplans and frameworks, the next several years will be critical in terms of implementation. There is a danger that masterplans secure planning permissions but get diluted through the development process. The public sector alone cannot implement good urban design ,and more work is needed to convince more people in the property market of its value.

The tight and expensive housing market is an issue that affects the whole city region, with the provision of affordable housing a continuing challenge. The limited infill sites mean that peripheral areas, including the waterfront and existing housing estates, must meet the bulk of the demand, creating an unarguable relationship between affordable housing and transportation. Spatial segregation has meant that many of Edinburgh's peripheral areas have suffered in the past. As at Craigmillar and the waterfront, growth opportunities must be seized delivering mixed communities of sufficient quality to attract new residents. Growth within the city served by good public transport will help alleviate pressure on outlying areas to meet Edinburgh's expansion needs. Too many regeneration efforts have produced a limited range of private housing, leading to gentrification and an imbalance of beneficiaries and choice. Again, the market needs to be convinced of the value of mixed communities, uses and house types.

Turning to the public realm and environmental issues, there are examples of both good and poor quality, but the trend seems to be improving generally. There was no evidence of clear, consistent, continuous improvement on the ground as a result of the design initiatives, but encouraging signs in the process. It is still too early to give a definitive view on qualitative results but the growing emphasis on the public realm is to be welcomed. Initiatives such as investment in urban design skills have started but need to be more pervasive. The council needs to have clear strategic aspirations given its key coordinating role. There is a danger that there are so many different initiatives that work becomes fragmented.

The rejection of congestion charging through a referendum was a major blow to sustainable transport. The new tramline linking Leith, the city centre and the airport will join up many key expansion areas with the centre, but the bulk of the city will not be served and the tram is no panacea for an end to congestion. Edinburgh is a good example of a compact city and there is no reason why policies limiting car dominance should not be pushed to their limit if the climate change imperative is to be taken seriously. Sustainability aims are evident in recent masterplans and planning policies. As in the case of the design initiatives discussed above, the watering down of these during implementation phases needs to be resisted. There is no doubt that densities have increased, but there is a worry that the pendulum might have swung too far, with too many flats crammed on sites poorly served by facilities.

In terms of governance, Edinburgh illustrates the complexity of interests that need to work together. Architecture + Design Scotland is in a key position to guide good practice nationally but is poorly funded in relation to CABE, thereby limiting its effectiveness. Genuinely and consistently engaging the public, so critical to successful urban design in the long term, remains a challenge. Confusion and cynicism over different waves of plans and proposals have characterised significant areas of change. It is unlikely that consensus will ever be reached but current debates are healthy. Despite major efforts, it is very difficult to overcome a 'them and us' dichotomy between existing and new areas. Gentrification is an easy trap. The case studies make the point that urban design in itself can never pretend to tackle wider economic and social problems.

Overall, Edinburgh shows just how complex and difficult urban design is. There are positive signs of progress, but no room for complacency. Much more evidence is needed to convince people that good quality can consistently be achieved on the ground.

References

Art in Architecture (2008). Online. Available at: http://www.artinarchitecture.co.uk (last accessed 12 September 2008).

Bramley, G. and Morgan, J. (2003) Building Competitiveness and Cohesion: The Role of New Housebuilding in Central Scotland's Cities. *Housing Studies,* 18 (4): 447–471.

Carley, M. and Ferrari, S. G. (2007) *The Cool Sea: Waterfront Communities Project Toolkit* (Edinburgh: Waterfront Communities Project) (Final report of EU Interreg IIIB North Sea Programme project).

Carrell, S. (2008) UN Threatens to Act Against Britain for Failure to Protect Heritage Sites. *Guardian,* 8 September: p. 3.

CEC (City of Edinburgh Council) (2002) *Urban Design and the Planning System,* Report to Planning Committee, 7 February (Edinburgh: City of Edinburgh Council).

CEC (2003a) *The Quality of Urban Design: Report of the Urban Design Working Group,* Report to Planning Committee, 6 February (Edinburgh: City of Edinburgh Council).

CEC (2003b) *Edinburgh Standards for Urban Design* (Edinburgh: City of Edinburgh Council).

CEC (2005) *Leith Docks Development Framework* (Edinburgh: City of Edinburgh Council).

CEC (2006a) *The Edinburgh Standards for Streets* (Edinburgh: City of Edinburgh Council).

CEC (2006b) *Tram Design Manual* (Edinburgh: City of Edinburgh Council).

CEC (2007a) *Edinburgh City Local Plan Deposit Version* (Edinburgh: City of Edinburgh Council).

CEC (2007b) *Edinburgh Standards for Sustainable Building* (Edinburgh: City of Edinburgh Council).

CEC (2008) *The (draft) Edinburgh Waterfront Promenade Design Code* (Edinburgh: City of Edinburgh Council).

CEC, PARC Craigmillar, Llewelyn Davies Yeang (2005) *Craigmillar Urban Design Framework* (Edinburgh: City of Edinburgh Council).

Congress for the New Urbanism (2008) *2008 Charter Awards: Masterplan for Western Harbour.* Online. Available at: http://www.cnu.org/node/1773 (last accessed 12 September 2008).

Dawson, E. and Higgins, M. (2009) How Planning Authorities Can Improve Quality Through The Design Review Process: Lessons From Edinburgh. *Journal of Urban Design,* 14 (1): 101–114.

DSP (Development Services Partnership) (1993) *Holyrood Project North Site* (Edinburgh: Development Services Partnership).

Edwards, B. and Jenkins, P. (eds) (2005) *Edinburgh: The Making of a Capital City* (Edinburgh: Edinburgh University Press).

Farrell, T. (2008) Twelve Challenges for Edinburgh. *Prospect,* 130: 1–49 (special supplement).

Forth Properties Ltd (2007) *Regenerating Leith Docks: A Framework for Development, Planning and Design Statement* (Edinburgh: Forth Properties).

Hague, C. (2005) The Changing Role of the Planner Before and After The Second World War and the Effect on Urban Form. In B. Edwards and P. Jenkins (eds) *Edinburgh: The Making of a Capital City* (Edinburgh: Edinburgh University Press) pp. 168–179.

Higgins, M., Walton, R., Douglas, M. and Devlin, D. (2005) *Health Impact Assessment of Craigmillar Urban Design Framework* (Edinburgh: Public Health and Health Policy Lothian NHS Board and South East Edinburgh Locality Health Care Cooperative).

Jenkins, P. and Holder, J. (2005) Creation and Conservation of the Built Environment in the Later 20th Century. In B. Edwards and P. Jenkins (eds) *Edinburgh: The Making of a Capital City* (Edinburgh: Edinburgh University Press) pp. 185–203.

Kerr, D. (2005) Preparing For the 21st Century: The City in Aa Global Environment. In B. Edwards and P. Jenkins (eds) *Edinburgh: The Making of a Capital City* (Edinburgh: Edinburgh University Press) pp. 204–216.

PARC (Promoting and Regenerating Craigmillar) and SEPA (Scottish Environment Protection Agency) (2008)

Technical Visit to Edinburgh's South East Wedge, unpublished paper from 11th International Conference on Urban Drainage, Edinburgh, September 2008.

Rosenburg, L. and Johnson, J. (2005) 'Conservative Surgery' in Old Edinburgh 1880–1940. In B. Edwards and P. Jenkins (eds) *Edinburgh: The Making of a Capital City* (Edinburgh: Edinburgh University Press) pp. 131–149.

Scottish Executive (2001) *Designing Places* (Edinburgh: Scottish Executive Development Department).

Turok, I. and Bailey, N. (2004) Twin Track Cities? Competitiveness and Cohesion in Glasgow and Edinburgh. *Progress in Planning,* 62: 135–204.

15 Glasgow

Renaissance on the Clyde?

Steve Tiesdell

Introduction

Glasgow has proved a resilient city. Keating (1988) referred to it as 'the city that refused to die'. A great industrial city of the nineteenth century, it suffered prolonged deindustrialisation during the twentieth century and only began to become 'miles better' during the 1980s. The twenty-first century sees the city remerging with a new economic base in knowledge-intensive services, such as finance and the cultural and media industries; retail, tourism and education are also significant components of its new economy.

The city's present economic resurgence is stronger than in the 1980s and 1990s. Between 2000 and 2006, its employment rate – the proportion of the working age population in work – increased from a scarcely believable 55 per cent to 65 per cent, though it remains below that of Scotland (75 per cent) and the core city average (67 per cent). With almost 80,000 new jobs locating in the city between 1995 and 2006 and an additional 40,000 city residents having found work, it has also been one of the UK's fastest growing cities in terms of rate of job creation (all figures from GEF 2007: 3). Economic growth has translated into modest population growth. In 2006, 581,000 people were living in Glasgow: a net increase of 4,000 on 2000 but a stark contrast with the haemorrhage of population for decades prior to this. Nonetheless if the foreground is apparent economic success, the background is major social problems – poor health, persistent worklessness, violent crime and increasing social polarisation (see MacLeod 2002; Turok and Bailey 2004a,b; Friend of Zanetti 2006; Hassan *et al.* 2007).

This chapter focuses on the physical transformation of Glasgow's central area and on competing conceptions of a 'design-led' urban renaissance. Urban design is about making 'good' places for people, key elements of which include mixed uses and diversity; connectivity and animation; public realm and accessibility; density and viability; identity and character; and sustainability. Place-making can be understood as a design and as a governance activity, which Varkki George (1997) termed first-order and second-order design. First-order design is similar to architectural design, involves the direct design of a component of the built environment, typically a building or a complex of buildings, and is usually undertaken by the private sector. Second-order design is similar to planning, and more generally to governance, and is generally (though not exclusively) undertaken by the public sector. It involves shaping the decision environments of key development actors, typically by means of plans, strategies and frameworks, but also by deployment and modulation of incentives/disincentives, such as financial subsidies, discounted land or infrastructure provision.

Second-order urban design can be place shaping or 'formative'. Occurring before the design of the development proposal, it shapes the design/development process by creating a frame for first-order design. It might consist solely of broad design policies/principles, but it can also be developed in greater depth through spatial strategies, development frameworks and site-specific design briefs.

The challenge faced by cities such as Glasgow, is to facilitate development while insisting on high-quality design. In the prevailing neoliberal era, many cities have been reluctant to engage in formative urban design with the consequence that design quality must be addressed, perhaps 'rescued', through the threat of refusing consent to poorly designed development. Reactive second-order urban design through development control is, however, intrinsically limited because – usually by omission – more fundamental and strategic design decisions have already been made and constrain what can be achieved.

After a brief setting of the context of Glasgow, this chapter outlines urban design and development in the city prior to 1999, when public agencies played a major role in facilitating and guiding private sector development. This provides a foundation for discussion of the post-1999 period, when there was a shift towards a more market-led approach.

The Glasgow context

Glasgow city centre's main north–south thoroughfare is Buchanan Street, which, with Sauchiehall Street and Argyle Street, forms the city's retail 'Z' (Plate 15.1). To the west of Buchanan Street lies the main business district – Blythswood – south of which is Broomielaw, a rundown, former industrial but emerging office area. To the east lies Merchant City. Previously a warehouse area, it has recently become a more mixed area with residential and entertainment uses. To the south is a more rundown mixed-use area, interspersed with large areas of dereliction and brownfield car parks.

Glasgow's morphology derives from three distinctive periods of city development, each leaving an infrastructure frame – a capital web. The oldest frame derives from organic growth around two key nodes, an ecclesiastical centre to the north and a commercial centre around Glasgow Cross to the south, linked by the High Street. The second frame derives from street grids laid out during the eighteenth and early nineteenth centuries: one to the north-west of Glasgow Cross, forming the area now known as Merchant City; two others further to the west at Meadowflats (1792) and on the Blythswood Estate (c. 1800); and three south of the Clyde at Tradeston, Laurieston and Hutchesontown (c. 1800). Deriving from the late 1960s, the third frame is the partial development of a 'motorway box' around the city centre, of which only the north and west elements were ever built.

Concurrent with building the new road system, the city's economy collapsed as chronic deindustrialisation combined with a flight of people, firms and investment. By 1979, the city's population had fallen from more than 1 million in 1961, to 700,000. The result was a shrinking core city fringed with vacant buildings, temporary brownfield car parks, creeping dereliction and abandonment.

Regeneration – pre 1999

The 1970s saw a policy shift away from slum clearance, comprehensive redevelopment and road building, and towards rehabilitation. Cleaning of the city's extensive stock of Georgian, Victorian

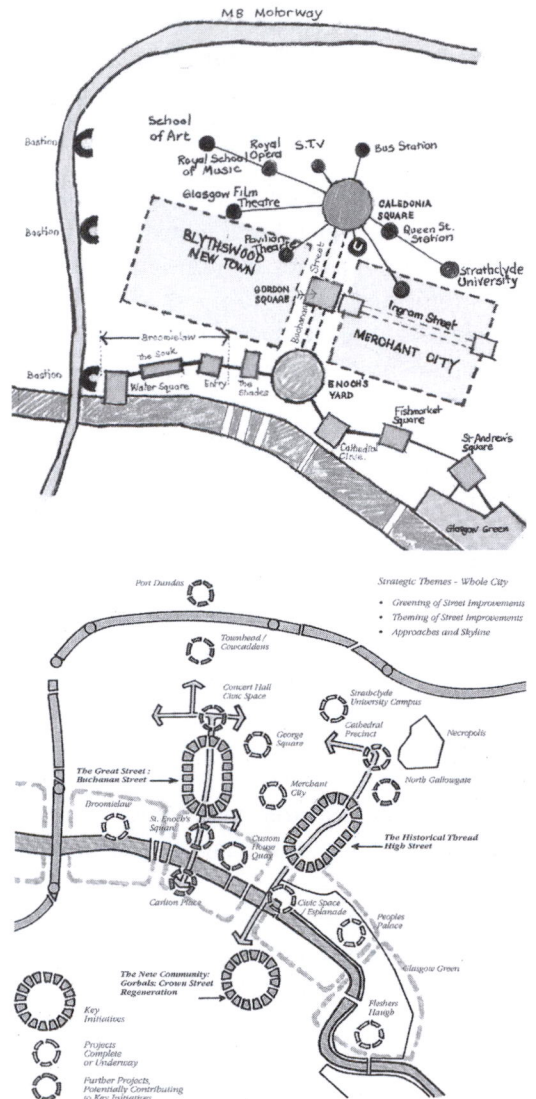

Plate 15.1 Glasgow: Spatial Development Frameworks. Spatial development frameworks for Glasgow city centre by Mckinsey/Cullen (1985) and Gillespies (1990) (Courtesy of Gillespies).

and Edwardian architecture revealed a city of honey and red sandstone, while redirection of public resources, from a New Town at Stonehouse to the Glasgow Eastern Area Renewal (GEAR) project, heralded an era of regeneration and renewal. Local public agencies played a leading role by undertaking place-marketing campaigns (e.g. Glasgow's Miles Better); launching community-based housing schemes; supporting rehabilitation of tenements and conversion of warehouses; promoting cultural events and festivals (e.g. Glasgow Garden Festival, 1988; European City of Culture, 1990); investing in tourist and visitor attractions (e.g. the Burrell Gallery, 1982; Scottish Exhibition and Convention Centre, 1985); and, of particular interest here, developing a spatial development strategy for the central city.

Contributing to a 1985 report and drawing upon ideas already current within the city, urbanist Gordon Cullen offered a vision and direction for future development in which Buchanan Street would become a 'great city street', flanked by 'two sturdy characters' – Blythswood and Merchant City – and counterpointed by a 'string of pearls' along the Clyde (Mckinsey/Cullen 1985; see Plate 15.1). Developing and extending Cullen's ideas, Glasgow-based consultants Gillespies (1990) proposed four spatial development themes:

- the Great Street Project – the Townhead–Buchanan Street–River Clyde axis;
- the Historical Thread – the Cathedral–High Street–Glasgow Cross–Gorbals axis;
- the New Community – creating a new neighbourhood in the Gorbals;
- the Marine Quarter – focusing on the Kelvin/Clyde confluence and suggesting a Byres Road–Partick Cross–Clyde–Govan axis.

Focusing on key places and linkages between those places, Cullen and Gillespies' work has been influential on all subsequent plans and strategies for the central city. Although the early 1990s property recession would slow the pace of regeneration, a coherent spatial development framework was in place.

The challenge for the city centre was to enhance its position as a retail centre and to develop its position as a business centre. The development of two major shopping malls – first the St Enoch Centre (opened 1989) and subsequently Buchanan Galleries (1998) – at the angles of the retail 'Z' made Buchanan Street the city's pre-eminent shopping street (see Plate 15.2). These developments were a mixed blessing, reinforcing the city centre's retail offer, but also making it spatially more concentrated, internalised and privatised, depriving it of identity and vitality, and reducing its permeability. Nonetheless, retail has been an increasingly important component of Glasgow's economy, with the city vying for position as the UK's leading retail centre after London's West End.

The commissioning of a public realm strategy (Gillespies 1995) fleshed out the ideas and concepts proposed by Cullen and Gillespies. Two demonstration projects were undertaken in 1997: the first focused on Candleriggs in the heart of Merchant City; the second involved pedestrianisa-

Plate 15.2 Glasgow: Buchanan Street. More consumerist than Cullen intended, Buchanan Street now has the highest footfall of any UK street outside central London.

tion of Royal Exchange Square between Merchant City and Buchanan Street. An international competition, the Great Street Project, for comprehensive public realm improvements to Buchanan Street, was held in 1997. Won by local consultants Gillespies, the project was completed in 2000.

Two projects – Merchant City and Crown Street – epitomise good practice in terms of design-aware and place-sensitive development facilitation. Begun in the early 1980s, the Merchant City Project demonstrated how public investment in infrastructure and development subsidies and public–private partnerships for flagship development projects such as Ingram Square (240 units) could revitalise a rundown but historic area, reinventing it as a new residential and entertainment quarter (Jones and Patrick 1992; Tiesdell *et al.* 1996). The majority of development projects in the area during this period were heavily grant aided, with developers also often receiving discounted transfers of public land and buildings. The city also invested in new infrastructure, including multistorey car parks.

Begun in 1990, the Crown Street Project – a mixed development of 1,000 residential units, plus associated uses, on a sixteen-hectare plot in the heart of the Gorbals – demonstrated how a high-quality 'new' place could be produced through a design-aware procurement strategy that harnessed political commitment, agency and community buy-in, organisational and financial resources, and had command over the provision of new infrastructure and the strategic disposal of land and other assets. Key elements of the 'Crown Street Model' included (Tiesdell and Macfarlane 2007):

- a dedicated public sector agency – the Crown Street Regeneration Project (CRSP) – to lead and coordinate development;
- a masterplan/development framework and prescriptive design briefs to coordinate and control development;
- public investment in infrastructure and development subsidies to 'prime the pump';
- development control exercised through land ownership and land transfers; and
- gradual release of land parcels, so that the agency could benefit from the uplift in land values resulting from the success of the initial phases.

In addition to significant upfront public sector investment, the model also required a willingness to forgo an immediate capital receipt, incur development risk and commit agency time.

The wider design challenge in the Gorbals was to create a framework within which desirable new mixed-use and mixed-tenure neighbourhoods could develop. Based on the spine of a reconstituted Crown Street (which connects to Glasgow Cross and High Street), the new street pattern remade the historic grid pattern and offered new connections for wider reconstruction of the Gorbals, with the use of open-ended street grids facilitating a coherent joining-up of subsequent development projects at Gorbals East (350 units from 1993) and Queen Elizabeth Square (600 units from 1998).

The period to 1999 showed public agencies taking a leading role in facilitating and guiding private sector development, with the local authority playing a central role. In 1975 a two-tier system of local government had been introduced, with Strathclyde Regional Council becoming the strategic tier, operating over a wider area, and taking powers and responsibilities from the City Corporation. The former Glasgow City Corporation had been a traditional managerialist and paternalistic authority, with politicians keen to control what happened in their city and suspicious of the motives of 'outsiders', be they from the private sector or other tiers of government

– a culture that has endured. The regional council's abolition in 1995 returned the lower-tier authority, Glasgow District Council, to its cherished unitary status – with the new Glasgow City Council becoming responsible for both strategic and local planning. Within the new council, planning and development and economic development became a single integrated department.

Nonetheless, in whichever manifestation, the Glasgow local authority has had to work in partnership with other major public agencies. The principal agencies were the Scottish Development Agency (SDA) (established in 1975) and its local body, Glasgow Development Agency (GDA), responsible for economic development and investment; and subsequently their successors, Scottish Enterprise, formed in 1991, and its local enterprise company, Scottish Enterprise Glasgow (SEG); and, after 1989, Scottish Homes, the national housing agency (Figure 15.1). As well as providing specialist expertise and focus, these national agencies were a means for central government – always mistrustful of Glasgow's political leadership – to put resources into the city, while by-passing the local authority and retaining some control. With the exception of some residential projects, the city council and GDA/SEG had to work together on almost every project of any scale. The city council and SEG have coterminous boundaries, thereby removing some of the territorial complications that afflict other partnership arrangements. The private sector has traditionally had, and continues to have, less significance in the city – although for a short period in the late 1980s, a public–private partnership, Glasgow Action, was active in the city (see Boyle 1989).

Glasgow's designation as UK City of Architecture and Design in 1999 signified its status as an innovator and leader in terms of urban design and development practices (Carmona 1996). A valuable outcome of this was Homes-for-the-Future (100 units) near Glasgow Green, which, among many design attributes, demonstrated the use of a masterplan to coordinate nine firms of architects each designing a development parcel. Another legacy was the establishment of The Lighthouse, Scotland's national centre for architecture and design.

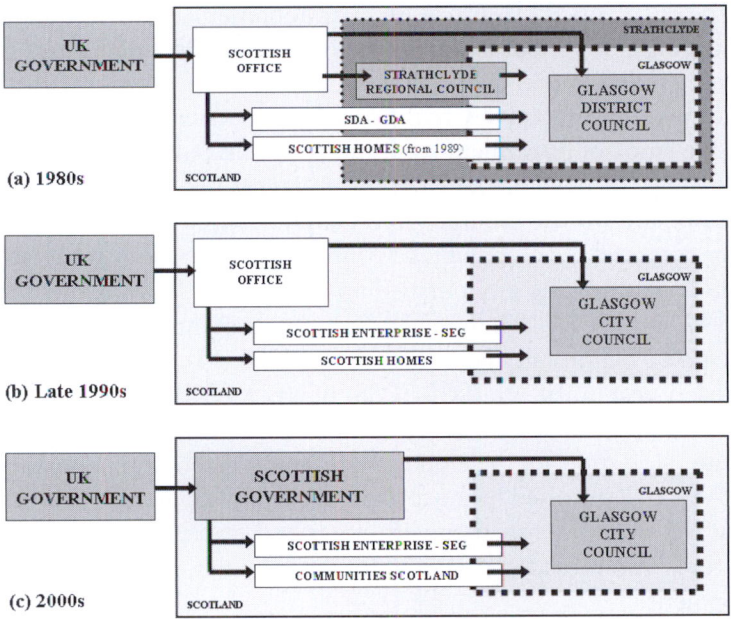

Figure 15.1 Glasgow: principal public agencies operating in Glasgow.

Renaissance – post 1999

With a deep tradition of urban living and exemplar projects such as Merchant City and Crown Street providing a foundation and model for subsequent development, Glasgow seemed in tune with the key elements of the design-led renaissance policy agenda as epitomised by the English Urban Task Force report (UTF 1999a). The subsequent development of an explicit urban design policy agenda at the national level, in both England and Scotland, involved catching up with practices in cities such as Glasgow.

Governance

The public agencies most significant to development in central Glasgow after 1999 remained Glasgow City Council, SEG and Scottish Homes (becoming Communities Scotland after 2001). Although less significant in the central city, a new agency – Glasgow Housing Association (GHA) – was established in 2003 to receive transfer of the city's remaining council housing stock (approximately 81,000 units) (see Kearns and Lawson 2008). What was new, however, was Scottish devolution in 1999, which introduced a new tier of elected politicians. As the Labour Party in Scotland has its roots and strongest support in the west of Scotland, a Labour government at Holyrood should have been favourable to Glasgow. But, despite a Labour-controlled city council and (until 2007) a Labour–Liberal Democrat coalition at Holyrood, Labour Party in-fighting, combined with the personalities and political histories of central actors, resulted in a power struggle regarding who could and should shape Glasgow's future (Crichton 2003). The Scottish government controlled much of the funding, both through transfers to the city council and through its executive agencies, Scottish Enterprise and Communities Scotland. But these agencies often had to work with the city council, whose considerable land holdings and planning and other powers enabled it to slow down and frustrate progress. The city council and SEG had especially strained relations during the early 2000s (Crichton 2003; Low 2006).

Significantly, the city council's shift to a more entrepreneurial ethos and market-led approach also accelerated during this period. Whereas the Merchant City and Crown Street projects had benefited from being rolled out gradually, now there was a new urgency. Passionately committed to the city – his city – the combative Charlie Gordon was council leader from 1999 until 2005. The city's extensive stock of brownfield land, much of it in public sector ownership, has always offered an ample stock of development opportunities. What had been missing was demand. Keen to get development on the ground soon, Gordon sought to broker deals with developers; reluctant to fetter potential development, anything that might delay it represented an obstacle. From the late 1990s onwards the city pursued an increasingly 'development-friendly' approach. Between 1996/1997 and 2002/2003, annual private investment development activity in the city was typically around £2 billion (all figures from GCC 2008: 15). In 2003/2004, it rose to £2.6 billion, increasing each year until, in 2007–2008, it was £4.3 billion.[1] This development boom provided a window of opportunity to get things done in the city.

To provide a 'one-stop shop' for development consents, internal reorganisation within the city council during 1999–2000 resulted in the formation of Development and Regeneration Services, bringing property and planning together, with roads and transport subsequently added in 2008. These new structures also provided potential for more joined-up thinking and decision-making regarding development.

In 2005, the more consensual Steven Purcell became council leader. While remaining avidly development friendly, Purcell (2008) has sought to broaden the development agenda to address social inclusion. Subsequent design-related reforms and innovations included the formation of the Glasgow Urban Design Panel (GUDP) as a forum for design review, appointment of a city design advisor (CDA) and commissioning of a detailed digital model of the central city as a tool for design, development management and communication. The city council has also developed better relations with the Scottish National Party government elected in 2007. Scottish Enterprise and Communities Scotland were both reformed in 2007/2008 in ways that, inter alia, returned some powers to local authorities.

In the core

The post-1999 challenge for the city centre was to consolidate and enhance its position as a centre for consumption (especially retail and leisure), strengthen its position as a business centre and grow its city centre population, especially in Merchant City and along the disused waterfront. By the end of the 1990s, much of the core city was well placed for development.

Significant retail investment has occurred, with the city centre witnessing a continuing spatial concentration of retail activity. Despite being substantial components of the overall retail offer, Buchanan Galleries and St Enoch Centre, compete with each other and with the wider city centre. The St Enoch Centre is currently being refurbished and extended, which will take it to over 90,000 square metres, while Buchanan Galleries proposes doubling its retail floorspace to 120,000 square metres. Despite bolstering the city's overall retail offer, these developments will result in further concentration (and internalisation) of retailing to the detriment of the wider city centre, especially if major stores are induced to relocate from Sauchiehall and Argyle Street. The retail spend has already been dissipated by the development of Braehead Shopping Centre (80,000 square metres, with 6,500 free parking spaces, opened in 1999) four miles to the west and Silverburn Shopping Centre (90,000 square metres, with 4,500 free parking spaces, opened in 2007) five miles to the south-west of the city centre.

A rolling programme of public realm improvements has been undertaken throughout much of the retail core, in Merchant City and in the International Financial Services District (IFSD), largely funded by a combination of European, national and city money, plus contributions from developers. Rather than extending into fringe areas and/or encouraging new development in new locations, however, this has largely been a physical upgrading and character reinforcement of the core city's public spaces and streets. Furthermore, apart from pavement widening and some additional pedestrianisation, there has been no remaking of public spaces through innovative design. The city's principal civic space, George Square, needs modernisation. To provide a durable and unobstructed surface for hosting trade and other events, it was controversially relaid with red tarmac in 2002. More positively, a 'café-in-the-square' design competition was held in 2004/2005. But, by demonstrating the need not just for a café, but also for a wider design rethink, Studio KAPS's entry effectively subverted the competition and, as yet, no further action has been taken.

As well as retail investment, substantial residential and commercial investment has occurred in the core areas of Merchant City and Blythswood/Broomielaw. Throughout most of the core city, development occurs within the established frames of their grids and benefits from positive spillover (synergistic) and agglomeration effects. The established context – the location's physical, social and economic infrastructure – also provides a frame for any development. The design challenge is thus largely one of reinforcing the existing context through sensitive urban architectural design; the land use challenge involves ensuring an appropriate mix of uses across the area. Provided certain 'rules' of good urbanism – respecting the street line and height datum, active frontages at ground floor level, etc. – are followed, design and development is relatively unproblematic.

Capitalising on the earlier investment, new development in Merchant City has primarily consisted of private projects, the majority without need of direct public subsidy – though significant public investment in environmental improvements throughout the area should be acknowledged. New developments are either conversions of existing buildings (albeit many are new-builds behind retained façades), infill development of gap sites or new-build following demolition. The intensity and volume of development are epitomised by recent residential developments along the area's main west–east spine, Ingram Street (see Plate 15.3). Nonetheless, Merchant City is only thinly animated and is not (yet) a vibrant urban neighbourhood. Despite the amount of residential development, many units have been bought as investment properties and have remained unoccupied. Planning consents require provision for active uses on the ground floor, but many such units remain unlet.

Just three larger brownfield sites remain in Merchant City – the most prominent of which is the so-called 'Selfridges site'. With extensive frontage onto Argyle Street, Candleriggs and Wilson Street, it is a major blight on the area. A number of category B listed buildings have already been demolished and others are deteriorating.[2] Subdivision of the site within a development framework would probably facilitate development, while also limiting the scale of development and providing variety. Once these sites are developed Merchant City will be substantially complete as a development project and the development challenge will be to extend the positive context southwards across Argyle Street and eastwards across High Street.

New office development in the core city has primarily occurred in the IFSD, a ten-year initiative designated in 2001 covering an area of approximately one square kilometre in the south-west of the city centre and intended to attract international financial services companies and to provide a relocation option for existing Glasgow-based companies. As demand for grade A

Plate 15.3 Glasgow: Ingram Street, Merchant City. Merchant City's main east-west thoroughfare, Ingram Street has developed as an up-market fashion street, while new residential development has brought vacant buildings into active use.

office space and rising office rents (peaking at £305 per square metre in 2007) made demolition and redevelopment viable, most development north of Argyle Street has been infill development within the Blythswood grid. The design challenge is again largely one of sensitive urban architectural design, and several new buildings stand comparison with the best Victorian and Edwardian commercial buildings. But, while previous redevelopment retained the original plot subdivisions, demand for larger floorplates has led to plot amalgamation and much larger buildings – the largest being Aurora on Bothwell Street at 16,500 square metres – changing the area's visual and physical scale and often creating a blander street scene.

During the 1990s, Broomielaw – the IFSD south of Argyle Street – had been changing from an industrial and warehouse area to an office location. After 2000 the area continued to develop incrementally through progressive and largely contiguous development from the eastern (city centre) end. Compared with the more regular Blythswood grid, the Broomielaw grid has elongated north–south street blocks. The larger street blocks allow, and perhaps require, the creation of new public spaces and east–west crossings within the block. Atlantic Quay and the proposals for Atlantic Square, by the same developer, illustrate the evolution of design and development. Begun in 1990, the initial phases of Atlantic Quay were seven- to eight-storey monolithic office blocks. At twelve storeys, the final building, Capella, is taller and has provision for active uses on the ground floor. The public spaces at Atlantic Quay are simply spaces between buildings, but at Atlantic Square it is intended to introduce mixed uses and to create a public square between two office buildings rising to twelve storeys and a residential building, with retail and leisure uses at ground floor.

The IFSD's southern and western edges – the Broomielaw waterfront and the M8 corridor – provide opportunities for a more powerful urban statement. The office buildings completed so far on Broomielaw have been in scale with the nine-storey datum of the existing city, but have not risen to the challenge of the setting. Proposed developments (ranging from fourteen to thirty storeys) to the west suggest a significant scaling-up of ambition that will dwarf the existing buildings. Despite a series of tall building proposals, sites along the M8 corridor remain undeveloped.

On the edge of the core

Alongside burgeoning development activity in the core city, there is continuing dereliction and vacancy on the city centre fringe, with key areas around the core city – east of High Street, the Clyde Street waterfront and alongside the M8 – remaining undeveloped. This reflects the difficulty of both development and design outside core areas. Rather than simply responding to an existing context, the design and development challenge is typically one of 'healing' a degraded or fragmented context or, in some instances, making a new context. The design and development tasks are more difficult in two key ways: first, because the locations are riskier and, second, because a context needs to be extended or established. Formative place-shaping urban design, including investment in infrastructure, can aid these tasks by establishing a frame for development, by ensuring critical mass and synergy between developments, and by reducing development risk.

Recognising that the Crown Street model cannot be resourced on multiple sites across the city, alternative and more economical ways of facilitating and managing development have been sought. These are important because some 15 per cent of land in the city, much of it in some form of public or quasi-public ownership, is in line for development. In the New Gorbals a different procurement method was adopted at Oatlands, a development of 1,275 residential units on a thirty-two-hectare site, which started on site in 2005. The land was sold by the city council following a design competition requiring a masterplan to be developed in accordance with a detailed council brief, and the signing of a master development agreement by the lead developer. But early impressions suggest Oatlands' design quality compares unfavourably with that of Crown Street and Gorbals East in terms of construction quality, the design and detailing of the public realm, and the intrusiveness of car parking. The later phases of Queen Elizabeth Square also show a loss of design quality.

Other approaches are being tried elsewhere in the city. Masterplans prepared to a city council brief are a common prerequisite of sales of larger land parcels, such as Collegelands, east of High Street – but there are continuing debates about how prescriptive developments briefs should be. With Scottish government encouragement a high-profile design and development competition was held at Bellgrove in the near East End. The Glasgow Canal Partnership, consisting of the city council, British Waterways and a private developer (Isis Waterside Developments), is engaged in developing a series of masterplans/development frameworks for the Forth and Clyde Canal corridor to the north of the city centre. As none of these projects is yet out of the ground, judgement of quality would be premature, but the processes provide some hope for twenty-first-century equivalents of Crown Street.

On the Clyde waterfront

Glasgow's major development challenge of the post-2000 period has been the Clyde waterfront (Figure 15.2). Collapse of its shipyards left the city with an extensive legacy of waterfront land. Presenting problems of dereliction and blight, it was also a major opportunity to effect strategic transformation. Until 2000 the city had other issues to the fore, and the Clyde had regressed from being Europe's most industrialised and exploited waterfront to possibly its most neglected.

Some waterfront development had occurred by the early twenty-first century. The first was the Scottish Exhibition and Convention Centre (SECC, opened in 1985), together with extensive car parks to the east and west, built on the site of the in-filled Queens Dock. An eighteen-storey hotel was added in 1989 and the 'iconic' Clyde Auditorium, known as The Armadillo, opened in 1997 (see Plate 15.4). Rarely place-making, such iconic architectural projects are

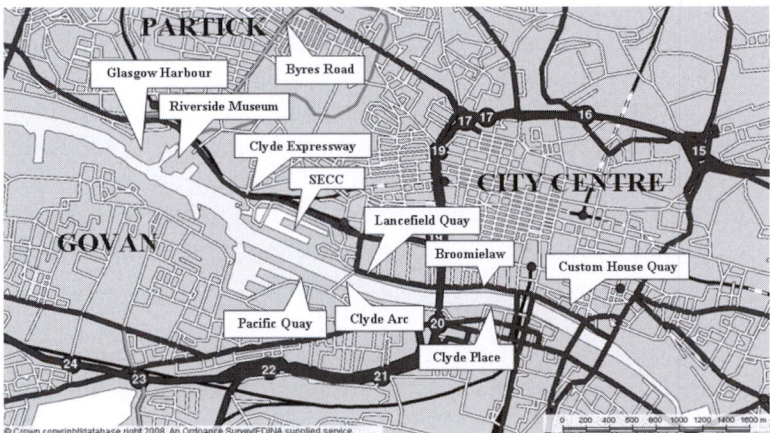

Figure 15.2 Glasgow: development sites and projects along the Clyde waterfront. © Crown Copyright and/or database right. All rights reserved. Licence Number 100049043.

Plate 15.4 Glasgow The Clyde Auditorium, SECC. Plonked in a sea of tarmac, neither appropriating nor commanding external space, the Armadillo 'signifies' but fails to create a meaningful place.

typically place-signifying – they make a site distinctive and put it on the map. Except for its elementary functions, the SECC does not invite or reward engagement. It lacks a mix of uses and its public spaces are of poor quality. South of the SECC is Pacific Quay, the site of the 1988 Garden Festival. Scheduled for development following the festival, but, located on the south side and lacking good vehicular connections to the north side, it lay vacant until development of the Millennium Commission-funded Glasgow Science Centre (GSC). Opened in 2001, these buildings – a titanium-clad, crescent-shaped science mall, a bean-shaped IMAX theatre and a slender viewing tower (originally intended for St Enoch Square) – provide more iconic forms on the waterfront. But lacking a mix of uses and active frontages that would promote and stimulate animation of the waterfront and with public spaces that are merely perfunctory, they offer little substantive place quality.

Another potential icon under construction near the Clyde/Kelvin confluence is the city council's new Riverside Museum, the outcome of an international design competition. Designed by Zaha Hadid, it is a long, narrow building, open to the 'city' and the 'river' at either end, with a complex, multigabled cross-section, due for completion in 2011. What gives it complexity and interest is the dramatic 'crumpling' of the plan. There are two major concerns: the building's design quality may be compromised by steadily rising costs and, if it is to be place-making rather than merely place-signifying, the animation and quality of the external public spaces is vital.

By 2000, the range of development projects coming forward along the tidal river required a more strategic approach to ensure that the whole would be greater than the sum of the parts. After a troubled gestation, when an urban development corporation was threatened (see Gough 2003), Clyde Waterfront Regeneration was formed in 2002. Charged with bringing together public and private sectors to regenerate the thirteen-kilometre stretch of waterfront from Glasgow Green to Erskine, it is a strategic partnership of the Scottish government, SEG and Glasgow City, Renfrewshire and West Dunbartonshire Councils (CWWG 2002).

Given scarce resources, the Clyde waterfront's size and scale presented the city with the classic regeneration dilemma between alleviating social need and exploiting economic opportunity, and deciding whether scarce resources should be deployed in the East End or on the waterfront. The reality, however, was that the city had few resources available anyway and so was heavily dependent on the private sector. The waterfront was championed by council leader Charlie Gordon,

Plate 15.5 Glasgow Harbour: With phase one complete and phase two nearing completion, Glasgow Harbour remains an exclusive, car-based and mono-functional development.

who was particularly influential in securing the largest single project – Glasgow Harbour (see Plate 15.5). Covering some fifty-two hectares, with three kilometres of waterfront, and proposing 2,500 residential units plus new business, retail/leisure space and some twenty-one hectares of public open space, the fact of its development is undoubtedly a significant achievement.

Public transport and other infrastructure are essential to open up and provide access along the waterfront. Clyde Fastlink was envisioned as a light rapid transit system, running from the city centre to Clydebank, on the north side of the river, and to Glasgow airport on the south side. The first phase will now be a dedicated bus rapid transit – albeit future-proofed to allow upgrade to a tram system. It will run from the city centre, via the IFSD and SECC, and terminate at the western end of Glasgow Harbour. First announced in 2000, it is scheduled to be operational by 2010; but has been delayed by disputes about who should fund it – the city council or the Scottish Government. This delay is problematic as the existing roads provide access but also make development car based; early provision of public transit allows people to build more sustainable lifestyles around it. A larger question is whether Fastlink is conceived merely as a transport engineering project or, more expansively, as a vital element of place-shaping infrastructure. It will not be place-shaping if it follows development.

As suggested in Gillespies' 1990 report, a key spatial development theme of the local plans of the 1990s and of the 2003 *City Plan* (GCC 2003a) has been to conceive the river as connecting, rather than dividing, areas. Thus, in plans and strategies, Broomielaw/Tradeston, Partick/Govan, etc., are considered as single areas. To give this concept substance, however, this approach needed a set of concrete actions: new bridges/connections; public places on the waterfront; activity on the water itself; and, in most cases, substantial development on the less favoured south side. Few of these have yet been forthcoming. The Clyde Expressway is another source of severance on the north side, frustrating connections between the previously industrial waterfront and the neighbourhoods to the north.

Clyde Waterfront Regeneration has pledged to build six new bridges between Glasgow Green and Erskine. As new bridges not only improve connectivity but can also bestow new character on an area, the intention has been to create visually distinctive 'identity bridges'. The first – the £20 million Clyde Arc, popularly known as Squinty Bridge and the first road bridge over the

Clyde to be built in Glasgow since Kingston Bridge (1970) – opened in 2006. Providing much needed connection to the more affluent north side, its construction had been a precondition for the BBC (British Broadcasting Corporation) and independent broadcaster STV relocating to new headquarters at Pacific Quay. Their presence also boosts an emerging digital media quarter in Govan. A design competition for a proposed Tradeston Pedestrian Bridge and attendant public realm works was held in 2003, with a £40 million budget. Featuring a sweeping horizontal curve, Richard Rodgers's Neptune's Way was judged the winner. Rising costs (estimated at £60 million) caused it to be abandoned and a new fixed-budget design-and-build competition was held. The new design, nicknamed Squiggly Bridge (currently being installed), is less dramatic but provides a more direct crossing.

Public realm improvements will be associated with Fastlink, but much more investment is needed. A good model is provided by a public realm project currently on site at Broomielaw/ Clyde Place, where the city is engaged in proactive place-shaping through public realm works, infrastructure provision and assistance with land assembly. Along Broomielaw, the 2008 proposals were for a series of pavilions beneath a continuous, undulating canopy – essential in a rainy city – with restaurants and bars (2,800 square metres) at first-floor level. First-floor level bars may inhibit natural animation of the waterfront, but a more significant flaw might be the four-lane carriageway, a median strip and then the Fastlink dual carriageway, which will separate the north side of Broomielaw from the waterfront. On the south bank, infrastructure and public realm works are being undertaken at Clyde Place (Tradeston) and a private developer, with public assistance with land assembly and consolidation, is due to develop a first phase of three waterfront perimeter blocks of eleven storeys with over 1,006 residential units in all.

Since 2004, an annual River Festival has been held, with attendances now reaching 75,000. This demonstrates interest and potential, but it is natural rather than cultural animation which involves considerable effort and organisation that is required. A consistent water level would facilitate more natural activity on the water surface, and a weir has been proposed since the early 1980s, driven by the desire to encourage leisure use of the river by stabilising water levels, hiding the areas of silt currently exposed at low tide and improving visual amenity and helping stabilise the quay walls. A weir, however, seems to have disappeared from the development agenda.

Despite two substantial development strategies for the Clyde (Llewelyn-Davies 2000; CiDRE/ EDAW 2001), there seems little commitment to implementing them in any meaningful way. Contrasting with the verve and authority of Mckinsey/Cullen (1985) and Gillespies (1990), the city council's *River Design Framework* (GCC 2003b) is an insipid document, overly focused on detail and reluctant to commit on more strategic issues. Its impact on development is open to debate. Rather than, as Mckinsey/Cullen and Gillespies suggested, identifying and creating focal places and connections between them, the emphasis with the present waterfront strategy seems to be on a series of large property development projects, which may – or may not – connect with the established neighbourhoods further inland and may – or may not – join up to create a coherent and integrated waterfront experience.

With a history of industrialisation rather than of urbanisation, larger waterfront sites in a single land ownership provide an opportunity for innovative design, but they also need a new infrastructure frame and appropriate subdivision to allow incremental urbanisation and the creation of significant diversity. Development proposals and masterplans exist for almost all sites, but almost all are 'large lump' developments with little consideration given to enabling smaller, more incremental development, which may in fact be easier to achieve. Many of the masterplans are merely layout plans or, alternatively, blueprints for 'Big Architecture' projects. What is needed, by contrast, are infrastructure and three-dimensional development frames able to accommodate varying intensities of development and types of land use, together with a procurement strategy able to deliver development incrementally and coherently.

It is difficult to replicate the complexity and synergy built up over time in the core city. But, for this reason, strategic planning and formative urban design of the waterfront become more important. With no active means of ensuring focus and critical mass through spatial concentration of (smaller) projects, development has been scattered. Developers cherry-picked sites that could easily be acquired, for which planning consent would be forthcoming, and within which they would be able to sell the resulting development. This was facilitated by a rising, investment-led and relatively undiscriminating property market. But the 'pioneering' developments, such as the fourteen-storey Lancefield Quay (335 units) and eleven-storey River Heights (ninety-two units) and, indeed, Glasgow Harbour, remain isolated. 'Urban' in terms of house type and density, they lack a mix of uses and activity generators capable of creating an authentically urban setting – there are few convenient places for residents to get dry-cleaning done or have a haircut, nor any choice of places to have a drink (coffee, alcohol, etc.) or something to eat. Glasgow Harbour is a particular case in point. One phase has been completed and a second is nearing completion; over 1,500 residential units will have been built, but, as yet, no shops, restaurants, bars, or other amenities. It is essentially a car-based, monofunctional 'suburban' estate on a rather barren quayside.

This may be true of many new developments for a period of time, but the key urban design question is whether there is scope for greater diversity of land use and enterprises to develop over time. Because there is greater existing variety of land ownership and land use in the immediate area, smaller developments, such as Lancefield Quay and River Heights, will probably become better urbanised over time. But again Glasgow Harbour presents a more difficult case. The place-making question is whether the development will ever become a well-connected and integrated part of the city. To increase connectivity and provide a major boost for regeneration in the west and south of the city, the strategic city-making move would have been to develop the potential of the Byres Road–Partick Cross–Glasgow Harbour axis, with a bridge link to Govan (see Frey 1999: 136). Equally bold moves are required to reduce the barrier effect of the Clyde Expressway. A pedestrian bridge across the expressway, lowering a section of the expressway by four metres and creating a new pedestrian 'boulevard' to Patrick Interchange, are insufficient, and Glasgow Harbour remains an inaccessible, and hence exclusive, enclave.

By late 2008, despite boosterist accounts acclaiming the new waterfront, results on the ground are underwhelming. Significant physical change has happened as noted, but the main impressions remain of a disused waterfront, with isolated developments rising among derelict land and vacant sites and iconic buildings standing among extensive surface-level car parks. At present, the waterfront is little more than a set of isolated, individual projects. The whole is less than the sum of its parts and, several years into the project, there are still no 'good' places.

The city might claim the waterfront as a work in progress, and that the recession has caught it at a particularly bad time, which is testimony not only to the continuing difficulty of attracting development to the city, but also to the sheer scale of the area. But it could have been different. At the SECC, for example, the public sector could (and should) have played a more instrumental place-shaping role by commissioning a development framework; installing the core infrastructure, including multistorey car parks to release the land for development; and subdividing the land into development parcels for disposal with design briefs or a design code. This approach would have enabled incremental, smaller-scale development, creating more opportunities, especially in the event of a market downturn.

Overdevelopment

Overdevelopment of small residential units suiting a limited range of population groups is a UK-wide problem and evident in the core city and on the waterfront. New residential developments tend to consist almost entirely of one- and two-bedroom units; larger units are typically penthouse units. Most new flats are relatively small – of a size that may suit first-time buyers, but much less attractive to those down-sizing, who may also want space for friends and family, especially grandchildren, to stay. But, given that 85 per cent of identified housing demand in the city is for single-person units, developers can argue, somewhat speciously, that they are merely responding to identified housing need. Faced with the difficulty of selling two-bedroom units in earlier phases of development, some developers have sought to change planning consents to include more one-bedroom units in later phases. Given surplus social housing stock within the city, there is no requirement to include social housing as a component of new housing developments. Thus, arguments for a greater range of house types and the inclusion of social housing have to be made on the grounds of ensuring more mixed and more sustainable communities. But, the end result is that only a limited range of social groups will occupy the size and type of residential unit built, while overprovision of a single housing type also means that these areas suffer disproportionately in any housing market downturn. Furthermore, beyond mere dwellings, commercial and community services, parks and good schools are essential for families and for more sustainable 'lifetime communities', able to accommodate and attract a wider range of social and age groups. The absence of these facilities guarantees population churn.

Conclusion

The overarching lesson from Glasgow's experience of renaissance is an obvious one: markets need direction to create well-connected, functioning places. The development boom was an opportunity to capture a quantum of development of benefit to the city. The result has been that much of the core city has seen infill development; that the fringe areas still lack development; and that, where development has occurred on the waterfront, it is highly fragmented. Recession means that much that is presently in the pipeline will not be built, at least not in the shorter term. The core city is likely to be most resilient, but bigger questions arise regarding the Clyde waterfront. If public infrastructure projects, especially public transport and public realm improvements, go ahead and precede development, a slowdown may be beneficial for place quality and the area may be more favourably positioned for a market upturn. More generally, a more prescriptive design and development strategy is needed, which addresses the severance caused by the Clyde Expressway, improves connectivity across the river, and which creates a critical mass of development and desirable places from which future development can be successfully extended. A more prescriptive design strategy should guide the physical character of places along the waterfront.

More specifically, practices that had worked well in the core city and at Crown Street were either not transferred or were not transferable to centre-fringe areas or to the waterfront. In part, lack of resources has prevented their deployment across a larger number of projects and areas and compared with the 1990s, a number of factors are different: development is no longer occurring only in core areas; the scale and geographical extent of development activity is much larger; the context is more arbitrary and ill-defined; development has become more fragmented and lacks necessary infrastructure; and, most importantly, public funding and other key resources are more thinly spread. The Crown Street model, and others like it, depended on control of land ownership. Public ownership of a development site is an opportunity for an immediate capital receipt, but also a means to structure and control development over time. Land ownership is useful in two ways: first, to allow direct public intervention in the targeted area and, second, to benefit from a subsequent uplift in land values, enabling either a larger capital receipt or scope to subsidise desirable (but otherwise not viable) development in later phases. But, in an era of retrenchment and downward pressure on Council Tax and in a city with high levels of social need, immediate capital receipts from land sales are a key source of income to supplement funding of mainline services. This imperative frustrates the ability to deploy or dispose of land more strategically and with more development and design requirements. It is much easier for the public sector to sell sites to the private sector (albeit with a requirement to prepare a masterplan), avoiding development risk and 'controlling' subsequent development through planning powers. But, lack of resources, especially given the size of the task, also suggests a need to prioritise, which, in turn, means directing the market to certain places rather than adopting a scattergun approach to maximise annual receipts.

Despite the fact that Glasgow remains a city that has to work hard to secure investment, and has a lack of public resources to manage the land development process, it is still difficult to account for the city's apparent retreat from 'formative urban design' after 1999. Since the early 2000s, apparently as a means of facilitating development, the onus has increasingly been placed on developers and their designers to initiate development proposals, and then for the CDA (after 2005) and others to work with them to improve development quality and content. Despite more joined-up governance, strategies and masterplans being commissioned, and latterly quality design advice from the CDA and the GUDP, the quality of development outside the core city has declined, most conspicuously on the Clyde waterfront.

It can also be hypothesised that a political and operational choice has been made: instead of design/development prescription in advance of the design process, and careful management of land disposals and development and design content to maximise quality and value in the long term, the decision has been made to maximise development potential, to unfetter both development content and design, allowing designers to design and encouraging development innovation. Freeing designers to design, however, is delusional: developers pay designers to design, developers dictate form and content and development becomes inexorably market led. Moreover, as developers 'push the envelope' in terms of development density, seeking to maximise profitability with little regard for the wider area, the outcome is overdevelopment.

Acknowledgements

The author would like to thank John Punter, Willie Miller and Kevin Murray for their constructive comments on earlier versions of this chapter.

Notes

1 A useful website on contemporary design and development in Glasgow can be found at www.futureglasgow.co.uk.
2 The city's drive for development has often been at the cost of conservationist concerns. Demolition of category B listed buildings, for example, seems negotiable.

References

Boyle, R. (1989) Partnership in Practice: An assessment of Public–Private Collaboration in Urban Regeneration – a Case Study of Glasgow Action. *Local Government Studies,* 15 (2): 17–28.

Carmona, M. (1996) Controlling Urban Design – Part 2: Realising the Potential. *Journal of Urban Design,* 1 (2): 179–200.

CiDRE (Cities Divided by Rivers in Europe)/EDAW (2001) *Clyde Corridor Regeneration Strategy, Cities Divided by Rivers in Europe Phase Two: Pilot Project* (Glasgow: EDAW).

Crichton, T. (2003) The Trouble with Glasgow. *[Glasgow] Sunday Herald,* 9 November.

CWWG (Clyde Waterfront Working Group) (2002) *The Clyde Waterfront Regeneration Plan: A River Reborn* (Glasgow: CWWG).

Frey, H. (1999) *Designing the City: Towards a More Sustainable Urban Form* (London: Spon).

Friend of Zanetti (2006) Constructing Neoliberal Glasgow: The Privatisation of Space. *Variant Issue 25.* Online. Available as: http://www.variant.randomstate.org/25texts/neolib25.html (last accessed 28 April 2009).

GEF (Glasgow Economic Forum) (2007) *Glasgow Economic Audit 2007: Summary Report* (Glasgow: report prepared by SLIMS for the Glasgow Economic Forum).

Gillespies in association with Price & Cullen, P A Cambridge Economic Consultants; Dougall Baillie Associates and Drivers Jonas (1990) *Glasgow City Centre and The Clyde: Continuing the Renaissance* (Glasgow: Report for Scottish Development Agency and Glasgow District Council).

Gillespies (1995) *Glasgow City Centre Public Realm Strategy and Guidelines* (Glasgow: Report for Strathclyde Regional Council, Glasgow City Council and Glasgow Development Agency).

GCC (Glasgow City Council) (2003a) *City Plan* (Glasgow: Glasgow City Council).

GCC (2003b) *River Design Framework* (Glasgow: Glasgow City Council).

GCC (2008) *Glasgow Economic Review June 2008* (Glasgow: Department and Regeneration Services, Glasgow City Council).

Gough, J. (2003) Mutiny on the Clyde. *Sunday Herald,* June 29.

Hassan,G., Mean, M., and Tims, C. (2007) *The Dreaming City and the Power of Mass Imagination* (London: Demos).

Jones, C. and Patrick, J. (1992) The Merchant City as an Example of Housing-Led Regeneration. In Healey P., Davoudi S., Tavsanoglu S., O'Toole M., and Usher D. (eds) *Rebuilding the City: Property-Led Urban Regeneration* (London: Spon) pp. 125–144.

Kearns, A. and Lawson, L. (2008) Housing Stock Transfer in Glasgow – the First Five Years: A Study of Policy Implementation. *Housing Studies,* 23 (6): 857–878.

Keating, M. (1988) *The City that Refused to Die – Glasgow: The Politics of Urban Regeneration* (Aberdeen: Aberdeen University Press).

Llewelyn-Davies (2000) *Clyde Riverside: A Framework for Development* (Glasgow: Glasgow City Council).

Low, S. (2006) Scotland: Lack of Enterprise? BBC News Channel, 19 June. Online. Available at: http://news.bbc.co.uk/1/hi/programmes/politics_show/5080952.stm (last accessed 1 June 2009).

Mckinsey/Cullen (1985) *The Potential of Glasgow City Centre* (Glasgow: Report for Scottish Development Agency).

MacLeod G. (2002) From Urban Entrepreneurialism to a 'Revanchist' City? On the Spatial Injustices of Glasgow's Renaissance. *Antipode,* 34 (3): 602–624.

Purcell, S. (2008) Council Leader Pledges to Make Glasgow Most Development-Friendly City in the UK. *Glasgow City Council Press Release,* Friday 2 May (Glasgow: Glasgow City Council).

Tiesdell, S. and Macfarlane, G. (2007) The Part and the Whole: Implementing Masterplans in Glasgow's New Gorbals. *Journal of Urban Design,* 12 (3): 407–433.

Turok, I. and Bailey, N. (2004a) Glasgow's Recent Trajectory: Partial Recovery and its Consequences. In Newlands D, Danson M, and McCarthy J (eds) *Divided Scotland? The Nature, Causes and Consequences of Economic Disparities within Scotland* (Aldershot: Ashgate)pp. 35–59.

Turok, I. and Bailey, N. (2004b) Twin Track Cities: Competitiveness and Cohesion in Glasgow and Edinburgh. *Progress in Planning,* 62 (3): 135–204.

Varkki George, R. (1997) A Procedural Explanation for Contemporary Urban Design. *Journal of Urban Design,* 2 (2): 143–161.

Wales

An introduction

An urban renaissance has not been an explicit part of the Welsh planning agenda, with the Welsh Assembly government (WAG) conscious of the disaffection this would arouse beyond Cardiff, Swansea and Newport. The Welsh planning system was not significantly different from the English prior to devolution, and the main difference in regeneration was the positive national role played by the Welsh Development Agency, which had important land assembly and reclamation powers. Since devolution in 2000, distinctive differences in planning and regeneration have developed. The vast majority of Wales became eligible for European Union (EU) Structural Funds and Objective 1 and 2 regeneration projects (including a small swathe of south central and east Cardiff). In 2001 the Labour-led assembly adopted a Communities First regeneration programme, their version of the English New Deal for Communities/National Strategy for Neighbourhood Review (NDC/NSNR). It focused on the 100 most deprived wards with bottom-up, community-based partnerships, improved service delivery and capacity building (including four neighbourhoods in Cardiff; WAG 2001).

WAG's Department for Enterprise, Innovation and Networks, which absorbed the Welsh Development Agency in 2005, continues to play an important role in major urban regeneration projects in the larger Welsh cities and towns, with three major projects in Cardiff, and others in Swansea and Barry, plus support for Newport's Urban Regeneration Company. Of increasing importance is the *Wales Spatial Plan* (WAG 2004: revised 2008), which coordinates local authority planning at the strategic level, particularly housing allocations and (the very limited) transport investment. It recognises the importance of the capital city-region (of which Cardiff is the focus) to the national economy, but favours the dispersal of new family housing to the South Wales valleys to drive wider regeneration, a policy that Cardiff Council supports. Cardiff now plays a more positive role in collaborating with its adjacent local authorities, but it benchmarks itself against the English 'Core Cities' to frame and promote its wider economic renaissance.

Sensibly Wales made far less radical changes to its development plan content and processes than England, though it did adopt the idea of core strategies. It consolidated its planning policies into a single document, *Planning Policy Wales* (WAG 1999: revised version in press), supported by technical advice notes (TANs). *TAN 12: Design* (WAG 2002), adopts the positive principles and practices of *By Design* (DETR/CABE 2000; Punter 2002), while WAG established the Design Commission for Wales as its national design advisor in 2003. But it did not introduce any equivalent of Planning Policy Guidance Notes/Planning Policy Statements 3 (PPG/PPS) to drive residential intensification, though the volume house builders imported its norms from the outset. Wales is pressing ahead with its commitments to energy efficiency in buildings and attempting speedier implementation of the Code for Sustainable Homes than England (WAG 2008a), and it is also giving close attention to the problem of affordable housing with a target of delivering 6,500 affordable homes by early 2011 (WAG 2008b).

References

Punter, J. V. (2002) Devolution and Urban Design: Wales, *Urban Design Quarterly*, 84: 29–31.

WAG (Welsh Assembly Government) (1999) *Planning Policy Wales* (Cardiff: WAG).

WAG (2001) *Communities First Guidance* (Cardiff: WAG).

WAG (2002) *Planning Policy Wales: Technical Advice Note 12: Design* (Cardiff: WAG).

WAG(2004) *People, Places, Futures: Wales Spatial Plan* (Cardiff: WAG).

WAG (2008a) *Affordable Housing in Wales: An Independent Report to the Minister of Housing* (Cardiff: WAG).

WAG (2008b) *Minister for the Environment: Further Consultation on Planning for Climate Change* (3 July 2008) (Cardiff: WAG).

16 Cardiff

A renaissance city 'with a reputation for imaginative architecture and iconic urban design?'

John Punter

Introduction: 'Europe's youngest capital'

Cardiff is the UK's tenth largest city with a population of 314,000 (2005). It has, until recently, marketed itself as 'Europe's youngest capital', following devolution and the establishment of the Welsh Assembly government (WAG) in 1999. Ironically, devolution deprived it of participation in the urban renaissance policy initiatives introduced in England that year, and has excluded it from membership of the English Core Cities grouping, though the council constantly benchmarks itself against these cities (CC 2007a). In a number of respects, Cardiff is the archetypal 'urban renaissance' city: competitive ethos, resurgent growth, high-density and entirely brownfield development for the next decade. But its self-acclaimed reputation for 'imaginative architecture and iconic urban design', a key part of the archetype, deserves close scrutiny.

This chapter will explore the origins of Cardiff's contemporary 'urban renaissance', the emergence of the council's boosterist mentality and 'megaproject' (by provincial standards) strategy in 1996, and the creation of a local planning regime with very limited design policy but increasing amounts of guidance. It will examine how changes in the property market and longstanding planning policies drove central retail and residential expansion. It will illustrate how these are combining with a pro-growth planning regime to produce a fragmented, but much higher density, city across south Cardiff. The chapter will explain how these changes in urban form are being reinforced by resistance to suburban intensification and extensions in the new local development plan (LDP), and assess the latter's design aspirations. In particular, it will examine the implications of the apartment boom for the future character and sustainability of Cardiff, and make the case for a much stronger level of design intervention to create a qualitative renaissance worthy of the nineteenth-century city and its landscape setting.

The chapter is based on recent collective academic research on planning in Cardiff (Hooper and Punter 2006), close analysis of city documentation, and the author's 'participant observation' in Cardiff Initiative, Cardiff Vision Forum and, since 2003, the design review panel of the Design Commission for Wales (DCfW 2005, 2008). It also benefits from local contributions to the ESRC seminars, and comments on a draft by senior planning officers in the council.

Twentieth-century history

The 'Coal Metropolis' of the world by the end of the nineteenth century, exporting the coal and iron of the South Wales valleys (Daunton 1977), the city gradually diversified its economic base, though its growth was modest in the first three quarters of the twentieth century. As the coal trade declined, the city turned its back on the waterfront and south Cardiff, to concentrate upon a service economy fostered by capital designation in 1955. Massive modernist redevelopment plans for the city centre fell foul of the 1973 property crash, and piecemeal redevelopment ensued. With the coal docks falling into dereliction, and the East Moors steel works closing in 1978, the city and, especially, the county councils turned their attention to urban regeneration in south Cardiff as the main area for city growth. Subsequently, large-scale regeneration was driven by the Cardiff Bay Development Corporation (CBDC), established in 1987 and wound up in 2000, with Cardiff Council assuming control of the regeneration thereafter (though WAG retained certain responsibilities). Cardiff Council continued to follow CBDC's place-marketing and iconic building strategy, seeking to deliver a range of 'megaprojects' to maintain its economic momentum. Like CBDC, it has found delivering high-quality urban design very difficult, not least because of market conditions and developers' low aspirations.

The arrival of the M4 in 1980 gave the city a clear northern boundary for suburban expansion long term, but strong restraint policies within the structure (deposited 1995) and local (deposited 1992) plans limited even this greenfield development, except in the north-east (Cardiff Gate). Strengthening, localised resistance to further expansion, since 1995, has stopped housing expansion and given further impetus to medium- to high-density residential development south of the city centre in Cardiff Bay, where there is much derelict land (Figure 16.1). This redirection of development reflects strong containment and countryside protection policies, allied to extensive landscape and conservation designations (Figure 16.2), but also emphasises Cardiff's social polarisation. The mature northern suburbs contain nine of the ten most socially advantaged wards in Wales whereas a southern arc of older housing contains ten of the most deprived wards

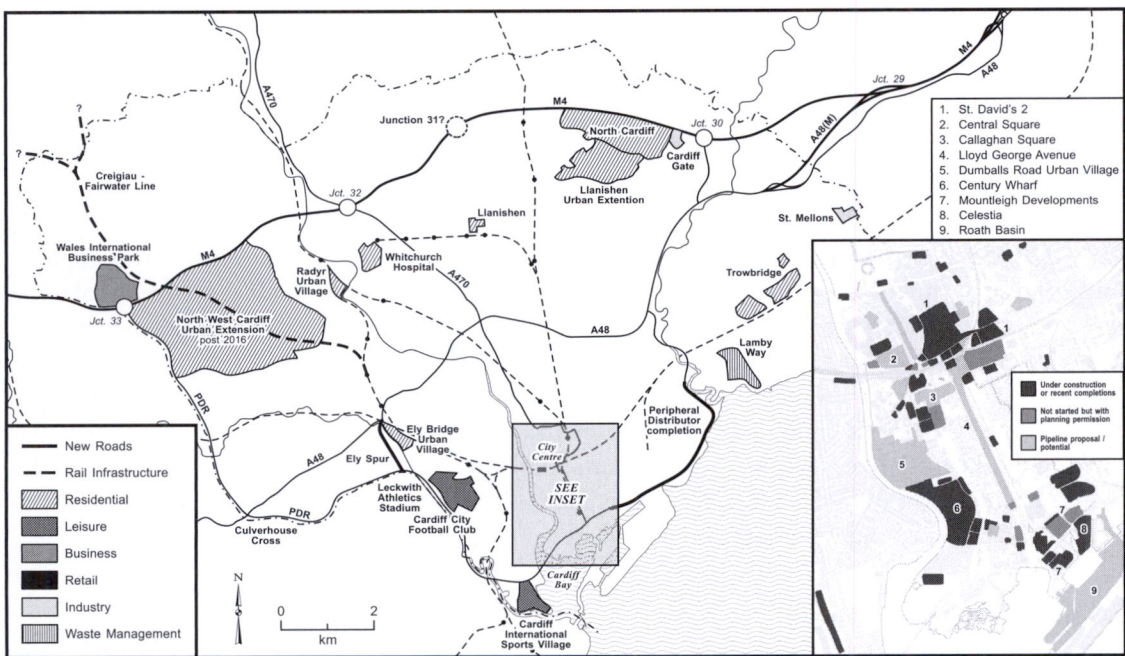

Figure 16.1 Cardiff: major development projects 1999–2015. This map identifies the major development projects, and those in the pipeline, by development type (redrawn by Jan Edwards: Courtesy Cardiff Council). © Crown Copyright. All rights reserved. Licence number 100049043.

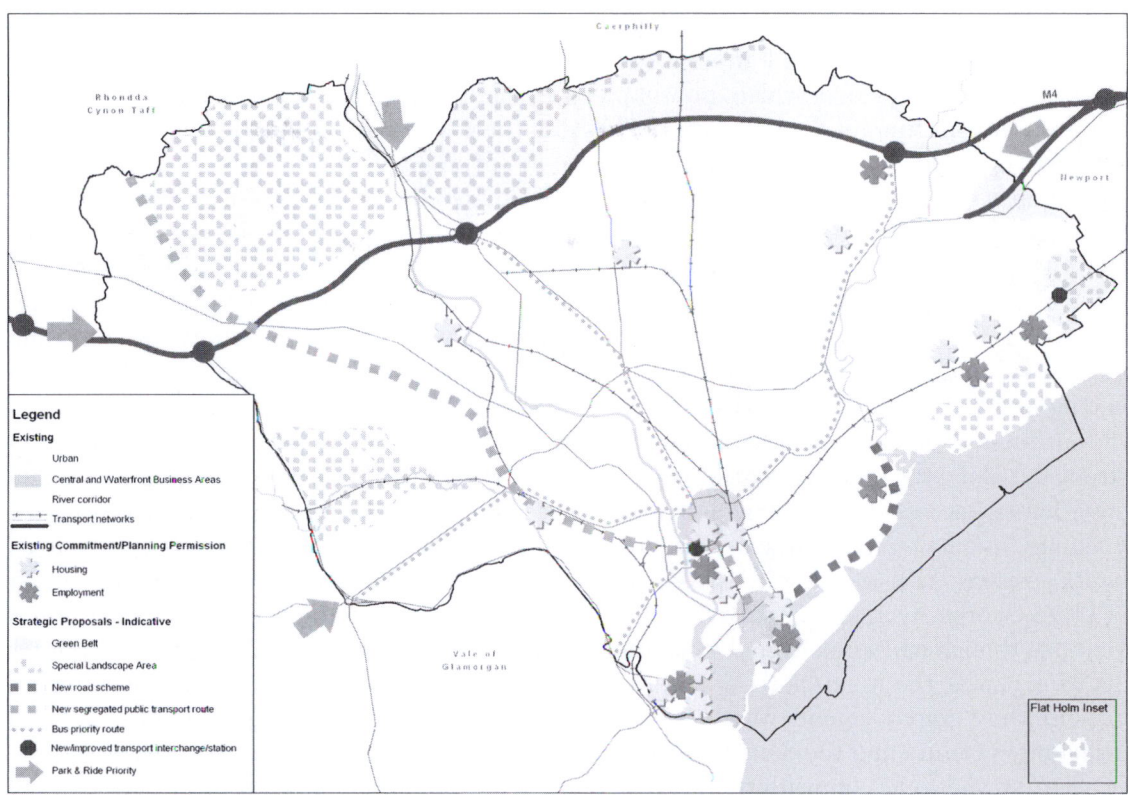

Figure 16.2 Cardiff: Local Development Plan Preferred Strategy Key Diagram 2007. This shows the main foci of development until 2021, and the land protected from development until then. Note the 'new segregated public transport route' north westwards (Courtesy Cardiff Council). © Crown Copyright. All rights reserved. Licence number 100049043.

nationally (embracing some 50,000 residents). Perhaps this social geography also explains the lack of public scrutiny and critique that is currently applied to development projects in south Cardiff.

Urban priority area designations helped tackle the worst housing conditions in south Cardiff, and large tracts of inter- and post-war council estates, and much of the Victorian/Edwardian inner-city neighbourhoods, have been carefully maintained by longstanding neighbourhood improvement programmes (CC 2007b). This has given Cardiff a generally well-maintained housing mix and neighbourhood coherence which would be the envy of many larger British cities, and constitutes a considerable regeneration and conservation achievement worthy of any urban renaissance. Meanwhile, since 1996 the volume housebuilders have been constructing a very different city in the former docklands of south Cardiff.

The first renaissance, 1989–2000: the redevelopment of Cardiff Bay

Cardiff's 1970s urban renaissance aspirations were focused on the derelict docks with the regeneration of Atlantic Wharf delivering a new County Hall, a peripheral distributor road (PDR) to access south Cardiff and campaigns for a barrage to replace the tidal mudflats (a Site of Special Scientific Interest) with a freshwater lake. The Cardiff Bay Development Corporation (CBDC) was established in 1987, but not fully operational until 1989, because of citizen and European Union (EU) opposition to the Barrage, by which time the property market had collapsed. CBDC was given six key objectives which, unusually, included the 'highest standards of design', a mix of housing, reconnection of the city with the bay and the creation of a 'superb environment', and £512 million in public funds to achieve it. Unusually, for an urban development corporation, the city retained development control powers, working closely with CBDC which, equally unusually, produced a raft of design policies and guidance and established a design review panel to complement its ambitious regeneration strategy (CBDC 1988; CBDC 2000; Punter 2007).

However, the size of the regeneration area (1,092 hectares), the difficult development climate, risk-averse developers and the need to achieve development targets in a short space of time meant that much of the design advice was progressively disregarded and subsequently discredited among CBDC executives. Contrary to its extravagant 'place-marketing', much of the bay became the antithesis of good urban design, a form of 'edge city' (Garreau 1991) of free-standing projects strung out along the motorway-standard PDR, with the highway engineers delivering a 'drive-in' environment across the bay. There was, however, a proliferation of architecturally distinctive buildings, usually replete with maritime analogies, though urban design was largely conspicuous by its absence. This was despite MBM, (from Barcelona), being commissioned for the design of Lloyd George Avenue (Cardiff's 'Ramblas') and Ben Thompson (from Boston) for the Inner Harbour, though neither delivered locally appropriate or functionally workable solutions (Punter 2007). By 2000, the Inner Harbour and the Oval Basin did possess a high-quality public realm, but elsewhere improvements were very fragmented. The subsequent completion of the Wales Millennium Centre and the Senedd, two national projects, gave the bay two genuine icons (see Plate 16.1), and some compensation for the failure to build the Zaha Hadid competition-winning

Plate 16.1 Cardiff: Oval Basin and Lloyd George Avenue. The avenue is not a direct, legible link and remains a one sided street. The Oval Basin provides the setting for the Wales Millenium Centre, but its scale is problematic except when hosting major events (Courtesy Cardiff Council).

Plate 16.2 Cardiff: Bay Pointe. Three double towers of 31-41 storeys (450 du/ha) were subsequently reduced to two (31-34 storey: 300 du/ha.) by the Planning Committee. The underground parking and landscaping were positive but the park would have been a wind tunnel (Courtesy Bay Pointe).

opera house (see Crickhowell 1997). But this enclave (and that of Scott Harbour) was scant compensation for the absence of coherent urban design elsewhere in the bay.

It was the revival of speculative house building in the mid-1990s that gave the bay the development impetus it needed, but unfortunately CBDC had little experience of housing development. The early schemes were 'compact suburban' in character, but from 1995 changed to much denser urban apartments. Notions of residential streets, a high-quality public realm, attractive communal amenity space and a broad mix of units were abandoned to a 'slab block in a car park' formula (see Plate 16.2), with some very large gated and near-gated communities in more remote locations, and this pattern of development has subsequently intensified as densities have been ratcheted up. The fragmentation of development, the introversion of projects, the increasing monoculture of one- and two-bed apartments and the absence of neighbourhood facilities have all conspired to deprive bay residents of an urbane, liveable environment. Remarkably, 31 per cent of the housing built under CBDC was affordable, at least twice the proportion city-wide over the last decade, and much of it was family housing, in sharp contrast to post-2000 developments. The bay, including the area south of the main line railway, which is a critical physical and functional divide, continues to be the principal focus of the city's development activity, and will be until at least 2021.

A new unitary council with a 'competitive ethos'

In 1996 the County of South Glamorgan was abolished and Cardiff became a unitary authority. County politicians took over the city council, and their greater development ambitions, signalled by the rescue of the Millennium Stadium project, underpinned a much more focused growth strategy. County visions of a vibrant, entrepreneurial and competitive European capital anticipated the EU Competitiveness White Paper (CEC 1993), and became the foundation of the city's 'megaproject strategy', designed to place the city on the European stage. When New Labour came to power, the city's Labour leaders installed the epitome of a strong mayor and cabinet with a 'presidential style' of leadership and (initially) weak debating and scrutiny mechanisms. The county Labour group had already developed a 'boosterist' place-marketing agenda, similar to that of CBDC, a competitive city ethos, a long list of megaprojects preoccupied with tourism, leisure and sports facilities, and an obsession with notions of 'moving into the Premier League of European cities' (SGCC 1993) despite a ranking somewhere around 211th. For the leader of the council, Russell Goodway, the aims of the megaprojects 'were not simply to add glitz to Wales' capital city . . . but to . . . provide meaningful employment opportunities for the people and communities we serve'(quoted in Morgan 2006: 39), particularly for the high concentrations of unemployed in the south of the city.

Top of the list of the megaprojects was a major expansion of retailing in the city centre. The success of the Millennium Stadium, and the happy accident of the demise of Wembley, provided the city with priceless publicity and temporarily boosted its hospitality industry. A strong sports and tourism agenda was developed initially embracing the Cardiff International Sports Village (CISV) on the bay, but then football/rugby, test cricket and a new athletics stadium. There were longstanding commitments to a revolutionary personalised public transport system (ULTra), which was never likely to be feasible, and a major convention centre. These schemes were given to a special projects team to deliver, partly to avoid conflicts of interest when it came to a planning application, but also to ensure that they were not delayed. Inputs from the planning service were limited with inevitable results.

The new council inherited a new (but old-style) 'Local Plan' that had been six years in gestation. It was very weak on development control and design policies, and its land use allocations and urban form controls were permissive in the crucial zone between the retail core and the inner suburbs. A good *City Centre Design Guide* existed (CCC 1994), but was not equipped for the changing scale of development post 1999. In 1999 development control was separated from planning policy and treated as a service activity (until 2006), and in 2001 the central planning team was disbanded into these separated functions. A new unitary development plan (UDP) was always 'in preparation', but was clearly not a council priority, and was eventually aborted, though its few policies were adopted for development control purposes. So development controllers had only weak statutory policy instruments to manage the residential property boom on the edges of the CBD (Central Business District), and only outdated CBDC briefs and policies in the bay. A periodically updated *City Centre Strategy* (CC 2007c) monitored development but lacked both vision and strategy, leaving the planning authority in reactive rather than proactive mode.

The New Labour/Goodway era ended with New Labour's biggest reverse in Wales at the 2004 local elections. The council had been reeling from strong press attacks on the leadership and a damning inquiry into its political leadership by the Lyons Commission (Morgan 2006: 40–42). A Liberal Democrat minority took over the leadership, but the megaproject agenda and pro-development planning regime have persisted for a variety of internal political reasons, but principally to ensure that the city maintains its growth momentum as the national capital and economic driver of the South-East Wales 'Capital Region' (CC 2007d; WAG 2004).

In the publication of a set of glossy corporate policy/marketing documents, the growth agenda has been repackaged as a vision of a highly competitive city, building on decades of regeneration success, and driving forward a series of exciting megaprojects. Each document has been given a sustainability spin to express the Liberal Democrats' stronger environmental aspirations. *Cardiff: A Proud Capital* (CC 2005a), launched at the city's centenary, was the 'new' vision, and it contained much city-marketing-speak. It claimed six pillars of excellence for the city embracing innovation (economic development/service delivery), opportunity (social inclusion/education/ skills), vitality (sport/culture), streetscape (transport/waste), sustainability (environmental/ social/design) and delivery (megaprojects/labour market planning/development). A key claim as regards the urban renaissance was that the city had taken a lead in 'intelligent and iconic urban design', was seeking to become a city recognised for its 'innovative architecture', and intended to develop 'a centre for excellence' (CC 2007a: 16, 20).

The new Liberal Democrat-dominated council has followed up this vision with a new *Community Strategy 2007–17* (CC 2007d) for a 'competitive city-region', which seeks to extend the city's recent high rate of employment growth (27 per cent during 1998–2004). The *Community Strategy 2007–17* (CC 2007d) emerged from a very truncated consultation relying on focus groups (a method regrettably repeated on the LDP), and contained a stronger environmental and overall 'quality of life' message. There was a commitment to a best practice, city-wide model of engagement and consultation to improve service delivery. The city had developed a local strategic partnership (LSP) with a range of other partnerships and forums, of which the business partnership is by far the most important. Within the *Corporate Strategy* (CC 2006) there are a number of new commitments to energy efficiency, high-quality urban design, recycling and sustainable transport, hinting at shifts in development aspirations, and at least an intention to use planning powers more creatively in future (CC 2007c). The first Strategic Planning Business Plan (CC 2008a) has recently been issued.

There is a new coherence to all these documents and promises of concerted action to raise design standards. Meanwhile, the planning service has been reunified, a new chief planning officer appointed, more than twenty supplementary planning documents approved (see below), and the service has recently won three Wales Quality awards. There is now the potential for a more design-conscious urban renaissance, but little confidence in its delivery given recent experience, which is now examined.

The Cardiff property market and density increases

Like English provincial cities, by the late 1990s Cardiff was enjoying a housing boom but office growth was far less buoyant, reducing rental growth to a minimum. Far from having enough business growth to feed two office cores, in the bay and the city centre, there has only been enough to keep one growing at a slow rate. There has been little sustained interest in the prime office locations available in Callaghan Square (developed as a Public Finance Initiative project at the end of CBDC's life), just south of the main line railway, but three large and rather poorly designed regional headquarters and one call centre have been developed immediately south of Central Station. Outline approval was given for eleven major office buildings behind the Wales Millennium Centre in the bay in 2005, but there was no obvious demand for such space (Figure 16.1).

The secondary office market, of twenty- to thirty-year-old buildings in the city centre, collapsed at the end of the 1990s, as it did in many provincial cities, and buildings were sold on for institutional use (universities) or converted into apartments or hotels, leading to new residential towers on the southern and eastern edges of the city centre. The first conversion of a thirteen-storey tower was completed in 2000 and its successful marketing encouraged a spate of high-density residential schemes on what were previously considered marginal commercial sites. Building heights increased to seventeen, twenty and twenty-three storeys as white-rendered slab blocks suddenly appeared on the city skyline.

Significantly, council land disposals and property deals helped drive up densities and building heights, whether it was the St Davids 2 shopping scheme with four to nine storeys of housing above the retail mall, the sale of the site of the city planning offices for a thirty-two-storey tower and twenty-two-storey slab block adjacent to the stadium, or the proposal for three thirty-four- to forty-one-storey double tower apartment blocks to cross-fund the Sports Village on the bay (see Plate 16.3). So developers have been able to double the building height, and perhaps treble the density, of apartments over the last eight years, driving up land values. They have produced a density of development that is largely detrimental to, and arguably inappropriate in, a city of

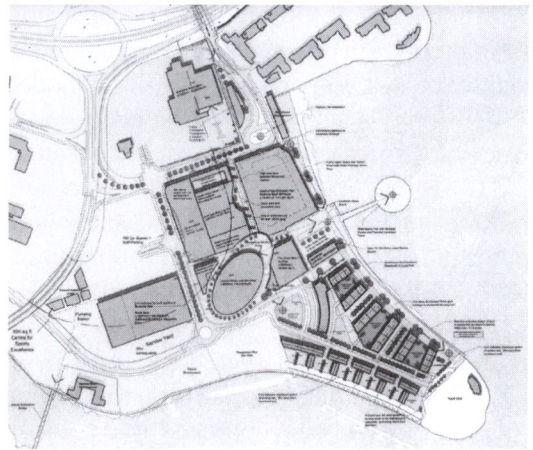

Plate 16.3 Cardiff: Celestia and Century Wharf. Two of the poorer residential schemes in the Bay, the former largely turning its back on the waterfront with its suburban wooden fencing, while the latter is a 550 unit gated community on the River Taff.

Cardiff's size and growth trajectory, creating false hope values which prevent smaller-scale and more bespoke mixed-use developments.. This ratcheting up of densities and values took place without any public debate, or any policy framework for the location of tall buildings (now in draft; CC 2008b), their design quality or their energy efficiency. A council resolution early in 2003 provided some locational control over tall buildings, and invoked the English Heritage/ Commission for Architecture and the Built Environment (CABE) criteria, but it did not ensure any environmental assessment, while affordable housing quotas were often resisted by developers.

Retail investment, public realm and the wider city centre strategy

The city centre has suffered from the competition of a second business, cultural and administrative centre in the bay. With the assembly rejecting City Hall as a home, the Wales Millennium Centre taking the prestige concerts/opera, and the Inner Harbour offering a major concentration of eating and drinking venues, the centre has not increased its vitality, and its public realm has become very tired (Parkinson and Kareecha 2006). There have been small-scale design/development successes, of which the prize-winning Brewery Quarter (a small bar/restaurant/residential scheme) is a notable development control achievement.

Major retail development in the city centre was slow to materialise despite being top of the city's megaproject aspirations. City land holdings were critical to facilitate large-scale investment, and a large tract of poor-quality retail and car parking projects from the late 1970s and early 1980s was the obvious site for redevelopment. When the new shopping centre was announced in 2004, a partnership with Land Securities, strong support had already been registered by a series of focus groups, leaving the consultation process to rubber-stamp detailed design. A two-level covered mall (one of the last of its kind?) with 100 new shops opens late in 2009, linking the 1970s St Davids Centre on Queen Street (also owned by the investor/developers) to a new John Lewis store to the south, increasing central shopping floorspace by almost a third (Figure 16.3).

The new shopping centre will rebuild the very poor public realm of the main north–south shopping street(s), creating a new axis to rival the ever successful east–west Queen Street (repaved and refurnished in 2004). The developers have taken responsibility for repaving and refurnishing five city streets and seven city spaces, some well beyond the margins of the scheme, in all a £12 million 'planning gain' (Figure 16.3). Fears about the commercialisation of public space are offset by the fact that the council could not fund anything approaching this level or quality of public realm investment (though Section 106 monies continue to be used for numerous small-scale public realm enhancement schemes).

In permeability terms, the new mall fits reasonably well into the pedestrian network (Figure 16.3), but its scale is overbearing, especially with up to nine storeys of residential (331 units, 8 per cent affordable) and six storeys of car parking, above what is effectively a three- to four-storey mall (Griffiths 2008). Much of the design, sustainability and public realm features had to be taken on trust in the absence of strong planning control over design details, and sustainability features such as those imposed (to good effect) on the same developers in Exeter. The promises of different teams of architects to diversify the design has been fulfilled with different practices for the shopping, housing and a new energy-efficient, landmark public library.

Spinning off the new public realm improvements will be a long overdue public realm best practice guide (including a materials guide). This is one of the key commitments set out in

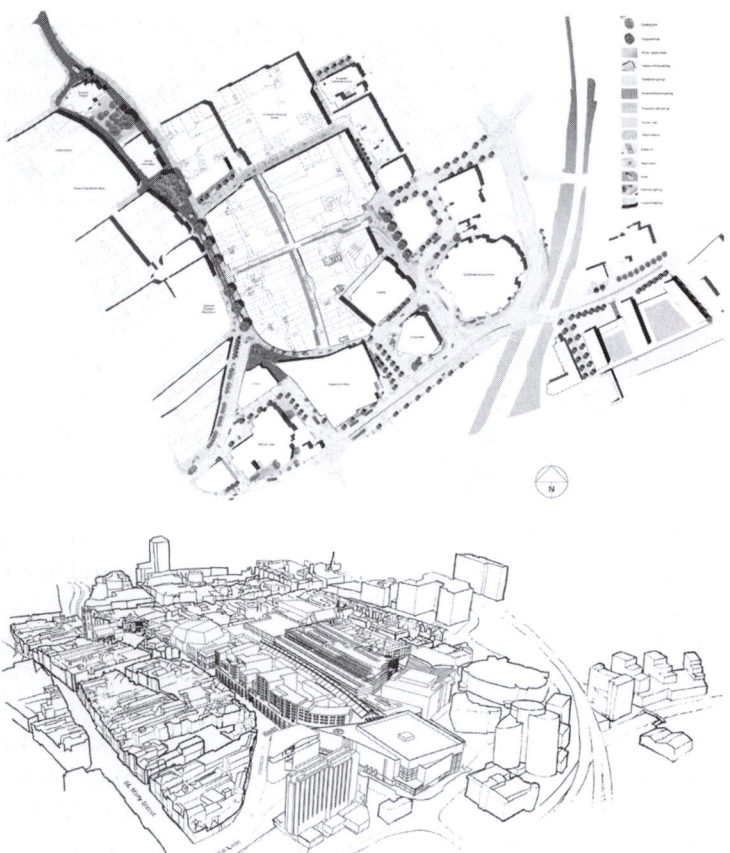

Figure 16.3 Cardiff: St Davids Two shopping centre. The map shows the mall and the extent of the refurbished public realm. The axonometric seriously underestimates the height of the housing and the car parking (Courtesy Land Securities).

the latest version of the *City Centre Strategy 2007–2010* (CC 2007c), alongside a consistent approach to Section 106 agreements to deliver environmental improvements, and further area appraisals as the basis for the identification of future improvement projects. Further public realm improvements include the pedestrianisation of most of historic St Mary Street (finally) and improvements to eight small areas of the public realm north of Queen Street. These are very much to be welcomed, as is the attention being paid to pedestrian and cycle links and new bus routes between the city centre and the bay.

The new shopping centre will change the circulation system of public transport in the city, and a new 'bus box' is being discussed to go around the centre, the challenge being to create a system that will work when the stadium is in use so that the centre remains accessible to non-spectators. Shrinkage or removal of the bus station will create more public space in front of Central Station, but there is no clarity about the future of this site or the method of procuring its redevelopment. A new convention centre is being promoted to link with the stadium facilities, while on the northern edge of the city centre the heritage lottery-funded restoration of historic Bute Park will follow on from the recent restorations and improvements to visitor facilities at Cardiff Castle, and will include a new public walkway through the walls.

To the south of the city centre the barrier of the main-line railway and the embankment of the bay link continue to make better links to the bay problematic. Failure to resolve transit links to the bay, to complete Callaghan Square and to remove the Butetown rail embankment further impair connections, leaving the one-sided Lloyd George Avenue in limbo. Buried in the strategy is a commitment to the removal of the Bute Street embankment (by the end of 2010), implying some new kind of (extended?) public transport link (train-trams are under consideration) between the centre and the bay (Figure 16.2). Whatever transport mode is chosen, there is an urgent need to physically connect the racially mixed community of Butetown (the second most deprived community in Wales in 2008) with the new apartment complexes to the east and west (see Plate 16.1). A linear park is mooted, but what is needed is a series of new blocks of mixed-tenure housing and mixed-use/live–work premises that can simultaneously reinvigorate and connect the two existing north–south streets, and create well-linked and serviced neighbourhoods between the city centre and the waterfront.

Overall, the new *City Centre Strategy 2007–10* (which incorporates the core of the bay) is a valuable reflection on recent achievements in the city centre, but it remains an inventory of developments in the pipeline and small-scale initiatives rather than a positive urban design strategy (CC 2007c). Like the city vision, it feels the need to assert that 'the city centre is becoming a focus for high quality buildings, setting new standards of sustainable development', while this is patently not the case (CC 2007c: 24). It states an intention 'to develop internationally renowned buildings and landmarks reflecting Cardiff's status as the Capital City of Wales' and makes a commitment to ensure the 'quality and sustainability . . . (which) are vital in achieving future success' (CC 2007c: 4). But delivery of these promises depends on establishing a new design policy framework and a much more challenging, more proactive and better skilled development control regime.

The wider transport network

A key problem for strategic planning in Cardiff, as in most British cities, is how to fund an adequate transport network after decades of underinvestment, and how to integrate it with land use planning/development. The Cardiff Transportation Partnership, established in 2004 to find innovative ways of funding new transport infrastructure, has made little progress in finding partners and developing a strategy. It would require some £500 million to complete what the council considers to be the necessary road and public transport improvements, and this would constitute five years of the WAG's current national road budget! Local congestion charging has been mooted, but the council now appears to have gone cold on the idea because of retail opposition and the potential risks to any political party proposing it. At the heart of the council's strategy is the completion of the PDR to the east, to improve access to the city centre and the bay. This is justified on the basis of major environmental and public transport improvements in east Cardiff, but commercial development aspirations in the bay seem a more powerful driver.

There is an enigmatic reference to a new city–bay transport link that would extend to the new business park in the Local Development Plan Preferred Strategy (LDPPS), but otherwise park and ride and bus priority are the principal public transport strategies, and they are at least affordable. Outline walking and cycling strategies have been developed recently, and the successful Sustrans Connect 2 bid for lottery funding promises to fund the bay shore and Barrage links for cyclists and pedestrians, a new bridge across the River Ely, and connections to regional recreational and commuter routes (Sustrans 2008). Implementation of this network would be a major step forward for open space/landscape planning strategies and boost the parks and green space and rivers strategies, also starved of adequate funding (CC 2007e,f). These elements of the 'capital web' are critical to the design quality and environmental sustainability of a rapidly intensifying city.

A new 'preferred strategy' for planning and development 2007

The property boom in the city 1999–2007 was facilitated by a generally permissive planning regime and a clear desire to attract whatever property investment was going, a reflection of the council's longstanding economic insecurities and 'boosterist' mentality. While the economic strategy has not changed, the Liberal Democrat council, elected in 2004, has begun to strengthen the planning regime, as previously noted. The *Local Development Plan Preferred Strategy* (LDPPS, or Core Strategy in LDF terms) is the first stage in developing the city-wide plan for 2006–2021 (CC 2007g), and it contains the basis for stronger planning and design policies, and a greater commitment to a sustainability agenda. However, it is not strong on vision and lacks any detail in terms of spatial strategy. Its most striking feature was a negative: the rejection of a long-mooted greenfield suburban extension in the north-eastern suburbs in favour of concentrating all new residential development on brownfield sites in the bay, and on the south side of the CBD (Figure 16.2). This was justified on the basis that the *Wales Spatial Plan* (2004) and its South East Wales Regional Strategy seek to encourage housing development in the valleys of the former South Wales coalfield (as a means of regenerating extant communities).

In many ways, the new preferred strategy was an archetypal urban renaissance response, pushing the proportion of development on brownfield land up from 70 per cent (1991–2006) to virtually 100 per cent in 2021, almost all of it in the bay area south of the main-line railway. But it was sold as suburban containment/countryside protection rather than an urban regeneration strategy to mollify key suburban constituencies campaigning against greenfield housing. Almost two-thirds of the allocated housing units (to 2021) have been approved already as high density, the vast majority one- or two-bedroom apartments (some 13,079 units including those awaiting Section 106 agreements; CC 2008c: 10), emphasising the scale of the recent boom. This raises doubts about whether the residential environment projected by mass house builders for south Cardiff will meet the needs of a wide section of the community in terms of unit choice, quality, amenity and affordability. In fact, the house builders themselves are already suggesting that the consents cannot be implemented post 'credit crunch'.

The LDPPS made a number of significant statements on housing strategy. It affirmed a policy to seek 30 per cent affordability on all housing schemes, but noted that only 14 per cent of the permitted/banked stock was actually affordable (CC 2007g). It required sustainable construction embracing energy and water efficiency, but two-thirds of the provision was seeking to avoid that by gaining early approval. Finally, it emphasised the importance of not overdeveloping sites, despite the council having already granted permission for a range of 'superdensity' projects (see Plate 16.4).

In the event, the LDPPS had to be revised in late 2008 because of higher population and housing projections. The planners recommended the addition of a small component of greenfield, family-oriented housing with a significant affordable element, responding to consultations. However, the executive chose to implement a far less flexible 100 per cent brownfield strategy that fails to acknowledge the nature of the housing waiting list (see below). This strategy also provides less opportunity to deliver key infrastructure and high-quality sustainable communities, and increases pressure on existing employment land and green space (CC 2008a: 6–13). It is a classic example of the all-brownfield high-density strategy that Peter Hall sees as the result of the

Plate 16.4 Cardiff: Sports Village and Roath Basin masterplans. The contrast between the two cannot be overstated. The first was a device to accommodate 'flexible uses': the second is a genuine 'masterplan in progress' that aims to be a European exemplar (Courtesy Cardiff Council and Igloo respectively).

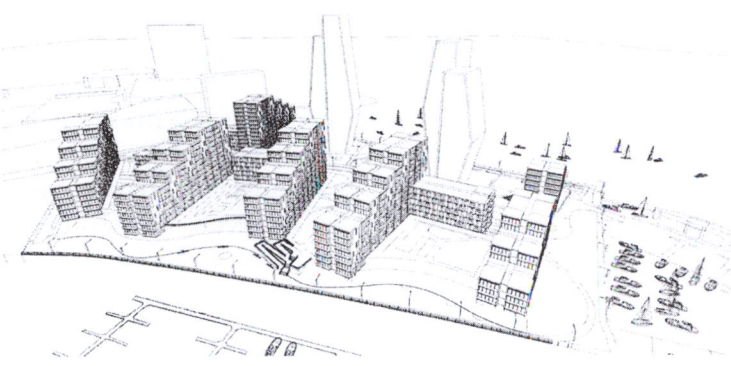

'land fetish' underpinning the urban renaissance–containment nexus (UTF 2005: 19). It is also remarkable for the low level of public participation, underlining points made previously about the 'democratic deficit' in council consultation.

Residential design quality: the liveability of super densities

The housing density issue is critical. There were particular concerns with the Bay Pointe scheme, on council-owned land, where gross densities of 450 dwellings per hectare were proposed with three double towers of thirty-one to forty-one storeys with reduced car parking (0.7 per unit) placed underground (Plate 16.4). A narrow park was provided between the two towers, and the waterfronts made fully accessible, with affordable housing pepper-potted through the scheme, green roofs included and some improvements to energy efficiency. Despite council desires to maximise land values in order to cross-subsidise its 'sports village', the planning committee subsequently reduced the density by a third, and the number of double towers to two, to acknowledge the gross overdevelopment. The developers have now gone bankrupt, but the precedent is established. On the Havana Wharf site, 500 metres south of Central Station, the rare production of a planning framework helped produce a concept design that is a much more considered approach to the triple issues of a high-quality public realm, good liveability and a sense of place/neighbourhood. Here, at densities of 180 dwellings per hectare, the developer proposed carbon-neutral, mixed-use and 15 per cent affordable housing on a network of urban streets, and after sustained negotiations agreed to undercroft parking and significant communal space for the apartments. The densities remain very high but the urban design is a much better model for south Cardiff than other recent housing schemes. However, the Section 106 agreement remains unsigned. The *LDP Preferred Strategy* promises 'Supplementary Planning Guidance to control the density of future housing developments and secure a better . . . "fit" between households and dwelling sizes' (CC 2007g: 46), and there are excellent guides around, which stress wider unit mix, energy efficiency, better soundproofing and private and communal space and participative management (e.g. Design for Homes 2007).

Residential design quality: suburban intensification

Minor residential intensification is evident throughout the city's suburbs, but larger-scale intensification remains largely confined to former industrial sites because resident opposition is much more muted in these locations. There have been prolonged battles to prevent residential conversion/intensification on a redundant hospital site and redevelopments of small groups of houses on large lots, and the council is reluctant to promote further intensification because of this opposition. WAG is promoting an exemplar sustainable urban village with a medium-density mix of family/apartment and live–work accommodation on a former industrial site (Ely Bridge) in the western suburbs, and this will be a welcome demonstration project. In some inner suburbs the emergence of bespoke student accommodation has become an urban design and development control issue of considerable importance, as student numbers in the city reach 28,000. On the one hand, its production offers some prospect of restoring key inner-city residential areas to family and year-round residential use, but on the other, high densities and mediocre design are of concern to adjacent residents. A *Student Community Plan and Partnership* has been established to better manage this issue (CC 2008d).

As for the city's council estates, predominantly low-rise and suburban in character, these have been well managed and maintained and not yet subjected to a drive towards greater mixed tenure, though there are extensive new private estates on some of their margins. So far the council has rejected the option of housing stock transfer, but there are doubts about its ability to fund their improvement strategy to meet the new Welsh Housing Quality Standards by 2012 (Hooper and Smith 2006). The council is now addressing housing renewal within a more comprehensive approach to neighbourhood improvement that is comparable to the English National Strategy for Neighbourhood Renewal, according to which mainstream service delivery will be adjusted to address social disadvantage (CC 2007b). Regrettably the length of the council's housing waiting list (6,555 homes, 70 per cent family) continues to increase exponentially, with average house price (£150,000) 6.75 times the average salary (2006 figures; CC 2007g: 8–10).

Three current megaprojects: contrasting design and sustainability credentials

Another factor requiring revision of the LDP was the proposal for the Wales International Business Park (WIBP) at Junction 33, north of the M4, in open countryside in the far north-western corner of the city (Figure 16.1). The WAG-supported proposal for 1.26 million square metres of floorspace is enshrined in the Wales Spatial Plan, to provide employment more for deprived Valley communities than for Cardiff. But it is clearly premature in terms of the development of the city, especially given the rejection of a north-westerly extension of the city until after 2021. The WIBP's 5,000 car parking spaces, and rather lame proposals for a bus interchange, emphasise the unsustainability of the concept, but it is being justified by its promoters as the *sine qua non* for major inward investment and/or new prestige business headquarters (ignoring perhaps twenty-five major sites with permissions, but few prospective occupiers in south Cardiff). The WIBP needs to be integral to a north-westerly 'sustainable urban extension', and to cross-fund the delivery of a new high-capacity public transport spine, connecting the western valleys to the city centre and the bay, and serving a sustainable urban extension (Figure 16.2). The subsequent sustainability appraisal of the plan fudged these issues.

WIBP contrasts sharply with another WAG-led megaproject, the brownfield, bioscience/creative industries and residential scheme for Roath Basin (see Plate 16.3), though it too is in danger of being ill-served by public transport. Here WAG sought an exemplar project, and ran a developer competition, won by an ethical developer (Igloo Regeneration), and with Sjoerd Soeters of Java Island (Amsterdam) fame leading the design team there are prospects at last of exemplary urban design and sustainable development. Mixed-use city blocks, strongly enclosed docks, lively public and communal spaces, high-quality inhabited streets with live–work and high standards of sustainable construction, significantly almost all in medium-rise blocks, are promised.

Roath Basin is a poignant counterpoint to the third current megaproject, the council's international sports village project and the whole regeneration of the Ferry Road peninsula (see Plate 16.3). The sports village was always problematic and overambitious, and not just because of the acquisition, remediation and piling costs (£60 million). Only the city's Olympic pool and a (temporary) ice-rink have been built of the original concept, and a series of sports stadia, commercial leisure, regional casino, mega-hotel and other resort attractions have failed to materialise (a white water canoeing facility is now assured). City land disposals and generous planning permissions (for apartment blocks, retail warehouse, supermarket and recently the Bay Pointe project: see Plate 16.3) have attempted to defray the costs and complete the infrastructure. But each has only emphasised the lack of coherent masterplanning and urban design, and the complete disregard of wider liveability, accessibility and sustainability considerations to which we now turn.

The sustainable city: eco-footprint issues

Despite its limited progress in promoting sustainability, and notwithstanding its new 'carbon-lite' mantra, Cardiff is one city which has pioneered eco-footprinting, in collaboration with Cardiff University (Collins and Flynn 2006). The results are revealing, and emphasise that living in a compact city, well served by public transport, does not necessarily reduce the eco-footprint. The average Cardiff footprint is 5.59 global hectares, three times the average earth share, and 0.24 global hectares above the English average. The key components of the high footprint are the use of catering services (eating out/drinking), private car travel (which one would expect to be less in a small city), air travel (particularly high), consumption of domestic energy and the generation of waste. The analysts conclude that a rising number of small households, living in apartments which do not have low energy ratings, and eating and drinking out more than the average, are likely to increase the Cardiff footprint significantly in the foreseeable future, as will a tourist and sports strategy (the eco-footprint of a tourist in Cardiff is 2.91 global hectares greater than that of a resident). Such footprints are primarily driven by consumerist lifestyles, but they can be reduced through planning and design, most obviously through energy-efficient dwellings, walkable/cyclable cities and services that are accessible on foot. All these are currently conspicuous by their absence in the new communities in south Cardiff, though some key infrastructure links may be emerging, while the network of protected landscapes within the city is crying out to be better connected. There are important lessons here for all British cities and for the renaissance at large.

Conclusions

Unable to take advantage of the English urban renaissance policies and programmes, Cardiff has nonetheless closely followed the English Core Cities' patterns of competitiveness, urban entrepreneurialism and place-marketing. Cardiff is one of the few large cities which has adopted the strong mayor and executive model advocated by the Urban Task Force, but the ensuing development dynamism has to be offset by evidence of a democratic deficit, and a relegation of planning to a service rather than a strategic function, at least until recently. While the council ensures that it maximises the value of its land disposals to raise capital for major projects, at the same time it has ratcheted up residential densities to metropolitan levels, and failed to ensure a high standard of design to humanise urban form. This is an all too common 'urban renaissance' trait, and it has been left to WAG to demonstrate how to use its land assets to progress higher design and sustainability standards in private development (e.g. Roath Basin and Ely Bridge).

Unlike many of the Core Cities, Cardiff has not focused most of its development and enhancement efforts on its city centre. Rather, it has sought to complete the regeneration of the bay by promoting a second business district, and a second major waterside sports/leisure focus. These ambitions seem simply too great for a relatively small, if steadily growing, city, particularly given the failure to resolve connectivity, and direct public transport links between the bay and city centre. The result has been the dissipation of regeneration impetus and a fragmentation of urban form. In terms of development outcomes the city now achieves very high proportions of brownfield development (88 per cent in 2007) and high-density apartments (70 per cent of completions in 2007), delivering a key quantitative element of the urban renaissance agenda. But it is the design quality and sustainability of this development that is at issue. The volume house builders have been allowed to build a monoculture of small apartments with only 14 per cent affordable, and little or no neighbourhood facilities or inhabited streets. Where a higher proportion of affordable is achieved, the developers drive up the density but not the design quality (e.g. Celestia, Plate 16.2i). These design outcomes have to be improved.

On a more positive note, within the inner suburbs and the council estates the council has pursued neighbourhood renewal with considerable success, while resisting the pressures to transfer its housing stock to housing action trusts. But like most cities, it has not developed proactive suburban intensification policies, and it has sought to stop suburban extensions because of suburban protest, thereby reducing the supply of land for family housing. A more balanced supply of family versus small household dwellings, and of social and private housing ,is urgently required, as it is across other cities.

In terms of urban design, the council's claims for 'innovative architecture and imaginative and iconic urban design' can be interpreted charitably as the flights of fancy of the city marketing team, or more critically as a collective design illiteracy. The alliteration in the claim suggests the former, but the pursuit of iconic buildings, replete with maritime architectural references, is deeply embedded in Cardiff's recent development history, and is now being reinterpreted as a 'city of towers'. As for iconic urban design, the megaprojects such as Callaghan Square/Lloyd George Avenue/the Flourish (Plate 16.1), and now the sports village (Plate 16.3), demonstrate the failure to civilise road engineering and create well-used streets and public spaces. Better integration of highway and planning functions and more urban design awareness are urgently required.

Meanwhile, the lack of real innovation in architecture is manifest in generally low levels of sustainable construction and energy efficiency (the Assembly's Senedd, and the new city library being honourable exceptions). Fortunately, from April 2009, WAG has required Code for Sustainable Homes Level 3, BREEAM (Building Research Establishment Environmental Assessment Mechanism) 'very good', and renewable energy provision for all but the smallest developments, with progress to carbon-neutral buildings by 2011 (WAG 2008b; see Figure 16.1). Its two exemplar projects (Roath Basin and Ely Bridge) promise very high levels of sustainability.

Does this chapter provide an unduly harsh verdict on the planning and design efforts of the city over the last thirty years? Does it fail to acknowledge the scale of dereliction that the city faced in the 1980s and the difficulties of integrating the myriad of development ambitions in what was, until the mid-1990s, a largely unfavourable development climate? In its focus on the megaprojects does it underplay the large number of individual planning achievements – parks, public spaces, sensitive infill and environmental enhancements – that have been achieved through patient and persistent development control negotiations and the extraction of Section 106 monies (£30 million in the last five years)? Senior Cardiff planners would argue that it does.

There is no doubt that most of the positive improvements to schemes negotiated by development control go unseen and unacknowledged, but without a proactive approach to design quality they can often only alter design at the margins. The planners argue forcibly that the city was never in a position to demand high-quality development as a right, and have always had to negotiate it in circumstances in which market conditions and developer finances severely limited the scope for improvement. They would argue that it is only now, from a platform of development success generated by council single-mindedness, that the city is able to demand higher design standards. Some support for, but mainly contradiction of, this view will be found in the qualities of the 13,000 or so residential units recently given planning permission (or awaiting legal agreements), some of which have been described in this chapter (see Plate 16.4).

International experts on design review would agree that 'the appropriate degree of regulation . . . [is] dependent upon prevailing economic conditions and social considerations, not to mention the political climate prevailing in the community' (Lai 1988: 429). But they would also judge a city by whether its design outcomes live up to its visions and place-marketing, and the (international) design standards which it repeatedly invokes. They would conclude that it is time that place-making was given priority over place-marketing

Much depends on the new planning regime that is being constructed, and its ability to deliver on the promises made in both the planning and city marketing documents to uplift design quality and standards of sustainability. Successful delivery depends principally on the *political* and *corporate* commitment to design quality and environmental objectives in the council's growth agenda. Both are now threatened by the severe downturn in the property market, the increased development costs of carbon reduction, and the parlous state of council finances (Cardiff loses 40 per cent of its business rates to the rest of Wales and generally receives one of the lowest annual settlements from WAG). But the economic downturn is also an opportunity to rethink the recent spate of apartment permissions, and the whole question of appropriate densities, mixes and forms of housing for the city, while acknowledging the absolute imperatives of keeping up with household growth and reducing waiting lists for affordable accommodation. Emerging policies and guidance have to be consulted on, tested, adopted and translated into positive and proactive control practices, and new corporate design standards have to be set for streets, spaces, green areas and public buildings, all easily said but in practice very hard to deliver. And by ignoring the results of public consultation on the LDPPS the council executive have fallen at the first hurdle (CC 2008a).

Simplistic notions of proportions of brownfield and higher-density development can no longer serve as an adequate planning response to sustainable communities and climate change, as the city's own eco-footprint studies show. This is a key lesson for the 'urban renaissance' strategy at large. While WAG initiatives on sustainable construction, and their exemplar projects in the city, are to be welcomed, much more radical action on the part of the council is necessary to give meaning to their new mantra of a 'carbon-lite' city, and to reduce carbon emissions to meet government targets (see RICS Wales 2008: 16–17).

References

CBDC (Cardiff Bay Development Corporation) (Llewelyn Davies) (1988) *Cardiff Bay Regeneration Strategy* (Cardiff: CBDC).

CBDC *(2000) Renaissance: the Story of Cardiff Bay 1987–2000* (Cardiff: CBDC).

CC (Cardiff Council) (2005a) *Cardiff: A Proud Capital; Beyond 2005* (Cardiff: Cardiff Council).

CC (2006) *Corporate Strategy* (Cardiff: Cardiff Council).

CC (2007a) *Competitive Capital: The Cardiff Economic Strategy* (Cardiff: Cardiff Council).

CC (2007b) *Cardiff Community Strategy: Neighbourhood Improvement Programme* (Cardiff: Cardiff Council).

CC (2007c) *City Centre Strategy 2007–10* (Cardiff: Cardiff Council).

CC (2007d) *Cardiff: A Proud Capital: Community Strategy 2007–17* (Cardiff: Cardiff Council).

CC (2007e) *River Ely Action Plan* (Cardiff: Cardiff Council).

CC (2007f) *Parks and Green Spaces Strategy* (Cardiff: Cardiff Council).

CC (2007g) *Cardiff Local Development Plan 2006–2021-Peferred Strategy Report* (Cardiff: Cardiff Council).

CC (2008a) *Executive Business Meeting 2–10–08: Progressing the LDP: Agenda Item 5* (Cardiff: Cardiff Council).

CC (2008b) *Draft Tall Buildings Supplementary Planning Guidance* (Cardiff: Cardiff Council).

CC (2008c) *LDP Preferred Strategy Consultation Responses*, April 2008 Planning Department (Cardiff: Cardiff Council).

CC (2008d) *Cardiff Student Community Plan: A Partnership Action Plan* (Cardiff: Cardiff Council).

CCC (Cardiff County Council) (1994) *City Centre Design Guide* (Cardiff: Cardiff County Council).

CEC Commission of the European Communities (1993) *Growth, Competitiveness, Employment: the Challenges and the Way Forward into the 21st Century,* White Paper, Supplement 6/93 (Luxembourg: Bulletin of the European Communities).

Collins A. and Flynn A. (2006) A City's Consumption: The Ecological Footprint of Cardiff. In A. Hooper and J. Punter (2006) *Capital Cardiff 1975–2020: Regeneration, Competitiveness and the Urban Environment* (Cardiff: University of Wales Press) pp. 242–264.

Crickhowell (1997) *Opera House Lottery: Zaha Hadid and the Cardiff Bay Project* (Cardiff: University of Wales Press).

Daunton, M.J. (1977) *Coal Metropolis: Cardiff 1870–1914* (Leicester: Leicester University Press).

DCfW (Design Commission for Wales) (2005) *Design Review 03–05* (Cardiff: DCfW)

DCfW (2008) *Design Review 05–07* (Cardiff: DCfW). Online. Available at: www.dcfw.org/designreview (last accessed 15 June 2008).

Design for Homes (2007) *Recommendations for living at Superdensity* (London: DFH).

Garreau, J. (1991) *Edge City: Life on the New Frontier* (New York: Doubleday).

Griffiths, M. (2008) Against the Grain. *About Wales (The Civic Trust for Wales)* (December): 4–5.

Hooper, A. and Punter, J. (2006) *Capital Cardiff 1975–2020: Regeneration, Competitiveness and the Urban Environment* (Cardiff: University of Wales Press).

Hooper, A. and Smith, R. (2006) Housing and Regeneration in Cardiff, 1974–2020. In A. Hooper and J. Punter (2006) *Capital Cardiff 1975–2020: Regeneration, Competitiveness and the Urban Environment* (Cardiff: University of Wales Press) pp. 97–117.

Morgan, K. (2006) Governing Cardiff: Politics, Power and Personalities. In A. Hooper and J. Punter (2006) *Capital

Cardiff 1975–2020: Regeneration, Competitiveness and the Urban Environment (Cardiff: University of Wales Press) pp. 31–46.

Parkinson, M. and Kareecha, J. (2006) *Cardiff: A Competitive European City?* (Cardiff: Report for CC).

Punter, J. (2006) A City Centre for a European Capital. In A. Hooper and J. Punter (2006) *Capital Cardiff 1975–2020: Regeneration, Competitiveness and the Urban Environment* (Cardiff: University of Wales Press) pp. 122–148.

Punter, J. (2007) Design-Led Regeneration? Evaluating the Design Outcomes of Cardiff Bay and their Implications for Future Regeneration and Design. *Journal of Urban Design*, 12 (3): 375–405.

RICS Wales (Royal Institution of Chartered Surveyors Wales) (2008) *The Climate Challenge: Your city, Your Responsibility* (Cardiff: RICS Wales).

SGCC (South Glamorgan County Council) (1993) *South Glamorgan: Eurocapital 2020 Vision: Social Development: Preparing the Ground* (Cardiff: SGCC).

Sustrans (2008) *Big Lottery Fund Project*. Online. Available at: www.sustrans.org.uk/biglottery (last accessed 12 July 2008).

WAG (Wales Assembly Government) (2004) *People, Places, Futures: The Wales Spatial Plan* (revised 2008) (Cardiff: WAG).

WAG (2008a) *Affordable Housing in Wales: An Independent Report to the Minister of Housing* (Cardiff: WAG).

WAG (2008b) *Minister for the Environment: Further Consultation on Planning for Climate Change*, 3 July (Cardiff: WAG).

Northern Ireland

An introduction

In Northern Ireland, as a result of prolonged sectarianism in national and local politics, the national government undertakes virtually all government activities, leaving local government to perform a range of minor functions. Planning, regeneration and transport are administered by the Northern Ireland Office and housing by the Northern Ireland Housing Executive. Planning is undertaken by the Planning Service Agency of the Northern Ireland Office, which consults with the twenty-six district councils. A Belfast City-Region Strategy was established by the Department of the Environment Northern Ireland (DoENI) in 1995, and a statutory plan produced for the city and its region linking transport and spatial planning strategies for the region.

As in England, there was a longstanding Urban Programme offering positive discrimination to the most deprived areas, and this was bolstered by a regional Peace Programme of investment in 1998, as well as long-term regeneration strategies for multiagency partnerships across five areas of Belfast (operating since 1995). An aspirational Belfast City Vision was completed (BCVPB 2001) with a twenty-year time horizon, and a national strategic planning framework published in 2002. In 2004, the Belfast Local Strategy Partnership published its strategy statement (BLSP 2004). Given Belfast's loss of half of its population over the last half-century, and its continuing inner-city clearances against a backdrop of large-scale urban sprawl and retail dispersal, urban renaissance policies have a particular relevance to the city as it seeks to pursue a new trajectory and put 'the Troubles' behind it.

In 1996, a national Quality Initiative (similar to John Gummer's initiative in England) was launched to improve the quality and sustainability of housing developments, and timed to provide better guidance for large-scale land releases around Belfast (Jenks 2002). The publication of *Creating Places* (DoENI 2000) meant that Northern Ireland was the first of the home countries to fully integrate national design advice on highways and planning. More recently, a national Architecture and the Built Environment Policy has been drafted, and a Ministerial Advisory Group for Architecture established, that will act as a design watchdog. Belfast's current pattern of development will provide a very stiff test for this body as it operates within a highly fragmented system of urban governance and development strategies, and a highly politicised development climate.

References

BCVPB (Belfast City Vision Partnership Board) (2001) *Belfast City Vision: Our City, Our Future, Our Vision* (Belfast: BCV).

BLSP (Belfast Local Strategy Partnership) (2004) *Helping to Build a Sustainable City at Peace with Itself: Strategy Statement* (Belfast: BLSP).
DoENI (Department of the Environment Northern Ireland) (2000) *Creating Places* (Belfast: DoENI).
Jenks, M. (2002) Devolution and Urban Design: Northern Ireland. *Urban Design Quarterly*, 84: 22–25.

17 Belfast

Rebranding the 'Renaissance City': from 'the Troubles' to Titanic Quarter®

William J. V. Neill

Introduction

In the wake of the Good Friday Agreement in 1998, opening the way for a cessation of thirty years of low-grade civil war, and taking some inspiration from Lord Rogers's Urban Task Force (UTF) report the following year, Belfast, at the turn of the millennium, proclaimed itself as the 'Renaissance City' (BCC 2002). The city can be forgiven for the oversight that this epithet had already been claimed by Detroit in the rebuilding drive that eventually followed its image collapse after the urban riots in 1967. Events in that city were subsequently to mock such a rebranding of place (Neill 2006a). Belfast, as this chapter will argue, has more hope, but remains afflicted with a lack of real self-confidence and a poverty of aspiration in asserting its identity as a unique place. A kinder critic might point out that expectations must be tempered with an awareness of the road already travelled. As late as 1992 the Belfast novelist Glenn Patterson, in his book *Fat Lad*, described the city's tourist image as a 'ghoulish fairground with a murderous significance ascribed to every street corner' (Patterson 1992: 203). This is in stark contrast to at least the physical renaissance, which Belfast, over fifteen years later, presents to the world. The new Belfast brand logo, launched in 2008, celebrating this turn around, but with lack of original-ity in the concept (a red welcoming heart sign with echoes of New York's brand), was justifiably met with an ambivalent response (O'Hara and Wilkie 2008).

The chapter proceeds by way of some preliminary comments on the Rogers's UTF agenda, of particular relevance for Belfast, involving the culture of cities. This is followed by reflection on the particular governance context in Belfast, which makes the realisation of a coordinated renaissance vision for the city especially difficult. A brief periodisation of development strategy since 'the Troubles', where conflict management and the projected 'feel-good' influence of city centre projects became closely entwined, is briefly outlined. On the basis of this, by the turn of the century, Belfast possessed an infrastructural launch pad underpinning a period of future property developments eventually incorporating a speculative bubble, which the 'credit crunch' since 2008 now threatens to deflate. Three facets of the 'urban renaissance' in Belfast are subse-quently examined: housing and planning, design and development and evidence of cultural shift.

Urban Task Force report

A useful and comprehensive overview of the discursive framework of New Labour's urban renais-sance agenda, strongly influenced as it has been by the architect Richard Rogers, has recently been provided by Colomb (2007). Identified among the cornerstones are high-quality urban design, public spaces and streetscape; the importance of higher densities with social mixing combined with attracting suburban knowledge workers to the city; and an embrace of the European Union (EU) notion that cities are the key to competitiveness, cohesion and environmental sustainability. As Colomb points out, this 'Third Way Urbanism' conjures up the construction of a new urbanity or urban idyll where linguistic strategies are deployed by key actors to sell the allure of a 'British metropolitan bohemia' (2007: 6). As will be outlined later, the transposing of this urbanity to Belfast presents its own problems, not to say credibility. It is the 'rural idyll' that continues to hold cultural sway in Northern Ireland, with Irish nationalism and unionism both rooted in a rural idealism that limits representations of place (Allen and Kelly 2003: 8). However, this may not necessarily prove insurmountable. As Colomb puts it, drawing on the work of Hoskins and Tallon (2004):

> The process of constructing a new 'urban idyll' involves the reinterpretation in an urban context of a number of themes traditionally associated with the countryside – such as the 'local community', 'nature', 'heritage', the 'village' – in order to create an appealing vision of urban living through association with traditional concepts.
>
> (2007: 7)

What is evoked are the possibilities associated with a culture of civilised urbanity with good design, providing appropriate spaces of socialisation associated with continental European cities. This evocation is not just through government policy. Colomb rightfully underlines that this reimaging of the city is actively pursued by the development industry and the media, which hypes, in Pine and Gilmore's phrase, the 'experience economy'(Pine and Gilmore 1999) and a new aesthetic of consumption. All these phenomena exist in the Belfast context with the added twist that, whereas the discourse on 'urban renaissance' privileges the 'civilised middle class' as new city pioneers and saviours (Atkinson 2003), in Belfast they are tasked with incubating a post sectarian urban culture as well.

Governance context

The city of Belfast, with a population of 277,000, is the centre of a much larger metropolitan region, bringing the total population to over 600,000. The city, increasingly Catholic in composition, has been in population decline for many years (a process which is now slowing) mirrored by population increases in surrounding local authority areas. The overgovernance of what is a relatively small core European city has recently been commented upon by Belfast City Council's Director of Development:

> The city, governed by eleven government departments and numerous quangos, has a council with few powers. Over the last few decades there has been a further proliferation of 'partnerships' to do everything and anything . . . While partnerships can be very positive for development, it is clear that Belfast has become encumbered by the sheer number and volume of such arrangements, so much so they are now an impediment rather than a help. There are currently fifty-five separate strategies operating in Belfast covering the area of 'development'. The architecture of governance is dominated by a single-focus mentality, a lack of cohesion and consensus, which has led to empire-building and lack of trust.
>
> (McGivern 2006: 339)

The impending reorganisation of local government in Northern Ireland and return of planning powers to the local level, may go some way to addressing this concern. The context is one in which a plethora of intermediate participative arrangements promoting so-called institutional thickness were put in place under direct rule to attempt to compensate for the local 'democratic deficit'. It would be wrong, however, to exaggerate the implications. A central guiding hand has steered, if imperfectly from a design point of view, development strategy towards the centre of Belfast over the last quarter-century or so as an adjunct to general conflict management.

Charting the discourse of development in Belfast from the Fortress City of the 1970s, four phases can be identified. Preceding this, the city centre was under a sustained IRA (Irish Republican Army) bombing campaign that a security 'ring of steel' only imperfectly thwarted.

- 1980–1994: towards first IRA ceasefire – development and the possibility of 'normality';
- 1994–1998: towards the Good Friday Agreement – key public infrastructure comes to fruition;
- 1998–2007: towards agreed devolution – 'urban renaissance' reaches to private sector;
- 2007–: towards a new brand for Belfast – development demonstrates that devolution is delivering.

Towards 'normality': Belfast 1980–1994

Physical planning in Belfast in the 1980s, through the mobilisation of development, became related to the management of 'the Troubles' in two major ways. First, the strategy to radically improve social housing in the city spearheaded an equality agenda and, second, development in the city centre took on special symbolic significance in the non-military battle with political violence. In 1981 housing was elevated to the number one priority among social and environmental programmes in Northern Ireland, and within this special priority was given to the housing needs of Belfast (Singleton 1987: 159). Unpopular tower blocks in Belfast were subsequently bulldozed, including most of the notorious Divis Flats complex, and in the 1980s Belfast saw new traditional terraced housing based on good-quality design standards come on stream. One reviewer commented in 1987 on how Belfast had been deliberately spared the harsh social policy rigours of the Thatcher years:

> Much has been achieved in alleviating the appalling housing legacy in Belfast during the last ten years. While new-build and other programmes have been drastically pruned in cities throughout Britain, in Belfast the largest ever public sector programme is now under way in the city and it is complemented by large scale rehabilitation and other related programmes aimed at tackling disrepair.
>
> (Singleton 1987: 167)

The planning and development of Belfast city centre in the 1980s and early 1990s complemented the British government's equality agenda with a parallel and complementary normalisation agenda. An invitation was extended to common civic pride with the possibility of the pooling of difference in a shared identity wrapped up in consumption. The seeds of this policy can be detected in a package of measures 'to spell the rebirth of Belfast', announced by the British Secretary of State for Northern Ireland in 1978. The government looked forward to the spread of 'oases' through the central area and 'the creation of a new Belfast of which all its citizens can be proud' (NIIS 1978). This is, in reality, the true date for the commencement of 'urban renaissance' in Belfast.

The city centre became an official symbol of a common prosperous future counterposed to the perceived wanton destruction of terrorism. The British Northern Ireland Environment Minister, Richard Needham, who is most closely associated with this period, characterised himself in 'rebuilding Belfast' as 'battling for peace' and, while the design strategy may be criticised, the city has not had a design champion with clout since. A new Castle Court shopping centre, which Richard Needham 'demanded' should be faced in glass, threw down a gauntlet to terrorism as 'the defining landmark of the city's new confidence' (Needham 1998: 171). Unfortunately, this project involved the demolition of the intact High Victorian Head Post Office of 1886. Castle Court, as a new symbol of a more normal city, complemented the refurbished Opera House which, located next to the infamous Europa Hotel (the most bombed in the world), had reopened in 1980. A new development corporation with ample resources was established to lead the physical transformation of Belfast's riverfront, renamed as Laganside.

A concept plan for the River Lagan in 1987 drew design inspiration from Salford Quays. A Belfast Urban Area Plan, published in 1990, presented positive images of newly built or planned developments in the 'new' Belfast, counterposed with anaemic toned panoramas of the 'old' backward-looking city. This reimaging of Belfast has been criticised elsewhere (Neill 1993). In embracing almost any development as 'good', much third-rate architecture and design was accepted, albeit for understandable reasons. 'Lipstick on the gorilla' in hindsight was perhaps too harsh a metaphor for this planning period, given the ultimate success of conflict management in general. The legacy, however, has been an urban design benchmark set too low.

Towards the Good Friday Agreement: public investment 1994–1998

Major public infrastructural investments which came to fruition in Belfast during these years, often with considerable European funding, must lead to the question of whether the peace process was the handmaiden to development or whether, in fact, the reverse was true. Pregnant optimism (punctured temporarily by the Canary Wharf bombing in February 1996) was to lead to the production of various 'visioning' plans for Belfast at this time (Neill 2004: 196–197), but it is four major developments clustered around Belfast's riverfront that were to underpin 'renaissance' in the late 1990s and beyond (Figure 17.1).

The new Lagan Weir, ushered to completion in 1994 by the Laganside Corporation, has been of instrumental importance in opening up for development riverside frontage in the heart of the city. This attractive infrastructural addition to Belfast enables high water level to be maintained, thus covering the odiferous aroma of previous mudbanks. The Cross-Harbour Road Bridge was opened the following year courtesy of the impetus provided by 'Belfast's Minister for Development', Richard Needham. The M3, when floodlit alongside the weir, provides an attractive addition to the Belfast nightscape, even if the opportunity to make a bolder and more unique design statement was lost. While its construction contravened wider spatial orthodoxy, which eschewed new urban motorway construction at the time, this link has proven extremely beneficial in linking the east and north sides of Belfast, diverting such traffic away from the town centre and opening up vacant land for development in the harbour area. It is surprising that alongside such a major investment in road infrastructure no rapid transit plan for Belfast has ever risen far up spending priorities, in a place which 'is today the most car-dependent medium-size city in Western Europe' (Smyth 2006: 118).

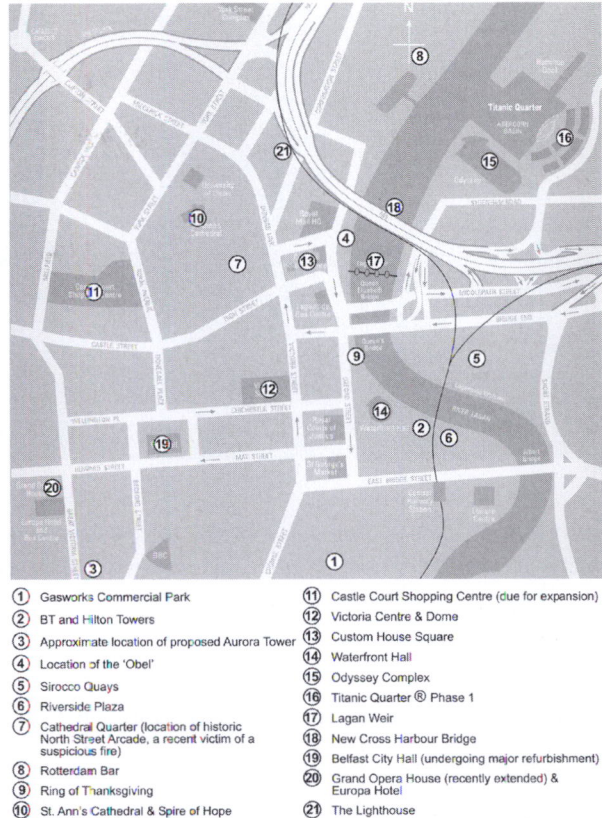

Figure 17.1 Belfast: Renaissance projects in the city centre. © Crown Copyright. All rights reserved. Licence number 100049043.

①	Gasworks Commercial Park	⑪	Castle Court Shopping Centre (due for expansion)
②	BT and Hilton Towers	⑫	Victoria Centre & Dome
③	Approximate location of proposed Aurora Tower	⑬	Custom House Square
④	Location of the 'Obel'	⑭	Waterfront Hall
⑤	Sirocco Quays	⑮	Odyssey Complex
⑥	Riverside Plaza	⑯	Titanic Quarter ® Phase 1
⑦	Cathedral Quarter (location of historic North Street Arcade, a recent victim of a suspicious fire)	⑰	Lagan Weir
⑧	Rotterdam Bar	⑱	New Cross Harbour Bridge
⑨	Ring of Thanksgiving	⑲	Belfast City Hall (undergoing major refurbishment)
⑩	St. Ann's Cathedral & Spire of Hope	⑳	Grand Opera House (recently extended) & Europa Hotel
		㉑	The Lighthouse

By 1998, Laganside Corporation had brought to completion the reclamation of twelve hectares of the most contaminated land in Northern Ireland with the opening up of the Belfast Gas Works site for future reuse. While this public pump priming would underpin the development of a private hotel and offices, the inevitable price paid was the removal of two huge defining gas holders from the Belfast skyline, which for a generation were a prominent signature of this 'dirty old town'.

A harbinger of the new Belfast, however, was a trio of buildings on Lanyon Place on the riverfront, which opened in 1998. The Waterfront Hall, sponsored by Belfast City Council, has won modest design accolades, which is not something that can be said of either the adjacent BT (British Telecom) tower or Hilton Hotel, labelled by one local design critic as 'blockish and bland' (Brett undated; see Plate 17.1). Compounding this is the total lack of attention to how public space works as an aesthetic ensemble. As Charles Brett, a prominent Belfast architectural historian, argues: 'It is a great pity . . . that a contemporary building [Waterfront Hall] of so much architectural merit should be so brutally overshadowed by its unneighbourly neighbours' (Brett 2001: 98). In 1998, design was less of a consideration than the sheer presence of such first-rank logos in the first place.

Towards agreed devolution: 1998–2007

In the aftermath of the Good Friday Agreement, the pulse of private development in Belfast was to quicken. As a former director of planning in the city points out, it was only after the

Plate 17.1 Belfast: Renaissance 'scrum' on the Lagan. From left to right: Offices of Price Waterhouse on 'Riverfront Plaza', Hilton and BT towers and the Waterfront Hall.

Provisional IRA ceasefire in 1994 that there was any sustained interest in major private investment in the heart of the city (Morrisson 2006: 152). Housing strategy, planning, design and development are now considered in the context of the rhetoric of the urban renaissance agenda, which found fertile soil in the 'post-conflict' city of Belfast.

Urban renaissance: housing strategy and planning

Both the former director of planning responsible for Belfast and the present director of development for Belfast City Council acknowledge the influence of the urban renaissance agenda in Belfast from the late 1990s onwards. The former draws attention to the fact that the Regional Development Strategy for Northern Ireland, adopted in 2002, accepted European compact city arguments (Morrisson 2006: 152). On a visit to Belfast in 1997, the European commissioner for regional policy expressed pleasure in the similarities between the Regional Development Strategy discussion paper and the European Spatial Development Perspective drafted that year (Wulf-Mathies 1997). The latter highlights the importance of the renaissance agenda to competitiveness and success for the modern city (McGivern 2006:332). The new Belfast Metropolitan Area Plan, long in gestation, will not change this aspiration.

The densification of Belfast is most apparent on the Lagan, where a plethora of apartment buildings of varying quality has mushroomed over the last ten years or so in fashionable reimaged locations such as Gregg's Quay, Laganview and St John's Wharf. This has truly changed the physical face of the city. Such urban renaissance manifestations, however, exist cheek by jowl with the continued underdevelopment of many vacated locations in the city, which have experienced Protestant exit to outer suburbs and dormitory settlements. Given sectarian realities, redevelopment of these sites for Catholic housing needs cannot be assured. As Boal points out, 'the proportionate increase in Catholics in the City is not, in the main, due to the growth in the number of Catholics, but to a decline in the number of Protestants' (Boal 2006: 71). With different spatial processes in operation, and under the constraints exerted by containment policy, Belfast provides a variegated residential profile. Town cramming is a serious issue. With considerable Catholic housing demand in the south of the city, historically less segregated, modern apartments are replacing detached Edwardian homes in spacious gardens. This is also changing the face of Belfast. The grip exerted by containment policy, also, until recently, a contributory factor to house price escalation in Belfast and a housing crisis for many first-time buyers, is presently causing a rethink of strategic policy. A review of the Regional Development Strategy was announced in June 2008 with some relaxation of containment policy expected.

Urban renaissance: design and development

At the turn of the century, Belfast's leading architectural critic, Sir Charles Brett, pointed out that only thirty years previously the city was predominantly Victorian and Edwardian, with a strong character of its own. He reflected on destruction and building over the intervening years: 'The architectural legacy of Belfast, today, is something of a plum pudding. There are many excellent ingredients; but the result is pretty indigestible' (2001: 98).

It is probable that current developments would have reinforced Brett's assessment. The character of Belfast's built fabric is changing at a rapid pace but there are, of course, those who like plum pudding. 'Drivers' of development include:

- demographics: population increase, 'post-conflict' returnees and a preference for city centre living by younger groups across the sectarian divide;
- compact city ideas and redevelopment of industrial sites with the disappearance of the manufacturing city;
- 'developer charter': close relationship between government and private sector, preferred developer status to major players and streamlined planning for major projects;
- oversized public sector economy;
- Celtic Tiger: availability of investment capital, speculative buy-to-rent investments and the influence of 'property buccaneers' (Brown 2008);
- public apathy towards many commercial development projects and design considerations, thus smoothing implementation;
- the 'post-conflict' emergence of Belfast as a popular tourist destination, spawning new hotels and ancillary services.

The 'post-conflict' city, in design terms, celebrates a better future with the shock of the new. Here the major parting shot from the now wound-up Laganside Corporation, which has led Belfast's riverfront reimaging over the last fifteen years, was a new glass skyscraper for the city, at twenty-six storeys destined to become the tallest building in Northern Ireland when construction is complete. The complex, which is intended to transform the Belfast skyline, will incorporate hotel, entertainment, apartment and office uses, and, according to the developer, by being 'breathtaking in its stature . . . will become an icon for the city' (Blackbourne, quoted in *Ulster Architect* 2005: 23). The building comes with its ready-made nickname, the Obel, apparently a short form of obelisk. Glass is now the representational form of choice for development in the 'post-conflict city', as an obvious contrast to the brutalist 'terrorproof' buildings of 'the Troubles'. The massive new Victoria Centre retail complex in the city, which opened in 2008 and connects the riverfront with the city centre, sadly saw demolition of the old Kitchen Bar, an irreplaceable time capsule of the now unfashionable Belfast of yesteryear (see Plate 17.2). That the city council participated with the Department of Social Development in a developer selection process that permitted this seems particularly lamentable. The Victoria Centre is topped with a glass dome, which looks like a scaled-down version of the Reichstag cupola.

A newly planned 'Hope and History Centre' in Belfast will be dominated by a glass enclosure,

Plate 17.2 Belfast: Victoria Centre with ersatz Kitchen Bar on the right and the restored Jaffe Fountain in the foreground. This seeks unsuccessfully to make amends for the deception.

as will a new extension to the Opera House. That the design of the 'post-conflict' city is insufficiently reflective of the character of Belfast has not gone without comment. In 2005, a fifteen-metre-high statue appeared on the banks of the River Lagan, courtesy of the Laganside Corporation and intended to be yet another icon for post-Troubles Belfast. Entitled 'The Ring of Thanksgiving', and looking like what appears to be a girl holding aloft a hoop while standing on a ball, one brave local journalist remarked on the £200,000 artwork:

> If Belfast is to have a huge statue that is in some way meant to speak for the city, shouldn't the people of the city have had a say in it? That way we might have had something that looks better than a sketch lifted from a child's storybook.

(O'Doherty 2004)

This was to bring a swift imperious retort from the president of the government-appointed committee responsible for commissioning the 'symbol of hope', that the critic was ignorant in not understanding that the statue 'contains all the symbolism of the feminine principle in mythology, including the Classical Greek and the Celtic traditions' (Appleton 2004). Some urban design additions, however, do exude unpretentious quality, which was a belated preoccupation of the Laganside Corporation in its dying days. The refurbished Customs House Square, a traditional Speakers' Corner in a former Belfast incarnation, has been rescued from traffic to provide, since opening in 2005, an attractive new square for a city sorely lacking in public space. An even more impressive Laganside project, the result of a latter-day design competition in 2004, has been the recent addition of a new spire to Belfast's St Anne's Cathedral. The stainless steel 'Spire of Hope', rising seventy-two metres from the innards of the cathedral, makes a truly dramatic statement on the new Belfast skyline and is considered one of Northern Ireland's best new design projects by the Royal Institute of British Architects (Pauli 2008). However, perhaps the greatest lost design opportunity during these renaissance years was the mediocre Odyssey complex, Belfast's 'landmark' millennium project, opened in 2001 (see Plate 17.3). Lying in reclaimed harbour land and 'neutral space', just north of the M3 road bridge, the commercial success of this cinema/ entertainment and concert arena (host to the equally neutral Belfast Giants ice hockey team), proves that, while this chance to produce a home-grown iconic building has lapsed, no one ever went broke underestimating the design tastes of the Belfast public. Thirty years of 'the Troubles' have, in the meantime, put aesthetics in its place. And as a Belfast City Council report put it in 2007, there are other concerns in the city:

> Evidence suggests that, while regeneration policies have gone some way towards improving the physical form of the city, they have had only a modest impact on areas of disadvantage. Indeed, in some cases, the gap between the poorer areas and the rest of the city has actually increased.
>
> (BCC 2007: 207)

2007–: Towards a new brand for Belfast – development demonstrates that devolution is delivering

In the context of what looks like more secure government devolution in Northern Ireland, the City of Belfast in 2007 turned to the international brand consultants Lloyd Northover to design a new logo for the city. The outcome, launched in July 2008 to underwhelming acclaim, does little to differentiate Belfast from many other cities starting with 'B'. In fact, the heart sign, already a cliché, apes a similar logo recently adopted by both Barrow and Blackburn. In Belfast the image floats free from the product, making little connection with the realm of emotion, the level at which, as the global director of Interbrand points out, true branding works (Swystun 2007: 35).

Here, Belfast has no set piece of modern architecture, art or design, despite many opportunities to be more adventurous, which can symbolise the path travelled and the struggle to

Plate 17.3 Belfast: Odyssey Arena and adjacent Titanic Quarter ® 'ARC' under construction in 2008. The completion of this skyline lies in the balance in the current financial climate.

define the road ahead where cultural tension is handled non-violently. This truly is a sign for the times. Only the spire on Belfast cathedral comes close, but was presumably discounted given the denominational bias. In 2008, Belfast has major development projects in the pipeline hyped by politicians eager to demonstrate that devolution is delivering. While the residential housing market lies dormant in Belfast at the time of writing in late 2008, the knock-on effect of more credit chastened times on the commercial sector remains to be seen. What is certain is that Belfast still lacks an overall design strategy or design champion, despite the best of intentions of the city council in funding PLACE (a drop-in centre giving information on design and architecture), the recent establishment of a Northern Ireland design panel, or the ongoing initiatives of the Department of Social Development in its Belfast Streets Ahead initiative to improve the public realm. Here, one academic comments rather harshly on the 'piecemeal reclamation of seemingly randomly selected sites':

> Licensed privateering is the order of the day, and the public agencies seem content to act as the city's pimps, parcelling up and branding the different 'Quarters' for the convenience of developers.
>
> (Jewesbury 2007: 2–3)

Nothing could be more random than the current planning application, seeking again to reach for the sky by building a tower block to exceed in height that of the Obel presently under construction. With claims to iconic status by the developer (Smyth 2007), the Aurora project, as presented in the brochure, would accommodate, on thirty-seven floors, 291 luxury apartments, residents' spa and gym, exclusive roof garden, twenty-four-hour concierge, valet parking, prime commercial space and signature restaurant. Without a tall buildings policy giving a context for assessment, this proposal for the new Belfast to the south of the city centre can be decided only on a piecemeal pragmatic basis.

The Northern Ireland construction industry is tied to a long list of development projects, either on the drawing board or taking shape on the ground, to raise up this new Belfast before the clouds of recession threaten. On the retail front, mention can be made of a planned 3,200 square metre extension to the existing Castle Court complex which helped to kick-start renaissance and the nearby Royal Exchange project with the usual mixed development blend of premium shops, restaurants, cafés, and so forth. The Lighthouse, developers tell us, will be yet another iconic mixed-use building for the northern side of the city centre. An upbeat promotional supplement to the *Belfast Telegraph*, on the occasion of a major USA investment conference in the city in spring 2008, summed up the situation thus:

> When America's corporate elite draw back the curtains of their hotel rooms they will see a skyline dominated by cranes. Not the great yellow Samson and Goliath cranes of the shipyard, but the workhorses of the construction industry that is rebuilding Belfast. There is barely a street corner where there is not some concrete evidence of the peace dividend . . .
>
> Belfast, in particular, is a city which has had to redefine itself. Once it was an industrial powerhouse with a huge shipbuilding industry, the largest ropeworks in the world, a world famed textile industry and a glut of heavy engineering plants. All those are virtually extinct. But a new Belfast is arising from the sites of those former industries.
>
> (White 2008; see Plate 17.4)

Plate 17.4 Belfast: The Rotterdam Bar, whose restoration was an early sign of renaissance, is temporarily saved from demolition for an apartment complex by the 'credit crunch'. 'The renaissance devours its children...the future looks bleak'.

Even if this new Belfast survives the punctured speculative bubble of the peace dividend and credit crunch, one cannot help but feel that underneath the hype is a buried lament for the passing of the old manufacturing city from which 'the Troubles' were an unwelcome diversion, a passing experienced earlier in other 'British' cities. Design, rebranding and renaming are for many of a certain generation but a thin disguise. The Belfast Sirocco Works once produced three-quarters of the world's tea processing machinery and was the world leader in ventilation equipment. Today, recast as Sirocco Quays, it is marketed as a 'unique riverside community', the location of 2,000 apartments and a niche shopping and leisure venue that is planned for construction over the next ten years (Carson 2007). In proximity to the gas works site, the first industrial clearance to set the renaissance rolling, now with its 'off the rack' office buildings, call centres and service jobs, the Sirocco development gives rise to the thought of how names that represented world-class achievement become reduced to image traces in a developer's brochure. Nowhere, however, has a developer's usurpation of industrial heritage been taken so far as in the development of Belfast's 'Titanic Quarter'®.

The Titanic Quarter®: A brand to remember

The centre of attention here is a 185-acre site, formerly part of the Harland and Wolff shipyard, now a pale shadow of its former self (Figure 17.2). Here, in the biggest property development scheme ever undertaken in Northern Ireland, the developer on the official website entices entry with the words: 'Welcome to Titanic Quarter . . . a new brand emerging on the horizon' (see www. titanic-quarter.com). The idea to create a new precinct for Belfast, described as a 'city within a city', dates from the aftermath of the Belfast Agreement and originated with the privately owned shipyard, itself faced with rapidly disappearing orders for ships, but with the prospect of large profits from land development. The project concept and brand launched in 1999 and based on the salvage of *Titanic* heritage has been embraced with gusto by all official place promotion agencies in Belfast, including the Northern Ireland Tourist Board and Belfast City Council. That a city should promote its heritage for profit is, of course, unremarkable given present place promotion imperatives. What is remarkable in 'post-conflict Belfast' is that the city, in less than

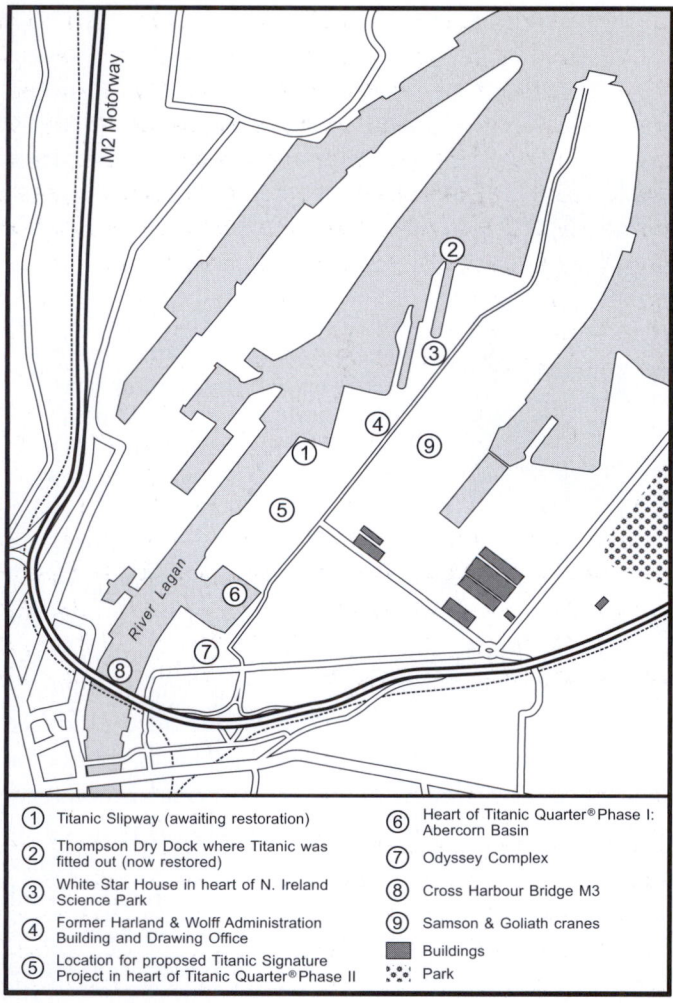

(1) Titanic Slipway (awaiting restoration)

(2) Thompson Dry Dock where Titanic was fitted out (now restored)

(3) White Star House in heart of N. Ireland Science Park

(4) Former Harland & Wolff Administration Building and Drawing Office

(5) Location for proposed Titanic Signature Project in heart of Titanic Quarter® Phase II

(6) Heart of Titanic Quarter® Phase I: Abercorn Basin

(7) Odyssey Complex

(8) Cross Harbour Bridge M3

(9) Samson & Goliath cranes

■ Buildings

⋰ Park

Figure 17.2 Belfast: Renaissance projects in the Titanic® Quarter (redrawn by Jan Edwards). © Crown Copyright. All rights reserved. Licence number 100049043.

a decade, has gone from leaving the memory of *Titanic* 'on a sunken plain of the psyche', not wishing to draw much attention to its 'ambiguous pride and embarrassment' (Foster 1997: 15, 70), to active celebration in representing the post-conflict city through association with the greatest of all twentieth-century symbols of human hubris, the lost confidence of modernity and the existential self-comprehension, to use Heidegger's phrase, of the self as a 'being-towards-the-end' (Middleton and Woods 2004: 69). The Oscar-winning 1997 film starring Leonardo Di Caprio and Kate Winslett, popularising 'the brand', is part of the explanation. Hill makes an important point:

> What evidence there is suggests that the appeal of the film extended across the sectarian divide in Northern Ireland. In this respect, the film's postmodern depthlessness helped to depoliticize the ship's legacy and facilitate its exploitation within local heritage and tourist culture.

(Hill 2004: 21)

The massive east Belfast landmark shipyard cranes of Samson and Goliath, now in their relative impotency symbolising the decommissioning of the yard as Protestant space, leave the way open for a joint appropriation of the project of bringing the legacy of the *Titanic* home.

This project picked up momentum in 2004 when the leasehold of the Harland and Wolff land was sold for a reported price of £48 million by its Norwegian owner Fred Olsen, with Belfast Harbour Commissioners, which administers the Port of Belfast, holding the freehold and the right to a share of future increases in development value. Nevertheless, the purchaser, with lead responsibility for the *Titanic* 'brand', is the Dublin-based development company, Harcourt Developments. The latter, through a wholly owned subsidiary, Ivy Wood Properties, now has the development rights to the Titanic Quarter®. In March 2005, Harcourt Developments launched its plans for the new city of Belfast, which will arise over the next fifteen to twenty years, not in Belfast itself, but at an international property exhibition in Cannes. The plans, which amount to a vast extension of Belfast city centre eastwards, involve mixed use of 3,300 new homes and waterfront apartments (which from artist drawings incorporating balconies and sun umbrellas look as if they belong in Cannes itself), around 3.3 million square feet of new business/office/research and development and other commercial space, a cruise liner berth and a large-scale leisure development featuring restaurants and hotels. The concept architect for Titanic Quarter, appointed by Belfast's self proclaimed new city builders, is Eric Kuhne from Texas, credited with the futuristic Bluewater shopping centre in Kent. A promotional video for the Titanic site invokes ample references to nature and the village idyll of community. Harbour villages, with maritime design motifs, echoing the craftsmanship of naval artisans, are to be connected by an 'emerald necklace' of parks, gardens and orchards. Belfast sees an appropriation of its ship-building heritage appropriately scrubbed and sanitised in the discourse clothes of the urban renaissance. That Belfast was in the ocean liner business of 'democratising luxury for a new century' would have come as some surprise to the poor souls in steerage class on the *Titanic*. In a condescending fashion, a counterfeit representation of Belfast, portraying a shipyard with a united workforce led by visionary captains of industry, both with an accepting 'tolerance for mixed values', is sold back to its inhabitants in the interest of profit via the dulcet tones of a mid-American accent (see www.ivicarts.com).

Phase 1 of Titanic Quarter, 'The Arc', now on release, is situated around the Abercorn Basin, which also provides the setting to the existing Odyssey complex. It involves 475 apartments, a hotel and office buildings, with the financial services company, Citi, recently agreeing to occupy with the allure of £2 million provided by government through Invest NI (Morton 2008). Overspill jobs from the successful Dublin financial services sector were seen as a possibility. The promotional material for the apartments reaches new heights of cultural cringe, at least for Belfast, wrapped around the language of urban renaissance. The appeal is to young professional colonisers to embrace 'European-style urban living' and the 'cosmopolitan atmosphere' on offer. A 'new way to live' is promised, with 'couples lingering over al fresco meals at superb restaurants, friends catching up over cappuccinos at chic cafés or fine wines at stylish bars' (Titanic Quarter® 2007). The references to collective but private (gated) gardens, and the paraphernalia of security are firmly if subtly implied. The financial backer for 'The Arc' is Ulster Bank, a subsidiary of Royal Bank of Scotland, which in 2008 announced record financial losses. Much hangs on the confidence needed to keep The Arc afloat in a deteriorating economic climate.

Phase 2 of Titanic Quarter, which received outline planning permission in late 2007, will be a harder sell, located as it is closer to the sounds of George Best Belfast City Airport, and a diminutive but still functioning shipyard involved with ship repair and salvage and the manufacture of wind farm units. In October 2007 the Titanic Quarter® developer was forced into an embarrassing public apology to Harland and Wolff after a model, perhaps wistfully, showed the area occupied by the shipyard as apartments. It also depicted the shipyard's cranes straddling a marina (Cassidy 2007). Phase 2, facilitated by a streamlined planning process for major projects, will again involve mixed uses, but with the emphasis on 2,000 residential units on a 16.5-hectare site. Admirably, the scheme will involve restoration of the old *Titanic* slipway to complement the completed restoration of the dry dock where *Titanic* was fitted out, but more controversial is the developer's design proposal for a Titanic Signature Project (TSP) to mark, in particular, the looming anniversary in April 2012 of the sinking of the ship. In a city which has one last chance to get an iconic design project right, the omens do not look good (see Plate 17.5).

Eschewing an international design competition for such a large-scale project and an important aspect of western memory and psyche, the developer, in 2007, brought forward a proposed building twice the size of Belfast City Hall, to sit at the head of the restored slipway. The seemingly 'take it or leave it' angular shimmering glass and metallic structure, deemed unilaterally to be Belfast's future 'Bilbao effect', invokes in its façades the bow of a ship, at least as far as can be discerned from published representations.

Amidst a maritime museum, the TSP would give visitors the vicarious thrill through a 'flying theatre' of recreating a dive to the *Titanic* wreck. While the Belfast public is awash with design indifference, the Big Lottery Fund's Living Landmarks Programme was not convinced. In late 2007 it turned down a £25 million application for funding. A former director of the Northern Ireland Housing Association, reflecting on the low commitment of the Titanic Quarter® to social housing and mindful of the development gain involved in the TSP, simply commented: 'Let the big property developers fund their own signature project' (Holmes 2007).

In late 2008, approaches from Titanic Quarter® to Belfast City Council and the Northern Ireland Executive to make up the shortfall eventually bore fruit with a combined contribution of £53 million dressed in the guise of a counter-recessionary stimulus, rather than a developer lifeboat for apartments that are not selling as planned. For a time in mid-2008, events were complicated by an imposter Titanic Signature Project sailing into the frame and also requesting

Plate 17.5 Belfast: Titanic Signature Project, as proposed by Harcourt Developments.

major public funds. Owners of the Odyssey complex, in partnership with Florida-based exhibition specialists WLM Inc, proposed to build a life-size replica of part of the *Titanic* complete with four funnels, as an extension to the Odyssey itself. A room with a view, promised in the Titanic Quarter® Arc development, would thus have taken on a different hue. Belfast seems destined, one way or another, to sell its *Titanic* birthright for a mess of potage in a design scenario which has descended into the farce of who can build the best theme park.

Meanwhile, the former administration and office block of Harland and Wolff, the truly historic iconic building in Titanic Quarter® within whose presently crumbling but magnificent interior the *Titanic* was designed, like a Cinderella uninvited to the TSP ball, contemplates a fate earning its keep as yet another Belfast hotel.

Urban renaissance: cultural shift?

While the promotional rhetoric of Titanic Quarter® carries the usual developer hyperbole, it can, nevertheless, be located as a part of a broader discursive strategy that attempts to soften the language of conflict. This has been integral to the peace process itself, where spatial planning has had its own role to play with visions of a shared and prosperous future. Some academics have applauded this communicative strategy interpreting it as open and discursive in facilitating agreement (Healey 2004), while others have emphasised its manipulative qualities and the papering over of the fissures of difference (Neill and Gordon 2001). The danger is that, with the vagueness of rainbow visions, more critical faculties can be set aside. In relation to the obfuscation of class issues and the displacement aspects of gentrification in particular, the cultural geographer Neil Smith comments that: 'European 'regeneration' policy optimistically imbibes the post-structuralist phlogiston of the age, namely that if one changes the discourse the world will follow' (Smith 2008: 196). Whether the cultural outlook in Belfast will follow the discourse of renaissance remains to be seen. Academic opinion is divided on the possibilities residing in the fluidity of identities between those taking an optimistic slant, emphasising, for example, the greater safety felt by people in moving around Belfast these days (Anderson and Shuttleworth 2007), and those pointing, pessimistically, to 'a decline in a middle ground within Northern Irish society' and the false presentation of Belfast as a 'normalising place' (Shirlow and Murtagh 2006: 1–2). Indeed, the view has credence that Belfast now remains located within a cultural war of attrition where spatial mixing is not the same as social mixing. It is a city far removed from any renaissance idyll, existing in a tension that is kept in check by the formal institutionalisation of agonism (to use the term currently in planning fashion) through the necessary padded cage of the Belfast Agreement (Neill 2006b). Belfast is not London or Berlin, being essentially a large town where incubation of more hybrid cosmopolitan identities will always be constrained and strangled by links to wider society. It is not just the architectural legacy which, to use the words of Brett, is a 'bit of a plum pudding', but the intractable cultural legacy as well. As expressed by the director of the Northern Ireland Community Relations Council 'both sides are still not ready to lose to each other' (Morrow 2008). In this context, as the artist David Evans has alluded, Northern Ireland has produced an architectural culture that 'tends towards introversion' (Evans 2006: 22). The city needs more 'itinerant or migrant architects' (Larmour 2006: xv) as a matter of urgency.

References

Allen, N. and Kelly, A. (2003) Introduction. In N. Allen and A. Kelly (eds) *The Cities of Belfast* (Dublin: Four Courts Press) pp. 7–18.

Anderson, J. and Shuttleworth, I. (2007) Spaces of Fear and Hope in Belfast. In *Belfast Ordinary* (Belfast: Factotum) pp. 14–15.

Appleton, R. (2004) Sculpture Will Be Stunning Addition To Belfast Skyline. *Belfast Telegraph*, 27 December.

Atkinson, R. (2003) Misunderstood Saviour or Vengeful Wrecker? The Many Meanings and Problems of Gentrification. *Urban Studies*, 40 (12): 2343–2350.

BCC (Belfast City Council) (2002) Development Committee Minutes, 18 November.

BCC (Belfast City Council) (2007) *Development Committee Response to Consultation Exercise on Inquiry by N. Ireland Assembly Committee for Social Development Regarding Town Centre Regeneration.* Adopted at Development Committee meeting, 12 December.

Boal, F. (2006) Big Processes and Little People: The Population of Metropolitan Belfast 1901–2001. In F. Boal and S. Royle (eds) *Enduring City: Belfast in the Twentieth Century* (Belfast: Blackstaff Press) pp. 56–83.

Brett, C. (2001) Victorian and Edwardian Belfast: Preserving the Architectural Legacy of the Inner City. In W. J. V. Neill and H. -U. Schwedler (eds) *Urban Planning and Cultural Inclusion: Lessons from Belfast and Berlin* (Palgrave: Basingstoke) pp. 85–99.

Brett, D. (undated) What Did They Build That For? – The Hilton Hotel. *The Vacuum,* Issue 4 (Belfast: Factotum).

Brown, J. M. (2008) Lucre of the Irish. *Prospect*, January, pp. 32–36.

Carson, H. (2007) Making Waves . . . City's New River Quarter. *Belfast Telegraph*, 28 September.

Cassidy, M. (2007) Titanic Apology to City Shipyard. *N.Ireland BBC News website*, http://news.bbc.co.uk/1hi/northernireland/default.stm, 5 October.

Evans, D. (2006) Modern Movement Architecture in Ulster 1950 to 2005. In L. Latimer (ed.) *Modern Ulster Architecture* (Belfast: Ulster Architectural Heritage Society) pp. 22–35.

Foster, J. W. (1997) *'The Titanic Complex': A Cultural Manifest* (Vancouver: Belcouver Press).

Healey, P. (2004) The Treatment of Space and Place in New Strategic Spatial Planning in Europe. *International Journal of Urban and Regional Research,* 28 (1): 45–67.

Hill, J. (2004) The Relaunching of Ulster Pride: The Titanic, Belfast and Film. In T. Bergfelder and S. Street (eds) *The Titanic in Myth and Memory: Representation in Visual and Literary Culture* (London: I. B. Tauris Press) pp. 15–24.

Holmes, E. (2007) Lottery Right to Sign Off Titanic. *Belfast Telegraph*, 24 October.

Jewesbury, D. (2007) Public Art, Architecture and the Overproduction of Spectacularised Happiness. In *Belfast Ordinary,* (Belfast: Factotum) pp. 2–3.

Larmour, P. (2006) Introduction. In L. Latimer (ed.) *Modern Ulster Architecture* (Belfast: Ulster Architectural Heritage Society) pp. xii–xv.

Larmour, P. (2008) A Venue to Remember. In *Royal Society of Ulster Arts Catalogue for 127th Annual Exhibition* (Belfast: RSUA).

McGivern, M. (2006) Belfast: The Way Ahead. In F. Boal and S. Royle (eds) *Enduring City: Belfast in the Twentieth Century* (Belfast: Blackstaff Press) pp. 328–341.

Middleton, P. and Woods, T. (2004) Textual Memory: The Making of the Titanic's Archive. In T. Bergfelder and S. Street (eds) *The Titanic in Myth and Memory: Representation in Visual and Literary Culture* (London: I. B. Tauris Press) pp. 63–72.

Morton, R. (2008) Citi Jobs a Vote of Confidence for Titanic. *Belfast Telegraph*, 8 July.

Morrison, B. (2006) Planning the City; Planning the Region. In F. Boal and S. Royle (eds) *Enduring City: Belfast in the Twentieth Century* (Belfast: Blackstaff Press) pp. 141–154.

Morrow, D (2008) Remark expressed at conference entitled *Conflict in Cities and the Contested State*, School of Sociology, Queen's University Belfast, 26 September.

Needham, R. (1998) *Battling for Peace* (Belfast: Blackstaff Press).

Neill, W. J. V. (1993) Physical Planning and Image-Enhancement: Recent Developments in Belfast. *International Journal of Urban and Regional Research,* 17 (4): 595–609.

Neill, W. J. V. and Gordon, M. (2001) Shaping our Future? The Regional Strategic Framework for Northern Ireland. *Planning Theory and Practice,* 2 (1): 31–52.

Neill, W. J. V. (2004) *Urban Planning and Cultural Identity* (London: Routledge).

Neill, W. J. V. (2006a) Selling Detroit. In P. Oswalt (ed.) *Shrinking Cities: Volume 2: Interventions* (Ostfildern: Hatje Cantz Publishers) pp. 730–736.

Neill, W. J. V. (2006b) Identity and Difference: Does Canadian Multiculturalism have lessons for Northern Ireland? *British Journal of Canadian Studies*, 19 (2): 191–200.

NIIS (Northern Ireland Information Service) (1978) *9 Point Package to Spell the Rebirth of Belfast* (Belfast: NIIS).

O'Doherty, M. (2004) 'Symbol of Hope' a Pathetic Icon of the Spirit of Belfast. *Belfast Telegraph*, 20 December.

O'Hara, V. and Wilkie, K. (2008) Feelings are Mixed over a New Heart Symbol for the City. *Belfast Telegraph*, 1 July.

Patterson, G. (1992) *Fat Lad* (London: Chatto & Windus).

Pauli, A. (2008) Our Best Buildings – as Voted by Architects. *Belfast Telegraph*, 13 June.

Pine, B. and Gilmore, J. (1999) *The Experience Economy: Work as Theater and Every Business a Stage* (Cambridge MS: Harvard Business Press).

Singleton, D. (1987) Belfast: Housing Policy and Trends. In R. H. Buchanan and B. M. Walker (eds) *Province, City and People: Belfast and its Region* (Belfast: Greystone Books) pp. 151–168.

Ulster Architect (2005) Obel, New Landmark for Belfast. *Ulster Architect*, 21 (3): 22–25.

Shirlow, S. and Murtagh, B. (2006) *Belfast: Segregation, Violence and the City* (London: Pluto Press).

Smith, N. (2008) On 'The Eviction of Critical Perspectives'. *International Journal of Urban and Regional Research*, 32 (1): 195–197.

Smyth, A. (2006) Belfast: Return from Motown? In F. Boal and S. Royle (eds) *Enduring City: Belfast in the Twentieth Century* (Belfast: Blackstaff Press) pp. 99–121.

Smyth, L. (2007) How Ulster's Tallest Tower will Change our Views. *Belfast Telegraph*, 25 September.

Swystun, J. (2007) Going Global. Global Branding Risks and Rewards. In H. Minamiyama and the World Branding Committee (eds) *World Branding: Concept, Strategy and Design* (Corte Madera: Gingko Press) pp. 34–37.

Titanic Quarter® (2007) *The ARC: Abercorn Basin*, Sales Pamphlet, Belfast.

White, L. (2008) It's Boomtime in Belfast. *Special Supplement for US/Northern Ireland Investment Conference, Belfast Telegraph*, 5 May.

Wulf-Mathies, M. (1997) Shaping our Future: the European Perspective. Paper at *Shaping our Future Conference*, 27 November, Belfast.

Conclusions

18 Reflecting on urban design achievements in a decade of urban renaissance

John Punter

Introduction

Urban renaissance has been a 'defining feature of contemporary urban policy' (Porter and Shaw 2009: 1) globally for perhaps two decades, but the explicit development of the English variant of this policy was not formulated until 1999 in the Urban Task Force's (UTF) report to the UK deputy prime minister. As Chapter 1 explained, the report drew its design inspiration from renaissance exemplars in Europe, particularly Barcelona and various Dutch cities but also, as other chapters in this volume have argued, from 1990s regeneration efforts in London, Birmingham, Manchester and Glasgow. While most of the report's recommendations were rapidly implemented, some took several years to be legislated (e.g. new-style development plans (LDFs) introduced in 2004) and others have still not been enacted (particularly reforms to local government finances and VAT reforms). So in many respects the full panoply of UTF renaissance frameworks and policies have yet to be put into place, and individual cities have been selective in what policies and processes they have chosen to adopt.

Arguably, what the case studies in this book have evaluated is perhaps less the outcomes of urban renaissance policy and more the impacts of the 1993–2007 property boom on British cities. Michael Edwards (Chapter 11) describes the 'rentier economy' that prevailed and operated globally over the period, driven by the pursuit of underpriced assets in land and property, where dramatic differentials in value could be quickly achieved for very little outlay – albeit often with a reckless amount of borrowing. The length of the boom lured almost everyone in Britain, and perhaps especially the current prime minister, to view 'boom and bust' as a thing of the past, and encouraged an unprecedented amount of speculative development activity, particularly in the form of 'buy-to-let', and 'buy-to-leave' practices in the housing market. These activities capitalised on rapid house price inflation, and in the process subverted the benefits of increased supply, eliminating improvements in affordability. Property improvement and speculation became a key component of prime-time TV entertainment, as homeowners became obsessed with the exchange, rather than use, values of homes and with their own (paper) housing wealth. The scale and unsustainability of 'buy to let' accounted for the collapse of one major British building society. Meanwhile, the speculations of British financial institutions and their profligate lending, along with rampant national consumerism and unsustainably high levels of personal debt, played their full part in precipitating the 'bust' and the deep recession now being experienced, notwithstanding the US subprime and toxic debt precipitation of a global financial crisis.

City governments welcomed the property boom as a long-awaited opportunity to repopulate their central cities; to remove dereliction; to reinforce service employment, particularly in the high gross-value-added financial service sector; to expand their shopping centres and widen their catchments; and to expand their appeal as cultural, party, entertainment or 'city break' destinations. Most city councils had already developed explicit competitiveness agendas and entrepreneurial strategies to attract investment, deliver major regeneration projects and public realm improvements. Maximising the value of council land assets and planning gain receipts were very important means of supplementing meagre capital budgets, and improvements in the property and business tax base were similarly welcome. The hegemony of business and property interests was reflected in the number and scale of public–private partnerships, in the influence of major investor-developers on local strategic (or transport) partnerships and in the ways in which councils managed major development projects.

The planning system was subjected to multiple pressures to facilitate, intensify and increase the scale of redevelopment, to speed up approvals, to ratchet up densities and to extract as much planning gain as possible to meet affordable housing targets and/or to pay for wider environmental improvements and infrastructure. It was also under pressure to deliver as many housing units as possible on brownfield land, to relieve the pressure on the suburban edge where public opposition to house building was increasingly vocal. In the UTF agenda these pressures were to be managed by strong, visionary, strategic planning to shape the direction of development, and by proactive development control helping to deliver design quality, a corporate commitment to place-making and high-quality service delivery. Although it is in times of intense development pressure that the planning system is best able to negotiate design improvements, the weakened position of planning within local government, the preference for entrepreneurialism over statutory development planning and the haemorrhage of planning and design skills from the public to the private sector all contributed to a situation where the influence of planning and urban design was more limited than the UTF intended. Furthermore, while the system was able to deliver a number of very high-quality and very stylish set-piece developments, it was far less successful in developing inclusive places or mixed communities, and without the direct power to build social housing councils were unable to effectively counter the increasingly widespread effects of gentrification. Once again, land use planning failed to act as much of counter-cyclical force in boom conditions, and the huge stock of consents is testimony to a failure to negotiate hard on affordable housing, energy efficiency or design quality while there was the chance.

In 2006 the *State of the Cities Report*, commissioned to assess the progress of the urban renaissance, noted what an 'opportune time' it was for renaissance policies to 'build on the market trend and lead to a virtuous circle of future investment and growth, and how cities were poised to be the 'motors of national advance' (ODPM 2006a: 63; 2006b: 154). As the UK enters what is predicted to be the deepest and longest recession since the early 1930s, these words have a very hollow ring, and the 'extra difference' seems to be merely the scale of redundancies in financial services (the primary 'motor of national advance'), the oversupply of commercial office space in London and the surplus of prime retail and small apartments in many regional cities.

Research focus and questions

The financial services/property boom has reshaped the urban renaissance and its complex, multifaceted policy agenda outlined in Chapter 1, and distorted many of its intentions and preferred development and design outcomes. Their design impacts have been examined through the lenses of more than sixteen different local government contexts, each with their own economic and demographic trajectories and particular responses to both market and policy. Each city has evolved a distinctive renaissance strategy, often predating, but also absorbing many elements of the UTF report. To add to the complexities of interpretation it is important to remember that the 'Celtic Cities' experienced the same property market trends, but were not directly subject to the renaissance policies that were developed in England.

To summarise and evaluate the reshaping of urban design as public policy over the last decade, and the emerging urban forms in the major cities, we return to the research questions that launched this collective enquiry. These were as follows:

- What are the most significant changes in the built form, public realm and urban character of British cities? Is there an appreciable improvement in the quality of the built environment?
- How has the property market responded to the urban renaissance? Are developers recognising 'the value of urban design'?
- Is local government adequately equipped to lead the urban renaissance? Do new city visions and partnerships demonstrate a deeper commitment to public participation and design quality? Is there evidence of a collective corporate commitment to good design?
- What is the effectiveness of the new statutory plans/frameworks alongside design strategies, masterplans, briefs, design policy and design control. Do they have adequate political support, resources and skilled support?
- Have local planning authorities been able to establish quality urban design as a foundation of planning policy, and been thus able to positively shape urban form?
- What are the emerging critiques of the new urban landscape?
- What are the sustainability implications of the emerging urban forms? How might a deeper, more sustainable urban renaissance be created?

A concluding section summarises the positives and negatives of the renaissance experience in the UK from a design perspective, and reflects very briefly on the prospects of addressing these negatives in the near future.

Significant change and improvement in built form, public realm and urban character?

Two headline measures of significant change in the form of development as a result of renaissance policies have been the increased proportion of development on brownfield sites, up from 56 to 77 per cent (1997–2007), and the increase in average residential densities, up from 25 to 44 dwellings per hectare (1997–2007) (DCLG 2009: 28). But in all the case study cities the urban renaissance's most dramatic physical impacts have been concentrated in the *city centres* and their immediate fringes. The typical combination is greatly expanded central retail, hotel, leisure and eating/drinking sectors, a reflection of the growth in consumerism, and dramatic increases in the number of apartments in areas skirting the commercial core. The city centre has clearly been the 'engine of growth' in every city, and the scale of redevelopment has been unprecedented in modern times, with several cities reporting 15–20 per cent of their central area under development in 2006. Meanwhile, sites with permissions or active development interest (in 2006) accounted for nearly twice that proportion.

Most city centres have recaptured their share of retail provision that had been gradually eroded by out-of-town development, a direct result of national planning policy changes made in 1996 (DoE 1996a). Most city centres were projected to have captured almost half of retail floorspace city-wide when the current schemes were completed (BCSC 2005), though oversupply was looming well before the 'credit crunch' (Stewart 2008) and shrinkage in off-peak locations was imminent. The *large-scale shopping centre* has been brought back into the heart of the city centre, and a more urbane approach to retail design has emerged, as shoppers, developers and local authorities eschew malls and seek to create traditional shopping streets with freestanding retail blocks (Coleman 2006). Manchester's Millennium Quarter began the trend in 1997, and Liverpool followed, creating a well-connected, mixed-use quarter, the work of sixteen different architects on twenty-six different sites. Sheffield plans a similar, if more modest, project, whereas Bristol has developed a hybrid and Birmingham, Cardiff and Belfast have completed what might be the last of the in-town malls. This 'return to the street' has reinforced urbanity, enhanced the vitality and quality of the public realm, reconnected the pedestrian movement network and the urban fabric, and spread the pedestrian footfall to revitalise a wider area.

Missing from many provincial city centres over the last decade have been *major office developments*, while unlettable second-hand stock has been selectively converted into apartments and hotels. The City of London and Canary Wharf have increased their near-monopoly of financial services and become the locations for a new generation of office complexes, and now very tall buildings, created by star architects keen to take advantage of invitations to build high with 'world-class architecture'. The first phase of Canary Wharf has been largely built out, while over a quarter of the City has been redeveloped over the last decade (Murray 2004). London's office boom has been driven by levels of take-up seventeen times those of the second city Edinburgh (CBRE 2006), emphasising the 'financification' of the economy and the intensified regional imbalances created by the spectacular growth in high-level financial services. Only four other cities – Manchester, Leeds, Bristol and Glasgow – show consistent, but modest take-up and development rates. Manchester's new Spinningfields Quarter and Sheffield's Heart of the City Project were both successfully masterplanned public–private partnerships, creating new squares and refurbishing key spaces. The best shopping and office projects have recognised the importance of creating a high-quality *public realm* in the city centre to attract office workers, shoppers, revellers and tourists, and have made significant contributions to the stock of city spaces, even if many such places retain a strongly corporate feel (e.g. More London, Canada/Jubilee Squares, all in London).

A key objective in many cities has been a desire to *significantly repopulate and extend the city centre*, increase its critical mass, *diversify its character* and to revitalise the areas immediately beyond the Central Business District (CBD). This has often been spurred by ambitions to expand the city's cultural industries, catering and entertainment offer and support services, to fill the gap left by the contraction of warehousing and industrial uses by reusing the best of the old buildings, and to bring residents back into the very edges of the city centre to foster a twenty-four-hour city culture. '*Quarterisation*' strategies, first developed in Birmingham, have been used to help regenerate fringe areas of the core and expand city centre uses and attractions. They have been criticised as agents of gentrification and for their emphasis on 'theming' as destructive of identity (Jayne and Bell 2006), but in most of the cities studied there was a vacuum in terms of use, occupation and investment, and care has been taken to retain character. Certainly the management of gentrification and residential intensification in such areas has been a major challenge, but exemplars – such as Glasgow's Merchant City, Liverpool's Ropewalks, Nottingham's Lace Market and Birmingham's Jewellery Quarter – have all used conservation designations positively, and maintained historic character and mixed use, though delivering social diversity has been a challenge dependent upon housing association investment. Generally, high-rise/high-density apartment investment has been concentrated in declining commercial areas (the zone of discard) on the edges of the city centre or in previously industrial/warehouse areas (the zone of discontinuity), along waterfronts and other areas of higher amenity. Between 1998 and 2006, some 5,000–9,000 apartments were built in the fringes of the city centres of Manchester, Leeds, Birmingham, Liverpool, Cardiff and Bristol (Unsworth and Nathan 2006; Barber 2007; Lambert and Boddy 2008). Now accounting for more than half of all local housing production, these apartments have become the focus of extensive design criticism, but the repopuation of the city centres has brought major benefits in terms of increased urban vitality, and met the housing demands of many small households.

The other major change in housing form has taken place on inner area *council estates* – a product of New Labour's programme to improve the quality of council housing and to provide more 'mixed' estates. The Decent Homes Programme has delivered extensive renovation programmes upgrading the existing stock and the estate at large, but more radical transformations have resulted from housing stock transfer and the injection of private capital into new house building on these estates, the transformation of Lee Bank into Park Central in central Birmingham being particularly dramatic. Further changes in some of the most monolithic 1960s council estates will ensue through demolition (Aylesbury Estate, Southwark), privatisation (Park Hill, Sheffield) or regeneration (Ocean Estate, Tower Hamlets), but in the last of these cases the tenants have not voted for stock transfer so improvements have ceased (Watt 2009), threatening the significant gains in health, education, crime, worklessness and community cohesion achieved under these New Deal for Communities projects (see Toynbee 2008; but also Manzi and Jacobs 2009). In both Edinburgh (e.g. Craigmillar) and Glasgow (e.g. Easterhouse) peripheral estate renewal and diversification continues.

More widespread residential renewal is being progressed in the northern English cities through the twelve *Housing Market Renewal programmes* set up in 2002 in areas of 'market failure', aiming to renew half of the low-demand properties. By 2006 more than 10,000 homes had been demolished but four times that number had been refurbished, with over a thousand new homes added (NAO 2007b). Small-scale design successes have been celebrated in Salford, Nelson and Oldham, but there are concerns about the general quality of outcomes and the durability of improvements. Liverpool's experience has been instructive, with major concerns being expressed about design quality and the Commission for Architecture and the Built Environment (CABE) sending in 'enablers' to work with the community and developers to raise standards. They continue to press for stronger place-making with design, heritage and sustainability commitments within each of these programmes (CABE 2006e). The case studies reveal few large-scale, comprehensive inner-city regeneration projects, but the New East Manchester experience has positive design elements. It has markedly improved resident satisfaction, but not the main deprivation measures, demonstrating the limitations of physical renewal (Parkinson *et al.* 2006).

Turning to the *public realm*, local authorities have invested very selectively relying on limited highway and Section 106 funding. Again city centres have been the main beneficiaries, leading some authors in this volume to comment on the stark differences in the quality, management and policing of space in the city centre as opposed to the immediate suburbs. Extensive efforts have been made to calm traffic, to share space, to extend pedestrianisation and to improve public spaces, all with better signage, lighting, furniture and public art – though often using advertising companies to fund furnishings and maintenance with a consequent proliferation of illuminated adverts. A major thrust of public realm investment has been to remove or reduce the severance of inner ring roads to reconnect city centres and inner neighbourhoods, and to spread footfall and investment potential. Where Birmingham led in the 1990s, Nottingham and Sheffield have successfully followed, each with tram projects – the former completing nine new spaces with twelve more projected, the latter focused on creating three high-quality pedestrian routes traversing the city centre. New pedestrian bridges have been among the most successful pedestrian amenities and generators of new footfall, as evidenced in Newcastle–Gateshead, Manchester and Central London/South Bank.

Nonetheless, even in London it has proved difficult to fund large-scale, high-quality investments in public space – as the abandonment of the mayor's 100 World Squares project illustrates. Central London shows the benefits of small-scale partnerships and private initiative projects some funded by Business Improvement Districts (BIDs), others by a combination of planning gain and Single Regeneration Budget (SRB) funds, e.g. Bankside): 'streetscene' policies and programmes have also significantly decluttered and improved public realm quality, though as previously noted cloned corporate spaces also proliferate.

Debates continue about the increased private control of public space in city centres throughout the case studies, whether it be evidence of stronger security cordons and the 'fortification' of space (City/Canary Wharf; see Coaffee 2003), the omnipresence of CCTV camera surveillance (Newcastle), the level and visibility of private policing (Liverpool/Sheffield; see Minton 2006), the commercialising of public space through café culture (Atkinson 2004), the 'corporatisation' of space by business (Central London) or the increasingly permanent cluttering of space with digital screens, fairground equipment and markets/promotions (Birmingham/Manchester). Despite the evidence that its impact is limited (Briggs 2006) and its disproportionate share of the crime prevention budget (78 per cent; House of Lords 2009), it has to be acknowledged that the majority of city centre users are reassured by widespread CCTV coverage, especially in the wake of the London bombings of 2005, while the private management of public space is to a much higher standard than the public sector can deliver. There are concerns that pedestrianised city centres are becoming increasingly exclusive, catering primarily for the more affluent consumer, and carefully managed to this end (Jayne 2006; Carmona *et al.* 2008). Fortunately, teenagers continue to appropriate their own socialisation spaces in the less commercialised spaces of the city centre at the weekends, creating real poles of sociability (e.g. Urbis, Manchester).

Particular problems have arisen with managing the 'evening economy' to prevent a clash of 'binge' and café cultures, and to allow city centre residents tolerable living conditions (Roberts and Turner 2005). Westminster has led the way with its definition of 'stress areas' and the establishment of far more sophisticated licensing and entertainment policies to manage the concentrations of drinkers that are now widespread in London and other major cities. Active management and high-level maintenance of the public realm are critical to maintaining high-quality space, but apparently affordable only where the private sector is prepared to contribute significantly, thus largely in city centres. Nonetheless, there is some general evidence of improvement in the condition and maintenance of the public realm with the proportion of 'unsatisfactory' neighbourhoods falling from 68 to 53 per cent (2001–2008: DCLG 2009: 28).

Overall it is possible to conclude that there has been an appreciable improvement in the quality of the built environment and the public realm in the centres of the major British cities. These centres have been significantly expanded and diversified over the last decade, with new 'quarters' added that provide more choice for businesses, residents, consumers and citizens. Beyond these enlarged city centres, however, evidence of renaissance and of improved environmental quality is sporadic. In many cities, the precise point at which high-level refurbishment and maintenance for well-heeled consumers and the tourists ends and the minimal expenditure for the residents begins is all too evident. Chapter 1 noted that the *State of the English Cities* report (ODPM 2006a,b) gave 'a cautious yes' to the question as to whether the urban renaissance has enhanced city-wide improvement in liveability (see Table 1.4). But it also acknowledged the failure as yet to extend the improvements across wider urban areas, and this will be the real challenge to urban renaissance policies over the next decade. It is already recognised as such in Nottingham and Leeds, where the issue is how to tackle the 'rim of discontinuity' beyond the city centres, and extend regeneration and enhancement into the inner cities working alongside both the National Strategy for Neighbourhood Review (NSNR) and Housing Market Renewal (HMR) programmes respectively.

The property market response to the value of urban design

The property market response to 'urban renaissance' development opportunities has been dramatic, but the response to its urban design agenda has been uneven. Huge development interest was expressed in all manner of sites during the 1993–2007 property cycle, particularly from the late 1990s onwards, with the number, size and nature of planning consents testifying to a decade of intense speculative development activity, easy profit and often permissive development control. Densities were ratcheted up as each project sought to outdo the last and councils sought to maximise numbers of housing units, affordable components and land receipts, despite the original UTF advocacy of medium-rise, ground-oriented schemes (UTF 1999a: 62–63). Proposals for thirty tower blocks around Liverpool's Central Docks, or thirty-four- to forty-one-storey double towers on Cardiff Bay, provide the ultimate examples of this driving up of development expectations and their complete departure from economic and demographic realities.

The best commercial developers have absorbed the messages of the 'value of urban design' strongly propagated by CABE (2001, 2003a, 2006a), particularly those investor-developers who take the long-term view (e.g. Argent, Canary Wharf Group, Grosvenor, etc.), and some of these have ventured into the provincial cities to undertake major schemes (e.g. Allied London in Spinningfields, Manchester). But the stagnation of office markets in regional cities points to London-centric views of the property market on the part of *institutional investors* in commercial property (Guy and Henneberry 2004: 227), and a view that most of the regional cities are too small and insufficiently profitable for institutional investors to bother with. This helps to explain the dramatic mismatches between supply and demand, the significant overpricing of assets and performance in London and the South-East, and underpricing elsewhere. However, this myopia has delivered a design bonus in that independent, often local, investors/developers have been able to exploit opportunities 'where institutions fear to tread' on the margins of the regional city centres.

Many of these *independents* are local developers delivering much cheaper space in off-centre locations with little commitment to good design. But others have views that are the polar opposite to those of institutional investors, preferring mixed to fixed use and vernacular to universal image, recognising socio-economic and environmental rather than purely economic value and being risk positive rather than risk averse and design sensitive rather than design blind (Guyand Henneberry 2004: 232–233). As a consequence, they produce better-designed development showing more sensitivity to the locale, more design innovation and more synergy, with local entrepreneurs who constitute the lifeblood of local regeneration. This recognition of design as a positive component of business strategies is essential to the generation of good places and diverse urban quarters. It also provides the 'gradual', rather than the 'cataclysmic' money (Jacobs 1961), essential to sustainable regeneration and to creating urban diversity.

The rise of design-led *niche developers* committed to quality design, conservation and imaginative reuse, and their shift to the national scene, has been one of the most positive elements of the urban renaissance in the regions. Examples include Urban Splash (Manchester/Liverpool and now national) as well as more local architect-developers such as George Ferguson (Bristol) and Pollard Thomas & Edwards (PTE 2005) (London) and entrepreneurs such as Carol Ainscow (Manchester) and Bennie Gray (Birmingham). If the inner cities are to be regenerated in more straitened times there will need to be many more small investors and socially committed architectural practices to take on small-scale projects in marginal locations (see Bauman Lyons Architects 2008: 98–108) that can meet community needs and act as catalysts to wider reinvestment. Bristol revealed a number of such initiatives linked to artists' communities and fledgling creative industries that needed to be nurtured to ensure room for diversity and to incubate new enterprises.

To these pioneers should be added a new breed of design- and sustainability-conscious companies and partnerships that adhere to a longer-term view of regeneration and financial returns. Mention should also be made of the Prince's Foundation, which has helped to deliver high-quality design in projects across the UK, and developed more inclusive development practices (e.g. enquiry by design) in the process.

Before it went into free-fall the *housebuilding industry* was becoming increasingly divided between those bespoke housing companies for whom good design is an essential part of their business strategy, those middle-of-the-road volume builders who vary design quality according to location and local market and those who deliver standard products on standard layouts for the lower- and middle-income markets. Studies of housing design awards (Biddulph *et al.* 2004) have revealed how few go to volume house builders (one-sixth). Many more (one-third) go to niche house builders (Urban Splash, Crosby, Countryside), and a similar proportion to social housing providers, notably Guinness, Ujima, but particularly The Peabody Trust, which has distinguished itself with experiments in sustainable housing. But the overall standard of housing design remains mediocre as CABE audits reveal (see Table 1.3), while over a fifth of all new homes in 2006 had construction defects (*Guardian* 2007a). CABE's more recent survey of social housing has shown only very slightly better performance levels for affordable housing over market housing (CABE 2009 forthcoming). The Building for Life (BfL) ratings underpinning these evaluations (CABE 2005f) are now recommended by government as monitoring tools to be applied to all but the smallest housing schemes in planning authorities' annual monitoring reports. The government has recently set housebuilders (private and public), and local planning authorities the task of halving the proportion of 'poor' schemes ad doubling the proportion of good/very good schemes, very ambitious targets.

The UTF also set out to raise standards of public buildings by requiring design competitions for all significant developments, but these have remained relatively rare events despite a major health care and schools building programme. Positive initiatives include the prime minister's annual Better Public Building Award (CABE/HMG 2006) and the Treasury's requirement for all public buildings to be assessed on whole-life rather than capital costs. CABE has taken responsibility for providing a flow of advice on clienting (CABE 2003c) and the special needs of educational, health and now school buildings (CABE 2008a), but the general experience with the quality of health buildings has not been positive in England or Wales. Reliance on *Private Finance Initiatives* (PFI) for the delivery of public buildings and infrastructure has been part of the problem (CABE 2005c), and there are real fears that the longevity of buildings (which revert back to the public sector after thirty or more years) is being compromised.

In conclusion, despite a substantial increase in the number of schemes with exemplar design, the overall performance of the development industry – especially the volume house build-ers – on design remains very disappointing. Remarkably quick to exploit the city centre/fringe development opportunities presented by the urban renaissance, few have displayed consistent commitment to raising design standards. This has been left to the long-term investor-developers, niche developers, architect-developers and select housing associations who have exploited the 'design dividend' and delivered improved products for clients and communities. The message of the 'value of urban design' (CABE 2001) has clearly had a positive effect but, even in property boom conditions, has been far from universally accepted by trader-developers and large-volume house builders. Meanwhile, the extent to which development control has been able to 'add value' in design terms has frequently been limited by local development imperatives.

Local government: 'collective corporate commitment to good design?'

A research question explored whether local government has been adequately equipped to lead the urban renaissance, and the extent to which it has been willing or able to pursue design quality as a corporate objective. New Labour's local government reforms emphasised micro-management of local service delivery, strong central fiscal control, (especially of increases in Council Tax), joined-up government programmes, and a multiplicity of partnerships with the private and voluntary sectors (Wilson and Game 2006: 361–388). For its part, the UTF focused on leadership, regeneration partnerships and improved funding, not only for regeneration but, more generally, for local authorities to allow them to drive the urban renaissance.

The UTF recognised the need for major improvements in the *political and professional leader-ship* of local authorities. Like the government, it strongly supported the appointment of city mayors and strong executives able to develop coordinated planning and regeneration strategies. There have been few strong mayors apart from Ken Livingstone in London, who was strongly committed to design quality, public space, affordable housing and the environment, and Rus-sell Goodway in Cardiff, who was not. Livingstone's delivery of congestion charging is arguably the single biggest renaissance achievement in a UK city over the last decade. Elsewhere, such design leadership has been noticeable by its absence or loss: council leader Jon Trickett is much missed in Leeds, as is an environment minister (Richard Needham) prepared to act as a design champion in Belfast.

The design sensitivities of the broader corporate leadership are critical to successful urban design. The 'Manchester model' is instructive: here a powerful central executive, led by a long-serving chief executive and council leader, has appointed from within to build a capable team of senior officers and have used development partnerships with private enterprise very successfully. 'Famously entrepreneurial, opportunistic and market oriented' (Chapter 3), Manchester's is not a leadership constrained by strong plans or design policies, though it has adhered to the broad design principles of its development code to good effect. Much of its design advice is received away from the public eye. Although project-by-project deal-making has set some unfortunate design precedents, and ratcheted up land values, it has also created a dynamic urbanism that is widely envied. Sheffield too has enjoyed the strong leadership of an able chief executive for the past decade (now chief executive of the Homes and Communities Agency), but its decisive (pre)'renaissance' moment – the initiation of the Heart of the City project – was engineered by senior officers in conjunction with the council leader. Liverpool has had similar positive experiences with a new council leader and chief executive and the establishment of an Urban Regeneration Company – 'market facing, business friendly and private sector oriented' – but also committed to design thinking. These examples of strong leadership backed by high-quality design advice at a high level are encouraging, but this is exactly what is missing in so many local authorities.

Vision is considered a necessity for both successful leadership and strategy development. Visioning has become an integral part of corporate governance in the UK, and a key feature of civic entrepreneurialism, supporting business development and aimed at increasing the effectiveness of place-marketing. But, arguably, its more important role is to build public consensus on desirable urban futures, and to ensure that this is embedded in statutory plans and design strategies. Good examples are hard to find, and the inclusiveness of such visions, and the extent to which they have sought and received the inputs of the citizenry, has long been a moot point. Birmingham's 1988 Highbury Initiative, which kick-started its urban renaissance, was a rather exclusive affair but its outputs were exemplary and have stood the test of time (Wright 1999). It is to be hoped that the 100 key stakeholders visioning the new Birmingham City Centre Masterplan (prepared by consultants) are equally far-sighted. Leeds is belatedly attempting something similar in the wake of tensions between the development strategies of the Urban Regeneration Company (Yorkshire Forward) and those of the council.

In England and Wales visioning is now a requirement for the development of (Sustainable) Community Strategies (SCS), providing an opportunity for the wider public to articulate their aspirations for the future. In addition, in England each LDF requires a vision and a core strategy informed by the SCS, but the reality of this connection needs much more scrutiny. EDAW (2008) argued for integrating the SCS and the LDF processes so that the former can be 'honed by the necessity of deliverability into meaningful and robust and unique visions' (Cheesbrough and Ledward 2008: 16–17). The city case studies provide few examples of this new approach, perhaps because limited progress has been made on many of their LDFs. The fate of Newcastle's Going for Growth Strategy (2000) is instructive. Its demise demonstrated not only failures of consultation and of mechanisms for local control, but also the difficulties of balancing top-down and bottom-up perspectives, local and city-wide issues, and the needs of new households versus existing occupiers (Cameron 2003). Significantly, its successor Housing Market Renewal programme has been praised for the quality of its community participation (SDC 2008: 77–78).

As indicated above, debates over visions and strategies often hinge on the nature and extent of *public participation*. There are increasing doubts about the breadth and depth of participation in the preparation of SCSs and LDFs, despite the promotion of a joined up community engagement approach across the local authority's remit with the introduction of duty to involve as part of Comprehensive Performance Assessment at national level. Bristol Civic Society forced a fundamental rewrite of Bristol's 2006 Statement of Community Involvement (SCI) for its LDF, and, with several local amenity groups, galvanised over forty similar bodies to form the Bristol Neighbourhood Planning Network (BNPN) (subsequently given an RTPI national award). BNPN has rewritten the ground rules for community involvement (now adopted in the Bristol 2008 SCI), enabling resident groups to build the capacity to be effectively involved in the LDF process and in pre-application discussions (David Farnsworth, personal communication; see also Bristol Civic Society 2007: 4–7). In Cardiff, by contrast, similar groups are not even on the list of consultees for the draft Local Development Plan (LDP) strategy. A decline in citizen and amenity group activism (of the non-NIMBY kind) in planning/design matters seems to have been widespread, though Bristol, Leeds and Manchester civic societies continue to give good accounts of themselves. Overall, the government's drive for more civic engagement and local empowerment (DCLG 2009: 31–33) has a rather hollow ring.

Turning to implementation, *public–private partnerships* are integral to corporate governance and have become a major feature of renaissance practices since the early 1990s. Key partnerships in Manchester have delivered the Commonwealth Games and associated infrastructure and new retail, office and residential quarters, while in central London three partnerships have been working with various landowners and different boroughs to improve the public realm to good effect. Sheffield's city centre partnership has been particularly successful, but questions have been raised about accountability and control in its operations and in the broader, city-wide local strategic partnership (LSP). By contrast, Belfast labours with its fifty-five separate partnerships working in the development field – a consequence of the democratic deficit that has existed since 'the Troubles'. Overall, the experience with public–private partnerships appears positive, but questions persist about transparency and about whose interests are represented in the various partnership arrangements.

The inadequacy of *local government funding* looms large in all debates about the urban renaissance and in all the case studies. None of the funding measures suggested in the original UTF report, nor those in the more recent Lyons report (2007), have been implemented. As a result of below-inflation settlements with central government, many local authorities have been forced to make swingeing cuts in revenue and capital budgets to fund even basic services, with associated cutbacks in non-statutory functions and maintenance programmes and significant labour-shedding. Capital for investment in enhancement and regeneration programmes locally remains scarce, though central government have found significant funding for new housing areas under the Sustainable Communities Plan and the New Growth Points Initiative (DCLG 2008a). The government has finally moved to legislate for the Community Infrastructure Levy (CIL), but a recent survey suggests that fewer than half of local councils will implement it (*Planning* 2009), which is very discouraging. The fund could help local authorities to address gaps in infrastructure provision – 'schools, parks, health centres, good public transport and provision for cyclists and pedestrians' (DCLG 2008c) – and the contribution to better design in the broadest sense could be considerable, but the CIL may well be a victim of the recession.

More needs to be done to *reduce both the complexity and fragmentation of regeneration funding* (Leunig and Swaffield 2007: 28–30). The UTF (2005) and the All Party Urban Development Group (2007) have focused on the particularly vexed issue of transport infrastructure and mechanisms to allow local authorities to borrow against future revenue streams without additional taxation, a facility which would allow Birmingham and Leeds to develop their tram/light rail schemes. Both support local congestion charging, and workplace parking levies are obvious sources of revenue with which to improve public transport and promote modal shift, but clearly local referenda are not the way to progress such measures (e.g. Manchester). The significance of European programmes for the pursuit of integrated regeneration strategies, drawing inter alia on good practice from elsewhere in the EU, should not be underestimated. The current Structural Funds Regulations provide for devolved management of European Regional Development Fund (ERDF) programmes by urban local authorities – an option yet to be taken up in the UK (EC 2008).

The *use of Section 106 agreements* and their effects on the quality of development received little attention in the city studies, but were a major issue for amenity interests and developers in the seminars. Evidence suggests that council demands for affordable housing through Section 106 has been a major factor driving up residential densities in the larger cities (Murie and Rowlands 2008) and in reducing design quality (e.g. Plate 16.2). The government's dependence upon the private sector to deliver affordable housing, and the particular success of this mechanism in London (34 per cent delivered from a target of 50 per cent of all units), has meant that in current reforms (alongside the introduction of the CIL) the use of Section 106 agreements has been narrowed to deliver affordable housing and the mitigation of site-specific impacts. This should address part of the issue of 'too many snouts in the trough' (Leeds developer) in Section 106 agreements, but the recession is already leading to widespread renegotiation of agreements, and the deferral of payments until the developer has achieved rentals or sales (which may well be a sensible way forward).

Finally, as regards local government leadership of the urban renaissance, the notion of '*collective corporate commitment*' to good design and sustainability is critical (Blaesser 1994; Punter 2007). All spheres of public action, from highway design to signage and lighting, from municipal landscaping to local authority land disposals, need to be treated as essential components of the drive for design quality and environmental improvement. While many councils are capable of achieving the necessary joined-up approach on individual projects, few seem able to sustain it across a wide range of interventions. Nottingham's particularly impressive 'design renaissance' has been facilitated by the retention of highways, transportation and planning functions within a single directorate over thirty years, with a single director from 1997 to 2007. Long-term adherence to primary planning principles (public transport, pedestrianisation, conservation, etc.), continuity of personnel and policy, and consistency of approach have been established. Corporate and partnership working with the private sector began early and has been extended into regional transport and regeneration partnerships, and now a neighbourhood renewal programme. Few other cities can display such far-sightedness, joined-up thinking and long-term commitment to design quality at the heart of a local authority, though both Westminster and Camden set similar standards in London.

Land disposal is an area where it is particularly important that councils display collective corporate commitment to good design and to sustainability (UTF 2005: 16), a point recently reiterated by central government (DCLG 2009: 45). Glasgow developed the 'Crown Street model' in the 1990s, to deliver a series of exemplar schemes. Under less patient political leadership, eager to take advantage of the 1999–2006 property boom and generate significant land receipts, the model has withered. Brief competition–masterplan–development agreement processes have been tried with disappointing results, and key sites have been disposed of without adequate development frameworks. In Cardiff, the cash-strapped council has used capital receipts in a bid to finance an ill-fated leisure project, but has succeeded only in setting precedents for ultra-high-rise and high densities, in the process driving up hope values to the point at which anything except the densest development is 'unprofitable'. The Leeds city centre rim study revealed that 50 per cent of the land on the edge of the city centre is owned by the city council. Used creatively, land disposal powers could ensure the adaptation of this inner ring to meet the twin challenges of climate change and social disadvantage (Bauman Lyons architects 2008: 168–171).

The government's planning reforms since 2004 have sought to secure a strong corporate role for planning as the key '*place-shaping activity*' at the heart of local government. Such a role assumes close working with the LSPs in England (and community planning partnerships in Scotland) and local communities, with a focus on the delivery of quality outcomes. In England, a more devolved approach to performance management has recently been introduced by central government using local area agreements (framed by LSPs) to become the key delivery agreements to drive wholesale improvements in planning practice (through specific improvement targets and indicators). These arrangements could offer planning departments a far more important role within the local government system, and an unprecedented opportunity to increase their influence over the way that localities are shaped in the future. The English planning White Paper (DCLG 2007a) recommends restoration of the chief planning officer to the local authority's management team (National Planning Forum 2007) and CABE (2006b) recommend a design champion role for the chair of the planning committee. All of these suggested innovations are necessary to reduce the marginalisation of planning within local governance, to create a system of development management capable of functioning in a more proactive way, and to allow urban design to play an influential role in place-shaping. The achievements of the Chair of Edinburgh Planning Committee (2002–07) and his wide-ranging Design Initiative indicate the potential (Farrell 2006), but such innovations have to be sustained to bring about a real change of design culture.

The effectiveness of new statutory planning frameworks and urban design tools

The previous section highlighted a challenging agenda for planning in corporate management to drive the government's place-making agenda, an agenda that only a few of the major cities or London boroughs have yet adopted. This section questions whether recent reforms in the planning system and the creation of stronger frameworks for design in the UK provide an improved basis for intervention and control, and whether planning at the local authority level is equipped to lead the urban renaissance in the way the UTF imagined. It examines the whole structure of what has been termed 'second order design' (George 1997) that provides the framework to coordinate built projects and ensure that collectively, they amount to more than the sum of the parts.

In Chapter 1 a key conclusion was that by about 2003–04 in England, Scotland and Wales a sophisticated national urban design policy framework had been established that gave local planning authorities (LPAs) the mandate and the supporting guidance necessary to drive forward a design renaissance. That framework came without any extra resources for LPAs and in advance of serious initiatives to raise design skills at the local level. As regards *the effectiveness of the new local planning frameworks* in facilitating urban renaissance, many cities have been slow to start work on the new LDFs and development plans, continuing to rely on regeneration strategies and Unitary Development Plans (UDPs) adopted in the early 1990s, which many considered could have been quickly updated to good effect (Cullingworth and Nadin 2006: 117). In England, the new plan-making process has already been streamlined (DCLG 2008d). Whatever the system, development plans can be remarkably ineffective regeneration vehicles, as the recent history of the Isle of Dogs shows.

Manchester's LDF was one of the first from the major cities to be completed, but it has been described as being 'as noncommittal as it can be about building density, height or land use, allowing hope values to roam freely and the city to negotiate developments case by case' (Chapter 3). The same might be said of Cardiff's draft strategy, which proposes a 100 per cent brownfield development strategy, but has nothing to say about desirable densities or urban forms, though high-density apartment permissions have already been negotiated for more than half the allocation to 2021. The Government Office for London rejected the first Core Strategy for Tower Hamlets because of its lack of a spatial strategy, whereas Bristol's draft strategy has been rejected by an alliance of amenity/neighbourhood groups on grounds of both process and substance.

The importance of a coherent core strategy to direct development and set appropriate densities that can withstand the cycles of boom and bust and deliver more sustainable urban forms has been clearly demonstrated over the last decade. However, the general prognosis for the urban design content of the new development plans, whether for strategic planning/design or development management, is not encouraging, yet they are the lynchpins of the place-making agenda. CABE has been conducting workshops with English LPAs to provide help delivering more design-literate core strategies, and its experience needs to be translated quickly into a briefing paper suggesting how clearer, more succinct and locally specific visions that embrace the dynamics of change can be developed. Meanwhile, CABE (2004e) is continuing to explore strategic urban design as a concept and process for use at both regional and district-wide scales. Terry Farrell's work with the Edinburgh Design Initiative Team illustrates some aspects of the approach required (Farrell 2006: esp. 32–38), as do his interventions in the London and Thames Gateway debates. Jon Thorp's work in Leeds links large-scale character analysis to necessary strategic interventions, but regrettably has not been developed into a fully fledged strategy.

The UTF report played a major role in the revival of *masterplanning* as a design tool, and CABE's (2004c, 2005a) advice consolidated this (see also new Scottish advice: SG 2008), but it remains one of the most misunderstood tools in the British planning and design lexicon. A masterplan should be detailed and three-dimensional, able to accommodate varying intensities of development and types of land use, the product of a multiprofessional team, the outcome of a thoroughgoing public consultation process and a deep developer–LPA dialogue. It should be fully tested for feasibility, and with agreed development allocations and control mechanisms for managing delivery, preferably with landowners or a long term investor-developer at the helm. Very rarely are these requirements met.

Notwithstanding disputes about the effectiveness of community participation (see Imrie 2009), King's Cross illustrates aspects of best practice in masterplanning processes, including creative engagement with the community, establishment of a social development fund and a broad Section 106 agreement covering community facilities, sustainability and management matters. It also provided a mechanism for flexible floorspace allocations within precise building envelopes. Canary Wharf, now almost completely built out, continues to demonstrate how masterplanning and the use of design codes adds value to development for a long-term investor-landowner and can help ensure a high-quality, though not always user-friendly, public realm. Newcastle is making good use of masterplans and codes in its housing market renewal (HMR) programme in both the Walker and Scotswood areas – the latter a particularly ambitious project. But it is Edinburgh that has made the most extensive use of masterplans over the past two decades, both to shoehorn new development into a heritage context, and to manage the large-scale developments on the waterfront, where the Western Harbour plan/code recently won a Congress for New Urbanism award. In Bristol there remains considerable dissatisfaction with the outcomes of all three of its key city centre masterplans, though two of the three have significant redeeming features.

Urban design strategies continue to play a positive role in cities such as Bristol, which regularly updates its 1998 City Centre Strategy (and will incorporate it into the new LDF as a Supplementary Planning Document), but less so in Glasgow, where the city council's Clyde River Design Framework has disappointed. Nottingham's new *Nottingham City Centre Masterplan 2005–2015*, the successor to the very successful *City 2000* vision (1990), synthesises ambitious public realm initiatives, and provides guidance for key sites in what is better described as an urban design strategy. The city's longstanding commitment to the use of *design briefs* (over 70 now) to maintain a proactive approach to development control is particularly impressive, and their relatively infrequent use elsewhere is to be regretted (but see Hall 2007 in Chelmsford).

Chapter 1 noted significant improvements in the efficiency of *development control decision making* since 1999, but also increasing doubts about its current resourcing, skills and staff morale (RIBA 2007). Concerted efforts have been made to revive and extend the use of pre-application discussions (PAS (Planning Advisory Service) 2006), and the recent Killian Pretty review (DCLG 2008e) sees this as fundamental to a more proactive, collaborative and efficient approach. But even the major cities have had difficulties in *securing appropriate design skills*, and their absence prejudices their ability to negotiate design improvements, especially when pitted against well-resourced developer teams. Impending retirements will rob at least four of the major cities (Manchester, Leeds, Bristol, Sheffield) of their most experienced and design-literate officers in the very near future, while others (Newcastle) have already lost their younger design talent to the private sector. As Holden and Iveson argue, in design as elsewhere 'planning is being re-made, as the location of expertise shifts from planners in Town Hall departments to private consultancies working as partners to deliver regeneration' (2003: 66).

Some cities have taken steps to address this de-skilling, finding ways to create a strong design culture within the planning department and the council at large. The Edinburgh Design Initiative led to the appointment of skilled designers for each area control team, and training for controllers and councillors (Dawson and Higgins 2009). Nottingham's continuing design programme brings all stakeholders together in a partnership supported by CABE and the Local Architecture Centre, emphasising training, design competitions and further design process innovations (Turpin 2007). Design for London (see www.designforlondon.gov.uk) has been particularly successful in establishing a bespoke design training arm to support all London LPAs. Opportunities also exist within URBACT (Urban Exchanges Between Towns) and INTERREG (Innovation and Environment Regions of Europe Sharing Solutions) to become part of European networks to develop design expertise and learn from best practice.

A number of cities and Regional Development Agencies (RDAs) have established *design review panels* to vet significant planning applications, and most cities make use of the national design review panels (though at the time of writing the Ministerial Advisory Group in Northern Ireland is not yet up and running). Recent CABE research has established that about 88 per cent of all English LPAs have access to either a local (64) or regional panel (270) (CABE, personal communication, 2008). However, the utility, timeliness and effectiveness of design panels, and the extent to which their advice is followed, are key issues. National design agencies are looking closely at their design review services to establish what design value they add to development (e.g. DCfW 2008) and CABE and Architecture + Design Scotland are pursuing 'enabling', but resources for this are limited.

A key question is to what extent the new systems of design review/support operated by the national design bodies, now widened and deepened by regional, *subregional* and local panels, compensate for the lack of staff resources and paucity of design skills at the local level. Panels are very rarely involved in the preparation of local policy and guidance and are often blissfully unaware of its content. Even if they do see a scheme at an early stage, and can offer excellent critiques of development proposals, it is hard to see how they are an effective substitute for proactive development control and positive local planning. They cannot interpolate between local politicians and the community, resolve the competing demands of all manner of consultees, or negotiate with developers and designers as the project evolves (unless some enabling relationship is set in place). The whole point of developing a sophisticated national planning framework was to empower LPAs to allow them to improve the quality, coherence and sustainability of development. Even among the major cities this is not happening on anything like a wide enough scale.

There was a concern that heritage-led regeneration was underplayed in the UTF report and the urban renaissance at large (exceptions such as Newcastle Grainger Town were noted). Various seminar contributors reported a lack of effective conservation programmes and significant funding, the weakening of *conservation controls*, and New Labour antipathy to the conservation lobby at large. Conservation activists in Glasgow, Sheffield and Belfast all cited evidence of loss of key historic buildings and insensitive development in conservation contexts as the scale of development increases – the new tower recently approved in Birmingham's finest conservation area, Colmore Row, being a case in point. Cases like that of the Vinoly Tower in London have helped to create an impression of an embattled and under-resourced English Heritage at odds with CABE, despite the fact that the two agencies have worked closely together to develop a range of conservation advice (EH/CABE 2002, 2003; POS/EH/CABE 2002). The government's failure to press for the reduction of VAT on all building repairs and renovations that would boost conservation (and rehabilitation/refurbishment/energy conservation of listed buildings) is a critical weakness (UTF 2005: 16–17; Hall 2009: 35) and there is an urgent need to reinvigorate conservation policy at large beyond the now delayed Heritage Bill.

In sum, there are concerns that the opportunities presented by the new development frameworks (LDF, LDP, etc.) are being missed, and that closer attention needs to be paid to the use of masterplans and design codes, urban design strategies and briefs, and the skills and quality of development management. Looking across the whole gamut of local design policy and practice and development management there is a general view that, whereas the national framework for urban design as public policy has been dramatically improved, urban design as local public policy remains underdeveloped and inconsistently applied in the majoity of LPAs. The reasons for this, and the differential levels of commitment to good design, are further explored in the next section.

Have local planning authorities established urban design as a foundation for planning policy?

Much progress has been made in refining national urban design policy and guidance, for which CABE, initially led by the secretary to the UTF, must take much of the credit as effectively the UTF's design arm. In Wales and Scotland the national governments and design bodies have also delivered positive advice. However, the effectiveness of local authorities' planning and design control practices is highly variable, both within and between cities, as has been seen. Gospodini's typology (2002) of varying European urban design practices has been cited in a number of chapters, and it offers a centre–periphery model to explain the different control regimes deployed across the urban hierarchy. It suggests differences between the pursuit of iconic and symbolic cityscapes in the metropolitan cities (the City and Manchester) and efforts to regenerate urban space and improve the city image in the major regional cities (Liverpool, Sheffield, Birmingham). It suggests the 'preserving or enhancing' of existing assets as part of tourist–culture–education strategy in 'special cities' (Edinburgh and Bristol), while those anxious to overcome peripherality seek to provide new bases for competitiveness through retailing and tourism (Cardiff and Belfast). But, despite some fit to the model, British cities' strategies strain against these categories.

There is a stronger base for characterisation in close scrutiny of the differing political economy of cities and the ways in which the level and consistency of urban design as public policy is 'dependent on economic conditions and social considerations, not to mention the political climate prevailing in the community' (Lai 1988: 429). Richard Lai sees 'a dynamic and ever fluid balance between public controls and pluralist economic determination' (1988: 353), which suggests a variety of different levels of design control, some stable, others in a state of flux, with stronger controls operating where local authorities are in a position to refuse poor development and weaker controls operating where they are especially anxious for development: all of them influenced by different political and officer regimes and by the vigilance or quiescence of the local public. A British 'renaissance' typology would suggest perhaps five groups of cities/boroughs operating, for the moment at least, in fairly consistent ways and under broadly similar constraints. These might be grouped into:

- those with strong, consistent control actively shaping development (Westminster, Camden, Edinburgh, Nottingham);
- those with similarly sophisticated controls but more entrepreneurial and in pursuit of development and signature architecture (Manchester and the City of London);
- those which have been highly focused on achieving particular design/regeneration projects as central to economic revival (Liverpool, Sheffield, perhaps Newcastle);
- those which once rightly prided themselves on a strong design ethos but which have found it hard to maintain for a mix of political, bureaucratic and economic reasons (Birmingham, Glasgow, Leeds and perhaps Bristol);
- those which have not created a strong design framework because they are anxious to capture all investment, if necessary without significant amelioration (Cardiff, Belfast, Tower Hamlets).

There are overlaps between the Gospodini and Lai models in terms of their expectations of cities at different positions in the urban hierarchy, and with different economic trajectories, but in the UK it would appear that the design regimes are much less stable than might be expected and, crucially, have not necessarily been strengthened by the urban renaissance agenda as intended.

The exemplars exercising strong, consistent control are Westminster and Edinburgh, which have the quality of heritage and the affluence and community influence to maintain their design standards. Edinburgh rediscovered its design ambitions through the leadership of a planning committee chair and his multifaceted, participative design initiative, but even here development pragmatism constantly threatens World Heritage Site status. Westminster maintains its clear development framework and conservation orientation and highly skilled and experienced planners (see also Raco and Henderson 2009). Lacking either the heritage or political capital of the other two, Nottingham is an even more impressive exemplar, a rare demonstration of what can be achieved with enlightened political and professional leadership, the real integration of land use and transport planning, and consistent delivery of conservation/pedestrianisation/design goals. It is the renaissance exemplar of this book although, significantly, it established its approach in the early 1970s. Like Edinburgh it has recently refreshed its design capacity and its control methods and widened its design collaboration, signs of a maturing of a design culture.

Design aware, but more entrepreneurial, Manchester is a particularly interesting case because it displays a complex mix of consistent design policy alongside regular resorts to fits of laissez-faire 'generosity'. Twenty-two successful major design appeals point to a serious commitment to design objectives, and its city-wide development code, a lesson in simplicity, has delivered a consistent 'return to the street' for development across the city. But alongside this, city leaders have ensured the approval of major schemes which undermine other design achievements – the Beetham Tower and the Green Quarter being the prime examples. Manchester displays the dynamic tension between 'pluralist economic determination' and planning vision that Richard Lai sees as necessary even within 'ideal' design regimes (Lai 1988: 353). Tentative comparisons might be drawn with the City of London, where there is often exemplary conservation control, but nothing seems to stand in the way of tallest towers, although many are refined through design negotiations (e.g. the refusal of the ninety-two-storey Millennium Tower (1997), which later became the forty-storey 'Gherkin' (2004; Plate 10.4).

Sheffield and Liverpool have both achieved major improvements in design policy and guidance, incorporated design panels, and worked well with their URCs and in close partnership with major developers to reconstruct their city centres. It is their particular focus on single central city redevelopment projects as the fundamental plank of their reimaging and regeneration efforts that marks them out from the rest (though Liverpool's Ropewalks is also a major achievement as a new mixed-use residential area). Together with Manchester, these three cities most closely fit Gospodoni's model in terms of larger cities focusing on the quality of central urban space as the essence of their reimaging and competitiveness. Meanwhile, Newcastle has delivered a wider improvement of its city centre and quayside with a strong conservation slant. It has also bravely tried to grapple with its wider residential renewal challenges in a more strategic fashion, being aware that the benefits of renaissance need to be spread more widely socially and geographically. But, like the next group of cities, it too has had to weather political shifts and professional upheavals that have undermined its design ambitions.

Glasgow, Birmingham, Leeds and Bristol have all struggled to maintain their 1990s reputations for strategic urban design, quality regeneration, and consistently good buildings. This seems to be largely a result of changes in political and departmental leadership, the loss of in-house urban design expertise and a failure to work corporately. But it is also a result of a dramatic increase in development pressure and opportunities to cash in (with land receipts, business rates, Council Tax and Section 106 receipts) on a private development bonanza. Glasgow promoted rapid and widespread private development with a new political leader, abandoning its public sector-led, patient urban renewal (it 'could no longer be resourced') in favour of more rapid land disposals. Birmingham failed to maintain its urban design leadership and expertise, and then, like Glasgow, experienced a more 'boosterist' leadership after a change of political control (there are hopes it is regaining some of this ground under new professional leadership). Political changes in Leeds have brought planning and design inertia just at the time of maximum development pressure, but, well before this, the city had failed to consolidate its planning/design framework around an up-to-date plan. A lack of significant regeneration funding has been compounded by not working effectively with the Regional Development Agency to deliver a definitive direction for urban design, and much valuable strategic design thinking has not been consolidated. Bristol has been similarly prosperous to Leeds and so also lacked major funding. As its design leaders have admitted, it has found it more difficult to maintain development quality, and failed to harness the wealth of local expertise in a more participative strategic design exercise (as in Edinburgh), or to define and fund a quality public transport strategy.

Finally, in Cardiff and Belfast, the facilitation of development has long been a corporate priority, but effective design policy is elusive in the former and a distant dream in the latter. Both might fit the Gospodini model as poorly resourced peripheral cities, and both struggle to maintain the kind of control over private development that might genuinely 'reinforce the city's development potential in the global system' (Gospodini 2002: 68). Cardiff has the 'innovative architecture' and 'iconic urban design' (Chapter 16) rhetoric in all its key documents, but it is developer led and lacks proactive policies and strategies. Meanwhile, despite the developers' rhetoric, Belfast is 'far removed from any renaissance idyll' (Chapter 17) with an architectural culture that 'tends towards introversion' (Evans 2006: 22). It is a much safer place to live than it was, but still a long way from being normal. It also conforms to a fundamental axiom of urban renaissance outcomes that spatial mixing is not the same as social mixing, but in a much deeper and more tragic sense than elsewhere in the UK.

So there are wide variations in each LPA's willingness and ability to shape urban form. Those cities with distinctive environmental quality, public pressure and political sensitivity towards design quality, and the ability to pick and choose between projects, all bolstered by strong planning leadership, highly skilled staff and good policy and guidance, are able to deliver strong quality control. Others with lesser assets, public awareness and political commitment to good design seem capable of delivering good design in particular projects, but struggle to maintain quality across the board. Still others feel that all major investment has to be facilitated and that their capacity to add value to design is limited. Design commitment has to be constantly renewed and refreshed, and it is easily dissipated by changes in both political and professional leadership as well as staffing, as a number of cities have discovered to their cost. In all cities proactive urban design needs to be extended beyond city centres into the inner cities and the mature suburbs to ensure the positive management of urban change.

Emerging critiques of the new urban landscape

The principal critiques of the urban renaissance as urban policy were set out in Chapter 1, and explored in many of the case studies. This section considers not only critiques relating to architectural outcomes, but also those linked to deeper social equity and community issues at the heart of the notion of urban renaissance. The arguments that the 'urban renaissance' is simply a more palatable term for 'wholesale *gentrification*', and that commitment to *social mix* and *neighbourhood* have been deliberately vague and generally neglected in the recolonised inner city, are examined. The case studies have generally not devoted much space to these critiques, being preoccupied with city centres, but they remain of critical importance to an evaluation of renaissance progress. The focus then switches explicitly to four related issues of built form, namely the *apartment boom as a large-scale design failure*, exacerbated by the failure to control the *density of development*, leading in turn to the *tall building* obsession and the preoccupation with '*iconicity*' at the expense of urban design.

There have been extensive academic debates as to whether the term *gentrification*, with its notions of the displacement of lower-income by higher-income groups in housing submarkets, is appropriate to describe either the intentions of the urban renaissance or the actual processes of 'recolonisation' (Atkinson 2004) of the inner city over the last decade (Lambert and Boddy 2008). Neil Smith (2000: 294) takes a wider view of the process, defining gentrification as 'the reinvestment of capital at the urban centre, which is designed to produce space for a more affluent class of people than currently occupies that space' (see also Sassen 2001: 225). This is a powerful definition that has much resonance with the first phase of the British urban renaissance as the central London, King's Cross, Sheffield and Bristol cases suggest. Lees *et al.* (2008) take this argument a step further and argue that gentrification can now be conceived as the leading edge of global neoliberal urban policy. They recognise gentrification hybrids such as commercial and tourist gentrification, 'studentification' (Smith and Holt 2007) and 'financification' (Lees *et al.* 2008: 129–161). There are some explicit, and a number of oblique, identifications of these forms in the city case studies.

It is 'new-build gentrification', coupled with industrial/commercial property conversions to residential uses on city centre fringes, waterfronts and other high-amenity sites, that has been so dramatic in British cities over the last decade and such an apparent outcome of renaissance policies. These medium- to large-scale apartment developments have been closely linked to, and (despite their significant under occupation) have supported, the reinvestment in retail, entertainment and culture in city centres, helping both to boost the evening economy and to create 'bridgeheads' of affluence (Lees *et al.* 2008: 140) from which the city is then 'civilised' and 'made safe' for middle-class occupation (Hoskins and Tallon 2004).

While these forms of recolonisation do not often result in the significant displacement of lower-income groups, and have sometimes delivered significant amounts of affordable housing (34 per cent in London, 21 per cent in Cardiff), they can hardly be described as delivering the kind of *socially mixed communities* promised by the UTF report. The private apartment complexes do not have large enough affordable component and do not provide the diversity of unit sizes, tenures and shared equity that the UTF envisaged (UTF 1999: 64–65). Nor do they make any attempt to accommodate larger households and families, and their frequent resort to gated designs expresses a distrust of the locality. A parallel programme of social housing, with a wide mix of tenure opportunities, would have to be mounted to counter the gentrification processes now under way and to deliver the kind of social balance that the UTF promised. This is the conclusion reached by the government late in 2007 when it set an (albeit modest) target of 70,000 affordable units per annum until 2014, two-thirds socially rented. Prior to that, more social housing was privatised annually (under the unrepealed Thatcherite 'right-to-buy' provisions) than was built anew (Shelter 2008), and New Labour determination to reduce welfare dependency in council housing precluded serious attempts to respond to the increasing unaffordability of housing, particularly in south-east England.

The issue of *social mix in the inner cities* was always a contentious element in the UTF report and in New Labour housing policy at large and, for many critics, was left deliberately vague (Colomb 2007). It combined the aspirations to desegregate council estates to reduce social disadvantage and welfare dependency, and to accommodate the new, smaller households in the inner city where they would be closer to work and to the full range of services. The actual scale and nature of social mix is, as many analysts have argued, deeply problematic. It depends on so many imponderables: the extent of the economic disparities (Hamnett 2003b), the extent to which mix facilitates social interaction, its actual ability to reduce disadvantage, whether shared services and facilities encourage mixing and whether perceptions and behaviours, and indeed disadvantage, are thereby changed (Williams and Daly 2005, quoted in Colomb 2007). To these conundrums can be added evidence that new apartment dwellers often choose 'convenience not commitment' in terms of locality, something especially evident in London Docklands (Butler 2004: 278). 'Mixed communities' of this type are characterised by voluntary segregation and social stereotyping, and they pose major challenges to notions of place-making and sustainable inner-city communities (Roberts 2007). Further research on these issues is an urgent policy priority

If the *proliferation of inner-city apartments* has been the most conspicuous new townscape feature of the urban renaissance, it has also been the most criticised from a design perspective. While in some cases well-designed apartment complexes have made exceptional contributions to city centres (e.g. The Edge in Manchester) and to the creative reuse of derelict areas of the inner city (Ropewalks, Liverpool), many new apartment blocks have had problematic impacts on waterfronts (Cardiff Bay, Glasgow Harbour) and riverside walkways (Thames-side; see Davidson 2009) and on inner areas at large (Leeds), often presenting significant problems in terms of liveability (Thames Gateway; Bernstock 2008) and neighbourhood amenity. Many apartment complexes have failed to engage with the public realm or to provide communal space, often devoting almost all of the ground level to surface car parking. They have often been too dense, poorly massed and cheaply finished, creating low-quality streetscapes and long-term maintenance problems. Once the complexes are tenanted by a wide range of owners, the problems of management, security, privacy and maintenance can become acute, further undermining liveability and wider regeneration aims (Wilner 2008). The collective result is a set of often oppressive projects, setting undesirable precedents in terms of density and design and making no pretence at contributing to the creation of a new neighbourhood. Developer inexperience and lack of design commitment have been compounded by lax development control.

As a response to this large-scale design failure and policy/guidance vacuum, various agencies have written design advice to improve the product (CABE/Corporation of City of London 2005; East Thames Group 2007; DfL (Design for London) 2007). These design guides have addressed aural and visual privacy, internal and external security, the quality of private and communal outdoor space, and the need to improve project suitability for larger households, especially families with children. They place a premium on professional and accessible management to handle the complexities of subletting and short-term occupation. Their recommendations need to be rapidly absorbed into apartment design and development control practice.

As the UTF (2005) argued, *more sophisticated controls on density* are also needed. Most density policies were judged 'overprescriptive' and were stripped out of development plans in the early 1990s, leaving LPAs without any policy or guidance. PPS3 (Planning Policy Statement; 2005) includes a recommendation that LPAs should develop a range of housing density policies in line with their spatial visions, appropriate to the capacity of local infrastructure and amenities, and to housing needs and availability (DCLG 2006c: paras 46–47). Most authorities have failed to follow this advice, not least because councils like to retain room for manoeuvre on major projects (e.g. Manchester, Cardiff). Density measures need to become more sophisticated and combined with more specific floorspace standards, along with floorspace indices to guide building volumes (East Thames Group 2002). Architects have warned against densities of more than 200 dwelling units per hectare, which are now regularly exceeded even in the smaller provincial cities, while the Royal Institute of British Architects (RIBA) has argued for a return to minimum space standards for apartments and wider mix of (ground oriented) unit sizes capable of accommodating families.

Finally, debates *about tall buildings and iconic architecture* have become major urban design issues in virtually all the cities, with over 300 proposals for very tall buildings in England's major cities by 2005 (though only twenty-seven constructed; Short 2007). The allure of the tall building for developers and city councils has increased over the last decade, height being equated with dominance, prestige, economic success and 'higher returns, rentals and unit prices' (Simon 2004: 27). Tall buildings are seen as putting locations 'on the map' and as the new landmarks signposting regeneration, indicating 'competition on the world stage' and 'expressing economic power'. However, the counter-view that they are 'a sign of political and economic immaturity' and 'symbols of political and cultural mismanagement' (Marsh 2004: 22) is gathering force, especially as many such towers now stand largely empty or are mothballed.

The debate has been most intense in London, where the former mayor was convinced of the need to secure some twenty towers of 200 metres plus over the period 2000–2015 (McNeill 2002; Strelitz 2005), though construction has started on only one of these. The London Tall Buildings Policy Framework has been tested almost to destruction, while the 2002 London Plan proposals were ruled overly permissive by the inspector (Velluet 2004: 33). Research in three English provincial cities has suggested that 'conservation planning concerns mitigated the worst excesses' of tall building, though the wider (particularly post war) townscape has been much less successfully protected (Short 2007: 192). Birmingham's new tower for Colmore Row suggests new threats to even prime conservation areas.

There is now excellent national guidance on tall building policy, which recommends an LDF-based approach to the identification of suitable areas, along with use of three-dimensional urban design frameworks (EH/CABE 2002). However, many councils find themselves trying to write policy as an *ex post facto* rationalisation of poor control decisions (e.g. Leeds), while others want the freedom to cherry pick proposals and to use them to lever in large Section 106 agreements to pay for all manner of social infrastructure, as is happening now in Southwark and Lambeth.

The obsession with tall buildings exhibited by architects, developers and council leaders has much to do with the relentless pursuit of the '*iconic*', and are often one and the same thing for the marketeers and boosterists (Sklair 2005). Both may be expressive landmarks competing with the public monuments of another age and creating a new urban skyline. But Morrison argues that,

> the true architectural icon is a building that is unmistakable, often provocative, and carries cultural signals far beyond its purpose . . . [however] as competition increases, each image has to be more extraordinary to eclipse the last . . . instantly memorable-more iconic . . . this oneupmanship . . . is a fatuous and self-indulgent game.
>
> (Morrison 2004; see also Jencks 2006a: 19–21)

He complains that the 'shock and awe' tactics of iconicity replace the practice of urban design with 'the contemptuous culture of consumerism and professional megalomania', 'designer labels' produced by 'starchitects', all wow factor and bling (Morrison 2004). Thus British cities have been largely spared the neo-modernist deconstruction, fractal geometry and contorted building forms, but spirals and shard skyscrapers are commencing construction in London now.

There are, of course, some very successful icons, many of them Heritage Lottery and Millennium Commission funded at the turn of the twenty-first century, though not all are good pieces of urban design (e.g. Selfridges, Birmingham), and much of what is labelled iconic is merely big or brash. In their tall buildings policy EH/CABE (2003) stress the importance of architectural quality, and considerations of scale, form, silhouette, top and technical credibility, while Jencks (2006a,b) argues for simple and complex metaphors, analogies and referents in iconicity. Many urban designers would agree with Morrison (2004) that 'it is the quiet strength of ordinary streets and unexceptional buildings that allows the icon to be special' and with Glenn Howells that the real challenge is 'to create a coherent fabric of modern buildings of lasting quality' (Howells 2004). Catterall warns of the dangers of 'symbolic devastation' if iconic design replaces overall urban design, and the overuse of 'landmarks' and 'gateways' in urban design strategies often contributes to this (2006: 2).

Sustainability implications

A final critique of the renaissance urban landscape would be the slow embrace of environmental sustainability issues in urban planning and design and corporate policy.

The chapters in this book and, to a lesser extent, the seminar debates have paid surprisingly little attention to issues of environmental sustainability, particularly the pressing need to respond to climate change, and how this might shape urban design. The UTF report was alert to some of the key sustainability issues, but its take on sustainable cities was all about creating 'compact, high quality urban neighbourhoods . . . to achieve more mixed and diverse urban areas . . . with sustainable transport options . . . and promoting equity and social solidarity' (UTF 1999a: 47). Four issues seem particularly important to sustainable urban design – *strategies for public transport, walking and cycling* and car restraint; attention to *green infrastructure* to ensure biodiverse and ecologically self-sustaining urban areas; building *energy- and resource-efficient buildings*; and integrating these and other measures into more *sustainable design, planning and local authority management practices*. Each is discussed briefly below.

Chapter 1 noted the slow progress towards *reducing car use in urban areas*, reducing carbon emissions, reclaiming space for pedestrians and improving walking, cycling and public transport, as recommended by the UTF. The government has continued to take a very short-term view of investment in light rail transit, but its emphases on improving urban bus travel and investing in the railways have been welcome (DfT 1999, 2004a). Notable public transport planning successes have been the establishment of Transport for London, capable of developing an integrated transport network for the capital and, of course, the Mayor of London's congestion charging experiment, which has been a major boon to bus transport, cycling and walking. Regrettably, the government has remained very timid on demand management measures, and its resort to referenda is playing into the hands of a vociferous car lobby (e.g. Edinburgh and Greater Manchester). City by city, the picture is one of very slow change and limited local capacity to initiate action on the scale required owing to lack of funding. The Royal Commission on Environmental Pollution (RCEP 2007) has pressed the government for an overarching urban health strategy to address the effects of urban air pollution, while CABE (2006e) has developed arguments for pedestrian/cycle initiatives to counteract the obesity epidemic. There is now widespread development of walking strategies (Middleton 2009), while cycling has been promoted in the DfT's recent £100 million Cycling City initiative, designating Bristol for extra funding (*Guardian* 2008).

The UTF report sought the development of comprehensive green pedestrian networks in towns and cities, and its Progress Report (2005) made specific recommendations as regards *environmental infrastructure*. PPS9 (ODPM 2005b) and the TCPA (2008) have developed useful guidance on this matter. CABE Space (2005d) and the Countryside Agency/Groundwork (2005) have demonstrated the potential of green space strategies. Regional spatial strategies and LDFs are expected to include broad locations and specific policies for their delivery within new development. A severe lack of funding and skills for this non-statutory activity continues to impair progress (CABE 2009), as evidenced in the Cardiff case study, but there is evidence of wider improvements and better management both in greenspace maintenace/improvement and in the number of 'Green Flag' parks, which have increased six-fold 2002–2008 (DCLG 2009: 28).

Turning to the question of *energy- and resource-efficient buildings*, the development of the Code for Sustainable Homes for new residential development is a belated but welcome initiative. This will take effect in 2010 in England (2009 in Wales), to achieve a 25 per cent improvement on current energy efficiency, progressing in two stages to zero carbon (in terms of the energy consumption in use) by 2016. It is a major advance in the management of climate change but, like transport policy changes, it will be very slow to deliver reductions in carbon emissions. It represents a huge challenge to the house-building industry, especially one emerging from a deep recession, because current cost estimates suggest that a 2016 carbon-neutral home (in energy use) will be 17–24 per cent more expensive than one with no energy conservation measures. Factoring in off-site renewable energy generation, to offset the overall carbon emissions from the actual development, could make the adjustment much cheaper (DCLG/DEFRA 2008). This would have interesting implications for urban design and integrated infrastructure provision, and it could encourage new forms of neighbourhood management.

In England, many of the *more ambitious 'sustainable design' agendas* are now spinning off the eco-towns initiative (DCLG 2007d, 2008b) – ten national demonstration projects for new settlements intended to make a contribution to local housing needs, but simultaneously to find ways to achieve zero carbon/sustainable living. Predictably, most of the fifty-seven proposals have met with fierce local protests and deep scepticism from many commentators, with sensible calls to bring the idea of eco-towns back into (or on the edge of) existing built-up areas. This may yet happen in Leeds and Birmingham, and the TCPA (2007a) has highlighted exemplar urban extensions (e.g. Great Park, Newcastle).

The eco-town initiative has led CABE to commission a set of sustainability indicators to challenge the promoters of each scheme to deliver exemplar projects. They link the (often conveniently ignored) necessity of households to live within planetary limits (using ecological footprinting) to the imperative of carbon reduction to counter climate change (taking the new 80 per cent CO_2 emissions reduction target for 2050). CABE/BioRegional's report (2008) defines the necessary reductions in both, converting these into reduction targets, broad masterplanning principles and environmental criteria. The intention is to use these standards, and ten 'process' criteria, to assess all new neighbourhoods and urban extensions.

CABE is also collaborating with the English Core Cities Group to develop a *Manual for Sustainable Cities* to be launched with a state-of-the-art website in March 2009 (www.sustainablecities.org.uk). This will seek to embed sustainable urban design in local authority practices, and will hopefully link up with the best European practice, especially the European Sustainable Cities and Towns Campaign. Ministers responsible for urban policy across the EU are currently working on a new common reference framework for sustainable cities (EC/French Presidency 2008). These initiatives could be critical to disseminating best practice and encouraging a more environmentally sustainable urban renaissance in UK.

To conclude, it is illuminating to refer to the *Sustainable Cities Index*, developed by Forum for the Future (2007, 2008; see Table 18.1), to assess the environmental performance of the twenty largest UK cities, thereby filling a gap in the *State of the Cities* evidence base. Its (annual) report emphasises that all British cities have large environmental footprints, and have a long way to go before they can claim significant progress towards sustainability. It offers the following pertinent comment in its 2007 report:

> The dominant model of city development over the past ten years of 'urban renaissance' has emphasized iconic architecture and grand projects to help re-brand and boost cities . . . The index would seem to indicate this formula is weak at delivering environmentally and [on] overall quality of life, and may distract from [a] broader set of criteria [as to] what makes a successful, sustainable, and liveable city.
>
> (Forum for the Future 2007: 13)

Table 18.1 Sustainable Cities Index 2008 (for twenty largest British cities: excludes Belfast)

2008 rank	City	Air quality	Ecological footprint	Environmental quality rank	Transport	Green space	Quality of life rank	Climate change strategy	Recycling	Future-proofing rank	CO_2
1	Bristol (3)	14	9=	2	20	1	2=	3=	1	2	2=
4	Newcastle (8)	5	17	6	15	6	8	16=	5	3=	16=
5	Cardiff (6)	15	6	9	16	5	6	14=	16	14=	20
6	Edinburgh (2)	9	19	18=	11=	12=	2=	14=	8	5	12=
7	Sheffield (7)	19	14	13=	14	17	9	16=	6	3=	19
9	Nottingham (11)	11	11=	8	2=	13	14=	6=	11=	10	10
10	London (10)	20	18	18=	9=	10	5	1=	10	12=	7=
14	Leeds (5)	16	15	20	16=	8	7	6=	14	11	12=
15	Manchester (12)	13	16	17	9=	4	10	6=	17	9	12=
17	Glasgow (15)	6	7	10	18	12=	20	14=	19	14=	7=
18	Birmingham (19)	7=	9=	13=	11=	7	14=	3=	18	18	4=
19	Liverpool (20)	17	11=	16	5	14	17	6=	20	19	4=

Note

Forum for the Future Sustainable Cities Index 2007/2008: www.forumforthefuture.org. Based on rankings of thirteen indicators (only six shown) amalgamated into three baskets: environmental quality, quality of life and future-proofing. These figures are all rankings whereas the original data was a mix. CO_2 figures are not integrated into the assessment, as standardised data are not yet available. Figures in brackets in column 1 are 2007 rankings.

The index (and the data) needs to be progressively improved. Clearly, they give smaller cities with considerable green space particular advantages over the older industrial cities, but it is the commitment to future-proofing against climate change which is the most critical factor, and Bristol's high ranking is confirmed by its shortlisting as one of eight cities for the European Green Capital award 2010 (in august company with Amsterdam, Freiburg, Oslo, Copenhagen and Stockholm).

Conclusions

In conclusion, it is perhaps most useful to summarise the major positives and negatives of the first decade of the urban renaissance the urban renaissance in the UK from an urban design perspective. The principal successes have been:

- the high profile now given to design in planning practice by national government and the devolved assemblies, and acceptance of its key role in promoting sustainable development;
- the creation of a national urban design framework of policies, guidance, processes and techniques developed from research on best practice, compiled by CABE with significant contributions from other bodies, continually updated and responding to new agendas, and now widening its scope into the key questions in sustainable development;
- the implementation of much of this design framework by a select number of authorities, in some cities in advance of the UTF report, and their continued efforts to improve their review practices and find new ways to promote design quality;
- a sharp increase in the proportion of development taking place on brownfield rather than greenfield sites, and in the average density of residential development;
- major design and environmental improvements in expanded city centres, particularly in the quality of the public realm, ensuring a wider mix of complementary uses and facilities, greater vitality and opportunities for residence, higher levels of public safety and better urban management;
- significant repopulation of the city centre and its margins with new apartment buildings, in some cities with the parallel delivery of significant components of affordable housing;
- widespread improvements in the quality of the council housing stock bringing it up to 'decent homes' standards;
- improvements in service delivery and community development on many of the most deprived estates and some success with social diversification and renewal;
- the emergence of a significant number of mainstream investor, niche and bespoke developers and social landlords for whom good design is a primary objective, and who demonstrate what is possible and set the standards for others to follow;
- the creation of a number of large-scale, sustainable urban extensions which set new standards for consultative planning processes, high-quality housing design and layout, integral employment and services, green infrastructure and positive estate management (vital to the renaissance but especially to the Sustainable Communities Plan).
- the widespread improvement of major city parks;
- a belated and incremental, but nonetheless firm, commitment to ensure the development of carbon-neutral housing (in use) by 2016 to reduce environmental impacts;
- and a final single but singular positive: the implementation of the London congestion charge

and its reduction of traffic and air pollution and improvement of bus transport, walking and cycling.

The negatives, or the key failures of the urban renaissance thus far include:

- the failure to develop a social housing programme to complement private development and ensure the creation of mixed communities, to counter social exclusion and gentrification, and to respond to lengthening housing waiting lists (acknowledging the government's commitment to building 70,000 social units per annum over 2007–10);
- the ratcheting up of building height and density to the point at which it prejudices good urban design and sustainable communities, and precludes the interventions of a wider range of development actors, entrepreneurs and community trusts;
- the general failure to develop clear density policies related to desired building typologies for areas undergoing change;
- the widespread design failures of high-density apartment complexes: the monoculture of small apartments, low space standards, poor communal space, intrusive car parking and poor relationship to street and neighbourhood;
- the slow improvement in the general quality of suburban housing layout and design despite the flow of positive advice and evaluation techniques;
- the frequent absence of proactive development control using design trained staff, pre-application discussions, strong design policies, design briefs and design panel advice to improve design;
- the failure to develop a good coverage of LDFs based on a graspable, strategic design vision with public support, translated into a core strategy with design principles and supporting policies;
- the need to improve public consultation processes in LDF formulation and the preparation of major planning applications (enquiry by design);
- the lack of planning and design leadership at council executive and corporate management levels, and the general absence of design champions (especially committee chairs) to fight for good design in high-level decision-making;
- the failure to reform local government finance (see UTF 1999a or Lyons 2007) to ensure that local authorities can deliver wider environmental improvements and forward-fund significant transport improvements to support land use planning and the drive for sustainable cities.

Renaissance in recession?

In the immediate future the response to these negatives will be deeply problematic given the likely depth of the recession and the spiralling public debt, which will lead to public expenditure cuts in all manner of government programmes. The revival of the construction, and particularly the house-building industry, will depend on the lead that the public sector can provide, both through its funding of social rented and intermediate housing and particularly through the activities of the new Homes and Communities Agency, a timely merger of regeneration and social housing agencies. The government remains committed to a major investment of £8 billion to boost the production of social and intermediate (affordable rent, shared ownership/equity) housing over the period 2008–14 to deliver some 400,000 homes (two-thirds social rented), but

Shelter (2008) now estimates that this programme needs to be increased by 70 per cent to meet current anticipated need.

At the time of writing the House and Communities Agency (HCA) is on the verge of initiating its first joint venture scheme with a major Registered Social Landlord to restart production, and there are discussions about further investment with institutional partners, as housing starts in 2009 seem destined to fall to 40 per cent of the government's annual target. The government is talking about further diversifying tenure choice, and shared equity/ownership opportunities, to address the realities of the 'credit crunch'. It is also on the verge of freeing up local councils to use housing receipts to fund social housing production on their own land. These constitute major opportunities to correct the imbalances inequities/iniquities in renaissance policies while simultaneously posing major challenges to production and design.

In the recession local government has the opportunity to rethink its economic ambitions, to development trajectory and planning strategies and to reflect on the development outcomes of the last decade and the priority it might accord to planning, design, conservation and future-proofing against climate change. There is an opportunity to complete their LDFs and development plans and to put in place strong design and sustainability guidance to accompany the progression towards carbon-neutral buildings. The biggest challenge remains to convert the increasingly vacuous mantra of 'place-making' into substantive corporate practices, linking development management with housing, transport and community services provision and environmental management, especially in the inner cities. The recent re-statement of the government's commitment to good design and quality place-making, and the sharpening of its focus for the recession, is very welcome in this regard (DCLG 2009).

There is no doubt that design quality will come under severe pressure, along with Code for Sustainable Homes levels and Section 106 agreements, as developers and house builders argue that they are entirely unaffordable in straitened economic times. Here the HCA have to take the lead and ensure that they maintain their commitment to design quality, energy efficiency, green infrastructure, social/tenure mix and lifetime homes in all the projects they fund. LPAs have to continue to insist that good design does not necessarily cost more money, frequently can offer a better environment for the same cost, and can often assist in maximising development potential while still respecting the context and contributing positively to the public realm. LPAs need to work closely with investor developers they trust, shortening procurement processes, buying land at existing use value, using compulsory purchase powers if necessary and using their often extensive land assets positively. Developers and local authorities can use open-book valuations to build trust, can defer Section 106 payments, lengthen the validity of planning applications and use other mechanisms to share risk and return in order to ensure project viability and design quality.

The deeper question for British society is what effect the depth and length of the current recession, and the different economic circumstances and lower levels of indebtedness that must prevail in its aftermath, will have upon consumerism, employment patterns, lifestyles and values. How deep will be the changes in the British economy and psyche, and will they lead to less consumerist and more sustainable lifestyles, and the acceptance of higher levels and more equitable taxation necessary to improve the provision of public goods and environmental improvements? Will there be the emergence of stronger communal values and more sustainable patterns of living that might support a more inclusive urban design and lasting urban renaissance? We live in hope.

Selected bibliography and references

All references to specific cities and groups of cities (e.g. Core Cities, Scottish cities) are placed at the end of the relevant chapter (Chapters 2–16) or introductions to the same. The references listed here provide a more comprehensive listing of government and other specialist reports which explore the urban renaissance policy areas and specifically its urban design dimension.

DCLG, Department for Communities and Local Government changed its name to Communities and Local Government in 2007: DCLG embraces both in this bibliography to avoid confusions.

All Party Urban Development Group (2007) *Loosening the Leash: How Local Government can Deliver Infrastructure with Private Sector Money*. Online. Available at: http//:www.allparty-urbandevelopmentgroup.org.uk (last accessed 26 February 2008).

Amin, A., Massey, D., and Thrift, N. (2000) *Cities for the Many not for the Few* (Bristol: The Policy Press).

ASC (Academy for Sustainable Communities) (2006) Mind the Skills Gap: The Skills We Need for Sustainable Communities (Leeds: Academy for Sustainable Communities). Online. Available at: http:// www.hcacademy.co.uk-mindtheskillsgapresearch (last accessed 7 April 2008).

Athey, G., Lucci, P., and Webber, C. (2007) *Two-Track Cities: The Challenge of Sustaining Growth and Building Opportunity*, Discussion Paper No. 11 (London: Centre for Cities).

Atkinson, R. (2004) The Evidence on the Impact of Gentrification: New lessons for the Urban Renaissance? *European Journal of Housing Policy*, 4 (1): 107–131.

Audit Commission (2002) *Development Control and Planning* (London: HMSO).

Baeten, G. (2009) Regenerating the South Bank: Reworking Community and the Emergence of Post-Political Regeneration. In R. Imrie, L. Lees and M. Raco (eds) *Regenerating London: Governance, Sustainability and Community in a Global City* (London: Routledge) pp. 237–253.

Bailey, N. (2007) Why is it so Difficult to Build Successful, Well-Designed and Sustainable Mixed Tenure Communities? Learning the Lessons from Housing and Regeneration Strategies in England and Scotland. Paper presented to AESOP Congress, Naples.

Barber, A. (2007) Planning for Sustainable Re-Urbanisation: Policy Challenges and City Centre Housing in Birmingham. *Town Planning Review*, 78 (2): 179–202.

Barker, K. (2004) *Review of Housing Supply. Delivering Stability: Securing our Future Housing Needs. Final Report – Recommendations* (London: HMSO).

Barker, K. (2005a) *Review of Land Use Planning. Interim Report: Analysis* (London: HMSO).

Barker, K. (2005b) *Barker Review of Land Use Planning* (London: HMSO).

Barnett, J. (1974) *Urban Design as Public Policy: Practical Methods for Improving Cities* (New York: McGraw Hill).

Barnett, J. (1982) *An Introduction to Urban Design* (New York: Van Nostrand Reinhold).

Bauman Lyons Architects (2008) *How to be a Happy Architect* (London: Black Dog Publishing).

Baxter, R. and Lees, L. (2009) The Re-Birth of High-Rise Living in London: Towards a Sustainable, Inclusive, and Liveable Urban Form. In R. Imrie, L. Lees and M. Raco (eds) *Regenerating London: Governance, Sustainability and Community in a Global City* (London: Routledge) pp. 151–172.

BCSC (British Council for Shopping Centres) (2002) *Urban Design for Retail Environments* (London: BCSC).

BCSC (2005) *What's in the Pipeline?* (London: BCSC). Online. Available at: http:// www.bcsc.co.uk (last accessed 15 September 2007).

Begg, I. (ed.) (2002) *Urban Competitiveness, Policies for Dynamic Cities* (Bristol: The Policy Press).

Bell, D. (2005) The Emergence of Contemporary Masterplans: Property Markets and the Value of Urban Design. *Journal of Urban Design*, 10 (1): 81–110.

Bell, D. and Jayne, M. (2003) 'Design-Led' Urban Regeneration: A Critical Perspective. *Local Economy*, 18 (2): 121–134.

Bell, D. and Jayne, M. (2004) *City of Quarters: Urban Villages in the Contemporary City* (Aldershot: Ashgate).

Bernstock, P. (2008) Homing in on Housing. In P. Cohen and M. J Rustin (eds) *London's Turning: The Making of the Thames Gateway* (Aldershot: Ashgate) pp. 169–188.

Biddulph, M. J. (2001) *Home Zones: A Planning and Design Handbook* (Bristol: Policy Press).

Biddulph, M. J., Hooper, A. J., and Punter, J. V. (2004) *Evaluating the Impact of Design Awards for Housing* (London: RIBA Enterprises).

Blaesser, B. W. (1994) The Abuse of Discretionary Power. In B. C. Scheer and W. Preiser (eds) *Design Review: Challenging Urban Aesthetic Control* (New York: Chapman & Hall), pp. 42–55.

Boddy, M. and Parkinson, M. (eds) (2004) *City Matters: Competitiveness, Cohesion and Urban Governance* (Bristol: Policy Press).

Booth, R. (2008) £35bn Revamp will Produce Generation of Mediocre Schools. *Guardian*, 21 July: p. 1.

Bramley, G. (2007) The Sudden Rediscovery of Housing Supply as a Key Policy Challenge. *Housing Studies*, 22 (2): 221–241.

Brand, R. and Gaffikin, F. (2004) Collaborative Planning in an Uncollaborative World. *Planning Theory*, 6 (3): 282–313.

Brenner, N. and Theodore, N. (2002) *Spaces of Neoliberalism: Urban Restructuring in North America and Western Europe* (Oxford: Blackwell).

Brenner, N. and Theodore, N. (2005) Neoliberalism and the Urban Condition. *City*, 9 (1): 101–108.

Breheny, M. (ed.) (1992) *Sustainable Development and Urban Form* (London: Pion).

Briggs, R. (2006) *Invisible Security: The Impact of Counter-Terrorism on the Built Environment* (London: CABE).

Bristol Civic Society (2007) *Annual Report 2007* (Bristol: BCS).

Buck, N., Gordon, I., Harding, A., and Turok, I. (eds) (2005) *Changing Cities: Rethinking Urban Competitiveness, Cohesion and Governance* (London: Palgrave).

Butler, T. (2004a) The Middle Class and the Future of London. In M. Boddy and M. Parkinson (eds) *City Matters, Competitiveness, Cohesion and Urban Governance* (Bristol: The Policy Press) pp. 269–286.

Butler, T. (2004b) Gentrification. In N. Buck, I. Gordon, A. Harding and I. Turok (eds) (2005) *Changing Cities: Rethinking Urban Competitiveness, Cohesion and Governance* (London: Palgrave) pp. 172–187.

CABE (Commission for Architecture and the Built Environment) (2001) *The Value of Urban Design* (London: CABE).

CABE (2002a) *Protecting Design Quality in Planning* (London: CABE).

CABE (2002b) *Paving the Way: How We Achieve Clean, Safe and Attractive Streets* (London: CABE).

CABE (2002c) *Streets of Shame Campaign* (London: CABE). Online. Available at: http://www.cabe.org.uk/files/streets-of-shame.pdf (last accessed 1 June 2008).

CABE (2003a) *The Value of Housing Design and Layout* (London: CABE).

CABE (2003b) *Councillors' Guide to Urban Design* (London: CABE).

CABE (2003c) *Creating Excellent Buildings: A Guide for Clients* (London: CABE).

CABE (2003d) *Survey Results: Review of Local Authority Planning Departments* (London: CABE).

CABE (2004a) *Design Reviewed: Urban Housing* (London: CABE).

CABE (2004b) *Regional Planning and Design* (CABE Discussion Paper) (London: CABE).

CABE (2004c) *Creating Successful Masterplans* (London: CABE).

CABE (2004d) *Design Coding: Testing its Use in England* (London: CABE).

CABE (2004e) *Housing Audit: Assessing the Design Quality of New Housing: London, the South East and the East of England* (London: CABE).

CABE (2005a) *Design Reviewed: Masterplans* (London: CABE).

CABE (2005b) *Housing Audit: Assessing the Design Quality of New Housing in the North East, North West and Yorkshire and Humber* (London: CABE).

CABE (2005c) *Design Quality and the Private Finance Intitiative* (London: CABE).

CABE (2005d) *Greenspace Strategies: A Good Practice Guide* (London: CABE).

CABE (2005e) *Start with the Park: Creating Sustainable Urban Green Spaces in Areas of Housing Growth and Renewal* (London: CABE).

CABE (2005f) *Building for Life: Delivering Great Places to Live: 20 Questions You Need To Answer* (London: CABE).

CABE (2005g) *Physical Capital: How Great Places Boost Public Value* (London: CABE).

CABE (2005h) *What's it Like to Live There? The Views of Residents on the Design of New Housing* (London: CABE).

CABE (2005i) *Design Champions* (London: CABE).

CABE (2005j) *Design Policies in Local Development Frameworks* (London: CABE).

CABE (2005k) *Design with Distinction: The Value of Good Building Design in Higher Education* (London: CABE).

CABE (2006a) *The Costs of Bad Design* (London: CABE).

CABE (2006b) *Local Authority Design Champions* (London: CABE).

CABE (2006c) *How to do Design Review: Creating and Running a Successful Panel* (London: CABE).

CABE (2006d) *Creating Successful Neighbourhoods: Lessons and Actions for Housing Market Renewal* (London: CABE).

CABE (2006e) *Physical Activity and the Built Environment* (London: CABE).

CABE (2006f) *Design at Appeal* (London: CABE).

CABE (2006g) *Design and Access Statements: How to Write, Read and Use Them* (London: CABE).

CABE (2007a) *Housing Audit: Assessing the Design Quality of New Housing in the East Midlands, West Midlands and the South West* (London: CABE).

CABE (2007b) *Paved with Gold: The Real Value of Good Street Design* (London: CABE).

CABE (2007c) *Sustainable Design, Climate Change and the Built Environment* (London: CABE).

CABE (2007d) *Actions for Housing Growth: Creating a Legacy of Great Places* (London: CABE).

CABE (2008a) *Designed with Care: Design and Neighbourhood Healthcare Buildings* (London: CABE).

CABE (2008b) *Campaigns and Research: Health*. Online. Available at: http://www.cabe.org.uk (last accessed 19 November 2008).

CABE (2008c) *Housing Market Renewal: Action Plan for Delivering Successful Places* (London: CABE).

CABE (2008d) *Inclusion by Design: Equality, Diversity and the Built Environment* (London: CABE).

CABE (2009) *Greenspace Skills Survey* (London: CABE).

CABE (2009 forthcoming) *Housing Audit: Social Housing*.

CABE/BioRegional (2008) *What Makes an Eco-Town? A Report from BioRegional and CABE inspired by the Eco-Towns Challenge Panel* (London: CABE).

CABE/British Council for Offices (2005) *The Impact of Office Design on Business Performance* (London: CABE/BCO).

CABE/Corporation of the City of London (2005) *Better Neighbourhoods: Making Higher Densities Work* (London: CABE).

CABE/HMG (Her Majesty's Government) (2006) *Better Public Building* (London: CABE).

Cabinet Office (2001a) *A New Commitment to Neighbourhood Renewal: National Strategy Action Plan* (London: Social Exclusion Unit).

Cabinet Office (2001b) *Preventing Social Exclusion: Report by the Social Exclusion Unit* (London: HMSO).

CAG Consultants (2006) *In-Depth Review of Sustainable Communities Policy: Report to the UK Sustainable Development Commission* (London: Sustainable Development Commission).

Callinicos, A. (2001) *Against the Third Way* (Cambridge: Polity Press).

Cameron, S. (2003) Gentrification, Housing Redifferentiation and Urban Regeneration: 'Going for Growth' in Newcastle upon Tyne. *Urban Studies*, 40 (12): 2367–2382.

Carmona, M. (2001a) *Housing Design Quality: Through Policy, Guidance and Review* (London: Spon).

Carmona, M. (2001b) Implementing Urban Renaissance: Problems, Possibilities and Plans in South East England. *Progress in Planning*, 56 (4): 169–250.

Carmona, M. (2008) Urban Design and the British Urban Renaissance, part 4: King's Cross, Central London, Docklands and the Thames Gateway. *Urban Design*, 109 (Winter): 9–13.

Carmona, M. and Sieh, L. (2004) *Measuring Quality in Planning: Managing the Performance Process* (London: Spon).

Carmona, M. and de Magaelhaes, C. (2006) Public Space Management: Present and Potential. *Journal of Environmental Planning and Management*, 49 (1): 75–99.

Carmona, M., Punter. J., and Chapman D. (2002) *From Design Policy to Design Quality: The Treatment of Design Policies in Community Strategies, Local Development Frameworks and Action Plans* (Tonbridge: Thomas Telford).

Carmona, M., de Magaelhaes, C., and Hammond L. (2008) *Public Space: The Management Dimension* (London: Routledge).

Carr, S. (2008) Can We Deliver Zero Carbon? In J. O'Rourke (ed.) *Placemaking: Celebrating Quality and Innovation in Urban Life* (London: RUDI/Academy of Urbanism) pp. 20–21.

Catterall, R. (2006) Editorial (Iconic buildings). *City*, 10 (1): 1–2.

CBRE (CB Richard Ellis) (2006) *UK Cities Offices: Market View*. Online. Available at: http://www.cbre.co.uk (last accessed 12 April 2008).

Centre for Cities (2008) *Cities Outlook* (London: CfC).

Chatterton, P. and Hollands, R. (2002) Theorising Urban Playscapes: Producing, Regulating and Consuming Youthful Nightlife City Spaces. *Urban Studies*, 39 (1): 95–116.

Cheesbrough, H. and Ledward C. (2008) Leading Questions. *Planning*, 4 July, pp. 16–17.

Clark, J. (2004) Historic Landscape Characterisation: A National Programme. *Conservation Bulletin*, 7 (Winter 2004–2005): 20–22.

Coaffee, J. (2003) *Terrorism, Risk and the City: The Making of a Contemporary Urban Landscape* (London: Ashgate).

Coaffee, J. and Wood, J. M. (2006) Security is Coming Home: Rethinking Scale and Constructing Resilience in the Global Urban Response to Terrororist Risk. *International Relations*, 20: 503–517

Cochrane, A. (2000) New Labour, New Urban Policy? In H. Dean, R. Sykes and R. Woods (eds) *Social Policy Review 12* (Newcastle: Social Policy Foundation) pp. 184–204.

Cochrane, A. (2009) London: Regeneration or Rebirth? In L. Porter and K. Shaw (eds) *Whose Urban Renaissance: An International Comparison of Urban Regeneration Strategies* (London: Routledge) pp. 313–322.

Cohen, P. (2008) Stuff Happens: Telling the Story and Doing the Business in the Making of the Thames Gateway. In P. Cohen and M. J. Rustin (eds) *London's Turning: The Making of the Thames Gateway* (Aldershot: Ashgate) pp. 99–124.

Cohen, P. and Rustin, M. J. (eds) (2008a) *London's Turning: The Making of Thames Gateway* (London: Ashgate).

Cohen, P. and Rustin M. J. (2008b) After London's Turning: Prospects and Legacies for Thames Gateway. In P. Cohen and M. J. Rustin (eds) *London's Turning: The Making of the Thames Gateway* (Aldershot: Ashgate) pp. 293–314.

Coleman, P. (2006) *Shopping Environments: Evolution, Planning and Design* (London: Elsevier/Architectural Press).

Coleman, R., Tombs, S. and Whyte, D. (2005) Capital, Crime Control and Statecraft in the Entrepreneurial City. *Urban Studies*, 42 (13): 2511–2530.

Colomb, C. (2007) Unpacking New Labour's 'Urban Renaissance' Agenda: Towards a Socially Sustainable Reurbanization of British Cities. *Planning Practice and Research*, 22 (1): 1–24.

Colomb, C. (2009) Gentrification and Community Empowerment in East London. In L. Porter and K. Shaw (eds) *Whose Urban Renaissance?: An International Comparison of Urban Regeneration Strategies* (London: Routledge) pp. 157–166.

COMPETE (2006) *The Compete Network: Final Report, Messages for Competitive European Cities* (Sheffield: Compete).

Cooper, D. (1998) Regard Between Strangers: Diversity, Equality and the Reconstruction of Public Space. *Critical Social Policy*, 18 (4): 465–492.

Countryside Agency/Groundwork (2005) *The Countryside in and Around Towns: A Vision for Connecting Town and Country in the Pursuit of Sustainable Development* (Cheltenham: Countryside Agency/Groundwork).

Crookston, M. (2001) Urban Design: The 'New Agenda' in Practice. *Journal of Planning and Environmental Law*, SUPP (Occasional Paper): 90–100.

Cullingworth, B. and Nadin, V. (2006) *Town and Country Planning in the UK* (14th edn) (London: Routledge).

Cuthbert, A. (2004) *The Design of Cities: Critical Readings in Urban Design* (Oxford: Blackwell).

Cuthbert, A. (2006) *The Form of Cities: Political Economy of Urban Design* (Oxford: Blackwell).

Davidson, M. (2009) London's Blue Ribbon Network: Riverside Renaissance along the Thames. In R. Imrie, L. Lees and M. Raco (eds) (2009) *Regenerating London: Governance, Sustainability and Community in a Global City* (London: Routledge) pp. 173–191.

Dawson, E. and Higgins, M. (2009) How Planning Authorities can Improve Quality through the Design Review Process: Lessons from Edinburgh. *Journal of Urban Design*, 14 (1): 101–114.

DCfW (Design Commission for Wales) (2007) *10 Points for Primary Care* (Cardiff: DCfW).

DCfW (2008) *Design Review in Wales: The Experience of the Design Commission for Wales' Design Review Panel*. Online. Available at: www.dcfw.org/designreview (last accessed 21 September 2008).

DCLG (Department of Communities and Local Government) (2005) *Planning Policy Statement 1: Delivering Sustainable Development* (London: DCLG).

DCLG (2006a) *Planning Policy Statement 1 (PPS 1): Delivering Sustainable Development* (London: DCLG).

DCLG (2006b) *Preparing Design Codes: A Practice Manual* (London: RIBA).

DCLG (2006c) *Planning Policy Statement 3 (PPS 3): Housing* (London: TSO).

DCLG (2006d) *State of the English Cities: The Competitive Performance of English Cities* (London: DCLG).

DCLG (2006e) *State of the English Cities: Liveability in English Cities* (London: DCLG).

DCLG (2006f) *State of the English Cities: The State of American Cities* (London: DCLG).

DCLG (2006g) *Code for Sustainable Homes: A Step Change in Sustainable Home Building Practice* (London: DCLG).

DCLG (2006h) *Building a Greener Future: Towards Zero Carbon Development: Consultation* (London: DCLG).

DCLG (2006i) *Review of Sustainability of Existing Buildings* (London: DCLG).

DCLG (2006j) *Strong and Prosperous Communities: The Local Government White Paper*, Cmd 6939–11, London: HMSO.

DCLG (2006k) *From Decent Homes to Sustainable Communities: A Discussion Paper* (London: DCLG).

DCLG (2006l) *State of the English Cities: The Changing Urban Scene: Demographics and the Big Picture* (London: DCLG).

DCLG (2006m) *Review of the Sustainability of Existing Buildings* (London: DCLG).

DCLG (2006n) *Delivering Affordable Housing* (London: DCLG).

DCLG (2006o) *Housing and Planning Delivery Grant: Consultation Paper* (London: DCLG).

DCLG (2006p) *The Callcutt Review of the Housebuilding Industry* (London: DCLG).

DCLG (2006q) *Lessons Learnt 2006: Designed for Manufacture* (London: DCLG/EP).

DCLG (2007a) *Planning for a Sustainable Future* (White Paper), Cmd 7120 (London: HMSO).

DCLG (2007b) *Homes for the Future: More Affordable, More Sustainable* (Housing Green Paper), Cmd 7119 (London: HMSO). Online. Available at: http://www.communities.gov.uk/documents/housing/pdf/439986.pdf (last accessed 1 June 2009).

DCLG (2007c) *Indices of Deprivation 2007*. Online. Available at: http://www.communities.gov.uk/communities/neighbourhoodrenewal/deprivation/deprivation07/ (last accessed 23 July 2008).

DCLG (2007d) *Eco-towns Prospectus* (London: DCLG).

DCLG (2007e) *Negotiating New Local Area Agreements* (London: DCLG).

DCLG (2007f) *Strong and Prosperous Communities: The Local Government White Paper Implementation Plan: One Year On* (London: DCLG).

DCLG (2007g) *Planning Policy Statement: Planning and Climate Change: Supplement to PPS 1* (London: DCLG).

DCLG (2008a) *New Growth Points Initiative: Partnership for Growth with Government* (London: DCLG).

DCLG (2008b) *Eco-Towns: Living a Greener Future* (London: DCLG).

DCLG (2008c) *The Community Infrastructure Levy* (London: DCLG).

DCLG (2008d) *Planning Policy Statement 12: Creating Strong Safe and Prosperous Communities Through Local Spatial Planning* (London: DCLG).

DCLG (2008e) *Planning Applications: A Faster and More Responsive System: Final Report Executive Summary and Recommendations* (The Killian Pretty Review) (London: DCLG).

DCLG (2009) *World Class Places: The Government's Strategy for Improving Quality of Place* (London: DCLG).

DCLG/DEFRA (Department of Environment, Food, Rural Affairs) (2008) *Research to Assess the Costs and Benefits of the Government's Proposals to Reduce the Carbon Footprint of New Housing Development* (London: DCLG/DEFRA, report prepared by Cyril Sweett/Faber Maunsell and Europe Economics).

DCLG/RTPI (2007) *Planning Together: Local Strategic Partnerships (LSPs) and Spatial Planning: A Practical Guide* (London: DCLG).

DCMS (Department of Culture, Media and Sports) (2007) *Heritage Protection for the 21st Century*, Cmd 7057 (London: TSO).

De Magalhaes C. S (2004) Centres of Excellence for Urban Regeneration: Promoting Institutional Capacity and Innovation or Reaffirming Old Ideas? *Planning Theory,* 5 (1): 33–47.

DEFRA (Department of Environment, Food, Rural Affairs) (2005) *Securing the Future: Delivering UK Sustainability Strategy* (London: HMSO).

DETR (Department of the Environment, Transport and the Regions) (1997) *Planning Policy Guidance Note 1 (PPG 1): General Policy and Principles* (London: DETR).

DETR (1998a) *Planning for the Communities of the Future* (White Paper) (London: HMSO).

DETR (1998b) *New Deal for Communities: Phase 1 Proposals: Guidance for Pathfinder Applicants* (London: DETR).

DETR (2000a) *Our Towns and Cities: The Future: Delivering an Urban Renaissance* (White paper) (London: DETR).

DETR (2000b) *The State of English Cities* (London: DETR).

DETR (2000c) *Planning Policy Guidance Note 3 (PPG 3): Housing* (London: DETR).

DETR (2000d) *Transport 2010: The 10 Year Plan* (London: DfT).

DETR/CABE (2000) *By Design: Urban Design in the Planning System: Towards Better Practice* (London: DETR).

DfL (Design for London) (2007) *Recommendations for Living at Superdensity* (London: DfL).

DfT (Department for Transport) (1999) *Transport; The Way Forward* (London: DfT).

DfT (2003) *Managing our Roads* (London: DfT).

DfT (2004a) *White Paper: The Future for Transport* (London: DfT).

DfT (2004b) *Walking and Cycling Action Plan* (London: DfT).

DfT (2005) *Home Zones: Challenging the Future of our Streets* (London: DfT).

DfT/DCLG (2007) *Manual for Streets* (London: Thomas Telford). Online. Available at: http://www.dft.gov.uk/pgr/ sustainable/manforstreets/pdfmanforstreets.pdf/ (last accessed 1 June 2009).

DoE (Department of the Environment) (1978) *Inner Urban Areas Act*. Department of the Environment, Circular 68 (London: HMSO).

DoE (1992) *Planning Policy Guidance Notes 1 (PPG1): Planning Policy and Principles* (London: DoE).

DoE (1993) *Action for Cities: Evaluation of Urban Development Grant, Urban Regeneration Grant and City Grant*. Inner Cities Research Programme (London: HMSO).

DoE (1994) *Quality in Town and Country: A Discussion Document* (London: DoE).

DoE (1995) *Quality in Town and Country: Urban Design Exhibition* (London: DoE).

DoE (1996a) *Planning Policy Guidance Note 6 (PPG 6) Town Centres and Retail Development* (London: DoE).

DoE (1996b) *Planning Policy Guidance Note 13 (PPG 13) Transport* (London: DoE).

DoE (1997) *Planning Policy Guidance Note 1 (PPG 1) Planning Policy and Practice* (London: DoE).

DTLR (Department for Transport, Local Government and the Regions)/CABE (2001) *Better Places to Live By Design: A Companion Guide to PPG3 (Housing)* (London: DTLR/CABE).

Durning, B. (2007) Challenges in the Recruitment and Retention of Professional Planners in English Planning Authorities. *Planning Practice and Research*, 22 (1): 95–110.

Durning B. and Glasson J. (2006) Delivering the Planning System in England. *Town Planning Review*, 77 (4): 470–484.

East Thames Group (2002) *High Density Housing in Europe: Lessons for London* (London: ETG).

East Thames Group (2007) *Delivering Successful High Density Housing: A Toolkit* (London: ETG).

EC (European Commission) (2008) *Fostering the Urban Dimension: Analysis of the Operational Programmes Co-Financed by the European Regional Development Fund (2007–2013)*. Working document of the Directorate-General for Regional Policy (Brussels: DG).

EC/French Presidency (2008) *Final Statement by the Ministers in Charge of Urban Development and Final Appendix to the Final Statement* by the Ministers in Charge of Urban Development for Implementing the Leipzig Charter, Marseilles, November.

Egan, Sir, J. (Chair) (2004) *Skills for Sustainable Communities* (London: RIBA).

EH (English Heritage)/CABE (2002) *Building in Context: New Developments in Historic Areas* (London: EH/CABE).

EH/CABE (2002) *Guidance on Tall Buildings* (Revised 2007) (London: EH/CABE).

Entec (2002) *Delivering Affordable Housing through Planning Policy* (London: TSO).

EP (English Partnership) (2006) *Car Parking: What Works Where* (London: Design for Homes/EP).

EP (2007a) *Places, Homes, People: Policy Guidance* (London: EP).

EP (2007b) *English Partnership's Approach to Community Engagement* (London: EP).

EP (English Partnership)/HC (Housing Corporation) (2001) *Urban Design Compendium* (London: EP/HC).

EP/HC (2007) *Urban Design Compendium 2: Delivering Quality Places* (London: EP/HC).

Evans, G. (2003) Hard-Branding the Cultural City: From Prado To Prada. *International Journal of Urban and Regional Research*, 27 (2): 417–440.

Falk, N. (2006) Smarter Growth and Sustainable Suburbs. *Built Environment*, 32 (3): 328–341.

Farrell, T. (2006) Twelve Challenges for Edinburgh. *Prospect*, 130: 1–49 (special supplement).

Fernandez-Galiano, L. (2005) Spectacle and its Discontents; or, the Elusive Joys of Architainment. In W. S. Saunders (ed.) *Commodification and Spectacle in Architecture*, A Harvard Design Magazine Reader (Minneapolis, MN: University of Minnesota Press), pp. 1–8.

Fitzpatrick, S. and Pawson, H. (2007) *Welfare Safety Net or Tenure of Choice? The Dilemma Facing Social Housing Policy in England. Housing Studies*, 22 (2): 163–182.

Florida, R. (2002) *The Rise of the Creative Class, and How it's Transforming Work, Leisure, Community and Everyday Life* (New York: Basic Books).

Flyvberg, B. (2007) Policy and Planning for Large Infrastructure Projects: Problems, Causes, Cures. *Environment and Planning B*, 34 (4): 578–597.

Forum for the Future (2007) *The Sustainable Cities Index Ranking the Largest 20 British Cities* (London: FfF).

Forum for the Future (2008) *The Sustainable Cities Index Ranking the Largest 20 British Cities* (London: FfF). Online. Available at: http://www.forumforthefuture.org.uk (last accessed 14 December 2008).

Gallacher, P. (2005) *Everyday Spaces: The Potential of Neighbourhood Space* (London: Thomas Telford).

Gallent, N. and Tewdwr Jones, M. (2006) *Decent Homes for All: Planning's Evolving Role in Housing Provision* (London: Routledge).

George, V. R. (1997) A Procedural Explanation for Contemporary Urban Design. *Journal of Urban Design*, 2 (2): 143–161.

Giddens, A. (1998) *The Third Way: The Renewal of Social Democracy* (Cambridge: Polity Press).

Gillman, S. (2007) Councils Shape up for Tests. *Planning*, 16 February, pp. 16–17.

Goode, D. (2006) *Green Infrastructure: Report to the Royal Commission on Environmental Pollution*. Online. Available at: http://www.royalcommissiononenvironmentalpollution.org.uk (last accessed 15 May 2008).

Gospodini, A. (2002) European Cities in Competition and the New 'Uses' of Urban Design. *Journal of Urban Design*, 7 (1): 59–74.

Gospodini, A. (2004) Portraying, Classifying and Understanding the Emerging Landscapes in the Post-Industrial City. *Cities*, 23 (5): 311–330.

Guardian (Newspaper) (2007a) Watchdog Starts Investigation into Housebuilding Industry. (*Guardian Financial*), 23 June: p. 37.

Guardian (2007b) Building the Future. (*Guardian Society*), 18 April: pp. 1–8.

Guardian (2007c) Housing. (*Guardian Society*), 2 May: pp 1–2.

Guardian (2007d) Promised Lands. 14 March: pp. 1–8.

Guardian (2007e) Buy to Let: The Winners and Losers. (*Guardian Money*), 23 June.

Guardian (2008) Bristol Wins First Cycling City Title in £100 m Plan to get Britons Pedalling. 20 June: p. 17

Guy, S. and Henneberry, J. (2004) Economic Structures, Urban Responses: Framing and Negotiating Urban Property Development. In M. Boddy and M. Parkinson (eds) *City Matters: Competitiveness, Cohesion and Urban Governance* (Bristol: Policy Press) pp. 217–236.

Gwilliam, M., Bourne, C., Swain, C., and Pratt, A. (1998) *Sustainable Renewal of Suburban Areas* (York: Joseph Rowntree Foundation/Civic Trust).

Hall, P. (1999) The Unfinished Agenda: Jobs, Jobs, Jobs. *Town and Country Planning*, 68 (9): 268–269.

Hall, P. (2002) Urban Renaissance/New Urbanism: Two Sides of the Same Coin? *American Planning Association Journal*, 66 (4): 359–360.

Hall, P. (2009) Planning London: A Conversation with Peter Hall. In R. Imrie, L. Lees and M. Raco (eds) *Regenerating London: Governance, Sustainability and Community in a Global City* (London: Routledge) pp. 24–39.

Hall, T. (2007) *Turning a Town Around: A Proactive Approach to Urban Design* (Oxford: Blackwell).

Hall, T. and Hubbard, P. (eds) (1998) *The Entrepreneurial City: Geographies of Politics, Regime and Representation* (Chichester: John Wiley).

Hall Aitken (2006) *The Social and Economic Impacts of Regional Casinos in the UK* (Glasgow: Hall Aitken).

Hamnett, C. (2003a) *Unequal City: London in the Global Arena* (London: Routledge).

Hamnett, C. (2003b) Gentrification and the Middle Class Remaking of Inner London: 1961–2001. *Urban Studies*, 40 (12): 2410–2426.

Hannigan, J. (1998) *Fantasy City: Pleasure and Profit in the Postmodern Metropolis* (London: Routledge).

Harvey, D. (1989a) From Managerialism to Entrepreneurialism: The Transformation in Urban Governance in Late Capitalism. *Geografiska Annaler. Series B, Human Geography*, 1 (71): 3–17.

Harvey, D. (1989b) *The Condition of Postmodernity* (London: Blackwell).

Harvey, D. (2002) *Spaces of Hope* (Berkeley, CA: University of California Press).

Haughton, G. (1999) Environmental Justice and the Sustainable City. In D. Satterthwaite (ed.) *The Earthscan Reader in Sustainable Cities* (London: Earthscan) pp. 62–79.

Healey, P. (2004) Towards a Social Democratic Policy Agenda for Cities. In C. Johnstone and M. Whitehead (eds) *New Horizons in British Urban Policy* (Aldershot: Ashgate) pp. 159–172.

Hebbert, M. (2008) Urban Design and the British Urban Renaissance Part 2: Manchester, Newcastle, Sheffield and Leeds. *Urban Design*, 107: 10–13.

HC (Housing Corporation) (2007) *The Williams Report: Quality First: The Cost and Quality of Affordable Housing in the Thames Gateway* (London: HC).

HM Cabinet Office (2001) *Preventing Social Exclusion: Report by the Social Exclusion Unit* (London: Cabinet Office).

HM Government (2007) *Planning for a Sustainable Future: White Paper*, Cmd 7120 (London: TSO).

Holden, A. and Iveson, K. (2003) Designs on the Urban: New Labour's Urban Renaissance and the Spaces of Citizenship. *City*, 7 (1): 57–72.

Hoskins, G. and Tallon, A. (2004) Promoting the 'Urban Idyll': Policies for City Centre Living. In C. Johnstone and M Whitehead (eds) *New Horizons in British Urban Policy: Perspectives on New Labour's Urban Renaissance* (Aldershot: Ashgate) pp. 25–40.

Howells, G. (2004) Making the Ordinary Extraordinary. In L. Kennedy (ed) *Remaking Birmingham: The Visual Culture of Urban Regeneration* (Abingdon: Routledge) pp. 41–44.

House of Commons (1999) *Integrated Transport White Paper: Report of the Environment, Transport and Regional Affairs Committee: Session 1998–9, HC 32* (London: HMSO).

House of Lords (2009) *Constitution Committee. Surveillance: Citizens and the State* (London: House of Lords).

Hull, A. (2004) Major Housing Developments: Density and Design in Appeal Decisions 2000–2003. *Journal of Environmental and Planning Law*, 379–393.

Hutton, W. (1998) *The Stakeholding Society* (Cambridge: Polity Press).

Imrie, R. (2009) An Exemplar for a Sustainable World City: Progressive Urban Change and the Redevelopment of King's Cross. In R. Imrie, L. Lees and M. Raco (eds) *Regenerating London: Governance, Sustainability and Community in a Global City* (London: Routledge) pp. 93–111.

Imrie, R. and Raco, M. (2003a) Community and the Changing Nature of Urban Policy. In R. Imrie and M. Raco (eds) *Urban Renaissance? New Labour, Community and Urban Policy* (Bristol: Policy Press) pp. 3–36.

Imrie, R. and Raco, M. (2003b) *Urban Renaissance? New Labour, Community and Urban Policy* (Bristol: Policy Press).

Imrie, R. and Thomas, H. (1999) *Urban Policy: An Evaluation of the Urban Development Corporations* (2nd edn) (London: Sage).

Inch, A. and Marshall, T. (2007) A Review of Recent Critical Studies of UK Planning. *International Planning Studies*, 12 (1): 77–86.

IPPR (Institute for Public Policy Research) (2007) *City Solutions: Financing Urban Growth: Towards a Supplementary Business Rate* (London: IPPR).

Jacobs, J. (1961) *The Death and Life of Great American Cities* (New York: Random House).

Jayne, M. (2006) *Cities and Consumption* (London: Routledge).

Jencks, C. (2006a) *The Iconic Building* (New York: Rizzoli).

Jencks, C. (2006b) The Iconic Building is Here to Stay. *City*, 10 (1): 3–20

Johnstone, C. (2004) Crime, Disorder and the Urban Renaissance. In C. Johnstone and M. Whitehead (eds) *New Horizons in British Urban Policy* (Aldershot: Ashgate) pp. 75–94.

Johnstone, C. and Whitehead, M. (2004) *New Horizons in British Urban Policy* (Aldershot: Ashgate).

Jones, M. and Ward, K. (2004) Neo-Liberalism, Crisis and the City: The Political Economy of New Labour's Urban Policy. In C. Johnstone and M. Whitehead (eds) *New Horizons in British Urban Policy* (Aldershot: Ashgate) pp. 143–158.

Julier, G. (2005) Urban Designscapes and the Production of Aesthetic Consent. *Urban Studies*, 42 (5–6): 869–887.

Kearns, A. (2003) Social Capital, Regeneration and Urban Policy. In R. Imrie and M. Raco (eds) *Urban Renaissance? New Labour, Community and Urban Policy* (Bristol: Policy Press) pp. 37–60.

Keith, M. (2008) Daring to Plan? Concepts and Models of Urban Regeneration in Thames Gateway. In P. Cohen and M. J. Rustin (eds) *London's Turning: The Making of the Thames Gateway* (Aldershot: Ashgate) pp. 53–66.

Keith, M. (2009) Figuring City Change: Understanding Urban Change and Britain's Thames Gateway. In R. Imrie, L. Lees and M. Raco (eds) *Regenerating London: Governance, Sustainability and Community in a Global City* (London: Routledge) pp. 75–92.

Kintrea, K. (2007) Policies and Programmes for Disadvantaged Neighbourhoods: Recent English Experience. *Housing Studies*, 22 (2): 261–282.

Kochan, B. (2007) *Achieving a Suburban Renaissance: The Policy Challenge* (London: TCPA).

Lai, R. T. (1988) *Law in Urban Design and Planning: The Invisible Web* (New York: Van Nostrand Reinhold).

Lally, M. (2002) Devolution and Urban Design: England. *Urban Design Quarterly*, 84: 18–21.

Lambert, C. and Boddy, M. (2008) *City Centre Housing in the UK: Prospects and Policy Challenges in a Changing Housing Market*. Paper presented to ACSP/AESOP Conference, Chicago.

Landry, C. and Bianchini, F. (1993) *The Creative City* (Bournes Green: Comedia).

Lees, L. (2003) Visions of Urban Renaissance: The Urban Task Force Report and the Urban White Paper. In R. Imrie and M. Raco (eds) *Urban Renaissance? New Labour, Community and Urban Policy* (Bristol: Policy Press) pp. 61-82.

Lees, L., Slater, T., and Wyly, E. (eds) (2008) *Gentrification* (London: Routledge).

Leunig, T., Swaffield, J., and Hartwich, O. M. (2007) *Cities Limited* (London: Policy Exchange).

LGA (Local Government Association) (2007) *Energy* (London: LGA).

LGA (2008a) *Planning at the Heart of Local Government* (London: LGA).

LGA (2008b) *5 Million People Waiting For Social Housing by 2010*. LGA press release, 16 May. Online. Available at: http//www.lga.gov.uk (last accessed 20 May 2008).

Lizieri, C. (1999) Making the Investment? *Town and Country Planning*, 68 (9): 265–267.

Llewelyn-Davies (1998) *The Use of Development Briefs* (London: DETR Research Programme).

Lock, D. (1999) Not an Election Winner. *Town and Country Planning*, 68 (9): 258–260.

Loftman, P. and Nevin, B. (1998) Pro-Growth Local Economic Development Strategies: Civic Promotion and Local Needs in Britain's Second City. In T. Hall and P. Hubbard (eds) (1998) *The Entrepreneurial City: Geographies of Politics, Regime and Representation* (Chichester: John Wiley) pp. 129–148.

Lyons, Sir M. (2007) *Lyons Inquiry into Local Government: Place Shaping – a Shared Ambition for the Future* (London: HMSO).

McNeill, D. (2002) The Mayor and the World City Skyline: London's Tall Buildings Debate. *International Planning Studies*, 7 (4): 325–334.

McNeill, D. (2006) Globalisation and the Ethics of Architectural Design. *City*, 10 (1): 49–58.

MacCormac Jamieson Pritchard (2005) *Sustainable Suburbia: Work in Progress* (London: MJP).

Macdonald, R. (2008) Architect in Paradise? *Urban Design*, 104: 24–27.

Madanipour, A. (2006) Roles and Challenges of Urban Design. *Journal of Urban Design*, 11 (2): 173–193.

Manzi, T. and Jacobs, K. (2009) From a 'Society of Fear' to a 'Society of Respect': The Transformation of Hackney's Holly Estate. In R. Imrie, L. Lees and M. Raco (eds) (2009) *Regenerating London: Governance, Sustainability and Community in a Global City* (London: Routledge) pp. 273–288.

Marsh, G. (2004) Tall Buildings – A New Era: Do We Need Tall Buildings? *Urban Design Quarterly*, 90: 22–24.

Marshall, T. (2004) *Transforming Barcelona* (London: Routledge).

Middleton, J. (2009) The Promotion of London as a 'Walkable City' and Overlapping Walks of Life. In R. Imrie, L. Lees and M. Raco (eds) *Regenerating London: Governance, Sustainability and Community in a Global City* (London: Routledge) pp. 75–92.

Miles, M. (1997) *Art, Space and the City* (London: Routledge).

Miles, S. and Miles, M. (2003) *Consuming Cities* (Basingstoke: Palgrave).

Mills, E. (1998) Sustainable Urban Development in the European Union: A Framework for Action, Com 98: 605 (Brussels: EC).

Mills, L. (2005a) Sources of EU Funding for Urban Environment Activities in the UK: Note in Evidence for the Royal Commission on Environmental Pollution Study on the Urban Environment. Online. Available at: http://www.rcep.org.uk/reports/26-urban/urbanenvironment-evidence.htm (last accessed 2 August 2008).

Mills, L. (2005b) Going European with Sustainable Communities. *Town & Country Planning*, 74 (11): 334–335.

Minton, A. (2006) *The Privatisation of Public Space* (London: Royal Institution of Chartered Surveyors).

Minton, A. (2008) In the Right Direction? *Architect's Journal*, 7 February: pp. 24–29.

Morphet, J. (2008) *Modern Local Government* (London: Sage).

Morrison, G. (2004) 'Look at Me!' *Guardian*, 12 July 2004. Online. Available at: http://www.guardian.co.uk/artand-design/2004/jul/12architecture (last accessed 8 June 2008).

Murie, A. and Rowlands, R. (2008) The New Politics of Urban Housing. *Environment and Planning C: Government and Policy*, 26: 644–659.

Murray C. (ed.) (2007) The Economics of Design: Transforming England's Core Cities. *Urban Design* (Special issue) 107: 16–35.

Murray, P. (ed.) (2004) *Architecture and Commerce: New Office Design in London* (London: Wordsearch).

NAO (National Audit Office) (2006) *Office of the Deputy Prime Minister: Enhancing Urban Green Space*, HoC 935 (London: HMSO).

NAO (2007a) *How European Cities Achieve Renaissance* (London: NAO).

NAO (2007b) *Department of Communities and Local Government: Housing Market Renewal*, HC 20 Session 2007–2008 (London: NAO).

Nathan, M. and Urwin, C. (2005) *City People: City Centre Living in the UK* (London: Institute for Public Policy Research).

National Planning Forum (2007) *Delivering Inspiring Places: The Role and Status of Planning* (London: Idox Group).

Neal, P. (ed.) (2003) *Urban Villages and the Making of Communities* (London: Spon).

Observer (Newspaper) (2007) *Planning and Placemaking.* (Observer Special Report), 27 May: pp. 1–8

Oc, T. (2002) People and Urban Renaissance. *American Planning Association Journal*, 66 (4): 364–5.

ODPM (Office of the Deputy Prime Minister) (2000) *The Urban White Paper* (London: ODPM).

ODPM (2002a) *Living Places: Cleaner, Safer, Greener* (London: HMSO).

ODPM (2002b) *Delivering Through Planning* (London: HMSO).

ODPM (2003a) *Planning for Access* (London: ODPM).

ODPM (2003b) *Sustainable Communities: Building for the Future* (London: HMSO).

ODPM (2004a) *Living Places: Caring for Quality* (London: ODPM).

ODPM (2004b) *Competitive European Cities. Where Do the Core Cities Stand? Urban Research Summary 13* (London: ODPM).

ODPM (2004c) *Making it Happen: Urban Renaissance and Prosperity in our Core Cities: A Tale of Eight Cities* (London: ODPM).

ODPM (2004d) *Government Response to the Egan Review: Skills for Sustainable Communities* (London: ODPM).

ODPM (2004e) *The Planning Response to Climate Change* (London: ODPM).

ODPM (2005a) *Sustainable Communities: People, Places and Prosperity: A Five Year Plan from the ODPM*, Cmd 6425 (London: HMSO).

ODPM (2005b) *Planning Policy Statement 9: Biodiversity and Geological Conservation* (London: ODPM).

ODPM (2005c) *State of the Cities: A Progress Report to the Delivering Sustainable Communities Summit* (London: ODPM).

ODPM (2006a) *State of the English Cities: Volume 1: A Research Study* (London: ODPM).

ODPM (2006b) *State of the English Cities: Volume 2: A Research Study* (London: ODPM).

ODPM (2006c) *Enhancing Urban Green Space*, HC 935 (London: HMSO).

ODPM (2006d) *A Framework for City Regions* (London: ODPM).

ODPM (2007) *Place Shaping: A Shared Ambition for the Future of Local Government: Final Report* (Sir Michael Lyons Inquiry into Local Government) (London: HMSO).

ODPM/CABE (2001) *Better Places to Live: A Companion Guide to PPG3* (Tonbridge: Thomas Telford).

ODPM/HMT (Her Majesty's Treasury)/DfT (Department for Transport) (2003) *Cities, Regions and Competitiveness: 2nd Report for the Working Group and Government Departments* (London: ODPM).

ODPM/HMT/GOER (Government Office for the English Regions) (2004) *Our Cities are Back: Competitive Cities Make Prosperous Regions and Sustainable Communities.* Third Report of the Core Cities Working Group (London: ODPM).

ODPM/HO (Home Office) (2004) *Safer Places: The Planning System and Crime Prevention* (London: Thomas Telford).

Oswalt P. (ed.) (2001) *Shrinking Cities: Volume 1 International Research* (Ostfildern-Ruit, De: Hatje Cantz).

Parkinson, M., Simmie, J., Clark, G., and Verdonk, H. (2004) *Competitive European Cities: Where do the Core Cities Stand?* (London: ODPM).

Parkinson, M., Evans, R., Meegan, R., Karecha, J., and Hutchins, M. (2006) *New Evaluated Manchester: Interim Evaluation of NEM* (Liverpool: European Institute for Urban Affairs, John Moores University).

Parkinson M., Ball, M., Blake N., and Kay T. (2009) *The Credit Crunch and Regeneration: Impact and Implications* (London: DCLG).

PAS (Planning Advisory Service) (2006) *Constructive Talk: Investing in Pre Application Discussions* (London: PAS).

PAS (2008) *Advisory Team for Large Applications* (ATLAS). Online. Available at: http://www.pas.gov.uk/ATLAS (last accessed 6 November 2008).

Planning (2009) Councils May Eschew Levy. *Planning*, 23 January, p. 1

Planning Inspectorate (2008). Local Development Frameworks. Online. Available at: http://www.planning-inspectorate.gov.uk/pins/appeals/local_dev/dpd/submitted_dpd's (last accessed 6 November 2008).

PTE (Pollard Thomas Edwards Architects) (2005) *Out of the Ordinary* (London: Black Dog Publishing).

Porter, L. (2009) Whose Urban Renaissance? In L. Porter and K. Shaw (eds) (2009) *Whose Urban Renaissance? An International Comparison of Urban Regeneration Strategies* (London: Routledge) pp. 241–252.

Porter L. and Shaw K. (eds) (2009) *Whose Urban Renaissance? An International Comparison of Urban Regeneration Strategies* (London: Routledge).

POS/EH/CABE (Planning Officers Society/English Heritage/CABE) (2002) *Moving Towards Excellence in Urban Design and Conservation* (London: POS/EH/CABE).

Potter, S. (1999) Travelling Towards Urban Renaissance. *Town and Country Planning*, 68 (9): 280.

Power, A. and Houghton J. (2007) *Jigsaw Cities: Big Places, Small Space* (Bristol: Policy Press).

Price, G. (2002) Another Crack at the Suburbs. *American Planning Association Journal*, 66 (4): 361–2.

PRP (2002) *High Density Housing in Europe: Lessons for London* (London: East Thames Housing Group).

Punter, J. V. (1987) A History of Aesthetic Control Part 2. *Town Planning Review*, 58 (1): 29–62.

Punter, J. V. and Carmona M. (1997) *The Design Dimension of Planning: Theory, Content and Best Practice for Design Policies* (London: Spon).

Punter, J. V. (2007) Developing Urban Design as Public Policy: Best Practice Principles for Design Review and Development Management. *Journal of Urban Design*, 12 (2): 167–202.

Punter, J. V. (2008) Urban design and the British Urban Renaissance: comparing Birmingham, Bristol, Cardiff and Nottingham. *Urban Design*, 106: 10–12.

Raco, M. (2003) New Labour, Community and the Future of Britain's Urban Renaissance. In R. Imrie and M. Raco (eds) *Urban Renaissance? New Labour, Community and Urban Policy* (Bristol: Policy Press) pp. 235–250.

Raco, M. (2005) Sustainable Development, Rolled-Out Neoliberalism, and Sustainable Communities. *Antipode*, 37 (3): 324–347.

Raco, M. and Henderson. (2009) Local Government and the Politics of Flagship Regeneration in London: The Development of Paddington. In R. Imrie, L. Lees. and M. Raco (eds) *Regenerating London: Governance, Sustainability and Community in a Global City* (London: Routledge) pp. 112–131.

Raco, M., Parker, G., Doak J. (2002) Reshaping Spaces of Local Governance? Community Strategies and the Modernisation of Local Government in England. *Environment and Planning C: Government and Policy*, 24: 475–496.

Ravetz, A. (1999) Local economies first. *Town and Country Planning*, 68 (9): 279.

Rawnsley, A. (2007) The Reckoning. *Observer: The Blair Years* (Special Colour supplement), 6 May: pp. 16–29.

RCEP (Royal Commission on Environmental Pollution) (2007) *26ʰ Report, The Urban Environment*, Cmd 7009 (London: HMSO).

RIBA (Royal Institute of British Architects) (2007) *Improving the Planning Process* (Practice and Policy paper) (London: RIBA).

Richards, D. and Smith, M. J. (2002) *Governance and Public Policy in the United Kingdom* (Oxford: Oxford University Press).

Roberts, M. (2007) Sharing Space: Urban design and Social Mixing in Mixed Income New Communities. *Planning Theory and Practice*, 8 (2): 183–204.

Roberts, M. and Turner, C. (2005) Conflicts of Liveability in the 24 Hour City: Learning from 48 Hours in the Life of London's Soho. *Journal of Urban Design,* 10 (2): 171–193.

Roberts, P. and Sykes, H. (2000) *Urban Regeneration: A Handbook* (London: Sage).

Robson, B. (1999) Bold Platform for the White Paper. *Town and Country Planning*, 68 (9): 278.

Robson, B., Parkinson, M., Boddy, M., and MacLennan G. (2000) *The State of English Cities* (London: DETR).

Rogers, R. and Fisher, M. (1992) *A New London* (Harmondsworth, Middlesex: Penguin).

Rogers, R. and Power, A. (2000) *Cities for a Small Planet* (London: Faber & Faber).

Rowlands, R., Murie, A., and Tice, A. (2006) *More Than Tenure Mix: Developer and Purchaser Attitudes To New Housing Estates.* (Coventry: Chartered Institute of Housing:, Joseph Rowntree Foundation).

RTPI (Royal Town Planning Institute) (2007) *Shaping and Delivering Tomorrow's Places: Effective Practice in Spatial Planning: Report, Findings and Recommendations* (London: RTPI/CLG).

RUDI/Academy of Urbanism (2008) *Placemaking* (London: RUDI/Academy of Urbanism).

Rudlin, D. and Falk, N. (1999) *Building the 21st Century Home: The Sustainable Urban Neighbourhood* (London: Architectural Press).

Sassen, S. (2001) *The Global City: New York, London and Tokyo* (Princeton NJ: Princeton University Press).

Saunders, W. S. (ed.) (2005) *Commodification and Spectacle in Architecture* (A Harvard Design Magazine Reader) (Minneapolis, MN: University of Minnesota Press).

SDC (Sustainable Development Commission) (2008) *Building Houses or Creating Communities: A Review of Government Progress on Sustainable Communities* (London: SDC).

SEU (Social Exclusion Unit) (1998) *Bringing Britain Together: A National Strategy for Neighbourhood Renewal* (London: SEU).

SG (Scottish Government) (2008) *PAN 83 Masterplanning* (Edinburgh: SG).

Shaw, K. and Porter, L. (2009) Introduction. In L. Porter and K. Shaw (eds) (2009) *Whose Urban Renaissance?: An International Comparison of Urban Regeneration Strategies* (London: Routledge) pp. 1–8.

Shelter (2008) *Homes for the Future: A New Analysis of Housing Need and Demand in England* (London: Shelter).

Short, M. (2007) Assessing the Impact of Proposals for Tall Buildings on the Built Heritage: England's Regional Cities in the 21st Century. *Progress in Planning*, 68 (3): 97–199.

Simmons, R. (2008) *More Than Wires and Windmills.* In RUDI/Academy of Urbanism (eds) *Placemaking* (London: RUDI/Academy of Urbanism) p. 24.

Simon, R. (2004) Mayor and Prince. *Urban Design Quarterly*, 90: 26–27.

Sklair, L. (2005) The Transnational Capitalist Class and Contemporary Architecture in Globalizing Cities. *International Journal of Urban and Regional Research*, 29 (3): 485–500.

Sklair, L. (2006) Iconic Architecture and Capitalist Globalisation. *City*, 10 (1): 21–48.

Smith, D. and Holt, L. (2007) Studentification and 'Apprentice' Gentrifiers within Britain's Provincial Towns and Cities: Extending the Meaning of Gentrification. *Environment and Planning A* 39 (1): 142–161.

Smith, I., Lepine, E., and Taylor M. (eds) (2007) *Disadvantaged by Where you Live? Neighbourhood Governance in Contemporary Urban Policy* (Bristol: Policy Press).

Smith, N. (1996) *The New Urban Frontier: Gentrification and the Revanchist City* (New York: Routledge).

Smith, N. (2000) Gentrification. In R. J Johnston, D. Gregory, G. Pratt and M. Watts (eds) *The Dictionary of Human Geography* (4th Edn) (Oxford: Blackwell) pp. 294–296.

Smith, N. and Derksen, J. (2002) New Globalism, New Urbanism: Gentrification as Global Urban Strategy. *Antipode*, 34 (3): 427–450.

Spaans, M. (2004) The Implementation of Urban Regeneration Projects in Europe: Global Ambitions, Local Matters. *Journal of Urban Design*, 9 (3): 335–350.

Stewart, H. (2008) From Building Sites to Sofas, the Crisis Starts to Hit Home. *Observer: Business and Media*, 6 July: p. 8.

Stoker, G. (2005) *Transforming Local Governance: From Thatcherism to New Labour* (London: Palgrave Macmillan).

Strelitz, Z. (2005) *Tall Buildings: A Strategic Design Guide* (London: RIBA Publishing).

Swanstrom, T. (2002) Are Urbanism and Fear at War? *Urban Affairs Review*, 38 (1): 135–140.

Swyngedouw, E., Moulaert, F., and Rodriguez, A. (2002) Neoliberal Urbanization in Europe: Large Scale Urban Development Projects and the New Urban Policy. *Antipode*, 34 (3): 542–577.

TCPA (Town and Country Planning Association) (2004) *Biodiversity by Design: A Guide for Sustainable Communities* (London: TCPA).

TCPA (2006) *Permission to Plan* (A Stakeholder Report by TCPA and PricewaterhouseCoopers) (London: TCPA).

TCPA (2007a) *Best Practice in Urban Extensions and New Settlements* (London: TCPA).

TCPA (2007b) *Eco-Towns: Scoping Report* (London: TCPA).

TCPA (2008) *The Essential Role of Green Infrastructure: EcoTowns Green Infrastructure Worksheet: Advice to Promoters and Planners* (London: TCPA).

TCPA/Buchanan (2008) *Planning Community Needs* (London: TCPA/RTPI/EPF/Rayne Foundation).

TCPA/Friends of the Earth (2006) *Planning Policy Statement 26: Tackling Climate Change through Planning: The Government's Objective* (London: TCPA).

Thornley, A. (1993) *Urban Planning under Thatcherism* (2nd edn) (London: Routledge).

Tiesdell, S. (2008) Urban design and the British Urban renaissance, Part 3: Glasgow, Belfast, Liverpool and Edinburgh. *Urban Design*, 108 (Autumn): 16–19.

Tiesdell, S. and Allmendinger, P. (2001) Neighbourhood Regeneration and New Labour's Third Way. *Environment and Planning C: Government and Policy*, 19: 903–926.

Tiesdell, S., Oc, T., and Heath, T. (1996) *Revitalizing Historic Urban Quarters* (Oxford: Architectural Press).

Toynbee, P. (2008) The Labour Idealism that Saved Clapham Park is Dead. *Guardian*, 12 July: p. 35.

Transport for London (2005) *Improving Walkability: Good Practice Guidance on Improving Pedestrian Conditions as part of Development Opportunities* (London: Transport for London).

Turok, I. (1999) Squeezing Surrey to Sustain Sunderland. *Town and Country Planning*, 68 (9): 268–269.

Turpin, N. (2007) Design 07 – Nottingham's Design Campaign. *Urban Design*, 103: 34–35.

UDG (Urban Design Group) (2002) *Urban Design Guidance* (London: Telford).

UK Government (1999) *A Better Quality of Life: A Strategy for Sustainable Development in the UK*, Cmd 4345 (London: HMSO).

Unsworth, R. and Nathan, M. (2006) Beyond City Living: Remaking the Inner Suburbs. *Built Environment*, 32 (3): 235–249.

Urban Design Skills Working Group (2001) *Report to the Minister for Housing, Planning and Regeneration* (London: DTLR/CABE).

UTF (Urban Task Force) (1999a) *Towards an Urban Renaissance* (London: Spon).

UTF (1999b) *Urban Renaissance: Sharing the Vision* (summary of responses to the Urban Task Force Prospectus) (London: Urban Task Force for Department of Environment Transport and the Regions).

UTF (2005) *Towards a Strong Urban Renaissance: An Independent Report by Members of the Urban Task Force* (London: Richard Rogers Partnership).

URBED (Urban and Economic Development Ltd) (2006) *Tomorrow's Suburbs Best Practice Guide: Tools for Making London's Suburbs More Sustainable* (prepared for GLA, LDA, ALG and TfL) (London: URBED).

URBED (2008) *Regeneration in European Cities* (London: URBED/Joseph Rowntree Foundation).

Velluet, P. (2004) The English Heritage Perspective. *Urban Design Quarterly,* 90: 32–33.

Ward, S. (1998) Place Marketing: A Historical Comparison of Britain and North America. In T. Hall and P. Hubbard (eds) (1998) *The Entrepreneurial City: Geographies of Politics, Regime and Representation* (Chichester: John Wiley) pp. 31–53.

Ward, S. (2007) Cross-National Learning in the Formation of British Planning Policies 1940–1990: A Comparison of the Barlow, Buchanan and Rogers Reports. *Town Planning Review,* 78 (3): 369–400.

Watt, P. (2009) Social Housing and Regeneration in London. In R. Imrie, L. Lees and M. Raco (eds) *Regenerating London: Governance, Sustainability and Comminuty in a Global City* (London: Routledge) pp. 212–236.

Whitehead, C. M. E. (2007) Planning Policies and Affordable Housing: England as a Successful Case Study? *Housing Studies,* 22 (1): 25–44.

Whitehead, M. (2003) (Re)analysing the Sustainable City: Nature Urbanisation and the Regulation of Socio-Environmental Relations in the UK. *Urban Studies,* 40 (7): 1183–1206.

Whitehead, M. (2004) The Urban Neighbourhood and the Moral Geographies of British Urban Policy. In C. Johnstone and M Whitehead (eds) *New Horizons in British Urban Policy* (Aldershot, Ashgate) pp. 59–74.

Williams, K. (1999) The Wrong Starting Point. *Town and Country Planning,* 68 (9): 263.

Williams, G. and Daly, P. (2006) *Mixed Communities as Outcomes of Regeneration Strategies? Lessons from Hulme City Challenge for the Housing Market Renewal Agenda.* Paper presented to the National Planning Research Global Spaces, Local Spaces Conference 2006, University College London.

Wilner, T. (2008) Ongoing Problem. *Regeneration and Renewal,* 22 August: pp. 18–19.

Wilson, D. and Game, C. (2006) *Local Government in the United Kingdom* (4th edn) (London: Palgrave Macmillan).

Wright G. (1999) Urban Design 12 Years On: The Birmingham Experience. *Built Environment,* 25 (4): 289–299.

Zukin, S. (1995) *The Cultures of Cities* (Oxford: Blackwell).

Index